Human Reality

Who We Are *and* Why We Exist

Anonymous

HUMAN REALITY—Who We Are and Why We Exist

HARDBACK
ISBN 978-0-9785264-9-8

SOFTCOVER
ISBN 978-0-9785264-8-1

Library of Congress Control Number: 2009937830

Worldwide United Publishing
an imprint of Pearl Publishing, LLC
2587c Southside Blvd, Melba, ID 83641
http://pearlpublishing.net—1.888.499.9666

Printed in The United States of America

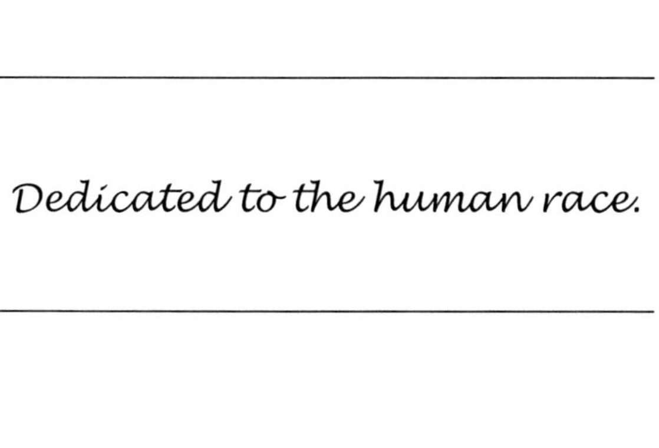

Dedicated to the human race.

He...who approaches the object [of knowledge] with thought alone, without associating any sight with his thought, or dragging in any sense perception with his reasoning, but who, using pure thought alone, tries to track down each reality pure and by itself...Will not that man reach reality...if anyone does?

—Attributed to Socrates in Plato's Phaedo, 65d-e

If you would understand anything, observe its beginning and its development.

—Attributed to Aristotle

TABLE OF CONTENTS

AUTHOR'S NOTE

Many of the facts presented in this book have never been explained to all of the inhabitants of this earth. Although there have been a few who have been privy to this information, none has made a worldwide attempt to make these things known to their fellow human beings. This book, a first of its kind, introduces many profound concepts that the reader is likely to have never considered before; therefore, a natural intellectual and emotional resistance can be expected.

As humans, we often find it difficult to accept something that conflicts with our established personal perceptions, opinions, and beliefs. When we decide to read a book that might disagree with our personal views and ideas, we are to be commended. Although many consider themselves to be open-minded, most people find it quite difficult to follow the intentions and thoughts of an author, once they encounter concepts that challenge what they currently accept as their own personal truths.

After initially reading something that is disagreeable to us, it is human nature to question everything that follows. Because our minds have layers upon layers of intellectual caution and personal prejudice embedded within, our reading comprehension may deteriorate as we struggle with concepts that increasingly conflict with our own. Subconsciously, we don't want our personal perceptions of our *own reality* to be challenged—we don't want to be proven wrong! Consequently, this can lead to mounting barriers of mistrust and disbelief in what is written. This results in an avalanche of prejudice that forms a slippery slope upon which our minds slide negatively against the new ideas and concepts being presented.

Anticipating this, I have intentionally written this book in a way that may appear to be redundant. Redundancies by definition are needless and excessive; however, I can assure the reader that my repetitiveness is both expedient and necessary. It is my hope that upon repetitive exposure to new concepts, the intellectual mind might expand and remove some of the barriers that prohibit it from acknowledging new ideas.

With rhetorical purpose, I repeat words and phrases throughout the book, which meaning might have already been conveyed to and understood by the reader in an earlier paragraph or chapter. Those with an open mind, who recognize their personal prejudices, will humbly admit that they have them and can be affected by them; and it is my hope that they will sincerely attempt to understand a different point of view than their own. These readers will not benefit as much from the superfluous, but purposefully intended, redundancy. There is immense significance in many of the explanations and details included in this book, which purposefully need to be repeated to give the reader clarity and proper understanding. Therefore, I will place literary emphasis and *reemphasis* on these most important points.

Besides the open-minded and sincere truth seeker (who might simply become mildly annoyed by this repetition), those whose reading skills are more proficient and advanced than others' might also find cause to criticize my intentionally repetitive writing style. To the more "sophisticated" readers, the continual repetition of words and phrases, along with the use of many *italicized and* ***bold*** *highlights*, might appear to be a reflection of insecurity in my ability to explain a specific point. However, I can assure these "highly educated ones" that I have no personal insecurities in presenting the concepts in this book exactly as I know them to be and in the way that I know they should be presented.

It became a very difficult task to put into writing what I know about HUMAN REALITY, desiring to ensure that all readers (scholarly or less-educated alike) were considered fairly in the composition of this book. It is my hope, therefore, that those who engage themselves in the task of reading this book might have compassion towards my weakness as I convey what I know through the written word. I have used my limited vocabulary and unorthodox writing style to convey a *description of things that have never been explained or shared upon this earth by any other person.* I make no excuses for my inadequacies; yet I also maintain that I am an expert on the subject matter and at tackling difficult and controversial subjects, despite my less-than-expert writing skills.

Because our minds comprehend and retain better when presented with fragmented bits of information (rather than lengthy explanations), I have segmented the book into numbered subheadings within each chapter. Each subheading is titled in an effort to help the mind transition from one concept to the next with greater ease and understanding. Also, for those so inclined, the numbered subheadings will serve as an easy reference tool.

Although faced with the challenges outlined above while writing this book, I remain hopeful that the most impenetrable, hardened mind might be softened, if that mind is so willing; and that the most prejudiced reader might grasp the most complete and comprehensive answers to our HUMAN REALITY that have ever been given to the human race upon this earth.

Upon obtaining these answers, each individual, as well as all of us as united human beings, will benefit—simply by applying our new understanding to our plight here upon this earth. To this end, it is my hope that all who read this book will come to understand WHO WE ARE and WHY WE EXIST.

—Anonymous

INTRODUCTION

My crown is called content: A crown it is that seldom kings enjoy.

—William Shakespeare

All of us have felt lost and alone, existing in a dreary world that shows little promise of providing us with any type of lasting peace and happiness. Feeling lost, we often seek for isolation away from others by withdrawing inside of our own minds.

Our mind is ours to control. It is our individual kingdom, surrounded by high walls and secure gates. Our kingdom is governed by its own crowned ruler, a powerful dictator of *one*. It is a city of refuge and peace where no person or thought is allowed inside its gates unless the king or queen within *permits* entrance. When a threat to our personal security (or better, our individuality) arises from without the walls of our kingdom, we shut and fortify the gates to ensure that the ruler within reigns supreme and gives up no power to the other kings and queens of the earth.

Yet being alone in our own kingdom does not satisfy us; nor does it bring us a fullness of joy and contentment. We often sit alone in our royal position of power, wondering what the purpose is for being the ruler of a kingdom of **one**. We have a distressing desire to share our kingdom with others, even though we are not even sure ***why***.

Other kings and queens living outside of our walls in their own kingdoms threaten to wage *war* against us. Many of them do not respect our kingdom, but instead want to make us a part of theirs so that *they are not alone*. These kings and queens are called parents, teachers, leaders, friends, and peers. The harder they try to get us to become part of their kingdom, the more we fortify the walls protecting our own. The more they pound on the gates to gain entrance, the tighter we hold them shut.

Once in a while, however, we come in contact with another king or queen who does not want to wage war against us and make us a part of his or her kingdom. These "few" want to open up their gates so that we can visit them from time to time and enjoy their kingdom with them as they in return enjoy ours. When not faced with the threat of "war," we become more inclined to open up our gates and allow others to enter *our kingdom* and enjoy it with us. And when we have enjoyed each other's, we both return to our own kingdom in peace and with a sense of fulfillment that we have found a ***true*** friend.

Nevertheless, here we sit in our own kingdoms, isolated away from each other and afraid to open the gates. The problem is, we realize that we are alone; and we do not even know **why** we are alone, or **how** we got here. In solitude, we ponder many universal questions about our existence—questions that have not been answered either within or without the high walls of our kingdom. Many have approached the gates of our city and knocked, wanting to share *their* truths with us. *Their truths* however, have only led to more questions, and have done little to convince us that their answers are any better than our own. They cannot satisfy our longing to know:

Why am I here upon this insignificant planet spinning around in space?

How did this planet get here?

Is there a purpose for my existence? If so, what is it?

Is death the end of this existence?

If death is the end, then shouldn't I be taking advantage of life?

Is this lifetime the **only** chance I get to experience consciousness?

What creates consciousness?

Why do I randomly and effortlessly dream when I am not conscious?

Why do humans appear more aware of themselves than other animals?

If we evolved from animals that once were not aware of themselves, then why aren't other animals becoming more like human beings and evolving to become increasingly aware of themselves?

Do animals ponder and question their existence as humans do?

If animals do not question their existence, then why not?

Is there a higher, more intelligent power than that of the human being?

How can human beings have the capacity for such great love and compassion and yet, at the same time, create such misery for each other?

Will the human race become extinct?

Is the life-giving sun burning out and will our planet eventually die?

What is the Universe?

Where did all of the stars come from, and more importantly, what are they?

Was our earth's creation just a natural occurring "accident"?

Does life exist elsewhere in the Universe?

Why do children seem happier than adults?

Is there such a thing as a soul and do I have one?

Why is peace and happiness so temporary and elusive?

Why is life such a struggle?

Did we ask to be born into existence?

What exactly is consciousness?

As stated above, we are given many answers to these questions, each individual (king or queen) trying to convince us that his or her idea is correct. When the answers are not straightforward and logical, some of us invent theories, beliefs, and opinions based on our own best speculation. Still, most of the answers remain *mysteries* and have remained so since the foundation of this world. Therefore, in order to be soundly convinced of **true reality**, we must be presented with explanations that make sense and do not lead to other questions.

Humans have attempted to answer many of these questions by using their *imagination.* But just what exactly constitutes our "imagination"? We must first solve this *mystery* correctly in order to understand **true reality**. With our unique ability to ***imagine***, we have invented an enormous genre of science and conceptual fiction. Nevertheless, today's science fiction could very well become tomorrow's human reality.

But what if we could understand future human reality TODAY? How would acquiring this knowledge affect our world? Would the *correct* answers to all of our questions improve humanity's plight? Or are we afraid that this **true reality** would destroy the established perceptions we have of ourselves—our *kingdom within*, which currently gives us our personal value and security? Being afraid to face the fact that we might all be wrong—and the conditions found in our world seem to prove this—how long are we going to remain scared and consequently loyal to our bad judgment and ignorance? What will it take before we accept the error of our ways and decide to change our current path? **True reality** will take away our fears and show us the way.

In ancient times, human imagination influenced the concept of "learning and study." Finding the answers to life's mysteries became a source of value to both teacher and student alike. The teacher, who thought he or she knew the *correct answers*, was valued by the student who did not. If the teacher convinced the student that his or her answers were the truth, the student then valued the learning experience.

There were natural phenomena that couldn't be explained; but it is human nature to want to understand ourselves and the world in which we live. Ancient teachers, therefore, gave their personal understanding of events and phenomena through the written word. Their writings eventually became respected bodies of literature. However, as humans progressed through experience, these ancient works became modern mythologies. These myths extend beyond the borders of the known earth into the Universe, and somehow gave the people who believed in them a safe concept of themselves and a hope that kept them satisfied with their existence. As we have advanced in thought and discovery, though, we are less and less satisfied with the answers that our teachers have provided us. We are getting tired of myths, hypotheses, and theories. We want the **real truth**!

In the 20th Century, science fiction began to replace mythology as a source of reality for many people. Human imagination began to provide a new hope for the human race. Advanced technology and understanding opened our minds to possibilities that extended beyond the limited and now seemingly ridiculous beliefs of our ancestors.

Now in the 21st Century, we find ourselves inundated with cinematic theories that create a sense of our incredible capabilities and human potential. We are advancing (at least in our minds) into realms of reality that we often find hard to accept, until they happen right before our eyes. Who would have thought, for example, that Dick Tracy's telephone-picture watch of the 1940's would be a reality in the 21st Century? Those living in the 1940's surely didn't!

The genre of science fiction-laced movies developed by our creativity and imagination pit *imperfect* humans against more advanced (but often more evil) beings, which in most cases are not human. Even the aliens we create through our imagination that are sympathetic to the human race, are not presented as creatures similar to us. Equally, it's hard for even the most creative and imaginative mind to envision an *advanced human being* (in contrast to an alien creature) helping to save the human race. This is because *reality* (based on the way human beings treat each other on earth) seems to be leaning towards humans causing their own eventual destruction. Therefore, it appears that a non-human, *alien being* would be a more logical choice to be the savior of the human race.

Science fiction aside, what if there really *are* more advanced human beings living on other planets throughout the Universe? And what if they are *solely* interested in our well-being and happiness, rather than seeking to dominate or destroy us? What if the idea of a "Supreme Creator" is in fact the simpler concept of caring, advanced human beings—parents who created us in their perfect world—sending us here to this earth to let us find out what we would do on our own, without them? Don't teenagers learn to appreciate what their parents provide for them by leaving a secure home life? Free-willed individuals cannot accurately learn *reality* unless they live it for themselves.

What if *human reality* is not about myth and fiction at all, but rather about "science," based on the work and intelligence of benevolent, highly advanced, perfected human "scientists"? If this is so, then why are they not interceding to help us and prevent us from destroying each other and the planet where we live? Most people would agree that part of **true humanity** *should* be the tendency to step in and offer assistance to others in need. So, if more advanced humans than us do exist, and they are aware of us, why aren't they interceding into our affairs for our benefit? They are humane, aren't they? They understand **humanity**, don't they?

But if someone who does not live on our planet has to step in and offer this assistance to us, then what does that say about *our* humanity? How can we prove that we deserve to be free-willed humans, if we lack the humanity that should separate us from all other animals in our world? Isn't it true that there are other animals who act more *humanely* than we do? Wouldn't we want to be given the chance to prove our humanity before having a civilization more advanced than our own step in and save us from ourselves?

As our world becomes more connected, we become more aware of the problems facing other cultures of people existing throughout the earth. It seems that the more technology advances, the more interconnected and interdependent we become. We are no longer separate parts of individual nations, but are becoming citizens of planet Earth.

Considering our progress in technological advancements, our future will undoubtedly include the ability to visit other planetary systems in the Universe. What will we do if we encounter other civilizations of human beings that need our help? Wouldn't our compassion and natural human propensity to help, compel us to step in and do whatever we can to assist these people? WE are humans! And if we have the power and the ability, we *should* help those in need!

But what happens when the whole of the human race upon this planet becomes needful of assistance? Who is out there in the Universe to offer us the help that we need? Are there any other civilizations of people with the same human nature (humanity) as our own? If these advanced societies have existed thousands, millions, even billions of years longer than we have, wouldn't their technology and advancements allow them the ability to be aware of us and our needs? Again, if they could help, wouldn't they?

For us to believe that we are the only human race that exists in the Universe is thoughtless, irresponsible, and illogical. Even if we began our existence as evolving bacteria (as some speculate), doesn't our ability to reason suggest the probability that there exist other bacteria somewhere in the Universe that have evolved to where we have, and beyond?

Some people have been searching all of their lives for some viable proof that other human civilizations do exist somewhere "out there." None has come up with any conclusive and hard evidence that would support the fact. Some have wondered why other, more advanced civilizations haven't made contact with us yet. What are they waiting for?

Well, maybe they don't think we need their intervention…just yet!

Without them actually making physical contact with us—what other way could we know that they exist? What proof would satisfy our skepticism? What about knowing what they know? Would that understanding and knowledge satisfy our disbelief?

What if they *have* made contact with us, but do not physically reveal themselves to us so as not to interfere with our own development and learning? If they did reveal themselves, wouldn't the whole world listen to what they have to say about the Universe and what is happening beyond our tiny planet? Wouldn't we depend on *them* to solve all of our problems and teach us how to live in peace and harmony with each other? Wouldn't they stop us and keep us from destroying each other?

If those who would help are indeed *advanced humans*, then they *would* step in and assist us. But they would not do so before giving us a chance to prove our right to *free will* and the right to have the power associated with being human. With the power of human reason and free will, we have the capability to control our environment, to have dominion over the plant and animal kingdoms of the world, and to do whatever it is that we want to do. As we advance our abilities through technology and understanding, can we be trusted with ultimate human power and capabilities? Can we individually be trusted to continue to advance into future realms of human-based knowledge that will eventually allow us to do things that we can only *imagine* today? Will we use our extraordinary free will and reason to perpetuate and support the human race or to destroy it?

These are questions waiting to be answered in the future.

The premise of this book is that advanced beings, who know *true* **HUMAN REALITY**, are subtly intervening in our lives and giving us the answers to the questions that we all yearn to know. They are doing this to aid us in our continual journey to prove our own humanity and make claim to all the rights and powers associated with existing as a human being. Some of these powers and rights have the ability to make us extremely happy or extremely miserable, depending on how we use them.

The most constant influences and motivational parts of our human nature are our sexual disposition and our will to survive. The majority of the problems of *humanity* come about as a result of actions that can be traced to some connection with one of these two physical influences. Although hard to accept and admit for some, this fact cannot be ignored as we consider **true human reality**. The downfall of societies can be traced to, first, how humans dealt with their sexual natures and, secondly, how they dealt with each other as they were forced to provide themselves with the basic necessities of life. These two motivating factors have been a course of study and observation by many of the world's greatest minds. Their conclusions generally agree that the vast majority of our *inhumane* history upon this earth has been the result of sexuality and our individual desire to survive.

This being the case, the logical solution to most of our problems would appear to be for us to gain a proper understanding of **why** these motivational forces cause so many problems for humans; and then to explain **how** we can eventually eliminate both sexuality and the struggle for survival from our existence. Although suggesting the elimination of human sexuality proposes intellectual suicide, eliminating the struggle for survival is humankind's greatest hope! To show why and how to accomplish both of these endeavors would be profound! It would literally be the salvation of the human race! The proof given throughout this book will overwhelmingly demonstrate that one day, the elimination of sexuality for *most* of us, along with the elimination of the constant struggle for survival for *all* of us, will both have to become **human reality**, or we will be faced with our own extinction.

In addition to the physical forces that have motivated and influenced our existence, the desire for equality and mutual respect has been the greatest emotional challenge that we have faced throughout our history upon the earth. It seems to be an emotional condition that we will always encounter during our *imperfect* state as human beings.

In order to create value for themselves and gain a sense of equality with everyone else, human beings have developed their own individual belief systems. Sometimes, they have even pretended to possess personal powers associated with the supernatural and paranormal. To address all of the ways that humans create personal value for themselves would create a voluminous work. Such a work would only lead to a further deluge of information that individual readers (according to their own perception) might find insignificant and unrelated to their own personal quest to understand *true reality*.

The *real truth* is that there is no true human reality in any belief system invented by humankind—not even one! There is no such thing as the "supernatural" or the "paranormal," or any other mysterious occurrence that cannot immediately be understood by the human mind, if the correct explanation is given. "Mystery" and "phenomena" are simply acknowledgements that we can't understand something about our reality.

As disquieting as this proclamation might be for most, its substance and veracity will unequivocally be proven by the end of this book. If the reader will have patience concerning those things which are currently accepted as "mysterious" and "phenomenal," and also maintain a sincere desire to understand more about his or her existence than he or she can honestly admit that he or she presently knows, then the reader will be astonished at how much emotional peace and security he or she will find by having all the mysteries of life explained in plainness. The **true reality will surely set one free!**

This book will give the direct, sensible answers to all of life's most difficult questions. Those responsible for this book will never pollute the sanctity of the reader's own kingdom. They will always respect the *king or queen who sits upon the throne.* They are knocking at your gate. They will go away if you do not want to be bothered. But they will leave this book outside the gates and walls of your kingdom, hoping, for your own sake, that you might one day open the gate just enough to grab the book and pull it back into your kingdom—the kingdom that is built within you.

In the solitude and security of your own world, engaging the power of your own mind, you are now presented with the opportunity to read a book that will finally help you understand

HUMAN REALITY—Who We Are and Why We Exist.

Human Reality

CHAPTER ONE

If you would be a real seeker after truth, it is necessary that at least once in your life you doubt, as far as possible, all things.

—Rene Descartes

1. THIS BOOK CONTAINS THE WHOLE OF HUMAN REALITY

This book answers many of life's most important questions. These answers transcend most views, opinions, and perceptions of humankind's current understanding of reality. As a result, they provide a stark contrast to the preconceived notions of truth many accept as their individual *reality*. Most established conclusions believed to be truth produce unanswerable follow-up questions. If a conclusion produces further questions then it cannot be based on **true** *human reality*.

Human reality is a totality of the events that impact our existence. Its scope includes those things that **actually** happened, those things that **are actually** occurring presently, and those things that **actually will** come to pass at some time in our future. **True** *human reality* seldom agrees with the false notions of our currently *accepted* realities that continue to change over time. *True reality* does not change—it never has and it never will! It resolves all questions with answers that leave no follow-up questions on which to speculate or debate. The only debate that will ever occur regarding *true reality*, is when it encounters the false notions of currently accepted reality.

2. ONE FACT IS KEY TO UNDERSTANDING WHO WE ARE

To understand the reality of *who we are*, we must first be willing to accept one basic fact about ourselves. This fact can be logically accepted from our present experience:

HUMAN BEINGS ARE THE MOST SIGNIFICANT FORM OF LIFE IN THE UNIVERSE.

Taking into account all of our experience upon planet earth, there should be no question in our minds that we, as human beings, are favored with more of life's opportunities, abilities, and choices than any other life form—including plants, animals, and other elements of existence.

3. HUMANS ARE AT THE TOP AND CENTER OF THE UNIVERSE

Stated again, and to finally get at the truth of *who we are*, we must recognize that the human being **is the most important and significant life form, not only upon earth, but throughout the whole Universe**. We exist at the top of the intelligence chain (the "top link in the chain") because we are the organism that has the greatest possible advantages in experiencing life.

In the realm of ***true*** "Human Reality," a human birth has the same significance as creating a whole new Universe. Without the human being and its ability to consider the implication of its own existence, what meaning or significance would a Universe have? No other life form is cognizant of the concept of a "Universe" except for the human being. When a new human life is created, it has the free will and capacity to comprehend and react to its surroundings according to its own unique perception; therefore, a *completely new* Universe is formed. The known Universe and the way that it is understood and accepted resides in each of us individually. The **only** Universe that exists is the one that is conceptualized by our own personal experience.

4. WE HAVE THE MOST ADVANCED INTELLIGENCE

Considering our experience upon earth, we have come to the realization that survival of the *smartest*—not the *strongest*—is the *real* way the natural world works. As humans, we find ourselves at the top of this "chain of intelligence," not because we are the largest or the strongest life form upon earth, but because we are the smartest. Understanding how we became the most intelligent and found our place at the top of the chain will provide us with more pieces of the puzzle in understanding our existence.

How did we get at the top? If our brains naturally evolved over many years and eventually placed us above all other animals advancing intellectually, why aren't there other species of animals upon the earth that are advancing like we have?

The simple answer is that humans *have always been* at the top. We have always been smarter than any other creature in our world (even in spite of our propensity to kill each other for no apparent justifiable reason, and to destroy the beautiful and natural design of our environment). Science has never conclusively and convincingly proven that there was ever a time when humankind was not the top link in the " chain of intelligence" while humans have been found upon the earth. Science theorizes that some kind of humanoid might have existed on earth for millions of years, but erroneously concludes that these first *humanoids* were not as intelligent as modern humans. These theories leave many unanswered questions and have created a "missing link" that science cannot explain.

If there is something to be said and respected about the *supposed* universal law, "the *strongest* survive," it nonetheless has its limitations in regards to the human species. It is obvious, for example, that much *smarter* animals have outlived the much *stronger* dinosaurs. Alligators, crocodiles, and many insect species are examples of life forms that have survived in spite of their inferior strength compared to others that are now extinct.

If the law of natural selection ("the strongest survive") was correct, we would have to accept that, unless the *smartest* human also becomes the strongest, the demise of the human species is inevitable. Indeed, for the human species to continue its prominence as ***the most significant form of life in the Universe***, it must be established as a ***true reality*** that the smartest and most significant life forms in the Universe (humans) are also the strongest and most powerful. This would ensure not only the consistent order found throughout the Universe, of which only humans are aware, but also the infinite continuation of the human race.

5. ONLY HUMANS SEEK A MEANING FOR THEIR EXISTENCE

As humans, we have the opportunity and choice to question our existence and to act upon the conclusions we accept as the answers (unlike other life forms that don't have the ability to worry about their existence). Because of this, we are constantly striving to give meaning to our own lives and the lives of all other life forms. We continually seek development and improvement, focusing our human nature on whatever provides for and benefits our unique "self." Our incredible minds have placed us within our own individual "Universe," set apart from everything and everyone else around us.

Instead of our environment mandating what we can and cannot do, we use our intelligence to subdue everything that surrounds us, attempting to have complete dominion over it. Sometimes our desire to control our environment benefits us and sometimes it acts as a detriment to our existence. Even now, the earth is jeopardized by our unique desire to control everything about our world. The earth in all of its beauty, strength, and greatness is no match for *human* free will. The earth's environs were established long before we began to subdue and change them. Regardless of how we use our intelligence to subdue the environment in which we find ourselves, the fact still remains that we can. Having this choice and the power to act upon it illustrates our unique significance to the earth and the Universe.

6. WHILE ON THIS EARTH WE PURSUE OUR INDIVIDUALITY

We attempt to find and take advantage of all that can possibly contribute to the experience of the individual "self." We are aware of our self as a separate entity, each of us with our own unique idea of what is personally satisfactory and what is not. That which is satisfactory to us, makes us happy. That which is not, makes us unhappy.

In our pursuit of individual fulfillment, we use the unique power of our free will to do all that we can to find this self-fulfillment we call "happiness." Because the Universe revolves around us, anything that we choose to do in pursuit of this happiness becomes the right thing to do; or at least we justify it as being the right thing, as long as it makes us happy.

7. HAPPINESS IS THE REASON WHY WE EXIST

As we develop the foundation of understanding that will lead to the correct answer (the ***true reality***) of *who we are*, we will come to understand ***why*** *we exist*. Until then, the latter question (why we exist) can approximately and generally be answered by using the term "happiness" as the purpose for which we exist, or as that which we seek to gain out of life. Therefore, ***true reality*** establishes that obtaining *happiness* is **WHY WE EXIST**.

HUMAN LIFE is simply a compilation of our experiences, based on various exposures to different events, people, and environments. A wide variety of many different experiences consequently lead to an increase of knowledge and opportunities that provide us with the potential of fulfilling our individual needs, or better, experiencing happiness.

8. HAPPINESS REQUIRES AN EQUALITY WITH OTHER HUMANS

We have, or should have, no other motivation in our life (our existence) other than being happy. Yet, for many of us, this pursuit is reduced to a *motivation of survival* instead, because of the physical requirements that our existence demands from us (i.e., food and shelter). Even when these basic needs *are* met (unlike every other non-human life form), we still desire something more from our existence. Having our physical needs met might enable us to experience life without worrying about dying from lack of food or shelter, but it *does not* bring us the fullness of happiness we desire.

We find that being alone in our "own Universe" cannot bring us a complete sense of happiness. We seek the companionship of other humans and are dependent on them to help us experience our own happiness. Although we need others, we find no joy in *not* being equal to them, or rather, in not being as happy as they are. Our inability to find and experience long-term happiness leads to the logical conclusion that we all have an innate desire to be happy and we all desire to be as happy as everyone else. We want equality.

If we see someone else with something that *appears* to make that person happy, and if we don't have what that person has, we begin to desire it. Regardless of whether that "something" is a material possession, a physical attribute, or a mental state (i.e., education and knowledge), if we *perceive* that others are happier than we are or live a more satisfactory life than we are living (because they have the "something" that we lack), we attempt to do whatever is necessary to acquire the *same thing* so that we can share in the same sense of satisfaction.

9. EQUALITY IS IMPORTANT, BUT NOT ALL THAT WE NEED

Ironically, when we acquire a sense of equality by possessing the same things as everyone else, we find that we are *still* not completely self-fulfilled and satisfied. This is because we have lost the uniqueness of our "self." Because it is in our nature to establish our "self" apart from everyone else, feeling equal to another takes away from our individuality and causes us to become unhappy with who we are.

We want to be valued equally by others yet still maintain our uniqueness with respect to everyone else. Said another way, at the same moment we desire equality, we also desire the inequality that makes us unique. This paradox creates the dilemma of the human being, which in turn creates most of our emotional problems and causes us to be forever searching for the answer to the question: **What must I DO to be happy?**

10. HAPPINESS SHOULD NOT BE OUR PURSUIT, BUT OUR RIGHT

It is repugnant to our sense of logic and contrary to the very core of our shared human nature that happiness here on earth is a *pursuit* instead of the *purpose* for why we exist. How can we be guaranteed *life*, *liberty*, and the *pursuit* of happiness, when we are constantly protecting the very life and liberty that are supposed to establish who we are? Who caused us to have to pursue that for which we exist?

Those on this earth who created us (our parents) should also bear the responsibility of aiding us in achieving the purpose for which we were created. Instead, they have introduced us into a world of struggles and insecurities that keep us constantly *pursuing* something that we should have been guaranteed upon our creation—the right of happiness.

11. IN OUR HASTE TO "GROW UP," WE LOSE OUR HAPPINESS

Lyrics from a contemporary song outline the premise of how simply and joyfully our life began. It profoundly expresses the ***true reality*** that as we grow up, life becomes more and more complicated. We are forced to learn how to *pursue* happiness instead of being able to enjoy it. Our life is one in which we are ever learning from our experiences, but never able to reach a point of self-fulfillment. While we started out life with all the abilities and potential of being true to our "self" and living happily, we come to the point where we lose our happiness and are left with the most basic of all questions—a question we ask ourselves over and over again: Who am I?

When I was young
It seemed that life was so wonderful
A miracle, oh it was beautiful, magical
And all the birds in the trees
Well they'd be singing so happily
Oh joyfully, oh playfully watching me

But then they sent me away
To teach me how to be sensible
Logical, oh responsible, practical
And then they showed me a world
Where I could be so dependable
Oh clinical, oh intellectual, cynical.

There are times when all the world's asleep
The questions run too deep
For such a simple man
Won't you please, please tell me what we've learned
I know it sounds absurd
But please tell me who I am

I said, now watch what you say
Or they'll be calling you a radical
A liberal, oh fanatical, criminal
Oh won't you sign up your name
We'd like to feel you're
Acceptable, respectable, oh presentable, a vegetable!

But at night when all the world's asleep
The questions run so deep
For such a simple man
Won't you please, please tell me what we've learned
I know it sounds absurd
But please tell me who I am, who I am, who I am, who I am.

Supertramp, "The Logical Song" (© 1979 A&M Records: Los Angeles, CA); on Breakfast in America [CD].

12. EXPECTATIONS OF THE WORLD HINDER OUR HAPPINESS

In our quest for happiness, we lose ourselves to the oblivion of what others have already defined as "happiness," a definition not created of our "self" but determined long before we were born into this life. Few adults experience life as a "wonderful thing." The world has transformed its children into material, "*sensible, logical, responsible, practical, dependable, clinical, intellectual, and cynical*" beings, whose only happiness comes from fulfilling the expectations and responsibilities established *for* us, not *by* us.

We started out on our journey in life with our own individual outlook of what made each of us happy in the new environment in which we found ourselves as children. We were once self-motivated little ones who possessed *only* the desire to satisfy an innate need to find happiness—each of us having a completely unique and individual idea of what this happiness and self-fulfillment meant to us.

13. IMPERFECT ADULTS SET OUR STANDARDS ON EARTH

Without any concern for our instinctive nature and predisposition to maintain our individual uniqueness, our earthly parents set standards *for us* and forced ***theirs*** upon us. Those who became our teachers taught us their standards. And those we were eventually trained to accept as our leaders imposed their values and standards upon us. Most destructive to our individuality and self-esteem are those with whom we form relationships and to whom we endear ourselves.

We reserve the right to choose with whom we associate on an intimate level, while our parents, teachers, and leaders have been forced upon us. In these close and seemingly most important relationships, standards are set that we are required to meet in order to be loved and accepted by those we have chosen to be our intimates. We try much harder to meet these *standards* than we do to meet those established by our parents, because these relationships are more important to us. They become the most important relationships in our lives because we are allowed to choose them for ourselves without having them forced upon us.

Through our relationships (both those that are forced upon us and those which we choose for ourselves) we develop our cognitive paradigms (the different ways we've been trained to think). The paradigms that are forced upon us establish a core of beliefs, which takes away the unique individuality we had as *little* children. When the *standards* that are set and forced upon us differ from the standards of those with whom we *choose* to have personal relationships, we become unbalanced and unhappy. To find our balance again, we usually desire those relationships we choose for ourselves over those that are forced upon us. For this reason, it is easy for a person to rebel against one's parents and their "core standards" when one "falls in love" with someone else. But when the object of our affection (the relationship choice we made for ourselves) does not fulfill our expectations, we often return to our parents and are forced once again to choose between their *forced* standards and those we desire for ourselves.

Why didn't our parents, teachers, and leaders just leave us alone and not mandate *for us* what was "right" and "wrong," "good" and "bad"? We would have figured it out on our own. How did *they* figure it out? And if what they concluded is really what is *best for us*, why is it that happiness remains as elusive for them as it does for us, and even as it was for those who set the standards and rules *for them*? We are not happy, they are not happy, and *their* parents were not happy—what a world of unsuccessful standards that have failed and are still failing to provide happiness!

14. SOMETHING IS "WRONG" WITH THE RULES OF "ORDER"

Those who set the standards for us will argue that, if everyone in the world did whatever they wanted to do to find their own happiness, the world would eventually collapse into utter chaos, anarchy, and eventual destruction. The world leaders who establish and maintain control over us claim that having rules, laws, and responsibilities in place brings some semblance of *order* to the world. This argument is as flawed as the supposed "order" that the "rule of law" has produced for our human race. If the purpose for our existence is "happiness," then why does the rule of law imposed upon us create such inequality and misery?

Sure, by brute strength and threats, free-willed individuals can be subdued and forced into submission to any rule or law. But exactly to what do our leaders expect us to submit? What kind of "order" is found in knowing that there exists the capability and availability of thousands of nuclear weapons, and that just one could destroy an entire culture of people? What kind of "order" is there found in the plight of the hungry, the homeless, the naked, the sick, and the impoverished—the state of existence of the majority of the human race? What kind of "order" is there in the racial and cultural separations and prejudices that cause one, supposedly "equal" human being, to hate or disparage another?

The very standards, laws, and rules that are restricting our personal freedoms, and are being forced upon us to maintain this "order," are having the opposite effect on our individual peace and happiness. The world leaders are steering humanity into chaos and anarchy; and if they remain unchallenged, we could ultimately be led to our own destruction.

But long before we are *physically* destroyed from without, we will be *emotionally* destroyed from within, stemming from our inability to find our own individuality and fulfill our individual needs. The kind of "order" that was established *for us* and not *by us* has created hopelessness and inequality that are a far cry from the happiness that is supposed to be the purpose for ***why*** *we exist*.

15. PARENTING CAN NEGATIVELY AFFECT OUR DEVELOPMENT

Those who argue against our free will to become who we want to become have failed us. We are intelligent enough to know, and more importantly to *feel*, that the established "semblance of order" is a way for a very few people to rule over the rest of us for their *own* benefit without any regard for what their "rule of law" does to our individuality.

As we have experienced different periods of human existence, we have learned that parents do their children a great injustice in welcoming them into the *parents*' world. Parents are selfish. They do not create children for the benefit of the child, but to satisfy some part of their own need to create value for themselves, through their children. A selfless parent would consider the state of the world in which their child would have to live. Why would someone do such an injustice to another human being by bringing them into a world where the ability of realizing their own happiness (i.e., the purpose for which we *should* exist) is virtually impossible?

16. "ACCEPTED NORMS" KEEP US FROM OUR *TRUE* REALITY

When we are first born into the world as children, we are generally allowed to live life carefree and according to our innate need to actualize our *self.* We soon find out that our self-centered parents (who gave us life for their own pleasure and agenda) take away the security of the environment that they provided us at birth. Our first environment was one of security, love, and complete dependence upon those who *chose* to create us. But in less than two decades of existence, our "creators" find it their "duty" and prerogative as parents to force us to provide for ourselves and become just as indentured to life's inequalities and miseries as they are.

We are born *free*. Shortly thereafter, we are forced into slavery and into a lifestyle and world that we had nothing to do with creating. Once we are forced into a condition of involuntary servitude (which is fueled by our own desire to continue to live and find happiness), our sense of *self* and *purpose* are submerged and dissolved into a toxic mixture of an impersonal and abusive world that poisons our individuality.

Personal happiness, which comes from freedom of self-expression and choice, is controlled by those who have enslaved us. All of us, young and old, rich and poor, small and great, free and bond, are forced to submit to the "rule of law" that feeds us, clothes us, cares for us when we are sick, and imprisons us when we seek our individual freedom and a sense of self apart from the "rule of law." These all add to the dilemma of being human and greatly multiply our emotional problems. How then, can we be thankful for the "blessing" of life in this world?

17. WE MUST SET NEW STANDARDS SO THAT WE CAN FIND OURSELVES

The only way we will ever free ourselves and keep from being emotionally destroyed from within is to come to a conclusive *reality* and understanding of *who we are* and *why we exist* in the first place. We do not want to make the same mistakes that our parents made, nor do we want to continually perpetuate their bad judgment. Upon understanding things that our parents never understood, we will be in a better position to make changes to the world, and be more comfortable introducing new human beings into it. Our selflessness will keep our own children from asking themselves what we often ask ourselves, "What kind of selfish parent would bring me into this kind of a world?"

With greater knowledge and insight into *human reality* (as given in this book), we will be able to change the "semblance of order" that has caused the abuse of the "self" in our world. Because we have not set personal standards that are uniquely our own, we must change the established societal standards so that they begin to conform to the true purpose for which we exist: to experience greater happiness and self-fulfillment than our ancestors did. To do this properly, we must come to a more conclusive comprehension of *who* or *what* human beings actually are. We must understand ourselves better than our ancestors did.

18. BEING FREE HELPS US ACTUALIZE AS AN INDIVIDUAL

As little children, it is acceptable to *act like* little children. But once we are considered human adults, if we attempt to establish our own set of standards, or even maintain the ones we once had as children, we are branded by others as "childish" or as "*radical, a liberal, oh fanatical, criminal.*"

None of us has *actually* achieved the "self" who we started out to become. If we were happy as little children, we are not now. Our self-actualization is hindered by two things: our need to provide ourselves with the *necessities of life* (or better, the *security* our parents now withhold from us) and our inability to completely understand our individual *self.*

Because of the influence of others, we have lost the ability to recognize who we truly are. We are not satisfied with ourselves because we are not pursuing our own values based on what *we* really *want* for our (own) **true** selves. We have lost who we *really* are to the expectations of others. To find ourselves again and become *who we **really** are*, we must be willing to return to our beginning and find out *how* we developed and became *who we are not*. Once we understand what caused us to develop in opposition to our ***true reality***, we must find a way to ensure that we do not have to worry about acquiring the *necessities* that support our life, so that we can concentrate our energy on becoming our **true** selves again. Without this worry, we will be able to find ourselves. Once we do, we will then be able to enjoy who we ***truly*** are.

19. WE ARE NOT THE ONLY HUMAN BEINGS IN THE UNIVERSE

We are the *only* life form that looks out into space and wonders *who we are* and *why we exist*. All other organisms exist in the environment in which they are created and are satisfied with their terrestrial predicament. Because we sense our value and significance in our world, and this *value* is not supported by our experiences on this earth, we are compelled to exclaim, "There must be more than this!"

When we look away from this earth, celestial lights beckon us to ask, "*Are we the only humans who exist in this enormous Universe? Are there other humans looking up into their own night sky and wondering the same thing? Do they feel just as lost as we do?*"

True *human reality* confirms that this earth is *not* the *only* planet in the Universe upon which human beings are found. There are human beings throughout the Universe at different levels of development. Besides those human beings who currently live on our planet earth, there are other human beings who live on their own "earth-like" planets who are *less*-advanced than we are, others who are just as advanced as we are, and still others who are far *more* advanced than we find ourselves today. For example, there are an infinite number of "earth-like" planets in the Universe whose inhabitants are approaching their year (according to their own calendar) 2012.

No matter in what stage of development human beings are found throughout the Universe, all humans have the same equal opportunities, advantages, and abilities to reach the fullest potential of the most advanced human beings. The most advanced human beings live in an existence of perpetual happiness. They are fulfilling the purpose of their creation in all aspects of their personal self-fulfillment.

20. SCIENCE IS A HUMAN INVENTION THAT GUESSES REALITY

Even the most subjective scientists admit to the possibility of life beyond our world. If we can't accept at least the possibility, then we reject the "objectivity" of our own science. In an attempt to understand *who we are* and where we began, even what is out there in the Universe, we have invented a means of observation, experimentation, and assumption called *science.* Using archeology, anthropology, genealogy, linguistics, psychology, and other human life-based scientific studies, we have attempted to form an idea of how our ancestors lived and where they came from, hoping that upon understanding them, we will have a better understanding of ourselves.

But none of these studies have been successful at creating a clear picture of *who we are.* Although we can learn by studying humans of the past (both their successes and their failures), we cannot figure out *who we are* from these studies because we are *not* our ancestors. They lived in a completely different world and environment than the one in which we currently live. Our descendents, those humans who will live upon the earth in the future, will also experience a completely different world than the one in which we currently live.

21. SCIENTIFIC "FACTS" OF TODAY ARE MYTHS TOMORROW

Our world changes every day. It is hardly the same today as it was 1000 years ago; in fact, it is not even the same as it was *five* years ago. The ever-changing world will continue to transform the scientific "facts" of today into the "myths" of tomorrow. Continual change does not allow us to determine and establish a **true** reality. As our *reality* remains in a constant state of change, our societies and cultures, along with our expectations and standards, also change.

With these constant changes, we are forced to make continual adjustments to our already-lost, *true* sense of self. If we arrive at some sense of balance by conforming to our present world, we are thrown off balance as things change around us. What happened in the past helps us to conclude that we will never arrive at a complete understanding of *who we are* by only studying our past, because who we were then is not who we are now. Furthermore, everything that we think we know today—all of the education, the theories, the laws, and the so-called *realities* that we accept and establish as our core beliefs—will one day be nonsense to those who live in the future. For example, all of the technology and innovation upon the earth today (*circa* 2012) will one day be viewed by advanced societies of human beings living in 3012 as we now view the Neanderthal technology of rubbing two sticks together to make fire. The greatest scientific minds of today will appear to future scientists as uncivilized and foolish "cavemen."

22. THE EARTH IS STILL NOT FLAT

An example of human ignorance is the historical *reality* that the some of the greatest scientific minds upon the earth once proposed the "fact" that the earth was flat and that it was the center of the Universe around which all other planetary systems revolved. No matter how absurd this might seem to modern scientists and physicists, these can rest assured that one day in the future, **many** of their modern-day theories will seem just as ridiculous to a more advanced mind.

This is a very humbling revelation of *reality* that most close-minded scientists and researchers, who have spent their entire life studying their own theories and postulations and those of their mentors and peers, will find very hard to accept—such is the case with the human ego. But whether we can accept it or not, this type of ignorance of the **real truth**, and our inability to admit that we might be wrong, are parts of *human reality* that keep us from discovering *who we are*.

23. SCIENTISTS AND SCHOLARS ARE NO WISER THAN OTHERS

To the avid scholar or professional who has dedicated his or her entire life to the study of humanity, the mere mention that all of their time and efforts are completely meaningless causes tremendous offense and disagreement. They would argue that these studies have helped shape and define better cultural, political, economical, emotional, and philosophical changes worldwide.

Yes, indeed, these well-read "wise ones" certainly have contributed to the shaping of our world. But it is the *shape* that this world is in that authenticates the "worthlessness" of their lives' studies. They study each others' theories and discoveries, only to continue to forge the same ironclad manacles and chains that have continued to keep human beings enslaved and incapable of reaching their full potential. They spend endless hours of research along with countless amounts of money exploring the space beyond our planet, when the same amount of money and time could instead be used to solve worldwide hunger and need. In the effort to discover *who we are*, we forget that **we are hungry, naked, sick, afflicted, and imprisoned**.

Whether the educated and trained like it or not, **none** of their conclusions and prideful dissertations of "fact" about this Universe will ever stand the test of thousands of years of human progression. If we can accept this fact, then it might help us to start concentrating our efforts on helping each other to find out who *we really are*.

24. WISDOM SHOULD NOT BE MEASURED BY HOW COMPLICATED IT IS

By the end of this book, humankind will know more about the Universe and our purpose therein than ever before in the history of the earth. We will no longer need to waste time and effort on studying space, because we will find that our **true happiness** can only be experienced upon this earth.

Owing to how this book is laid out in presentation, it might serve some "wise ones" well if we included a detailed and comprehensive bibliography wherein were referenced many of the statements of so-called "fact" made within its text. Some of the most unhappy and close-minded among us will not even read a book that is not cross-referenced and annotated according to the guidelines and rules set by the elite academia. They also want their books "peer-reviewed," though their peers know no more about ***true reality*** than they do.

There is no need to publish endless and useless bibliographies that subject the text of a book to endless and useless peer review; for, unless the information presented agrees with the prejudices associated with the reader's mind, he or she will disagree with it no matter what the content is or how much extensive research has been completed to prove its truthfulness.

Once again, it is important to keep in mind where this "elite" group of humans has led the rest of the human race with their brand of intelligence and study: to more stress and unhappiness. The *reality* of the truths given in this book transcend what the world has taught us, and beckon us to reflect on the innermost vestiges of our subconscious minds.

25. ADMITTING IGNORANCE HELPS US TO FIND TRUE REALITY

All of the knowledge contained in every book, in every library, in every University, and in any part of the world, will one day be considered hieroglyphical babble to the students of the future. Before any of us can accept *human reality*, we must be humble and submit to the fact that we really don't know anything of **real truth**, *despite all we have learned and all we are presently learning.*

Current scientific laws, facts, and all other knowledge that has the possibility of changing, cannot be considered *real truth*. **Real truth** is the ultimate reality of how things **really are**, how they have **really been**, and how they will **really be**. **Real truth** *cannot* be changed or amended in any way. Once we can accept this fact about ourselves—that we are ill-informed of *true reality* (real truth)—we will then open and expose our minds to possibilities that we would have never considered otherwise.

26. THOSE CLAIMING TO BE WISE LACK AN OPEN MIND

If we individually *think* that we have found or are in possession of the ultimate and unchangeable truth, what could possibly motivate us to look for something that we believe we already have (unless perhaps it was the realization that our accepted "truths" are not making us happy)? If we are close-minded, we will not accept other ideas. If we are open-minded, we will be receptive to other possibilities, which will expose us to new realities and allow us to find **real truth**.

By modern standards, "cavemen" are considered to have been close-minded and ignorant. At one time in our development, our ancestors believed that rubbing two sticks together was the most efficient way to create fire. More advanced human beings would never accept the idea that the "two stick" method is the best way to make fire. With the little that we presently do know, it becomes possible to imagine that one can create fire from a simple thought.

Upon reading the last sentence, one might say, "*How can a human being create fire with a thought?*" If you (the reader) thought this, you might forever remain a "caveman," because you do not have an open-mind. And while your current prejudices and paradigms of thought are rejecting the possibility, there is another open-minded scientist somewhere who is developing a technology that captures the electromagnetic forces produced by the brain when one thinks, and transforms them into a spark that can ignite a fire. Seemingly impossible technologies (as we would view them today) could very well be the basic technologies of an advanced future world.

27. IT IS DIFFICULT TO ACCEPT NEW IDEAS OF REALITY

Because we are conditioned to believe and accept only that which is available to us in our modern world, the truths set forth in this book might not agree with our current cognitive paradigms (again, the different ways we've been trained to think). These paradigms are responsible for how we perceive ourselves and each other. Because there are as many ways of thinking about things as there are people, a simple answer to our **true** *human reality* might be very difficult to agree upon universally.

The reader must keep in mind that most of what we understand comes from the limited (less-advanced) knowledge and accepted traditional prejudices passed on to us from the culture in which we are born and raised. If one is able to set his or her current knowledge aside and consider the *new facts* presented in this book, a completely different light than how we presently view ourselves will illuminate the open mind.

If we are willing and able to accept these facts, then we gain the advantage of opening up our minds to other realms of information and possibilities that we personally have not yet discovered or considered—realms that more advanced human beings on other worlds already understand. We will also come to understand how more advanced human beings who exist throughout the Universe view us. Looking through this new open window of reality will help us establish a proper foundation of **real truth**—something that we can all agree upon and finally accept as *human reality—who we are and why we exist.*

The conclusion we will reach, based on the systematic observation and experimentation of the vast *potential* of our rational and intelligent minds, will assuage our yearning and answer the question of the awakened inner soul caught in a world asleep. As stated in the lyrics above:

"PLEASE TELL ME WHO I AM, WHO I AM, WHO I AM!"

28. TRUE REALITY QUESTIONS STANDARDIZED WISDOM

Understanding the mysteries of life depends upon the innate human ability to reason that is referred to as "common sense." The "wise ones" among us will question the ability of this book to solve the mysteries of life without consulting with them or depending upon their wisdom and conclusions.

"What?" they will inquire. "Training and education are not necessary to solve the mystery of life? Impossible! A person cannot understand that for which he or she has not studied and received an accredited degree!"

These "learned ones" will close their minds to the possibility that a comprehensive and conclusive answer *does* exist, although it is not associated with their "learning." However, the answers given in this book not only support most scientific conclusions, but will also expand many of these conclusions into realms where science has dared not go for fear of peer scrutiny and alienation.

Once again, it matters not what the scientific, expert, professional, and academia fields have to say. We have tried their ways and submitted to their conclusions, only to find ourselves stuck in a never-ending quagmire of human ego, misery, and complete confusion.

29. THERE IS MUCH TO LEARN THROUGH "FUTUROLOGY"

Included in this book is the application of the relatively new science of futurology—the science, art, and practice of postulating (imagining) the possible, the probable, and the preferable future based on the past. However, we will use an appropriate twist:

> The focus of our attention will not be on predictions based on the likely outcomes of current trends and experiences of the *past*. Instead we will focus on the potential of the human mind and what this mind can **imagine** for the *future*.

Accepting our ever-changing world, we concede that in order to arrive at a more accurate understanding of *who we are*, we must focus our attention on *who we are becoming*. Although the acceptance of who we *have been*, based on our past, allows us the ability to make an educated guess as to *who we might be*, the prediction cannot develop into a complete and true picture unless we consider the potential of who we can *become*.

Making the future instead of the past the focal point and direction of our thought and effort will help us to arrive at a better understanding of our destination, which in prospection (the opposite of retrospection), will allow us to see ourselves more clearly as who we really are. Once we have a better understanding of our future, our ability to enjoy the present will increase substantially as we understand the purpose and impact that our experiences today might have on who we will become tomorrow.

30. THE HUMAN MIND IS THE KEY TO THE FUTURE

The basis for what we will become in the future originates in the human mind. Our unique ability to imagine and contemplate things we have not yet experienced allows us the potential to expand and change our current way of thinking into realms that our ancestors could never have imagined.

But how is it possible that our minds can form an image or an idea of someone or something that we have not yet met or experienced, or to which we have not been exposed at some point in our past? These questions cannot be answered unless we accept the possibility that perhaps there exist other human beings somewhere else in the Universe who have already experienced our past and present, as well as our future. As they live in what will become our future reality, we currently live in their past reality. We must also consider that we have lived before and that those things which we *imagine* are simply the recollection of the experiences of our past.

31. ADVANCED HUMAN INTELLIGENCE IS PROVABLE

The point in human history upon this earth at which we currently find ourselves is a considerable improvement in advancement over the many years of our past human existence (at least for a few of us). Even as we have progressed, there remains a possibility that there are other human colonies existing in other parts of the Universe that have advanced many, many years beyond the point we have reached. Although this seems impossible to the closed-mind that has been conditioned by others—who have centered their perspective only on the past (those who are logical, responsible, practical, intellectual, and clinical)—to the imagination of a *little* one's mind (who sees life as wonderful, beautiful, magical, a miracle), it makes perfect sense.

We have already proven that we can attain levels of knowledge and technological advancements that once seemed impossible to those who lived in our past. Now the question remains just how far we can progress in the future and how high we can reach into the vast possibilities that we have yet to discover. With the future as our focal point, we will consider what we have learned in the past and combine it with both what we presently know and experience today and what we can imagine to be in the future. Upon doing so, we will arrive at a better understanding of *who we are* and *why we exist*.

32. WE HAVE MUCH TO LEARN ABOUT LIFE AND DEATH

Our focus on the future takes us to one inescapable conclusion about life and death. At this current state of human development upon this earth, we must accept the fact that we are going to die someday. However, the twist in our study of human life includes the potential of what the human mind can *imagine*—including beyond, or even in place of, the seemingly inevitable event of death.

Our ability to imagine a life *without* death has made many discoveries and technologies possible (including the development of new ways to combat disease), which will eventually lead to the engineering of our DNA makeup in such a way that we will stop aging. Then, after we stop killing each other, we will have a good chance at living indefinitely. The possibility of never growing old and eliminating all deformity and disease is not a question of *if* we can do it, but *when* we will.

Our current understanding of "death" ends with the process of our physical bodies breaking down into the elements of the earth to become what they once were—food for other organisms. Death brings on decomposition, which leads to bacterial consumption, which adds nutrients to the earth. A carrot, for example, needs these nutrients from the soil in order to grow properly. Through natural processes, our bodies eventually become the same foods that they once needed to construct and maintain themselves. Our bodies are more connected to our ancestors than we would like to think (i.e., the carrots that we eat could once have absorbed the body of a decomposed ancestor).

But is our body *who we are*? Or is it simply some sort of a receptacle for holding the **real** us?

We know that our thoughts are generated and our memories stored in our brain. Current technology has proven absolutely that the *essence of who we are* (i.e., our thoughts, sensations, memories, and the ability to think) resides in our brain. Modern science has the ability to isolate the head from the body and, with artificial means that pump blood to the brain, keep the *essence* of the individual (animal or human) completely alive and conscious. Those humans with deformed bodies or who have no sensation or any use of the body from the neck down are still considered human and just as "alive" as the rest of us. So, our body is certainly not *who we are*. But is our brain?

33. ONLY THE HUMAN BEING IS CONSCIOUS OF BEING ALIVE

Consciousness is the state of being awake and aware of what is going on around us. It begins and is acted upon in our brain. "Waking up" or "becoming alive" is the first thing that happens to us when we are born. Yet, this seemingly simple human act (of becoming a conscious, breathing human) is one that all the "Great Minds" (in their own minds) of the world have never been able to explain.

Science thinks that it has solved many questions of physics. It believes and defends its position that its experiments and observations have led to extraordinary discoveries that have affected human life enormously. But the simple reality of consciousness still eludes its understanding. Will science ever be able to measure the onset of consciousness in newborns? It has speculated that consciousness might be similar to what physicists call a "phase transition," which, in this situation, would be an abrupt and sudden transformation resulting from microscopic changes in the brain's structure.

Science has witnessed this transition in chemistry and in other scientific observations, but has still made no attempt to prescribe a *law* to the phenomenon of what makes an infant transform from an unconscious, non-breathing, heart-pumping fetus, into a breathing and conscious human being. Again, it takes us back to the question of whether *we* are the body that forms inside the womb, or if *we* are something outside of the body that enters therein upon taking our first breath in a new environment.

The study of consciousness has always been considered too abstract, too subjective, or too difficult to study scientifically. But as we begin to properly understand *who we are*, it will emerge as a viable and necessary field of study and observaton. Consciousness can no longer be set aside and relegated to superstition and the invention of its own making—human imagination. It must be the first question solved, as it is the first thing that occurs once we become *alive* upon our first breath outside of the womb.

We not only need an answer to the mystery of human awareness, but also a proper understanding of dreams, sleep, the phantom feelings felt by amputees, our biological clock (*circadian rhythm*), memories, and last, but certainly not least—the most unique and self-fulfilling part of our human consciousness—the sense of humor associated with laughter. Having an answer to these mysteries of the mind will contribute to a complete and better understanding of our "self" and our **true** "essence."

34. OUR CONSCIOUSNESS SUPPORTS THE IDEA OF AN *ESSENCE*

Human imagination has tied consciousness to the idea of a soul—the concept that in each of us there exists an immaterial *essence* that survives death and perhaps even predates birth. It is believed that the *soul* allows us to think and feel, remember and reason, and that our individual personality, individuality, and humanity originate from it. Perhaps the first step is to understand "imagination," including where it comes from and how it is associated with our consciousness. Then we can arrive at a better understanding of exactly how we have *imagined* another part of us that is *separate* from our physical body, which body takes its first breath at birth and exhales its last breath at death.

From what science has surmised, the operations of the "soul" are attributed to physical processes in the brain. But exactly how these chemical and electrical processes send signals between trillions of brain cells and are transformed into the actions and experiences of the *human soul* (thoughts, emotions, and a sense of self) is still unknown.

No one can doubt that a strong correlation exists between the brain and consciousness. In understanding who we are, we need more than just a correlation; we need an explanation. How and why brain processes give rise to consciousness is the question that needs to be answered.

35. OUR HUMANITY WAS ESTABLISHED BEFORE OUR LIFE ON EARTH

Our common humanity was established within each of us long before this solar system came into existence. To gain a proper understanding of how this happened, it is necessary to use logic and common sense as we consider a *possible* human scenario based on what we know about our current world.

36. WE CAN IMAGINE THE PERFECT HUMAN WORLD

Imagine for a moment, that in the future we eventually figure out how to live with each other in peace and harmony. As science and technology advances, we learn to use these advancements for the mutual benefit of the human race, and at that same time, we learn to live in harmony with the natural environment of the earth. We learn to correct both our social and environmental mistakes of the past, and the earth becomes a wonderful place for humans to live.

With our increased knowledge and advancements, we learn to engineer the DNA makeup of our bodies and eliminate aging and death altogether. We learn to live as vibrant, healthy human beings with equal opportunities to enjoy our individual lives. Imagine that this existence then becomes an eternity.

Imagine that we finally develop and live in a perfect human world. Although *improbable* with the current forms of governments and socioeconomic systems we allow to control our lives, it is *not impossible* to **imagine** that we can accomplish this goal as a unified human race. It is not impossible to *imagine* a perfect world. In fact, it is what we hope for. "Hope" is the intrinsic measure of our humanity, or better, that which we feel can be *possible* in spite of the *improbabilities* that seem to be part of our present experience.

37. HUMANITY IS FOUNDATIONALIZED IN A PERFECT WORLD

As mentioned above, this "measure of our *humanity*" (hope), was established within us and is one of the main differences between the human life form and all other forms of life.

This is a brief overview of how this "measure" was established:

Once a human society perfects itself, it no longer allows a human being to suffer from unhappiness, pain, or sorrow of any kind—it creates a perfect world! Existing in such a state of joy motivates humans to create other human beings like themselves, who can also enjoy what they are enjoying. When a child is created and introduced into a perfect world, its first and only experiences are of everything that is ***good*** about being a human. Therefore, its **humanity** is established!

38. NEWLY CREATED HUMANS HAVE NO SENSE OF HAPPINESS

However, the newly created human has no **true** sense of enjoyment or happiness because it has nothing with which to compare its **perfect human reality**—the only experience it has ever had. Once the new human becomes aware that the Universe revolves around it and that everything in the Universe exists for its enjoyment, it begins to realize just how powerful it is. It understands that it has dominion over every other life form (every piece of matter) that exists.

There is a stark distinction, however, between the newly created humans and their creators. The creators (the advanced human beings) seem to have a concept of joy and happiness that the new humans do not and cannot appreciate. Though the creators try to explain how wonderful and **perfect** the world and Universe is, the new humans cannot fully comprehend such things. Consequently, they need to be allowed the experience of contrast and opposition in all things. They must be given the opportunity to find out for themselves what is so wonderful about their perfect world.

39. WE ALL DESIRE OUR OWN PIECE OF THE UNIVERSE

Furthermore, every human being wants their own piece of the Universe, a part that they can call their own. A *perfect* human society cannot continue to create human beings without providing enough space for them to live and experience life, according to the individual desires of each free-willed human.

40. OUR SOLAR SYSTEM WAS CREATED ESPECIALLY FOR US

Advanced creators have the technology and intelligence to travel to places in the Universe where there are no planetary systems. The purpose is twofold: to provide a place for the experience of opposition (the contrast to the **perfect human world**) and to establish a place in the Universe for each newly created individual human being. In this expanse of space, they create enough worlds for the new batch of human beings, who were originally brought into existence on *their creators' own planet* in their creators' own solar system. They know how to create a Sun, moons, and planets that will accommodate the needs of this *new group* of human beings.

One of the newly created planets is then provided for the enlightenment of the *advanced*, *perfect offspring*, to help them experience everything opposite and in contrast to their perfect life in a *perfect world*. On this planet, the newly created humans are provided human bodies that are *imperfect* and unable to remember anything beyond their current feeble few-years-at-a-time lives on their now ***imperfect*** world.

This is basically *who we are* and *why we exist* in this current world that we call Earth.

41. THIS BOOK ANSWERS THE VITAL QUESTIONS OF OUR EXISTENCE

Spontaneously, especially during times of deep reflection when we are not affected by the current struggles of living in an *imperfect* world, our minds are prone to reflect upon subconscious memories—real energy patterns emitting from somewhere inside of our heads that seem to directly affect our emotions. These seemingly irretrievable memories cause us to long for, hope for, and crave a *better world* than the one in which we now live. They affect our perception of how we and others are treated, and make us constantly aware that our human society is far from what it *should* or *could* be.

How do we know how our society *should* or *could* be? How is it that we can mentally create a *measure* (a hope) by which we determine that there has to be something better than what we currently have in our world today? What causes our humanity? Now we know.

But as logical and probable as it may seem (that we are actually *advanced, perfect human beings going through an imperfect experience*), there are still pieces of the puzzle that keep us wondering if it could actually be true.

This book, **HUMAN REALITY—Who We Are and Why We Exist**, will give the people of the world every piece of the puzzle needed so that everything about our existence makes perfect sense!

SUMMARY

Once one has read this entire book, he or she will know **human reality**—*who we are* and *why we exist.* Once we understand who we **really** are, who we **really were**, and who we **really will be**, we will be able to reshape our world into an environment where we can be guaranteed that we will all have the potential to become who we really choose to be.

This book answers many of life's questions in a way that has never before been presented for human consideration. If read with an open mind, a whole new perspective of *human reality* will unfold and, with the new insight, we will gain a better understanding of ourselves—both individually and collectively. With this understanding, we will be free to experience the reason ***why*** *we exist* and to become a lot happier!

The reader will conclude that the reason **why** we all exist is to experience happiness; and that the struggle to survive limits the amount of happiness that we can experience in this life (because we have no proper understanding of **what** we are struggling for). The answers given in this book will help one to increase his or her happiness by explaining the purpose of the life that we try so hard to preserve.

This book, however, was not written for the reader's happiness alone. One of the main purposes for this book is to unify us, as a race of human beings. If we will learn **true reality** as a group, representing *all* human beings on this planet, we can transform our world into one of peace and security wherein happiness is no longer a pursuit, but rather a guarantee. We can achieve happiness together as THE HUMAN RACE, which will bring greater joy and happiness to each individual. By living **true** *human reality* TOGETHER, we can demonstrate our *true* and collective HUMANITY, which in reality is the *essence* within all of us.

Universal Reality

CHAPTER TWO

If there has been a first man he must have been born without father or mother—which is repugnant to nature. For there could not have been a first egg to give a beginning to birds, or there should have been a first bird which gave a beginning to eggs; for a bird comes from an egg.

—Aristotle

1. THEORIES DO NOT SOLVE THE HUMAN QUESTION

The age-old mystery, "Which came first, the chicken or the egg?" is a logical question to consider as we ponder our existence. More broadly—which came first, the parents or the child? Philosophers and scholars have never been able to conclusively solve this puzzle.

Science has attempted to prove that life started, not as anything like a chicken or an egg, but as some kind of unknown bacterium. Scientists call their theory "Evolution." This theory suggests that somehow something similar to either the chicken or the egg came into existence by means of this bacterium going through a lengthy process of adaptation and transformation over millions of years. This theory was later expanded to include the "Big Bang theory." This generally accepted theory proposes that the Universe started from a single point and expanded from there.

In considering both of these theories, especially the "Big Bang theory," many questions remain unanswered; therefore, they cannot be **real truth**. A reasonable explanation cannot be given for how **some***thing* can start from **no***thing*. If there was a big bang, then how did it start? Where did the elements that were necessary to create the "big bang" exist at the time of the explosion? If there was a big bang that was responsible for forming the

Universe, then we are forced to accept the possibility that another big bang *might* end it.

Many other theories have been developed by the human mind in an attempt to arrive at a comfortable balance. We have continually searched for a reasonable conclusion about how we came into existence since the time we were old enough to consider our individual existence apart from everyone else. We search out any explanation that gives us some semblance of assurance that our life has a valid meaning. This search has led to a wide variety of different speculations. But with each new theory, more questions arise; and in an attempt to answer each new question, another theory is proposed.

"**Real truth**" is the final answer. It gives a conclusive and ultimate explanation that requires no further discussion or change. **Real truth** debunks all ideas and beliefs that are formed through speculation or conjecture devised in the human mind. It ends our search and gives us the comfort we need to be assured that life does, indeed, have a purposeful meaning.

Based on the actuality of **real truth**, it follows that there must be a conclusive and clear answer to the mystery, "Which came first, the chicken or the egg?"

2. THE UNIVERSE AND ALL THINGS HAVE *ALWAYS* EXISTED

The simple answer to the mystery of "the Chicken and the Egg" is: **Neither came first**. They have both **always** existed. There has never been a time when either a chicken or an egg could not be found in some part of the infinite Universe. Every chicken started as an egg, which was laid by a chicken, which started as an egg, and so on *ad infinitum* (endlessly).

Likewise, the Universe has always been. The most basic and fundamental components of every piece of organized matter have always been. Although matter can be found in many different forms, there has never been a time when it (in one of its present living or non-living forms) could not be found somewhere in the Universe.

Using water as an example of a form of non-living matter, there are places in the Universe where it exists as a solid (ice), a liquid (water), or a gas (steam)— a simple compound of the known elements, hydrogen and oxygen. There has never been a time when water has not existed. There has never been a time when the known and *unknown* elements have not been present somewhere in the vast Universe. There is no such thing as empty space or "nothingness." Where there are no elements, there exists instead all of the components (protons, neutrons, and electrons) from which all elements are composed.

3. SCIENTIFIC THEORIES CONFUSE MORE THAN ENLIGHTEN

Of course, this "new" information counters the explanations and theories of science, which have continually failed to lead us to any sensible answer to the question of *who we are*. Most modern-day scientific theories do not fully answer our questions, nor do they agree with our common sense. Even the power of human imagination has a very difficult time providing a reasonable answer to this question of the chicken and the egg.

4. REAL TRUTH OFTEN CONTRADICTS CURRENT KNOWLEDGE

Real truth does not leave any unanswered questions. To be accepted as the final and unquestionable authoritative answer, **real truth** must be easily understood by everyone and leave none of us with a follow-up question to consider. And most importantly, we must feel comfortable with the answer.

The difference between **real truth** and accepted *knowledge* is that the latter is what we have been taught to accept as truth (i.e., the earth is flat) and the former is how things *really* are (the earth is round). Although some of us would like to think of ourselves as more *knowledgeable* than the average person, thus maintaining a claim of superior intelligence over others, *true reality* supports the fact that all of our modern knowledge will one day be replaced with completely different knowledge. The smartest and most intelligent of today will be the "cavemen" of tomorrow. Nothing, therefore, that we suppose we know today is actually **real truth**.

This "evolution" of knowledge will continue until all of the questions and "missing links" are discovered. Each **real truth** discovered will not necessarily support the current knowledge, but it will make *complete* sense and leave no room for questions. And it will never change.

5. THE UNIVERSE HAVING ALWAYS EXISTED MAKES SENSE

Some speculate that a so-called "explosion" or "expansion" created the galaxies of the Universe with a "Big Bang," which was caused by certain elements reacting with others. If this were the case, then the elements that created the explosion existed *before* the big bang; therefore, the explosion could not have created them.

If elements make up the Universe, and these same elements existed *before* the Universe was created, then they must have been present in some sort of environment in order for them to interact and explode or expand to create a Universe. In other words, if a big bang created all the elements of the Universe, then what created the "bang"? The whole theory leads to a mass of confusion. It just doesn't make sense (and it never will)! Few of us are comfortable with this conclusion of how we came to be.

In contrast, the idea that the Universe has always been, and that the organization of matter into new living and non-living substances is and always has been going on, makes perfect sense. The proposition supports some scientific conclusions that most elements (the matter that makes up all substances) cannot be created or destroyed. Advancements in science and understanding, however, prove that elements *can* be destroyed and changed because they are *made up* of other sub-particles. Therefore, it is these "sub-particles" that cannot be destroyed and have always existed in their natural form in the Universe. (Throughout this book, these "sub-particles that cannot be destroyed" will be referred to as "protons, neutrons, and electrons.")

6. THE CREATION OF NEW GALAXIES EXPANDS THE UNIVERSE

One thing current scientists have gotten right is that the Universe *seems* to be expanding (and to a scientific mind, this gives credence to the theory that it is expanding away from the point of the "Big Bang"). As new galaxies with solar and planetary systems are created in the endless *dark matter* of space, where none were found before, it would *appear* as if the Universe is continually expanding. It also *appears*, from our Earthly vantage point, that some galaxies are colliding with others. However, it is the "vantage point" from which we make our observations that creates the false perceptions of what is actually going on in the Universe.

It isn't hard to comprehend a Universe that has no boundaries, borders, or limitations of space, and which appears to expand as new galaxies and solar systems are created. The outside Universe, apart from this earth, would not exist if we could not observe matter from our "vantage point." If there were no lights in outer space, then it would appear that nothing else exists "out there" except for us. Science has been very sloppy in proposing theories of truth that are based on its limited observational vantage point, especially when we consider that it has only been a relatively very short time period in which humans have been observing the expanse of space and speculating on what all of those lights actually are.

If we observe that the lights found in space change over time, by increasing in number and intensity for example, we would detect an expansion of observable matter; in other words, our Universe would appear as if it is expanding. It has always been this way and will continually be this way forever. It is what we can call "Universal Infinite."

7. ACCEPTING "UNIVERSAL INFINITE" ANSWERS WHO WE ARE

The hardest thing for the human mind to conceive (because the mind currently exists on a plane of thought that *begins* with birth and *ends* with death) is that **everything** has **always** existed in one form or another. Although it makes sense—and even though it would answer many of the mysteries humans cannot solve with their limited view of the Universe—it still remains a premise that is not *easily* comprehended.

The idea that human beings have **always** existed contradicts the known fact that each of us, as a mortal individual upon this earth, had a beginning. To our finite minds, it is impossible that we could have existed forever, and if we have not, then how could it be that other human beings have existed forever?

In developing a correct understanding of *who we are*, we need to consider everything that we currently know about our *self*. None of us can remember a time when we did not exist; because of this, it is easier to accept the fact that we might have existed **forever**. Even though the human mind cannot comprehend **Universal Infinite** in this manner, it does not necessarily change the fact that it is *true reality*. Furthermore, if we are willing to accept as **real truth** that everything has always existed, we will place ourselves in a better position to fully comprehend *who we are* and answer many other questions about our existence.

8. INTELLIGENT REASONING SUPPORTS NON-EARTH LIFE

If water (the basis for most forms of life) has always been, though in different forms throughout the Universe, then it should make reasonable sense that human beings (another form of living matter) have always been, and can also be found in different stages of development in all parts of the Universe.

Let's hypothetically suppose that, theoretically and statistically, we randomly evolved from bacteria. If this is the **real truth**, then it is **probable** and **possible** that the same thing could happen and has happened already in other parts of the vast Universe. To say it couldn't happen anywhere else would be intelligently unreasonable and irresponsible. Our own existence proves its probability!

9. HUMANS ARE THE HIGHEST LIFE FORM IN THE UNIVERSE

In order to come to a complete understanding of who we are and why we exist, we must be willing to accept the following:

First: **Human beings are the greatest and most significant life form** (or any other compilation of matter) **in the Universe.**

Second: **All human beings, no matter in what stage of their development they are found throughout the Universe, are indisputably equal in their potential to optimize their existence as free-willed life forms.**

It is a false idea that higher forms of intelligent life above humans exist in the Universe. Ideas such as "aliens," science-fiction "creatures," or non-human monsters or machines will be expelled from our thinking once we learn more about how our creative thinking process and imagination work. For now, we must consider what we know to be the **real truth** by being honest about what is happening upon this earth: humans are indeed the most intelligent and complicated life form in existence here. There are no other forms of life that are comparably close in intelligence, or better, that have the same *potential to optimize their existence*, as human beings.

10. ADVANCED HUMANS EXIST THROUGHOUT THE UNIVERSE

If humans have always existed, it would logically follow that advanced societies of human beings also exist and can be found throughout the Universe in infinite numbers. How far do human beings need to *advance* until they know all that there is to know? How long before we know about **every atom** that makes up **every element** that makes up **every molecule** that makes up **every cell** that makes up **every part** of **every** living and non-living particle of matter that exists and has *always* existed in the Universe? Regardless of how long we think it would take, only human beings (and no other life forms) will ever attain a complete knowledge of the source of all matter. Furthermore, human beings are the only life form that seems to care about attaining this knowledge.

There are human beings who have this knowledge and understand it as a **real truth**. Along with this knowledge, they have the capability (the power and ability) of using it to do *whatever* they desire. Consequently, HUMAN BEINGS CONTROL EVERY ASPECT OF THE UNIVERSE. THE UNIVERSE EXISTS EXCLUSIVELY FOR HUMAN BEINGS AND SUPPORTS THE DESIRE OF HUMAN BEINGS TO OPTIMIZE (make the best of) THEIR EXISTENCE.

11. ADVANCED HUMANS CREATE MATTER FOR ENJOYMENT

What is it that highly advanced humans, who *know* it all, have *experienced* it all, and have the *power* to do it all, would *want* to do? It would seem that in such a state of existence they would find themselves quite bored with their lives. What more could they experience than what they already have? If they already know how all matter is going to act or react in any given circumstance, what else is there to stifle their monotony and boredom?

If, on the other hand, they organized matter in such a way that they *did not know*, even with their infinite intelligence, how it was going to act or react, they would succeed in creating for themselves an interesting, exciting, and often entertaining diversion (somewhat akin to our current obsession and enjoyment in watching a "hidden camera" or home video show, where we are surprised at what humans do).

In order to accomplish this, these advanced beings would have to organize matter in such a way that the creation could have "free will" with the same ability to act and react to its environment as they do. In providing this opportunity to newly created human beings like themselves, they would be successful at enhancing their own enjoyment and happiness, thus *optimizing their own existence.*

12. HUMAN BEINGS ARE THE ONLY FREE-WILLED LIFE FORM

These highly advanced human "scientists" (using the term loosely) organize matter into other beings like themselves and allow their creations to have free will. "Free will" is the motivational force for action of all human beings, who do not have preprogrammed instinctual behaviors. Those with free will have the power to make choices that are unconstrained by external forces. Every other living organism is preprogrammed with instinctual instructions within its makeup, which information determines its actions and reactions to its environment. In other words, advanced human beings program (or command) a plant or animal to do whatever they expect of it, without the ability for it to respond with free will. Upon preprogramming matter in this way, a creator could certainly become bored by just watching the animals and plants, as their actions would always have the same outcome in similar environments and situations. However, this is not the case with other human, *free-willed* creations.

Advanced humans create galaxies and solar systems for these newly created, free-willed organisms (i.e., humans) patterned after the environments in which humans have always existed forever throughout the Universe. These "environments" are the worlds provided for the human beings to *optimize their existence* (i.e., to experience continual happiness).

Most life forms can be categorized and placed into two main kingdoms of "plants" and "animals." Human life, however, belongs in a completely different category all its own. Humans have the ability to act according to their *own* will without being controlled by perfunctory instincts. This ability results in humans having the most advantages of any life form in the Universe.

13. FREE WILL ALLOWS FOR INDEPENDENT CHOICES

The human being is designed by advanced creators to do pretty much what it wants to do. Because it cannot be programmed by any source other than itself, it becomes a uniquely individual, free-willed life form—there are no others like it anywhere in the Universe. This is what separates the human being from all other forms of life.

Newly created humans, therefore, are not preprogrammed in any way. They are allowed the same abilities and potential possessed by their more advanced creators (parents). Although our current *imperfect* human bodies have natural instinctual drives to survive and reproduce, we have the power to control these instincts and choose what each of us wants to do with our own existence.

We can choose to eat or not to eat, even until our body grows to excess or dies of malnutrition. We can choose to have sex or not. We can control the production of offspring that the sexual act produces through advanced birth-control techniques. In fact, our desire for sex has little to do with creating life, but all to do with satisfying the needs of our physical body; and there is no other life form that even comes close to enjoying the effects of sexuality in the same way that a human does.

No other life form can consciously make these kinds of choices. But because of our unique ability to make these choices, what we decide to do with our free will is completely unknown, even by our creators, *until* we do it!

14. FREE-WILLED INDIVIDUALITY ENTERTAINS OUR CREATORS

In our own lives, we are usually surprised and entertained by watching little children play. We enjoy watching them use their newfound freedom of movement and choice to experience new things and situations. Even advanced human parents, who have been around forever, will never become bored from observing the antics demonstrated by human free will and the situations into which we, as their children, place ourselves.

With our current technology, we can secretly videotape the actions and reactions of human nature and spend endless hours watching the unknown results of free-willed behavior. With much more advanced technology, we will one day be able to watch the behavior of other humans on other planets in other solar systems and be entertained forever by observing their interactions with different environments and situations. Likewise, one day, with the same advanced technology, we will be able to observe our own past actions and humor ourselves at our own antics, performed when we did not know that we were actually being recorded!

It is a wonderful experience of joy and happiness for advanced creators to give new human beings the potential to live as they once lived and become as they are now, and watch the "new humans" progress to where they have. This potential does not necessarily mean that most of us will become like our advanced parents/creators, but rather that we will have the ability to be completely content with whomever we *choose* to be through the use of our unconditional free will.

15. WE NEED NEW EXPERIENCES TO INDIVIDUALIZE

No matter in what stage of development humans are found throughout the Universe, they will always be the *only* "free-willed" life forms that ever exist. And as unique and as different as we are from any other life form, we can only be satisfied and find happiness by participating in never-ending *new* experiences.

We must be allowed to fully participate and take advantage of these *new experiences* with our exclusive free will in order for us to grow, individualize, and find joy in our existence. There are worlds without end in the Universe where the human experience is taking place at different stages of development and advancement. In each of these stages, human beings are taking advantage of their existence and *optimizing* their life to support their unique individuality. The culmination of all experience is to bring happiness to the individual (although the specific purpose here on earth seems to be opposite of that—this will be explained later). This is ***why*** *we exist.*

16. OUR CURRENT EXPERIENCE CAUSES US CONFUSION

The concept of Universal Infinite (again, that **everything** has **always** existed in one form or another) is hard for us to accept; this is because we have been conditioned to accept, as a consequence of our current existence, the conclusive fact that we were born and that we will die. This part of **real truth** leads many of us to question the proposed idea that humans have always existed.

Being born appears to have started our existence, and death seems to end it. So the idea that everything has always existed (though it can make sense of many things) still leaves us perplexed, as we are unable to fully comprehend it and find comfort with it. Our limited existence of having *only* one lifetime upon this planet would be sufficient if it were possible to learn all we need to know about *who we are* during the very short seven or so decades that we are alive in a mortal body. But that is not possible. And those who die at a young age would have even less time to learn about themselves. Therefore, these facts point us to the *reality* that we have all experienced **many lives** upon this earth, each one putting us in a position to *optimize our individual existence.*

17. EACH NEW LIFE EXPERIENCE HELPS US INDIVIDUALIZE

The law of Universal Infinite does not negate the fact that each of us had a beginning as a human, but also supports the reality that others *like us* have *always* existed. We did have a beginning, but we will have *no end.* If this is the case, and we know we are going to die and discontinue being the person we are recognized as while living in mortality, then *who we are* cannot be the part of us that dies. If *we* are not the part of us that dies, then we were not the part that was born either. Therefore, we are **not** just our body, or better, our current mortal body is **not who we really are**. All of this might not make sense right now, but it soon will, as the reader continues to learn **real truths** that have never been considered before.

SUMMARY

Matter has **always existed** and cannot be created or destroyed; therefore, it will **always exist** in **Universal Infinite**. Human beings, as organized life forms composed of matter, are the most advanced life forms found in the Universe and have **always existed and always will**. Human societies on worlds like our planet earth **have always existed and always will**.

Humans exist in these societies in different stages of development. The most advanced humans know all **real truth** and find joy in their existence by organizing matter, or better, creating other humans that have the power of free will to act and react without preprogramming. These advanced humans create environments where other "less-advanced" people (such as ourselves) can learn to enjoy their humanity through the experience of many mortalities.

The singular uniqueness of the free will provided to human beings alone (and to no other life forms), allows us to develop into individuals with our own sense of self apart from everyone else. We will eventually choose what will make us happy; and ultimately, we will **always be happy**. This is the **reality of Universal Infinite**!

The Human Essence

CHAPTER THREE

We are in fact convinced that if we are ever to have pure knowledge of anything, we must get rid of the body and contemplate things by themselves with the soul by itself.

—Socrates

1. THE ESSENCE IS THE FOUNDATION OF A HUMAN BEING

In the creation of a *new* human, the first thing that advanced creators/parents do is to provide this person with a body and a unique, free-willed *essence.* This "essence" constitutes the actuality of the self—everything that this newly created person will become. The *essence* establishes uniqueness and individuality and, together with a likewise *personally unique* physical body, distinguishes each of us from the rest of the human race in the Universe.

The responsibility falls upon the creators to ensure that this *new* human being is free to fulfill the purpose of its creation. This "purpose" is to experience life and to learn and decide what brings happiness to the unique, free-willed human being. A big part of this happiness is being valued as an individual apart from everyone and everything else in the Universe! And only a ***human*** *essence* has the potential to fulfill this *purpose*, or to experience continual and lasting personal happiness.

2. OUR ESSENCE IS AN ADVANCED RECORDING DEVICE

The human *essence* can be compared to a highly developed, memory-recording and storage device. Advanced human creators exist in a more technologically advanced society and utilize new blank *essences* to create other human beings, in order to continue human life throughout the Universe. Because the *essence* records and stores the experiences generated by the sensory receptors of sight, smell, sound, taste, and touch, it requires a body in order to become operational. All human beings, advanced and otherwise, have an *essence* that is identical to every other when it is created. The only difference comes from the variety of experiences recorded upon it in the course of each individual discovering their happiness in a human body. The recording and storage of our free-willed choices, as we use our body to respond to the environment in which we find ourselves, allows for a recollection of events. This "recollection" is an actual *collection* of what we record through our senses. It provides us with the ability to recall the experiences that give each of us our individuality and uniqueness.

Because we are free-willed life forms, nothing is preprogrammed in our essence. During our lifetimes, i.e., when our essence is inside a physical body, we are exposed to various environments in which we can use our free will and the functions of our body to create our own unique experiences. We record these experiences and play them back by using the sensory organs of our physical body. Our individuality is created by the wide variety of experiences we are exposed to and how we each choose to respond to them.

Only when our *essence* enters a physical body do we become a living *human*. We need a body to generate our experiences and an *essence* to record them, so that the body can play them back for us later and thereby express our unique individuality. This "playback" (recollection) allows us to enjoy our individuality, because each of us is the *only* one in the Universe who responds to our environment exactly the way that we do! Without either part (our *essence* or our body), we are not a *living* human being.

Our current *imperfect* body can be compared to a highly advanced computer with its own internal memory and processor (the brain). This "computer" contains the software applications of sight, smell, sound, taste, and touch. Our *essence* can be compared to a separate external hard drive that acts like a memory bank with an infinite storage capacity. It also has its own source of power apart from the power provided by the computer (our *imperfect* body).

When connected to the computer (our body), this powerful recording/storage device (our *essence*) is always on and records everything that the computer does. If the computer or any of its components fail (i.e., the body dies), the *essence* will be always available with a perfect recollection of all previous activity. Even though the *essence* will always work perfectly, the body in which it is placed does not have to work perfectly. If the computer is defective, it doesn't matter how *good* the "hard drive" is. The computer can only function within the limitations allowed by its efficiency and lack of defects. Until a *perfect computer* (perfect human body) is created that will never fail, other fallible computers (*imperfect* bodies) are made available to operate with the memory recorded on the external hard drive (our *essence*). When this "external hard drive" is finally plugged into a *perfect* "computer" that will never fail, the *new, perfect* computer will be able to use the memories that were recorded by all the previous *old* computers, *plus* create its own new memories.

Although the fallible computers (the *imperfect* bodies) can be constructed of materials that wear out over time and *can* fail, the separate hard drive (the *essence*) is constructed of materials that *never* wear out. Whether the computer (body) is fallible or perfect, the external hard drive (the *essence*) is programmed to *never* fail to do what it was intended to do. It was created and programmed to record and store the memories created by the computer (the body) in which it operates.

Our current technology allows us to create all types of computers, but only from materials that are subject to wear and tear, and that break down over time. All of the *known* elements (which make up the components of our computers as well as the material of our physical bodies) slowly give off their energy over time and eventually break down into their basic elementary forms. For example, a computer of today is actually an assembly of basic elements bound together by their energy levels to create the metal, plastic, and other materials from which it is constructed. Over time, the bonds that hold the elements together lose their strength and break down. These bonds can also be destroyed by external interactions such as the application of heat (fire) or solvents. This is what modern science calls the *Second Law of Thermodynamics*. That "law" mandates that all things not in equilibrium experience increasing entropy (a measure of deterioration or disorder) over time.

3. THE ESSENCE IS MADE OF UNDISCOVERED ELEMENTS

There are elements in the Universe that our scientists *do not know* exist, as they have not been discovered. These elements are formed from equally unknown atoms and make up the molecules that form the *human essence*. As stated, this *essence* is the most advanced recording device found anywhere in the Universe. Its ability to record and store information is as infinite as the Universe itself.

The bonds created by these unknown elements in forming the *essence* do not deteriorate over time. The Second Law of Thermodynamics does not apply to these elements. Once these elements are combined, their bonds become just as indestructible as each element itself. Only advanced human creators know what these elements are and how to use them.

The molecules that form our *essence* are preprogrammed to store recorded information, which, again, contains the sum and substance of our individual existence. The highly specialized (currently unknown) elements that make up the molecules forming the *essence*, are what provide the capacity to store and play back an infinite amount of information.

These specialized elements allow the structure of the *essence* to expand its memory capacity continually and infinitely. Thus, it can be best described, in modern terms, as a *perpetual memory disk of infinite capacity*. No matter how much information is recorded on it, its makeup and structure perform endless functions of storage, categorization, and defragmentation for future recall. This activity takes place by the *essence's* constant energy levels replicating themselves, very much like our muscle cells replicate when the need arises. However, the elements that form the *essence* expand on a subatomic *energy* level and always maintain the same mass, whereas the cells that make up muscle, for example, replicate themselves and create more mass. (Although modern scientists would love to know how this is done, they will not be given this information for the same reason they have not yet discovered all of the elements of the Universe. This reason will be explained later.)

The elements of the *essence* do not reflect light. Therefore, the *essence* remains as invisible to the human eye as the elements that make up the atmosphere of earth. It cannot be photographed, nor is its mass affected by the gravitational pull of any celestial body. In other words, it is weightless and remains at a constant mass no matter in what part of the Universe it is found.

4. THE EVIDENCE OF THE EXISTENCE OF THE ESSENCE

Science has failed to make any meaningful progress in understanding the human mind. This is because it doesn't consider the possibility that the physical human brain is not *solely* responsible for the ability of a human being to *reason*, *dream*, and *imagine*, which all offer evidence of the existence of the *essence*. Science stubbornly rejects the possibility that something might enter the brain region upon birth that is not only responsible for the body's ability to start breathing, but is also completely responsible for consciousness and for our partially accessible subconscious mind.

Science, with all of its pride and glory in its research and observation, rejects the existence of a separate *human essence* that exists apart from the human body. However, if science would just consider the possibility of the existence of the *essence*, then it would be able to solve all the other mysteries of the mind. Because science doesn't accept the possibility, we will solve the mysteries without the help of scientific observation and study!

5. BIRTH SUPPORTS THE EXISTENCE OF AN ESSENCE

Let's take a closer look at how our *essence* reacts with our body. The reader must now use the human ability to reason, wonder, create and imagine; one must also possess the ambition to understand something that he or she has never considered before.

Let's begin our exploration and understanding of the mysteries of life with the miracle of birth:

When a body is inside of the womb, it performs automatic functions that are controlled by the elements that make up the body and the womb. The heart, for example, develops before the brain, and pumps continuously as its muscles are instructed by the DNA patterns it is given. As the fetus progresses and develops, it remains in a coma-like state, unconscious of its surroundings. The movements of the fetus felt by the mother are the natural reflexes associated with the muscles and nerves of the body as it develops. Just as one cannot stop the automatic reflexes of the body outside of the womb (sometimes occurring even in a dead body), a fetus' reflexes *inside* the womb are likewise controlled by the body of either the developing fetus or the mother's own body. It is **not** a conscious act of the fetus' brain, because the heart begins to pump before the brain has even developed! This supports the *reality* that a fetus is *not a complete* and *conscious* human being until the *essence* enters the body upon birth.

Any time a movement is made, from the pumping of the heart to the sucking of the thumb inside the womb, a chemical change takes place. Elements react with each other to produce the result determined by the DNA instructions of the body. Therefore, we can conclude that every action or reaction that takes place in the fetus is the product of a chemical reaction (or when one element reacts with another), sustained in the environment of the mother's womb.

Science has appropriately theorized that DNA provides the regulations and instructions to tell the molecules of the body what to do, and that the plan each of these molecules follows is incorporated into the makeup of the DNA. However, what DNA does *not* tell the body, and what it is *not* preprogrammed to do, is to mandate when and how we breathe. A developing fetus does *not* have the function of breathing, but a *living* life form can control it at will with its conscious mind.

6. HOW THE ESSENCE ENTERS THE BODY

In all life forms that require oxygen to survive, breathing is a chemical change that takes place when certain muscles are *told* what to do by the elements that are programmed to produce the chemical change. To make the muscles of the diaphragm move, a chemical action must take place in the same manner as it does to make the same muscles move when we laugh. The difference is, the DNA instructions of our body do *not* control the chemical reaction that moves our diaphragm—our *essence* does.

Science has found it difficult to determine why oxygen-dependant life forms begin to breathe once the infant's body has left the mother's womb. It has not ascertained what causes human beings to breathe, because it has not yet discovered what elements participate in producing these reactions (nor will it ever). It does not understand the makeup of our *essence.*

Our *essence* has the ability to control breathing. We can stop breathing anytime we want. We can *willingly* force the stoppage of air in and out of our lungs until we pass out. If we pass out, however, our DNA programming continues to regulate our breathing. The *essence*, though extremely powerful when in a *perfect body*, has a very difficult time controlling any part of an *imperfect* human body that is being controlled by the perfunctorily set DNA patterns. These patterns were already preprogrammed with instructions of how to perform before the *essence* entered the human body. One can stop breathing simply by the will of the mind; this is possible because the *essence* is present. But it is impossible for one to *will* the heart to stop beating. Nevertheless, in some instances of enhanced mental focus, the power of the *essence* can indeed mildly effect other parts of the body that are normally controlled solely by the human body's DNA.

The body has no power to control the *essence*, but the *essence* can control the body. The *essence* and the body are each separate compilations of element structured to perform different functions for the human being. Unfortunately, the current human brain is incapable of allowing the *essence* to perform to its full capacity, or better, to perform to its full potential. In our current *imperfect* bodies, the *essence* acts more subconsciously by itself than it does consciously with the incapable brain.

Upon our initial, primordial creation, our *essence* was placed in a *perfect*, quintessential human body. Later on in our development as a human being, and for a very wise purpose, our *essence* is repeatedly placed in *imperfect* mortal bodies that get sick, grow old, and die. With our current, limited knowledge, and because of our inability to recollect at will what is recorded on our *essence*, we understand the *essence's* entrance into a body as "birth," and its exit from a body as "death."

7. THE ESSENCE IS NATURALLY ATTRACTED TO THE BODY

The matter from which the *essence* is created is naturally attracted to the body that is created for it. As far as current scientific understanding goes, magnetism works by the attraction of negative and positive forces. If the negative end of a magnet is placed near the positive end of another magnet, both will come together naturally without any outside force.

To gain a better understanding of how the *essence* enters the body, and taking into consideration what science seems to have theorized, we need to think of the human brain as having a negative charge and the *essence* as having a positive charge. When a newborn (negatively charged) body comes out of the womb, the closest *essence* (positively charged) will find its way to the brain once a pathway has been cleared. However, because the *essence* is made up of elements that do not have the limitations of the *known* elements, it can pass through much of the matter of which the materials of the earth are constructed. For this reason, the *essence* can find its way into the circulatory system the moment a baby is born, even if the birth takes place underwater. The only *known* element that remains impervious to the molecules of the *essence* is lead. The rest of known matter does not inhibit the ability of the *essence* to travel where it needs to go.

Because the elements from which the *essence* is created have similar characteristics to the gaseous elements in our atmosphere, these elements can enter the newborn body the same way oxygen does—through the nasal or mouth cavities. Our *essence* then travels from the lungs through the circulatory system to the brain. The *imperfect* human body is constructed so that the *essence* can only get to where it needs to be through the circulatory system, though it would be able to pass through the elements that make up the skull and brain in a *perfect* body. Once the body dies, the *essence* leaves the same way it came in, exiting with the last breath. This occurs when and because the dying brain no longer has a negative charge strong enough to keep the positively charged *essence* attracted to it.

However, the *essence* **cannot** pass through the cells of the mother's *imperfect* body into the fetus because of the way that her body reacts when pregnant. For illustration purposes only, the mother's body, in effect, becomes *positively* charged in relation to the baby's *negatively* charged body. The *positive* charge of the pregnant mother repels the *positively* charged *essence*. When she is no longer pregnant, the mother's body returns back to its former negatively charged state.

Some might argue that if the mother's body becomes positively charged when pregnant, then her own positively charged *essence* would be repelled by the magnetic change. One must note, however, that the miracle of pregnancy and birth is being presented in this book the only way that our *imperfect brains* can comprehend it. "Magnetism," and "positive/negative" forces were invented by *imperfect* humans to explain things according to their very limited understanding. The use of these terms in this book is completely illustrative. What is important is that the reader understands what is taking place according to his or her ability to reason and comprehend.

8. MEMORIES OF THE ESSENCE DIFFER FROM MEMORIES OF THE BRAIN

The *essence* never changes. There are major differences, however, between the physical body we have now and the body that an advanced human being possesses. Throughout this book, our current body will continue to be described as an *imperfect body*, and the most advanced human body possible as the *perfect body*. Later, the differences between the two will be described in more detail; for now, we need to focus on how the *essence* reacts with each.

The *perfect* advanced **brain**, as a part of the *perfect body*, DOES NOT record experience. Experience is ONLY recorded in the *essence.* In the *imperfect body*, however, experiences are recorded **both** on the brain's structure AND in the *essence.* Because of the "double recording," the way we recall experiences (remember) is much more difficult in the *imperfect body* than it is in a *perfect* one.

9. ENERGY IS REQUIRED TO PRODUCE MEMORIES

In an *imperfect body*, recalling stored memories requires different levels of energy that are generated by the body. If we want to remember what we ate for breakfast this morning, for example, then less energy is used than what would be required to remember what we ate for breakfast yesterday. Remembering the meal from breakfast two days ago requires even more energy. There are some memories, however, that we can recall rather easily with very limited expenditure of our energy, even in an *imperfect* body.

The more frequently the experience is repeated, the less energy our brain uses in recalling it later. This happens because of the way our brain compartmentalizes repeated experiences upon recording them. In addition, as information is stored, if we spend more energy in concentrating on the experience and forcing it to be recorded, then less energy will be required to recall it. Consequently, the more the experience affects us (the more traumatic), the easier it is to recall. For example, all those who were old enough to be aware that the World Trade Center in New York City was attacked on September 11, 2001, are able to recall with very little effort what they were doing at the moment they heard of the attack. However, they cannot as easily recall what they were doing a year after the attack (in 2002) on the same day.

With our current *less*-developed and poorly utilized brains, the greater the energy it takes to record the experience, the less the energy it takes to recall it. Therefore, we are forced to consciously concentrate (the cerebral expenditure of energy) on something if we want to retain it in the forefront of our brain's memory banks and be able to recall it easily in the future.

10. ENERGY LEVELS OF THE ESSENCE ARE CONSTANT

Unlike our less developed brain, our *essence* is set up in such a way that it records all experiences on *equal* energy levels. The structure of the *unknown* elements that comprise the human *essence* is always equal and stable. In this balanced environment, there is very little expenditure of energy in recalling memories. In the *perfect body*, we can recall any experience as if it happened just a moment ago.

The way that our *imperfect brain* records experience and gets in the way of our ability to instantly recall memories is very different from the ease in which it can be done with the *perfect brain*, which *does not* record experience. The *perfect brain's* only function is to take the energy levels stored on the *essence* (our memories) and allow the sensory receptors of sight, smell, sound, taste, and touch to react with the energy, thereby giving the advanced being an incredibly detailed recollection of every experience. Our recollection of past events will be remembered (played back), upon our desire to remember them, with the exact same physical sensations that were produced when the event first transpired.

11. ENERGY LEVELS OF THE BRAIN FLUCTUATE

Let's attempt to simplify it even further:

A different level of energy is produced from each experience. These "levels of energy" are what we consider our "emotions." We prioritize our emotions by the level of energy we use in experiencing them. For example, let's assume that the energy levels of all experience fall between 1 and 10, with 10 being the constant energy level that is required for our brain to recall an experience. Because we eat breakfast every morning, we do not expend a lot of energy trying to remember what we are eating. So let's assign the number 2 to the experience of eating breakfast. When a loved one dies, however, we expend a tremendous amount of emotional energy experiencing the event. So let's assign the death of a loved one the number 7.

On the day that we learn of the death of our father, we eat something for breakfast. Our brain records both experiences at a level 7 and a level 2, respectively, according to the energy levels produced by each experience (and as allowed by the *imperfect* brain's capacity). When recall is attempted, by illustration, it would only take an energy level of 3 to remember our father's death, but a level of 8 to recall what we ate for breakfast the same day.

In contrast, all experiences are stored *exactly the same* on our *essence* at the highest, most stable, energy level. Because the *essence* has its *own* energy source that does not fluctuate as the *imperfect* brain does, it always records the experience in a balanced state of equilibrium. This supports its immunity to the *Second Law of Thermodynamics*, the law that maintains that the entropy (or breakdown) of an isolated system *not in equilibrium* will tend to increase over time. In other words, an *essence* will *never* break down and will always record every experience *perfectly*. This is due to the stability and equilibrium of the *essence's* perfect energy and environment.

There are some anomalies of the physical brain structure, however, which do allow some people to have a near-photographic memory; but it is impossible for any less advanced brain to be as *fully* photographic as an advanced brain. Nevertheless, the fact that we have developed varying degrees of ability to recount what we experience, supports the conclusion that the human brain is indeed capable of much, much more than we currently are able to utilize.

12. ONE DAY WE WILL ALL HAVE A PERFECT BODY

The more we advance, even with our *imperfect bodies*, the more we will understand the workings of the human brain and consequently, be able to use it more efficiently. Keep in mind that advanced societies of humans who know how to create a human *essence* have *always* existed, and human beings inhabiting *perfect bodies* have always been. There has never been a time when one of these societies has not been found somewhere in the infinite Universe. Furthermore, as more human beings are created and go through the stages of their own development, the number of these advanced civilizations increases. Eventually, each of us ends up with a *perfect body* that can react in *perfection* with our *essence*.

In other words, in a few thousand years from now, we will be the advanced societies of the future. With the technology and information that will be available then, some will choose to be parents and continue to perpetuate the human race. These *creators* will do this by first creating a human *essence* and then creating a body in which this *essence* can fulfill the purpose for its creation. (Again, this purpose is to record life's experiences and store them as memories at emotional energy levels, thus producing the sensation of happiness.) These advanced humans choosing to be creators will have the knowledge to create other solar systems; and in these new solar systems, *new* humans will compile experiences until they, too, become as advanced as their creators.

13. THE UNIQUE ABILITY TO IMAGINE OUR FUTURE

As we accept the fact that undiscovered, advanced human societies exist in other parts of the Universe, it's not hard to imagine other human beings who have progressed far beyond the point we're at upon this planet. Just picture how our own mortal ancestors would have viewed us in their day, if they had seen what we know and understand today. Surely, they would have seen us as far more superior and advanced to themselves, at least in terms of "worldly" knowledge and technology.

Take, for example, the musicians of early Greek societies, known for their musical advancements of the time. Could they have even imagined that one day their descendents would be carrying around a device the size of an apple slice (pun intended for the Apple iPod TM) that could play literally thousands of songs—songs that were masterfully recorded by instruments that didn't even exist at that time?

Likewise, it shouldn't be very difficult for *us* to imagine a future where these exact same songs, and millions of others like them, are no longer recorded upon a device that we carry *outside* of our body. Instead, the songs' melodies and rhythms will be recorded and played at will *inside* of our heads. This will be accomplished by the sensory receptors of our brain cells being connected to the audio nerves or our ears, which will allow us to *listen* to the music from inside. When we have brains that are properly developed, we will not only be able to hear the words playing in our heads, but we will also hear the sounds of the instruments that create the harmony and rhythm. This will bring the songs to life and cause the joy we experience by listening to them. At that point, what need would there be for a 21st century-made iPod, when the technology and know-how exist to record any song we hear and play it back anytime we desire, just by thinking about it?

It's easy to *imagine* these things. They seem very reasonable, especially in light of all that has been discovered about the brain and how *nanotechnology* works. Enormous amounts of information can now be stored on tiny objects such as the integrated circuitry of the modern iPod music player. Despite this, modern scientists can be among the most ignorant and hardened against the *true reality* of the existence of our human *essence*—the *ultimate* recording and playback device ever created!

14. DREAMS ARE ACCESSED MEMORIES OF THE ESSENCE

One realm of evidence for the existence of the *essence* in which science has failed to make any significant conclusions is that of dreams. Science speculates that dreaming is necessary and vital to our emotional health. It proposes that one who does not dream might descend into some sort of insanity. In *reality*, however, this is not the case. A more comprehensive understanding of what a dream actually is and how it takes place in the mind will show that those who dream less are emotionally more at peace with themselves than those who dream more. And those who take their dreams *too* seriously often become more out of touch with reality than those who do not.

Dreaming and imagining are simply the random recollection of stored memories from either or both our *essence* and our physical brain **that our conscious mind is attempting to organize into *reason*able and recognizable experience.** Unless some outside manipulation is taking place, such as hypnosis, all dreams materialize from the random, fragmented parts of our actual experiences in our recent or long ago past. When our *imperfect* brain attempts to organize our memories of past experiences into something we can consciously understand, our dreams become subconscious compilations of completely unrelated instances we have a hard time explaining or figuring out.

A perfect night's sleep consists of one in which we go to sleep and before we know it, we wake up the next morning, not having had any dreams or restless periods, just pure, unadulterated, deep sleep. As stated above, those who currently experience more emotional stability and peace dream less and are able to sleep more soundly.

Although dreams are not necessary, they *are* an inescapable part of how our *imperfect* brain functions. This is because the brain (our *imperfect* body) cannot consciously access or control the subconscious (the *essence*). When we dream, we are not *completely* in a *subconscious state.* Our brain is working hard during a dream as well as are the rest of the sensory systems of the body. As we dream, our conscious mind tries to make sense out of the dream, causing an expenditure of energy that takes away from a *good* night's sleep.

15. WE ALL NEED TO SLEEP

Sleeping is our brain's way of telling our subconscious to be quiet and get some needed rest, which, of course, the *essence* will never do. The *imperfect* brain, being a major part of the *imperfect* body, needs rest because of the constant imbalance of energy fluctuations. In other words, the brain can become as exhausted as any other part of the body if it does not receive as much energy as it uses up, or if it is underused and atrophied. As the *imperfect* brain attempts to rest, it rejects the continual wavelengths of the energy levels (memories) coming from the *essence.* When this occurs, the person's capability to reason is not fully utilized and therefore, it cannot organize the memories into *reasonable* experiences. Thus, the fragmented and nonsensical experiences associated with dreaming are created.

Insomniacs (those who find it difficult to fall asleep) have a hard time getting the brain to stop thinking about their present realities. It's good advice for these people to "count sheep" jumping over a fence. This is why: If one can concentrate (direct the energy levels of the *imperfect* brain) on something that is *not* very realistic (sheep continually jumping over a fence in perfect order), but makes perfect sense (counting one, two, three…makes sense), then the energy it takes to *reason* will shut down much more readily.

If insomniacs pick up a fictional novel to read at bedtime, and they have already determined that they will experience no *reality* in the story (therefore, they do not expend energy trying to *reason* and figure it out), they will fall asleep quite easily. This happens because our *essence* does not require sleep or a "recharge of our energy levels." When a person concentrates on something that *reason* does not have to deal with (fantasies), the energy level produced by *thought* is automatically diverted to the part of us that has no need for any "recharge" from our body (the *essence*). This allows the part of us that *reasons* and needs to rest (our *imperfect* brain) the ability to do so.

16. AS WE DREAM, OUR ABILITY TO REASON IS INHIBITED, YET THE ESSENCE REMAINS ALERT

Most people have similar dreams. For example, many of us have dreamed that we can fly. Some of us might have envisioned ourselves as a falling leaf drifting gently down to earth. Many of us have dreamed of attending school half-naked. We might have even dreamed that we saw a one-eyed giant living on another planet. All of us have had nightmares in which monsters have invaded our dream world to threaten our life. We have the potential of dreaming impossibilities that make no sense to our *reality*. So, how can this be? Did we once fly? Were we once a leaf, or did we actually see a one-eyed giant? Did all of us make the same mistake of not getting fully dressed to attend school? Are there such life forms as monsters that chase us and threaten our lives?

As we are dreaming, our ability (mental capacity) to *reason* is greatly inhibited, along with many of the other functions of our *imperfect* body; therefore, we can dream some very weird and nonsensical things. Dreaming is a product of our *imperfect* brain's inability to control our subconscious mind, where our human *essence* continues to exist as it always has since we became a conscious, fully living human being, without the need to sleep or the need of energy from our body.

The *essence* has its own source of energy—much like the charged battery of an iPod, only the "batteries" of the *essence* never run out. Therefore, as the "always-turned-on" energy from the subconscious attempts to interact with the brain (which has been forced by the need to rest to turn off its energy in a state of sleep), *reason* cannot play a part in the conscious recollection or understanding of the mental images that are produced. (Keep in mind, "reason" is an energy expenditure of the brain, not of the *essence*.) Because our *imperfect* brain only allows us to remember fragments of our past experience, it tries to make sense of the energy (memories) affecting it when we are asleep. This becomes our dreams.

17. WE DAYDREAM WHEN WE ARE NOT IN NEED OF SLEEP

The natural phenomenon of dreaming also takes place while we are fully conscious, in what we consider "day" dreaming. When we make no conscious effort to shut our brain off through sleep, we are continually affected by either the energy of our brain (as we *reason* our way through life), or by the constant energy of our *essence*. Without any *willingness* on our part, memories from our subconscious seep into our conscious mind. Again, this occurs because the energy of our *essence* cannot be turned off. Our *imperfect* brain, therefore, creates the random, nonsensical *imaginations* that come into our mind during daydreaming the same way it creates the *dreams* when we are trying to sleep.

Daydreaming occurs when we are not fully utilizing our brain's current energy levels; in other words, we are not allowing our current environment to affect our conscious need to reason. Stated another way, if our brain is not engaged in interacting with the world around us and we stop "thinking," we will begin dreaming. If our *imperfect* brain is in need of sleep, the moment we stop using it to *reason*, we will drift off into a state of sleep. If it does not need sleep, we will begin *day*dreaming.

18. THE BLIND DO NOT DREAM IN VISUAL IMAGERY

Those who are blind from birth do not claim to have the same dreams as fully sighted people. When asked to describe their dreams, they find it very difficult, almost impossible, to relay a description of them in any type of detail that a sighted person would understand. Science has concluded that people who have been blind from birth do not experience visual imagery during their dreams. How can science conclude this? How is a congenitally blind person (blind since birth) going to be able to describe something to another person who has experienced it in a completely different way?

For example, if a blind person actually does see the color red in a dream, how can it be described to a person who has been taught what to call "red" in the sighted-person's visual experience? The blind person would have no reference point from which to draw a proper description.

The fact is, a blind person wouldn't be able to describe a visual experience even if one occurred in a dream. Because blind people have visual experiences stored in their *essence*, they have dreams they cannot explain in their current experience. What they can do, however, is **attempt to organize the random expressions of their stored memories into reasonable experiences** that make sense to them; thus causing them to dream.

19. ALL NEAR-DEATH EXPERIENCES ARE DREAMS

Consider this scenario:

Let's say that a man having an operation wakes up after the operation and can vividly recall things about the operation that would seemingly be impossible to recall if he did not have an "out-of-body" experience. Let's suppose that the man remembered seeing the surgeon flapping his arms at times to stretch his muscles and loosen the stress and tension in his arms during the surgery. Let's assume, as is customary, that there was a sheet draped between the man's range of view and the surgeon. Having his vision blocked would seemingly eliminate the possibility that the man became conscious or semi-conscious during the procedure and was then able to see the surgeon's behavior. Also, assume that the man was conscious before he was wheeled into the operating room, and that he met with the surgeon before being put to sleep.

Just as we dream when we are asleep, a person *dreams* while their physical brain is undergoing a traumatic event. The person creates the *dream* from the traumatic experience itself and from the stored memories that affect the unconscious mind. When awakened from the trauma, the brain attempts to organize the recorded memories into *reason*able experience.

During any operation, for example, though the *imperfect brain* is affected by the anesthesia, the *essence* **is not**! Although the man's eyes are closed, there are still energy patterns of smell, sound, taste, and touch that are entering the man's sensory receptors and being recorded upon his *essence*.

One's eyes can be closed and another person in close proximity can give a distinct groan or yawn while stretching and moving their arms. This action causes a discernable release of energy and is then recognized for what it is—a man stretching. When our physical brain is put to sleep either artificially or naturally, the power of our *essence* continues to record any and all experience created in the surrounding area.

If the surgeon had on rubber boots, for example, the man lying on the gurney does not need to actually see the boots to know they're rubber. He might deduce the *reality* by hearing the sound the boots make on the floor (which creates a sound that the man recognizes as rubber-on-floor), or by the distinct smell of the rubber itself.

All near-death experiences are dreams.

20. THERE ARE NO TRUE "OUT-OF-BODY" EXPERIENCES

During any normal dream sequence, we routinely have an "out-of-body" experience. We are actually viewing ourselves going through whatever dream event we are having. We always perceive the dream as if we are viewing our own body performing the actions of the dream. We do not dream using the eyes of our own body in the dream. We participate in dreams as a third person viewing our own actions.

There is no difference between an out-of-body experience one might have in a dream, and the experience one has who believes he or she has died and come back to life. The *true reality* is that once the *essence* leaves the body, there are no sensory receptors working to record experience; thus, there can be no true "out-of-body" experience, as some believe. The *essence* does not necessarily have to leave the body immediately when the heart stops or when the *imperfect brain* stops functioning. But when it does leave the body, then, and only then, can a person truly be pronounced dead; and at that point, there is no way for the individual to record a literal out-of-body experience.

Fortunately for the human race, one day we will never *dream* again. Subconscious and conscious thought will not exist. Instead, all thought and experience will be perfectly stored and perfectly controlled and accessed by our free will through the power of our *essence* that resides in a *perfect* human body. But for now, we have to dream and imagine, then use our *reason* to figure out what is *real* and what is not.

21. THE ABILITY TO DREAM, IMAGINE, AND REASON

The difference between the way humans dream, imagine, and reason is the mental state in which they do these things. We *dream* in an unconscious state, such as sleep, or in a state in which we place our mental thoughts outside the realm of our current reality—such as daydreaming while we are supposed to be working.

The difference between dreaming and using imagination is that *imagining* is a <u>deliberate</u> mental process, while dreaming is an <u>involuntary</u> mental process that begins in our mind randomly. While both dreams and imagination are often artful, whimsical, and associated with a relaxed thinking process, *reasoning*, on the other hand, stresses our mental capacity to its limit.

The process of reasoning, or figuring things out, is simply utilizing the process of imagination, or better, dreaming up a way to solve a problem by concentrating a proportionately greater amount of energy on the thought than we would while actually *imagining* or *dreaming*. The mental energy used to reason is much more demanding than that which is needed to dream or imagine. This is why some people can't *reason* as well as others. It is not that their *human essence* is any less "human," but rather that their particular *imperfect* brain might not be capable of producing the "mental energy" needed to *reason* appropriately.

The genetically inherited, *imperfect* brain can only produce the "mental energy" provided by the instructions passed on from its parents. Our widely differing abilities to use our brains are dependent upon the physical makeup of our individual brains. Due to genetic differences, some people have the capability of reasoning much more quickly and efficiently than others. This says nothing of *who we are*, however, because if the individual *essence* of a slow-learning person was placed in a body where the brain functioned more proficiently, they would be just as "smart" as everyone else. The degrees of so-called "intelligence" found among human beings have nothing to do with the *essence*, but all to do with the physical limitations of the *imperfect body*.

22. SOME MEMORIES NOT PART OF OUR CURRENT REALITY

All of us *imagine* at one time or another. Many of us have experienced the insecurity of going to school on the first day and wondering if we were going to fit in, thus accounting for our dream of attending school partially dressed. And there isn't a monster imagined that doesn't have its body parts taken from an animal that we have seen or are aware of in our experienced reality. It's easy to imagine a "kangaphant." Just think of an elephant that stands on its hind legs, has short front legs and a pouch with a baby kangaphant tucked inside. Now picture it with big shark-like teeth!

Some have noticed a leaf falling from a tree and wondered what it must feel like to be a leaf and fall slowly, gently down to earth. We've seen birds fly with uninhibited freedom in the sky and imagined what it would be like to be a bird. Given that we can *imagine* these things, it is logical that there is an experience locked in our subconscious mind (*essence*) of a time when we actually could fly. And there is! It was in the advanced world where we came from, where technology exists that we have yet to discover.

The point is, there are some memories stored in a part of us that are not a conscious part of our current reality. Although our brain is incapable of accessing these subconscious "stored" memories upon demand, when we relax our minds and begin the process of dreaming or imagining, we access this unconscious realm and attempt to organize what we retrieve into a part of our current reality through *reasoning*.

23. DELUSIONAL REALITIES ARE SELF-INDUCED

One of the biggest dilemmas of our human experience, therefore, takes place within our own minds. The problem occurs because we are incapable of determining exactly when our brain is using its *own* energy to *reason* a solution to its environmental situations, versus when we are actually *dreaming*. As a result, we can be led into a delusional reality that is not shared by anyone else but ourselves.

The conclusions we come up with by "day" dreaming exist *only* in our *own* mind, unless, of course, we are successful at convincing others that our dreams are reality. Our current reality can be especially distorted by our dreams when we convince ourselves that what we dream (either in a state of sleep or when we are fully awake) is *real* experience. As we ponder our unrealistic dreams and use our unique ability to *reason*, we try to formulate some kind of order to make our dreams fit into our reality. This distorts what is *really* happening in our environment into a convoluted form of our own *unreal*istic world.

A work that defines and delineates each and every human mental aberration known (such as ESP, superstitions, placebo effect, etc.) would be voluminous and continually incomplete because of the differing circumstances in which the mind phenomena is experienced by each individual person. By applying common sense and reason, the reader will be able to see the similarities between most mental anomalies, both real and not. For an example, we will discuss a few below:

24. WE ALL HEAR "VOICES IN OUR HEADS"

Some people with mental disabilities (fragile minds) express their dreams and imaginations as their conscious mind perceives them, without having the ability to utilize their *reason* to form them into rational thoughts. Others hear voices in their heads, or perceive that they are communicating with someone or something outside of their own body. In reality, these people are limited genetically in the use of their ability to *reason* and cannot make the distinction between current reality and stored memories.

As explained, the energy level of the *essence* is constant and does not fluctuate as the brain's does. When our conscious mind has energy fluctuations, or better, ebbs at a lower wavelength of energy, the consistent higher energy of the *essence* provides the "thoughts" (energy) that come to our mind. In these instances, because we are completely conscious, our mind interprets stored memories as current thoughts, as our *imperfect brain* tries to make sense out of them. This is the best way to describe the "voices in our head."

Here's an example: If we leave our car keys somewhere and forget where we have put them, the memory is still stored in our brain of where we put them, but just at a much lower energy level than the level at which it was stored in our *essence.* Our conscious mind can be concentrating on other things, when suddenly the memory of where we left our keys, comes to mind. Our brain is so inefficient in its use of memory, that the more we concentrate on where we left our keys, the harder it is for us to remember. But the *essence's* energy level is consistent and will fill in the gaps created by our *imperfect* brain. These mental "gaps" can vary depending on individual physical ability, due to inherited genetic flaws of the brain. The more "gaps" there are, the more mentally disabled the person appears to be.

Another example of "voices in our head" happens when we believe that a dead relative or another disembodied soul is speaking to us. When this happens, we are simply applying our *reason* to what we *imagine* could happen. We take actual memories of the person (as in the case of a relative), or imagine someone outside of ourselves, and construct a conscious reality of the experience.

The unpolluted mind of a child has considerably more "gaps" than an adult, whose conscious mind is continually concentrating on many different current realities that use up all of the *imperfect* brain's energy potential. Therefore, invisible friends are a common experience for many children, as well as their ability to imagine more freely. This is caused by the *essence* filling in the gaps of their immature brain. Consequently, little children can pull memories out of their *essence* much easier than adults can.

25. ABNORMAL AND NORMAL THINKING PATTERNS

Some of us may appear mentally retarded, insane, schizophrenic, or otherwise emotionally disturbed; however, the *dreams* and *imaginations* of all *imperfect* humans, if acted upon without using our ability to *reason*, can seem very unrealistic to others. This is why the dreams we have in a subconscious state can be compiled experiences of unrelated incidents (or even fantasies) that would never happen in *reality*. A good example of this happens to many of us when we experience a nightmare. After watching a particularly disturbing movie, we may find ourselves in a dream that incorporates parts of the movie into a personal situation we might be experiencing in our current reality; thus, we can be equally disturbed by the fantasy created in our mind by the unrelated events.

Another example is the way we view a person who walks down the street talking into thin air. The only difference between this person and someone who does the exact same thing in private is the accepted standard that we have placed on the action. Although the act is the same in both situations, talking into thin air might be considered socially acceptable as the personal supplication of a pious person to his or her chosen deity, or the purposefully directed energy of thought used by one who is meditating. On the other hand, one who does the act in public is socially branded as "schizophrenic." The accepted difference is in what we *reason* can be *expected* of those who talk into thin air. We have been taught, and therefore use our *reason*, to differentiate between allowable "sane" acts and those we consider "insane" acts.

26. THE ESSENCE STORES OUR MEMORIES AND DEFINES WHO WE ARE

Many factors in our current experience lead us to a logical conclusion of the existence of the human *essence*. At this point, we need to use our best <u>reason</u> and <u>imagination</u> to take us into a realm of *reality* to which few humans have ever ventured with their conscious minds. We need to reach into the subconscious realm of dreams and creative and imaginative thinking. It is in this cognitive realm that we will come to a better understanding of how our *essence* is a crucial part of *who we really are*.

All of us dream and all of us imagine. The problem is that when we do, we have no idea that what we are dreaming or imagining is simply recollection of our experiences stored in our subconscious memory. It is this "memory" that stores all of our experiences (both in this world and in previous worlds) and defines us as individuals based on these past experiences. This is our *essence*. This, apart from whatever shape or size our body turns out to be, is who we *really* are.

But before we can properly understand exactly what our human *essence* is and how it works, we need to consider *how* we think. To do this and therefore be successful at learning the **real truth**, we must be willing to open our minds to possibilities that we have never considered before.

27. WE CANNOT IMAGINE WHAT WE HAVE NOT EXPERIENCED

In considering the human mind and how it thinks and processes information, the first thing we need to understand is that we cannot think or achieve something that we cannot *reason*ably conceive could happen. In fact, we cannot think or achieve anything unless we can first *imagine* that it could happen, or at least *dream* of the possibility of it happening. And we cannot *imagine* or *dream* of something that we have not yet experienced, because we would have no memory from which to draw out the things we are imagining or dreaming about. Therefore, everything that we think or *believe* that we can achieve (imagine or dream), we have experienced before.

This does not mean that we have experienced everything ourselves; perhaps instead, we have witnessed someone else having the experience. Imagining that we can be eaten by a wild animal doesn't mean that it had to have happened to us personally, only that the situation did take place as we saw it, and as the event was recorded as a memory from our own experience. For example, a little child has no fear of snakes until (through experience) the fear is embedded in the child's psyche, either personally or by being taught by someone whom the child trusts. The fears and phobias we possess at birth aren't necessarily genetically inherited from our parents. More likely, they are experiences recorded upon our *essence*. For this reason, long before they learn fear or acceptance from their parents, some infants are afraid of scary masks while others are not. The infant might associate the non-human facial expression of a mask with something that caused a stressful situation in a past life experience. There is no way to know why some infants react differently to certain extrinsic stimuli than others unless we were able to view all of the past memories stored in their individual *essences*.

Because all of us have the extraordinary and exclusively human ability to *imagine*, it is no wonder that we are so disillusioned with each other. Other life forms do not have the ability to *reason*, which is the *reason* it is impossible for them to come up with the disjointed ways of dealing with their environment and each other, as humans do. This is not to say that animals do not dream, because they do—but they *do not **imagine*** as we do because they cannot *reason* like a human being.

28. OUR IMAGINATION SEPARATES US FROM ANIMALS

The fact that we can call upon ideas that are *not* part of our current reality (imagine them) separates our thought processes and abilities from those of all other animals. However, it would be offensive to animal lovers to maintain the opinion that humans are far more intelligent and more *humane* than every other life form. It would be equally insulting to the other side, to support the idea that we are not much different from animals, believing that our ancestors were once wild animals themselves. To take sides in this debate would mean either the alienation of the readers who receive much more companionship and love from their pets than they do from other humans, or the alienation of those who have had a friend or relative mauled or killed by the very same animals the victim once protected and adored. It is just as hard for the victim of an animal attack to see the similarities between animals and humans, as it is for the victim of war or crime to see the differences.

No matter how hard one might try to defend the animal lover and humble the human, the *reality* remains that no other animal uses reason, language, inquiry, wonder, longing, morality, aesthetics, creativity, imagination, and ambition as proficiently or as often as we do. There are those who ascribe to some species of animals the use of all of these attributes. Nevertheless, it takes a *reasonable*, *inquisitive*, *wondering*, *longing*, *moral*, *creative,* and *imaginative* mind to make the comparison make sense to those who do not see any similarity.

Think about this: Ranchers keep tens of hundreds of pounds of pure horse and cattle muscle from escaping by simply installing a thin wire with a small amount of electricity running through it. The horses and cattle do not *long* to eat the greener grass on the other side of the electric fence, nor do they *wonder* or *reason* and *inquire* about the smell of distant fresh clover. But even *if* they did, they still do not have the capability, the *creativity*, or the *imagination* to realize that it would only take a simple step to break the flimsy boundary and become free (even after many years of experience of being corralled behind the fence).

29. ANIMALS LIVE BY INSTINCT WITHOUT REASON

Like us, animals must *first* experience something before they can conceive that it can be completed. However, they have no ability to *reason*, because they have no way to access any experience that is not part of their current consciousness. Again, our ability to reason is our ability to conceive something in our mind by calling upon past experience (even an experience that might not be part of our current reality) and then find a way to accomplish it. To begin the process of reasoning, we must *imagine* that we can do something and then *concentrate* our mental abilities on finding a way to do it.

For example, a chimpanzee that uses a stick to extract termites from a small, deep hole does not imagine, dream, or reason that it can be done. First, it is driven by the need to eat. Observing that termites sometimes come out of the hole and crawl up on nearby sticks, the primate learns (upon first seeing the action) that termites will cling to sticks. The animal then finds that picking up the stick with a few termites on it is an easier way to get a meal. The chimp next discovers that by putting the stick in the hole, it can extract termites that cling to the stick.

However, the chimp didn't make this discovery until experience first taught it that putting the stick next to the hole, then into the hole, would produce the desired result. It might notice the termites climbing on nearby grass blades. When it pulls up the grass to put the termites in its mouth, it might discard the grass blade near the entrance of the termite nest. As other termites climb on the discarded blade of grass, the chimp realizes that this is an easy way to get a meal, and utilizes what it experiences to gain what it is after. However, no infant chimpanzee will ever pick up a blade of grass or a stick and put it into a termite hole unless the behavior has first been learned by observing an adult chimpanzee do the same first.

If a human being were in the chimpanzee's position, he or she would *subconsciously* know that there is a much more efficient way to extricate the termites from their nest. Without waiting to see them climb out onto a blade of grass or a stick, we would start imagining all sorts of ways to get them out and then would use our *reason* to make what we imagine a reality. For this reason, it is easy to keep animals in captivity; but it is very, very difficult to keep humans likewise confined. There is not a human alive who could be kept in captivity by the same, thin electrical wire that can keep a thousand pounds of horse muscle from running free.

30. ANIMALS HAVE PREPROGRAMMED ESSENCES

Animals do have *essences*. However, these storage devices (as they have been described above) are fully programmed and do not allow for free will. During its lifetime, no other experience is recorded upon the animal *essence*. Nevertheless, the brain of the animal **does record experience**, just like the *imperfect human* brain.

But the animal *essence* **does not record any experience**. The best word to describe what is recorded on an animal's *essence* is "instinct."

Let's use the relationship between a pet and a human being as an example to further illustrate the differences between human and animal *essences*:

If Bridgette develops a loving and endearing relationship with her dog Spot, when Bridgette's *essence* is placed in her *perfect* body, she will be able to relive all of the experiences she once enjoyed with her beloved pet. Spot, on the other hand, will not go on to live another life time. Even if a *perfect body* was created for Spot, putting an animal's *essence* into the body would not allow Spot to recall any event it experienced with Bridgette. Why? Because Spot's *essence* would be full with instinctual programming that makes Spot a dog. However, because the new Spot is the same type of dog that was the *old Spot*, its interactions with Bridgette would be very similar.

All animal *essences* are preprogrammed by advanced human beings who have the technology and expertise to do so. Animals are used to serve the needs of humans and maintain a balance in nature on *imperfect* worlds. (This concept will be explained in much more detail in another chapter.) Some might wonder if a dog's essence, once a dog dies, comes back to the body of another dog. In most cases, this would be true. However, because the animal's *essence* is programmable, a dog's *essence* could very well be re-programmed to provide the instinctual behavior needed for a cat or a mouse. Advanced beings make these judgments.

31. PLANTS DO NOT HAVE AN ESSENCE

Plants, on the other hand, do not have *essences*. Each plant carries within it the ability to reproduce itself infinitely without any outside influence telling it what to do. In other words, the seed contains all of the plans for the plant's behavior. Nothing enters the plant's body upon birth, because a seed is not born; it grows. Advanced beings are also responsible for what plants and their seeds do and do not do.

32. CHILD PRODIGIES AND SAVANTS GIVE EVIDENCE OF PREVIOUS EXISTENCE

Although animals can only learn through behavioral conditioning, we see human instances where young children do extraordinary things that they have never seen an adult do in their current life experience. Amadeus Mozart, one example of many, could read and write music at a very young age far beyond the capabilities of his musically inclined parents. How did he know how to do this?

Somehow, Mozart's mind could conceive that it could be accomplished because he had stored memories of it being attained, whether they were memories of himself in another life or memories of being around others who had. Then, he imagined himself doing what he conceived, and with his abnormally advanced ability to *reason*, Mozart accomplished it without any influence except his own intrinsic motivation and desire to do so. But if he had never had any current life experiences wherein he was exposed to the learning that it takes to read and write music, how did he learn how to do it? The answer is that Mozart learned how to compose and recognize music as a child because he had experienced these abilities in one of his previous lifetimes. The memories from his past lives were recorded upon his *essence*, which in turn, gave him his prodigious talent as a young child.

Savants are likewise those who can do extraordinarily complicated things without any previous training or education. The examples of their seemingly supernatural powers are widely known and documented. Although they are inefficient at demonstrating normal human behavior in most other areas, their unique abilities have proven the great potential hidden in the human brain. But how do they do what they do? Who taught them these things? Why can't a "normal" brain do these things?

Most savants are mentally impaired so that it is virtually

impossible for them to reason—that is, to make a conscious effort to rationally solve a problem by using their own imagination based on their experience. The ability to do the extraordinary things that they do comes from what is already recorded in their eternal memory banks (*essence*). It is an involuntary (subconscious) expression of something they have already experienced in the past, before their current mortal existence.

There has been a great amount of research effort put in to attempting to understand the brain structure and mental capacity of a savant compared to that of a "normal" brain. Science has yet to explain this phenomenon and easily concedes that it is far from solving the mystery of the human brain and its full potential. And until science understands the *essence*, it will never solve this mystery.

It should now make sense why a human savant can do extraordinary things with the brain that "normal" people cannot. It is not that most people don't have the same capabilities of all savants also recorded on their *essence*, but they do not have the proper brain alignment to access these past experiences; or rather, their *imperfect brain* gets in their way. A savant's brain is an anomaly; and although the way it functions shows the brain's potential, without the rest of it functioning correctly, the individual has difficulty *optimizing the human experience* and living in a society that requires learned social and other mental skills.

33. WE RECOGNIZE BEAUTY BECAUSE OF PAST EXPERIENCE

The recognition of beauty is further evidence of unconscious memories stored in our *essence*.

Let's say that a blind person should not know the difference between a non-attractive person and an attractive one. For those blind people who regain their sight, why is it that they can perceive beauty seemingly instantaneously? What if they regained their sight and everyone around them had a facial deformity? If a beautiful person stood next to one with a deformed face, would the blind person choose the beautiful face as the one that is accepted by all sighted people as being "beautiful"; or would the newly sighted person not be able to tell the difference? The fact is, they *would* be able to tell the difference, just as newborn infants, who also have very limited visual imagery experience, can.

Scientific research has shown that babies look longer at faces that are rated as attractive by adults than at faces rated as unattractive. Excluding parents, babies respond differently to strangers based on the stranger's physical attractiveness. Toddlers, who are more involved in play, show more positive affect toward an attractive stranger than an unattractive one. Likewise, when the stranger is unattractive, they withdraw from the stranger more often than an attractive one. Infants bring an understanding of what is and what isn't beautiful from somewhere other than their current experience. They make the assessment based on subconscious memories stored on their *essence*.

34. LAUGHTER AND HUMOR ARE OUR MOST DISTINGUISHING ATTRIBUTES

The one thing that cannot be attributed to any animal in any way, and which prominently certifies the extreme difference between animals and humans, and further substantiates the existence of the *human essence*, is the sense of humor that causes laughter. Although we can train a chimpanzee to smile and make the expressions of laughter, they do not (nor does any other animal) have the ability to experience the full effect of a hearty laugh or a sincere smile.

Laughter is a reaction to a failure to meet an expected and reasonable outcome. Only humans experience laughter, because they are the only ones who have expectations. For example, it is not funny to see someone walk down a sidewalk and step around a discarded banana peel—this is what a reasonable mind would expect a person to do. But if a person steps on the banana peel and slips, now that is funny!

The brain reacts to these ironies by releasing a hormone similar to adrenaline. Hormones are catalysts that affect other chemical changes at the cellular level, which cause muscles to contract and glands to produce what the body needs. The reaction starts in the brain and results in the compulsory effects of laughter, which is the emission of forced air from the lungs passing over the tightened muscles of the voice box, the shaking of the diaphragm, and in some cases, the flow of tears.

The release of the hormone stimulates the effects of laughter. But *what* causes the reaction that releases the hormone? Never known before, it is caused by the energy levels of the *human essence*, and is the trait that distinguishes the human being from all other animals. Although laughter can be observed and measured, science has not answered what actually causes it and why it only occurs in the human species. It has proven that animals also have similar brains and produce similar hormones to humans. But a chimpanzee (the animal proven to be the closest relative to the human) would never be seized with genuine laughter upon witnessing a failure to meet an expected and reasonable outcome.

Whereas all chimpanzees make similar noises and grunts, the way humans express laughter is as unique as each individual is. This exclusivity comes from the uniqueness of each human brain, each human voice box, and each human diaphragm, which produces a distinctive and recognizable laugh for each of us.

What science has not effectively studied, and cannot study with its existing rudimentary tools, is the chemical change that takes place just before the reaction occurs that produces a laugh. A "chemical change" is the effect of one element interacting with another. For the sake of simplicity, we will define a "chemical" and an "element" as the same substance. With what we now know about our *essence*, we can understand that the "chemical change" is created by the ex*change* of energy levels between our brain and our *essence*.

As mentioned, laughter is controlled by the *essence* reacting with our brain. It is this *essence* that causes the chemical change to the prefrontal cortex, which produces the hormone that causes the body to perform the laugh. As laughter is the reaction to a failure to meet an expected and reasonable outcome, it is the *essence* that provides the memory of what is *expected* and *reasonable*.

35. CHILDREN LAUGH AND SMILE AT MONKEYS

An infant smiles and reacts to certain stimuli that would not make a monkey (which does not have a *human essence*—thus no human experience) react in the same way. The smile is a reaction to an experience that the *essence* already has stored, is able to recall, and then react to with the brain.

The reason why some people smile and laugh less than others is not necessarily that their *essence* is flawed, but that their *imperfect* brain might be. The main reason why some might laugh at a person slipping on a banana peel, while another gasps in concern, has to do with what is stored in the *essence*. If there is no previous record of a person slipping on a banana and hurting themselves, then the "failure to meet the expectation" is confirmed and the individual laughs. On the other hand, if an experience is recorded that a person was *hurt* slipping on a banana peel, then there *is* an expected outcome, thus producing a reaction that generates the effects of concern. A monkey wouldn't react either way.

SUMMARY

We laugh because we are human. We are human because we possess a human *essence* that no other life form has. Other life forms, such as all animals, insects, etc., have an *essence*; but theirs is always preprogrammed, thus eliminating the possibility of free will.

Our individuality is defined by our unique *essence*. It makes us *who we are* and allows us to answer the question of *why we exist*. In possession of this *essence*, our abilities are limitless and our potential immeasurable.

Because we have an *essence*, we are motivated to ponder and wonder about our origin, our past, and our future. We go to school, read books, develop mathematical theorems, and then try to solve them. We celebrate life through birthdays and holidays. We invent ways of answering our questions, but can only accept the answers as **real truth** if they match with what is recorded in our *essence*.

Our *essence* also gives us the moral foundation that *should* separate us from all other animals and make us humane and civilized.

It is the **true reality** of the human being. Without stored experiences (memories), we would have no expectations; therefore, we would not know how to be human, nor would we be compelled to act on our humanity.

A newborn infant can be placed in an environment where it has never seen another human smile or laugh, and yet it will still exhibit these uniquely human attributes without being shown any example of how to do them. An infant smiles and laughs without any current life experience because it obviously has the experience and know-how to do so recorded on the human *essence* that entered its body upon birth. In contrast, if an infantile chimpanzee is placed in an environment where humans laugh and smile, no effort on its part will be made to mimic the human action; the chimpanzee will *not* smile or laugh during its lifetime.

Now that we know that a sense of humor is something unique to the human being, and that a hearty laugh and a pleasant smile are reactions to previously recorded experiences, the next question that must follow is, "Where did the experiences for the recorded memories of the *human essence* come from?"

Our Foundationalization Process

CHAPTER FOUR

The only source of knowledge is experience.

—Albert Einstein

1. ADVANCED PARENTS ARE RESPONSIBLE FOR THE FOUNDATION OF OUR HUMANITY

Long before we were born into a body upon this earth, we were brought into existence as free-willed, separate individuals by advanced human beings. These highly developed humans, whom we can appropriately call our first parents, or creators, organized an *essence* for each of us out of elements that have existed in the Universe forever. This *essence* was void of any preprogramming or remembered experience. As explained previously, it is a *perpetual memory disk of infinite capacity*. This is important to understand because the most significant part in becoming a human being is the foundation of the very first experiences recorded in the *essence*.

Our first parents "formatted" our *essences* to become human beings by providing an environment where universal standards of humanity would be the first thing we recorded as our individual memories. These first experiences set the balance, or better, became the "measuring stick" with which we would compare all of our future experiences. These primordial experiences established our human conscience and provided a *foundationalized alignment* that will keep us in balance for the rest of our existence. The process of aligning a newly created *essence* can best be described as the ***Human***

Foundationalization Process. Through this process, the particular way each individual determines and experiences happiness—the reason *why* we exist—is established. It creates our humanity and allows us to become free-willed human beings and makes us unique from all other life forms in the Universe.

2. WE WERE FIRST CREATED WITH A PERFECT BRAIN

When we were first created, our *essence* was placed in a *perfect* human body with a *fully functioning* human brain. Advanced parents know exactly what constitutes the *perfect* human body. With the knowledge and power they possess, they created the ideal human biological form in which to place the newly created *essence*.

While in the *imperfect* bodies we have upon this earth, we only use a very limited part of our mortal brain. When we were first created though, we used every part of our primordial brain. We did not require sleep or rest, and all of our experiences were recorded in a fully conscious state.

Because we existed in a continual, fully conscious state of mind, we were able to utilize our *perfect* brain to its full capacity. In contrast, when our *essence* enters the *imperfect* bodies we currently have, it (the *essence*) becomes our *sub*conscious. Our *imperfect* brain has only limited access to the *essence*. Our current need for sleep and rest and the continual influences of life's stresses and expectations inhibit our brain's ability to function to its full capacity. In addition, our *imperfect* brain is not constructed the same as a *perfect* human brain; nor was it intended to do what a *perfect* human brain can do.

3. PERFECT BODIES PROVIDE OPPORTUNITY FOR EXPERIENCE

The *essence* must be placed in a physical body that can see, hear, feel, smell, and taste in order for it to record the experiences provided by our sensory receptors. Our first (primordial) body was *perfect* and allowed us to develop in a *perfect* human world where our creators/parents lived. Once these *perfect experiences* are recorded, all of our future experiences will be *measured* by, or compared to, these foundational ones. If the experience of the present *aligns* with the *foundationalized* experience of the past, we will sense what is recognized as calmness, comfort, and balance.

For example, when a newly created human in a *perfect* body first tastes a *perfectly* grown and engineered apple, the sensation produced by the stimulus of the taste buds will be forever recorded in the *essence*. The first sensation of *taste* is now permanently programmed in the *essence* and becomes a part of who the person is and will always be. The other sensations associated with the experience (such as when the person first *sees* the apple, *feels* it, *smells* it, and *hears* it crunch between their teeth) are likewise recorded. Every other apple that the person will eat will be compared to the level of quality set by the first. No other apple of the same type (and there are many, many, many different varieties) will ever taste, feel, smell, or sound better to the person unless the experience of eating it matches the first experience *perfectly*. The same **foundationalization process** occurs with each new experience that the person has.

The process of foundationalization is similar to what modern psychologists describe as "imprinting," where a person goes through a phase of learning that is independent of the consequences of behavior. This process includes everything that the new human sees, hears, feels, smells, and tastes. It also includes the experience of association, where the individual sees another person, hears their voice, smells their distinctive smell, feels their touch (or *feels* the energy of their presence and/or thoughts, in some cases), and creates an experience with them. These stored memories will always be associated with each individual with whom the newly created human comes in contact. This "association" also occurs with everything else (plant, animal, or element) in the developing human's surrounding environment. Each new experience will be permanently associated with something that was seen, heard, smelled, felt, or tasted during the foundationalization period.

As to taste, newborn mortal (*imperfect*) infants instinctively put everything that they see, touch, hear, and smell into their mouth. They subconsciously are making a comparison to their foundationalized experiences by using <u>all</u> five of their senses. Likewise, when we become adults, we kiss each other on the mouth as our first *taste* of the person to whom we are physically attracted, after we have seen, heard, touched, and smelled them. All of our physical senses are utilized so as to confirm compatibility with and enjoy the experience of physical bonding to another.

Another example of our uniquely human *foundationalized essence*, when compared to other life forms, is our use of the sense of smell in evaluating breath; we are the only species that seems to have a problem with the bad breath of one of our own species. Although at times we ignore it, nothing is more unpleasant than kissing someone with bad breath. It offends our established sense of smell. It creates imbalance from our previous experience with advanced human beings. This is because, just as newborn babies have the freshest and most delightful breath, so did the advanced human beings around whom we first established our sense of smell.

4. OUR PERCEPTION OF BEAUTY WAS FOUNDATIONALIZED

The *primordial foundational process* also set the standards of beauty that will stay with us throughout our eternal existence. Every advanced human being is a very beautiful person. They each possess the ability to choose for themselves what their physical body looks like. Although each is individually unique, each is also the quintessential example of human beauty. Therefore, when a newly created primordial human first opens its eyes and sees the people surrounding it, the standard of what a human being should look like is permanently established within the *essence*.

Rest assured that there are no uncontrollable, powerful "monster-like," big-headed, or green creatures with tentacles anywhere in the Universe that are going to one day take over or destroy the human race; having an established measure of all that is beautiful confirms this. The ultimate and most advanced life form in the Universe is a *beautiful* human being.

Even as the most beautiful examples of the human body are part of our first experiences, so are the most pristine and picturesque environments possible in the natural world. The perfectly beautiful mountains, plains, rivers, lakes, oceans, forests, and jungles of our primordial environment add to our foundational alignment of natural beauty and far surpass our present *imperfect* environment, even in its most glorious splendor.

In our primordial *perfect* world, our advanced creators had the knowledge and capability of creating the most exquisite architecture ever imagined. Once we experienced its magnificence and beauty, our own *unique* sense of architectural style and design was established. As a result, our mortal ability to recognize symmetry of lines and forms now allows us to build buildings and construct engineering marvels through the use of our *imagination* and *reason*. Likewise, our sense of rhythm, synchronicity, tempo, and timing, all established during our foundationalization, enables us to recognize the soothing melody of the sounds of both the natural world and the music we create by using our *imagination* and *reason*.

5. HUMANITY IS A LEARNED BEHAVIOR

In the primordial world, along with the values (*measures*) we uniquely determine for ourselves based on everything we see, hear, taste, smell, and touch, we also establish our first perceptions and cognitive paradigms (thinking experiences or patterns). A "paradigm" is best described as a very clear or typical example, or archetype. "Cognitive" means conscious intellectual activity. Therefore, the first "cognitive paradigms" (perfect examples in our consciousness) that are established during the foundationalization process of our *essence* are responsible for creating our *humanity*. They set the alignment for the way in which we interact with other people in our environment and with everything else that exists outside of ourselves.

For example, the ***uniquely human*** emotion of *compassion* was foundationalized in us through our first experiences. No other organism in the Universe shows the same type of sympathetic consciousness of all others' distress, along with a desire to alleviate it, as humans do. Not only do we show this emotion towards each other, but we also demonstrate it in our concern for all other animals and plants, and for every other aspect of our natural environment. In fact, we have the capability to feel as compassionate about a polluted ocean as we do about a sick neighbor.

Granted, there are animals that demonstrate a propensity for sympathy, but not in the same way as humans. As explained in the last chapter, an animal's *essence* can be programmed to instinctually do whatever the advanced human being who created the animal wants it to do. If an advanced human wants a dolphin, for example, to show an instinctual compassion for anything that is being subjected to a shark attack, then the programming for such instinct will be provided in the dolphin's *essence*. But the dolphin does not have a choice of whether to react or not; it does so instinctually. Humans, on the other hand, **can choose** to be compassionate or not.

Our ability to sense equality, justice, peace, and joy is also directly related to the recorded memories of the experiences we had around advanced humans who exemplified the *perfect* human beings. These beings expressed all of the positive emotions associated with ***humanity***. By sensing (using all of our sensory receptors) their example, our individual ***humanity*** was foundationalized. This "humanity" was the principal catalyst to ensure that we would use our free will for our own personal benefit *without* impeding the free will of another to exercise theirs for ***their*** own personal benefit.

6. HAPPINESS IS A COMPARATIVE BALANCE BETWEEN OUR ESSENCE AND OUR CURRENT EXPERIENCE

Our advanced creators/parents *smiled* when we did something no other being had ever done in quite the same manner. They *laughed* at our actions when our free will motivated us to act and react to our environment in totally unexpected ways. They *chuckled* when we exercised our free will and our actions failed to meet expected and reasonable outcomes. Their positive encouragement allowed each of us to develop unique personalities. They did not tell us *who* we should become. They guided the imprinting of our characteristics so that we could make our own choices. Their guidance during our *Foundationalization Process* ensured that all other humans were protected from our actions and guaranteed their right to become who they wanted to become. In other words, they did not allow us or provide us with any opportunity to think that another's choice of individuality was any better or worse than our own. They established the basis for unconditional human equality.

Just as we enjoy observing the funny things that mortal infants and small children do as they learn to use their physical body in our world, *advanced beings* receive similar pleasure watching us grow and learn. Because we are not preprogrammed to act or to be acted upon, we have the infinite capability of surprising even the most advanced parent—even one who has witnessed an immeasurable number of new human beings grow and develop.

Our advanced parents taught us how to smile. They taught us how to laugh. They taught us how to experience happiness. As happiness is the reason *why we exist*, it follows that our existence is based on our ability to feel happy. And it is the responsibility of our creators/parents to ensure that we fulfill the purpose of our human creation and experience continual and lasting happiness forever.

"Happiness" is simply feeling a sense of conformity. It exists naturally when the actions of our free will are in line with the first experiences we recorded as primordial human beings. When we use our free will to act or react to the stimulus of our current environment, our actions are automatically (subconsciously) compared with what is recorded on our *essence*. When the comparison is not consistent with what is *foundationalized* in our *essence*, the resulting feelings of imbalance in our life are those that we associate with unhappiness.

As explained above, the proper alignment of our primordial experiences establishes our humanity. Throughout our existence, the foundationalization we received will ensure peace and order all through the Universe, which exists for and is controlled by advanced, free-willed human beings. To allow us to act on our own, but ensure this peace and order, when we do something that makes us unhappy, we are naturally motivated to try to change the course of our actions so that we feel happy again. Therefore, our foundationalized experiences act as an "inner gauge" or an emotional meter of sorts, warning us when we are not acting as a free-willed human being was foundationalized to act.

7. FEELINGS ARE BASED ON OUR MEMORY OF EXPERIENCE

We develop "feelings," including the *feelings* of happiness and unhappiness, based on our recorded experiences. A "feeling" is the way our consciousness attempts to figure out whether or not what we are experiencing is in balance with what we have stored in our *essence.*

When we are around someone who looks suspicious, for example, we can get a "feeling" that something isn't right, as if the person doesn't fit into our expectations of what a "trustworthy" person *should* be. We make the judgment based on what we can remember, which is generally only what we have been taught since our mortal birth. This is because our *imperfect* brain cannot consciously recall experiences recorded in our *essence.* Although no prejudices or judgments of others were part of our primordial *foundationalization*, in our *imperfect* world, they become the *imperfect* foundation of our current reality. Our *true humanity* is altered here upon this earth, and we often treat others ***inhumanely***, contrary to how we were reared on a *perfect* world.

If, for example, we have always heard since our mortal birth that dark people cause problems, when we see a person with dark skin, our conscious mind creates a *feeling* of imbalance. If, however, we had the ability to immediately remember *all* of the experiences stored in our *essence*, we might discover that we ourselves were once dark-skinned in a previous life, or that we once had a good friend, or even lived around an advanced creator/parent, who was. This would then eliminate any feeling of suspicion or prejudice.

Although our initial "feeling" might be negative toward another person while existing in this *imperfect* world, if we used our *reason* (which again, is our ability to determine what is *real* and what is not), we could conclude, in the example used above, that we should not judge a person merely by the color of their skin. To live in ***true reality*** and create the peace and order intended for the human race, we must temper our *feelings* with our ability to *reason*.

Current scientific understanding defines a "feeling" as a chemical reaction that starts in the brain and causes the body to respond. But, if this were the case, then out of the millions of other animal species upon the earth, one surely would have developed a somewhat similar array of feelings to those which human beings exhibit. None has, because none has a *human essence* inside of its body, providing it with a guide on how it should feel. Being happy is a human feeling. Smiling and laughter are human responses to the feeling of happiness. We have already explained why humans smile and laugh and other animals do not. Our feelings are distinctively *human* because of the energy exchange between our *human essence* and our brain, an exchange that animals do not experience.

All other human feelings, positive or negative, are produced exactly the same way that "happiness" is produced—through these exchanges. The only difference between a negative emotion and a positive one is the *way* our body responds to each. These "emotions," though not considered a physical part of us, are more powerful than might be supposed. They can greatly affect the physical state of our body, causing sickness, disease, and even death. Many cases have been documented where a close partner dies leaving the surviving one emotionally affected. The surviving partner soon dies from no known physical reason. Emotions are just as physical as every other aspect of our existence. Just as it takes energy emissions from our brain to move our muscles, emotions are likewise emissions from our brain of the exact same energy.

When our *human essence* was foundationalized, it reacted with a *perfect* and *fully functional* brain that did not allow (what we know as) *negative* "feelings." A negative feeling causes an imbalance in our body, whereas a *positive* feeling causes balance in our body. Whenever something occurs in our current experience that is *not* part of our *human foundation*, our *imperfect* brain responds by producing levels of energy (chemical reactions) that are not balanced with the levels of energy stored in our *essence*. When our body produces these energies, we feel what can best be described as "stress," which leads to anxiety, tension, and discomfort. It could be stated that positive feelings create *high* energy and negative feelings create *low* energy; thus, the free-willed human has *some* control over their environment in order to create the balance that is felt as "peace and happiness."

When we were being "foundationalized," our body was *perfect* and literally made to be part of our *essence*, just as our *essence* was made to be part of our *perfect* body. Either way, there were no negative or positive forces involved in the union. The *essence* and the *perfect* body were one. Being one, everything we experienced with our positively charged body was perfectly recorded on our positively charged *essence*, with little expenditure of energy.

Because our *imperfect* brain cannot connect with all of our past memories, our mind is *subconsciously* trying to place itself in balance with a memory of an experience that caused us to feel happiness. Using the example from above, prejudiced parents seem (in the child's eyes) to be happy when their children distrust dark-skinned people; therefore, when the child sees a dark-skinned person, the first *positive* memory that comes to his or her mind is that of doing what made the parents happy.

Our current life experience upon this earth is full of negative "feelings" because of the prejudices and in*human*e examples of others, especially the parents responsible for our *imperfect foundationalization*. Until we can remember *all* of our multiple lives' experiences, including our extensive life in a *perfect* body, we will always be susceptible to negative feelings and the stress they cause to our bodies.

8. EMOTIONS ARE THE WAY WE EXPRESS OUR FEELINGS

An emotion is not the actual feeling. Emotions are the way we express our feelings. One person might be more emotional than another, even if both are experiencing the exact same feeling. Using the example from above, even if two people have been taught the *same* prejudice concerning dark-skinned people, one might react completely opposite of the other to the feeling of "suspicion."

Emotions, or the way that we express our feelings, have all to do with the mortal body we have been given. Unique genetic patterns can determine different levels of emotional balance and produce a wide range of varied emotional expressions. Some people cry to express negative emotions, while others cry to express positive ones. Negative emotions offset the naturally balanced state of our body, whereas positive emotions support the body and enhance its capacity to function.

The *essence* has nothing whatsoever to do with our emotions. Only our physical body can determine how we express our feelings. For this reason, having a *perfect human body* is the only way we will ever be able to completely eliminate negative emotions. In addition, because we were not provided with a *perfect body* while on this earth, it was not intended for us to be continually happy. We were meant to experience unhappiness.

9. WE HAD TO LEARN HOW TO SMILE

In our primordial stage of human development, we had no *negative* feelings to express as emotions. This is because in a *perfect* world, nothing was out of balance. The life and environment provided by our first, *perfect* parents allowed for only *positive* "feelings" to be instilled in our *essence*. "Negativity" is produced only when the energy levels we expend in our actions and thoughts do not align with our *foundationalized* ones.

Our advanced parents taught us by their example how to express our feelings. They taught us proper *emotions*. However, because we had nothing to compare them to, we did not understand *why*, for example, our advanced parents laughed and smiled; we only knew that they did. We mimicked what they did. We learned that it was an expression of positive feelings—the only feelings we understood. Without prior learning or previous experience with expressing emotions though, it was impossible for us to express inappropriate or negative emotions.

Our creators taught us how to smile, which is the physical demonstration of balance or contentment. The "smile" is distinctly human and is not found anywhere else in any other life form. A genuine and sincere smile is a universal and unmistakable sign of balance and comfort. When we are comfortable with an experience, or when the experience fits into our subconsciously established "comfort zone," we demonstrate the effect by smiling. We learned this from observing perfect parents smiling at us as we began to respond and react to our perfect environment in their world. When we smile in our *imperfect world*, we create an energy pattern (or better, an experience) that matches what is recorded in our *essence* and makes us feel happy.

10. PARENTS PLAY THE MOST IMPORTANT ROLE IN THE HUMAN FOUNDATIONALIZATION PROCESS

As humans advance and become experienced with different societies and cultures in which they associate with each other, they recognize the effect that proper parenting has on the emotional outcome of a new human being. A child who is reared in an environment of fear, insecurity, inequality, abuse, or ignorance (or who in any other way is trained contrary to what a productive and contributory member of a society should be), can cause many problems as an adult. The way a child is reared by those with whom it has contact for the first foundational years of its life is paramount to its ability to fit in with and feel a sense of personal balance around the rest of humanity. Our *imperfect* experiences as mortals with many failed human societies have confirmed that being a parent is *not a right* that should be granted to everyone.

11. IT IS A PRIVILEGE TO BE A PARENT

Even the most successful of the less-advanced, modern human cultures upon this earth have determined that it is necessary for their citizens to obtain permission for many of the privileges that people are allowed to have. To drive, for example, one must have a license. To do any specialized task that can affect the whole of society, individuals must prove themselves capable of performing the task without producing a result that could potentially harm society.

One must have permission to gain the privilege of being a doctor, for example. One is required to obtain a license in order to participate in the construction trades, thus ensuring the building of safe structures. Modern cultures have determined that permission from the majority must be granted for almost every aspect of human interaction wherein the actions of one have the potential of affecting the life experience of another.

Ironically, however, none of our current modern civilizations has determined the need to issue special permission to an individual to produce another human being. One does not need any particular training, understanding, or ability to become a parent and provide the care and nurturing necessary to a new member of the human race. Although childhood experiences can be linked to almost every problem affecting the security and balance of a successful society, no government has figured out the necessity of making sure a parent has the ability to rear a child properly.

For this very reason, all societies upon this earth have failed. But once the effect of *improper* parenting finally takes its toll on even the most modern human cultures, humans will begin to realize the importance of *proper* parenting. The determination will then be made that parenting must be regulated; and *only* those individuals with the proven capability of proper parenting will be granted permission to do so.

No matter how much food is available, no matter how much specialized education one has, no matter what kind of opportunities are afforded to a human being, if one receives faulty or insufficient training during one's foundational years, that individual has the potential of negatively affecting the rest of society during his or her adult years. Although contrary to the ways *imperfect* human societies operate upon this earth, it is vital to the peace and order of the entire Universe that, ultimately, no free-willed being is allowed the ability to create other beings, unless found capable of and competent enough to do it correctly.

12. ADVANCED PARENTS MUST FOLLOW STRICT GUIDELINES TO RAISE CHILDREN

Through their own extensive experience, advanced parents have already learned the proper way to rear children. They acquired a lot of experience during the different stages of their own human development and concluded for themselves that being a parent was what would bring them the most happiness. Those who choose to provide and be responsible for the foundational experiences of new human beings are well-versed and experienced in the proper way children need to be reared, so they (the children) can become integral and productive members of a perfect human society.

Because human beings have always existed throughout the Universe, there have always been strict laws and instructions established to ensure continual order. The instructions on how to rear a newly created child have also always been, and must be followed precisely. It can be said that these instructions (the "recipe" for *all* life, including plants and animals) are contained in an eternal "*Book of Life*" that all humans must use and follow, if they are allowed to be responsible for the creation of life.

There is a governance structure set up that ensures that all established eternal laws are followed as they have always been. The Universe is assured that a newly created human being will receive the proper foundationalization and be taught the proper way to interact and behave with other humans. Thus, only those whom the Universal Government allows will have the power and knowledge to create and foundationalize humans. This is consistent with the laws of the

Universe. These creators/parents must first desire the responsibility, and then prove to the rest of us that they will fulfill their obligation correctly. They prove this by the way they use their free will.

Becoming a parent and having parental responsibilities is **not** how most of us would like to spend the rest of our eternity. An advanced creator's/parent's personal freedom is restricted in a similar manner to the restrictions placed on mortal parents, who are required to provide for the physical and emotional needs of the children they produce. It takes self-discipline and personal sacrifice to follow the strict guidelines that have been established for foundationalization parenting.

13. ADVANCED PARENTS MAKE A CHOICE TO HAVE CHILDREN

During our foundationalization as humans, we are free to choose what guidelines and laws we wish to follow. But because we are foundationalized in a *perfect human society*, we learn, without any contrasting experience, to agree with and support the established guidelines. After eventually going through the different stages of our development (especially the stage we are presently going through on this earth), we will come to the conclusion that the society in which we received our primordial foundation is indeed the *perfect human society*. We will then **choose** to follow the guidelines and laws of that society.

While going through these different stages of our human development, we will learn that improper parenting creates the problems associated with the aberrant behavior that is counterproductive to the peace and happiness that *should* exist in a human society. Through our own experience, we will learn that the government, laws, and instructions contained in this universal "*Book of Life*" on how to rear a human being are indeed the *only* formula that will maintain continual peace and order as it has always existed.

Because of the strict requirements of advanced parenthood, no one is forced to be such a parent. Some choose the responsibility—most do not.

14. WE DEVELOP OUR FREE WILL AND COMMON SENSE IN A PERFECT WORLD

Although a child in an advanced *perfect world* can be trained to think, act, and react to its environment, there is a noticeable difference between free-willed children and *restricted* children, who are not allowed to develop free will. The former are allowed to roam free and experience different aspects of their individual liberty by interacting in various environments. The latter are isolated in a strict, enclosed environment of learning.

Those who are uninhibited in the choices available to them develop a sense of ***free** will* that allows them to individualize and become quite different from their parents. On the other hand, those who are secluded from different choices and given a structured environment, in which only specific and specialized instructions are provided, never establish a sense of *free* will and become exactly as their parents expect them to be. In specific terms, the "son" raised in this particular environment, becomes exactly like the "father."

In our *imperfect* world, children often rebel against their parents and society because they are not allowed to experience a life consistent with the experiences recorded in their *essence*, which allowed uninhibited free will. It is seen as "rebellion" *only* because the action doesn't fulfill the expectations of the *imperfect* parent and society. Advanced children, however, could not "rebel," because they had no other experience recorded in their *essence* that would motivate them to act a certain way. Furthermore, advanced, *perfect* parents and societies didn't place the same restrictions on free will as *imperfect* parents and societies do; therefore, there was no such thing as "rebellion" there. "Rebellion" is a state of our mortal *imperfect* body, which is in constant opposition to our *essence*-empowered desire to exercise our free will.

In advanced societies, newly created children are provided an open environment, which allows each of them to grow and develop a sense of individualism and free will. The few exceptions to this are those few children intended to become a "public servant" or "government overseer" (a specialized human who oversees what all other free-willed beings do in a particular solar system, and who *does not* develop with this sense of free will). An animal adapts to its environment based on the instinctual behavior provided for it by its preprogramming. Conversely, a human child freely *uses* its environment to produce its own distinctive behaviors and instincts and records these as new *experiences*.

It is easy to predict how an animal will respond to its environment; because of this predictability, most animals can be easily trained to adapt to almost any environment in which they are placed. A human being, on the other hand, attempts to *change* the environment to adapt to what the person *expects* from it. These expectations come from the human's ability to *imagine* and *reason*, which we have already properly defined as the ability to think about an experience until it makes *sense*. We also refer to this as "common sense." It is a general *sense* of conformity to what our past experience has already *reasoned* is best for us. The *Human Foundationalization Process* establishes our common sense regarding what is ***humane*** and what is not.

15. ADVANCED MOTHERS ARE RESPONSIBLE FOR OUR BODIES AND FOUNDATIONALIZATION

The parent who is responsible for determining what the physical body is going to look like (what color of skin, hair, eyes, etc.), in which the *essence* is placed, is the female mother. Because she is the one responsible for ensuring that the child is foundationalized correctly, she retains the right to choose her children's appearance. The mother provides the materials and environment in which the body is created and prepared for the newly created (i.e., blank) *essence*. Although this process takes place inside the mother's womb on our current *imperfect* world, the advanced mother, with greater knowledge and superior powers and abilities, is not required to go through the pain and stress of childbirth. The process in an advanced human world allows a mother to program the exact *DNA patterns* (for want of a better term) that will create the body she desires for her child.

The number of children that a mother creates is her choice. Generally, because the process of foundationalization is so important, a mother will only rear one child at a time. These advanced mothers know when a newly created human has had "enough" experience, at which point it then needs less attention and care. The mother will ensure that the child has been properly *foundationalized* before creating another one.

During this time, a strong bond is created between the mother and the newly created child; and until she is sure that this everlasting bond is formed, the mother will concentrate on one child at a time. This bonding period is similar to the way a mother on this earth might wait two or three years before having another child. In advanced worlds, where there is no concept of time, this bonding period could last for thousands of years, if necessary.

16. OUR INITIAL BOND WITH OUR MOTHER IS VITAL TO OUR HUMAN DEVELOPMENT

Our advanced mothers have bodies with breasts that carry a "milk-like" substance that becomes the first *taste* experience for the child. Though this "mother's milk" has no nutritional value for a *perfect body* that does not require any outside nutrition, the experience of breastfeeding enhances the bonding period. Advanced mothers breastfeed without the pain sometimes associated with it in mortality. Human *bonding* is an emotional result of our relationships with each other. Each of us developed our *first* bond with our own *first* mother much the same way an infant in this world creates a bond with its mortal mother. These intimate moments will forever solidify a personal bond between mother and child. This bond also adds to the reasons why an advanced human desires to be a parent-mother—for personal enjoyment.

In addition to this *emotional* bond, we also have a *physical* bond with our mothers. This is because each individual mother was involved in the creation of our *first* physical bodies and copied some of her own "DNA patterns" into each of our unique bodies. Our mothers created each of our bodies to look uniquely different from the rest of our siblings. This was not so that *they* could tell us apart, but to help *other* human beings value our uniqueness. Even if we all looked the same, our mothers could tell us apart, because *their* advanced *senses* would always recognize the differences.

When each primordial mother copied her own "DNA patterns" into the makeup of each child's body, she allowed energy patterns to transfer that were part of *her own* and, therefore, easily recognizable by the power of her *essence.* When our cells perform their functions, they give off energy patterns unique to the specific action each performs. Each of our bodies as a whole also has an energy pattern that is unique to the individual. These energy patterns are physically tied to our mother's *own* body.

If a mortal mother had an advanced mother's brain, she would be able to "tune in" to each of the children to whom she has passed on some of *her own* "DNA patterns," even in this *imperfect world.* Although this effect is currently experienced at times between a mortal mother and child, it is not as readily available to the conscious mind of an *imperfect* brain as it is to an advanced mother's brain.

The role of the advanced female is the most vital and important part of the *Foundationalization Process.* Although advanced males play an important role later on in the developmental stages of the human being, without the principal role of the mother, human life throughout the Universe would not succeed. The main reason why there are so few advanced males involved in the production and foundationalization process of new human beings is because they are not needed. On this earth, the purpose of the much stronger male is for the protection and support of the female and her offspring. In a perfect world, women do not need to be supported or protected. Advanced women have all the powers and abilities of any advanced male.

17. ADVANCED FATHERHOOD IS ACHIEVED WITHOUT SEX

Once the perfect body is created and has reached the size of a normal infant (which only takes a few moments), the *essence* is prepared to be introduced into it. The advanced humans who gather the required matter and know how to create an *essence* are best described as advanced fathers. Advanced procreation follows similar patterns to the natural patterns on Earth. Although the *imperfect* women's body is programmed to only produce one child at a time (except in the abnormal anomaly of multiple births), an *imperfect* male can father many children with many different women at the same time. Likewise, in advanced societies, it takes only *one* advanced male to create many *essences* for the mothers who have created bodies for their children. The biggest difference, however, is that the entire procreation process is done asexually. No advanced human in the future, male or female, will have physical sex in order to produce a child. With the powers and knowledge possessed by advanced creators/parents, sex will become obsolete for the purpose of producing the perfect human being (although not obsolete for its enjoyment to those advanced human beings who will possess sex organs).

Sex, as we know it in an *imperfect world*, is not an instrument for advanced procreation in a *perfect world* for two main reasons:

- First, procreating asexually removes any chance of an unintended imperfection in what the mother wants the body to look like. She is solely responsible for the production of the physical body.

- Second, polygamous relationships in the procreation of children, by one male having sex with multiple females, would cause the human emotions of lust, jealousy, and inequality. This would also result in all the problems that arise from emotions associated with the imperfect human notion of "love."

Advanced human societies have learned how to live appropriately so as to eliminate *anything* that causes stressful negative emotions. Those choosing to become parents responsible for continuing the human race *will* be able to experience the physical, emotional, and intimate enjoyment of the sexual experience; but they will not have any of the negative emotions currently associated with our natural desire to have sex. The *imperfect* emotion of "love," is a comparative value that we place on something (or someone) when compared to something (or someone) else less desirable. This comparison does not exist in a perfect world, where all people are treated equally and everything provides the ultimate human experience.

18. OUR FOUNDATIONALIZATION IS CARRIED OUT ON AN ISOLATED PLANET

As mentioned previously, a child is greatly affected by its first experiences in life. It was also mentioned that advanced societies have determined that it takes special training and understanding to make sure that all newly created human beings have the right environment provided for them during the time they are recording their first experiences. Advanced "parents" isolate themselves from the rest of humanity so that they can fulfill their responsibility to foundationalize their children correctly, which includes concentrating entirely on parenting each child properly. These parents have distinct planets upon which they can utilize isolated environments to foundationalize their children.

All of the children and their mothers reside on these *parenting* planets, but are not isolated from each other nor separated into family units. The whole *parenting* society is one big communal happy family. You've undoubtedly heard the statement, "It takes a village to raise a child." Well, it's *true*! Although there *is* a unique bond created between each mother and each of her children, the absence and division of what we currently call the "family unit" aids in the proper foundationalization process of equality and free will.

There should be no question now as to who and what is responsible for the majority of the inequality and misery found in the *imperfect world*: It is *imperfect* parenting and the value *imperfect* humans place on their *own family unit* above any other human beings in the world. If we only realized that we are all part of a universal family and are all siblings of other advanced humans, our society would transform overnight. While it is impossible in this life for any of us to be a ***true parent***, we can rest assured that those advanced humans who are, promote and ensure universal human equality in all things.

19. DIFFERENT PLANETS FOR REARING CHILDREN

In advanced societies, there are two main classifications of "parenting groups." One group consists entirely of women who have determined for themselves that rearing children from infancy to adulthood brings them the most joy in their existence. The other group is made up of male and female couples. To best describe these two types of parental groups, it is necessary to envision them as they existed in our past when we were first created, and how those of us who choose to be responsible for children will exist as advanced parents in the future.

As mentioned above, to rear a perfectly balanced child, the parent and child must be isolated from the rest of the human race (or from those who want nothing to do with parenting), so that the child can be foundationalized without other distractions. The way that advanced parents rear their children does not create a very interesting and desirable environment for those who choose not to be parents; therefore, other planets exist that allow a more desirable situation for non-parental adults.

Using our current solar system as an example, there are basically *nine* main planets. In the future, these planets will become habitable. Those of us who inhabit this particular solar system will live upon one of the planets, based on our personal desires of happiness and wanting to be around others who share similar interests.

20. MERCURY—THE PLANET FOR MALE/FEMALE COUPLES

Mercury (using the names of our known planets ***only*** as examples, as the names of each does not matter) will become a planet upon which will live those humans who desire to live together as a couple—one male and one female. The purpose for this partnership will be expounded upon later. For now, it should be understood that males create other solar systems and oversee the different stages of human development. They do not want to work alone; they desire a companion.

With their female companion's help, these fathers produce children who are not allowed free will, but are instead reared to become "sons" who will become the "public servants/overseers" of each new solar system. These couples will reap the benefit of their choice to serve others in becoming parents by sharing a sexual relationship. Their individual DNA patterns will be adjusted so that each partner is only capable of being attracted to the other. In this way, it becomes impossible for either partner to experience the challenges and distractions that can be associated with monogamy in an *imperfect* world (jealousy, lust, etc). All other advanced beings of the opposite sex will have the same appeal to the advanced male and female as the non-sexual attraction between modern-day brothers and sisters.

21. VENUS WILL BE THE PLANET FOR FEMALES

Venus will become the planet upon which live *only* women who desire to be mothers and who do not cater to the needs of anyone (including men) except their children. These women are the principal progenitors of the next batch of newly created humans. Although children are not created through the act of sex, these women retain the ability to enjoy sex by sharing the experience with other women or from self-manipulation. As many modern-day women will attest, few sexual experiences match those that are created *by* other women. And, although many will try to deny it, less-advanced *imperfect* males are very comfortable with two women enjoying sex together. In fact, most find it enticing to their own sexual nature.

This is a reasonably natural response, when one takes into account the experiences that are recorded in our *essences*, which were foundationalized around women who lived together and associated sexually with each other or by themselves. Because we had no sense of sexuality during our foundationalization period, we did not equate the relationships between our mothers as anything but the natural way of how things were. Although we never saw our mothers engaging in the act of sex, we saw the love and tenderness they demonstrated toward each other in our presence.

These "Venus" women do not associate sexually with the "fathers," who live in the partnerships mentioned above as being on the planet Mercury. These women are completely self-sufficient, and have the power to create anything and everything for themselves and their children on this world, without the help of a "male." As mentioned and as will be discussed later in greater detail, a significant role of the male is to create new solar systems for these women's children and to oversee the second stage of their children's development.

Upon this earth, we are currently in the *second* stage of our development. Other civilizations found throughout the Universe are also experiencing their *second* stage. Still others exist in the *first* stage of human development (known as our Primordial Foundationalization) or in the *third* stage, where they permanently reside on advanced planets. No matter in what stage of development humans are found throughout the Universe though, all of us were foundationalized on what are best termed as *parenting* planets similar to Mercury and Venus, which are found in all parts of the Universe where human creation takes place.

22. EARTH WILL BE THE PLANET FOR SERVANTS

Our Earth will eventually accommodate those people who will be the "working" servants of everyone else. Earth will become the "servants quarters," for want of a better term, for all of those humans who have the knowledge and the power (and most importantly, the desire) to serve the needs of other human beings.

These advanced humans in servitude will have no gender, because they will choose not to be involved in the creation of life. Their primary responsibility will be to work with the parents and ensure that the purpose for which humans are created is fulfilled. Because they will have all the knowledge and powers of advanced creators (except the ability to enjoy sexuality), they will be a great support to the fathers and mothers, who are ultimately responsible for their children's happiness. They will be the fathers' and mothers' servants, and consequently, the servants of the entire human race.

Their home planet (Earth) will be a base from which they are assigned and given instructions on their various missions for each new batch of children in each new solar system. When a new solar system is created, they will work under the direction of the "father" and the "public servant/overseer" of that solar system.

In relation to our solar system, once our planets have become "advanced," these servants will serve the needs of those of us who do not desire to become parents. Some of these types of human beings are also actively involved with us while going through our *imperfect* mortal stage of development, again, always under the direction of the male father or "overseer" of this solar system. According to our current understanding, and some generally accepted but often erroneous beliefs, this type of human being could be called an **A**dvanced **N**omadic **G**enderless **E**nlightened **L**ife form (**ANGEL** for short).

23. THE PLANETS OF EACH SOLAR SYSTEM SERVE INDIVIDUAL NEEDS

Most of us want to be left alone to pursue our own desires of happiness. We want to serve ourselves, establish our own environment, and create our own plants and animals, according to our own needs and wants. The planets of Mars, Jupiter, and Saturn will provide all the space needed for the majority of us who wish to serve ourselves. Uranus, Neptune, and Pluto, however, will be inhabited by those of us who have no desire to serve ourselves and want servants doing everything for us. Those of us on these planets will love the idea that all of our needs will be provided for without any effort on our part, except to enjoy all the experiences that advanced life has to offer.

The advanced human (male/father) who was responsible for creating each of our *essences* and our solar system counseled with our mothers to find out what our needs would be so that each of us could experience ultimate happiness in our *own* way. Our mothers knew what our desires of happiness were and would be, because they reared us and watched us grow, as well as having an emotional bond with each of us.

Our mothers, therefore, counseled with our "father," who then created the precise number of planets, each exact in size, to accommodate every single one of our personal preferences. Because we existed for eons of time and experienced all there is to being a perfect advanced human being, our *Foundationalization Process* established and solidified *who we are*. We became ***who we will always be*** in this perfect primordial world. Because we will not change our desires of happiness, our solar system has a precise number of planets with predetermined sizes to fit our needs perfectly.

24. THREE MAIN STAGES OF HUMAN DEVELOPMENT

There are basically three stages of our human development:

1st Stage Our primordial foundational existence upon the planet of our creators.
2nd Stage Our mortality upon this present earth.
3rd Stage Our final residence upon one of the planets in our own solar system.

We can describe ourselves (which will also describe our final state of existence—the 3rd Stage) as each belonging to one of three main categories or "humanity types":

1) **Those who want to serve others**
2) **Those who want to serve themselves**
3) **Those who want to be served**

In planning our solar system for the batch of children we all belong to, our "father" created three different sets of planets to accommodate each category, which, for want of a better word, we can call "estates." The three main estates each have three "sub-estates," for a total of nine *main* planets.

Although three of the planets (Mercury, Venus, and Earth) exist *solely* for the purpose of creating and serving the human race and ensuring each person's individual happiness, there will be another planet created and assigned as the "governing body" of our solar system. This *tenth* planet will be the place where the one who is *anointed* to oversee the government of our solar system will reside.

25. GENDER IS A CHOICE, NOT A MANDATE

During the first stage of our development, every primordial human body that is produced to house a blank *essence* is genetically constructed to be genderless, without the ability to have children and without sex organs. No newly created body has the innate hormonal desire to create its own kind; therefore, none has a sex drive. The DNA patterns of an advanced human child do not allow for gender or any type of sexual nature. The person first must have enough experience without gender to determine whether or not they want to be a parent.

We make the determination of whether or not to be a parent long before we go through our second stage of development upon this earth. However, our mortality here allows us the opportunity, through multiple earth lives, to confirm and solidify this decision by having the temporary ability to experience sex and the responsibility of parenthood. During our second stage of development on the earth, most of us will experience lives both as a male and as a female. We have these differing gender experiences so that we will be convinced that neither gender fits our desire of happiness (for those of us who did not choose to be parents), or which gender we enjoyed the most (for those of us who will become parents).

In general, because the experiences of both genders are recorded in our *essence*, there is a possibility, for example, that we might obtain a male body in one of our lives upon this earth that allows us to be physically attracted to other males. This occurs because we use our *reason* to find a consistent balance between the energy of our *essence* (our latent memories) and our current experience. This is the case for those who are homosexual.

There is no abnormal or *unnatural* attraction that occurs between homosexuals. In fact, they are usually more "in tune" with the power of their *essence* than *imperfect* heterosexuals are. Their brains allow them to make a stronger and more direct connection to the memories stored in their *essence*, causing them to feel a balance when they have a *current* experience that matches a *past* experience. A man, therefore, who does not have this kind of "direct connection" with his *essence*, will not easily remember that in one of his past lives, he lived as a woman.

The man or woman who has the stronger, more *direct connection* will be more affected by the energy of the past experience stored in the *essence*, thus causing his or her physical body to react more spontaneously to what makes it feel comfortable. Because of this more direct connection with their *essence*, homosexuals by nature are generally more compassionate, kind, nurturing, and tender than those humans who have no such *connection*. They are more connected to ***true humanity*** than those whose *essence* has little effect on their *imperfect* brain.

26. SEXUALITY ADDS TO THE PROBLEMS OF HUMANITY

There is no doubt that our sexual natures cause the majority of our problems. Psychologists who have long studied human nature and its associated dilemmas often agree that there is an underlying sexual aspect to almost all of our psychological and emotional issues. To avoid these negative aspects of our emotional awareness, there are no sexual functions or desires given to newly created, primordial human beings.

This is important to ensure the necessity that our first experiences do not include any negativity that would set a precedent for later actions. If, for example, the desire to satisfy a sexual appetite became a part of our foundational experience, we would then crave to satiate the sexual longing during mortality and in our 3rd stage of human development in order to maintain conformity with our subconscious, regardless of the problems associated with it. It is also necessary that our experiences in our permanent 3rd stage of human development do not include such negativity.

Our sexuality will be explained in greater detail later, as we discuss our life here upon this earth during our second stage of development. Here it is important to understand that our sexuality has *nothing* to do with our pre-earth experience and is not a part of our *essential* recognition of happiness. It is purely a functional aspect of the physical body we currently have upon this earth. In the situation of mortality on the earth in which we currently find ourselves, we often battle the sexual desires of our body, attempting to subdue them to correlate with our humane belief that these desires *should* be controlled.

As is logically concluded, in an *imperfect* world, sexual abilities are necessary to perpetuate life. Here on earth, the organs of the body associated with sex perform the way they do for no other purpose than to create life. Although there are emotional benefits felt by humans in experiencing sex, the fact still remains that the purpose for the physical act is to create another human being. In a *perfect world*, if one does not have the desire to create life, that person does not need the body parts necessary to do so. The sex organs and the feelings that they produce are part of the process of perpetuating life. Therefore, in advanced, *perfect* worlds, they are not necessary or available to those who do not want to be parents.

As reasonable as this might seem to our *common sense*, the fact that we enjoy the ability to have sex (which is now enhanced by our current technology to do so without creating life) leaves us wondering why all humans shouldn't retain the ability to experience sex forever. Why shouldn't it be part of human nature to enjoy sex simply for the sake of the enjoyment alone? Although we would like to argue this point, later it will be shown why the laws of the Universe mandate that having sex as advanced human beings must be limited to those who have determined to be advanced parents.

Regardless of whether we are genderless or have the ability to enjoy sex, in the end, all of us will be completely happy and content with the type of human each of us has chosen for ourselves, for we had the choice from the beginning.

SUMMARY

All life forms in the Universe, with one exception, are programmed and specialized to do something that contributes to the environment in which they live. Their environment determines the way that they exist and ***if*** and ***when*** they are needed for the sake of the environment. If they do not perform the function for which they exist, they become extinct. Some of this "programming" is instinctual according to the makeup of the body, and some is learned as the organism *adapts* to its environment. In this way, the Universe retains its extraordinary beauty, order, and balance. These life forms exist ***for*** the Universe.

There is **one** life form, however, that exclusively *controls* its environment, making changes to its surroundings according to its own personal desires. This life form does *not* adapt to its environment, but has the power to force its environment to *adapt* to it. Its dominion can destroy its environment if its personal desires are not being met. It is the only organism in the Universe that has not been programmed to react to its environment. Instead, this life form has the power and free will to act upon it. The Universe exists ***for*** this life form. This specialized life form is the **Human Being**.

The Universe provides the most advanced planets with the most complex and sophisticated technologies available to ensure that the human being has the ability to experience the most fulfilling existence possible. The needs of the people residing on advanced planets are provided for freely and equally. Nature (the term used to describe all other living and non-living things) works in its perfected state upon these advanced planets. Trees and plants bear the most succulent and delectable fruit ever tasted or imagined by human beings.

In these advanced societies, new humans are being created continuously. These newly created life forms are given the same power and free will over their environment that their creators enjoy. Each new human being establishes the unique propensities of **humanity** in these advanced worlds that are without need, without sorrow, and without negativity—worlds where everyone is treated and respected equally. It is in this type of world where our first experiences were recorded in our *essence.*

From these first experiences, we measure and judge every future experience we will ever have. This is how we develop and maintain our unique ability to *reason*. All we are doing in our current experience upon this earth is trying to figure out how to reproduce the feelings of balance that we recorded during our primordial, foundational life. We can succeed in this quest, however, only by relying on our *common sense*—that innate part of our human *reason* that we use to seek balance, until things make *sense*. Our *common sense* was established in our *essence* during our foundationalization.

Our ability to *imagine* and *reason*, which is associated with our pursuit of and longing for happiness, is simply our conscious mind trying to find a way to make us feel comfortable with our current environment. Our *common sense* is the "measure" of our imagination and reason. If an action we are considering "makes sense" to us, we do it. Unlike other organisms that have no ability to reason, and which react and adapt to their surroundings, we find ways to *change* the environment so that it reacts and adapts to *us*—until it fulfills our desire for happiness. It is within *us* where we find our individual happiness, the *measure* of which was established through a perfect **Human Foundationalization Process**.

The responsibility of our advanced human creators/parents was to ensure that we had the appropriate environment, where the proper human conscience, our *common sense,* could be foundationalized. The way that they lived and interacted with each other, and with us, gave us an example of how we should treat others and expect to be treated by others throughout our existence as human beings.

During our first experiences, we stored memories in our *essence* of all that we saw, smelled, heard, tasted, and touched. Because everything that we experienced in a perfect world produced the ultimate, perfected outcome of all things, we established a sense of what we will forever recognize as beautiful, fragrant, soothing, satisfying, and pleasant.

Our basis for what we will always recognize as happiness was established upon these advanced planets, as we bonded and engaged with our perfect mothers. All advanced people are the most beautiful specimens of human form and beauty. There are no noxious weeds that irritate us, or any insects or other animals that bite us, scare us, or make us feel uncomfortable. The animals that do exist in these perfect environments interact with us as playfully and gently as a newborn puppy. They are preprogrammed instinctually to be the best animal companions a human being could possibly desire.

Only in this perfect environment could we become *free-willed* beings. It was as wonderful there as we can possibly imagine it to be; and it is only possible to *imagine* it because we once experienced it. The human mind cannot imagine or conceive something it has not yet experienced.

Life in our *imperfect* world creates unhappiness, through the experiences that are inconsistent with the ones that we recorded upon our *essence* during our foundationalization in a perfect world. None of us likes to be told what to do. We want to do what *we want* to do. When one takes authority over us and demands something of us that we don't agree with, we feel "unhappy." This feeling arises because doing what we *really* don't want to do is not how we were foundationalized.

The advanced creator/parent never told us what to do, who we should become, or how we should interact with our environment. There are absolutely no expectations in a perfect world. We were allowed to experience anything we wanted. There, we interacted with our environment and created new experiences that would eventually make us a separate and unique individual apart from all other human beings. However, because there is nothing except human perfection in an advanced world, we only had the opportunity to record *perfect* experiences.

During this perfected **Human Foundationalization Process**, because we only experienced everything that was good about being human, our *personal experience* did not allow us to know the difference, for example, between "good" and "bad." Nothing we experienced in our primordial, advanced world allowed us to make a comparative value. Consequently, neither did we really know "happiness." All we knew was how things were in our present reality there. We didn't even realize that things were perfect! Our creators/parents consequently made possible an *imperfect* world (the one in which we presently exist) to help us learn to appreciate *who we are* and *why we exist*.

Our Primordial World

CHAPTER FIVE

Our birth is but a sleep and a forgetting: The Soul that rises with us, our life's Star, Hath had elsewhere its setting, And cometh from afar: Not in entire forgetfulness, And not in utter nakedness, But trailing clouds of glory do we come...

—William Wordsworth

1. ADVANCED PERFECT WORLDS HAVE ALWAYS EXISTED

Just like everything else in the Universe, perfect worlds have always existed. In these worlds, the most highly advanced technologies exist and are utilized to allow human beings to experience individual happiness. The term "technology" used throughout this book refers to the means and ways that human beings act upon their environment with their free will. Therefore, "the most highly advanced technologies" are the ways and means that the most advanced humans in the Universe act upon their environment. The state of the environment in which humans live upon these *perfect* worlds cannot be improved upon with any higher form of intelligence or technology. In other words, there is no greater means and ways that human beings act upon their environment than how they utilize technology in *perfect* human worlds. Everything is in its perfect state of existence, and it is *impossible* to make improvements upon *perfection*.

It is possible for each of us to picture what the perfect world could be like. We just need to consider what each of us conceives as being *perfect* by using our imagination. We now know that our *imagination* is simply our ability to reflect upon things that we have experienced in our past, even though our conscious mind cannot fully pinpoint when, where, or even *if* we actually experienced what we are imagining.

The foundation of who we are was established on a *perfect* world. All of our experiences on that primordial world are embedded in our *essence* as memories. Because of the fully functioning and highly advanced human body we possessed at the time, we were always *conscious* of all that we did. In that world, we did not have the ability to *imagine* and we experienced no ***sub****conscious* state of mind. In that *perfect* state upon a *perfect* world, we began our existence as human beings. (More about the perfect human body and mind will be discussed in chapter 11.)

2. OUR ESSENCE INFLUENCES US TO IMPROVE OURSELVES

Further proof that we existed and established memories in a world apart from the one in which we currently live is the fact that we have a subconscious part of us that we do not completely understand. Not only have we forgotten everything before our current life's early childhood (having *imperfect* brains), we sometimes even find it hard to remember what happened yesterday. And as our *imperfect* body grows older, we eventually find it hard at times to remember what we did a few seconds ago. Nevertheless, no matter how inhumane and undesirable the environment is into which we are born, all humans long for a better state of existence. One might think that a newly created human being who is born into a certain environment (even one that is inconsistent with human happiness) would adapt and find a way to deal with the given situation, *without* desiring to improve his or her only known state of existence. But this is never the case with human beings. All of us are continually searching for ways to manipulate our environment in order to bring us more happiness.

The fact that we are able to recognize that we and the world in which we now live are far from perfect, distinguishes us from every other life form on our planet. None other considers that its state of existence is anything but *how it is*, nor contemplates how it *should* be. "Something" about being a human being makes us strive for a better life. We long for a better existence than what we are currently experiencing. This "longing" and our constant need to improve our situation are caused by what was recorded on our *essence* eons before we came to this planet.

3. FACING DEATH IS NOT A PERFECT HUMAN SITUATION

We can agree that our current world is far from perfect. In considering what a perfect world should be like, most of us would want to live in one in which we would not be facing the possibility of death on a daily basis. The fact that we are slowly dying on this earth shows just how *imperfect* our world is. One day, the individual whom we became during this lifetime will cease to exist. Death comes in a variety of ways—from our body wearing out, from disease, from random accidents and the acts of other free-willed humans—regardless, it comes. None of us is immune to death. Put another way, none of us is immune to non-existence, which is the end of all of us, *if* it is a *true reality* that our current incarnate in this world is all there is to our human experience.

Not to be outdone by the *imperfect* environment to which we are currently subjected, our *own* actions also cause a tremendous amount of death. Although there is nothing (presently) we can do about growing old, the main causes of premature death are our *own* fault. The exercising of our free will causes more death and misery in our lives than any other natural occurrence produced by our environment. Statistically, the causes of premature death from natural occurrences pale in comparison to what is actually ending our lives upon this earth.

Many of us die from starvation and pestilence because other humans use their free will to subject us to their economic policies and land ownership. The free natural resources of the world, which would otherwise provide us with food and shelter, are withheld from us by the force of others. In addition, many of us cause ourselves a premature death by overeating or by eating foods that are not naturally balanced and compatible with our bodies. Eating unnatural foods that are not meant by *nature* for human consumption neutralizes the body's natural defense mechanisms. This prevents it from doing what it is instinctively programmed to do—kill invading bacteria, viruses, and any other substance that is not part of a body's natural makeup. Anything that is processed and changed from its natural state of existence is "unnatural." And nothing more abruptly changes an element's natural state than the application of heat; cooking food changes its composition and makes it unnatural. Cooking our food is literally killing us prematurely. No other life form upon our planet cooks its food before eating it. Consequently, no other life form experiences the types and regularity of disease as do human beings.

Realizing that death ends our existence, our human *reason* causes us to wonder what the purpose might be for living in the first place. The thought of death causes us an enormous amount of stress and emotional imbalance that certainly does not add to a fulfilling life of happiness. And in our pursuit of happiness, we begin to look for any solution we can come up with that might take away the sting of death.

4. WE LONG TO PERFECT OUR WORLD AND LIVE FOREVER

We have a desire to better ourselves and live forever because of our *essence's* constant subconscious energy stimulation. The energy patterns of our brains seek to find a balance with the power of our *essence.* Without being consciously aware of it, we are continually encouraged to create experiences that are in line with our primordial existence. In the *perfect* world where we were first created, we did not die nor understand anything about the concept of "death."

The will to survive is the strongest innate desire that we have. Although we may be ignorant of all the causes of our premature death, we are motivated to do anything we can in order to prolong our lives. In our current world, with the limited technology that we do have, we are finding ways to save and extend our lives, without changing our free-willed actions that cause us the sorrow in the first place. Medical and pharmaceutical sciences provide us with some means of prolonging our lives *without* changing our lifestyles, where otherwise our lifestyles would have killed us. As technology improves and expands, we find ourselves living much longer than our ancestors did, even though we eat unhealthier and exercise less than they did.

The technological and biological advancements of the future will one day eliminate *natural* death altogether. For any disease that we encounter, we will develop an immunization that will defeat it. If our body is traumatized and harmed from accident, or if trauma is forced upon us, we will develop a surgical procedure that will keep us alive and restore us to new.

Our DNA contains plans for the development of each cell of each organ of each anatomical system that our body requires. Currently, it also includes instructions to stop reproducing perfect cells, which replace the ones that are damaged or lost over time; thus causing us to grow old and die. One day, our geneticists and bioengineers will be able to override those instructions and manipulate our DNA patterns to allow the cells of our body to continue to reproduce themselves indefinitely, thus eliminating death from a slowly deteriorating body. When our current scientists discover this technology, we will never experience the effects of old age again. At least in many ways, death will become a thing of the past.

5. WE DON'T WANT TO LIVE FOREVER IN A MISERABLE STATE

Our physical future is bright with the technological possibilities ahead of us. But what about our positive emotional health, the fruition of which, in reality, is *why we exist*? Although we might eventually avoid death from natural causes or from our errant eating habits, and though we might develop safety devices to prevent accidents and others from hurting us, it does not mean that the struggle to survive will end; nor does it mean that we will live in happiness.

We can have a perfect body that never grows old or dies, but if the struggle to live continues to cause us stress and misery, what purpose would there be in prolonging a miserable state of existence? We can outwardly become the most beautiful expression of human form possible, yet still remain void of the personal peace and happiness that creates inward beauty. This inner peace can only come from what some of our current psychologists call "self-actualization." This means that we are able to reach our full potential as individuals, or in other words, come to know *who we are* and act **true** to ourselves.

One of these so-called experts, Abraham Maslow, created what he called the "Hierarchy of Human Needs." He proposed that if our basic human needs were met, that we would be able to advance to the highest level of our individual potential. He has become famous among those who study human behavior because this part of his theory is profound.

Indeed, we cannot become *who we are* unless we meet the physiological needs of the body. In our current state of existence, however, the majority of us spend *all* of our conscious hours and physical and emotional energy trying to meet these needs. We are forced to rely on our subconscious state to supply us with what we can *dream* or *imagine* our self becoming. However, the time we spend *dreaming* and *imagining* is minuscule compared to the time we spend struggling to meet our physiological needs.

It is through hypnosis (the relaxing of the conscious mind) and drug use that our ability to reach into our subconscious state is heightened. Yet, who has time to do any of these in a natural way, with the current responsibilities and expectations placed upon us living in our *imperfect* society? Ever wonder why the greatest songs with the greatest meanings seemed to have been composed by those "high" on illegal drugs?

One part of Maslow's theory, however, is dead wrong! He postulated that our need to satisfy our physical body is *much stronger* than our need to find out and become *who we are* on an emotional level. Because he spent very little time studying those of us who continually struggle just to survive (the majority of his study being concentrated on the affluent and educated of the world), he missed the greatest determinant in "self-actualization"—our ***need*** to <u>feel</u> happy.

The subjects Maslow studied had all of their physiological needs met, but they still didn't have a clue who they were, and they certainly were not very happy. We base this general conclusion on the overwhelming evidence that many of the individuals who have become extremely wealthy in our world still remain extremely unhappy. Maslow rejected the existence of the human *essence* and the power it has in urging us to become the person we were *foundationalized* to be. Thus, his studies and work failed to help any of us find what we are constantly looking for—happiness! Maslow's studies failed to conclude that, in reality, the strongest need of a human being is to have a perfect balance between the body and the *essence*. This is happiness.

6. ADVANCED TECHNOLOGY SUPPORTS A PERFECT WORLD

The perfect world where our *essence* was foundationalized not only provided us with a perfect body that was impervious to any disease or to the effects of age, but also with everything we needed to live. There was *no* struggle to survive.

The "advanced scientists" who exist in these worlds know how to manipulate and control every aspect of their environment. They know how to cause specific pressure changes in the atmosphere that will cause it to rain on demand anywhere they choose. They know how to tilt the planet just the right way towards the life-giving sun to create constant temperatures that feel pleasing to our body—not too hot and not too cold. They know how to grow the right plants that provide the perfect foods that not only agree with and completely satisfy our taste buds, but also delight the body's senses of sight, smell, and touch, and all the while support the healthy nature of the *perfect* human body.

7. PERFECT PLANTS AND ANIMALS WERE PART OF THE ULTIMATE SENSORY FOUNDATIONAL EXPERIENCE

There were no noxious weeds or irritating plants upon our perfect planet. There were only those plants that were pleasant to the sight, smell, taste, and touch, all of which provided the ultimate in human experience. The grasses were lush to the touch of the bare feet, and one could run without fear of stepping on a thorn or thistle, which were nowhere to be found. Fruits and flowers grew spontaneously, and there were no seeds to produce the thorns, thistles, briars, and noxious weeds that now afflict and torment our senses.

With the advanced technology available on *perfect* planets, horticulturists, farmers, and even simple personal gardeners can develop whatever type of plant they want for whatever purpose they desire. In fact, in our *imperfect* world, there is nothing that anyone will ever come up with that does not *already* exist somewhere else in the Universe. Through our ability to *reason*, *dream*, and *imagine*, we have created species of plants and animals that serve our needs. Just because we live in an *imperfect* world, does not mean that we do not demonstrate all of the human propensities we had while living in a *perfect* one. We were created to be like our creators, or better, to exist as the *perfect*, advanced human beings we were when our existence began. We have the same desires as they have and we will use our environment to seek to satisfy these desires just as they do.

In our primordial world, there were no animals (from the largest dinosaur to the tiniest insect) that afflicted or threatened human beings; nor did they threaten each other. The killing of another living organism and the consumption of its flesh is a thing of uncivilized, *imperfect* worlds, where it is necessary for humans to experience the *opposite* of a *perfect* world.

The perfect *Animal Kingdom* in our primordial world existed solely to assist the perfect *Plant Kingdom* in perpetuating itself, and vice versa. Both of these "kingdoms" existed solely for the experience of the *Human Kingdom*. Every animal was as comfortable with humans as a puppy is with a child, and as a child is with a puppy. No creature existed that could hurt or destroy another. There existed, for example, no animals with the huge teeth and digestive system needed to destroy another. The DNA patterns of all animals were programmed to coexist in a symbiotic state of perfection.

Advanced technology and genetic engineering of plants and animals allow these organisms to live forever. They continually perpetuate themselves so as to maintain the perfect natural balance of all things. For example, the sweat of a laborer's brow is not needed to ensure a plant's fruitfulness. Instead of a human laborer, who is hired in an *imperfect* world to pinch off the right amount of buds from a fruit-producing bush so that it can yield just the right amount of fruit, a beautiful deer that enjoys the bush's buds was created and genetically programmed to nibble off just the right amount and keep the bush trimmed properly. So the human being enjoys not only the fruit of the bush, but also the companionship of the deer. Advanced humans have the ability to create whatever plant or animal they desire to fulfill their own personal needs for happiness.

8. WE ATTEMPT TO CREATE PERFECT ENVIRONMENTS

The perfect world so far described above should be easy to visualize and imagine when we take into account what we can and have already accomplished upon this earth. With the right amount of resources, a person generally can control *what* vegetation grows *where*, thus adorning any environment according to the beauty in the eye of the landowner. Herbicides eliminate unwanted plants and insecticides eradicate undesired bugs. Crossbreeds of many different animals can ensure that a person is surrounded by the most docile breeds of what would otherwise be *wild* animals. Our current ability to organize our world into what we want it to be is limited only by our resources and our imagination to create it.

No other organism seeks to manipulate its environment so that it *appears* beautiful. All other non-human organisms only use their environment to provide for their physical needs. These other life forms have no sense or perception of order or beauty, except as it relates to the needs of their own species. Human beings behave unlike any other living organism because they have what all other living things do not—a human *essence* that was *foundationalized* to recognize beauty and perfection, even in other species. A lion does not contemplate the beautiful skin and muscle tone of a gazelle. The lion simply wants to eat the beautiful gazelle to satisfy its hunger.

9. IT'S EASY TO VISUALIZE THE PERFECT ENVIRONMENT

The advanced human beings who were responsible for our foundationalization had limitless resources available to them. The only limitation placed on what they could do with their environment was its physical expanse (that is, for those who did not venture into the uninhabited realms of the Universe and create their own planets, solar systems, and galaxies). And the only reason they limited the size of their own world was because they only needed a specific amount of space in which to do what makes them happy.

The majority of advanced human beings are very satisfied to *not* be responsible for other human beings, and to simply enjoy the planet on which they live. They are surrounded by those who have similar personal interests. Each has everything possible available to them in order to fulfill each of their individual desires of happiness. If they desire their own country, for example, the space will be provided. (Consider the space that would be available on a developed life-bearing planet the size of Jupiter or Saturn, for example.)

Again, it should be easy for the reader to visualize this. Just think what you would do if you had unlimited resources. What kind of house would you build? What kind of gardens would surround your house? What kinds of pets would you keep, both inside your house and outside in your gardens? There would be rivers, creeks, hills, and mountains to beautify your surroundings and bring joy to your senses, all according to your *sense* of experience.

It is easy to imagine these things. Relax your mind for awhile. Forget about everything you are doing for a moment. Reach deep within the corners of your seldom-explored *essence* and you will come up with the perfect environment. The description is perfectly recorded there and because it is, we do not need to spend much time describing a world with the perfect environment.

10. IT'S NOT EASY TO VISUALIZE THE PERFECT SOCIETY

What is not so easy for us to visualize is a *perfect* society of *people*. It's hard for us to imagine these things because our current experience is void of any known example. Although we can find those in our *imperfect* world who have the means to surround themselves with what seems *to them* to be the perfect natural environment of flora and fauna, there exists no mortal person upon the earth who exemplifies the *perfect* human being.

While these very few with landscaped, seemingly *perfect* personal environments hide behind their gated "worlds," millions more of us suffer from poverty, hunger, homelessness, sickness, and a pitiful state of existence. Most of us are constantly struggling to provide ourselves with the basic necessities of life.

This wasn't the case in our perfect world. There we became who we *really* are as we witnessed and recorded in our memory (*essence*) the ideal example of humanity. The qualities and characteristics of the human beings in that world presented humanity in all of its full glory and splendor. Again, this is the reason why we long for "utopia." We *dream* of a perfect society that would create a peaceful world, which we will recognize immediately when we experience it again.

11. UNCONDITIONAL EQUALITY IN OUR PRIMORDIAL WORLD

Our first experiences were in a world where everyone was treated unconditionally equal in all things. All people with whom we associated were equally beautiful and equally intelligent and knowledgeable.

Knowledge, as we currently view it, is the accumulation of information. Intelligence is the ability and way that we use this information. Because we were all exposed to the exact same things in the first stage of our existence on a perfect planet, we all had the exact same knowledge. During our formative period of foundationalization, our intelligences were also equal, in that we all had the capability of utilizing the knowledge that we gained according to our *own* individual free will; thus, each of us developed our own unique personal intelligence.

In other words, no one forced us to use our knowledge in any specific way. Our mothers did not establish expectations of how we should use the information that we were acquiring from our new experiences. Initially, therefore, because there were no expectations, there were no classes or grades of intelligence. We were all equally intelligent because we used our knowledge as *each of us* wanted, thus becoming the most intelligent person that existed according to our *own* experience. No one else used *their knowledge* like each of us did individually; therefore, there was no one as intelligent as we were. Likewise, we were not any more intelligent than anyone else was. Thus was established our human yearning to be treated equally with everyone else. Why? Because we saw ourselves as being *completely* equal with everyone else in all things—because we were.

Throughout the Universe, however, there will always be those who have more power or abilities than others. (In other words, there will always be some who have a greater ability to make use of their knowledge than others.) Only in this way could we say that some are more *intelligent than others*, but **never** more knowledgeable. Where there are two beings, one having more *intelligence* than another, there always exists another having more *intelligence* than them.

However, those humans who gain the ability to utilize all the knowledge that is available to them and all other humans in the Universe will be those who are the creators. And in using their knowledge as they do, they are *more intelligent* than all others. Moreover, because our creators have a creator, there will always be someone in the Universe more *intelligent*, by *use* of their knowledge, than us. But in spite of the semantics in the way we perceive knowledge and intelligence, it can be properly concluded that the human being who is the most happy, is indeed, the most intelligent, as happiness is what all humans seek.

12. THE UNIVERSE REVOLVES AROUND EACH OF US

Since we were foundationalized with equality, we were conditioned to understand that the entire Universe exists for each of our own personal sakes. We can correctly say, "Without me, the Universe would not exist! Because I exist, so does the Universe! The Universe was created for me! I am the most important thing in the Universe!"

All of these statements are true, because that is how we were treated by the advanced parents/creators who brought us into existence. Without us living and being able to recognize our *self* as a separate part of everything else that exists, what purpose would the Universe have? If we cannot conceptualize the Universe, then it would mean nothing to us. Moreover, if we cease to exist, so does our Universe.

From the very moment that the first light reflected off our mother's face and into our eyes, when her image was recorded by our *essence* as our very first memory, we were treated as if the Universe revolved around us. Is it any wonder then why human beings appear so arrogant and self-centered in our current world? Doesn't it bring us a tremendous amount of happiness to know that we are the best in the world, and that no one else is as good as we are, or at least we are just as good as everyone else?

Unfortunately, our current state does not allow us to *actualize* the potential of our *true* selves, nor does it allow us to believe that we are just as good as everyone else is. Thus, we are out of balance with who we *really* are and subject to feelings of unhappiness. From our current *imperfect* experience, there always seems to be someone stronger, smarter, more successful, more beautiful, or happier than us.

Those who establish themselves in our current world as being better than others are the most insecure with themselves. These continually try to maintain an inequality because they are afraid another is going to come along who is perceived as being better than them. If they could only remember how we were all *created and treated equally*, and that each of our experiences will always be different from everyone else's, then their *perception of* "better" would change. They would understand that none of us will ever achieve a state where we can truly perceive our self as being "the best" or better than anyone else.

It is possible, however, to come to a sense of peace and happiness in knowing that we are *just as good* as everyone else. This is possible because the Universe exists to support this ***true reality***. We experienced it on the world where we were foundationalized as human beings; and we will experience it again, once we transform our world into what we know is the best for *all* of humanity.

13. OUR DEVELOPMENT IN ISOLATION ENSURED OUR SENSE OF SELF-WORTH

We have already learned that when we went through our *Foundationalization Process*, we were isolated from other human beings. We did not foundationalize around those who were not parents and who lived in their own state of continual happiness doing whatever they wanted, *without* the responsibility of worrying about the development of another. One of the main reasons for this isolation was so that our mothers could control how we developed our sense of self, or in other words, our self-perception and self-worth.

If we had started out our existence around advanced humans who were more interested in what made *them* happy than what made us happy, we would have developed an inferiority complex, which would have marred our otherwise perfect view of ourselves. If our sense of self had been foundationalized around parents who were more concerned about their *own* self-image and value of happiness than ours, we would have been inclined to measure our own sense of value by theirs. And if we didn't measure up, we would have been convinced that the Universe is not *really* about us, but rather about them.

In this situation, we would never have developed a pure sense of **free will**, because we would have begun our experience by mimicking the experience of those who seemed to be completely satisfied with their own sense of self and the happiness they were experiencing.

Instead of becoming unique individuals, we would have become clones of our parents, which would not have led to a proper human experience, where individuality brings the highest level of joy possible to both our parents/creators and to ourselves. We would never have been able to find happiness in becoming like someone else. Fortunately, we are instead free to be the best that *we* can be, rather than worrying about how to become the best that another *thinks* we should be.

Those who chose to be our parents in our current *imperfect* world generally destroyed our self-esteem and drastically diminished our chances of becoming who we *really* wanted to become. There is a huge contrast between advanced human parents, who know what they are doing, and mortal parents, who have no training or proper experience in parenting. Our *imperfect* mortal parents create the unhappiness and inequality we experience in our current state of existence upon this earth.

Untrained parents have children for their *own* sake, without considering the environment into which they are introducing a child. They do not consider the fact that their children are individuals with their own free will. *Imperfect parents* seldom understand that children are *not*, nor should they be expected to be, just like them.

Unlike *imperfect* parents, our advanced mothers ensured that each child developed equally and that all of us were endowed with a sense of self-worth, which allowed us to mature into self-assured and *perfect* human beings, around whom the whole Universe revolves. What better sense of personal empowerment could any of us have possibly desired?

In no way did those who helped us foundationalize our *self*, tell us or continually remind us what we *should* do with our free will. As we later discuss the ramifications of the way children are presently reared upon this earth, it will become very apparent that much of our unhappiness is a direct result of poor parenting.

14. IN A PERFECT STATE, WE WERE AWARE OF OTHERS' IMPERFECTIONS

We mentioned that we were continually acquiring information in that perfect world, but not all of the knowledge we acquired was of the experience of existing as a *perfect* human. In these advanced societies, the technology that is available allows anyone to watch what is happening on any planet in the Universe (much like using the computer effects of a Universal Google™, or watching a documentary about a foreign country in real time on the Discovery Channel™).

As we matured and surpassed the ability of our perfect world to provide us with experiences that we hadn't already stored in our memories, our mothers encouraged us to watch what happens on less-advanced worlds. On these worlds, other humans were going through their second stage of development on planets similar to the earth on which we currently live.

We were able to see what happened when a new solar system was created, so that children like us could go through their second stage of development. Upon these planets, everything was the opposite of our safe and orderly perfect world. We didn't understand death any more than we understood old age; yet right before our eyes, in phenomenal video-type holographic presentation, we saw human beings killing each other, hurting, abusing, and taking advantage of each other, and creating societies of the most inhumane natures, which were completely out of balance with our foundationalized sense of humanity. We could not *imagine* how other human beings, who appeared to be like us, could act this way. We could not *imagine* it because we had not yet experienced it for ourselves.

15. MANY OF US WANTED THE SAME POWERS OF CREATION THAT OUR CREATORS HAD

As we watched these things take place on other worlds, none of us could admit that we would ever do the same things that we saw other humans doing to each other if we were placed in their exact situation. We were reared to believe that we were the best kind of life form in the Universe. We could not *imagine* ourselves doing anything unbecoming of how we were taught a human being should act. We could not *imagine* it because we had not yet been placed in a situation where our humanity could be tested.

Part of our foundationalized "sense of self" included the desire to possess the power and the *intelligence* to do what other advanced human creators could do. We saw how they could manipulate the very elements of the Universe to do whatever they wanted these elements to do. We saw that their *intelligence* (the use of their knowledge) was indeed much different from our own and that they were capable of doing things that we had no power to do. We saw how they interacted, unseen, with the less-advanced worlds, so that they could monitor the free-willed humans who had no idea that more advanced humans even existed.

These advanced beings did not let the less-advanced humans know that, with their advanced knowledge and technology, they were the ones making sure that the balance of nature on the *imperfect* planets was being maintained. If these advanced beings did not monitor and sometimes intervene in what the unaware and *imperfect* humans did, the less-advanced civilizations would have killed themselves and destroyed the planet they were placed on, long before its purpose was fulfilled.

We saw examples of power and control that convinced us that in order to be the happiest human possible, we had to have these *same* powers. We saw that some of them experienced a great amount of physical joy from the sexual abilities they possessed—sensations and abilities that we couldn't understand. Although we weren't expected to be like our primordial parents, it was a natural propensity for us to *want* to be just like them.

Although most of us would choose not to take upon us the responsibility of creating new human beings, we still wanted to experience the fullness of joy that our parents did. We realized, however, that we did not know if we could be *trusted with these powers*, or what would happen if we were. Our creators informed us that during the second stage of our development we would be endowed with the power to create other human beings and experience uninhibited sexual desires. We would be able to use our free will without condition and restriction. By being allowed to have the power of a creator (to a certain extent) during our 2nd stage in life, many of us would come to realize why we *should not* be allowed to have these powers and abilities.

16. OUR ADVANCED MOTHERS HELPED US TO ESTABLISH AND UNDERSTAND OUR UNIQUE INDIVIDUALITY

We existed in this perfect world for eons of time. Because there was no death, there was no accounting of time. We existed for what seemed to us to be the only measurement of time available: forever. Each of us developed propensities and characteristics uniquely our own. We each acquired personalities that fit into one of the three *humanity-type* categories mentioned previously:

- Some of us wanted to serve others by being creators and parents.
- Some of us wanted to serve ourselves and develop and create our own world to satisfy our own desires of what brought us happiness.
- Some of us wanted others to continue to serve us forever.

Our mothers helped us to understand that *most* of us would never be endowed with the *intelligence* that would allow us to have the power that advanced human parents and creators possess in order to carry on the creation process of expanding human life. Our mothers helped us to understand and accept whom we had chosen to be.

However, what they could *not* help us understand, because we had no experience beyond the *perfect* human situation, is why those of us who did not want to serve others couldn't have the same powers and abilities to control and manipulate the elements of the Universe that they have. Nor could we understand, at the time, why those of us who didn't want to serve others would never be able to experience what seemed to be the ultimate physical sensations a human being could experience—sexual pleasure. We couldn't understand why we couldn't at least have all of the sensory pleasures possessed by our advanced parents.

17. ULTIMATE POWERS ARE RESTRICTED TO CREATORS

During our *Foundationalization Process*, we developed a keen sense of equality. We were taught that all human beings have the exact same potential and opportunity. Yet, when we realized that only those who chose to become parents and continue to create other human beings possessed the *ultimate* powers of the Universe, we were naturally confused. It didn't make sense with respect to the idea of perfect equality. "Why couldn't we all have the same power?" we questioned.

Our parents/creators understood our confusion. We were taught that if this incredible power to create anything we wanted was given to those of us who wanted to serve *only ourselves*, or to those of us who wanted to be served *by others*, it would be misused. They explained to us that because all human beings are free willed and cannot be forced to act or to be acted upon, being able to use the power (except for the sake of others) would allow situations to exist that are not conducive to an orderly and peaceful Universe.

By watching the experiences of human beings going through their second stage of development (upon planets like this earth), we received a sure witness of how they acted, regardless of their *perfect foundationalization*. When those who wanted to serve themselves or to be served had the ability to create other human beings (not for the sake of the newly created person, but for their own sake), great unhappiness and inequality were and are the result.

18. DIFFERENT BODIES ARE CREATED FOR EACH INDIVIDUAL

We have discussed "free will" as being unique to human beings, who are the highest life form of all. We are the ultimate form of existence found anywhere in the Universe. We always have been and we always will be. Part of what gives us our unique nature is our ability to think, act, and react by our *own* power, without any outside force mandating what we do. This is free agency. It is the most protected right of all the laws of the Universe.

All other matter is subject to a Universal law that *allows* it to act or react to an outside stimulus according to how it has been programmed. Only human beings retain their own individual power to not be affected in any way by anything outside of their own free will. This will, this power, is generated and resides in the human *essence* and is properly exhibited *only* with a perfect human body.

This exclusive *human power of free will* is developed and fostered by those who use their own free will to make sure our development takes place properly and that the power within the *essence* becomes *human*. All *perfect* human bodies are constructed to fulfill the need and potential of the *essence*. Therefore, no free-willed being has the power to create the *essence* and the appropriate bodies that will work best with it, unless they do so *only* for the sake of the human beings so created. In other words, if one doesn't want the responsibility of **ensuring** the happiness of another's creation, one will not have the power to create.

Those who have the ultimate power of creation possess the body, with all the appropriate parts, that allows them the capacity to use this power properly. Without the appropriate body, an advanced human is not able to use the power. Therefore, to ensure that the power is not misused, those who choose *not* to be responsible for the creation of other human beings have a *different* body from those who do.

All perfect bodies look human. Those with the power to create have sexual body parts associated with males and females. Those without the power to create have no sex organs. But the greatest difference between a human body that can create and one that cannot is the way the body responds to the energy levels and frequency generated by the brain.

19. SCIENCE HAS LIMITED CONTROL OVER THE ELEMENTS

Understanding how this power to create works will give us a better understanding of why it is *only* given to those who use it wisely and appropriately. Currently, our scientists have only limited power to create. They can use the elements available to create different things according to the natural laws that control and determine what the elements can do. In other words, modern-day scientists can only create what the elements allow them to create. They must work within the potential of each element and the established parameters of its structure.

20. SCIENTIFIC UNDERSTANDING OF MATTER IS RUDIMENTARY

Before we can understand what knowledge and powers an advanced human creator has that the most knowledgeable modern-day scientist does not, we must first understand some basic conclusions or hypotheses current scientists have made about matter.

Science has determined that all matter is made up of elements that are comprised of atoms, which contain varying numbers of subatomic particles called protons, neutrons, and electrons. (Now, don't get lost here; it will all begin to make sense.) The number of protons an atom has determines what element it is. For example, hydrogen is hydrogen because every one of its atoms has a single proton. It is theorized (which means it makes sense, although no one is positive) that for each proton, there is an electron that balances the atom. There are elements that exist naturally, that is, science had nothing to do with their creation; and there are elements that scientists have created.

Science has learned to create its own elements by changing the number of protons. It does this through the use of energy. Although elements can be destroyed, their protons, neutrons, and electrons cannot. In simple terms, when scientists add energy or take it away, they can cause one element to turn into another.

As far as current scientific theory concludes, it is a common natural phenomenon for elements to continually be created and destroyed. The best example of this is our own sun. The energy of the sun is so strong that, at its center, atoms of hydrogen (containing only one proton) are forcefully compressed, so that their protons combine to create helium, which has two protons, again, according to current scientific theory. Thus, the hydrogen is destroyed and helium is created (at least according to what science can determine is taking place).

However, the more protons an atom has, the more energy it takes to change it into another element. Because science has reached this conclusion, it believes that to create carbon and iron, for example (which have considerably more protons than hydrogen and are the fundamental elements needed to create a new earth), it would take much more energy than even the sun could provide in order to create them.

The sun appears to be the greatest source of energy in our solar system. As discussed, science has theorized that both the sun and the earth were created when a massive star exploded in an event known as a "supernova." They speculate that the star blew itself apart, and that this provided the energy needed to create the more dense atoms (those with more protons) that make up planets and suns. From this conclusion emerged the so-called "Big Bang theory" of creation, which has been accepted as the explanation of *how* all things exist.

But this theory leaves a reasonable mind wondering: If a star exploded, or a big bang created the star that exploded, and that created the earth and this solar system, then what "big bang" created the elements that reacted to create the big bang? Where did the energy come from that caused the very first big bang? Needless to say, science has left too many questions unanswered; therefore, their conclusions cannot be the **real truth** that humans so desperately seek to find. **Real truth** provides answers that leave no other questions to ask.

21. A LIMITED AMOUNT OF ELEMENT CAN CREATE TREMENDOUS ENERGY

What science doesn't appreciate is that it has already helped answer these questions without even realizing it. Our scientists have learned how to create elements. They have learned how to utilize the energy contained in the makeup of the elements. They have demonstrated this very well in the creation of nuclear bombs that give off a tremendous amount of energy from a very limited amount of element. It takes just a few pounds of enriched ("enrich," meaning **human intervention** to increase the proportion of a desired ingredient) uranium, for example, to create enough energy to destroy an entire country.

So, if our current scientists know how to create new elements and control the energy contained within them, why is it so hard to accept that advanced human beings have developed the knowledge and power to manipulate and control elements in ways that current scientists could never dream of doing at the present time? Why can't current scientists accept that they and their past mentors have absolutely no idea what the *true* potential of elements actually is? Furthermore, why can't they admit that they do not understand, nor are they aware of, many other more powerful elements found in the Universe?

If someone would have told those early *imperfect* pioneers who first discovered and began to experiment with elements that one day future scientists would be creating their own elements that would be used to destroy the earth, they would probably have responded, "Oh, that's the fantasy-thinking of science fiction. It will never happen!" But it did! And more advanced humans have the ability to control elements that current scientists could never imagine, according to their limited and *restricted* knowledge and experience.

22. MYSTERY OF CREATION IS FOUND IN "DARK MATTER"

It should not be hard to theorize and accept that an advanced human scientist has the means to travel to different parts of the Universe, where there is space without a sun or a solar system and, with the knowledge and power to do so, create a completely new solar system. This advanced one can then create more new solar systems, until he has created a whole new galaxy, and then even more new galaxies, until he has become the creator of a whole new part of the Universe. This is accomplished by using advanced technology controlled by advanced human beings who have the answer to a question that modern scientists cannot solve: "What is dark matter?"

Dark matter is all the matter that fills the gaps in the Universe where science cannot place any *known* matter. Scientists have hypothesized that it is matter that does not interact with any other matter and has no electrical charge or transference of energy patterns.

The answer to the question, "What is dark matter?" is as simple as the answers to all of the questions posed in this book. To illustrate exactly what dark matter is, let's take a look at the color "black." The color black appears to be a combination of every known color.

Likewise, the dark matter or *black* matter of the Universe is a compilation of all of the potential energy (or better, all the protons, neutrons, and electrons) needed to create any element in the Universe.

"Dark matter," therefore, is a collection of *everything* needed to create *anything* in the Universe. The secret lies in knowing *how* to transform dark matter into the elements that make up all other matter—or in other words, create something new that didn't exist before. This is achieved by forming energy patterns where none existed before.

In "dark matter," the mass of protons, neutrons, and electrons is already there, but these subatomic particles are not yet configured properly to create the force of energy generated when they interact inside the atoms of matter that form everything in the Universe, from rocks to the cells of the human brain. Advanced human scientists know exactly how to perform the proper configuration. They know how to control energy levels to create anything they want. In other words, every proton, neutron, and electron found in the Universe is at their command!

23. OUR LIMITED ABILITY TO CONTROL ELEMENT

To further understand the vast power of advanced science, we need to take a look at the abilities of modern scientists to create and control element and then distinguish these abilities from those of advanced creators. To begin to comprehend these things, those of us who are not scientists need to understand that each of us has a limited power to control the elements.

To raise one arm above our head, our brain sends out an energy impulse that contracts our muscles, which are made up of elements, and causes our arm to move as we want it to. Our arm will *not* move until, by the use of our free will, we make it. Each time we do this, we are manipulating elements with the energy generated by our mind. Yes, even the extremely limited power of our own mind can control element!

Our current scientists can actually measure the energy that is generated by our brain any time we think or move by simply placing electrodes on one's head. This means that there is obviously a measurable degree of energy transference given off by our brain that is powerful enough to go through the thick bones of our skull each time we raise our arm above our head.

24. CURRENT SCIENTIFIC THEORY IS INCOMPLETE

Current science does not understand all there is to know about protons, neutrons, and electrons. In fact, none of these things have ever even been seen by modern-day scientists. The existence of these subatomic particles is the product of scientific experimentation and theories based on what scientists can observe with the senses of their body. If current scientists cannot see it, smell it, taste it, touch it, or hear it, these "learned" and self-perceived "wise ones" will not accept what is possible beyond their *non-advanced* human perception. Without empirical evidence, science is forced to develop uncertain theories and hypotheses of what it observes.

Here is the great hypocrisy of the scientific mind: No scientist has ever seen, smelled, tasted, touched, or heard a proton, neutron, or electron. Therefore, how do they know these things exist? The answer is, they actually don't. Scientists have created these ideas and theorems in their minds to explain things that they don't understand; and it is a personal blow to a scientific mind when it cannot find some way of explaining why things are the way they are. For this very reason, it can be properly, even *scientifically*, postulated that what scientists know today will be proven incorrect or insufficient compared to what will be known by future humans.

25. ADVANCED SCIENTISTS CREATE WITH THE POWER OF THEIR THOUGHTS

Again, we have presented the fact that there exist and have always existed societies of advanced humans who have developed a true and complete understanding of all there is to know about the Universe and how it works. Some of these advanced human beings (those who are trusted with the knowledge and power of creation) have the type of brain that allows them to manipulate protons, neutrons, and electrons and create any element outside of their bodies. Just as easily as we can command the elements that make up the muscles of our body to raise our arm above our head, they can cause the creation and destruction of any element in the Universe by their thoughts alone.

Elements do not even need to exist for advanced creators to create something! All protons, neutrons, and electrons are compositions of specific energy levels—levels that can be measured and controlled and found anywhere in the Universe. The creator's *perfect* brain can put these energy levels together from the actual energy emanating from their own brains, and accomplish what our current minds can only envision (erroneously) as "creating something out of nothing."

26. THE *ESSENCE* PRODUCES PERPETUAL ENERGY

The energy of thought is produced by the power of our *essence*. As mentioned previously, modern science does not understand, nor has it discovered, all of the elements of the Universe. In other words, there exist elements of energy levels (mass) different from those of which scientists are currently aware. And just as a nuclear reaction takes place and releases extraordinary amounts of energy from a relatively small mass of element, the human *essence* is made up of elements that can release an even more powerful energy.

The difference between the way energy is released during a nuclear or atomic reaction of the elements, as manipulated by modern science, and the way the elements of our *essence* react, is in the containment of the energy. A nuclear reaction of enriched uranium, for example, continues until the energy of the element has completely dissipated. But in addition, the reaction can also give off a harmful byproduct called radiation.

The reaction that gives power to our *essence*, however, exists in a completely contained subatomic vacuum (for want of a better term to explain it), where it is confined within the boundaries set for a *human essence*. The byproduct of the reaction creates the energy needed to continue the reaction. In other words, our essence is a perpetual energy factory.

27. ALL ELEMENTS ARE EQUAL TO ADVANCED SCIENTISTS

Advanced scientists can command energy levels to produce 79 protons, 79 electrons, and 118 neutrons, *which would cause pure gold to appear out of nowhere.* For this reason, *to them*, gold is worth about as much as the nitrogen, oxygen, argon, carbon, neon, helium, methane, krypton, hydrogen, and xenon that make up most of the air we breathe.

But what modern-day scientist, if he or she had the knowledge and the power, would create air instead of pure gold? What modern-day scientist would keep his or her knowledge and ability to understand and control the energy levels of atoms away from those who would use it to create an atomic weapon that can destroy life?

Although they cannot create gold, our current scientists trade their knowledge and abilities *for* "gold," known and valued as "money"; and as long as someone offers them enough gold, they do not have much personal concern for what the buyer of their knowledge does with it. The power of creation and control on earth goes to the highest bidder. For this reason, modern-day scientists who would sell their knowledge for money could *never* be trusted as advanced human creators.

28. ADVANCED HUMANS CONTROL THE ENVIRONMENT

Everything associated with *human perfection* is created and controlled by advanced human beings who know how to do it properly. The *perfect* planet on which we went through our Human Foundationalization Process had the *perfect* food to eat and taste, the *perfect* clothes to wear, the *perfect* architecture for the *perfect* houses, the *perfect* animals and the *perfect* plants, etc. It provided us with the perfect environment in which we developed the *perfect* sense of sight, smell, sound, taste, and touch. All of this was controlled and maintained by advanced human beings who knew exactly what *perfection* should be.

29. WE NEEDED TO EXPERIENCE IMPERFECTION

Being around this seemingly omnipotent, advanced society of humans in our primordial childhood, we were provided with the opportunity to choose to be like them or not. There has never been a free-willed human being who would not want the incredible power of creation described above. However, very, very few will ever be trusted with it. Again, during the time we were experiencing life as a perfect human being, we couldn't understand *why* we couldn't be trusted with the power if we were properly trained how to use it. In a *perfect* world, we would never understand why.

Our creators explained to us that the only way we would ever understand this would be for us to go through our own *second stage* of development and see for ourselves how we would react when allowed to exist on our own without the intervention or the help of our advanced parents/creators. We needed to experience the *opposite* of a perfect world and place ourselves in the same situations as the other less-advanced humans we observed on other planets, whom we thought we would never act like.

In addition, our mothers explained that, for us to truly appreciate everything we had experienced in a perfect world, we would have to experience the opposite. To truly appreciate our own *perfect* existence, we had to experience an *imperfect* existence. We cannot appreciate something we have always had. The only way to truly appreciate it is to have it taken away from us. To help us appreciate our perfect world, therefore, our first parents created an *imperfect* one for us.

SUMMARY

Advanced worlds have always existed. These worlds establish the precedent for the ultimate human experience. We were created on these worlds as individuals. Because our humanity was foundationalized there, we developed an inner sense of what our existence should be like. Our *essence* causes us to long for what we had; but we can't consciously remember what it was like to live in this type of a world.

In our current state, we realize that simply living and dying is not conducive to a perfect situation for us—it confuses our sense of humanity. We find it hard to accept that, once dead, our existence is finalized. However, what we do know for certain is that we do not want to live forever in the *imperfect* state in which we currently find ourselves.

We realize that the more we advance through technology, the easier it is to exist, but it does not necessarily mean that we are going to become any happier. We find that we have the power to change our environment and control many aspects of our existence. With our knowledge, we attempt to create a better world for ourselves, so that we can experience more happiness—which is finding a balance between our current state of existence and the life we subconsciously long for. We want and expect unconditional equality and the guarantee that each of us can become who he or she wants to become.

In our primordial state, we saw the powers and abilities that our advanced human creators had, and many of us desired to have the same. Yet, the laws of the Universe restrict these creative powers and associated abilities only to those who choose to continue human life. We realized that our personal choice not to serve others and be responsible for their happiness would limit our human abilities.

During our *foundationalization stage of development*, we were of the opinion that we *could* be trusted with these quintessential human powers. We rejected the option that we would act as we observed other human beings acting, who were going through their experience in an *imperfect* world. Only our own experience in such a world could convince us that our chosen humanity type could *not* be trusted with these powers. This is one of the main purposes for living in our own *imperfect* world as we do now.

Living in a Perfect World

CHAPTER SIX

The divine principles within us are the thoughts and revolutions of the universe. These each man should follow, and correct the courses of the head which were corrupted at our birth, and by learning the harmonies and revolutions of the universe, should assimilate the thinking being to the thought, renewing his original nature, and having assimilated them should attain to that perfect life which [was] set before mankind, both for the present and the future.

—Plato

1. THE PERFECT WORLD EXHIBITS THE OPPOSITE OF OUR CURRENT WORLD

During our current lifetime upon this earth, most of us long for world peace, good health, the elimination of world hunger, poverty, and desperation, and safety from all types of harm—that caused from the forces of nature as well as that caused by other humans. We long to be secure in our personal relationships and to be valued by others for our individuality. This longing comes from our desire to create experiences in our current world that align with the memories stored in our *essence*.

We now understand that memories are specific energy patterns that are produced when we have an experience. Each experience is recorded as a distinct *wavelength of energy* that distinguishes it as a unique event that is stored as a memory. We know that our *human essence* is a compilation (or storage) of all of these different wavelengths (memories).

We are individuals separate from everyone else, each having our own unique compilation of memories. Most importantly, we now know that the reason why we feel *unhappy* at times in our current world is because the energy patterns (the things that we experience upon this earth) do *not* match what we have recorded in our *essence* (the things that we experienced upon a *perfect human world*). This causes a physical feeling of imbalance that we recognize as "unhappiness."

2. WHAT WE IMAGINE TO BE THE PERFECT WORLD, IS A REFLECTION OF REMEMBERING A PERFECT WORLD

With what we have now learned about ourselves, it becomes easier to envision what it must have been like when we lived in the perfect world where we were *foundationalized.* Everything that brings us a sensation of wonder, peace, and the thought of, "Wouldn't it be nice if…" brings to our conscious mind what living in the perfect world might have been like. Anything that we can conceive and recognize "deep down inside of us" as *how things should be* is a reflection of the perfect world where we used to live.

All of us have asked at one time or another, "Why can't we all just get along? Why can't we all smile at each other, hug once in awhile, and accept each other for who we are?" These questions are really statements about our own humanity. They create a sense of longing and hope that one day we might reach our potential as *human* beings. To fulfill the yearning of our *inner-humanity*, however, we must confront the things in our current world that do *not* bring us a sense of balance (those things that cause us stress) and eliminate them.

We can *imagine* a world of peace and order where none of us experiences stress, and can wish that it existed. But we will never achieve this ideal and perfect state, unless we learn to listen to the gentle persuasions of our *internal emotional core.* Within this core we will find the correct pattern for the perfect world for which we strive and from whence we came.

3. THERE IS NO CYCLE OF DAYS AND NIGHTS IN THE PERFECT WORLD

In a perfect world, there are no values of measurement, no numbers, and no quantitative expressions with which we experience our day-to-day activities. In that world, even the concept of day and night does not exist.

Logistically, a perfect world is situated in position and tilted towards the sun so that most of the planet's surface is always exposed to the sun's light. Our *imperfect* planet makes a full revolution, exposing only half of its surface at a time to the sun. However, there are *small* parts of our earth that stay light, though the sun appears to "go down." This phenomenon is caused by the shifting tilt of the earth as it travels in its orbit around the sun.

In contrast, as a *perfect* planet revolves, it simultaneously tilts appropriately along with its rotation to keep the *greater* majority of the planet's surface always in the light. There is little purpose for "nighttime" because the perfect body does not require sleep. Our eyes need light to produce an experience; therefore, of what use would there be for a place where no light existed for half of the time?

There is always an area on a perfect planet, however, to where the habitants can travel to enjoy the beauty of the night and the experience that it creates. The small part of a perfect world that is always in the dark can be compared to a planetarium, of sorts, where one can go to look beyond our planet into the sky and observe the natural beauty of the wonderful lights of the rest of the Universe. This natural planetarium provides the perfect view (and thus the perfect experience) of a starlit night. We had this "nighttime" experience recorded in our *essence* when we were going through our *foundationalization stage* living in a *perfect* world. For this very reason, *only humans* enjoy looking up at a clear night sky and watching the stars. We care because of what is stored in our *essence*. Other animals could care less.

4. THE PERFECT BRAIN PERCEIVES ALL THINGS AS THE PRESENT

The very first physical body and brain that we possessed were created to be completely compatible with our *human essence*. With this brain, we lived fully aware of what happened in the past and what was happening in the present, as if all experiences were one and the same experience. We developed a perfect concept of the present, because anything that we did in the past and recorded as memory was instantly accessible to our physically perfect brain. We would recall (or better, re-experience) the memory as if it just happened a moment ago. Because we are free-willed beings, our future does not exist until we experience it and cause it to happen by the choice of our free agency. But the past can become, once again, our present with the abilities of the perfect human brain.

Unlike our current brain, our primordial brain was perfectly balanced with the energy patterns shared with our *essence*. We had only *one* memory storage unit—the *essence*; whereas, we currently have *two*—our physical brain (our conscious mind) and our *essence* (our subconscious mind). Although we have touched upon it previously, it is important to gain a better understanding of how we store memories both with a *perfect* body and with an *imperfect* one. Keep in mind that the purpose of having an *imperfect* brain while on this earth is so that we can experience the *opposite* potential and abilities of the ultimate human brain. We develop appreciation by having the comparative experiences.

5. OUR IMPERFECT BRAIN HAS AN IMPERFECT MEMORY

The cells of our brain currently record and store our memories. (Although we could discuss the exact scientific terms of dendrites, synapses, axons, nerve endings, etc., for the purpose of easy comprehension, we will combine all of these terms and call them the "cells of our brain.") If the cells of our brain are damaged, we lose the memories stored on those cells and are not able to consciously recall the experiences we recorded. This is what modern science calls "amnesia." What science cannot answer, however, is how a person who has damaged the cells upon which memory is recorded, can start to *remember* those events, people, and places again. If the cell upon which the memory was stored is damaged beyond repair or regeneration, wouldn't the memory also be gone forever?

For example, if the image of an individual's mother is recorded on the cells of his or her brain, and through accident or surgical procedure those cells are damaged or removed, according to what current science understands, that person should never be able to regain memory of his or her mother again. How then, can a person one day *recover* the memory of his or her mother (in this example), if the cells of the brain upon which the memory was recorded no longer exist? The true answer is simple: by the power of the *essence*, the existence of which current scientific conclusions overlook or dismiss.

Science theorizes that in the case of brain damage causing amnesia, the part of the brain where the memory was stored could *not* have been fully destroyed, and that the brain eventually found a way to access the memory through other undamaged connections. What scientists do not know is that, in our current brain, all of our experiences are recorded twice: once on the cells of our brain *and* once in our *essence*. The memory recorded on our *essence* **cannot** be destroyed or damaged in any way. Its construction and the elements from which it is made render the *essence* virtually indestructible.

Previously, we discussed that our *essence* stores memory at a different, *higher* energy level than our current brain does. Our *imperfect* brain has a hard time recalling a memory if it is recorded at a *lower* energy level. It has an easier time recalling a memory if it is recorded at a *higher* energy level consistent with the *perfect essence.*

Our current physical brain can easily lose memories and even invent memories that were never stored on it, deceiving us into believing something happened that never *really* did. Our *essence*, on the other hand, will never deceive us. It records our experience *exactly* as it occurs. An example of how easily our *imperfect* brain can be deceived is when we are deprived of sleep or food. When so deprived, we begin to hallucinate, because our brains are not functioning properly.

Hallucinations are simply our deprived and delirious physical brain being unable to handle the energy levels given off by our constant and perfect *essence*. Hallucinations, like dreams, are often disconnected and random parts of our *real* experience, put together by our physically *imperfect* brain in a way that we can *reason*ably understand them. Our *imperfect* brain can also be affected by stimulating drugs, actual mental disabilities, or a self-induced willingness to produce *imagined* thoughts and feelings, and then make these *imaginations* part of our current "reality."

6. A PERFECT BRAIN DOES NOT ALLOW SENSORY DECEPTION

A *perfect* body will never deceive us through dreams or hallucinations, because it has a *perfect* brain. Its energy levels are *always* constant. A perfect body does not need sleep or food because it receives its energy from the perfectly balanced and consistent energy of the *essence*. (A full description of the *perfect human body* and how it works will be given in chapter 11.)

Again, the *essence* can be compared to an encased nuclear-energy facility that provides itself with its own perpetual energy. The *essence* is the source of the energy needed to operate the perfect body. Food is not needed. Sleep is not needed. No outside energy is needed for the perfect human body.

This can more easily be conceptualized by visualizing the *essence* as a generator that supplies a constant stream of energy to the brain and to the other parts of the body, each part performing its own specific function. Through sensory input, each function of the body adds to the sense of joy felt by the human being. Having its own source of perpetual energy, the perfect body does not need any outside source of energy. Taking this a step further, the *essence* provides the necessary energy that all the cells of the body need. Easily put, the entire construct of the perfect body is like a human being having a nuclear reactor inside one's head—one that provides all the energy a person will ever require in order to live and act human.

7. AN IMPERFECT BODY CREATES DISCOMFORT

Our current bodies need food and sleep because they do not have their own source of energy. Although our *essence* is a part of us, our *imperfect* bodies were constructed purposefully so that they couldn't fully utilize its energy. In other words, our current bodies do not have the "wiring" to deliver the constant and perpetual energy of our *essence*.

We are forced to take a variety of steps to provide the energy that we need. These "forced steps" do not add to the joy of being a human. We are forced to labor to plant, then labor to harvest, then labor to prepare, and then labor to chew and swallow. We then have to *further* labor to get rid of the excrement remaining from the parts of the food that our body cannot utilize for its energy! It's a laborious process that all of us wish we could eliminate. One need only consider how our *imperfect* body rids itself of excrement to understand the *opposition* of a joyful sensory experience. In this one necessary bodily function, we experience the exact opposite of what our senses enjoy smelling, seeing, tasting, touching, and hearing. We will one day laugh together as we recall how our *imperfect* bodies once expelled waste.

8. IN THE PERFECT WORLD WE ATE ONLY FOR PLEASURE

If the perfect human body does not need to eat to survive and function, then what would be the use of eating the perfect foods grown in the perfect world? During our foundationalization, we ate *only* to experience the sensation it provided to our body. Taste is one of the ways a human body experiences joy. It is one of our sensory receptor systems, along with sight, sound, touch, and smell. These systems allow the outside environment to provide us with experiences that we recognize as enjoyable.

As previously discussed, our *sense* of happiness was established in our *Foundationalization Process*, during which the ultimate human standard of what tastes good was set. Because of this, we are the only life form in the Universe that eats purely for pleasure. This *pleasure* is the balance we reach when what we put into our mouth touches the receptors of our tongue and creates an energy transmission that conforms to the memory stored on our *essence*. These memories are what were stored when the first substances from our primordial environment came into contact with the taste buds of our perfect body.

It would not be correct to call the first substances that foundationalized our sense of taste "food." We currently view "food" as a source of energy for our body. In the perfect world, the substances we take into our mouths provide our taste buds with sensory pleasure, but we are not dependent upon them in order to survive. Although food will not be necessary to survive in the perfect world, we will continue to enjoy tasting those things that provide a sense of pleasure to us.

9. OUR SENSES ARE PARAMOUNT TO OUR DEVELOPMENT

Infants use *all* of their senses to foundationalize themselves in our current world. As stated, they utilize their sense of taste more often than any of their other senses. They love to put things into their mouths. During our *Foundationalization Process*, we also put many things into our mouths as newly created humans. However, just as parents on this earth do not let their infant children put things into their mouths that would harm them or taste bad, our creator mothers did not allow us to put things into our mouths that they knew were not the perfect foundationalization substances for our sense of taste. Without any prior mortal experience of taste, a poisonous plant not intended for human consumption, for example, would have forever tasted good to us, had our advanced mothers allowed us to eat it and establish it as a palatable substance.

Using the sensory receptor systems of the physical body is the natural way that we experience our surrounding environment. During our *Foundationalization Process*, nothing outside of the human body could be experienced and recorded as a memory unless it passed through one of our five sensory systems. This is the way our physical bodies allow us to gain experience, both in our current world and in the perfect world where we became human beings.

Humans also possess a *sixth* sensory system that allows us to receive outside stimulus that is not produced by sight, smell, sound, taste, or touch. This sixth sense can best be described as our ability to sense electromagnetic wavelengths of energy generated by other humans and recognized by our own brain. This is how we sense "feelings" or emotions of another person, without seeing, smelling, touching, hearing, or tasting them.

10. IN THE IMPERFECT WORLD, WE USE ALL OF OUR SENSES TO FORM RELATIONSHIPS WITH OTHERS

We use these sensory systems to choose what brings us happiness and what does not. An example of how we use *all* of our sensory receptor systems to find happiness is the way *imperfect* humans choose the person with whom they desire to have sex (which is the ability to utilize all of our senses for the greatest amount of pleasure). Our eyes determine that what we see of the person is desirable. Our nose determines if the person's smell is acceptable. We draw close to them to hear them speak and breathe and so that we can touch them. Then, just as an infant child would do, the last thing we do in courting the object of our affection is to introduce the person to our mouth.

There has never existed a person who has chosen a sexual partner who did not have the desire to *taste* the object of their affection. This accepted form of tasting is known as "kissing." This is why human beings gain a great amount of pleasure from kissing on the mouth. Kissing allows us to use *all* of our senses to choose the person with whom we have a desire to share the ultimate of all human physical experiences—the joy of sex. The physical courting process involved in attempting to introduce another person into one's personal experience is like an infant finding a bug on the ground and trying to fit it into the infant's reality: the infant sees it, might have heard it, touches it, smells it, and then—**tastes** it!

11. MORTAL "LOVE" DID NOT EXIST IN THE PERFECT WORLD

Now that we have mentioned how we find a person in our *imperfect* world to be the object of our affection, it is a good time to discuss "love." Keep in mind that everything we experience in this *imperfect* world is the *opposite* of what we experienced in our foundationalization stage of development. Therefore, we need to understand how "love" affects us in an *imperfect* world.

"Love" did not exist in our perfect world as we understand and experience it in our *imperfect* world. There was no word that was used in our communication that meant what "love" means to our current understanding. On this earth, "love" is a way we measure the effect that outside stimuli have on us. The more something makes us happy, the more we *love* it.

Love ***cannot*** *be part of our* ***true perfect*** *reality*, because it is not something that lasts, nor is it something that we can experience with one or more of our five senses. Although we can enjoy what we see, smell, touch, hear, and taste, the experience that our senses provide us is not actually "love." In our *imperfect state*, love is the measure of the effectiveness of our senses to react with our environment to bring us happiness.

Based on this understanding, feelings of compassion or empathy for another cannot be considered "love." These "feelings" are examples of our ability to generate electromagnetic wavelengths of energy that can be *felt* by other humans, but have nothing to do with our physical senses. Our brain recognizes and senses these wavelengths of energy without actually seeing, smelling, touching, hearing, or tasting another person. These types of feelings cannot be equated with "love," because they do not bring us personal happiness. It is not enjoyable to recognize and sympathize with the unpleasant plight of another. And the reason these feelings do not bring us personal happiness or balance is because when we lived in a *perfect* world, there was no need to have compassion for or empathize with another.

In our *perfect* world, everything was *perfect*. Therefore, because everything was in its perfected form, what measure of "love" could we have placed on anything we experienced there? Our *Foundationalization Process* established the standard of perfection for us, thereby eliminating any other standard of measurement by which we graded our experiences there. It also provided the standard of measurement by which we would grade our experiences of the future. Everything we did in our perfect world is what we will later recognize as the ultimate experience of human happiness, once we have experienced the *opposite* of perfection here. We need to experience an *imperfect* world so that we have a contrast with which to compare our *perfect* foundationalized experiences.

Here is another way of looking at it: If we love something, then it follows that we must hate something else (as a measure by which we *devalue* something in comparison). Because "hate" cannot exist in a perfect world, then "love" cannot exist there either. Through our current experience, we understand how hate produces negative emotions that throw our body out of balance and cause us unhappiness. When we hate, we experience something that is not part of who we really are or who we are striving to become. We do not feel comfortable hating something.

Stated again another way: We do not "like" (a softer word for love) an apple that tastes bad. The experience of biting into an apple that tastes bad is physically unpleasant and leads us to conclude that we "hate" the apple. It's not much different in our experiences with each other. Some people make us feel comfortable and we "love" to be around them. Others make us feel uncomfortable, so we "hate" being around them.

Although love seems to provide us with a great amount of joy here, the opposite effects of the feeling can also cause us a great amount of misery. During our *Foundationalization Process*, we did not learn how to be miserable; therefore, we did not learn how to love. And although love seems to be a natural and beautiful expression of feelings in our *imperfect* world, when considered honestly, it is the value we place upon it that causes most of our emotional problems.

Most of our mental frustrations are a cause of being disappointed by someone or something we value (love) or of losing personal value we once received from others. It is a known fact that many people who thought they were once "in love" with each other can develop a "hate" for one another that is just as strong as the "love" they once shared.

12. A PERFECT WORLD IS VOID OF PREJUDICES

In the perfect world, there were no personal relationships formed where we felt a *measure* (love or hate) of comfort that told us whether a relationship was healthy or not. We did not *love* to be around some people and *hate* being around others. We interacted with all people and used our free will to choose with whom we wanted to associate. This "choice" depended more on logistics than it did upon picking and choosing different people. The perfect world where we were created was large enough so that each of our mothers had their own home, centralized with others in a location where their children were foundationalized. Therefore, naturally, we developed bonds of familiarity with those who spent most of their time near where we lived.

The choices we made were not from *comparing* our experiences with those of others and developing a sense of "mine is right" and "yours is wrong." Everyone's personal choices in life were just as "right" as everyone else's. Again, we knew that the Universe revolved around each of us, as it did the same around everyone else. Each of us was considered and treated "special." What gave us a *sense* of *equality* was that all of us were treated the same way—we were all "special," so none of us were. We were not uncomfortable around those with whom we did not choose to associate any more than we were around those with whom we did. We were foundationalized to accept all people and the way that they each exercised their individual free will. We were comfortable with everyone's actions and made no judgments of others.

13. MUCH MISERY COMES FROM THE JUDGMENT OF OTHERS

In our *imperfect* world, however, we are conditioned to judge what others do with their free agency. We form personal opinions and choose whom we want to be around based upon whether or not what they are doing brings balance to our own life. If what others are doing does not conform with what we think is the "right" thing to do, then we judge them as being wrong, develop a sense of hate for what they are doing, and alienate ourselves from them. In this *imperfect* world, we often justify our *hate* by saying, "I don't hate the person; I just hate what they do." In *reality*, however, we truly do "hate" those whose actions we hate.

The bulk of human misery comes from one group of people judging another group as being inferior or making inappropriate (wrong) lifestyle choices. To protect their own "***right***eousness," one group of people will expect others to see things *their* way and adapt to *their* way of thinking. If the others refuse, physical force is often used to compel them. This is the main cause of the creation of nations and borders that separate the human race and promote the inevitable wars that ensue between them.

This human misery is also exacerbated because the natural resources of the earth are limited and controlled by only a few people who believe that the needs of their own group (family, community, or nation) take precedence over everyone else's. These human-invented prejudices are very successful at providing us with a stark contrast between a *perfect* world and an *imperfect* one.

14. OUR HUMANITY WAS FOUNDATIONALIZED IN EQUALITY

In the world where we foundationalized our humanity, we made no judgment or measure of what another did. During that time, we were all equally experiencing everything that was perfect. There were no *families* formed behind "white picket fences" where parents foundationalized their children completely differently than their neighbors did who lived just a few feet away, behind their own "white picket fence." The living arrangements of the mothers who were responsible for rearing newly created children were open communities where children wandered freely throughout the environment.

The mothers of the community each reared their children in the exact same way, according to what these advanced parents accepted as the rules and procedures for proper parenting. These *perfect* parents had no personal possessions that belonged to any particular person. Everybody owned everything equally. Everything existed in that highly advanced environment to provide the newly created human being with the *perfect* example of how humanity should be, or better, the standard was set for acting humane.

However, as we developed and learned to interact with our environment, we *did* begin to make things and accomplish things that we associated with our own personal free will. We began to value the things that we made and accomplished as personal "possessions," only because as an individual, apart from all others, we made the choice to do something that no one else did. But everyone else also had the *same opportunity and ability* to do anything that we did or anything else that they wanted to do with their free will. Thus, our accomplishments were not valued any more or less than anyone else's. They simply became an expression of our individuality.

15. THERE WERE NO TRADITIONAL FAMILY UNITS IN THE PERFECT WORLD

Because we had no need to eat or sleep in this perfect state, there was no need to construct houses where eating and sleeping took place, which are the main purposes for individual housing units in our current world. During our *Foundationalization Process*, we were constantly engaged in exercising our free will in an open and completely equal environment. However, each advanced mother or partnership had their own domicile where they could isolate themselves, if desired, from all others and maintain their own individuality.

The society in which we were foundationalized was the perfect form of a communal living arrangement. However, there was no need for communal houses or buildings in which we needed to congregate for any specific purpose of foundationalization. The technology existed that enabled us to experience anything we wanted whenever and wherever we found ourselves. The world itself was like an open community with no locked doors or closed businesses, where everything was available for the sake of developing individuality while associating closely with other humans.

16. BOREDOM DOES NOT EXIST IN PERFECT WORLDS

Although we have already discussed the absence of time in a perfect world (because there is no day or night), it is almost impossible to completely understand the time frame in which we existed and developed in our primordial world. The best answer that can be given is that we existed there before we came here for as long as we needed to establish a perfect sense of humanity.

There was plenty to do there. It was impossible to become bored living in the perfect world because we had no contrasting experience to be able to comprehend boredom. All of our experiences were *new* to us; therefore, our limitless capacity to store these experiences eliminated boredom. In our *imperfect* bodies we experience the feeling we associate with boredom when our freedom to act as we want is limited or restricted. But in a perfect world, we could do whatever, whenever we wanted; and we had an unlimited choice of things we could do.

17. PERFECT MOTHERS EXPERIENCE PERFECT "BIRTHS"

As explained previously, our experiences in a perfect world were not categorized as a timeline of events where we recognized our experiences as the past, present, and future. We existed only in the present. Our advanced human brains kept all of our memories continually present in our minds as if everything that happened and was happening to us was taking place "right now" in the present.

To understand this better with the limited capacity of our current brains, we need to discuss how a newly created human being came into existence and experienced the *Foundationalization Process* on the "day-by-day" timeline with which we are familiar. Our current timeline on this earth started with our birth. So using our need to follow a timeline scenario to understand, the following is typically how a *birth* took place in a *perfect* human world:

A mother who wanted to create a child stood anywhere upon the planet. She usually chose a place where she could be isolated by herself, either in her own home or alone surrounded by the natural beauty of the perfect world. With the power of her own thought, she visualized what she wanted the child's body to look like. She did this visualization by accessing the database of her own body, or what we would consider as her DNA patterns. From these familiar patterns, and having a perfect knowledge of what every one of her other children looked like, the mother chose what she wanted the new child to look like—what color of hair, eyes, skin, etc. No human child looked exactly the same.

The mother then commanded the subatomic particles of matter (protons, neutrons, and electrons) to create exactly what she was thinking. Everything was done by the energy provided from her own *essence* and the type of body (that of a creator) she possessed. The new body came together and materialized right in front of her. There was no need for embryonic development. The body was formed exactly how the mother chose it to be by the power of her thoughts. The body looked like an infant's body, but without a navel ("belly button") and without any sex organs or parts. There were also no or other major organs in the body, such as those required in an *imperfect* world to eat, digest, and eliminate food. (There are no dirty diapers to change in a perfect world!)

18. ADVANCED MOTHERS ORGANIZED THE ELEMENTS FOR OUR PERFECT BODIES

To relate to how the advanced creation of a human body is possible, as just described, we need only compare it to our current technology. Worldwide access to wireless Internet service demonstrates that a person can be anywhere in the world and, with a small handheld device, receive multiple downloads of a variety of different information. The human race upon this earth has only had this type of technology for a few decades, but each year, the ability to access different types of information becomes more and more advanced. Wireless transmission of information is accomplished unseen through the air by electromagnetic power, which, for all intents and purposes, is the power generated by the subatomic particles (protons, neutrons, and electrons) of all matter.

As explained previously, advanced human creators have a brain that can command the formation, structure, and instructions of all matter because of their ability to control these basic subatomic particles. We now understand that these subatomic particles are simply electromagnetic energy that has not yet been formed into recognizable matter. The advanced mother has the ability to form these particles into the elements needed to create a physical body.

In the creating process of a new human being, an advanced mother's brain can be compared to an advanced computer that has the capability of receiving wireless transmissions of electromagnetic energy directly from her environment. Using her advanced brain, she simply "downloads" the elements she needs to create the body she has previously designed in her mind. All of the elements needed to create the body come from the mother's ability to take protons, neutrons, and electrons (for want of an easier way to explain it) from her surrounding environment and form them into the necessary elements that make up the body.

The electromagnetic energy needed to create the body comes from the power of her *essence* through her perfected "creator-able" brain. She organizes the elementary makeup of the body in the air in front of her the same way our current technology projects holographic images into mid air. The source of current holographic imagery is generated by devices that project electromagnetic energy into a controlled space of air. The device used in advanced-holographic *reality*, which is far more superior than how current technology works, is the advanced human brain. The energy of thought generated through the perfect "creator-able" brain controls subatomic electromagnetic energy exactly how the person, who produces the thought, wants it to be controlled. Therefore, the body of the new human being is created in a matter of a moment with one thought.

19. ADVANCED PARENTS OVERSEE HUMAN DEVELOPMENT

With another *thought* (burst of electromagnetic energy), the mother telepathically "dials" the "number" of the male whom she has chosen to provide the *essence* for the child. This is the way she informs the father of the creation of the body for his *new* child.

The advanced male (father) has agreed to take the responsibility, along with the mother, to ensure that the newly created human develops and becomes a *perfect* human being. These two advanced beings, male and female, ensure that the child has every opportunity to reach its full potential as a human being. Because of this responsibility, the parents stay in contact with the child and monitor its development throughout all the stages of its existence, until it reaches full maturity and becomes an advanced *perfect* human being like themselves

20. ADVANCED PARENTS ARE ALWAYS CONNECTED WITH THEIR NEWLY CREATED OFFSPRING

It is in the energy patterns created by the *perfect* physical body that the mother is provided with the ability to be continually in touch with her child. Likewise, the creation of the *essence* allows the father the ability to keep track of his children by the energy each *essence* generates. In other words, the physical body of the child is connected genetically to the mother and the *essence* is connected to the father.

The father's brain is like a computer that stores infinite amounts of data. When the father creates a new *essence*, he places a personal file "tag" upon it so that he can access it at any time with the energy of his own *essence*. Each of our individual *essences* is "tagged" with a personal frequency of energy that is known and recognized by the father who created it.

Although the newly created *essence* is void of any recorded memories, its energy frequency level is created and uniquely tagged by the specific father who creates it. This is how he keeps track of us. If the father wants to access any particular *essence* to see how the child is doing in its development, all he has to do is to *think* about it. This brings the child's unique *frequency* to his mind, which allows him to make a direct connection to the child's *essence.*

In this way, the father will forever have the ability to connect with the newly created human being for whom he is responsible. The only reason why he maintains this connection is to make sure the child is receiving everything necessary to help the child become an advanced human and enjoy its existence. Likewise, the mother will always maintain her personal connection with each child through the energy patterns emitted by the physical body.

The mother has no direct connection with us while we live in an *imperfect world.* Once our *essence* was taken out of the body our advanced mothers created for us and placed in an *imperfect body* upon this earth, the direct connection was lost. This happens because the mother *does not* want direct insight to the pain, sorrow, misery, and suffering her children must go through during their necessary and important second stage of development in an *imperfect* world. What mother would?

The father, however, continues to maintain his direct connection with our *essence.* In this way, with the help of other advanced human beings, he can monitor our progression upon this earth in our quest to understand and appreciate our individual humanity type. Male creators, as well as those who help them (best referred to as A.N.G.E.L.S., as previously explained), can access our *essence* at any time. They can put an *essence* into any particular *imperfect body* being born anywhere in the world if, by so doing, it will enhance the individual's ability to succeed in understanding their humanity type.

For example, some people upon the earth are poor, uneducated peasants, who are forced to depend upon lives of crime in order to take care of their basic necessities. If someone spends their lifetime judging these "life choices" of another, then the one judging can be assured that after they die, their *essence* will later be directed to a body being born into a poverty-stricken, crime-laden community. The father has no problem seeing his children *suffer*, if it means that they will learn the lessons of ***true*** humanity.

21. OUR ESSENCE IS UNIQUELY TAGGED BY THE FATHER

Going back to our discussion on the creation of a new human being, the father knows what frequency level to "tag" the new *essence* with, based on the mother requesting it. Each mother has her own "tag" established between her and the father. Although it does not happen exactly this way, here is an example of how the process works, according to our current ability to comprehend what takes place:

If mother A wants a new *essence* from father A for her 265th child, then father A tags the *essence* with an energy frequency level of AA265. If mother B wants a new *essence* for her 578th child from father A, then father A tags the *essence* with an energy frequency level of AB578.

Each mother has her own frequency level, and each of the bodies she produces for her children has its own frequency level. The mother and the new child's body are connected by the mother's frequency level, because the patterns of the child's body *came* from the mother. She categorizes her children differently than the father, who is responsible for the children of many, many mothers.

In this rudimentary example, each of us would be easily recognizable from each other by the frequency level *tags* given to us by our parents. Child AA265 and AB578 both belong to the same father (A) but different mothers (A and B). Mother A recognizes her child as 265 and mother B recognizes hers as 578. Father A recognizes the child from mother A as A265 and the child from mother B as B578.

This is the easiest way to explain it with our current understanding. In reality, there are no numbers assigned to any human being. We are not a number, as there are no quantitative measures in a perfect world. We are an energy level whose frequency is fine-tuned in order to be unique from everyone else and directly connected to *our* creators.

Here's another way of looking at it: In our current world, everyone can own a cell phone with their own individual number. The way our parents call us is by dialing our personal phone number that, in *essence*, is simply a different frequency or wavelength of energy generated by our parents' phone that soars through the air and finds our unique number and rings our phone.

Even with the rudimentary technology we have today, a person can be found anywhere upon earth by tracing where the energy of the call ends up. In the near future, parents will have the ability to utilize the current GPS (Global Positioning System) to know exactly where their children are, at all times.

With this understanding, we can grasp how in advanced worlds (with far more advanced technology than we have today) children are created to be like *biological cell phones*, by each receiving, in effect, its own personal number (frequency level) when created. When advanced mother B wants to "call" her 578th child, for example, she simply "dials" the child's unique number stored in her memory and she is immediately connected with the child telepathically. When she creates a new body, she is creating a *new phone number* that she records in the *phonebook* stored on her *essence*. It's really that simple!

The father has his own phone number for the child, which he assigns to the newly created human being when he creates its *essence*. The father also stores the *phone number* in the *phonebook* on *his essence* and can telepathically access the *essence* of the child anytime he wishes. When he accesses the *essence* of his child, he will know all there is to know about the experiences the child is having. He does this by concentrating on and then accessing the energy levels stored as memories in the child's *essence*, much the same way he brings to mind his own memories. In other words, an advanced parent has the ability to read a child's mind and recall the child's memories as easily as recalling their own.

Because the *perfect* body and the *essence* exist on the exact same energy level (as explained previously), the mother can also access her child's *essence* with her own mind. From this, she can know everything there is to know about how her child is doing in its developmental stages on its way to becoming the perfect human being, ***but only* when the child's essence is in the perfect body *she* creates for it**.

22. OUR MOTHER'S SMILE AND KISS ARE OUR FIRST SENSORY EXPERIENCE EVER

Once the father creates the *essence*, he delivers it with pinpoint accuracy to the location on the planet where the mother has created the new perfect body. The *essence* is naturally attracted to the body and enters into it to bring life to the child held gently in the arms of its mother. Once the *essence* enters the body, the eyelids open and the first experience of all human beings is the tender kiss and warm smile of a caring mother. (Is it any wonder why we currently associate the pleasant feelings created by a kiss and a smile with our positive personal relationships?)

THUS BEGINS THE PROCESS OF HUMAN FOUNDATIONALIZATION

Each mother involved in the *Foundationalization Process* of a new human being determines the point in her child's development when the child can be left alone to continue the process without constant guidance. This determination is made once the child has developed the physical skills to care for itself. The new human being must be able to move freely throughout the environment at will, as it is from all aspects of the perfect environment that the newly created human will gain its foundational experiences.

Because the environment presents nothing but the perfect human situation in all things, our foundational parents had no concern that we would hurt ourselves or make a wrong choice of action. In this world, it was impossible to make a *wrong* choice. Our entire primordial world was set up to allow us to experience everything good about being human and establish what the *right* choices should be. There was nothing we could have done that would have given us anything but the ultimate human experience.

23. A PERFECT BODY ALLOWS UNDERWATER BREATHING

In our current stage of development with our *imperfect* bodies on our *imperfect* world, most of us have had dreams wherein we experienced ourselves being able to breathe underwater. These dreams come from actual experiences when we were first brought into existence in the *perfect* human world. We did not need oxygen to exist, even underwater.

Previously, we discussed how our *essence* is an enclosed vacuum of perpetual nuclear energy that provides all the energy the perfect body needs to exist forever. Our *perfect* bodies do not have lungs and do not breathe the surrounding air. The perfect body has none of the major organs our current body has, all of which are associated with blood.

Our current bodies use oxygen as a catalyst to begin the process of utilizing the energy of the nutrients our blood delivers to our cells. The energy that our current body uses comes from the foods that we eat, which are then broken down by various bodily functions. In our *perfect* body, the pure energy that our cells need is produced by our *essence* and delivered through a perfected and complete nervous system. Therefore, in our initial bodies, we could survive underwater.

24. WE ONCE KNEW HOW TO FLY

Most of us have also had dreams of flying. These dreams also come from actual experiences we had in the *perfect* world. We could fly there, though much differently than birds do.

Just as an infant on our current world learns to control its nervous system so that it can sit up, crawl, and then eventually walk, in the perfect world, we learned how to sustain ourselves in mid-air and then to propel ourselves through the air. To comprehend how a human being can do this, we must first understand what *prevents* us from floating in our current world.

Our scientists theorize that the gravitational pull of the earth keeps us from floating, or better, the mass of our bodies gives us weight. They also theorize that the earth has a gravitational force and a magnetic force and that each work separately to perform different functions.

It would confuse us (as science often does) if we tried to explain all that science claims to know about gravity and magnetism and about how they each function. To understand what is really taking place with both forces, we only need to understand their basic powers. Both forces can be traced to the exact same energy given off by subatomic particles (protons, electrons, and neutrons).

25. MAGNETISM KEEPS US ON THE EARTH

Let's make it easier to understand. If we take the positively charged end of a magnet and place it near the negatively charged end of another magnet, an invisible force causes them to come together and holds them tight. The same force that causes the opposite ends of magnets to come together is also the force behind gravity.

The earth can be compared to an enormous, positively charged magnet. All matter on the earth's surface can be visualized as being negatively charged, each part of matter having a differing strength of negativity, which creates "weight." This causes all things to stay stuck to the earth. The further away we place the negative end of a magnet from the positive end of another, the less force there is pulling them together.

Using this scenario then, each piece of matter upon the earth has its own unique negative force. The greater the density of the subatomic particles from which the piece of matter is made, the greater the negative force. For example, the density of iron is much greater than the density of salt; therefore, on the surface of the earth, a 4" x 4" block of iron weighs much more than an equal size block of salt. But size, mass and density are only indirectly related to weight.

Contrary to current scientific postulations, the density of an object is directly related to its negative polarity (i.e., the greater the density, the greater its negative polarity; and hence, the greater the negative polarity, the greater the weight). Thus, if object A, because of its greater density, has a greater negative polarity (charge) than object B, then A will weigh more than B if both are the same size. However, if one adds more of object B to the scale, then the negative polarity is increased, thus making it weigh more. Conversely, the weaker the negative force of the object because of its lesser density, the weaker the attraction (pulling force) toward the positively charged core of the earth.

If we place the positive (or negative) ends of two different magnets next to each other, there is an invisible, repelling force that prevents them from touching. The stronger the repelling force, the greater the distance forced between them.

26. OUR SOLAR SYSTEM IS BALANCED BY MAGNETISM

On the scale of our solar system, the positively charged earth is kept at a certain distance from the positively charged sun and the other positively charged planets based on the strength of their respective positive charges. For this reason, the earth never gets any closer to the sun or to any of the other planets than the distances established when the solar system was created. The earth, as it is now, was designed to have an appropriate tilt of its axis and fluctuations in its energy charge. This allows us to come closer to the sun at times so that we can experience the different seasons. Furthermore, the rotation of the earth and its orbit around the sun has all to do with its polarity in relation to the sun and the other planets.

The planets' polarity is also affected by the polarity of the moons that orbit each one. Each moon has a specific, intended polarity that keeps the planet doing what it was intended to do by its advanced creators. If we want to see a change in the basic natural patterns of our earth, all we would have to do is create another moon or eliminate the one we have.

Science has not identified one major cause of the weather changes (global warming, etc.) currently taking place upon the earth. These weather changes are largely being caused by all the metal (negatively charged) satellites and debris that humankind is forcing into the earth's orbit. This is affecting the earth's *natural polarity* and disrupting the perfectly balanced relationship between our earth and its only moon.

The advanced "scientists" who created our solar system knew what they wanted accomplished and how to do it. They understood the natural effects of polarity and utilized it for their own purposes. They knew how to create a human body that could be appropriately "polarized" by the mind to perform different functions of human propulsion.

27. WE LEARNED TO WALK, FLOAT, AND FLY

If we take a negatively charged magnet and touch it to a positively charged magnet, they will be stuck together. But if we change the polarity of the negative end to a positive charge, they will immediately be forced apart. Comparatively, our newly created bodies were negatively charged in relation to the positive charge of the planet on which we were created. Now here's the secret: The power of our *essence* can change the polarity of our *perfect* body.

By the power of thought, our perfect body can become positively charged in relation to the surface of the planet, thus allowing our body to float away from the surface. The more force we put into the thought, the greater the magnetic resistance between our body and the ground, thus allowing us to navigate wherever we want. If we want to walk on the ground, we simply change the polarity of our body to a negative charge and we will again be held to the ground, until we use some form of energy to lift one foot and put it in front of the other, then lift the other in a familiar "walking" motion.

To propel ourselves through the air, we also used the power of thought. We possessed the ability to change the polarity of our bodies not only in relation to the surface of the planet we were on but also with the surrounding atmosphere. This change in polarity causes motion by creating a repelling and attracting force with respect to the elements that make up the atmosphere.

Although the perfect world has an atmosphere that contains different elements than our current one, let's use oxygen and hydrogen in our example to explain how the perfect body can move through air:

Let's give oxygen a negative charge and hydrogen a positive charge. If our body is surrounded by oxygen and hydrogen elements, we need to first sense the presence of each, then change our body's polarity just enough to either repel us away from one of the elements or attract us towards the other.

The propulsion, or rather the changing of our body's polarity in relation to the surrounding elements, is caused by the power of the thoughts generated by our *essence*. By the power and energy of our thoughts, we can change the position of the elements that surround us. Simply put, to move forward we place negatively charged oxygen atoms behind us to repel our negative body away from them and positively charged hydrogen atoms in front of us to attract our body towards them.

A newly created infant learns to walk and float by the power of its *essence*. The coordination it takes to learn to control the polarity of the body takes time. Through trial and error (and the gentle guidance of an advanced, perfected mother who knew what she was doing), before long, we were propelling ourselves through the air as easily as we currently run through the lush grass of a meadow.

28. OUR PERFECT BODY FUNCTIONS WITH A PERFECTLY BALANCED NERVOUS SYSTEM

Our modern-day scientists have determined that we presently use only about 10% of our brain. If we compare our brain to a circuit board, where each circuit is connected to a part of the body that needs the brain's energy to function, then we could say that our body is *un*able to utilize 90% of its potential power source.

To deliver energy to our *imperfect* bodies, we have *imperfect* systems of delivery we call our circulatory, digestive, nervous, and lymphatic systems. Instead of having these systems and their particular organs, a *perfect* human body has only one: the nervous system. Where our *imperfect* body presently has capillaries, vessels, and veins in which to deliver energy to the cells, our *perfect* body is full of nerves, which are each connected to the brain and supplied with 100% of their energy from our *essence*. Our current bodies are purposefully built *improperly* so that they cannot utilize all of our brain's potential; thus fulfilling the purpose of experiencing an opposition in all things.

There is only one system in our current body that is not responsible for the disease and maladies that negatively affect us: our nervous system. The energy delivered directly from our brain cannot be corrupted or polluted. However, the nerves contained within the system *are* subject to disease and trauma, because they receive the energy to construct and maintain themselves from the other *imperfect* systems. In a *perfect* body, the nervous system delivers the energy provided by the *essence* and is also maintained by the same energy.

29. ENERGY IS THE BASIC NECESSITY OF ALL LIFE

The easiest way to understand what has been presented above about an advanced-human body is to understand that energy, in its most basic form, is the *only* thing that the cells of the body can use to maintain themselves. Unless the food we eat and the air we breathe is broken down into this basic form of energy, the *imperfect* body cannot use it. The main difference between the body we currently have and the *perfect* body in which we were foundationalized is the way energy is delivered to the cells that make up each body.

The *essence* produces the most basic form of energy, which is consequently delivered by a perfect nervous system to all the cells of the perfect body. It does this through the connections made between the brain and these cells. In the perfect body, we have at least 90% more brain connections with our nervous system than in our current body, and the *essence* never runs out of this energy.

In contrast, our current *imperfect* bodies get their energy from outside sources. We get this energy from the food that we eat and the light of the sun, which warms our body. Once we introduce these outside forms of energy into our bodies, we have other systems that are necessary to break them down into a form of energy that our cells can use. Our current bodies require energy to take in energy, break it down, and get it to where it needs to be to make our body function properly. The *perfect* body does not take in energy, does not break it down, and has the *perfect*, complete delivery system for its own perpetual energy.

30. MOTHERS EXPERIENCE THE JOY OF MOTHERHOOD

One might ask why advanced creators don't skip the developmental phases of the physical body and create mature adult bodies, which then could be foundationalized properly. The first reason is the choice a person makes to become a mother. Bonding with an infant, holding it close, watching it grow, and nurturing it provides a tremendous amount of joy to the mother.

The perfect infant's body grows and develops in size much the same way our current *imperfect* bodies do. However, once the body has reached the normal size of most adults, the body stops growing and does not age any further. A mother wouldn't experience the same sense of joy rearing an adult child, who looks exactly like she does, that she would otherwise experience if her child started out as an infant.

More importantly, the infant phase cannot be skipped because it is the natural and most effective way to foundationalize a human being. When a newly created *essence* is placed in the body, the *essence* has no experience and no memory or preprogramming that would allow it to work properly with the body. The body has no functional memories that are necessary for the coordination needed for movement. Infants need the time to become familiar with their bodies and to learn motor skills gradually, by creating an experience, memorizing it, then recalling the memory to make the action more smooth and stable. There is no other way.

In contrast, most animals have been preprogrammed *with* the coordination they need to move and act as an adult shortly after birth. This is another very significant proof that human beings are much different from all animals. Although there *are* animals whose newly born young are just as vulnerable as newborn human infants are, the animal parents have been preprogrammed with the strength and ability to protect their newborns from the surrounding environment.

In our *imperfect* world, a human parent can be as vulnerable as the infant. We have no preprogrammed knowledge of how to care for our offspring. If we existed in our current environment with only the things that nature has provided for us, we would not be successful as a species. No human male has the innate ability or natural strength to protect his offspring from predators or the natural environment.

The only way human fathers or mothers can protect themselves or their offspring is for them to *change* their natural environment by using their ability to *reason*. We do not have fur. We need clothes and shelter. We do not have the teeth, claws, strength, speed, or repugnant smells or poisons that would protect us from predators. We need weapons. We need the energy and ability of our unique *essence* to help us be successful at rearing children. This is the case in our *imperfect* world; but is not so in a *perfect* world.

31. IN A PERFECT WORLD EVERYTHING EXISTS FOR THE SAKE OF HUMAN BEINGS

Everything about the natural environment of the perfect world is about supporting the life of a human being. As mentioned, the plants and animals that exist in this type of world exist *for* the sake of the human being. The law of "survival of the fittest" is *not* the "law of the jungle," because there are no "strong" and there are no "weak."

We exist in these perfect worlds to take advantage of being human. The advantage we have over every other life form in the Universe is that no one can tell us what to do. We are left to ourselves to do whatever we want. Because the perfect environment is structured around providing us with the ultimate human experience, there is nothing that exists in this environment that does not do just that.

As we learned to use our physical body, we gained the ability to transport ourselves from one place to another. There are no cars to run over us, no steps to fall down, and no obstructions to our ability to exercise our free will and to do whatever our heart desires. A newly created child is allowed to wander anywhere it chooses. There are no expectations placed on the child by its mother of what it should be doing and when it should do it. The child exists for itself, not for the mother. The mother gains great joy in seeing her child develop into an individual by using its free agency to do things in ways different from any of her other children.

A perfect mother could never become bored from watching the use of free will in the development of her children. Because the human *essence* is *not* preprogrammed, the mother has no idea what the child is going to do with its new body or what type of human being it will choose to become. Part of the joy of being a mother is in the surprise of each new action.

32. A PERFECT WORLD HAS NO BOUNDS

Once we had mastered our means of movement, our ability to experience new things was only limited by our personal desire to do so. We explored the most perfect environment that any human being could possibly *imagine*. It is this *imagination* that can help us to visualize what we did with a *perfect* body in a *perfect* world.

There is no experience you can currently *imagine* in your mind that is not possible in the *perfect* world. We could fill volumes upon volumes of books describing what goes on there. Even so, the memories of our time spent on the *perfect* world where we were foundationalized are stored inside each of our *essences*. All we have to do is use our *imagination*. Nothing is impossible. Everything that we can dream and imagine that would be the perfect world...was and will be our perfect world!

SUMMARY

Our ability to imagine the perfect human world is simply our subconscious recollections of past events that appear completely disassociated with our current world. What we can *imagine* our human world to be is a direct connection to the experiences we had in the perfect world where we were created.

The abilities of our current bodies (though they appear similar in construct) are far from the abilities of the *perfect* human body. Having an *imperfect* body allows us the opportunity to go through experiences that we did not go through while being foundationalized as new human beings. We will value these experiences for the rest of our existence. The comparative value will afford us the appreciation for the *perfect* human body forever. This appreciation will provide us with continual and lasting happiness.

Our primordial advanced parents are directly responsible for our existence, as well as for our happiness. They are connected to us so that they can fulfill their responsibility towards us. We can live confident that, in all that we experience, they are aware of our plight and will ensure that, in the end, we have what they have—everlasting happiness!

Becoming Who We Are

CHAPTER SEVEN

Man's main task in life is to give birth to himself,
to become what he potentially is.

—Erich Fromm

1. WE ARE COMPLETELY UNIQUE FROM EVERYONE ELSE

There is a very good reason why siblings who share the same DNA and are reared in the same household by the same parents each turn out completely different. It is the same reason human beings are so widely varied in their personalities and characteristics, more so than any other species of animal. The reason makes us all unique individuals. The reason is this: we have the free will and right, and most importantly the ability, to become *who we are* of our own choosing.

2. WE ARE RESPONSIBLE FOR WHO WE CHOOSE TO BECOME

Our core personality was established long before any of us came to this earth and received an *imperfect* body. During the *Human Foundationalization Process*, we each individualized ourselves by using our free will to act and react within the physical and social environments of a *perfect* human world. Our primordial parents did not need to direct or guide our personal development. They ensured that the environment in which we received the foundationalization of our personality was such that the first *impression* or *imprint* we recorded upon our *essence* was one of quintessential humanity.

Unlike *imperfect* parents, who act as sculptors when they create a child (by outlining rules, goals, expectations, and a lifestyle for the child), *perfect parents* act as cultivators of free will. Advanced parents allow the child to develop without interfering into the experience of the child. Everything the newly created human does is the free-willed, uninhibited choice of the individual.

Rearing children in this way places the responsibility and outcome of a person's human nature *solely* on the individual. None of us will ever be able to blame *or give credit* to our creators for who we become and what we do with our free agency. We are completely responsible for *who we are* and what we do. This is only fair in light of the fact that *none of us asked to be created.* If we were created only to be told what to do, and had no other choice but to do it, then there would be no value or purpose in having free will. We would be no different from other animals that are created and programmed to act instinctually in specific ways in any given situation.

3. NO ONE CONTROLS WHO WE BECOME

Plants, animals, all other life forms, and every other bit of matter throughout our Universe, were organized with a specific purpose in mind. As explained previously, advanced human beings have *always* existed and have always been the ultimate overseers of everything in the Universe. All matter has always existed for the benefit of the human being. Those responsible for our creation and well-being determine what all matter does and how it is organized on our behalf. The only matter advanced human beings do not control is other human beings. Therefore, the need to ensure ***proper** humanity* is consistent with a continuing Universe of order. Otherwise, free will would result in chaos.

Although advanced creators do not control who a free-willed human being becomes, they *do* limit the power that each of us has over matter and over each other according to what we choose to do with our free agency. Because all things exist *for* human beings, it is important to ensure that all things continue to serve *human* needs. One of our greatest needs is to have the ability to remain empowered as individuals who have control over our environment and ourselves. Limitations of this empowerment are in place to ensure that the exercising of our individual free will does not impede another individual from exercising theirs.

4. WE WERE PROVIDED EVERYTHING NECESSARY TO INDIVIDUALIZE ACCORDING TO FREE WILL

In the perfect world where we were foundationalized, there was a perpetual abundance of everything we needed to experience the ultimate *human reality*. Our parents did not limit, in any way, what we did in that world. There were plenty of resources available for everyone. Whatever we wanted to do or whoever we wanted to become, the opportunity to do so was made available to us within the limitations set for our humanity. These limitations are all inclusive of one main consideration: What we would want others to do to us, we should do to them.

To list all of the experiences we could have while living in a *perfect* world would fill volumes. To understand all that we could do, even all that we did do, the reader needs only to use his or her *imagination*. Our imagination is the subconscious reflection of our past experience in a perfect world. Whatever we can imagine to be the *perfect* world for us *was* our perfect world during our foundationalization upon an advanced planet before we came to this earth.

5. THERE ARE THREE BASIC HUMANITY TYPES

Each of us is different from every other human. We each have our own perspective and experience that works uniquely for us as individuals. This individuality creates the basis and motivation for everything that we do; and what we do defines our personal *reality*. It is *who we are*.

The sum of *who we are* can be expressed as our **humanity type**, or better, the kind of person we are in relation to the Universe and everyone else in it. In general, there are three main *humanity types*:

- Those who depend on others to take care of them
- Those who take care of themselves
- Those who serve the needs and wants of others

6. FEW OF US FOUND HAPPINESS IN SERVING OTHERS

Our advanced parents/creators were an example of the humanity type that exclusively serves the needs of others; i.e., their children. As newly created beings, we all started out depending on others to take care of us. The role of a *service-oriented parent* was vital to our development. As explained above, if the parent created us for *their sake*, then our ability to become a unique individual would have been greatly hindered. As we grew and developed though, we began to realize that we could take care of ourselves and our own needs by using our environment for our own benefit.

Some of us enjoyed being taken care of by unselfish parents. These didn't see any reason why their creator's care over them should ever have to end. However, the majority of us were determined to serve ourselves and take advantage of our free will. We wanted to be responsible for our own happiness. We knew that our parents/creators were responsible for our happiness, because it was their choice to create us. But as we developed, we made the determination that it would be of greater value to our individuality if we were responsible for our own happiness (serve ourselves). This responsibility, we felt, would make us equal to our parents/creators, even if we didn't become parents ourselves.

We established our personalities and unique individual characteristics according to the ability allowed human beings to act for themselves. We gained the knowledge and had the power to interact and manipulate our environment in any way that we desired. However, we knew that there were limitations to our power, because we could *not* create other human beings. Although we had some reservations as to *why* we couldn't have all the powers and abilities of a human creator, there were nevertheless only a few of us who ultimately decided to become just like our parents and create and serve other human beings.

7. WE WERE ALL CREATED WITHOUT A SPECIFIC GENDER

Newly created humans are completely genderless, as none has had the experience to decide if becoming a male or female human creator is something they would freely choose for themselves. Had a specific gender been given us upon creation, we would have lost the freedom of choice and been destined to do what other gender-specific advanced humans do. Our free will would have been negated because we would have been foundationalized as a specific gender without being given a choice for ourselves.

We learned that there were both male and female creators. In the solar system where we were created, there were also other advanced humans living on other planets. We knew that these took care of themselves and chose not to be responsible for the lives of others. They were also genderless like us, as were those humans living on other planets, who had chosen to be continually served. *Only* those who chose to perpetuate human life and become responsible for rearing newly created life correctly, possessed a specific gender.

There is a difference between *imperfect* bodies that have gender and a *perfect, gendered body*. A "perfect, gendered body" does not have all the parts of the *imperfect human sexual reproductive* system. Advanced males and females only possess those parts that are responsible for providing sexual pleasure. There is no need for sperm or egg production or the parts of the body that support the growth and development of a body inside of a female. The ability to have sex is the greatest use of our sensory systems. However, sex organs, and the abilities associated with them, have always been directly tied to the promulgation of new life. (More about why this is the case in advanced human societies will be discussed in chapter 12 on human sexuality.)

Small children here upon this earth recognize the difference between their roles as children and that of their parents. They also recognize the differences between the bodies of boys and girls. Just as in these examples, we also recognized these distinguishable differences between our creators and ourselves. Although genderless at the time, we realized that we had the choice to become the same humanity type of any of the advanced human beings living in the solar system where we first came into existence.

8. EACH PLANET SUPPORTS A DIFFERENT HUMANITY TYPE

We were created in an advanced and perfected solar system. This solar system has a specific number of planets orbiting a sun. The exact number of the planets of any solar system in the Universe is directly associated with the *humanity types* of the advanced humans who live there. Advanced humans inhabit each of these planets according to the type of humanity they chose for themselves while going through their own *Foundationalization Process* while living in a completely different solar system with *their* creators.

Each of us chose what *humanity type* was best for us when we lived with our creators in *their* advanced world. After experiencing the perfect world on which we are created, we were placed in this *imperfect* world, where we are able to *confirm* that the *humanity type*, or the person we have chosen to be, is truly *who we are*. This *personal confirmation* is not to prove that our choice of *humanity type* is "correct," because we had plenty of time to figure out what was right for us while living in a perfect world. Rather, our experiences in our *imperfect* world help us appreciate forever whom we have chosen to be. After our creators are assured that we each have chosen our individuality, they prepare our own solar system with the appropriate number of planets to accommodate each person's chosen *humanity type*.

9. OUR CURRENT LIFE IS A PROBATIONARY EXPERIENCE

All human beings establish who they are and who they will always be in their first, primordial foundational stage of development. The second stage we need to go through (the one in which we currently exist) serves as a probationary experience, wherein we confirm to ourselves that we indeed made the *right* choice for ourselves during our primordial development. We confirm this by seeing how happy or unhappy we are when we experience the results of our personal choices. The probative experience further adds to our ability to accept the way we have chosen to use our free agency (the *humanity type* we have chosen). It helps us to realize that we will forever be satisfied with our choice and that it will fulfill all of our desires of happiness. We will never want to change *who we are* once we have experienced our probative experience!

Another important part of our experience in an *imperfect* world is to receive the confirmation that we would not be happy being responsible for the creation and happiness of others. Through this experience, we will come to accept that **only** humans who choose *to serve others* **should** have certain abilities that no other humanity type has. To confirm this in our minds, according to our own experience, we needed to see what would happen if all humanity types had the powers and abilities of human creators.

For this reason, during our current life upon this *imperfect* world, we all have the power to create and be responsible for human life. How we use this power and responsibility will convince us whether or not we find a fullness of joy in being entrusted with it. Most of us misuse the power by rearing children completely contrary to the Universal laws governing proper parenting. Many of us also abuse our personal power over others by limiting their free agency to whatever *we* determine is right. By experiencing how we misuse power, we will be convinced that we should not be allowed the ability in the future.

10. VERY FEW WILL BECOME HUMAN CREATORS

It is important to point out that during our probative state currently upon this earth, we will learn why it is that *only service-oriented* humanity types can be trusted with the responsibility of creating human life. Although all of us can have children in this life and rear them the way we believe to be correct, few of us realize that the responsibility of human life not only entails what we do for our *own* children, but also what we do for every other human being.

During our time upon earth, some of us might rise to positions of great authority and possess the ability to exercise power and control over the free will of others. Some of us will have much success with money and material things. Nevertheless, few of those who wield temporary power and control over others and *own* and control the resources of the earth will consider the plight of the least among us. Few will see the value in complete equality in all things. According to the laws and order of the advanced human societies throughout the Universe, those who do not consider the plight of the least human being and do not desire to create unconditional equality for all, by making the least among them as great as themselves can *never* be entrusted with the power and responsibility of being a creator of human life.

Those who are honest with themselves know whether or not the life of a stranger is as important to him or her as the life of his or her own child or "loved" one. Those who have chosen the humanity type that *serves themselves*, or that expects to be *served by others*, feels completely comfortable with and easily justifies the inequality created by *imperfect human associations*, such as family and friends. However, the memories in the *essence* (the subconscious) of a person who has chosen to be a creator *will not* allow him or her to tolerate inequality in any form. The power of creation is directly connected to the promotion and sustaining of complete and unconditional equality in all things for all human beings. Thus, we are all created as humans; but very few chose to create them and be responsible for their happiness forever.

We can figure out which humanity type we chose by being honest with ourselves. We can ask ourselves, "With which *human situations* are we most comfortable while living in an *imperfect* world, and with which are we not? What do we do about human inequality, in spite of what it might do to our own personal relationships with our family and friends? Are the lives of others just as important to us as the lives of our family and friends? If so, what are we doing to demonstrate that they are?" From our experiences in an *imperfect* world, it is easy to see just how few creator-type humans actually exist.

Nevertheless, the perfection of our creators' plan for us is not to condemn us for being who we are. Our creators want to help us realize just how important it is to have those who receive their joy by serving others, possess the ultimate powers of the Universe. Thus, those of the other humanity types are allowed to be our leaders, judges, and parents here upon earth. We are experiencing what their leadership, judgments, and parenting does to a human society.

11. WE CANNOT CHANGE THE FOUNDATIONAL CORE OF OUR HUMANITY

To understand how we individualized and chose our *humanity type*, we must have a better understanding of the three (3) different types that develop during our *Foundationalization Process*. Although advanced human societies have no quantitative measures such as time or measurement, as mortals, it helps our understanding to place a measurement on the amount of time we spent going through the *process* of becoming *who we are* when we lived in the advanced solar system of our creators.

In current time measurements, we spent about 5 billion years *becoming who we are*. In relation to this great amount of time, the short span of a few thousand years upon our present earth in a state of *imperfection* is not going to change any of our personal characteristics. We either receive happiness from being *served by others*, in *serving ourselves*, or in the *service of others*. No humanity type is any better or worse than any other—they are just different choices of personal behavior based on the free will to choose what makes us happy.

It is *impossible* for any human being to change who they are *after being foundationalized* for such a long period of "time." This is evidenced in the specific number of planets that were created for our present solar system. We were not created for any specific solar system; our solar system was created *for* us. The size of each planet in our solar system was determined by the number of people in our batch of newly created humans who chose a specific humanity type that corresponds to each planet. The size of these planets will not grow or shrink, because all of us have already chosen and outlined what we wanted our *perfect world* to be. Our creators made our solar system according to our desires.

12. SOLAR SYSTEMS AND THEIR PLANETS ARE ESTABLISHED TO ACCOMMODATE OUR HUMANITY

Although science will continue to argue the specifics of what constitutes a planet and what does not, for the sake of understanding how and why our solar system was planned, we will acknowledge the existence of nine (9) main planets. These planets were designed in size to accommodate the three degrees of human desire (*humanity types*) of those who are assigned to this solar system.

13. WE ARE DISTINGUISHED BY OUR HUMANITY TYPE

It is necessary to give a name to each *humanity type* to avoid the repetition of more lengthy definitions. Accordingly, we will use the following names for each type:

- Those who are served—Stellarian
- Those who serve themselves—Lunarian
- Those who serve others—Solarian

14. DIFFERENT PLANETS ARE CREATED FOR DIFFERENT HUMANITY TYPES

Using the current names we have given the planets of our solar system, we can categorize them to properly illustrate and give examples of the different types of human beings who will one day inhabit them, once they have been properly prepared for human life.

MERCURY
(Solarian)

15. MERCURY IS FOR MALE AND FEMALE COUPLES

This planet is designed to house *couples* consisting of one male and one female. These humans choose to be together for one purpose only—to serve the needs of others.

The male oversees the creation of new solar systems and the government administration of all *new* creation. He also oversees the creation of the human *essence* that advanced mothers put into the bodies they create, as explained previously.

The female's primary role on this planet is to be an eternal mate to the male creator and to ensure that a new human being is created to become the *overseer* for each of the new solar systems the male creates. This particular mother does not allow free agency for the child she rears to become an overseer. She prepares the child for a specific purpose. This purpose will be covered in the next chapter when we discuss how the government of the Universe is set up. However, she *does* have other children who are not predestined to become an overseer; therefore, these children are allowed complete free will to do what they want and develop into whomever they desire to be.

16. FORMING RELATIONSHIPS AFFECTED BY PROXIMITY

All newly created humans are genderless, and have not yet decided if they want to be a male or a female. While going through the Foundationalization Process, people can pair up (similar to how friends do upon this earth) and choose to associate with each other throughout the process. As previously discussed, although the concept of "love" is indiscernible in a *perfect* world, as there are no values placed on anything, people *do* have the choice of with whom they wish to associate.

It was impossible for us to get to know all of our newly created siblings. Even after over 5 billion years of existence, we still found ourselves in a closer physical proximity to a relatively few number of people. From these close physical proximities, we would form friendships with some whom we became more comfortable with the more we hung around them. From these "friendships," emotional *bonds* were formed between people that were stored in the *essence.* For this reason, we meet some people upon this earth with whom we feel almost immediately comfortable.

17. ETERNAL PARTNERSHIPS FORM ALLIANCES AND MAKE COMMITMENTS TO SERVE OTHERS AS COMPANIONS

When two people decided that they would be happiest in the service of others as companions in the work of creation, each of them chose to be related to the work in a specific way, either by choosing to become a male or a female. The actual companionship of an advanced male and female comes from a promise that two genderless humans make with each other during their foundationalization process. This companionship can be appropriately called "eternal mates."

After many years of witnessing the example of their male/father and female/mother creators, and deciding that service to others was what they wanted to do, two individual humans became *bound* together by the promise they made to each other to follow in the footsteps of their creators and become eternal mates. Because most humans are *foundationalized* around only mothers, the greater majority of human beings will not choose to be service-oriented *male* creators or the female partners that are companions to them.

18. SOLARIAN COUPLES HAVE A PRIVATE RESIDENCE

The couples on this planet each have what could be considered as their own home. These "homes" allow them to remain isolated from the other couples so that they can enjoy private sexual relations. The homes also help the mother to keep the children "corralled," so as to facilitate her control over the behavior of the "one" who is being prepared to be the overseer of the solar system that will be created for all of the children for which the male/father is responsible.

These living arrangements are similar to a modern suburb. This *Solarian* neighborhood consists of neighbors who are each doing the same thing as the other, creating new humans and the solar systems where these newly created beings will further develop and reside forever. In a very good sense of comparison, the male leaves home to do his job and the mother stays at home rearing the children.

When the *one chosen* sibling has developed enough to be able to maneuver throughout the environment, this *one* accompanies the male/father every day to his work (explaining it as we can understand it, using comparisons to what we do on this planet). From the father's example, the *one* is foundationalized to do exactly what the father would do in every instance. The other children are raised uninhibited and similarly to the children being foundationalized on Venus by their own mothers.

Besides the fact that all Solarians (whether living on Mercury, Venus, or Earth) have either a male, female, or genderless body, the physical brain of a Solarian is different from the brain of a Lunarian or that of a Stellarian. Lunarians and Stellarians are *always* genderless. Although the *essence* of all human beings is the same, a Solarian brain can utilize the *full power* of the *essence* and create and manipulate matter as has been explained.

19. COMMUNICATION WITH A ONE- OR TWO-STEP PROCESS

The Solarian brain can communicate telepathically with others. Because all Stellarians are in constant desire of being served, for example, the Stellarian brain allows the Solarian servant to read their thoughts at the very moment a Stellarian thinks of something. The Stellarian brain, however, *does not* have the ability to read the thoughts of any other human. There is no reason for it to do so. Stellarian and Lunarian communication consists of a two-step process. The thought must be generated by the *essence*, and then the energy is sent to the voice box, where it is expressed and received by vibration, much the same way we communicate now on this earth.

Solarian humans, on the other hand, can communicate with a *one-step* process. The Solarian brain has the ability to perceive the energy of human thought immediately. A Solarian also has the ability to read all of the memories of the human *essence* in all Stellarians, but they *do not* have the ability to read the memories of most Lunarians unless that person allows them. (This will be further explained later.)

Except for unnoticeable physical differences that allow a Solarian servant to utilize the full power of the human *essence* and the obvious gender differences, all advanced human physical bodies appear to have similar features. As explained previously, no advanced human body has digestive organs. The energy needed for the cells of the body is generated by the *essence* and delivered by a highly developed and complete nervous system.

20. ADVANCED HUMANS EAT ONLY FOR PLEASURE

When advanced humans desire to eat (which will always be purely for the pleasure of the sensation and not for sustaining energy), they put a *source of pleasure* into their mouth. Advanced human food dissolves completely in the mouth and is transformed into energy that is experienced as a sensation in the advanced brain, and then sent to the *essence* to be recorded as a memory. There is no excess fiber or byproduct from the chewing process, as there is nowhere for the food to go after it is chewed.

Chewing is part of an advanced body's tasting process. The teeth and tongue sense the texture and taste very similar to the way our *imperfect* bodies do. The biggest difference is that advanced human foods are created to maintain their texture and taste for whatever length of time the specific type of food has been genetically produced to last. Some foods take longer than others do to dissolve, all depending on what sensory effect the person desires when the food is chosen to be eaten. Some people like the smooth texture of pudding, which lasts only a few moments before dissolving. Others might like the more extensive process of chewing for a long time on something and relishing the pleasure of the taste during the mastication process. Whatever the desire, there will be all kinds of future foods that will bring a great amount of joy to the taste buds of the perfect body *without* the waste the *imperfect* body produces.

21. ONLY MALE AND FEMALE SOLARIANS HAVE SEX ORGANS

Only Solarians who chose to be male or female have sex organs. The male organs are similar to the ones of our current bodies, but no sperm is produced. The semen that is produced is a sexual stimulant for the benefit of the female. Once the semen is introduced into the woman's vaginal area, it is designed to attach to other advanced sensory receptors located in the vagina, which creates an intense orgasm for the woman. (The male has no prostate. Besides producing the stimulating semen, the testicles exist *only* as male sensory receptors.)

The way new human life is created has already been explained. The advanced woman does not have any internal organs presently needed by an *imperfect* woman to create a human body. The sex organs of an advanced woman exist solely for pleasure. The liquid produced by the female's vaginal cavity is like the semen produced by the advanced male. Advanced female vaginal liquid acts as a stimulant to both the male penis and the female vaginal cavity. Again, the sex organs of an advanced human body exist for one purpose only—pleasure.

The hardest thing for any free-willed human being to accept is that most of us will lose the ability to experience this pleasure, unless we made the choice during our *foundationalization period* to be Solarian creators and serve others. (This dilemma will be mentioned again and discussed in detail in chapter 12.)

VENUS
(Solarian)

22. VENUS MOTHERS FOUNDATIONALIZE THE MAJORITY OF NEWLY CREATED HUMAN BEINGS

The majority of advanced females reside on this planet. No males live here. These are the mothers of the majority of newly created human beings. Upon this planet, the *Human Foundationalization Process* takes place for most human beings. These women possess the characteristics, propensities, and skills to ensure that each newly created human being receives the correct foundational experience.

23. STRUCTURES PROVIDE PRIVACY FOR MOTHERING AND SEXUAL PLEASURE

It was mentioned previously that because we had no need to eat or sleep in this perfect state, there was no need to construct houses where eating and sleeping took place, which is the main purpose of individual housing units in our current world. It was also mentioned that during our *Foundationalization Process* we were constantly engaged in exercising our free will in an open and completely equal environment. However, the structures that do exist in a perfect "Venusian" world allow each woman her own private dwelling place. This allows her privacy to enjoy being a mother, as well as having a private place to exercise the right of a female to experience personal sexual pleasure.

These dwelling places are similar to each other, but each is constructed according to the individual designs of the woman. The exterior and interior décors are as individual as each mother. The flowers, plants, bushes, and trees are placed according to the desire of the woman's individual perception of beauty. The only thing that is exactly the same about each of these dwellings is the size. Because advanced creators have a perfect sense of equality, they do not require more land than another to do what each has chosen to do. The room required for personal privacy and for rearing children is the same throughout the planet.

A Solarian Venusian mother can use her privacy to breastfeed her children, if she so desires, which creates a physical bond with the child and can provide the ultimate joy of being a mother. Very few advanced mothers will ever deny herself or the child of the extraordinary sensation of joy that comes from watching an infant feed from her breast and smile thereafter in satisfaction. She uses this private location and time with a child to teach it away from others when the need for personal and intimate instruction is necessary.

These mothers understand child-rearing very well. Because of free will, we all foundationalize differently. Our mothers know when one of her children needs to be guided in a direction that will enhance the child's ability to foundationalize correctly. Usually, these gentle motherly persuasions are directed toward a child who is using its free agency in a way that affects the free agency of another. This reinforcing tutelage can be done in the intimate privacy of the mother's home or around others in that world. Either way, what the mother does in encouraging the child's development never impedes the free will of the child. It only directs it towards proper *humanity*.

24. IN THE PERFECT WORLD, SEX IS VIEWED AS A PERFECTLY NORMAL WAY OF EXPERIENCING PLEASURE

The Solarian Venusian woman does not have or need a man to satisfy her sexual needs. She does very well on her own and may also share the experience with other Venusian sisters. As explained previously, the vaginal fluid enhances the stimulation of the advanced woman's perfected body. When two women enjoy the sexual experience together, their vaginal fluids combine to enhance the experience even further.

As mentioned previously, there is no feeling of being "in love" with another person in this perfect world; therefore, there is no negative emotion of jealousy or possessiveness associated with love and sex as there are currently in our *imperfect* world. The sexual experience has nothing to do with valuing one person above another. It has only one purpose—*human pleasure.*

Because most of us were reared around Venus mothers and the experience of our primordial childhood is embedded in our *essence*, it is of no wonder that current female homosexual relationships appear more natural and acceptable to our *imperfect* senses. In fact, most mortal men prefer to see two women engaged in sexual contact and generally are greatly aroused by the act. In addition, the woman's breast adds to a mortal male's arousal because of the effect that the stored energy in the *essence* (in the form of memories of primordial breastfeeding) has on the male *imperfect* body. This natural attraction to breasts was established long before any of us were born into this *imperfect* world, where our natures have been changed from viewing sex as a perfectly normal way for a human being to enjoy a fullness of sensory stimulation and satiation, into a possessive, secret, and "immoral" act.

25. CHILDREN INDIVIDUALIZE BY LEARNING, GROWING, AND ENJOYING LIFE AND EXERCISING FREE WILL

A Venus-type world is set up to provide the perfect educational environment for newly created children. The children experience the ultimate beauty and perfection in all there is about being a free-willed human. They learn individualization by seeing the different styles of homes where their mothers reside and also from visiting other planets where different types of people live. They live in a neighborhood, of sorts, where Solarian mothers express individuality for a common purpose. With other mothers and their children, people on this planet congregate in parks and forests, beaches and sand dunes, and around oceans, lakes, and streams.

While in their infant stage, mothers outline proper and constructive experiences for the children. Once the child has learned to control its body in relation to the surrounding environment, the child ventures off by itself and learns about the many wonderful things that are available to a human being. These children can also visit the other planets in their particular solar system and see how other people experience life.

26. LUNARIANS AND STELLARIANS ENJOY THE PRESENCE OF DEVELOPING CHILDREN

Because all advanced human beings, regardless of humanity type, would never harm or disrupt the foundationalization process of a developing human being, the Lunarians and Stellarians welcome all children and enjoy a child's presence on their worlds. The childlike curiosity of each newly created being adds to the joy of the other non-creator advanced humans. Each visit by a foundationalizing child brings to an advanced human non-creator a perfect recollection of their own foundationalization process and the stages of development they each went through to arrive at an understanding of what they wanted out of life.

These non-creators answer the children's inquisitive questions and explain their own situation and give their opinion and perception of *why* they chose the *humanity type* that they did over the others. These planetary "neighborhoods" aid greatly in the child's ability to determine what type of world and happiness they will eventually choose for themselves.

27. VIRTUAL "TIME TRAVEL" IS POSSIBLE WITH ADVANCED TECHNOLOGY

By means of advanced video capabilities, the child also has the ability to view in real time any planet in any *other* part of the Universe where people are going through their second stage of development in mortality. They can tune in to any planet that is going through the period of early human development, *circa* before 5000 B.C.E. for example, to the later developmental stages of the 21st centuries C.E.

Although "time travel" is impossible, it can become an accepted reality in the sense that one can place oneself in any period of human history and vicariously experience the effects and outcome of these eras. And, although one's physical body cannot travel in time backwards or forwards in relation to one's own experience, with the advanced technology available to them, it *is* possible for foundationalizing humans to "virtually" travel to a world where others are experiencing many different "time" periods. So, in *essence* (pun intended), developing human beings, or any other advanced human, can travel throughout "time" anywhere in the Universe.

Because the solar system where we were foundationalized consists of the ultimate and perfect human worlds, we are essentially headed "back to our future." Hence, we have already lived in our future and create our past with each new experience on this earth. Although somewhat confusing to our time-based mortal brain, to a perfect human brain, it makes complete sense. A human being can only live in the present of one's own experiences—there's no going back to the past or visiting a future that hasn't occurred yet. Once the moment has passed, nothing can be changed in what was experienced in a moment in the past. The "moment" can, however, be re-lived by the power and ability of the memory capabilities of the *essence*. Only in this way can we re-visit our past, but upon so doing, we cannot change or affect what has already occurred.

Therefore, as developing human beings with the proper advanced technology available to us, we could observe what others were doing in their second stage of development. We saw life that was somewhat similar to the world that would exist in our future when we went through our *own* second stage of development. Although their *imperfect* worlds were different from our own *future world* where we are now experiencing *imperfection*, there are always very similar developments and experiences. This is because human nature is similar no matter where it is found in the Universe.

Because newly created beings do not have a past, they perceive the year 5000 B.C.E. on another less-advanced planet as their *possible* future. They also view their current *perfect* life as where they want to end up (the future), because that is how they were foundationalized—they know no other way to become balanced and experience happiness.

28. WE CANNOT UNDERSTAND "HAPPINESS" WITHOUT THE OPPOSITE COMPARATIVE EXPERIENCE

"Happiness" is actually unknown to newly created beings. Because everything they experience is perfect, they have no perception of what happiness is and what it is not. They do not know what is bad or what is good, or what is too much heat or too much cold. They do not know or appreciate their perfect situation. The physical sensations they experience are not "pleasurable," they are just how things are and have always been. Even the ability of their creators/parents to experience a sexual stimulation of their gendered bodies means nothing more to a newly created human than how things are and have always been.

Although the actual act of sex is not observed among their advanced parents, genderless children become aware of the physical joy experienced by their parents through sex. They do not understand, however, why a gendered human being reacts to the stimulation the way that they do. Although they do not observe their creators/parents in the act, advanced children *are* aware that the mortal humans in other less-advanced worlds (who they can see constantly engaged in or thinking about sex) seem to get a tremendous amount of physical pleasure from it. To children, the act of sex is nothing more than a physical act that they do not understand. So that they *do* understand, and so that they learn to appreciate and benefit from the perfect human body and world (even all of its ultimate sensory fulfillments), the newly created human beings must be placed in a world where everything is the opposite of what they have experienced up to this point in their development. This includes all of the effects of sex, both negative and positive.

This is the purpose for the mortal world or second stage of development—the one in which we currently find ourselves. The

Solarian Venusian Mother's ultimate responsibility is to establish all that is good in us so that we can compare it to all that is bad *without* them. Although we choose for ourselves what type of human being we want to become, all of our foundational opportunities were the same. Our mothers made sure we developed the proper human conscience that will forever separate us from animals. We are human *because of them*. We are different *types* of human beings, *because of us*.

EARTH
(Solarian)

29. GENDERLESS SERVANTS WORK UNSEEN

This planet houses those advanced human beings who choose not to be mothers or fathers accountable for the creation of new human beings and all that the responsibility entails. However, they still desire to serve other people. These people work with the male fathers in creating and helping to oversee the solar systems created for the children. These intervene (unseen) in the second stage of our development. They are very much involved, unperceived, in what we are going through presently upon this earth. When needed by advanced Stellarians, these also serve them.

These people are genderless because of their choice to *not* create human beings or be responsible for new human life. This planet acts as their home base, from which they are sent throughout the Universe to help in the creation of new solar systems. Again, these are servants who work alongside the male creator and are readily available to assist in overseeing the mortal *imperfect* worlds the father creates for his newly created children.

At a moment's notice, these Solarians have the technology and ability to go to the planet to which they are assigned and thereon interact (unseen) with humans as the need arises. However, for the most part, their interactions with other worlds are achieved through the highly advanced technology available to them on their *home planet.*

Although the technology is much more advanced, these beings act similarly to a person who sits in front of a security screen monitor and observes all activity taking place in their assigned areas. They monitor all situations occurring upon the earths where other humans are going through their mortal experience.

With their advanced technology and knowledge, they can see and hear anything that occurs at any time, anywhere upon the worlds they monitor, which currently includes our planet earth. And just as a security camera records the events that occur within the scope of its viewfinder, all actions on every *earth-like* planet are recorded. All of the actions of every human being going through their second stage of development in less-advanced worlds are viewed and recorded.

30. OUR ADVANCED "GUIDANCE COUNSELORS" MONITOR OUR MORTAL WORLD

These advanced beings ensure that things are carried out according to the will of the father who created the solar system and the earth-like planet on which the human beings he is responsible for are placed. They have the power to place an *essence* in a particular situation during mortality that will aid in the development of the individual human being.

Before any of us were sent to our "earth," we counseled with these *monitors/guidance counselors*, who sat down with each of us and helped map out what each of us wanted or *needed* to do to fulfill the purpose for going through our second stage of development in an *imperfect* world. And what was this purpose? To learn through our own experience the benefits of our particular *humanity type.*

For example (giving a hypothetical explanation), when *human AB6165* is ready for its second stage of development, the individual counsels with these advanced human servants and maps out its life, according to what that person wants to do and expects to gain from the experience. As we've discussed, before we came to our current world, each of us chose which humanity type we wanted to be. We had eons of time to make the decision after weighing all of the options and observing the actions of others.

Regardless, based on our personal desires, we counseled with a Solarian advanced servant on what would be the best way for us to get the most benefit out of our mortality and further our progression into our eventual Solarian, Lunarian, or Stellarian lifestyle. They helped us map out our desires based on what they knew (from their *perfected* experience) would be the best for us. These decisions were then recorded and placed on file under our "*tag*."

As we go throughout our existence in our current state upon this earth, our advanced "guidance counselors" ensure that we gain from the experience exactly what we expected and desired. They do this by monitoring what is continually being recorded and filed under each of our individual "tags." These advanced human beings can see, monitor, and record everything that happens to each of us individually as we live on our world. They are concerned with everything that happens to us during our second stage of development.

31. SOLARIANS UNDERSTAND THEIR SPECIFIC RESPONSIBILITIES IN OUR DEVELOPMENT

In contrast, the Solarian women who reside on Mercury and Venus are only involved in our first stage of development, or our foundationalization stage; and the creator males who reside on Mercury are responsible for both stages.

All Solarian people understand the correct recipe for human foundationalization and development found in what can be referred to as the "Book of Life." They understand the order of the Universe and of all the matter found therein. They know their specific roles in making sure, 1) that the Universe continues to exist as it always has; and 2) that human beings continue to benefit from their existence in it. Solarian advanced human beings are *our servants*. They do only what we want them to do, ensuring that we realize the reason why we were created in the first place—to experience happiness through the use of our free will.

MARS
(Lunarian)

32. CLOSE-KNIT FRIENDS ENJOY COMMONALITY AND INTERACTION WITH EACH OTHER

This is the first of three planets designed to house those who have no desire to be responsible for others, but who wish only to take care of and be responsible for themselves. During the *foundationalization stage*, many human beings became close friends and acquaintances. This planet is for those of us who wish to live in close-knit communities of friends and relations.

Although these people maintain their distinct independence, they are happiest being directly connected with others who share their same desires of happiness. This is the closest planet that could be compared to a communal living arrangement outside of a Solarian society. The people do not create fences or borders around individual parcels of land, but all people have everything in common—what is owned by one is owned and enjoyed by all. The societies on this planet are very similar to the society of the mothers on Venus, the biggest difference being that these people are not responsible for anyone but themselves.

This planet is much smaller than the Jupiter- and Saturn-sized planets, which accommodate other Lunarian individuals. This is because the people here enjoy constant interaction with each other. They gain happiness in sharing each other's experiences. They have the technology and ability to create their own space and environment according to each individual's wants, but do not mind if others come into their space uninvited. This world is a literal *open house* to all inhabitants.

Like all Lunarians and Stellarians, these people are genderless and have no sex organs; again, they do not have the ability to produce the bodily stimulations and satiations associated with sex. However, like all other advanced human beings, their bodies allow them to use their sensory functions to their fullest capacity. Without sex organs, however, they have no need or desire to experience the sensory input or output associated with sex.

These people do not need anyone monitoring them or serving their needs, because they take care of themselves. The thoughts generated by their perfected brains need not and, in fact, *cannot* be read or monitored by any Solarian servant. These people have the greatest level of personal privacy of any type of human being, because no one can read their thoughts.

JUPITER
(Lunarian)

33. SOME PEOPLE ENJOY ISOLATION THE BEST

The people who inhabit this planet are similar in every way to those who reside on Mars, but with some minor, yet important, social differences. Although this planet also houses those who want to take care of themselves, these people *do not* desire a close-knit community, but gain their joy in owning their own piece of land, usually as large as a country, where they arrange their surrounding environment according to their own will and pleasure.

These are the most physically isolated of all human beings. They do, however, have various places on this type of planet where they meet together often and compare notes and stories of how their personal "country" is doing. They gain joy in comparing notes on what they have done with their vast land, but none of them considers another's accomplishments of any value above their own. They do not seek praise or platitudes for what they do with their free-willed existence.

SATURN
(Lunarian)

34. PRAISE AND ACKNOWLEDGEMENT ARE GIVEN GENEROUSLY TO THOSE WHO DESIRE IT

This is the last planet designed to house those who want to take care of themselves. Like those living on Jupiter, these people also desire vast tracts of land to develop and create their own personal environments. Unlike the others, however, these *do* gain value from how their neighbor views what they have done. They visit each other's "countries" and give as much praise as they receive. Their existence is not only in pleasing themselves, but also in doing whatever it takes to impress their neighbor.

Because these people find joy in how their actions are praised, they desire the praise of their creators. Therefore, there is a slight difference between their physical bodies and those of the other Lunarian people. This difference exists in order to facilitate their thoughts being monitored by the Solarian individuals who live on the earth-like planets who serve others' needs.

These people like to accomplish personal feats and achievements, and appreciate acknowledgement and praise for what they have done. Knowing this, Solarian servants (usually, but not always from Earth) can visit these Lunarians in their world and express their sincere interest in what these type of Lunarians have accomplished. For the most part, it is to this world where the advanced mothers take the developing children on "field trips" to experience a *Lunarian* environment. The people living on Saturn enjoy the interaction they receive from the *foundationalizing* children. Especially when one of the children says, "I want my world to look just like yours someday!"

URANUS
(Stellarian)

35. ANYTHING WE DESIRE, WE CAN HAVE

This planet is the first of three designed to house those who want others to serve them. These types of Stellarian people are limited in what they can do with their own environment because they have no desire to cultivate or maintain their own world. This type of person takes full advantage of having been created to have joy, a guarantee granted to all of us by our creators. They have the attitude that everything that exists, does so for them personally, which, in this world as well as in all others, is an entirely appropriate attitude to have.

The most important thing to these types of people is how well they are served by their environment. They are served mainly by those who reside upon the planet Earth, as described above, as well as by non-human androids (for want of a better word to describe the advanced human-like machines that will serve all of their needs). Anything they want, they get, simply by desiring it. They do nothing for themselves. They live to enjoy all the physical pleasures (except sex) of being human. Because of these desires, Stellarians and their planets are monitored by Solarians much the same way these "monitors" oversee less-advanced, *imperfect* worlds.

The Stellarian physical body is like the Lunarians' residing on Saturn. They are genderless and their minds are an open book to any Solarian person. They are comfortable with the fact that those who serve them have access to all of their thoughts and desires, so that these servants can give them everything they need and want.

On this first of the three (3) Stellarian planets, the people *do* desire to have their own home and environment created for them and still be separate from others, but they also enjoy the companionship of close friends and the associations they developed during their foundational stage. They live similarly to, but without the pretentious attitudes of the extremely wealthy people in our current world. They enjoy parties and gatherings where servants attend to their needs, while their associations with other free-willed beings like themselves bring them happiness. They enjoy other people as long as their own needs are taken care of.

It is to this planet that the "foundationalization field trips" for newly developing humans are usually taken to experience a Stellarian existence. As we've discussed, once left to themselves, developing humans can travel to any planet within the solar system in which they were created in order to learn about how other people are enjoying their different human experiences. The people of this planet enjoy the children's presence, but are also glad that their mothers take them back to Venus or Mercury after the visit. These people are not very comfortable with anything or anyone that does not serve some personal need of their own.

NEPTUNE
(Stellarian)

36. WE CAN HAVE RELATIONSHIPS WITH FREE-WILLED BEINGS AND WITH ADVANCED ROBOTIC ANDROIDS

The only difference between the people who live on Neptune and those who live on Uranus is the personal relationships they desire. Neptunians do not have as great a social need as those Stellarians who live on Uranus.

These Stellarians have an equal ratio of relationships with other free-willed beings and with advanced robotic androids. They get just as much joy out of an android-type of being that is *programmed* to be their friend and do what they are programmed to do, as they do from being around free-willed beings who *choose* to be their friend. And as long as their needs are met, they are satisfied with either type of relationship.

PLUTO
(Stellarian)

37. A VIRTUAL UNIVERSE IS AT OUR FINGERTIPS

Plutonians have no need for other people, but depend on the advanced technology and know-how of Solarian servants to provide the relationships and associations they desire for themselves. Their desire can best be compared with those now upon earth who live primarily in isolation and who enjoy creating virtual worlds where imagined characters play out any reality the programmer and creator desires. In other words, these people limit their interactions with other *real* humans, choosing instead to create their own relations and associations with advanced robotic and virtual companions of their own choosing—beings without free will.

These people are *Virtual Creators*, whereas those who live on Mercury are *Reality Creators*. These can form any Universe, galaxy, solar system, planet, and any form of matter they desire within the realm of their *own* world, or better, by the power of the advanced computer programs and holographic-image technology available to them. They can do no wrong in their world. They pretty much receive all their joy in a virtual Universe created by their own mind. Whatever they want their world to be, it becomes!

These people enjoy the experience of *virtual* competition and reliving the experiences of an *imperfect* world, wherein humans destroy and kill each other in defense of themselves and their territory, or in defense of their culture or beliefs. Their attitudes and happiness reflect the human nature of most people who are going through their second stage of development in an *imperfect* world. These Stellarians love to watch "their" home team win a game against another. Some have a deep sense of patriotism for their own country and cheer and applaud the destruction of other human beings through war or despotism, but never in reality, only in their *virtual worlds*.

Some establish their own set of rules and standards and enforce these standards on others, and are "happy" when others accept their way as the "right" way.

In the *virtual* universes created by those who reside on Pluto-like worlds, these people relive the *inequality* that human nature creates when we are left to ourselves to create the world of our own choosing. If these types of people were given the *real* power of creation (instead of being relegated to advanced computerized *virtual* universes of their own creation), the *real* Universe would be a chaotic mess of warring civilizations and alien creatures fighting humanity—something similar to the science-fiction genre generated through the human imagination of our current world.

We would not want human beings of this type governing us, but we do want them to be able to utilize their free will in any way that brings them happiness. If they want to be creators, then they are allowed to "create," but only under the restrictions placed upon them. In this way, and because of this type of world, no one will ever be able to complain about not being allowed to do anything that they want to do with their free agency. The advanced technology of the future will be able to, in effect, "trick" the human mind into believing that a "virtual" world is a "real" universe when, in fact, it is nothing more than the computerized creation of a Stellarian creator.

---

38. DIFFERENT PLANETS HELP ACCOMMODATE OUR INDIVIDUAL DESIRES FOR HAPPINESS

From the above descriptions, it is easy to see why different *humanity types* need to be placed on separate planets according to their personal desires of happiness. There is no place in advanced worlds for an uncomfortable situation to arise as a result of being around another human with a completely different desire of happiness than our own. There will be no reason to discuss or argue opinion or perspective, as we will exist among those having similar ideas of how one "should" live to be happy.

Presently upon this earth, groups of people isolate themselves from others and promote their own perspective. Sadly, these groups each think that "theirs" is the proper way to live and attempt to force "their ways" upon everyone else. Throughout our history, we have learned that power in the hands of a person who does not support an individual's right to his or her own happiness causes a tremendous amount of human misery.

The cause of all of humankind's emotional problems on earth can be directly connected to Stellarian and Lunarian perspectives being forced on others through the process of social "law and order" and *imperfect* parenting. Solarians would never consider their opinion "right," but would allow and protect the unconditional right of each person to live as he or she so chooses.

39. EACH SOLAR SYSTEM DIFFERS IN THE NUMBER OF ITS PLANETS ACCORDING TO HUMANITY TYPES

In contrast to the nine planets of the solar system representing *our* future home, the advanced solar system where the planet is found upon which we received our foundationalization has only six (6) planets. Three of these planets are like our Mercury, Venus, and Earth and house our creators and those who oversee what is taking place upon our earth currently. Two of the other planets there are like our Jupiter and Saturn and one is like our Pluto.

The sizes of these planets were designed to house the batch of newly created human beings from which our creators/parents came. During their *foundationalization process*, these people chose their *humanity type* the same way we chose our own. Their Mercury-, Venus- and Earth-like planets are similar in size to our Jupiter, Saturn, and Uranus, indicating that more people in "their" batch of humans, when compared to "our" batch of humans, chose to do what our parents/creators do: serve others. Again, each solar system is uniquely designed in anticipation of the needs of those who will inhabit it, according to their humanity types.

40. EXPOSURE TO ALL HUMANITY TYPES GAVE US THE OPTION TO CHOOSE OUR OWN

To allow us the opportunity to foundationalize into a particular *humanity type*, it was necessary for us to be exposed to all three (3) types. We were able to do this by traveling to any planet we desired in our current solar system and meeting with the people residing there. We observed them and talked to them about what they do and how they made the choice to become who they are. If during our foundationalization experience we were not exposed to a certain type of person, then there is no way we could have possibly had the choice to be like them or not.

Obviously we were all exposed to the lifestyle of the Solarian people, as they were our creators and *foundationalizers*. Because they encouraged our complete free agency to become who we would become, our creators supported our efforts to become familiar with the lifestyles of the Lunarians and Stellarians who lived in their solar system in a *perfect* human setting.

We had the ability to visit the other planets of our primordial solar system at will. The advanced human races, regardless of humanity type, accepted us as observers and treated us as we currently treat inquisitive, curious little children who pose no threat to our individuality. Furthermore, the technology was available for us to observe what was going on in other worlds where Stellarians, Lunarians, and Solarians were going through their second stage of development on their own *imperfect* worlds. We could "tune in" to any learning "channel" on our advanced televisions and see in real time what was happening in other solar systems. With the ability to see the three different types of humans acting and reacting to their environments, both in a *perfect* setting and an *imperfect* one, we were affected and conditioned by the observations and chose which situation we would like to experience.

41. OUR FIRST EXPERIENCE WITH CONFUSION INVOLVED SEX

It was while we were observing the way in which advanced people live their lives that we began to form a cognitive dissonance about our existence. "Cognitive dissonance" is the feeling of uncomfortable emotional tension that comes from having two conflicting thoughts in our mind at the same time. We were taught through experience that all things are equal in the human realm of existence throughout the Universe, and that we all have the same opportunity to experience a fullness of ultimate human joy. Yet, we could see that our creators possessed powers and abilities that other humans did not.

We realized that these abilities were directly connected to serving the needs of other human beings and perpetuating life, and that we could experience great amounts of physical stimulation without the ability to have sex. It was also obvious to us, though, that Solarian parents possessed the ability to experience something that appeared to us to be the greatest, strongest, and most exhilarating feeling that the human *essence* could possibly produce in the perfect human body: the sexual orgasm.

42. SEXUALITY IS THE ULTIMATE HUMAN PHYSICAL EXPERIENCE

No other sensation created by the will of the mind and the sensory receptors of the body can be compared with the feelings brought on by sexual arousal and the final release of tension that this arousal creates. There is no other sensation in the Universe that compares with this experience; and *only* humans experience it to its full potential.

So why are some Solarians only able to experience it? This was one of the issues that confused us then (during our foundationalization stage), and will continue to confuse readers of this book. If all things are supposed to be equal, why can't we all experience this uniquely human physical stimulation forever?

This issue will be explained in considerable detail in chapter 12. It will be shown why Stellarians and Lunarians, or those who do not receive ultimate joy in serving others, do not have sexuality. We will come to the conclusion that this is how things have always been in the Universe. Knowing this, however, created one of the first discussions and arguments we had as newly created human beings.

43. WE ALSO QUESTIONED THE GUARANTEE OF PERFECT, UNCONDITIONAL EQUALITY

The *other* issue that added to our primordial cognitive dissonance was the realization that very few of us would have the opportunity to become a male and have the vast powers associated with a male's position. As has been explained, it takes many more female creators than males to create new human beings. The *Foundationalization Process* is overseen by mothers, whereas the father is solely responsible for the second stage of development, or life in an *imperfect* world, which we are currently experiencing upon this earth.

Because of the perfected technology associated with the power and knowledge of an advanced human race, it only takes *one* male to oversee the creation of an entire solar system. However, it takes *many* females to create the children and oversee their individualization during the *Foundationalization Process.* Every mother needs to take personal time with each of her children as each grows and progresses into adulthood.

Because few males are needed, most newly created humans are not exposed to advanced males. Using the current names of our planets as simple categorical descriptions, those children who are reared among the male and female couples on *Mercury* are usually the *only* ones who would ever have the desire to make a choice to become a male. One cannot desire to become something about which one has very little recollection or experience.

44. THERE ARE FEWER ADVANCED HUMAN MALES THAN FEMALES

Overall, there are fewer advanced human males than there are Solarian mothers, Solarian genderless servants, Lunarians, or Stellarians. Per capita, in fact, there are very, very, very few male human beings throughout the Universe. If we used an acceptable quantitative measure to fully understand just how few males there are in comparison to all other human beings, *less than* one percent (1%) would be the appropriate number.

By observing current human behavior on our planet, it is easy to understand why so few have the vast powers associated with a male creator. Most human beings throughout the Universe are Lunarian, as most people with the power of free will choose to serve themselves and rejoice in the empowerment of their own individuality. The proper quantitative measure of Lunarians in comparison to all others would be about eighty percent (80%).

Of those who are Solarian, most are female creators who live on planets like our Venus. As has been stated, many more female creators than male are needed to foundationalize the human race. Throughout the Universe, therefore, men are in relatively "low demand," although their functions and responsibilities are as important as those of any other advanced human being.

SUMMARY

Who we are correlates to the type of person we have chosen to be during our *foundationalization* in a perfect world. None of us is any better or worse than anyone else. We are completely and unconditionally equal because we all had the same opportunities as everyone else to choose which *humanity type* was best for us.

During the eons of time we were exposed to all aspects of humanity, we became who we will *always* be forever. We made the choice for ourselves after considering all the options. However, we did not understand at that time why there were some (very few) who had the opportunity to become a Solarian male creator, by being more exposed to that *humanity type* (living on Mercury around male fathers), while the rest of us didn't have the chance. Nor could we understand why we would not enjoy the emotional and physical fulfillment of human sexuality, unless we were Solarian creators.

These two issues did not make sense to us, and caused an emotional tension between the ideas of ultimate human potential and equality and the fact that most of us would not have certain abilities reserved only for a few. Our creators did ensure us, however, that after passing through the next stage of our development in an *imperfect* world, we would understand *why* these two significant exceptions to human experience were not only necessary, but also *vital* to the continuation of Universal order and happiness forever.

To understand more about how we became individuals during the *Human Foundationalization Process*, we need to discuss in detail the human experience in an *imperfect* world. It is in this state of imperfection that we will learn all we need to know to be able to accept the way things are and the way they have always been throughout the Universe. However, before we begin discussing our current world, it is necessary to explain how the government and control of the Universe is set up, who runs it, and how it is governed.

The Government of a Perfect Universe

CHAPTER EIGHT

The care of human life and happiness...
is the first and only legitimate object of good government

—Thomas Jefferson

1. PERFECT GOVERNMENTS ARE ESSENTIAL TO UNIVERSAL ORDER

A government generally makes laws and enforces them upon the people. The laws that govern this Universe have **always** existed; therefore, there is no need for a governing authority to make *new* laws for a *perfect* world that exists in this Universe. Although we have never experienced the *perfect* government during our experience on this earth, part of our *Foundationalization Process* was to understand the *Universal* laws and powers that establish order and stability. A universal system of government has always existed. This perfect government maintains the appropriate order in the Universe.

One of its responsibilities is to ensure that those who become parents/creators have the necessary knowledge and personal requisites needed to perform proper parenting of newly created human beings. This government will never allow a faulty *Human Foundationalization Process*. The reason why the Universe continues forever in order and perfection, is because its ultimate life forms (those that control it) are human beings. Those who are responsible for creating other humans do so according to the eternal laws that ensure continual Universal perfection.

2. THREE BASIC PRINCIPLES OF THE PERFECT GOVERNMENT

The perfect government is structured around **three basic principles**. These three principles establish the Universal Rule of Law that empowers all governing authorities:

POWER IS ONLY USED TO SERVE

The first principle and law of perfect government is that government will never be self-serving; or, in other words, it will never act of itself for the sake of its own existence. This government is restricted in its power according to the restrictions that are necessary to ensure that it always abides by this first principle and law. It serves those who benefit from its existence. Those who benefit from its existence are those who give it its power. And this power is *only* used to *serve* those who have given it its power.

GUARANTEED FREE AGENCY FOR ALL WHOM IT SERVES

The second principle and law of perfect government is that it guarantees the freedom, or the free agency, of all those it serves. The only restrictions it places on those whom it serves prevents any one of them as an individual from infringing on the free agency of another. It protects all people from having any other being infringe upon their free agency. Again, this government *will do nothing* that infringes upon the free agency of those whom it serves, except in the defense of individual free will where one person under its jurisdiction might infringe on the free will of another.

GUARANTEED OPPORTUNITY OF HAPPINESS FOR ALL

The third principle of the perfect government is that it provides the means whereby those whom it serves may have an equal opportunity to experience the happiness that each of them (those served) desires.

Because it was not the choice of those whom it serves to exist, this government is *required* to provide those things that are necessary to fulfill the purpose of their creation, which purpose is the fulfillment of their individual happiness. But, although the government provides the means whereby those whom it serves might experience happiness, it cannot compel them to use those things which it provides for them. If this government were to compel them to use the means it provides for their happiness, it would then break the second principle and law that empowers it.

3. WORLDLY GOVERNMENTS HAVE ALWAYS FAILED US

One thing that we have learned up to this point (in our current stage of development upon this earth) is that the governments we have produced have never been able to create and ensure equality, peace, and stability. Some of our *less*-advanced societies (compared to the advanced societies found elsewhere in the Universe) *claim* that they support the principle of free agency; but not <u>one</u> of them has guaranteed it unconditionally and equally to **all** people. Moreover, not one has incorporated all three of the above *universal* principles into its constitution. (A government's "constitution" is more than just a piece of paper; it is what "constitutes" the actions and purpose of the government.)

Many different forms of government have existed on this earth. We have already tried democracies, but they have only created degrees of class and inequality. This is because we always elect and give power to those who use that power to benefit themselves and their own political agendas, thus acting contrary to the first of the three principles outlined above. We have tried communistic governments, where the third principle of providing the basic necessities for all the people equally was corrupted by disregarding the first principle. The leaders of these governments use their power and authority for their own personal gain. Although dictatorships that openly abuse the first principle *have* achieved quasi-peace and order and have sometimes provided their people with the basic necessities of life, they destroy the free agency of those whom they control. From all of these experiences, we have learned that a proper government that protects everyone's rights equally ***cannot*** be controlled by *free-willed* beings.

4. ONE HUMAN BEING IS APPOINTED AS THE PERFECT GOVERNING HEAD

To oversee the perfect form of government, *one* human being is prepared before the implementation of any government in any planetary system. New worlds are created for each *new* batch of human beings. The person who is chosen to be the "overseer" of each new planetary system is not *foundationalized* in the same way as the rest of us. It is this **one** human being who is given more power and knowledge than any other. The purpose for this ultimate power and authority is to operate the government properly and ensure that the Universe continues in the order in which it has always existed.

Again, although it is somewhat difficult for a time-based, mortal mind to conceptualize, everything that exists has always existed, although at times in different forms of matter. But the order by which these things exist has always existed and has never changed or fluctuated in the slightest. It makes sense, that if the order of the Universe never changes, then there must be something "everlasting" that keeps it from changing. That "something" is the manner in which one advanced human being is *foundationalized* for each solar system, even the one who oversees what all other human beings do with their free will.

5. ONLY A SPECIAL OVERSEER CAN BE TRUSTED WITH THE "INSTRUCTIONS FOR LIFE"

Although the perfect government has always existed, one can imagine it this way: It could be supposed that, through years of negative experience, humans finally realized that they needed to create an ultimate being to rule over them. In this essential human being, they programmed (or foundationalized) all knowledge that is good, and bestowed all power. Doing this ensured that this being would *only do good* things that are consistent with human happiness.

Let's suppose that over millions of years of existence, advanced human beings sat down and composed a list, or better, published a book entitled *The Rules and Laws Pertaining to the Creation and Government of Life* (*The Book of Life* for short). In this book, everything was written that humans have learned through experience is *right* for humankind. Because it is the *perfect* "book of instructions" for humanity, it never changes. Nothing can be added to it or taken away to improve what it contains. It is complete, and contains the laws and instructions on everything associated with the composition and order of all matter in the human-based Universe. It also contains the important keys to absolute technology, or better, the most advanced information that exists.

Who could be trusted with this information? A *free-willed* human being certainly could not! They are created and allowed to set their *own* sense of what is right and wrong based on a lifetime of experiencing both. On the other hand, could a machine or a robot be created, into which the "*instructions for* life" could be programmed, so that it would *only* do what it was *programmed* to do and not make any mistakes? This would seem more reasonable.

6. FREE-WILLED HUMAN BEINGS CANNOT BE TRUSTED WITH POWER AND AUTHORITY OVER OTHERS—DEMOCRACY DOES NOT WORK

A free-willed being—who establishes who it is from the exercising of unlimited and uninhibited free agency—might one day determine for itself that its happiness should extend beyond maintaining the status quo forever. This being might determine that a little change here and there probably wouldn't hurt anything; in fact, it *might* create more happiness.

The history of human government in our current world should be all the proof we need to understand that it is impossible to trust any one of us or a group of us to treat all people equally and establish the perfect government. None of us can be trusted with power and authority over others, because it is part of our human nature to change our environment to fit our *personal* preferences. However, the Universe is an environment that cannot be modified to adapt or react to the opinions and perspectives of any one individual or of a majority. **All** opinions and perspectives must be respected and protected.

Most people who will one day make one of the planets of this solar system their eventual home are Lunarian and Stellarian, according to their individual desires of happiness (their *humanity type*). This means that if we were left alone in this Universe to govern ourselves (like we currently are upon this earth), those whom we elected by the voice of the *majority* would more-than-likely follow their "conscience," and establish a government that served them (*Stellarian*) or one that allowed them to serve themselves (*Lunarian*).

The current democratically elected and supported governments on our earth do not *serve the people*, but rather are *served by the people* by the taxes that the people are forced to pay. The citizens are expected to *serve* these governments through patriotism. Some governments are set up to support their citizens in their individual efforts to enrich themselves and their families. However, these governments set up systems of class based on economic status that afford more opportunity and success to those in the *higher classes*. No democracy has ever met the important criteria of *serving* (*Solarian*) the needs of *all* the people *equally*.

In an *imperfect* world, the majority is seldom right. Even in the first ostensibly *free* democracy of the United States of America, the majority once believed it was *right* and *proper* to own other human beings as slaves in order to enrich themselves and to deny women the rights of men. When this so-called "free democracy" was first established, its *majority* also believed that the Native American Indians were a *lower*-class people. This justified the *stronger majority* with the *stronger* weapons to steal the Native Americans' land and destroy their "savage" way of life. In more modern times, the *majority* believes that love shared by two free-willed beings of the same sex is wrong.

During a time in our recent history of this earth, a *majority* of the most respected, refined, and educated people believed that the world was flat. These ignorant ones were the same ones who ran the governments that controlled the people. Unfortunately, we have very little assurance that those who are the most respected, the most refined, and the most educated people of our *modern world* (those who currently control the governments of the world) are not just as ignorant as the *majority* of our ancestors.

All of these facts show *how* and *why* a democracy for and by the voice and vote of the *majority of free-willed people* will never lead to lasting peace and happiness for **all** free-willed people *equally*. The only *humanity type* that can be trusted to act solely for the benefit of others are those who are Solarian. Ironically, a Solarian servant wouldn't last a day as a leader or an official in any government or in any other institution that controls the lives of human beings in this *imperfect* world.

7. THE PERFECT OVERSEER MUST BE HUMAN

A *preprogrammed* robot, though eliminating negative *human* propensities, would be too impersonal as an *overseer of humans*. How would it ever smile or laugh? Nothing is more endearing to a human being, both now and in the future, than a good sense of humor. How could a robot possibly be programmed to understand us and laugh with us and about us?

None of us would ever feel comfortable letting a *non-human* entity direct us and have complete authority and control over us forever. We would not be happy, nor could we trust such a "machine." What if its functions became corrupt and it began to create other machines that were programmed to get rid of humans? (There are a few *imaginative* movies currently of this genre.) Our happiness is based on our *first* experiences, and none of these experiences included following orders or taking directions from a non-smiling, non-interacting, non-HUMAN! Considering all, it would appear that our only choice is to have a human being, like us, rule over us.

It is the responsibility of our creators to ensure that such a human being exists and is trained properly so that the person *cannot* fail in the purpose for which that individual is created; and that *one*'s only purpose is to support and perpetuate the perfect government. The power of the government must rest upon this person's shoulders alone. All power and authority must reside in this person's hands; and this human being must act alone so as not to be influenced by any other motivation or any other being that might cause the person to fail.

This human being, however, **cannot** be free-willed like those whom this person serves. This human will become the **one** who oversees and forever supports the principles of the ***perfect government***, which in exercising its powers, promotes the cause of human happiness throughout the eternal Universe. This human being can only accomplish this ***if*** the person is foundationalized ***not to fail***.

8. ADVANCED MALES ARE RESPONSIBLE FOR THE PERFECT GOVERNMENT

In advanced human societies, the male's role is different from the female's. The males (fathers) are the ones responsible for the upbringing and instruction of those who will become government officials. They *foundationalize* these newly created beings to become male like them; thus, the government overseers throughout the Universe are always male in gender.

This does not mean that there is an inequality between the genders. There is no inequality, only specialization. The terms *female* and *male* are designations given to human beings who have the body parts and ability to create life as was explained previously. Each has a specialized function to perform in the *Human Foundationalization Process*.

9. PERFECT OVERSEERS DO NOT HAVE FREE WILL

Although the thought of being an uninhibited, free-willed human being appeals to the sense of *individualism* in each of us, and logically seems to be the right way to *foundationalize* a human child, *one* who is reared to become an overseer is *foundationalized* differently. Therefore, there are advanced parents who do not allow these "selected ones" to develop a sense of free will. These "ones" are instructed and nurtured in such a way as to cause them to become *exactly* like the parent. However, they do *not* have the free will that the parent has. They have no choice of which *humanity type* might fulfill their desires of happiness. Their "desires of happiness" are *foundationalized* from the very beginning of their creation and provide these *specialized humans* with joy in serving others—*exactly* what their creators/parents do.

10. THE OVERSEER IS FOUNDATIONALIZED WITHOUT FREE WILL

With the help of their female mate, and with premeditation, an advanced male specifically creates a child whom he can teach and instruct in all the power, wisdom, and personal characteristics that he (the father) possesses. The child becomes both a father and a son—a son because his flesh was created by his mother, and a father because his *essence* is an exact reflection of what his father's has become.

One stark difference between the father and the son is that the father became who he is by exercising his free will and making the choice to become a creator. The *specialized* child, on the other hand, who is being prepared for the responsibility of an overseer, does not develop the willingness and desire to serve from the exercising of its free will. The *predestined overseer* is prepared from his foundation to perform specific functions determined by his parents/creators. The rest of us were created as genderless beings who would one day make the determination for ourselves—first, if we even wanted a gender, and secondly, whether that gender would be male or female. The predestined overseer was created as a male from the beginning.

These overseers are not allowed to experience the exercising of free will like all other children. Their strict upbringing and instruction prepares them for a life of service, like their parents, which gives them no choice of any other lifestyle. Because their *Foundationalization Process* is structured from the beginning, they have no other experience upon which to base their future actions. Their "*happiness alignment*" becomes the memories of what is instilled upon their *essences* as they are *foundationalized* to do what their parents intended for them.

The main difference between a child *foundationalized* to be an overseer, and regular, unrestricted human children, is that the parents of the overseer *intend* for the child to become like them (the parents). There are no such intentions or expectations for regular human children. There is no specialized training set forth for the other children. These *unrestricted* ones are allowed to experience all aspects of differing environments and experiences and choose which one best suits them individually.

11. AN OVERSEER IS A PERFECT EXAMPLE OF THE FATHER

This process of foundationalizing an overseer helps fulfill the advanced male's responsibility towards all the new human beings he creates. He is responsible for the way these beings will be governed forever. He is responsible to ensure that each of his children receives an equal opportunity to become an individual and to be able to express this individuality according to the free-willed nature of each.

In other words, our father/creator is responsible to ensure that we can do whatever we want, as long as what we do does not impede or inhibit what another of his children wants to do. To accomplish this, he creates a perfect example of himself, or better, an *overseer* of his responsibilities.

Because an advanced human male can create endless solar systems in which to place his children, he must make sure that there is an overseer for each of his new solar systems, because he himself cannot be present in each one at all times. Each new solar system is created for each group (or better, a batch) of newly created humans, along with their own overseer. The new overseer will remain under the advanced male creator's tutelage until the entire batch of children, to which the overseer is assigned, is ready to go to its appointed solar system and begin the second stage of human development in an *imperfect* world.

Once the batch of newly created humans to which we belong was placed in our solar system, our advanced father was free to prepare *another overseer* for a new batch of children to be placed in another solar system different from our own. This process continues on forever—worlds without end.

12. ONLY THE OVERSEER CAN END HUMAN EXISTENCE

Unlike his parents (who are advanced free-willed human beings who were given the choice and *decided* to become advanced parents), an overseer cannot and will not ever make a mistake by exercising his will. His parents *could* make a mistake according to their **free** will, but an overseer does not have the same free will or the capability to do so. Again, he was not given the choice of who he wanted to be as a human. His life was predestined from the beginning to perform a specific purpose.

He can be compared to, in some ways, a preprogrammed robot that can only do what its creator has programmed it to do. However, because he is human and was *foundationalized* around other humans who smile, laugh, have compassion, and experience joy, he has the ability to interact with us and appreciate our perspectives and experiences when we do what we choose to do with our free will. He also has a body and an *essence* like our own that is capable of sensory fulfillment, which provides happiness to a *human* being.

Only in this way, could we ever possibly trust our overseer's supreme judgment to make the right decisions in governing us. He is given all the power and knowledge that is available in the Universe. He understands every law that governs the Universe and also has the power and capability to do what very few advanced human beings will ever be able to do—disassemble (un-create) a human *essence*.

When our *essence* was created, a chemical bond occurred between the molecules of its elements that rendered it indestructible. No matter how much energy is forced into the atomic structure of our *essence*, nothing can cause the bonds to break apart. For this reason, if a person burns to death, no matter how hot the fire, the person's *essence* remains unaffected by any amount of heat. There is no chemical or any other substance anywhere, that can affect the structural makeup of the human *essence*—not a single thing in the Universe.

Nevertheless, the *essence can* be taken apart by an overseer. This being will have the knowledge and the physical body that will allow him to break the bonds of the elements that make up the *essence*, but only for a certain, very rare purpose to be discussed in detail in a later chapter. The only reason why he would ever do this is if a free-willed human being chose to end its existence by its own free will.

13. OVERSEERS APPROVE THE READINESS OF A NEWLY CREATED OVERSEER

Although our creators/parents have the knowledge of how an *essence* can be destroyed or "killed," and they can teach an overseer how this is done, they do not have the physical body to do it themselves. The overseers have specialized bodies that are provided only for those who will govern and *oversee* human society. Just as certain animals have specialized bodies that do things that other animals cannot, an overseer is provided with the body to be able to produce the appropriate command that can destroy the human *essence*.

The final say of who receives the type of body that has the ultimate power to destroy a human *essence* is the "overseer" who is responsible for what each *father* does. Every free-willed human being has an appointed overseer—they always have, they always will. The fathers' overseer ensures that those whom the fathers prepare for this power are properly trained and ready to perform the important responsibilities correctly. So, although fathers prepare the overseers, only other overseers can approve the final granting of *overseer power* and *responsibility*.

Because only an overseer has the power and knowledge of an "overseer," it is one of his responsibilities to create the bodies of all of the overseers created under his jurisdiction. The human *essence* placed in the male body is just like everyone else's. The only difference is the way that it is *foundationalized*, as has been explained. The body, however, has much greater capabilities than any free-willed human being has.

14. CREATORS CANNOT DESTROY A HUMAN THEY CREATE

There are two main reasons why advanced human creators, who are not overseers, are not allowed to destroy a human *essence* after they have created it:

First, because of free will, these beings can do what they want, when they want. A "mistake" is the exercising of free will that does not lead to what is best for the individual or for the whole of humanity. And because advanced creators were foundationalized differently than an overseer and have this free agency, they *could* make a mistake. They usually don't, but it is possible. Therefore, for the rest of humanity to feel safe and secure forever, we are assured that the ultimate power resides **only** in the hands of those who *cannot* misuse it and who *cannot* make a mistake.

The second reason is because of the compassion of these free-willed advanced human parents. Just as it would be very hard for any normal person to kill another person, especially one's own child, an advanced parent would have all kinds of *free-willed* justifications as to *why* their child should be given another chance or shown compassion and mercy. Justice can only be properly rendered by those who have no emotional ties to the person to whom justice is enacted, and who follow the law in spite of their personal feelings. Though an overseer can relate to our experience, because he is required to go through the vicissitudes of an *imperfect* world along with the rest of us, his conditioning ensures that he will never make a nepotistic or biased judgment.

15. AN OVERSEER SEES AND TREATS ALL PEOPLE EQUALLY

An overseer is isolated from all other people during his *Foundationalization Process*. He does not create bonds of friendship, close associations, or any familial bonds, except with the person, male or female, who will become his partner. To him, all human beings are exactly the same in relation to himself.

He exists so that he can serve all human beings equally. He exists to make sure each of them realizes the purpose for which they were created—to be happy—and to ensure that none of them impedes or inhibits the happiness of another. He learns how to do this by being around his father the entire time he is being *foundationalized*. He watches how his father serves others. He has very limited access to his other siblings, and when he does, it is only in the capacity of figuring out what would be the best way to serve them, as would his father.

Because he was *foundationalized* to a certain level of understanding and development by his mother, an overseer *does* have the ability to be a good partner to a female or another male, with whom he will be able to enjoy the fullness of joy through human companionship and sexuality. He will not be alone forever. He would not be happy alone, because there has never been a moment in his existence when he was not around either his mother or his father; thus he has a need for either a female or a male partner. Because overseers do not create new humans, there is no requirement that his partner be a female mother. Some overseers choose male partners. In any case, each overseer shall have the one who brings him the most happiness.

16. NO MISTAKES WILL EVER BE MADE BY THE PERFECT GOVERNOR

The greatest aspect of knowing that only *one* person in our existence will be able to govern our lives, is the assurance that our guarantee of life and happiness will remain secure forever. Under his watchful eye and guidance, the *one* created and prepared specifically for this purpose will never let us down. He will always be there. He will be the *only* human in the Universe who will have any authority and power over us. We will never have to worry about him exercising this authority and power over us unjustly.

SUMMARY

There is no way that free-willed beings can exist in peace and happiness if they do not have some aspect of control and restriction placed on their free will. The purpose of a ***perfect*** government is to exercise the appropriate power and authority over us within proper parameters of this control and restriction. This ensures that we are all treated equally and are all able to fulfill the purpose of our creation, by individualizing and benefiting from and enjoying our existence the way we want to.

A *true* and *right* government would never tell us what to do or establish laws that in any way would take away our right to do what we want to do. It exists to protect our rights from everyone else in the Universe, *including* those who created us, and provides us with the necessary opportunities to pursue our personal happiness, whatever our "desires of happiness" might be.

A *single*, powerful, human governing head is necessary for the continual peace and order of the solar system over which he is appointed; this ensures continued order in the entire Universe. The order by which the Universe is maintained has always been the same and will always be the same. An appointed overseer ensures this. In later chapters, we will discuss more of his role and how he governs and interacts with us in our own solar system.

The Creation of our Solar System

CHAPTER NINE

There follows Saturn, the first of the wandering stars....After it comes Jupiter....Next is Mars....An annual revolution holds the fourth place, in which as we have said is contained the Earth....In fifth place Venus....Lastly, Mercury....In the middle of all is the seat of the Sun....Thus indeed the Sun as if seated on a royal throne governs his household of Stars as they circle around him....We find, then, in this arrangement the marvelous (sic) symmetry of the universe, and a sure linking together in harmony of the motion and size of the spheres, such as could be perceived in no other way.

—Copernicus

1. ADVANCED MOTHERS DETERMINE WHEN OUR FOUNDATION IS COMPLETE

Advanced mothers make the decision of how many children they wish to have for each batch of children (during each foundational period). The length of time of each "period" differs for each batch of children, depending on how fast the newly created offspring determine who they want to be. Because the concept of time does not exist in advanced worlds, there is no specific set time period for humans to foundationalize. Whatever time we need, we get.

The number of children our parents create depends on how long it takes a batch of children to figure out who they want to be, or better, what *humanity type* they choose for themselves as part of the *Foundationalization Process*. An advanced mother does not churn out child after child after child that would eventually overpopulate a planet; neither does she create multiple children and care for them all at once. She has only one child at a time, and assists the child in adapting to its new environment before having another child. This exclusive individual attention to *one* is necessary, because of the responsibility the mother has for the newly created being's *foundation of humanity.* She must ensure that the process is satisfactorily started for one before moving on to another; and some children take longer than others do to adapt to their environment sufficiently in order to be left to themselves to continue their *foundationalization*.

All newly created humans will have enough time during their *foundationalization* stage of development to learn all there is to know about everything in the Universe. In order for us to make a fair determination of which *humanity type* is right for us, we must know all there is to know about being a human being. There were no "surprises" or something we might have missed or did not consider in weighing the options associated with each *humanity type*. By the time we were ready to choose who we would be for the rest of eternity, we knew just as much as our creators and every other advanced human being in the Universe. That's why it takes billions of years (according to our mortal accounting of *time*) for us to go through the *Foundationalization Process*.

Here's a basic example of what happens (all figures used in this example are strictly hypothetical):

2. THE SIZE OF EACH PLANET IS DETERMINED BY OUR HUMANITY CHOICES

If there are one million people who want to be mothers, then a Venus-like world (using our own solar system as an example) would be created with a diameter, let's say, of 8,000 miles. If there were two million people who want to be mothers, then Venus would be 16,000 miles in diameter. Likewise, if there were only 500,000 people who wanted to be mothers, then Venus would only be 4000 miles in diameter.

The planets that allow the creation of new human beings are limited in size according to the number of humans who made the decision to become creators. The size of the planet directly correlates to this particular number. There is a specific amount of room on these planets that is necessary to accomplish the *Foundationalization Process*.

The communities of advanced parents take up only a small part of the whole planet. The rest of the planet is available to be used by the developing humans according to their individual free will. After newly created humans develop into who they choose to be by using their free will, these "children" continue to live on their parent's perfect world (i.e., Venus- or Mercury-like), until their own solar system is prepared, where they will reside forever.

Because new human beings are not created all at once, there is plenty of *time* for each one to develop at their own pace. Those who were created *first* in our batch of humans, for example, waited until the *last* of all those created for our batch were created and *foundationalized* properly. Because there was no concept of time in our primordial world, the *first* to be created had no problem waiting on the *last.*

The "overseer" for our batch was the *first* to be created. This allowed him the opportunity to watch his younger siblings grow and develop over billions of years. Our male/father creator is connected to each of his children through the power of each uniquely "tagged" *essence*. Likewise, because of the unique power and ability of his body, each overseer develops the same type of connection with those humans who belong to the batch of children for which he was created. In this way, we are assured that our overseer will perform his responsibility with fairness and equity as he deals with each of us throughout eternity, according to our desires of happiness.

3. THE PLANETS ARE SPECIFICALLY DESIGNED FOR THE HUMAN FOUNDATIONALIZATION PROCESS

Using our own Venus as an example, and the same *hypothetical* numbers above, we can visualize the planet in this way:

Venus is about the same size as our earth. Therefore, a community of one million people would be a small dot on the entire planet, about the size of the city of San Diego in the State of California in the United States. The rest of the world is available for the newly created humans to explore and experience as they desire, after spending their first foundational years exclusively with their mothers.

According to an earth timeline, a mother would oversee and directly control the activities of the child (although always allowing for complete free will) for about 1000 years.

(Keep in mind that no time frames or quantitative measures exist in a perfect human world; therefore, 1000 years to us in our current world might seem like one day to an advanced human being. Because the concept of time has no application in a *perfect* world, a world that we'll become a part of in the future, creating time frames is only useful to put things into a perspective that we can mentally deal with in an *imperfect* state, in order for ***true reality*** to make sense.)

After spending this initial time with the child, the mother will withdraw from her direct involvement in the life of the child and will allow it to continue to develop on its own. By this time, the child has been properly directed and has its *humanity* established, but not necessarily its *type*. It takes many experiences and much time for the *humanity* ***type*** to be chosen.

Before the mother withdraws her direct involvement in the life of the developing child, therefore, she ensures that the child will act appropriately among other human beings. This ability to act appropriately is our *humanity*. This *humanity* is the core of all human beings, regardless of *humanity* ***type***. After the mother has released her responsibility over the child, she is free to create another one.

Using random numbers to elucidate what we are trying to understand about our primordial existence, let's say there are one million mothers who each have a child every 1,000 years. After 10,000 years, these mothers would have foundationalized 10 million children; after 20,000 years, 20 million; and so on.

Assuming that our current solar system was created to house 15 billion human beings and cater to every one of their individual desires for space, according to their *humanity type*, it took our 1 million mothers 15 million years just to complete the primary *Foundationalization Process* for the batch of children to which we belong. (Keep in mind that these numbers are hypothetical and are only used to help us visualize *reality*.)

Once we were each released from our mother's tutelage and direction, we each had the right to exist in our primordial world as long as everyone else, to further test our resolve at being who we chose to be (including our humanity *type*). Because the *Foundationalization Process* determines what type of person we are going to be for the rest of our existence, once we had finished the process, our creators then knew exactly what size and how many of each planet was needed for our own solar system.

4. THE EXPERIENCE OF AN UNCONTROLLED ENVIRONMENT

With their advanced knowledge and technology, our creators *could have* created the entire solar system in a virtual instant, patterning it after the perfect world where we were created. But in so doing, they would have negated the very purpose of our second stage of human development, which is to experience *imperfection*.

As explained before, **perfect** worlds have **always** existed and are intended for the human race—the ultimate life forms in the Universe. Perfect humans know how to create the perfect world. They could have used the *perfect process* (the one that has always existed) to create our solar system. But we would have never known that the process was perfect, unless we experienced an *imperfect* one.

The perfect process takes literally seconds. The *imperfect* process takes billions of years, during which time all kinds of variables come into play that are not conducive to a perfect human environment. Our creators wanted to show us what would happen if the natural laws of the Universe were left to do what they do, *without* advanced human intervention and the control of the power and authority of a *perfect* government.

An *imperfect* world would help us understand the necessity of the "overseer," as explained in the previous chapter. We were created with the expectation of being *completely equal* with all other humans in the Universe, and creating an "overseer" and giving him absolute power over us didn't make much sense at the time, if we were all intended to be equal. Further, it would help us understand why only human creators should be allowed the greatest of all the powers in the Universe—the ability to create and control matter, and the ability to have sex. We wondered why all of us, no matter what *humanity type*, couldn't have these extraordinary powers and sensations.

Part of this experience of *imperfection* is to observe the course of natural development and what comes of it with very little human intervention. Thus, our world was left largely to itself to develop according to the laws of nature, which are not the *perfect* laws that govern the Universe.

5. WE MUST AGREE TO CONFORM TO ALL UNIVERSAL LAWS

We needed to know for ourselves that the laws and procedures that have *always* existed in the Universe were just and true. We needed to be able to reconcile our free will to accept the fact that these laws couldn't be changed, and more importantly, *should not* be changed by anyone. Without being coerced or manipulated, we needed to experience for ourselves the results of the misuse of free will. An *imperfect* world would provide us with this experience.

Upon experiencing both a perfect world and an *imperfect* one, we would become convinced, without doubt, that we must allow ourselves (our free will) to become subjected to the Universal laws that govern all human beings. If we couldn't be convinced of this through the different stages of our human development, then we would not be allowed to continue to exist as a free-willed human being.

6. ADVANCED HUMAN BEINGS CONTROL THE UNIVERSE

Everything in the Universe exists for and is controlled by advanced human beings. Therefore, the creation of our solar system had to begin with the command of a human creator with the power and knowledge to do so. Even this first step in establishing our own piece of the Universe showed us that *nothing* in the Universe is done randomly or without a *specific* purpose. If it were not so, the Universe would be an uncontrollable and chaotic mess. Because it is not, some force must be behind its order. The force that holds the Universe together and in perpetual order is produced by the knowledge, power, and will of advanced human beings.

As we progress in our understanding of what is actually taking place in the Universe, we will find that the "laws of nature" as we currently understand them are simply conjectures and theories created by *imperfect* human beings who do not have all the pieces of the puzzle. There are not any so-called "laws of nature" that cannot be changed and manipulated by an advanced human being with the knowledge and power to do so. This should be of no consequence to our limited understanding, because we continually see our current technology usurping the laws of nature we once supposed could not be broken. This is how our solar system was created in an infinite Universe without beginning and without end:

7. MALES ARE RESPONSIBLE FOR THE CREATION OF NEW SOLAR SYSTEMS

Our father isn't the only male creator upon the planet where he resides. There are others just like him, who are each responsible for their own batch of children, created in unison with the women who have chosen each of them to be the father of their children.

As explained previously, many advanced human women only need one male to help in the creation of their children. Because there are a very limited number of people who choose to be male creators, or better, because there are so few who can be trusted with the job, each individual mother has only a few to pick from to help her with her children.

United under the same resolve to establish new planets for newly created human beings, these fathers find places in the Universe where there is no creation (or better, organized matter). They map out the area for a brand-new solar system, depending on the needs of those placed in their care and responsibility. Each male creator has his own galaxy which comprises of all the solar systems he creates for those humans for whom he is responsible. The galaxies throughout the Universe continue to grow and expand exponentially according to the needs of the newly created humans. There is no end or limit to the size of these galaxies. They continue to expand until they seem to become a whole new universe.

The size of a solar system, and therefore the galaxy to which it belongs, is determined by the needs of the children. The fathers know what their children require for their happiness. The area these fathers prepare for each new galaxy is connected to their own galaxy, by what current scientists would call a "wormhole" or a "black hole."

8. CURRENT SCIENTIFIC THEORIES ARE NOT REALITY

Although current scientific understanding and theory is far from the **real truth**, what scientists have theorized so far will help the reader understand more about what is actual *reality*. As explained in a previous chapter, human beings can imagine and conceptualize what could be true, although it may be disconnected from **real truth** by the limitations of an *imperfect* brains.

Now that it has been explained that our current mortal scientific theories and hypothesis could be only portions of **real truth**, but are usually *far* from perfected reality, we can use some of them and expand their proposals so that we can have a better grasp of **true reality**.

(We must always remember, however, that what we know and understand today upon our earth is far from the **true reality** of advanced human civilizations. Because of free will, we are allowed to act upon what we observe and can *imagine* in our *imperfect* world. With this allowance, we have made and will continue to make great strides in creating new theories and hypotheses. However, as we continue to learn, we must keep in mind that in our *imperfect* state, we will be ever learning and never able to come to a complete knowledge of ***true*** reality. We are going to need a *perfect brain* to come to this understanding.)

With what we do know and can imagine, let's take a look at what science theorizes about "black holes":

9. SCIENTISTS THEORIZE ABOUT BLACK HOLES

According to the limited perception of current scientific observation, black holes are the evolutionary endpoints of stars at least 10 to 15 times as massive as the Sun. Here is the current scientific theory:

> If a massive star undergoes a supernova explosion, it may leave behind a fairly massive burned out stellar remnant. With no outward forces to oppose gravitational forces, the remnant will collapse in on itself. The star eventually collapses to the point of zero volume and infinite density, creating what is known as a "singularity." As the density increases, the path of light rays emitted from the star are bent and eventually wrapped irrevocably around the star. Any emitted photons are trapped into an orbit by the intense gravitational field; they will never leave it. Because no light escapes after the star reaches this infinite density, it is called a black hole. (NASA/GSFC, Imagine the Universe! Dictionary, 1997–2009. NASA's Goddard Space Flight Center. 19 August 2009.)

Although the above explanation isn't entirely accurate, when the wording is changed appropriately, it can lead to a complete understanding of what "black holes" *really* are:

10. A BLACK HOLE IS A CONDUIT TO CONNECT THE CREATORS' GALAXY WITH THE NEWLY CREATED/CHILDREN'S GALAXY

Black holes can be considered both the endpoints and beginning points of galaxies. Galaxies are comprised of many distinct solar systems. A sun makes up the foundation for *each* new solar system. When a new sun is created, it begins with what might be termed as a "nuclear explosion," which could give some limited credence to the scientific "Big Bang theory."

The elements involved in creating a new sun come from the "dark matter" that exists in the place where the new solar system is to be formed. An advanced human being, who has the power to do so, organizes the basic components of the elements that are needed from the existing dark matter, in order to create a proper nuclear explosion.

He uses technology and understanding to form the elements that will create the initial reaction that leads to the *birth* of each new supernova, or sun (and not the *death* of one).

Advanced humans use energy from their bodies to perform the action of creation. However, before any energy is transferred from a part of the Universe where energy exists (in the form of light and heat or within the bonds that create matter) to a part of the Universe where there is none, a conduit is created that connects the two parts of the Universe to each other. This conduit is what scientists observe as a black hole.

11. BLACK HOLES ARE CONDUITS FOR THE TRANSFERENCE OF ENERGY FROM ONE GALAXY TO ANOTHER

These "holes" are the way that the energy from one part of the Universe is directed into another. They act somewhat like electrical wires that conduct electricity and carry it to its intended destination. So that our creators can keep track of what goes on in each solar system, the energy that is produced—by our thoughts, actions, and literally every bit of energy given off by every bit of matter in our solar system—is conducted through the "black holes" or "wormholes" connected to their own galaxy.

Every time a new galaxy is created, a new "hole" is created. This is so that all the energy produced from the newly created matter can be monitored and overseen by its creators in another part of the Universe. For this reason, science has correctly speculated that no light or energy can escape these "holes." Because their limited observation and technology only allows them to see energy being drawn into these holes, these scientists cannot conceptualize what happens to the energy once it enters, or observe that energy also comes *out* of them. They have found no logical perspective from which to formulate an observation of what comes *out of a black hole* at the other end. They are also unable to observe or measure the energy that is coming out of the black hole at the point where they are observing energy being drawn in.

12. BLACK HOLES CAN BE COMPARED TO SATELLITE TECHNOLOGY

Visualize a satellite dish mounted on your house that receives transmissions from a satellite orbiting the Earth and transfers the energy through wires to your television set. The top of the black hole can be compared to the function of a satellite dish, whose nature is designed to capture electromagnetic transmissions and direct them through wires to the receiver. The receiver transforms the transmissions into what your television can form into a visual and audio experience that a human being can understand.

Similarly, our creators can monitor everything that happens in our galaxy and solar system. The end of a "black hole" that we can observe from our earth is like a satellite dish that receives the transmissions of electromagnetic energy that occur in all matter, from a rock to an advanced human being. The black hole captures the energy from one galaxy and directs it to another. The receiver (Solarian advanced human brain) can transform the signal into a perfect replica of what was transmitted.

13. ALL MATTER GIVES OFF SPECIFIC AND UNIQUE ENERGY PATTERNS

Everything that exists gives off certain unique levels of energy, which are measured and defined by current science as "frequencies." These energy frequencies bind together the protons, neutrons, and electrons of all matter. This energy is discernable and measurable with advanced technology. An advanced human being who receives the transmission of all of these energy frequencies has the knowledge and technology to discern which particle of matter is creating which energy frequency or level, and exactly what action the matter is performing.

For want of a better term to describe it, let's call this advanced technology: **A**dvanced **N**uclear **G**enerated **E**nergy of **L**ife **S**pectrometers, or **ANGELS** for short. (*The term "technology," used throughout this book, refers to the means and ways that human beings* *act upon their environment with their free will.*) There is no actual machinery used in the process. The advanced nature of a Solarian brain allows the energy produced by an actual event to form in the Solarian advanced brain, just as a dream or a vision unfolds in our *imperfect* mind. For purposes of explanation, we will refer to this ability as the function of ANGELS.

14. THE TECHNOLOGY OF ADVANCED HUMAN BEINGS RECOGNIZES AND MEASURES ENERGY

ANGELS can pick up transmissions of any level of energy produced in the specific region of space where it is directed. The "black" or "worm" *holes* are specifically positioned to receive energy emissions from specific areas of the Universe. These specially designed receptors and conduits of energy are always aimed in the logistical direction intended to be monitored by the advanced human.

When a butterfly flaps its wings, or a bacterium replicates itself on someone's dirty hands, energy from each action is produced. All energy is picked up by a properly placed "hole," which then relays the information to ANGELS on the advanced planets in our creator's solar system. Whoever is working with the ANGELS knows where every single particle of matter exists and what it is doing.

15. ENERGY LEVELS ARE AFFECTED BY THEIR LOCATION IN THE UNIVERSE

The energy frequency emissions of all of matter are affected by their relative position to the ANGELS. (Each energy emission is different depending on its specific location.) Instead of the **G**lobal **P**ositioning **S**ystem of location currently used on our earth, advanced technology allows for a **Universal Positioning System**. This is how the ANGELS know exactly in which galaxy, in which solar system, on which planet, in which area of that planet, and on what person's hand a particular bacterium is growing. Every point of location in the Universe has a specific way of affecting the energy emissions of all particles of matter found therein, relative to the position of the ANGELS.

Here's a hypothetical example:

Let's assign the flapping of butterfly A's wings the frequency of Abfly105. Another butterfly with the exact same DNA makeup can be found anywhere in the Universe and will emit the exact same energy frequency. However, a butterfly that is flapping its wings on the *Eastern* Hemisphere of our earth gives off a frequency of Abfly105*a*, whereas its twin doing the same thing on the *Western* Hemisphere of our world would emit a frequency of Abfly105*ab*.

In addition, the same butterfly flapping its wings on a similar planet in the solar system next to ours gives off a frequency level of Abfly106a. By this illustrative "coding" and "mapping," the ANGELS know exactly what is taking place with all matter in the Universe.

16. ADVANCED HUMANS CAN MONITOR THE WHOLE UNIVERSE

Using the hypothetical example we used previously to describe the unique "tag" of the human *essence*, if a person in the Western Hemisphere had a butterfly sitting on his or her head flapping its wings, the ANGELS would pick up transmissions of AB6165 and Abfly105b. By these unique energy emissions, an advanced human being would then know exactly what kind of butterfly was flapping its wings on whose head and in what part of our world—it's really that simple!

If the butterfly stopped flapping its wings and rested on the head of a person, the butterfly would not be giving off the same energy emission any longer (although it would still be giving off energy that identified it as a certain species of butterfly). Therefore, the frequency would change and be interpreted as a "resting" butterfly sitting on a person's head in the *Western* Hemisphere of the world called Earth.

The ANGELS instantaneously transmits the energy patterns into the Solarian brain where it is transformed into visual imagery allowing the advanced human being to view what is going on. And because all sound, color, and smell are simply different frequency levels of energy, the ANGELS transmit the exact frequency levels of sound, color, and smell into a holographic-like virtual reality where the advanced human can physically participate in all that occurs, much like we actually participate in the dreams created in our *imperfect* minds.

The advanced human can participate in all that we do in this way, as if they were right next to us, when in fact they could be trillions of miles away. We live the experience in reality; they live the experience in a virtual vision-like world created by their advanced brain. In this way, they can theoretically "walk through walls, furniture, etc." since it is just an image in their brain.

17. OUR ENTIRE LIFE EXPERIENCE IS RECORDED

We can think of our life experience (as sent to advanced beings on a distant planet) as a continual series of energy emissions recorded, stored, and recalled by the power of our *essence*. Everything that we do, including every thought (which is also a production of energy), can be perceived by the advanced beings who oversee our world just as if we spoke the thought out loud. Before we speak, our brain releases energy to our voice box, which takes the thought's energy and transforms it into audible vibrations.

ANGELS (**A**dvanced **N**uclear **G**enerated **E**nergy of **L**ife **S**pectrometers) pick up the energy of our thought long before it reaches our voice box. Advanced beings generally know what we are going to say or do before we actually say or do it. It's as if someone is following us around with a video recorder all of our life and documenting everything that we do. And the ANGELS not only monitor all energy patterns, but also record and store everything—every thought, sight, smell, sound, taste, touch—everything! We will be able to review all of our life experiences when we are able to use the technology that advanced beings will bring to this earth during our *third stage of human development*. (We will discuss the purpose for reviewing all of our life experiences in a later chapter.)

Everything that we experience is recorded and stored on the advanced memory banks of the ANGELS, according to our specific *essence tag*. It is stored as the unique energy levels that each experience or thought produces. This storage is provided by the advanced brains of the Solarians who are responsible for us. As discussed earlier, the *essence* is an unlimited, perpetual recording device—there are no limitations on its capacity to do what it was designed to.

At any given time, these ANGELS can *download* into our brain the exact replay of our experiences. If allowed to with our *imperfect* bodies, we could download and view any part of our existence as if we were experiencing the event a second time as a *dream*.

18. A PERFECT BRAIN RECALLS AND RELIVES ANY EXPERIENCE

In the future, when we receive a perfect human body, we will no longer need the assistance or monitoring capabilities of the ANGELS. The same energy patterns that create all of our experiences, including sight, smell, sound, taste, touch, and thought, are also recorded upon the element of our own *essence*. In a way, our *essence* is our own individual ANGELS *without* the ability to collect and transmit the energy patterns created by others between galaxies—a power available only to Solarian servants.

With a perfect body, we will be able to recall any experience we have ever had and relive it in our mind in a similar, but more perfected, way to how we currently experience the events of our dreams while sleeping. Our dreams seem real to us at the moment we are *dreaming of the events*, but they are not a reflection of *our true reality* because our dreams are produced by an *imperfect* brain that is reacting with the power of our "veiled" *essence*.

As explained previously, the dreams produced in an *imperfect* state are disconnected experiences of our reality often put together in random nonsensical patterns. But the fact that *we do dream* demonstrates that we *have* the ability to experience an event in our mind that is not actually taking place in our current reality.

A *perfect* brain has the ability to produce dream-like situations in our mind that reflect *exactly* what we experienced in the past by reproducing the exact same energy levels of all of our experiences as they were recorded when the actual events took place. The reliving of our experiences is for our *own* good, and each experience will be relived according to our personal perception of the events that took place.

The ANGELS, however, record everything *without* a personal human perception. It is possible for others outside of ourselves to view our experiences and create their own perception of the event where they had no personal involvement. This ability is limited to the advanced Solarian humans, whose intent in viewing what we experienced will better aid them in serving our individual needs. But in the end, the only perception or opinion that will ever matter to any of us is what *we* each perceive, each of us creating our *own* reality based on these individual and personal perceptions, formed from the experiences in exercising our free will. In other words, we won't care what anyone else thinks about us. And why should we? It *really* makes no difference to our Universe!

19. CONCEPTS OF THE FUTURE CAN BE CONFUSING

The introduction of advanced systems of monitoring and recording can seem just as impossible to the people of our current world (*circa* 2012) as our modern technology would have seemed to humans who lived just a few decades or centuries in our past. Therefore, it should be very easy for us to rationalize and conceptualize what we are now learning about *who we are* and *why we exist*.

The comprehension of how and why the actions (energy expenditure) of all forms of matter in the Universe are monitored and recorded is vital to a better understanding of ourselves. Therefore, it is important that we repeatedly describe, explain, and build upon what we already know about basic technologies of which we are currently aware.

20. CURRENT VIDEO RECORDING IS INEFFICIENT

In our present world, a camera records what it sees by focusing light and storing what is reflected in the light as an image. Light is simply transference of energy from one particle of matter to another. Therefore, cameras record the energy patterns introduced into their lenses.

The techniques of recording images are continually improving as modern technology advances. However, our current technology is primitive in comparison to the advanced technology of our future. Advanced beings on other planets record everything that happens on our earth. Yes, everything—from the movements of the smallest oceanic plankton to the actions of every human being upon the earth—is seen, recorded, and stored by the advanced human beings who oversee our world, as has been explained.

21. SUBATOMIC ENERGY LEVELS ARE RECORDED

Current night vision technology works by collecting the tiny amount of light available (including the lower portion of the infrared light spectrum that is present, but may be imperceptible to our eyes) and amplifying it to the point that we can easily observe the image created. Current thermal imaging works by capturing the *upper* portion of the infrared light spectrum, which is emitted as heat by objects instead of simply reflected as light. Outperforming both of these techniques, advanced technology can measure and record *any energy level* given off by the electromagnetic fields produced by *any* form of matter. In other words, the energy that keeps protons, neutrons, and electrons together to form matter can be seen and recorded by the advanced technology of our future, or better, the current technology of advanced human beings.

22. ALL SCIENTIFIC THEORIES ARE FLAWED

Currently, we can view imagery as close as the makeup of a molecule with an electron microscope, or objects as far away as many light years with the Hubble telescope. This current (primitive) long-distance technology is based on *comparing* the energy levels given off by far away sources to the energy given off by *known* sources closer to the earth.

X-rays, microwaves, and other means are utilized by scientists to speculate as to what matter exists in the Universe and what it is doing. However, "speculation" is the key word here. Science creates hypotheses based on their observation and what they accept as truth. But what they know is minuscule, almost non-existent, compared to the **real truth** of how things really are.

Current technology has advanced from rudimentary cameras, capturing black-and-white photographs from just a few feet away, to satellite imagery being captured from dozens of miles away. And these extraordinary advances happened in the relatively short time span of about 100 years. Therefore, one can imagine what sort of advancements and improvements could be made to this technology in 10,000 years! Nevertheless, it is important to always keep in mind that the ultimate and perfect technology has always existed somewhere in the Universe. But, because our current minds cannot remember anything about perfection (as this is the purpose of our current stage of development), we can only continue to invent theories and hypotheses based upon what we can observe by less-than-perfect means and rationalized with our *imperfect* brains.

23. ALL ENERGY GIVEN OFF BY MATTER IS MONITORED

We can look into the night sky and see a point of light that we call a star (which could very well be an entire galaxy of billions of solar systems just like our own). In the same way, advanced technology can focus on the same point of light and see and record every bit of energy given off by the smallest bacterium to the largest dinosaur that exists on any of the planets in any of the solar systems in that galaxy. This has already been explained, but to further clarify this important concept, we will again use some redundancy and elucidate how this happens and why it is possible by using our current technology and understanding as an example:

24. ADVANCED TECHNOLOGY ALLOWS A REAL TIME VIEW OF ALL THE UNIVERSE

Current technology allows security cameras to zoom in or zoom out on any particular scene. For example, while zoomed out, one might see a group of people sitting at a table eating dinner. But when the camera zoomed in, one could see the unnoticed human hair that is floating in a bowl of soup. The view and perspective is limited to the ability of the camera to zoom in and out and the power of its lens.

If, on our current earth, we had the same technology that is available to advanced human beings, we could pick out any star in the sky and aim the advanced "camera" in that direction. "Zoomed out" it would appear as we currently see it, a simple star in the sky. But if we "zoomed in," the technology would work like a microscope, which would enhance any particle of matter anywhere within the image of "star light" on which we are focused. (For example, this could be the speck of dust on the wing of a fly sitting on a fence on such-and-such a world.)

25. ALL OF OUR THOUGHTS ARE RECORDED

Because our thoughts are also levels of energy created by our brain, these are also recorded. As mentioned previously, all of us have a "tagged" essence that is unique only to us. Our essence gives off electromagnetic frequencies that correlate to our exclusive individual "tag."

A thought is a pulse of energy that is given at a specific frequency level. When a person, (we'll call Tag No. AB6165 for example) thinks a thought, the advanced recording devices record and categorize it as a thought generated by AB6165. While it is being stored, it is also being monitored during our second stage of development by those advanced human beings who find a great amount of joy in watching the unpredictable things that we think and do as mortals.

By tuning into the frequency of Tag No. AB6165, an advanced human monitor can know exactly what the person is thinking and doing at any time. And because this "monitor" knows the frequency level associated with each of our unique *essences*, the being can, if desired, communicate with us by sending out a communication on the same frequency level, which we would then perceive as a "thought" coming to our mind.

26. ADVANCED HUMAN BEINGS CAN INTERVENE IN OUR LIVES

In rare instances, for specific purposes, we may receive this type of communication as a thought that randomly pops into our head. However, because we are not aware of the way our *imperfect* brain analyzes the input of energy, we would not know the difference between our own thoughts and those put into our head by an advanced human being.

Many *imperfect humans* believe that they are receiving thoughts from an outside source, when, in reality, it is their own made-up thoughts generated by their own mind. Because of our inability to distinguish the energy patterns of our *essence* from those produced by our *imperfect* brain, we often perceive our own thoughts as those coming from an outside source.

Advanced human beings rarely, if at all, communicate with us during our second stage of development in an *imperfect* world. They know that the few thousands of years that we live in an *imperfect* world are for our own good and for the purpose of experiencing an existence *without* their involvement. Therefore, the *only* reason why any advanced human being would ever put a thought in someone's head would be if 1) the action of the individual was going to make a great impact on the rest of us, or 2) the action would in some way impede the purpose for which we live in an *imperfect* world.

During our second stage of development on this world, they only intervene for the greater good of *all*. They never interact with one in a way that they would not interact with everyone else for the same purpose. They do not give "inspiration" and advice to one mortal, while disavowing the right of another to receive the same intervention.

27. HUMANS WERE KEPT FROM DISCOVERING TECHNOLOGY TOO EARLY

More about how and why advanced humans involve themselves in our world will be explained later. However, an example of their unperceived involvement will answer the question as to why our ancestors upon this earth, with all that their *imperfect* brains imagined and invented in their day, could not come up with the knowledge of how electricity works and then harness its power. We are the descendants of these *imperfect* humans and are no smarter or more gifted than they were; yet it has taken those of us in their future only a few relatively short years to understand the power and use it according to our free will.

Democritus (circa 400 B.C.E) was one of the first recorded humans who theorized that all matter is made up of various imperishable, indivisible elements that he called "atoma." If he was sitting alone one day thinking about the idea of electricity, an advanced being would have effectively clouded his mind with other random thoughts in order to keep him from making crucial discoveries or putting together vital pieces of the puzzle of electricity. In this way, advanced human beings kept the discovery of electricity from the earth's inhabitants for a time. This is because they would have done with it exactly what we are doing with it today, and would have destroyed humankind long before the time allowed for the purpose for which we live in this *imperfect* world was complete.

28. ADVANCED HUMANS' INTERVENTION IS LIMITED

To more easily visualize how all of this takes place, consider the following hypothetical situation. (Although the following is not exactly how it happens, it is reasonably close enough to allow the reader the ability to fully understand what genderless Solarian servants do):

Each advanced human servant is assigned a certain number of newly created human beings, let's say for example, Tag No.'s AA0001 through AA5068. Each of these "tagged frequencies" is recorded in the advanced brain of the servant. The servant-monitor is alerted to certain thought patterns given off by each of the individuals for whom the monitor is responsible.

If a thought pattern from one of the assigned "tags" comes in, for example, that the person is in distress, the monitor can engage a dream-like state in the advanced brain and visualize the events taking place with the distressed person and analyze the situation. The monitor can then determine if any action should be taken.

These highly advanced beings know what is the right thing to do in all situations. They are in the position of "monitor" because they have chosen this as their life's desire and gain a great amount of happiness from doing it. They know what is best for each of the human beings in their care. They know that non-intervention is essential during our time in an *imperfect* world, so that we can take full advantage of *imperfection* temporarily, in order to better appreciate *perfection* forever. For these reasons, they will not intervene in the free-willed affairs of our current world, unless their intervention will lead to an outcome beneficial for the entire human race.

29. EINSTEIN'S THEORY OF RELATIVITY IS NOT TRUTH

The *Theory of Relativity* developed by Albert Einstein ($E=mc^2$) does not work when applied to black holes. Part of Einstein's theory speculates that the speed of light in a vacuum is constant and is also an absolute physical boundary for the speed of all matter. In other words, nothing can go faster than the speed of light.

Einstein speculated that all matter moves within a range of motion, where the speed of light is the fastest that anything can move. If this were the case, then a transmission of energy from another galaxy just 20 light-years away (over 100 trillion miles) would take 20 years to reach our earth. Yet, if that is the case, then how could an advanced human "servant-monitor" have clouded the mind of Democritus the moment he was creating a thought? Again, the answer is found in a proper understanding of black holes and dark matter, which current science does not completely understand.

30. ENERGY IS TRANSFERRED MUCH FASTER THAN THE SPEED OF LIGHT IN A DARK MATTER ENVIRONMENT

Dark matter consists of every space where organized matter is not found. It is everywhere and endless in our Universe. The transference of energy through all dark matter in the Universe, of which a "black hole" is created, is always in real time. Although it would appear that there would be no need for "black holes" if the transference can be made through *all* dark matter, a "black hole" is like an energy condenser that makes the transference more efficient.

Although this concept is as hard for the *imperfect* brain to comprehend as is the fact that the Universe and advanced *perfect* human beings have always existed, it is nonetheless the **real truth**. The moment an advanced human being emits energy from 100 trillion or a trillion trillion miles from this earth, it instantly becomes part of our real time.

31. ENERGY IS AFFECTED BY ITS ENVIRONMENT

Sound is simply transference of energy. In our current world, sound travels faster underwater than it does through our atmosphere. Based on this realization, one can easily understand how the environment of dark matter (again, which includes black holes) can allow transference of energy much faster than anything our current *imperfect* brains, with their limited capacity, can comprehend.

One might question: If energy frequencies traveling *through* dark matter essentially travel at an "infinite" velocity, which in ***reality*** equates to "real time," then what about the energy that is traveling *outside* of dark matter? Is the energy slowed down once it comes into contact with other matter, such as a planet? Could Einstein's Theory of Relativity be considered true when we are upon a planet, but not when in space? How is the "infinite" or "real time" velocity maintained *outside* of a "dark matter transmitter interface"?

These questions are easily answered if we understand **true reality**. There is no difference between the basic components of *regular* matter and "dark" matter. The best and easiest way to define each is as "organized" and "unorganized" matter. Because energy, light, and heat are byproducts of matter, they (energy, light, and heat) do not really exist in and of themselves. There is only matter, either organized or unorganized, throughout the Universe.

Energy, light, and heat are a direct result of matter reacting with other matter, whether in its *organized* or *unorganized* state. Therefore, everything is created and maintained throughout the Universe on a subatomic, basic level of existence. The power of *all* matter resides in its basic components. Therefore, the *power of energy transference* resides in these basic components, regardless of whether the matter is *organized* or *unorganized.*

None of our current technologies can measure what occurs in the *transference of energy* on a subatomic level, or better, the way that energy is transferred through the basic components of all matter. Thus, we can conclude that science *cannot* measure the speed at which energy travels through "dark matter." Science measures time, speed, and distance using machines that transmit energy, light, or heat in very primitive ways. These "machines" are made of *organized* matter; thus, this primitive technology only allows the *imperfect human* to measure the transference of energy through *organized* matter.

In any event, no scientific advancements or understanding of dark matter will ever be given to any human being who is not a creator anyway. Only an advanced creator understands the *true* composition of dark (unorganized) matter and how to use it properly.

SUMMARY

The creation of our solar system that belongs to our galaxy was completed by advanced human beings in the following manner:

After newly created humans have decided what *humanity type* brings them the greatest amount of happiness during their *foundationalization* period, the father of these people creates a solar system specific to their needs; in this way, we are directly responsible for the creation of our own solar system.

To create these solar systems, these advanced fathers find an area within the infinite parameters of the galaxy assigned to house their children where there is no organized matter—"matter" being **everything** but dark matter. They create a conduit from their own *home* galaxy that harnesses the energy emitted from their own planet (even their own bodies) and conducts it to where the new galaxy of solar systems is to be located. They command the protons, neutrons, and electrons (again, using these basic nuclear components only as a reference) that exist in dark matter to produce the elements that are needed to create a new sun and new solar systems. These conduits, known currently as "black holes," allow the transference of energy between the two galaxies.

The speed by which energy travels is not restricted in the environment of the dark matter of the Universe. Advanced human beings who live in other galaxies can monitor and intercede into the life experience of human beings in other galaxies in *real time*, instantly. In this way, the creators responsible for human life ensure that all those who are going through their second stage of human development take from the experience what is intended.

The planets of our solar system will one day become the *home* residencies on which we will live forever as perfected human beings, according to our individual choice of what makes us the happiest. We made this personal choice long before our solar system was created. This solar system was created to accommodate the choices we made.

To enhance our ability to live with the choice we made for ourselves and enjoy it forever, we needed to add one more thing to our development as a perfect human being—the **opposite** of all that is perfect. We needed to live for a time upon a planet and experience all that is the opposite of the purpose of our existence—the opposite of human happiness. Our current world was created for this purpose. Our earth was allowed to go through an *imperfect* natural creation process with very little intervention by advanced humans. From our experiences on this earth, we are able to understand the difference between a world where the laws of nature are controlled by advanced human beings and one where the laws of nature *control human beings*.

From this experience, we learn to appreciate the control and order of the Universe and accept our place within it. One day we will be able to freely subject our free will to the laws that govern it and to those who administer these laws. We will one day be able to submit to the power and authority of the governing laws of the Universe because of our experience of living *without* them. We are learning to appreciate what we once had (a perfect world), so that when we have it again, we can finally enjoy it forever.

The Creation of our Imperfect World

CHAPTER TEN

The world itself...is the perfect manifestation of imperfection.

—Henry Miller

1. THE SUN IS A PERPETUAL ENERGY FACTORY

The sun was created from a direct command given by an advanced human being. The command caused the subatomic particles found in dark matter to form into a cluster of the required elements. These specific elements cause a perpetual chain reaction that releases enormous amounts of energy. This reaction is similar to a nuclear explosion created in the confines of our atmosphere upon this earth.

However, the "nuclear reaction" that was responsible for the sun was subjected first, to the environment in which the reaction took place, and second, to the types of elements used to create the reaction. The environment was a vacuum of empty space. Enriched uranium and plutonium are the *known* elements used in some of the nuclear reactions upon this earth. The elements used in the creation of the sun are generally *unknown* to current scientific classifications.

A sun's nuclear reaction does not spread beyond a predetermined boundary, thus creating its own atmosphere. This encapsulating atmosphere was created by the reaction itself. In other words, in empty space, or in an environment of dark matter, the reaction becomes perpetual and forms a spherical boundary that appears to us on earth as a huge ball of fire. The fireball gives off tremendous amounts of energy in the form of light and heat, which are given off in perpetuity (forever).

2. THE SUN CREATES ELEMENTS

From the limited conclusions of current scientific observations, the sun is made up of 70% hydrogen and 28% helium. Carbon, nitrogen, and oxygen make up about 1.5%, and the other 0.5% is made up of small amounts of other elements such as neon, iron, silicon, magnesium, and sulfur. These conclusions have led scientists to make assumptions about the sun that are not **real truth**.

The sun is NOT *made up* of these elements, it *creates* them! If you ask a scientist what created the nuclear reaction that created the sun, their responsive theories would differ, because they haven't yet figured out what space (dark matter) consists of, or better, which elements, if any, exist in the space between planets, solar systems, and galaxies.

3. THE SPHERE IS THE UNIVERSAL SHAPE OF ALL MATTER

When a group of molecules consisting of two (2) hydrogen atoms bound to one (1) oxygen atom (H_2O, water) are released into an environment of dark matter (space), it forms into a sphere or ball much like the shape of the sun. Yet, when the same combination of elements are introduced into the environment of our planet Earth, they do not form a sphere or a circle, but instead spread out indiscriminately, into what we observe as clouds, rain, rivers, lakes, and oceans.

All elements, when they occur in sufficient mass in the environment of dark matter (space), react according to one Universal law: they always form into a sphere, as evidenced by the sun, its major planets and their moons, and the spherical orbits in which these celestial bodies move. Nowhere in the open space of the Universe, where matter is massed together, will a rectangle or any other shape exist, or any other motion take place that does not reflect the form of a sphere. The perfection of the sphere as a *circle* or its imperfection as an *elliptical* shape (oval) depends on the forces affecting it. For this reason, some comets, for example, seem to have an *elliptical* orbit.

The round form of a sphere is caused by the *symmetrical* forces that are generated by the positive and negative charged particles that make up all matter. When these forces are allowed to act independently in space, without being influenced by another form of energy, they will always exist in a spherical form. In addition, all asteroids, moons, planets, solar systems and galaxies circumvent or rotate around a given point and form circles or rings called orbits. These orbits also result from the symmetrical forces caused by the environment of the dark matter throughout the Universe.

However, as other elements are created from the dark matter of space to form other planets, solar systems, and galaxies, other energy forces are subsequently created that can affect the shape of perfect spheres, which cause them to lose their perfection. The earth, for example, is round, but it is not a perfect sphere, because of the gravitational/magnetic forces of the sun and the other celestial bodies that are near it.

4. DARK MATTER (SPACE) CONTAINS THE ELEMENTARY PARTS OF ALL MATTER

We have already introduced the **real truth** that space consists of the subatomic particles that make up all matter. In addition, we have limited our description of these particles to being only protons, neutrons, and electrons, although science continues to create exotic new ideas and concepts of quarks, strings, and many other notions. Nevertheless, it is *only* important to understand that the basic components of all matter are what make up the vastness of space, or dark matter.

(We must always keep in mind that scientific classifications, theories, laws, and hypotheses are simply the manner in which primitive, *imperfect* scientists communicate with each other. Scientists make their observations, then conclusions, and then create names and titles for what they *believe* they have discovered. The subatomic particles called protons, neutrons, and electrons are some of these names, as well as even the term “subatomic.” **Real truth** has nothing to do with these terms. Advanced human beings do not use these terms. These terms are as *imperfect* as the minds that created them. Nevertheless, in order to come to some reasonable understanding of the **real truth** of how things actually work, we must use the words and terms that are most familiar to us.)

5. THE SUN GETS ITS ENERGY FROM DARK MATTER

As mentioned before, the sun was created from the environment of space by the command of an advanced human who has the power and knowledge to manipulate and control dark matter. As the sun uses the protons, neutrons, and electrons of space to create the hydrogen, helium, carbon, nitrogen, oxygen, neon, iron, silicon, magnesium, sulfur, and other elements that produce its energy, the next logical questions could be: Isn't the sun going to burn out? Or does the sun continually create energy?

Erroneous scientific speculation assumes that the sun will eventually burn out by running out of energy. Science is again wrong. How can the sun burn out when it is continually taking in the protons, neutrons, and electrons from a vast and endless space and transforming them into elements which create the energy that it produces?

The *reality* of the sun is that it is an advanced nuclear reactor that absorbs the surrounding space and creates elements. It will never cease to exist or do what it was "programmed" to do as long as the dark matter of space exists. And there is no end to the dark matter of space.

The sun is a perfectly balanced and pressurized sphere that endlessly regulates itself. When its energy levels decrease, the pressure of the sun's atmosphere also decreases, allowing the surrounding subatomic elements to enter from the higher pressure state of open space. In that unique sense, the Sun effectively "breathes." Its intake is dark matter and its exhaled breath is perpetual light and warmth.

As the earth and its environs use the energy created by the Sun, the byproducts of this exchange of energy are the basic components of matter that emit back into space, where they will eventually again be used by the Sun. These basic components (protons, neutrons, and electrons) cannot be destroyed, but are continually recycled throughout the Universe, as they perform the purpose for which they are used in the process of creation. Keep in mind that by themselves, these basic components cannot create energy. "Energy" is the byproduct of their interaction with each other.

6. SOLAR SYSTEM PLANNED ACCORDING TO OUR NEEDS

The plans for our solar system, its size, dimensions, and number of planets, moons, asteroids, etc., were made after the batch of newly created human beings, to which we belong, was properly *foundationalized* and ready for our *own* part of the Universe. This "part" is known as *our* solar system. The exact number of people who are going to inhabit each solar system, as well as the size of each planet on which they will eventually live forever, determine the size and power of its sun.

Each planet is created and perfectly balanced to move in a pre-designed orbital path around the sun. Moons are also precisely positioned as necessary to keep each planet where it should be. Properly placed asteroid belts aid in the stabilization of each planet's composition. The location and composition of all planets and their moons are preplanned when the sun, which is also preplanned, is designed for each particular solar system.

This process is no different (although much more highly advanced) than an architect and engineer considering the needs of a client then drawing up the plans needed to meet these needs. The plans are then given to a contractor, who proceeds to build whatever the plans entail.

7. GRAVITY AND MAGNETISM ARE THE SAME THING

To understand the **real truth** about how our solar system works, we need to combine the concepts of gravity and magnetism. In other words, there is no difference. Both forces are caused by the subatomic particles that make up matter reacting to each other and creating an energy force. Again, (quoting from above) by themselves, the basic components of matter *cannot* create energy. "Energy" is the byproduct of their interaction with each other.

To keep it as simple as we can, we are going to use *positive* and *negative* forces to explain *reality*. However, it should *again* be noted that using these terms is for the sake of understanding, and does not necessarily reflect the exact cause and effect of how things work in the Universe. But to aid in facilitating the reader's comprehension, these recognizable terms will work just fine.

8. POWERFUL INVISIBLE ENERGY FORCES KEEP THE PLANETS ALIGNED

A magnet has two poles, one positive and one negative. If we attempt to touch two positive or two negative poles together, an invisible energy force does not allow it, except with the application of considerable force (energy). Yet, a positive and a negative pole are attracted to each other with the same force. The easiest way to understand our solar system is to view all matter found therein as emitting certain levels of positive and negative energy, which either keeps substances together (positive-negative) or keeps them apart (positive-positive or negative-negative).

The sun can be viewed as the most powerful positive energy force in our solar system. Each planet can also be viewed as distinct positive energy forces, each with differing levels. To illustrate, let's call the positive level of Mercury (1), Venus (2), Earth (3), Mars (4), Jupiter (5), Saturn (6), Uranus (7), Neptune (8), and Pluto (9), with Mercury having the lowest positive energy level among the planets and Pluto the greatest.

Because Mercury's positive energy level is only (1), it is not repelled as far away from the sun as Pluto, whose positive energy level is much greater. If we were to change Pluto's energy level to a (1), then it would be found at the exact same distance from the sun as Mercury. The stronger the positive energy emitted, the further away the object is going to stay from another positive force. As long as the planets' positive levels remain unchanged, they will never get any closer to the sun than they presently are.

9. MOONS HELP KEEP THE SOLAR SYSTEM BALANCED

The moons of the planets help regulate and balance each of their energy levels, and ensure that each planet maintains its position and does what it was intended to do when the solar system was planned. The closest planet to the sun that has a moon is the Earth. Because of the Earth's moon and the subsequent changes required to allow life to exist on Earth (and thus, the unique energy forces that the Earth emits), the rotation of Venus is affected.

10. PLANETARY ROTATION AFFECTED BY OTHER PLANETS

Venus rotates backwards in relation to the general rotation of the Earth because it has not yet been transformed into a planet that allows the existence of living organisms. Living organisms need properly regulated energy from the sun to produce the products and byproducts associated with *life*. When a planet is changed to support life (by advanced humans who know what they are doing), the energy forces it emits are altered to accommodate that change. When Venus is transformed into a life-bearing planet, it will emit the same energy forces as the Earth, and will be the exact same distance from the sun that the Earth is. The two planets will never collide, however, because their orbital paths around the sun will be varied and regulated appropriately (as will the rest of the planets also).

As previously mentioned, any form of matter can be affected by other forms of matter in close proximity. Venus is situated between a planet that supports life (Earth) and one that does not (Mercury). If it were situated between two planets that supported life, it would rotate in the same direction as all life-supporting planets do. If it were situated between two planets that did not support life, its rotation would be the same as those planets.

For example, if we were to move Venus closer to the sun than Mercury, then both Mercury's and Venus' rotation would reverse, and Mercury would rotate backwards instead. Or if we placed Venus in between two other planets that do not support life, its rotation would reflect the rotation of those neighboring planets. This is the reason why all the planets in our solar system rotate on their axis in the same direction *except* for Venus. Venus is the only one situated between two planets of profoundly different charged forces.

One might ask why Earth (a life-bearing planet) rotates like every other *non*-life-bearing planet in the solar system, except for Venus. Earth is located between Mars and Venus, both non-life-bearing planets. When the solar system was first created, Venus rotated like all the other planets. The change in direction did not occur until Earth's energy levels were changed by advanced humans who intended for Earth to accommodate life. Upon changing the energy forces emitting from Earth, Venus' rotation was affected.

The planet Uranus appears to be rotating differently than the other planets. This is, however, just an optical illusion because of the way Uranus is situated between Saturn and Neptune.

Some might argue that Mars, like Venus, is located between a life-bearing planet (Earth) and one that does not support life (Jupiter); so why isn't Mars' rotation affected in the same way Venus' is? The simple answer: Because there is no asteroid belt between Venus and Mercury, as there *is* between Mars and Jupiter.

11. ASTEROID BELTS IMPACT THE PLANETS

Asteroid belts were put into place to regulate the positive and negative forces and to aid in the regulation of the composition of the planets. There are two main asteroid belts in our solar system—one that separates the four inner, solid planets from the four outer, gaseous planets, and another (called Kuiper) that separates outermost **solid** Pluto from the *gaseous* planets. Therefore, this is how our solar system is arranged:

Sun, Mercury, Venus, Earth, Mars, ASTEROID BELT,
Jupiter, *Saturn Uranus*, *Neptune*, ASTEROID BELT,
Pluto

If the asteroid belts were removed, the gaseous planets situated between them would become solid in composition. The asteroids create an energy field, which keeps the elements that make up the gaseous planets from becoming solid like those situated *outside* of the asteroid belts.

12. DISTANCE INFLUENCES PLANETARY MAKEUP

The gaseous planets (*Jupiter, Saturn, Uranus,* and *Neptune*) and the disputed Pluto do not have a constant and equal distance between them as do the solid planets (Mercury, Venus, Earth, and Mars).

As the solid planets orbit around the sun, the point at which each comes closest to the sun is separated by *equal* distances (of about 30 million miles): Mercury is about 30 million miles from the sun; Venus is about 60 million, Earth about 90 million, and Mars about 120 million miles from the sun. On the other hand, the gaseous planets vary widely in their distance when they come closest to the sun during their orbital journey: Jupiter about 460 million miles, Saturn about 840 million, Uranus about 1700 million, Neptune about 2700, and Pluto about 3600 million miles. The consistency of equal or unequal distances between each planet affects their energy forces and overall composition, or the way their *organized matter* reacts (solid or gas).

Matter comes in three basic forms that we can observe within the capacity of our human senses. These are: *gas*, *liquid*, and *solid*. The only difference between the three is the energy levels that influence the basic structure of the subatomic particles that make up the matter. Using the same advanced technology by which the solar system was created, all of the planets in our solar system will one day be changed so that they can support life. Until this happens, the larger planets will remain gaseous while the smaller ones remain solid in nature. All of this was precisely planned and determined by the advanced human creators who were responsible for creating our solar system and maintaining its order and balance.

13. ADVANCED HUMANS CREATED EARTH

Although science might dispute the *new realities* presented in this book, its lack of approval will not negate the fact that they are *reality*. Science *cannot* explain *why* our earth is the lone planet in the solar system that can sustain life, when it has conceded that all the planets came from the same source. What made the earth what it is today? Why is it a completely different planet from all the rest? The simple answer: Advanced human beings knew what they were doing and ***why*** they were doing it.

14. THE EARTH IS BILLIONS OF YEARS OLD

The solar system was created in a matter of what we would consider as just a few moments. It took only a few moments for the cities of Hiroshima and Nagasaki to be completely changed by the *primitive* power of limited nuclear technology. Therefore, it shouldn't be difficult for one to *imagine* an advanced technology *creating* the solar system in about the same amount of time, or less.

However, the earth as we know it today took billions of years to form. As mentioned previously, with their advanced knowledge and powers, the creators *could* have formed the earth and its environs in just a few moments, as they did the solar system. They could have formed it *perfectly* without any flaws by patterning it after the blueprint of the *perfect world* on which they live. They could have created each planet precisely as needed to house the different wants and desires of happiness of the batch of newly created human beings destined to become the eternal inhabitants of this solar system. They could have, but they didn't. Why?

They did not, because they wanted *us* to find out what would happen if natural law was left to itself *without* human involvement. Earthquakes, volcanoes, hurricanes, and all other natural disasters are <u>not</u> part of a human-controlled *perfect world*. They are the result of the forces of nature left to do what they would do if no outside intervention is used to control them.

As we advance in our current world in understanding these natural phenomena, we will begin to learn how to predict them. However, without the superior knowledge and technology of advanced humans, who have been around a lot longer than we have, the forces of nature will continue to create disasters beyond our control. On the other hand, in a *perfect*, *advanced world*, all aspects of nature are precisely controlled to fully benefit the human race.

15. WE NEEDED TO SEE THE EARTH DEVELOP IMPERFECTLY

As we were being foundationalized in a *perfect* world, we were guaranteed the right to exercise our own free will. One of the biggest dilemmas we were faced with at this time was the fact that we were *still restricted* in the use of our individual free will according to the boundaries set by the laws and order of the Universe, which have always existed. We came to understand that we were *not* completely free to do whatever, whenever we wanted.

There needed to be some controls and rules that would ensure that the order of the Universe would never be disrupted or changed. Still, for free-willed human beings who have the power to act as they wish for the sole benefit of themselves, this was a lesson that needed to be learned with patience. No one likes to be told what they can and cannot do.

It was necessary for us to experience a world and observe how its life forms (including us, as human beings) develop *imperfectly*. This helps us to understand the importance of advanced and perfect government control (as explained in chapter 8). Our experience in witnessing and participating in an *imperfect* environment would ensure our acceptance of this control and intervention in our lives, realizing it is the proper government to which we should subject our free will. We needed to be guaranteed the purpose for which we were created (happiness). We needed to experience for ourselves that those restrictions on our free agency are necessary, and that they will only lead to our individual happiness.

16. AN IMPERFECT WORLD PROVIDES VITAL EXPERIENCE

An *imperfect* world is one that provides the exact opposite of what a *perfect* world provides. Instead of absolute equality in all things, there must be inequality. Instead of a timeless existence without quantitative measures and values, there must be death and values and measures placed on all things. Rather than complete control of all aspects of our environment, nature must be initiated, and then left to itself to act on its own.

In other words, we needed to experience a world that would affect our happiness and expose us to heartache, pain, misery, depression, fear, stress, death, and everything else that contradicts the perfect human reality. We needed to experience an opposition in all things.

17. BACTERIA AND VIRUSES AID AN IMPERFECT ENVIRONMENT

One of the vehicles by which advanced creators control the environment of an *imperfect* world is through the unseen world of bacteria and viruses. Bacteria and viruses are programmed life forms that keep an *imperfect* world ("our world") *imperfect.*

The atmosphere and environment of *our world* were created so that bacteria and viruses could live and thrive. Once they were placed upon our world, plants were then introduced that created an environment favorable to higher life forms, i.e., animals. All plants are patterned after similar plants found in perfect human worlds. No life form can exist without first being created and introduced into its environment by the *highest* life form that exists in the Universe—advanced human beings.

Because advanced human creators were setting up *our world* to be *imperfect*, they created all types of *imperfect* plants from the environment created by bacteria, so that the plants could provide life for *imperfect* animals. The *imperfect* animals would then distinguish themselves unequally as the strongest to the weakest, thus establishing the hierarchy of a "food chain" that would add to the *imperfection* of our world.

18. NOTHING EXISTS WITHOUT INTERVENTION

Nothing can exist without the will of a human being—ABSOLUTELY NOTHING! It takes energy to produce the bonds that create any and all matter. These bonds *have always been* and *will always be* produced by the energy of a human being taking some sort of action. These actions establish energy bonds that start a perpetual event, which creates matter and then allows it to fulfill the purpose for its creation.

The purpose of this creation has been and always will be determined by human beings—the greatest and most significant form of life in the Universe. Again, to reiterate, the necessary energy for matter to exist ultimately comes from the actions of advanced humans who are responsible for the creation, perpetuation, and final end (happiness) of the human race. Therefore, although we needed to experience an *imperfect* world *without the intervention and control of advanced humans*, our world still needed to be created as an *imperfect* one *by them*.

19. NATURAL IMPERFECTIONS ARE NOT OUR FAULT; SOCIAL ONES ARE

Our creators are responsible for all the "opposition to happiness" that we find in our world, but ONLY the opposition (wrong) found in the natural environment. WE ALONE ARE RESPONSIBLE FOR EVERYTHING ELSE THAT IS WRONG IN OUR HUMAN WORLD. We cannot be blamed for the hunger of a stronger predator wanting to kill us for food. Nonetheless, WE ARE responsible for killing each other for no reason other than to protect and perpetuate our own inequality.

Our *imperfect* natural world can be blamed on our creators, but our individual problems can only be blamed on ourselves. However, it was always our creators' intention to have us live in an *imperfect* world. In an *imperfect* world we would be compelled to act *imperfectly* in order to recognize and appreciate the difference in how we feel when we act properly compared to when we act improperly. In *essence* (pun intended), our creators are partly to blame for our *imperfections*. Without taking away our *free will*, they gave us no *real* choice but to partake of life in an *imperfect world*, so that we would know that everything has its opposite.

Knowing that our creators are directly responsible for *setting us up to fail* in our world, makes failure in this *imperfect* world seem much less difficult to accept. *Failure* in an *imperfect* world is *success* for us as *perfect human beings*, who will one day learn to appreciate *who we are* and *why we exist* because of our failure as *imperfect humans*. The *imperfect world* that our creators created for us is a *perfect world* for the purposes of our second stage of human development.

20. THE EARTH'S LAND MASSES WERE ONCE JOINED

Simply put, our creators formed the plants on our world to support the environment so that the animals could live. This, in turn, helped the plants to propagate without overrunning the earth. To facilitate these events, in the beginning, the land of the earth was created in one great mass to aid in the propagation of all forms of life.

It would be very hard for a flower to be wind-pollinated across the huge distances of vast open ocean water. Likewise, the animals created to help the plants could not swim across the ocean. Many of these insects (animals) are still live today, and it is quite obvious that no species of insect can, on its own, traverse these great bodies of water.

21. OUR WORLD DOES NOT SUPPORT INDIVIDUALITY

Each plant is specifically designed to do something to keep perfect balance upon this earth *without* the intervention of continual human monitoring. The plants take the energy of the sun and replenish the atmosphere of this world, and also provide sustenance for the animals, which depend on the plants for survival.

The *imperfect* natural world does not allow an individual species of any kind to survive perpetually on its own for its own sake. Everything exists because or for the sake of something else. This interdependence creates a perfectly balanced symbiotic relationship that works for the benefit of all species as one. The only thing that has ever disrupted this *natural balance* is the free will of the human species and its desire for individuality.

The *imperfect* natural world does not provide an environment for the establishment of individual desires and experiences that serve just one being; that's what a *perfect* world is for. In an *imperfect* world, everything is dependent on everything else. Take away one thing and it will cause a ripple effect that will tip the natural balance that keeps things working in their proper order. In an *imperfect* world there is no respect for individuality, not in plants or in animals. One will eat the other to survive.

Therefore, it can be stated that the *imperfect* world is all about *natural selection* and the concept of the *survival of the fittest*. The problem, however, lies in the inability of plants and animals to thrive in their *natural state* when they are confronted with *higher forms of life* that are aware of their individual existence and will do anything to protect that **individual existence**. Animals do not ponder or concern themselves about survival or individuality. They simply do what they do—eat or be eaten.

As one of the species placed upon this earth, we humans are forced to work (contrary to the nature of our free will) in order to provide the things that we need to survive. Because of our intrinsic need to protect our individuality, we subdue all other forms of nature to fulfill our needs. This is how we "work"! We sense the need for individual protectionism and realize that our world's natural resources are limited. Therefore, we work harder than any other species and are constantly competing with them for what we need to survive, not only physically, but also emotionally, as individuals apart from the whole of nature.

In contrast, a *perfect* world allows and supports human individuality and provides all things necessary for our existence without the need to work for them. There are unlimited resources on the perfect world, thus eliminating any form of competition to get the things that are necessary for our physical and emotional survival.

22. OUR NATURAL WORLD DOES NOT MAKE SENSE

Creating something that will ultimately end up being destroyed doesn't make much sense. Watching a gentle and innocent baby antelope being devoured by a hungry pride of lions *doesn't make much sense* to human reason. Witnessing the devastation of a beautiful tree by the strong trunk of an elephant *doesn't make much sense.* Knowing that some insects have a short life span of a few days or even hours, and that some are even eaten the moment they're born, *doesn't make much sense.*

The *imperfect* world **doesn't make much sense**. Animals and plants, however, don't have "sense"; therefore, they don't care. We do! We have a sense of compassion that compels us to protect plants and animals and allow them to grow and prosper in their own individual environments. (Yet, some humans have been eaten by the very animals they were trying to protect.) This compassion comes from our human *essence* and the *humanity* that was *foundationalized* in us in our primordial, perfect world.

No matter how much we try to use our "sense" to understand the natural world, we will not make *sense* of it. And if we try to make our *imperfect* world a perfect one, by allowing *imperfect* creations of both plants and animals to exist, we will fail miserably. This would be like a compassionate paleontologist bringing back the meat-eating dinosaurs, who would not "sense" that their creators were compassionate, but would instead *sense* that they were lunch! Or, in the same token, it would be like a compassionate botanist wanting to protect noxious weeds!

The creation of this world has only one purpose that makes *sense*: it was created to help us appreciate the perfect world and the perfect plants and animals that exist there (which do not eat us or irritate us in any way, but rather bring us joy).

23. IMPERFECT HUMANS CREATE MORE IMPERFECTION

If our current program of science does not accept that the

purpose of this earth is to allow us to experience *imperfection* (which it does not), then it will continually strive to learn how nature works, how organisms function, and how it is all intertwined with human beings. In fact, with its learning and progression, science will always only produce more *imperfections*. Take, for example, genetically manipulated plants and animals, which science believes benefit humankind. No genetically manipulated apple can match the taste of one grown according to the established natural laws of the earth. In fact everything that *imperfect humans* create will *always* lead to some other type of *imperfection*, which will ultimately cause us more misery instead of more happiness.

This is not to say that we should not try. The purpose of this life is to experience the effects of the uncontrolled exercising of our free will. Go ahead, science! Create a Tyrannosaurus Rex and see what happens next! Not only will this gigantic meat-eater disrupt the already-confused natural balance of our current world, but there will also be those compassionate humans who will exercise their free will and attempt to protect the Tyrannosaurus (a respected form of life) and provide an environment in which it can exist with humans in a symbiotic relationship. And if these compassionate ones are not eaten by the very animal they are trying to protect, they will soon learn that there is not enough room on this planet for any life form that does not serve the purposes of happiness expected by a human being. Moreover, feeding an innocent cow to a T-Rex is certainly not an element of *perfect* humanity!

However, neither is killing a perfectly serene cow that keeps the wheat grass mowed in a field a show of our ***true*** *humanity*. We kill it and put its seared flesh between two pieces of the naturally matured and processed wheat grass that the cow was keeping in check (manipulated by *imperfect humans* into bread) and call it a hamburger! We would be much better off, and much more *humane*, eating wheatgrass like the cow!

24. PERFECT PLANTS AND ANIMALS EXIST FOR HUMANS

The *perfect* lion does not have fangs and claws to kill, rip apart, and devour another animal. Lions exist in a perfect world, but they have perfected bodies that allow them only to do what they were created to do: serve the needs of human beings. Perfect lions are like gigantic pets with big eyes and soft, strong backs upon which some people like to ride or snuggle up against. These lions have no need to eat, because they are created with a *lion's essence*, which is a perpetual energy factory that provides the energy a lion needs to fulfill the purpose for its creation. Thus, also are all *perfect* animals.

Perfect plants are the same. They exist only to serve the needs of human beings. They produce the *perfect* foods that advanced humans and newly created humans eat. However, only advanced humans appreciate the perfection of their taste and texture. Why? Because newly created humans have never tasted *imperfection*; thus, they cannot distinguish the difference. But they are given the opportunity in an imperfect world to make a comparison.

25. NATURE PROVIDES CHECKS AND BALANCES TO PROMOTE BALANCE

During the early developing stages of the earth, plant-eating animals were created to keep the plants in check or plants would have overgrown the earth. Flesh-eating animals were created to keep the plant-eaters and other flesh-eaters in check. And bacteria and viruses were created to keep them both in check.

The very first plants placed upon this earth created the atmosphere that supports all other forms of life. These "plants" were the algae and other less-advanced plants that did not need an "atmosphere" to exist. All they needed was the energy of the sun. The byproduct of their use of energy was the composition of our current atmosphere. Science knows very little of these primordial plant species. This is because once they fulfilled the purpose for their creation, they became extinct.

Once the atmosphere was in place, there was then a need for a large number of plants to get things going. Then enormous plant-eating dinosaurs were created that could consume large amounts of plants. Then, to eat the enormous plant eaters, enormous flesh-eating dinosaurs were created. The end of the plant-eating dinosaurs came when the flesh eaters ate them all.

26. THE DINOSAURS DIED OF NATURAL CAUSES

The end of the flesh-eating dinosaurs came when they couldn't catch the smaller and faster prey (such as crocodiles and alligators), so they ate each other or eventually died off from starvation. The idea that the dinosaur species magically disappeared or were instantly destroyed by some cataclysmic event thwarts the intelligence of beings with a "sense" that these theories leave too many unanswered questions to be considered *true reality*.

Science is said to be the study of the physical and natural world and phenomena, especially by using systematic observation and experimentation. If this is the case, then let's become "sensible" scientists and observe what happens in our present time when a particular species of animal becomes extinct. Do they simply disappear? Are they instantly destroyed by a meteorite? Is this what we have "systematically observed" taking place? No, it is not!

Extinction occurs from the destruction of natural habitat or by being eaten, such as by another species higher up the food chain, because a particular species does not have the ability to protect itself or its offspring. Extinction can also be caused by a bacterial or viral infection to the natural state of the species. So being the simple scientists that we are, and using systematic observation, we can conclude with great accuracy, as we have above, that the same thing happened to the dinosaurs.

27. THE THEORY OF EVOLUTION IS MISUNDERSTOOD

The second characteristic of science is experimentation. Yet it is through the experiments of modern bioengineers and hybrid breeders that we can debunk one of the greatest scientific errors of our time: **The Theory of Evolution**.

This theory generally proposes the following explanation of how all things upon this earth evolved to be what they are:

> In biology, evolution is the changes in the inherited traits of a population of organisms from one generation to the next. These changes are caused by a combination of three main processes: variation, reproduction, and selection. Genes that are passed on to an organism's offspring produce the inherited traits that are the basis of evolution. These traits vary within populations, with organisms showing heritable differences in their traits. When organisms reproduce, their offspring may have new or altered traits. These new traits arise in two main ways: either from mutations in genes, or from the transfer of genes between populations and between species. In species that reproduce sexually, new combinations of genes are also produced by genetic recombination, which can increase variation between organisms. Evolution occurs when these heritable differences become more common or rare in a population.
>
> (Wikipedia, the free encyclopedia. 2009 http://en.wikipedia.org/wiki/Evolution)

This is obviously *not* a scientific fact that was established by "systematic observation," because no one has been around long enough to actually *observe* these things taking place.

Some scientists might argue that science has *indeed* observed certain gene mutations and other elements of "evolution" of certain traits in species that have a short life span. What they do not realize, however, is that there are much more advanced scientists than they who are monitoring what these less-advanced scientists are doing.

Just as current scientists can modify the environment of the organisms, or the organism itself, used in their experiments, advanced scientists can modify *anything* they want to at *any time* they want. Nevertheless, through our limited perception of *systematic observation* (science), we cannot conclusively verify that evolution actually took place, because it happened over the course of millions of years.

However, we *can* "systematically observe" what scientists are doing today! Unfortunately for the proponents of the *Theory of Evolution* (because their theory is currently being disproven by their own science), we regularly observe the experimentation of their theory by other scientists who are continually creating *new* species of plants and animals; and it is taking them a few hours instead of millions of years! We can "systematically observe" scientists changing the inherited traits of a population of organisms from one generation to the next!

These changes are caused by the current technological advancements in bioengineering and hybrid breeding. We have observed how certain genes are isolated, manipulated, and passed on to an organism's offspring in order to produce the inherited traits, which are the basis of the error of evolution. We observe that these traits vary within populations with organisms showing heritable difference in their traits.

When bio- and genetic engineering take place, organisms reproduce and their offspring may have new or altered traits. These new traits arise because of the ability of scientists to use current technology to transfer genes between populations and between species.

In species that reproduce sexually, these technologies allow new combinations of genes that are also produced by genetic recombination, which can increase variation between organisms. Scientists and their technology can control when these heritable differences occur, so as to become more common or rare in a population, depending on the desire of the scientist.

28. ADVANCED HUMANS CONTROL THE BALANCE OF IMPERFECT WORLDS

Therefore, if current *primitive* scientists can use current technologies to create new species of flora and fauna virtually overnight, wouldn't it make "sense" that advanced human beings, thousands of years in the future, have the technology and ability to create new plant and animal species in an instant? This is exactly what takes place as those who monitor this *imperfect world* ensure that it remains *imperfect* for as long as is needed, in order for us to gain what is necessary from the experience.

We will continually discover new species of flora and fauna as the advanced humans who are responsible for our world continue to create them as needed. As explained previously, they monitor our world and the energy frequencies of every single life form and every single piece of matter. They have the ability, when needed, to introduce new species of plants or animals to serve the purpose of maintaining a perfect balance for an *imperfect world.*

We have discussed how they could have stopped the ancient scientist Democritus, for example, from understanding the basics of electricity—in order to keep him from discovering something that could destroy the world before the purpose for its creation was complete. In the same way, advanced human monitors of our planet also add bacteria, viruses, new insects, fish, plankton, or whatever else is necessary to keep the world in its *imperfect* state—everything for our own good.

It is important to understand that they will NEVER do anything to *really* harm us. The cause of most things that affect our happiness (disease, illness, etc.) is the exercising of our own free will. However, the bacteria and viruses, for example, which they have created and preprogrammed for our *imperfect world*, have the ability to mutate on their own and adjust to our ever-increasing need to invent antibiotics and anti-viral medications to fight them. If we were allowed to create the *perfect* medication for all of our ills, then the purpose for our *imperfect world* would be negated.

SUMMARY

The principal guideline by which those who oversee our world follow is the principal that they do not intervene into our lives upon the planet we call Earth, *except* to ensure that the purpose for our existence is fulfilled. The purpose of a *perfect* world is perpetual life and happiness for individual beings who are aware of themselves and their surroundings and use their environment to enjoy their individuality. In contrast, the purpose of an *imperfect* world is to allow death and the destruction of one individual entity so that another can continue to live and prosper.

Perfection leads to happiness. Imperfection leads to misery. And the greatest situation ever implemented to help us learn the difference between the two was the creation of our *imperfect world* placed in our own solar system.

The Human Body

CHAPTER ELEVEN

Take the human body alone—the chances that all the functions of an individual would just happen is a statistical monstrosity.

—George H. Gallup

1. PERFECT BODIES EXIST FOR THE PURPOSE OF PROVIDING US WITH JOY

To better understand the type of *imperfect* body we currently have on this earth, we need to consider the type of body that all advanced humans have throughout the Universe. They have a *perfect* body, the type of body that any of us would desire. If we considered which parts and functions of our body make us happy and which ones do not, we could *imagine* what a perfect body might be like.

The *perfect* physical body exists to ensure that its functions and attributes aid in the ultimate experience for the being that is utilizing it. More simply, a perfected human body exists to bring the most quintessential (ultimate) sense of joy possible to a human being—there is no other purpose. Because there is no other reason for human existence except to experience joy, it would make sense to only have body functions that served the purpose for which the body exists in the first place. Even with the primitive limited technology available to us currently, an individual can make the choice to change the physical body in a way that provides a more fulfilling sense of personal contentment. So, one can imagine what can be done by advanced human beings to the bodies they possess. Every human being in the Universe will end up with the type of body that provides the individual with the ultimate experience of human existence.

The purpose for our *imperfect* bodies, on the other hand, is to provide us with the *opposite* experience from that which we would receive from a perfect body. Experiencing an *imperfect* body helps us appreciate the **perfect** human body that each of us will possess forever.

2. OUR ESSENCE CREATES THE ENERGY NEEDED FOR THE PERFECT BODY

We have discussed how the human *essence* provides perpetual and everlasting energy to the perfect body. But it has not been explained *how* this *essence* creates the energy needed to support all of the body's functions.

Does the *essence* burn out over time? Based on the *Second Law of Thermodynamics*, upon which current science establishes many of its theories and conclusions concerning the entropy of all matter, it must! Regardless of what science proposes, however, our *essence* will never lose its ability to create and provide energy for the perfected body. To understand this concept, which upon first consideration appears to oppose the accepted *Laws of Thermodynamics*, let's take a look at other laws proposed by scientific "systematic observation" that *true reality* seems to contradict.

3. SCIENCE OPPOSES THE FUNCTION OF AN ESSENCE

The *First Law of Thermodynamics* basically proposes that any matter that produces energy can store or hold its own energy, and that this internal energy is conserved. The concept of "heat" (relating to the term "thermo") is a process by which energy is added to a system of composed matter from an outside source, or energy is lost to its surrounding environment.

The *Law* also stipulates that energy can be lost by the system (our body in this case) when it acts upon its surroundings, or conversely, it gains energy as a result of its surroundings acting upon it. For example, when it is cold outside, our bodies react to the cold environment by expending energy to keep us warm (this is how a "system" loses energy). When we eat something from our environment, we are providing our "system" with energy (this is how a "system" gains energy).

This *First Law* leads to the *Law of Conservation*. This law states that energy cannot be destroyed, but is consistently conserved throughout the Universe in the exchanges from one source of energy to another; thus, the total amount of energy in an isolated system (i.e., the body or the *essence*) remains constant. The *Law of Conservation* states, therefore, that the only thing that can happen with energy in an isolated system is that it can change form.

All of these so-called "laws" mandate that perpetual energy produced by any system of matter can only work **if** it delivers no energy to its surroundings, or if it does not expend more energy than is put into it. Because our *essence* does indeed expend energy to our body and then replaces the spent energy by creating the energy it needs for itself, its function seems to oppose all the known laws of science.

4. UNDERSTANDING DARK MATTER DISPELS SCIENCE-BASED "TRUTHS"

Based on these current scientific "laws," the **reality** presented for the first time in this book *could not be true*. Current scientific laws demand that, in time, the Universe will end just as it began. Therefore, science stipulates, or at least implies, that human beings are not entities of an eternal nature, but are just a small part of a Universe that is dying. Scientists come to this conclusion by observing the *imperfect nature* of not only our human body but also our environment. From everything we know about our experience on this earth, it seems that everything around us is slowly dying, including ourselves. These scientific conclusions are made because of science's inability to *observe* and accept the existence of an *essence*.

However, even as we are forced to accept the *reality* of death (the end of our existence), the very brain that postulates our eventual ending fights the inevitable, and creates a hope that it might not be ***true reality***. Fortunately, the **real truth** verifies and proves that the eternal nature of humanity is indeed **true**! The piece of the puzzle that keeps the conclusions made by scientific theories just "theories," instead of ***true reality***, is science's inability to completely understand dark matter (the *space* that makes up the Universe where there appears to be no matter), as explained previously.

If science wants to speculate that a "Big Bang" formed our Universe, then it must reconcile itself, according to the *Laws* that it has established, to conclude that one day there will be nothing in the Universe except for "space." What science cannot explain is exactly *what* acted upon the environment of the Universe to expend its energy to create the big bang. Accepting the Big Bang theory, that enormous amounts of energy were responsible for the formation of the Universe, then it follows that this energy must be in a state of entropy continually, meaning that the Universe itself is dying.

Was the "big bang," therefore, the *last* breath of a *dying* Universe that somehow created itself again? Again, scientific conclusions lead to irresponsible speculations (guesses) that only fit into the parameters of their own accepted conclusions (the laws of science). In almost every case throughout history, as the human race has advanced into the future, scientific *conclusions* have been changed, rejected, or proven to be inaccurate. (Consider again that science once accepted as fact that the earth was flat and that the earth was the center of the solar system.)

Building upon scientific *reason*ing and conclusions, **real truth** will show how "space" actually supports and allows our Universe to function as it does and allows it and the human beings who control it to exist forever.

5. DARK MATTER PROVIDES EVERYTHING NEEDED TO PRODUCE ENERGY

As explained previously, the sun is the factory that takes the substance of dark matter (space) and transforms it into energy. To accommodate scientific terms, it can be said, in the case of the sun, that the infinite dark matter of our Universe is *potential energy* that is turned into *kinetic energy*.

But again, dark matter *does not* contain any *actual* energy. It contains everything *needed* to produce energy, as has been stated; i.e., the protons, neutrons, and electrons that make up all things. Acting alone, a proton, neutron, or electron can do nothing. Yet acting together, they produce the necessary energy levels that make up all matter.

When the sun draws on the infinite environment of space to create its perpetual energy, it is acting in accordance with some of the accepted aspects of the *Laws of Thermodynamics*. "Dark matter" is brought into the sun in order to balance the energy that goes out.

6. OUR ESSENCE CREATES PERPETUAL ENERGY

The conclusions made thus far should help the reader understand the exact way that an *essence* is able to provide a perfected body with all the energy that it will ever need to function properly. An *essence* uses the same perpetual mechanics as the sun. It is a perpetual factory that takes *potential energy* from its surrounding environment and turns it into the *kinetic energy* that our sensory systems require to provide us with joy.

Currently, our *imperfect* brain creates energy as electromagnetic impulses whenever we think or act. It emits these pulses through our skull and scalp, which then take off into "space." The *perfect body*, on the other hand, allows the *essence* to *draw in* the components of the *potential energy* found in any surrounding environment and then transform them into *kinetic*, useable energy. If we are underwater, for example, the *perfect* body allows the two hydrogen atoms bonded to the one oxygen atom in the water molecule to permeate our skull and be transformed by our *essence* into the energy that our muscles need in order to swim at leisure on top of or underwater as long as we so desire.

If we find ourselves with a *perfect* body anywhere in the Universe, our *perfect human essence* has the ability to utilize <u>any</u> form of energy from <u>any</u> source of matter found in <u>any</u> environment.

It can utilize the subatomic particles of space and transform them into the energy that ensures that our body can fulfill the purpose of its creation and bring us joy! Although an *imperfect* body would not survive the most hostile environs of space, a perfect body survives just fine! Again, it can survive because the *essence* can utilize <u>any</u> form of matter from its surroundings in <u>any</u> environment and create the energy the body needs in order to function perfectly.

As explained previously, there are some differences between advanced *perfected* bodies depending on the *humanity type* chosen by the individual. Lunarian and Stellarian minds cannot manipulate matter at will. Their *essence*, however, is made of the same matter as the *essences* of all human beings, even Solarians. However, Solarians have *a type* of body that can use the full power of the *essence* at will. Lunarian and Stellarian bodies cannot utilize the full power of the *essence*. They cannot control the power of the *essence*. Their *essence* works with their body similarly to how the heart muscle works with the *imperfect* body. Without any thought or will of our own, our hearts keep our *imperfect* bodies supplied with energy.

No human *essence* in an *imperfect* body can, by using free will or the energy of thought, control the functions of the heart. The heart beats to keep the body alive whether its owner likes it or not. Similarly, the Lunarian and Stellarian body is kept alive and functioning by the power of the *essence*. Solarians, on the other hand, though their body is also kept alive by the *essence*, have the ability to utilize its power to manipulate the subatomic makeup of all matter.

The primary differences between advanced human body types have *only* to do with the body itself, not the *essence*. All human *essences* are of the same composition of element. What makes each *essence* different is not its makeup, but what is recorded in it. The experiences differ in each *essence* according to the free will of the individual whose physical body's sensory receptors created each experience. Although the experiences in each *essence* vary, each *essence* has the exact same potential of power. However, the potential of each experience is restricted or limited by the physical body in which the individual's *essence* is placed.

7. THE PERFECT BODY RECYCLES THE SUBATOMIC PARTICLES OF MATTER

When an *imperfect* body takes in energy from its environment, in the form of food for example, it uses what it needs and then expels the rest through excrement. To use what it needs, the *imperfect* body takes the matter and breaks it down into *other* forms of matter, which byproducts are sent back into the environment, such as in the form of perspiration and exhaled breath. So what is the byproduct of the *essence*, if any? If one takes in the subatomic particles from the environment, forms them into matter that produces energy, and then uses that energy, what is left over? If the subatomic particles of matter cannot be destroyed, then what happens to them after the *essence* gets done with them?

As mentioned earlier, our *essence* creates and gives off the energy that is needed by a *perfect* human body in order to function. Energy is always some kind of matter acting upon other matter, or being acted upon by other matter. When matter interacts, it creates a *reaction* of some kind. In our nose, we call the reaction a "smell"; in our eyes, "sight"; on our skin, "touch"; in our mouth, "taste"; in our ears, "sound"; and in our brains, "thought." The "reactions" themselves do not destroy or break down element. If an entity of matter (us) took in elements and didn't use them up, then the elements would remain in the isolated environment of our body and make us bigger and bigger and bigger. That is not the case in ***true reality***. Instead, this is what happens:

In a *perfect* body, our *essence* has the power to take apart the elements of our environment and change the protons, neutrons, and electrons into the elements that can create a reaction with our body's sensory systems. Once the action is complete, our *essence* then breaks down the element it created back into subatomic particles, which are *recycled* by our *essence* and used again. Therefore, as long as no energy escapes the body, the *essence would never need anything from its environment to provide the body with the energy it requires to function.*

As mentioned, the difference between advanced humans and their individual abilities is their body type, based on what *humanity type* they have chosen for themselves. Lunarians and Stellarians do not need bodies that would require their *essence* to do much more than take care of the needs of the Lunarian and Stellarian body. Therefore, these body types do not import a great amount of subatomic particles from their environment. All the energy they need is provided for their body by the power of the *essence*, which can recycle its own energy to maintain itself. Solarians, on the other hand, emit great amounts of energy from their *essence*, as they give commands to other matter. This, in return, requires a great amount from their environment.

8. THE ENERGY FROM NEW EXPERIENCES ARE STORED IN THE ESSENCE FOREVER

In the *perfect* body, the production and use of energy by the *essence*, especially in the Lunarian and Stellarian type bodies, is contained and recycled in the performance of the sensory systems of the body, but not in the formation of a *new experience*. In other words, when an advanced human is hearing, seeing, smelling, tasting, or touching something, the *essence* provides all the necessary energy to perform these functions. However, there is an expenditure of energy that cannot be *recycled*. This is the energy produced by a "thought."

"Thinking" is generally not accepted as part of our senses in either type of body (*perfect* or *imperfect*), although **real truth** categorizes it as such. It is the function that analyzes the energies that our senses produce and organizes them into experiences, which are then stored in the *essence as memories*. In a *perfect* body, for example, if we see and smell a flower, our *essence* provides the energy needed for the eyes to see and the nose to smell it. Once these two sensory receptor systems have taken energy from the *essence* to perform the action of seeing and smelling, the energy produced from these actions is given back to the *essence* in the form of a *new* experience. The *new* experience, however, will stay in the *essence* forever and will not be recycled by the *essence* for other experiences. This is when the *essence* needs to draw in more energy from outside of the body. This process agrees with the scientific law that matter cannot be created or destroyed. Neither our *imperfect* nor our *perfect* body destroys matter.

9. THE ESSENCE CREATES ONLY ONE TYPE OF ENERGY FOR THE NEEDS OF THE PERFECT BODY

Our *imperfect* body changes matter from food into basic sugars, for example, which the body can then utilize to create energy. This process *needs* energy to perform the functions of the *imperfect* body of biting, chewing, swallowing, digestion, and etc.

In a *perfect* body, the *essence* eliminates secondary processes that require energy and instead **creates** the matter that the *perfect* body's sensory organs can directly utilize. *Perfect* sensory organs do not "use up" any matter, but are acted upon by the matter. For example, when a person with a *perfect* body feels wind on their face, the matter that makes up the wind is not destroyed or changed in any way, but it does react with the sensory receptors of touch to give the person a sensation of feeling wind. Again, the only energy that is spent is *when* the *experience of feeling the wind*, if it is a *new* experience, is recorded in the *essence*. This energy alone then needs to be replenished.

Because the *perfect* body has only the nervous system as a delivery process connected to the sensory receptors, only one type of matter needs to be produced for the *perfected* senses to create sensation. The same matter that interacts with the *perfected* body's sensory organs also gives the cells of its muscles, tissues, and bones the stimulation they need to continue to do what they were created to do. This is why a *perfect* body does not get tired or need sleep.

Again, once the *essence* takes the basic components of matter from the surrounding environment and creates the energy that the body needs, it is passed through the nervous system to the cells of the *perfect* body. Once it interacts with the cells, the matter is again passed back to the *essence* to be broken back down into the basic components, which are then recycled or added to the *essence* as a new experience. Except in a Solarian body, which uses great amounts of energy in creation and in doing what Solarians do, energy does not leave the *perfect* body and its essence.

When we use the muscles of a *perfect* body, for example, energy is not "used up." The cells of the muscles are in their *perfect state* and will remain so forever. However, for a muscle cell to cause the bicep to contract, for example, it needs the stimulation from the energy that the *essence* creates.

10. THE PERFECT BODY SURVIVES IN ANY ENVIRONMENT

Let's assume that lead is an element that cannot be easily penetrated by most other elements. For the sake of this example, let's further assume that NO ELEMENTS can pass through it. If we make a lead box that no other elements can enter into or escape from and place a person with an *imperfect* body in it, that person would eventually die. This would happen because an *imperfect* body takes in oxygen and expels carbon dioxide. In other words, the element of oxygen enters into the body and creates a reaction, which produces a different combination of the elements already present (carbon dioxide from carbon and oxygen).

(Keep in mind that a carbon-based body must take in carbon through eating to produce the energy to function. If a carbon-based body did not get rid of some of the carbon it takes in after utilizing it as it needs, that body would grow bigger and bigger. Basically, this is why we exhale carbon dioxide—to keep our carbon-based bodies in equilibrium.)

In this example, the reaction of oxygen entering the body is that two oxygen atoms grab onto a carbon atom and pull it out of the carbon-based body, creating carbon dioxide (CO_2). Sure, the person can breathe in the CO_2 and use the two oxygen atoms to bind to another couple of carbon atoms and exhale again. But eventually there will not be enough oxygen atoms to take away the carbon atoms, and the person will suffocate and die.

This is not so with the *perfect* body! In an enclosed lead box (continuing this assumption for our example only) the *essence* will utilize whatever atoms are available, even the lead itself, and break them down into their basic components of protons, neutrons, and electrons; it will then form the appropriate elements that can react with the *perfect* body. A Lunarian or a Stellarian would have to stay in the box a lot longer than a Solarian, because their bodies would not immediately require a lot from their surrounding environment. Eventually, the lead element would be dissolved by the power of the *essence* as the Lunarian and Stellarian mind creates the *new experience* of being enclosed in a lead box. In the case of a Solarian, however, the Solarian mind can immediately change the composition of the lead into its subatomic particles and the lead box would simply disappear.

Without doubt, the *perfect human body* is the greatest bio-machine ever created, or rather, that has ever existed in the Universe!

11. OUR IMPERFECT BODY HELPS US APPRECIATE THE POTENTIAL OF A PERFECT BODY

To appreciate the extraordinary and seemingly miraculous potential of our incredible *essence*, we were given an *imperfect* body that does not allow our *essence* to draw upon the surrounding environment for *potential energy*. It's as if a covering or veil is placed over our otherwise powerful *essence* so that it is restrained from exercising its full potential. Consequently, we are forced to depend upon the *imperfect* features of our anatomy in order to get the energy we need to function.

We would never correctly perceive our *essence* as "extraordinary," "seemingly miraculous," or "incredible," if we only had the one experience of human perfection. It would just seem "ordinary." An *imperfect* body provides the contrast needed to develop the proper perspective of just how extraordinary, miraculous, and incredible the *perfect human body* is.

In an *imperfect* body, the *essence* must depend upon the energy provided to it in its enclosed environment, which is greatly limited; thus, the *essence's* incredible power is restricted. If it wasn't restricted, it would overwhelm the *imperfect* brain we currently have. It is also this restriction that keeps us from being able to utilize the *essence* to its full capacity and call upon its stored memories. If we could, we would remember everything about ourselves and the whole Universe and negate the *imperfect* experience we needed to go through during our second stage of human development. Keep in mind, in an *imperfect* body we store memories in both our *imperfectly functioning* physical brain and in our *essence*. The *imperfect* body was designed to keep the *essence* safe from us accessing its vast power.

12. A PERFECT BODY HAS ONLY A NERVOUS AND A MUSCULOSKELETAL SYSTEM

A perfect body does not have a digestive, respiratory, or circulatory system (which includes all other sub-systems such as the lymphatic system). It has only two basic systems: the **musculoskeletal system** and the **nervous system**. When we think about it, a human being can only experience joy through the nervous system. None of the other systems of the *imperfect body* aid the nervous system in delivering what our sensory organs produce, which are the only things that we care to experience anyway.

The fragrance of a rose that enters our nose does not, of itself, deliver any reflection of joy. The nerve endings known as "sensory receptors" in our nose are responsible for the wonderful smell of a beautiful rose. The sensory receptors of our eyes deliver the "beauty" of the rose. The sensory receptors in our skin allow the velvet texture of its petals to fulfill our desire for touch. And though the rose makes no noise to satisfy our sense of hearing, it can be tasted in conjunction with smelling it so as to provide a sensory experience through the receptors found on our tongue.

The *perfect* brain does not store memories, but is used solely for the accumulation and processing of the energy received through the sensory organs, much like our *imperfect* brains currently work. These perfected brains also produce the appropriate energy patterns of each sensory experience so that a memory can be created and stored on the *essence*. Sensory systems allow us to interact with our environment and en*joy* it. They sense the external world and transmit the information to the brain, where it is processed and interpreted. Therefore, we only need these few unique systems to fulfill the purpose of our creation.

13. IMPERFECT BODIES CAUSE US MISERY

The *essence* provides the energy needed to support the sensory systems of the perfect body. A complete and perfect nervous system delivers this energy from the *essence* to the musculoskeletal system and the subsystems of skin, hair, etc., and then delivers the sensations created back to the brain. But because our *essence* is "veiled" in our current *imperfect* bodies and cannot draw upon the surrounding environment as a source of energy, the other systems of our body are vital to our existence.

But what kind of existence is it? Our existing *imperfect* systems deliver misery and eventual death to us, at least until we (science) understand more than we currently do now. All disease is delivered through the circulatory, digestive, or respiratory systems. Bacteria and viruses that cause us so much pain and misery do not gain access to our bodies through the nervous and musculoskeletal systems; although these important systems can be greatly affected by them. However, in a *perfect* world there are no viruses or bacteria that affect an advanced human body. These pestering organisms were specifically engineered and designed for an *imperfect* world. They interact with our *imperfect* bodies in an environment that ensures us the probative and comparative experience intended for this life.

14. A HUMAN CONSISTS OF A BODY AND AN ESSENCE

Our brain is something completely separate from the *essence*, which enters our body at birth. The brain is what processes the input from the sensory systems and is what creates the energy patterns that are stored in the *essence* as memories. In other words, even the perfect body needs a brain. Without it, the human *essence* would be useless.

In addition, without the body, the *essence* would be like a sun that does not have an earth to give light and warmth to. What purpose would there be for the energy produced by the *essence* if there was nothing that could use its energy? We do not become a complete *human being* unless we have both a body and an *essence.* The absence of either one will never constitute a complete and individual human being.

When the *essence* enters the *imperfect* body, we become a conscious, living human being. When the *essence* leaves the body, we no longer exist as the individual person we were when our *essence* was in our *imperfect* body. But each life experience (incarnation) becomes an integral part of understanding *who we are.* Therefore, in *essence,* each individual is an anthology (collection) of different *imperfect* people who have lived upon the earth. But this anthology is not nearly the *complete* person. Because we existed for billions of years before the life-death-life-death scenario of our second stage of development, and we will exist forever thereafter, our short time in mortality adds very little to *who we* **really** *are.* Nevertheless, it is the most significant part of our existence that helps us later to fully **enjoy** *who we are.*

An argument often encountered from people who do not have a proper understanding of reality, is that a forming fetus inside of a mother's womb becomes a human being once the cells begin to divide and form the body. This shortsighted and narrow view does not come from *reality,* but from the inability of the "veiled" *imperfect* brain to recognize and understand the concept and function of the *essence.*

The revealing of reality given in this book should leave no argument: the only time a *human being* can exist is if there is a body **and** an *essence.* The *essence* enters into the body upon the first breath taken by the newborn and leaves with the last breath when the person dies as has been explained. There is no other reality.

15. UNDERSTANDING OUR ESSENCE CAN SOLVE MANY OF THE MYSTERIES OF THE MIND

Our *imperfect* brain's inability to respond to and communicate with our *essence* has already been discussed at length. We have explained how we store and work with the memories of the experiences gained from our sensory systems' input. We have explained the basic problems that occur when our *imperfect* brain is juxtaposed with our *perfect* essence. We have solved many of the mysteries of the mind that have eluded the understanding of science since humans began to "systematically observe" how the mind works. But there are some things that only an *imperfect* brain does (that a perfect brain would never do) that we have not covered yet.

The more we understand about the **true** nature of our physical body and our indestructible and eternal *essence*, the more we will understand about the *mysteries of the mind* that have baffled mortal humans from the foundation of our world.

16. OUR IMPERFECT BRAIN CREATES FANTASIES

One of the many problems of the *imperfect* brain is that it creates situations that are *not part of our current reality*. Our brain has a difficult time maintaining a consistent way of categorizing all of our memories into chronological and situational realities. What happened many years ago could influence our current reality because the *imperfect* brain might perceive something recorded in the past as something relevant or applicable to what is currently taking place. Our inability to maintain an accurate time line of events can cause our past to affect our present. Well have current psychologists concluded that some of our present emotional conditions are directly related to our past experiences.

If a small child, for example, experiences a traumatic event in childhood, even though as an adult the experience is not consciously remembered, the experience's energy presence in the subconscious can still affect the child's future emotions. This happens because the *imperfect* brain has a hard time putting events, especially those that are not forefront in the conscious mind, into sequential order. Although the past experience might have no significance or relation to current events, the *imperfect* mind subconsciously coalesces the two events as one and the same, very much like what happens when we dream in a subconscious state.

The *essence,* in contrast, keeps a consistent and perfect timeline of the events that we experience. Each event affects us **only** at the time it is experienced and does not influence any of our present behaviors, *unless* we bring the memory into our current reality. However, once we do, we are able to distinguish the events as completely separate from one another, never allowing one to influence the outcome of the other. In this way a *perfect* brain organizes all experiences and presents them as the conscious **now**, or better, presents everything consciously as the present.

The ability of the *perfect* brain to recollect experiences instantaneously contributes to our capability to make an immediate comparison in events so as to always have an appreciation of the experience. For example, if we have eaten a bad-tasting apple, we will remember how it tasted the very moment we are biting into a perfect-tasting apple, and we will be forever appreciative of the comparative experiences. If we couldn't immediately remember the opposing comparative values, we would not be able to appreciate how good an apple is supposed to taste, even after billions of years of eating perfect apples.

17. AN IMPERFECT BRAIN INHIBITS OUR ABILITY TO REASON PROPERLY

Our *imperfect* brain creates arguments and contentions that are not based on reality, but on our inability to understand *who we are*, *why we exist*, and *how we came to exist*. Part of the purpose of our *imperfect* life is for us *not to* understand these things so that we will have the desire to continue on in our imperfect state and gain by the experience. These "arguments and contentions" cause what we recognize as frustration, anxiety, and depression, which lead to anger, heartache, fear, and worry.

When we are confronted with a situation that we cannot control and that instead controls us and takes away our free will, our *imperfect* brain attempts to form a conscience acceptance and justification for the loss of our free will. This leads to the "argument and contention" of trying to figure out why things aren't turning out how we expected them to. If we understood and could remember the ***true reality*** of our individual existence and power, we would let no one control us, nor would we ever be confronted with a situation that we could not control by ourselves.

It is vital to our development and eventual human *perfection* that our minds are veiled—or in other words, that our *imperfect* bodies don't allow us to remember anything before our birth (and for most of us, anything before our late childhood). As our *imperfect* brain continues to deteriorate with age in our *imperfect* world, many of us can't even remember what we just experienced 10 seconds ago!

If we could remember all of our past lives and experiences, we would realize that we really cannot die. Knowing this as **real truth**, if we are experiencing a lifetime of sorrow, pain, misery, and everything opposite of what we would expect out of life, we would kill our body in the hope that the next time around things would be better for us. None of us would stand for an *imperfect world* that directly opposes our *true reality*; consequently, none of us would spend time going through the important second stage of our human development.

In addition to our inability to *reason* properly, there are many cognitive anomalies—some might call them phenomena—that occur because of our *imperfect* brain. These mental aberrations affect the way that we think about reality. We turn *reality* into *imagination*, or into things we desire to be true, but are not. It will not be necessary to cover all of them, for this would require volumes of useless scientific and philosophical words that would confuse and bore most readers. But it is important that we touch upon a few interesting ones that generally affect most people in the same way.

18. DÉJÀ VU IS THE MISFIRING OF AN IMPERFECT BRAIN

"Déjà vu" is a phenomena experienced by most of us. The term is associated with the experience of feeling sure that one has witnessed or experienced a new situation previous to the moment of the event. This gives one a sense that an event has already happened or has happened before. The experience of Déjà vu is usually accompanied by a compelling sense of familiarity and is often associated with what we feel as a strange or eerie sensation.

Here's how it works: The moment a new event takes place, our sensory systems act in unison to send their specific energy patterns to the brain to be compiled into a new experience and recorded as a new memory. In the *imperfect* body, the process of recording the event as a memory takes place **twice**—once in the actual physical structure of the brain, and once in the *essence*.

Usually this is done simultaneously, and no notice is given of the event being recorded twice. However, because the *imperfect* brain does not always work *perfectly,* it can misfire and produce the feelings associated with déjà vu. In this case, the event is first recorded in the brain and then, as the same event is being recorded on the *essence*, the brain senses the same energy patterns unique to the event a second time, thus causing the person to relive the event and experience déjà vu.

19. PHANTOM FEELINGS AND HALLUCINATIONS ARE THE RESULT OF AN IMPERFECT MIND'S CAPABILITIES

We have already discussed hallucinations and how they are formed in our mind. This is also why some amputees sense the phantom feelings that their limbs still exist. They continue to experience sensations from the exact location where their limb once was. When a man has used his legs all of his life and they are suddenly amputated, the memories (energy patterns) of being able to use his legs are still recorded in his *imperfect brain.*

Because our *imperfect* brain has the ability to store memories outside the *perfect nature* of our *essence*, it not only stores the information *imperfectly,* but also recalls and analyzes it with *imperfection.* At any time, a random sensation of "having legs" can be felt by an amputee simply by the experience being remembered. This occurs because our *imperfect brain* attempts to organize the events and categorize them into a perfect chronological order of past, present, and future. The remembered "feeling" that is stored in the *essence*, if felt, becomes the current *reality*.

Above, we touched upon the fact that experiences we had in the past can affect our present state of mind. For the same reason, most amputees experience dreams with their limbs intact. They are simply remembering what is recorded. Just because they might have lost their limbs, does not mean that they have lost the memories of the sensations they felt when they had them. For this very reason, there is much to be said of not trusting one's *imperfect* mind for the **real truth**.

However, by eliminating the double storage of memories, the *perfect* brain can only utilize the perfect memories of the *essence* from which to form its current sensations of reality. The *essence* categorizes and stores our experiences with perfection. If it were possible to amputate the legs of a perfect body, the person would not have "phantom feelings" because the present reality of "not having legs" would be the **only** reality present in the mind.

In that case, the only way the perfect brain could cause a remembrance of the sensations of "having legs" would be if the memory of the event was brought to mind by the concentration and free will of the person. But if the body didn't have legs, there would be no present source of sensory stimulation; therefore, there would be no *phantom feelings*. ONLY with a perfect body is it possible to trust one's cognitive perceptions to be *perfect* recollections of what happened in the past and what is happening in the present. We cannot trust the *imperfect* brain that we have here on earth.

20. MENTAL DISORDERS ARE CAUSED BY AN IMPERFECT BRAIN

Our *imperfect* brain also causes a variety of mental disorders that add to the miserable state we sometimes experience on this earth. There is not much joy taken in by our sensory systems when we are faced with a schizophrenic person whose *reality* can cause us or themselves harm.

Schizophrenia is properly defined as an emotional instability or detachment from reality and withdrawal into the self. In a sense, we are all currently subjected to this same mental disorder. Just as we find ourselves uncomfortable in the presence of a person suffering from schizophrenia, we also sense the same level of discomfort around "normal people" who have formed a reality that is different from our own. There are some people who make life choices that to others seem *unstable* and detached from reality. In *essence*, we are all schizophrenic in that, during our lifetime, we develop various *emotional instabilities*, such as depression, jealousy, envy, spite, anger, anxiety, and/or zealousness for our own reality, etc., that cause us to *detach from true reality and withdraw into our self.*

21. WE ARE ALL EQUALLY MENTALLY CHALLENGED

Most humans, if not all, live in their own little box from which they are sheltered from others who live inside their own little boxes. But to us, only our box is the "right" and "true" *reality*, while everyone else is living in a fantasy world. The **real truth**, however, is that we are <u>all</u> living outside of *true reality* in our current world, because of the *imperfect* state of our brains.

Human existence is a "true reality" that no one can responsibly and reasonably dispute. Some might lie to themselves and create a personal delusion for the sake of trying to make themselves seem different from the rest of us. The existence of the sun, for example, is a "true reality." However, a person's individual perception of the sun and their own existence is not necessarily a "true reality," but can very well be an invention created in their own mind based on their own individual experience. Thus, it becomes a *true reality* to them, but a delusion to the rest of us.

In past history, many people believed that the sun was turned off at night because their experience (i.e., what they were taught by their teachers and leaders) convinced them of the "fact." They could not conceive that the sun continued to shine brightly on the other side of the earth, because they didn't know that there *was* another side to the earth. Some even believe today that the sun is a reflection of another "greater light," like the moon, which we know reflects the light of the sun. However, if all other "normal" human beings throughout the Universe do not agree with a person's "perception of reality," then it cannot be "true reality."

In our *imperfect state* upon this earth, there are few things that we will all completely agree upon. Likewise, there are very few "true realities" known and recognized by *imperfect* humans. In this world, for a purpose we now understand to be in our best interest as developing human beings, it is IMPOSSIBLE for a person to live in *true reality*, which is what we experienced in the *perfect human state* in our primordial world, and which we will again experience after this mortal world.

In the end, when we receive a *perfect* body once again, we will recall all things we have recorded upon our *essence* with *perfect* recollection, in *perfect* chronological order and categorized *only* as the present, and with a *perfect* understanding. Only then will all of us be able to completely experience "true reality."

22. THE BRAIN CONVERTS ENERGY INTO EXPERIENCE

The perfect brain *does not record memories*. All memories are stored in the *essence*. In a *perfect* body, the organ we refer to as the "brain" has the primary purpose of receiving energy patterns and organizing them into the energy that each of our sensory receptors provide to make the experience happen in our mind. In a perfect brain, this process takes place both as we experience a current event and as we remember a past event. In either case, the energy must be sent first to the brain for processing. The energy patterns of each event are unique to the event itself. We distinguish one event from another by the uniqueness of the energy patterns each produces.

In our *imperfect* body, we can only experience the full event of each sensory response while the event is taking place. Although we might be able to remember a certain event, our sensory organs do not respond to the memory as they did when the event first took place. In our *perfect* body we not only experience the full effect of sensory stimulation *during* the original event, but also are able to experience the exact same stimulation when we *recall* the event from our *essence* in the future.

Advanced humans can hear, see, smell, taste, and touch anything in their past just as they did when they first had the experience. The sensory organs of their bodies react to the memory exactly how they did when the event first happened. In this way, we are able to appreciate all of our experiences, good or bad, without having to actually be present in the environment where the experience took place. In other words, we will forever appreciate the experiences we had in an *imperfect world* without having to live in one again.

All of the sensations of any event (including joy and pain) can only be experienced in the brain organ in both a *perfect* and *imperfect* body. In both cases, as an event is happening, all of the energy patterns produced by our sensory receptors are sent first to the brain where we are able to benefit from them. However, in an *imperfect* body, the brain not only takes the patterns of energy and creates the sensations that we experience, but it also records a memory of the event in what scientists would call a new dendrite. These dendrites are formed by the energy patterns of the sensory stimuli acting upon the cells of the brain.

With each new dendrite in place, a person can recall the event by concentrating energy on a particular dendrite, which upon being found, will cause the person to remember, but not ***re-live***, the event. If these dendrites are destroyed and damaged by trauma or disease, the person will not recall the recorded event. This is often referred to as amnesia (although their memory of the event may "return," as discussed previously, because of the record of the event in the *essence*).

23. AN IMPERFECT BRAIN ADDS DENDRITES FOR EACH NEW EXPERIENCE

In a *perfect* body, the brain reacts (causing us to experience the event) to the energy sent to it from the appropriate sensory receptors *as the energy of the event is being passed to the* essence *for recording*. A perfect human brain (the organ itself) would not be able to store all of the new cells/dendrites it produces for all of the events it will be required to record over trillions of years of existence into infinity. If a new dendrite were formed with each new experience, the human skull would have to expand to accommodate the new experiences, making the human head larger and larger as longer amounts of time went by. (Maybe this is what leads some in our current world to erroneously imagine advanced humans with very large heads.)

Because the *essence* is designed to store an infinite amount of experience, the *perfect* brain (the organ) does not need to store the events. Its only purpose is to make sure the event is properly experienced through the sensory receptors of the perfect body.

To understand this concept better, let's look at it this way:

Let's suppose that the event of eating an ice cream cone creates an energy pattern we will call IC58342. When we eat the ice cream, our taste buds contribute the energy level "5" to the energy pattern. Holding the cone contributes an energy level "8." Smelling the ice cream contributes the energy level "3." Seeing it contributes "4," and hearing the way our tongue and mouth react to it adds the energy level of "2" to the overall energy pattern of the experience.

All of these different energy levels are sent to our brain, where they are organized into IC58342, which we will remember as eating an ice cream cone. Once our brain has organized the patterns into a specific event, the *imperfect* brain creates a new dendrite that is distinct from all others, which is now *tagged* IC58342. The energy pattern is also recorded virtually simultaneously on our *essence* as IC58342.

If we were to suffer trauma to our brain that damages or completely destroys the IC58342 dendrite, then we will never be able to recall the experience of eating the ice cream cone again in our *imperfect* body. (Except as previously stated, that the memory "comes back" because it is stored on the *essence*.) However, **nothing** can affect the IC58342 energy pattern stored in our *essence*. The memory will last forever!

24. IMPERFECT BODIES DO NOT ALLOW US TO EXPERIENCE PERFECTION

How can we experience the perfect existence when we do not have the means to do so? The *reality* is that we cannot create the perfect human experience with an *imperfect* human body! So our creators have placed us in a conundrum where we find ourselves puzzled and confused in trying to find lasting joy in our current reality.

Let's say we are a sheep that is perfectly satisfied chomping on the green grass of a soft meadow. Nearby is a family of wolves that have a need to satisfy their hunger. They don't eat grass; they eat sheep! Therefore, so that one might live, the other must die. This reality might be appeasing to the wolves and those who live with them in their "little box," but to the sheep, this is unfair and is in complete opposition to the reason why they exist—"Just leave us alone in peace and let us eat our grass! Why were we created so that we could be violently eaten?!"

If the grass had a voice, it too would have something to say about this *imperfect reality*: "When the sheep are full, they defecate on us and kill us, or eat us down so much that it's hard to grow tall and full of the seeds we need to propagate ourselves! So we vote for the wolves' reality and their "little box" because it serves our own needs.

25. AN IMPERFECT WORLD SUPPORTS OUR IMPERFECTIONS

Humans are no different. Some of us are "sheep," some of us are "wolves," and some of us are "grass." If our surrounding environment supports our reality and the construct of our "little box," it doesn't matter to us if another's reality ends to support our own.

In addition, if someone else's reality helps our own, then we'll support their reality even if ours is different from theirs, but *only if* theirs continues to support our own. If the "wolves" start eating the grass because the sheep are all gone, then the grass is going to start to complain about the wolves just as it did about the sheep.

All in all, energy that is expended by all matter in an *imperfect* world is about *supporting the individual organism* without affording other organisms the same opportunities of survival. The "sheep" have no hope in an *imperfect* world. In contrast, in a *perfect* world, wolves do not eat sheep, nor do sheep defecate. Furthermore, the grass doesn't care, because it was created to be eaten by the sheep and will continue to grow forever without the need to propagate itself, thus all things fulfilling the reason for which they were created. **This perfect world allows to be done to all organisms what the individual organism would want done to itself.**

26. FEW EXPERIENCES CAN BE LABELED AS MISTAKES

Our current world and the bodies in which we exercise our free will and gather experience were set up so that we would *fail* to find lasting happiness, except through our willingness to reject our current reality and come to a knowledge of ***true reality***. We were set up to fail and, therefore, paradoxically, as described below, we *cannot* fail!

The enticement of a mortal experience is like the symbolism of our creators setting a cookie jar within our reach after we had been taught that cookies taste really good without being able to eat one and see for ourselves. They told us that in order to grow and become like them, we had to eat the cookies, but they forbid us to do so, explaining that if we decided to eat the cookies, we would have to go through all types of misery. Nevertheless, they gave us our free agency to decide for ourselves whether to eat the cookies or not.

In fact, they *expected* us to eat the cookies, because THEY themselves previously ate the cookies too. If they had chosen not to, they would not have advanced. So, if by design it is our current reality to fail, can we make a mistake in our current body? If we are failing to find and sustain a complete sense of happiness, are we failing? Or rather, are we fulfilling the purpose for which we exist in an *imperfect world*?

Does a wolf make an error in judgment or a mistake by killing a sheep to survive? The sheep never had a chance from the start. Likewise, do we make mistakes by the way we treat other people in an effort to support our own self-serving individuality, when this selfishness (everything exists for each one of us) was *foundationalized* into us on a perfect world? How can we make a mistake or be held accountable to anyone but ourselves for what we do during our time in mortality?

It is impossible to make an incorrect, unwise, or unfortunate act or decision caused by bad judgment or a lack of information. We shouldn't worry or stress about our "mistakes" when the bodies that have been provided for us upon this earth don't allow us to access the information to make any better judgment than what we do. No one makes a mistake! It is impossible in this world! The "mistake" as seen by one might very well be the "right" thing to do for another in order to protect individuality and support life. One of the greatest contributors to the misery we cause each other in our world are the judgments we make about how others exercise their own free will. We create judgment by defining human actions as mistakes or as *right* and *wrong*.

27. SERIOUS "CRIMES" ARE NOT EVEN MISTAKES

Some might propose that humans are more intelligent and much different from "sheep and wolves"; therefore, they would say that murder and rape, for example, cannot be excused. Advanced human beings who understand the problems associated with *imperfect* bodies in an *imperfect* world see things quite differently than we currently do. There is no such thing as "death," so how can murder be wrong? Are not the expected civilian casualties during war, really just murder? Yet, those who are responsible for civilian deaths during the exercises of war justify their actions and do not consider them a *mistake*.

Most people will not be allowed to have sexual abilities forever, so the creators very well knew that most people will misuse that ability in an *imperfect* situation. So how could they hold rape against a person? Our *imperfect* perception of how things are will change once we understand how things ***really*** are.

As mentioned previously, a *perfect* government ensures that our actions do not impede on the free will of another. Thus, we might assume that anything we do in our mortal life that takes away the free will of another, such as murder and rape, should be expressly condemned no matter what the situation—they must be "mistakes." Again, it depends on the perspective of the individual.

Millions of people are "murdered" by a very few when proper nutrition and health care are withheld from them because of unequal economic policies. Tens of thousands of young girls are forced (raped) into sexual experiences (prostitution) that they would never choose, except to provide themselves and their families with the basic necessities of life. Yet, many people turn away from this abuse and make no effort to solve the problem, considering it a vicissitude of a *Third World* country. Although there are millions of *imperfect* humans who are wont to judge murderers and rapists as those who should be punished for their deeds, they do not see that their own apathy and perpetuation of poverty through their own lifestyles are indirect causes of the same so-called "mistakes."

28. THERE ARE NO MISTAKES IN A PERFECT SOCIETY

The advanced human beings who oversee our mortal stage of human development in our current world understand the inconsistencies of our *true* humanity that are the result of living in an *imperfect* world with an *imperfect* body. There are none of us who do not affect the free agency of others and justify it in some way or another at one time or another in our current world. We go about our lives unaware of the harm that our actions indirectly do to another person. If we were all held to the standard of human behavior that is a condition of an advanced, *perfect* human society, we would all be criminals in some way or another.

There is no *mistake* in anything that *imperfect* humans do. It is when we are *perfect* and have all the resources and abilities associated with our humanity type that we then become accountable to our creators for how we treat each other. This is the reason why there are different *humanity types* and the specific powers and abilities associated with each. Our overseer is not going to allow any of us to make a "mistake" in a perfect world. That is why he exists with the power that he has. However, what we do while in an *imperfect* state is broadly overlooked because of the understanding of our creators, who are governed by their own overseer. Again, there are **no mistakes** made in an *imperfect* or a *perfect* world. The Universe is, has been, and will always be an environment of order without *mistakes*.

29. OUR INSTINCT TO SURVIVE COMES FROM THE CRAVINGS OF OUR IMPERFECT BODY

The *imperfect* human body allows for *imperfection* because of how it reacts to an *imperfect* environment. The strongest instinct of all organisms in our world is the fight for survival. In humans, who are the only organisms that recognize their own individuality, this survival includes maintaining this individuality at all costs. Only humans fight emotional as well as physical battles in order to survive.

This battle is caused by a human being's ability to recognize and pursue perfection. This concept of "perfection" is instilled in each of us. How this was accomplished was through our *Foundationalization Process*, as explained previously. When we experience an environment that is less than perfect, we are unable to sense the feelings of joy to the full extent of our perception of perfection, which is stored in our *essence*. We are continually motivated (called to battle) toward our individual state of perceived *perfection*. A big part of this drive for perfection in an *imperfect* world is in how we view each other and ourselves. Except for little children, there exists no human being in our world who does not see some personal flaw in their own physical appearance or character.

30. SEX PROVIDES BOTH PLEASURE AND MISERY

Our basic sense of physical beauty is greatly affected by the second most powerful instinct that motivates human responsiveness to any particular environment—sexual desire. As mentioned previously, this intense physical desire *only* occurs in the bodies of advanced human creators (Solarians who live on the Mercury- and Venus-like planets) and in the *imperfect* makeup of all of the bodies we currently possess during our second stage of development.

Once we have completed this stage of our development, or better, once we again live in a perfect world with perfected bodies, very few of us will have the desire for sex (only those who become creators of other human beings). *Why* this is, *how* it is, and why it will always be this way, will be explained in detail in the next chapter.

31. LUST IS CAUSED BY THE IMPERFECT BODY

The desire for sex causes extreme emotional variances in our mental state of balance, swinging our emotions from the feeling of ecstasy to that of frustration and sadness. To understand why this happens, we need to examine how sex affects the way we perceive beauty.

The most sensual or attractive body is one that appears to comply with all of the requirements of a good sexual experience that would lead to the production of human life. We can properly call these bodies "sensual" because, upon seeing them, our sensory systems are affected. When a man sees a woman with full lips, large breasts, or a perfectly shaped torso and buttocks, which encompass the body parts that are responsible for the creation and nurturing of life, his senses begin to respond without any conscious thought or will on his part. His breathing gets deeper in an effort to smell her better. His eyes adjust in an effort to see her better. His mouth produces more saliva to effectuate his sense of taste. And his sense of touch increases. These sensory changes within his body cause the *longing* he feels to have sex with her.

For a woman, a man who exudes physical strength, which would naturally protect her and her offspring, causes the same sensory reactions in her body. His sex organs, his torso, his arms, his chest affect her, as well as the overall appearance of strength reflected in his body. She too encounters an *involuntary* sensory stimulation to a man's outward appearance, just as the man does to a female's body.

32. MANY ACTIONS ARE MOTIVATED BY OUR SEX DRIVE

The animalistic propensity to mate is the same for all animals, including the *Homo sapiens*. The male and female seek out the most compatible partner with whom they can have sex. However, **only** humans desire the experience for something other than the propagation of their species.

In fact, other animals do not even know *why* they want to mate. An animal's existence only satisfies the longing that its sensory systems produce. Because humans are aware of themselves and can develop a *reason why* they *want* to have sex, they can control the "longing" and can choose to have or not to have sex.

Stated another way, animals do not *reason* out the process of sex in their minds; when the longing comes, they act on it. Humans, however, still have the "longing," and some never find a way to subdue and control it. Left unsatisfied, the longing causes the human being to become frustrated and unhappy with their surrounding environment. Being thus frustrated, we attempt to create the environment that will be more conducive to making sex happen; or else we encounter other emotional and psychological problems directly associated with our inability to satisfy our sexual needs.

33. WE MANIPULATE THE IMPERFECTIONS OF OUR BODY IN ORDER TO ATTRACT A MATE

Part of the environment that humans can change to have a better chance at experiencing sex is their own personal physical appearance. If bigger breasts and a fined-tuned torso and buttocks are what men want, then that is what women will strive for, thus ensuring their chances of satisfying the natural longing that occurs. Likewise, men may concentrate their efforts on their physical appearance by increasing the size and definition of their muscles (or other parts of their body).

It is no secret why *imperfect* people desire a "sensual" body: they want to satisfy the sexual longing they feel for each other. When they find a mate with whom they can satisfy this longing, they often stop worrying about their physical appearance as long as their mate will accept their "not-so-sensual" physical appearance and still give them sex.

34. IMPERFECT BODIES ARE NOT PERFECTLY BEAUTIFUL

Most of us in an *imperfect* world do not have a "sensual" appearance. This adds to the conflict and purpose of this world. If we all had a perfect physical mortal body, then our sexual longings would be less irritating to us because we would be in a better situation to have them satisfied by someone we would find "sexually attractive."

Our *natural* sex drive does not support monogamous relationships (one partner at a time). We use our free will to develop and support these monogamous relationships, however, because with this restriction, we are assured that we can satisfy our sexual desire. If we always have at least one partner around, we will most likely be successful at having sex. In addition, monogamy supports the *emotional* need of a human to be valued and appreciated as an individual above all others.

As human societies progressed in the *imperfect* world, they incorporated the idea of *marriage* and commitment into the moral structure of society in order to protect a person's ability to have sex. Less attractive and weaker males benefit from such standards of morality because it limits the competition from other, more sexually attractive males. If rules and laws are in place to punish a *married* partner for having sex with another more sexually attractive partner, this would decrease the motivation for infidelity.

In some societies today, the men mandate that their women cover their bodies from head to toe to eliminate other males lusting after them. They have established strict rules of chastity in their cultures with harsh consequences to dissuade sexual freedom. This enables the leaders and most of the men (who more often than not are not very sexually attractive) to enjoy the protection of *their women* and ensure themselves a continual sex partner. Ironically, these same societies also condone polygamy for the man, but vehemently restrict the woman's right to have more than one sexual partner.

In this world, sexual longings are "supposed" to irritate us and take away from our happiness. Nevertheless, the sexual desire creates an *unrealistic* perception of beauty. Why unrealistic? Because in an *imperfect* world, it is almost impossible, as intended, for anyone to have naturally perfect features *without* the help of surgery, make-up, or specialized concentrations of energy by the will of the individual (such as doing 1000 crunches a day to get the perfect abs).

35. THE PERFECT BODY IS NOT INFLUENCED BY SEXUALITY

In a perfect world, beauty is *not* based on sensuality. The sensory systems of a *perfect* body do *not* respond to any outside stimuli that is not introduced into the body by the motivation of free will. The perfect body was created to house our human *essence*; therefore, it is in complete balance and harmony with our *essence*, and we have no need to seek to create the balance that is disrupted by the cravings we feel in an *imperfect* one.

We eat, smell, taste, touch, and hear things because *we allow* our environment to provide these things, which causes our senses to react to them. Nothing in a perfect world causes our sensory receptors to react *unwillingly* as does our *imperfect* body when we see a sexually attractive person. The perfect body is either without sex organs or, in the case of advanced human creators, the sex organs do not produce the hormonal stimulus that is responsible for our craving of sex that we refer to as lust.

The only perception of beauty that exists in a perfect world comes from the power of the *essence* in comparing what we are seeing in the present with what was foundationalized within us in the past. The perfect body responds the same way to sexuality as a little child in our *imperfect* world responds—it does not.

36. WE ALL RECOGNIZE BEAUTY IN THE SAME WAY

As has been touched upon previously, little children are drawn to beautiful people. A small child's sense of beauty does not come from any memory recorded in their new mortal experience. Their perception of beauty comes from the limited power of their *essence* that produces the memories of the physical appearance of the advanced human beings associated with their *Foundationalization Process*. The subtle energy emissions of the *essence* are more readily available to little children who have not yet clouded the emissions with experiences recorded in their *imperfect* brain.

Our creators were beautiful people. Their beauty came from their own perception of what beauty is to them, MINUS any sexual attraction. In other words, they do not need to have big breasts, finely shaped torsos, or any exuding muscles to appear as perfectly beautiful. Symmetry was the common basis for the beauty they perceived.

37. PERFECT BEAUTY IS ANDROGYNOUS

Perfect beauty in the perfect body is androgynous (having both male and female characteristics). The perfect body (except for the bodies of those who continue to produce life) starts with a head that reflects the fine features of a woman combined with the subtle contour of the male's facial structure. Women in an *imperfect* body may need make-up to accentuate their beautiful features, whereas men have a natural construct to their face that doesn't require make-up. In an *imperfect* world, a woman can appear masculine without her make-up and some men with finer features can appear feminine with make-up. The *perfect* body will never need make-up or anything else to accentuate its features.

38. DIFFERENT SKIN COLORS ADD TO THE BEAUTY OF EACH INDIVIDUAL

Our visual perception of skin color depends on the way the reflected light bounces off a person and enters our eyes. The perfect body is neither too dark nor too light, but is made to fit the physical attributes of the face. A person's skin tone is another personal choice made by the individual. Some advanced human beings are white, brown, tan, or whatever color fits their individual perception of beauty.

Some people with certain features look better with lighter skin, while others with different features look better with darker skin. In our *imperfect* world, darker people want to be lighter with smaller features and lighter people want to be darker with larger features because, regardless of the skin color, the symmetry and size of the features creates beauty.

Many people think that a well-tanned body looks better than a white one. When our body becomes tan, its color base hides many of our imperfections, similar to how foundation hides the imperfections of a woman's face with the application of make-up. For some, many hours of basking in the sun to create the perfect tan adds to the individual's sense of beauty.

39. DESIRING "PERFECT BEAUTY" CAUSES PROBLEMS

Ironically, when humans bask in the sun, they currently wear sunglasses to protect their eyes from the sun and make it more enjoyable to be in its full power and glare. What humans fail to realize is that when they put on a pair of sunglasses, their body thinks that they are now in the shade. While in the shade, the body has no need to create the natural protective chemical reactions that it normally does to protect itself while in the sun. So, while the sunbathers are enjoying the sun with their sunglasses on, their bodies are not producing anything to protect itself from the natural rays of the sun's energy. Their bodies actually *think* they are in the shade.

This is just one of the many "mistakes" attributed to current human nature that no other animal on earth has ever made. One would be hard-pressed to find another natural living organism wearing sunglasses and cooking its food over a hot barbecue. This leaves little wonder why *only* humans are affected with the many physical diseases that destroy their bodies and cause them premature and unnatural death.

40. ADVANCED MOTHERS GAVE US OUR PERCEPTION OF BEAUTY

Our mother *foundationalized* our perception of what is beautiful to us by creating us the way that *she wanted.* She is *solely* responsible for how we viewed ourselves in that world. She created our first primordial body based on *her own* perception of beauty, usually drawing on the body patterns from her own experience to create a unique body for each of us.

Advanced mothers do not create male and female bodies. Their creations are the perfect reflection of what they know to be the perfect combination of both. Because our primordial bodies were neither male nor female, when we go through our experiences in this second stage of our development with only one of the two types of gender in each mortal life, we are never completely satisfied with our appearance. No matter what we do or how hard we try, we cannot recreate the perfection of beauty *foundationalized* in us by our mothers.

As we've discussed, sexual attraction is the main basis of beauty in an *imperfect* world. Again, we have a subconscious desire to create experiences that match those stored in our essence. When it comes to those memories in our *essence* concerning the creation of human life, we have only one example of perfection recorded: New human beings were created by beautiful human female mothers. Therefore, our mother's physical beauty set the standard for us regarding any future sexual experience we would have in mortality. This is because we saw their sexual features and abilities while being *foundationalized* around them.

However, we didn't have any sexual desire at that time; therefore, we were not in the least bit attracted sexually to our mother or any of the other mothers or fathers, or to our siblings. If we were allowed to associate with these women or men while in *imperfect* bodies with sexual desires though, we would see them as the most sexually attractive women and men imaginable.

41. OUR WORLD HAS TWO GENERAL TYPES OF BODIES

To give us the experience of the *opposite* of the perfectly featured and contoured body, our creators originally allowed two types of physical bodies on our *imperfect* world. The first was created to be darker, with larger, less-refined features. The second was to be lighter with smaller, more refined features. The first was given the greater "sensual" physical appearance and attraction, while the second was given less sensuality, but more symmetry and a stronger likeness to the perfect human form.

The first had bigger, firmer breasts, buttocks, muscles, and shoulders, fuller lips, and most other features to which an *imperfect* body is naturally attracted. Upon seeing these bodies in their natural state, as a whole, we might not consider them to be an example of the perfect human presentation of beauty; but their overall shape would resonate with our sexual desires. The second had smaller bodies and features, which was a form that would makes us feel more comfortable and exude what all humans relate to as natural beauty. Combined, these two body types would create very attractive human beings.

42. BEAUTY IS CREATED BY THE MIXTURE OF BODY TYPES

When these two types of bodies began to intermix upon this earth, they created the myriads of human shapes and presentations of beauty that we now find in our *imperfect* world. Without question or prejudice, the people who are recognized as the most beautiful and sexually attractive people in the world are those who are a combination of their lighter and darker ancestors.

Here's how this took place in the beginning of the human race on our earth:

43. ORIGINALLY THE TWO IMPERFECT BODY TYPES WERE SEPARATED

As explained previously, this world was prepared through natural causes and effects that, although initiated and overseen by advanced human beings, were allowed to exist and act and be acted upon with very limited advanced human interaction. In the beginning, all of the landmasses of the earth were one large landmass. This was necessary because plants prosper and grow best when they are in one group. However, over time (over millions of years—which doesn't matter to advanced humans, for time only matters to those who die), the land drifted apart, creating what we now recognize as hemispheres and continents.

When human beings were first allowed to exist upon the earth, the land had already separated into continents and islands. In the warm environs of Africa in the Eastern Hemisphere, the *first* type of body—the darker-skinned, less refined featured, more sensual body—was allowed to develop in mortality. In this part of the earth, the forces of nature had created an environment of balance with an established "food chain" of nature, over which mortal humans had very limited control. In other words, the success of any animal in this part of the world was due to its position on the food chain ladder. Human beings were certainly not on the top rung; therefore, they were susceptible to predators just as any other animal.

The stress of being a human being was great, and a stronger body construct was necessary to survive in that environment. In addition, a strong sexual attraction was vital to ensure that mating and producing offspring would create and maintain a foothold for humankind to survive in that natural, but hostile environment.

44. ADVANCED HUMANS OVERSAW THE CREATION OF THE *HOMO SAPIENS* RACE UPON THIS EARTH

It was in this Eastern part of the world that certain animals were allowed to breed with other species of animals until a body developed that could be inhabited by a human *essence*. We have already discussed how current genetic and biological engineering coupled with hybrid breeding techniques allow the creation of a particular type of animal that does what its creators want it to do. Therefore, it shouldn't be too hard for us to accept the fact that advanced human "hybrid breeders" had their hand in forming a human body out of the animals already upon the earth that they had also created and placed here. They did this through patient and subtle manipulation, without changing environments or any particular species of animal's natural propensities.

In time, a body had been created that was able to accommodate the human *essence* and live in the environment in which it was placed. This body can best be described as the earliest known *Homo sapiens* species.

The Theory of Evolution has already been explained and discounted. The *evolution* of the kind of physical body that could house a *human essence* was orchestrated and controlled in the environs of an *imperfect natural world*. The intent of our creators in producing a humanoid body in this manner was necessary to help us understand the need for human intervention in all aspects of nature, including how animals are formed for a specific purpose. In addition, they oversaw the creation of a body that was counter-productive to (the opposite of) the *perfect human body* and how it functions in its perfection.

45. CARNIVORES AND HERBIVORES WERE SEPARATED FROM EACH OTHER OVER TIME

The environs of the earth changed as natural land separation took place over time and as the landmasses acquired a different geographical location than where they originally developed. Initially, most animal species were created in mild climates where the temperatures remained stable and consistent throughout the year. Where a land mass might have originated as lush tropical gardens of consistent mild weather, once the land drifted to another part of the earth, it became subjected to weather conditions that were not suitable to maintain its original environment. This contributed to the extinction of many pre-historic species of plants and animals, but not all.

Along with the change in climate, a general migration of animals occurred, subtly directed by the advanced human beings who oversaw the creation and formation of the earth. These environmental changes eventually separated the main body of predators (carnivores) from the more docile herds of plant eaters (herbivores).

A southern migration was natural because of the cold winter days of the northern areas of the landmasses. The carnivores (flesh-eating predators) couldn't find much food in the winter, and their systems were not conducive to cold weather; so they went south. This is why in our current world, those main bodies of carnivores maintaining the higher rungs of the food chain ladder (such as tigers, lions, etc.) are usually found in the southern tropical climates, while the more docile creatures (such as the former larger herds of bison [buffalo], deer, elk, etc.) are generally found in the more temperate climates.

46. NORTH AMERICA IS WHERE THE LIGHT RACE OF THE HUMAN SPECIES ORIGINATED

In the Western Hemisphere, in the area currently known as North America, our creators found a place to introduce the *second type* of body upon the earth. These more refined, lighter-skinned, less sensual bodied people would never have survived in the imperfect environs and natural effects of the world without our creators' intervention.

It was here where the advanced mothers came and created bodies from the elements of the *imperfect* world that could house the *essences* of the children they had foundationalized on their planet. These *essences* were now ready to embark on their second stage of development—the experience of mortality in an *imperfect* world. These bodies, just as the bodies of the darker-skinned human beings who developed upon the African continent, were created with gender and the ability to perpetuate the human species.

It is important to understand that "these *essences*" brought from an advanced human world were also placed in the bodies of the darker-skinned *Homo sapiens* of the Eastern Hemisphere. There was and is no difference in value and importance between the *essences* that were placed in the different parts of the world. There was a need for *both kinds* in order to begin our human experience on this earth. The biggest difference between them though, was that one group was allowed to develop on its own *without* any initial intervention by our advanced mothers, while the others were taught how to act appropriately as human beings in an *imperfect world.* We needed the actual experience to see what would happen in each case.

Because every human being assigned to this solar system and earth has lived many lives during mortality, most of us have experienced an existence as both a *Homo sapiens* of a darker-toned skin and as a lighter-skinned human form. There is certainly no reason for any of us to assume that our present race or skin color is any better than or unequal to any other. We all have equal *essences*!

47. ADVANCED MOTHERS CREATED MORTAL BODIES

Every advanced mother who had created new human beings in the primordial world and led them through their *Foundationalization Process* left their home planet and came to this earth. Each produced *only one* child in the less hostile Western Hemisphere, together producing an exact number of females and males.

They reared them in this *imperfect* world much the same way that a mother rears her children in modern times—by restricting their free agency (unlike in the primordial world)—in an effort to teach them how to survive in an *imperfect* environment. They taught their children how to live with nature. They taught them when and how to migrate to habitable areas when the weather changed. They taught them to be gatherers and live off what was produced naturally; for these children were not taught to eat meat in the beginning.

Once the human *essences* were placed in the mortal bodies the advanced mothers created, their new bodies and brains could not access the memories stored therein. The only experience that the now-*imperfectly*-embodied humans could remember was what they were learning lots of new things in their new environment. This new environment included dangers that could affect the safety of the innocent children and harm their physical body as well as take away their experience of happiness.

48. ONE OF OUR FIRST EXPERIENCES OF SEPARATION ANXIETY WAS SAYING GOODBYE TO OUR MOTHERS

Advanced mothers reared their mortal children on this earth to adulthood, wherein the children could now take care of themselves, having had the experience for many years in their new environment.

Once this was accomplished, the advanced mothers went back to their own planet. The farewell experience was not one of tears or unhappiness for the mothers, but it was certainly the first experience of unhappiness felt by their now *mortal* children. A great anxiety of separation was felt and the first instincts of the unknown (fear) were experienced at that time. In parallel, the darker-skinned *Homo sapiens* created in the other hemisphere were also experiencing great amounts of unhappiness attempting to survive in the natural *imperfect* world, particularly after one of their close acquaintances was taken through death.

The advanced mothers knew that what was going to happen to their children was for their own good and development. The mortals could now only trust in what they were taught, not knowing for sure what was about to happen once their mothers were gone.

49. OUR ESSENCES WERE TRANSPORTED TO OUR NEW WORLD

The introduction of this second type of mortal body in the Western Hemisphere coincided with the advent of a human-compatible body being ready in the Eastern Hemisphere. All of our human *essences* that were foundationalized in our creators' galaxy and solar system were brought to this new world and placed in either dark or light bodies during this first period of mortality, except for one.

The one who was foundationalized as the *overseer* of this solar system stayed behind and did what he was created and taught to do: observe and oversee everything that happened in our solar system. To do so, he needed to have the advanced technology available to him as well as the ability to continue to be tutored properly. This continued mentoring and tutelage was overseen by his father (our father), and also by the overseer who was assigned to the solar system where our father was created.

Although the *chosen overseer* for our solar system was prepared before the foundation of our world, we were still not 100% convinced that he would *always* do the right thing on our behalf. The only way we would ever be convinced that he could be trusted to do for us what we couldn't do for ourselves was if he also became mortal and went through the experience of an *imperfect* world like we had to.

50. OUR FIRST EXPERIENCE WITH DEATH WAS OUR PRIMORDIAL SEPARATION FROM OUR CREATORS

In a sense, before we left our perfect primordial world, all of us were put to death, or better, our *essences* were taken out of the perfect bodies in which we were foundationalized so that they could be transported to our new world. It could be said that we experienced our *first death* when we were separated from our creators, the perfect world where they live, and from the perfect body that our mother created for us. Our creators literally took apart the elements of our primordial perfect bodies and allowed the subatomic particles that they were made of to go back to their original state, to again be used by our mothers in the formation of the bodies for the next new batch of children.

51. WE STRUGGLE TO FIND OUT WHO WE ARE

Once we were brought to our new world and introduced into our *imperfect* mortal bodies, we were in what could be considered a "fallen" state from the one that we were used to. And ever since we first realized that we could think and *reason*, we have been constantly struggling to figure out the sense of our mortal life, having a never-ending longing for something that we cannot figure out. We are constantly trying to figure out *who we are* and *why we exist.*

52. SOME NEW MORTALS LIVED IN INNOCENCE WITH A SEMBLANCE OF PERFECTION

After the mothers left the light-skinned humans, they (the children) lived very healthy lives as they began to take from the environment what naturally tasted good to them. They were herbivores, but found little joy in the taste of the grasses and other plants that the animals around them were eating. They were basically fruitarians, who ate only those foods that produced seeds within themselves and needed another animal (humans) to eat them and spread their seeds, so that they could promulgate their own plant species.

The mortals who developed in the Western Hemisphere did not cook or process food in any form. The mothers did not teach their children how to cook, or how to kill other animals to sustain their lives. In the beginning, they took their place in the food chain and only ate those things that needed to be eaten for our cells to continue to reproduce themselves. With symbiotic reverence, they lived in balance with the natural world that surrounded them.

53. PEOPLE IN THE WESTERN HEMISPHERE WERE NOT SEXUALLY ATTRACTED TO EACH OTHER IN THE BEGINNING

While in these first mortal bodies, we associated with each other the way that brothers and sisters associate with each other on this earth. Although we had the ability to have sex, we were not sexually attracted in the least to our "brother" or our "sister"! We lived for many years having about as much desire to mate and have children as we do with our own mortal siblings, with whom we have been reared with since birth. We observed other animals mating and producing offspring, and we were taught by our mothers that this is the way that humans also procreate. But with our brother and sister?! Forget it! We were not naturally attracted to them at that time.

54. OUR ESSENCE WAITS IN THE ATMOSPHERE UNTIL A BODY IS READY UPON BIRTH

The atmosphere of our world sustains the positive and negative forces that produce what we call gravity and magnetism. Our *essence* cannot escape the confines of the earth's atmosphere, as its positive energy is continually attracted to the negative energy created by the earth. (The terms *positive* and *negative* attraction are used hypothetically to illustrate opposing forces.)

As mentioned above, at the same time period that our human *essences* were brought from our perfect world and placed on this world, the other type of bodies (*Homo sapiens*) were ready to attract the energy levels of our *essences*. (This process was explained previously.)

At that time, all of the human *essences* brought to this world were either in a mortal body or hovering in our atmosphere waiting for the next human body to be created. These bodies cannot be produced except by the free will and choice of human mortals. Therefore, the mortals with the first type of body (*Homo sapiens*) living in the Eastern Hemisphere (those more sexually attractive and conducive to reproduction) began to have sex with each other and to produce bodies for the *essences* waiting in the atmosphere to inhabit them.

55. THE MORE SENSUAL PEOPLE INFLUENCED SEXUAL BEHAVIOR FOR ALL EARLY HUMANS

In a short time, the darker race of mortals found a means of travel across the ocean, and some of them eventually ended up encountering the lighter race in the Western Hemisphere. The lighter-skinned humans were in jeopardy of their own extinction because they still had not found it within themselves to have sex with a brother or a sister.

Our advanced mothers did not create all the people at once. There was a wide variety of age groups, because our mothers knew it would take us awhile to learn that there was no other way to propagate our species than through sex. As it is in most cases of emotional motivation regarding the perpetuation of life, the females figured this out before the males.

As old age set in, some of these lighter-skinned people began to die off without being replaced by new creations of mortals. Nevertheless, once the more sexually advanced darker races of humans found them, this began to change.

56. PROTECTIONISM LED TO SOCIAL DETERIORATION

Once in contact with each other, the lighter-skinned people were now sexually aroused toward the darker species. This led to indiscriminate sexual behavior, which began to separate brother and sister and once again caused fear. Soon, stress and discontent arose among a people who had never known such feelings.

To protect their new human emotions and maintain their sense of individuality from their darker-skinned neighbors, some of the lighter-skinned people did not mingle with them. Instead, they migrated with "their own kind" and began to see the benefit of becoming sexually active with each other so that they could perpetuate and protect what they saw at the time as "their own kind" of human being. The smaller, weaker, and less passionate, lighter-skinned people were threatened by the physical strength of the darker-skinned humans, and the fear and threat resulted in the first human murders upon our earth.

57. WE EXPERIENCE EACH DIFFERENT RACE WHILE IN MORTALITY

Because the purpose of our experience upon this earth is to experience all things, there was no definitive selection of which *essences* would inhabit which bodies, at first. In the beginning of our mortality, our *essences* entered the bodies randomly, according to the location of our *essence* in the atmosphere at the time a newborn body came out of a mortal mother. Nevertheless, each of us was eventually given ample opportunity to experience a life in the different types of bodies made available through our *imperfect* world.

In the beginning, some of us were the darker-skinned humans living in the Eastern Hemisphere and others were the lighter-skinned humans living in the Western Hemisphere. But, from the beginning and throughout the rest of our existence, we would remain equal human *essences,* each having chosen for ourselves what *humanity type* was best for us. Our choice of life experience in mortality would be influenced by what we desired before we came to this earth. As explained previously, there are advanced human beings who act as our "guidance counselors." These beings have the power to ensure that each of us has the life experiences that will best help us learn what we wanted to accomplish during this time of mortal probation.

58. DIFFERENT HUMAN RACES WERE FORMED: BLACK, WHITE, AND TAN

In time, the mixture of the light and dark DNA patterns produced varying tones of skin and human features. This is how the modern races of human beings came to be and became logistically and geographically located throughout our current world.

59. THE DIFFERENT RACES RELOCATED THEMSELVES

The darker-skinned people (we will refer to as the "black race") migrated from the Eastern Hemisphere to the Western Hemisphere, where they interbred with the light-skinned people (we will refer to as the "white race"). This created varying features and skin colors, which we will refer to as the "tan" race. The white race felt threatened and left the Western Hemisphere to the tan race, migrating across the ocean to the Eastern Hemisphere, where they found the fertile grounds of the rivers and tributaries that flowed into the ocean.

Having the knowledge of how to survive in the more harsh environs of a winter, the white race spread northward from the equator in the Eastern Hemisphere. The black race remained south of the equator in what is commonly referred to as Africa. Some of the black race also had migrated to the continent of Australia, instead of staying in the Western Hemisphere. By about 5000 B.C.E., the tan race occupied the majority of the northern part of the Western Hemisphere; the black race occupied the southern parts of the Eastern Hemisphere; and the white race occupied the northern parts of the Eastern Hemisphere.

60. THE TAN PEOPLE BECAME THE MONGOLIC RACES OF EASTERN ASIA

As human nature took its course on our emotions and our instinctive desire to maintain our independence and individuality, human wars and contentions began. The tan race was at continual war with itself in the northern parts of the Western Hemisphere (no one had yet discovered the southern parts).

To avoid these wars, some found their way further North, where they discovered the Bearing Strait that allowed them to rather easily traverse the narrow span of water to the Eastern Hemisphere. Following the course of the fertile lands that bordered the Pacific Ocean, these tan races eventually colonized the Eastern shoreline of the Eastern Hemisphere. They also ventured out into the ocean and colonized the islands of the sea. This is where the modern Mongolic races came from.

61. THE WHITES INHABITED NORTHERN EUROPE AND THE BLACKS DWELT IN THE SOUTH

With the advent of swords, spears, bows and arrows, armor, and other accouterments of warfare, the white race developed better ways to protect itself from the much stronger black race, eventually isolating the black race to the confines of the very southernmost regions of the Eastern Hemisphere. The white race overran the Northern parts of the Eastern Hemisphere, but rarely found it necessary to involve themselves with the Mongolic races of the East, as these people generally kept to themselves and their own cultures.

62. THE WESTERN HEMISPHERE WAS SOON FORGOTTEN

Over time, the white race had all but forgotten everything about a Western Hemisphere. However, small groups did return to the Western Hemisphere, where they stayed for a time; but because of their own internal wars and dissensions—that at this time had become an integral part of human nature—they decimated themselves to extinction.

Many years later, however, the white race would once again discover and overrun the Western Hemisphere, destroying the tan races and positioning themselves as the supreme rulers of the world. This racial ignorance and arrogance would create the prejudice and social deterioration that is the basis of our *imperfect* world today.

SUMMARY

The races of humans that cover the earth today are descendants of one of the three races we have described: black, white, and tan. Yet there cannot be found upon the earth any human being who does not have a mixture of the DNA patterns of *all of these races*. There are some who have maintained a more pure form of the tan race, or of the black or white races, but the bodies of all human beings are a mixture of each of the human races on this earth. There is no "pure" blood. The blood of the African was just as "pure," or better "*impure*," as the blood of the *imperfect bodies* created for the lighter-skinned people.

Because of the unevenness of the mixture, the majority of us are not good representations of ultimate human beauty and perfection. Most people are not that good-looking, although almost all of us, with a normal *imperfect* body, are intensely sensual creatures. The proper mixture in the beginning of a lighter-skinned, more beautiful mortal, combined with a darker-skinned, more sensual one, brought equality to us all, thus eliminating any excuse of racism. We are all just as much black as we are white. We are all *Homo sapiens*.

With wise intent and for the purpose of allowing us to see what it would be like to have the ability to experience human sexuality, the races that constitute the *imperfect* human body were planned by our creators. And because of the imperfection of our bodies and the constant "longing" of our sexual urges, we have used our *imperfect* bodies and our free will to create a world **completely opposite** in almost every regard to the perfect world where we once lived.

Consistent with what we have experienced in this *imperfect* world is the following wise rationale and logical conclusion we will arrive at. To transform our world back into a *perfect* one, and further conform our senses and emotions to the *foundationalized* perfect balance that brings us our individual happiness, we must eliminate (in most cases) the very aspect of our mortal nature that causes all the problems—sexuality.

The *perfect* human body has always existed in some part of the Universe. It is the ultimate biological form of matter that can work with the *power of the essence* to give a human being the best life experience possible. We started out our existence as a human being in these *perfected* bodies. But to learn to appreciate them, we needed something to compare them to.

Our creators organized our current world with the purpose of allowing us to store the comparative experience of a perfect world in our *essences*. These experiences will be available to us forever. Because a perfect body can recall each experience with the same sensation and magnitude as when the event was first recorded, we will always have a constant remembrance of what it was like to have an *imperfect* body in an *imperfect* world. And with this vivid recollection, we will be forever grateful and appreciative of the *perfect human body*.

Human Sexuality

CHAPTER TWELVE

It is the nature of desire not to be satisfied,
and most men live only for the gratification of it.

—Aristotle

1. EXPERIENCE IS THE STORAGE AND RECALL OF ENERGY

We have discussed how our humanity was *foundationalized* and how the balance was set by which we experience happiness. We are happy when we are using our body in a way that is in alignment with what is recorded in our *essence*. This "alignment" is *adjusted* according to the energy levels at which our first experiences were recorded in our *essence*.

The *essence* interacts with our body by first storing "experience" as energy patterns and then giving off these stored energy patterns as "memories." The totality of our existence and individuality comprises the events of our lifetimes stored in our *essence*. Each event creates specific and unique energy patterns. These energy patterns are produced by the sensory receptor systems of our physical body. With a *perfect* body, in conjunction with our individual *essence*, we have the ability to relive (re-experience or remember) the events of any of our lifetimes at will.

When the energy levels of our current experience match or align with the energy levels already stored in our *essence*, we feel a physical sensation of peace and balance. We recognize this physical sensation as joy. When the energy levels of our current experience do not match or align with those stored in our *essence*, our physical body reacts in a way that makes us feel sad, anxious, depressed, and emotionally out-of-balance. Because our individual *alignment* occurred during our *Foundationalization Process* in a *perfect human environment*, this part of our development is the *most important* part in becoming a human being. We would not be able to behave as a *human* if the qualities and characteristics expected of human beings (i.e., *humanity*) were not the core foundation of *who we are.*

2. SEXUALITY AND GENDER WERE NOT PART OF OUR FOUNDATIONALIZATION

Sexuality and gender were not forced upon us. In a *perfect world,* the free will and individual choice of each human being are respected and protected. In order to have a fair chance to choose which *humanity type* we wanted for ourselves, we existed in a *perfect world* for eons of time.

During this time, we were exposed to varied societies of people. Each of these groups of people demonstrated a *different humanity type.* We were able to travel to any planet in our primordial solar system and interact with the advanced humans who lived in these *perfect worlds.* For the greater part of our foundationalization, we were continually exposed to our *female* mothers; thus we had the opportunity to choose to become a *female* creator. We were also exposed to *male* attributes that our father/creator had; thus, we had the choice of whether to become a *male* creator. By observing all different *humanity types* for such a long period of time, we were able to set our own "alignment." This personal choice was based on the experiences we had in exercising our free will. No advanced human manipulated us, coerced us, or forced us to be anything but what *we chose to be.* We chose our own *humanity type* all by ourselves.

At the time of our initial creation, none of us were created as a *male* or as a *female*, because it is not consistent with a fair and equal *Foundationalization Process* to be given *inequalities in any form.* Had some of us been created as *male* and others as *female*, the gender would have been **forced** upon us without our consent.

During the process of our *foundationalization*, everything done to us and provided for us was unconditionally equal for all of us. None of us will ever be able to complain that the life we have chosen is not fair. In the *perfect* world, life is completely fair and equal. Had some of us been created as males and others as females, without being given the personal choice, there would have been no fairness and equality in this type of forced destiny. If this were the case, some females might have had the right to complain, "Why couldn't I have been a male?" Males could have complained, "Why couldn't I have been created as a female?"

3. SEX LEADS TO AN IMBALANCE BETWEEN OUR BODY AND OUR ESSENCE

Gender creates an emotional dilemma for us in an *imperfect* world. In this world, we are born into a body of gender that does not fit our *foundationalized alignment*. According to how our *essence* works in providing us with a physical sensation of joy, how in this *imperfect world* can any of us be happy with gender or the accompanying sexual desires when these things were NOT part of our individual foundation?

Sexual attraction and the feelings that we associate with gender are natural and instinctual and are NOT caused by the exercising of our free will. They are not part of the experiences recorded on our *essence*. They are caused by our *imperfect* body and affected by our gender.

The feelings of lust, jealousy, and sexual desire *do not* make us happy. They are a physical irritant to our overall balance. They *irritate* us because they cause a physical change in our body's chemistry that we did not desire by using our free agency. We do not understand where these feelings come from or how to eliminate them, except by acting upon them with our physical body. We can, however, control these feelings by using the power of our free will. But the fact that they arise in our bodies and offset our balance of happiness, *without our willing consent*, causes us frustration. If left to the natural urges of the body, without interference from our own will, these feelings would continue to irritate us until we satisfied them. Satisfying these urges could lead to consequences that we did not initially desire as part of the expected experience.

Sexual desires arise naturally and do not have to be "willed" by us. When we see a particularly sexually attractive person, for example, our body reacts before we have a chance to think about it. Most people in an *imperfect* world are given a set of moral guidelines concerning sex and how to control these *unwilled natural physical sensations*. Some of us might be taught that we should not lust after another person who is not our "married partner," for example. Nevertheless, the lust and desire seem to arise and affect our body whether we like it or not! And the physical stimulus is not so much what bothers us, but rather more often, it is our inability to conform to the moral guidelines instilled in us (and therefore our inability to immediately satisfy the sexual urge) that causes us the greatest frustration and concern.

4. ANDROGYNOUS FEELINGS ARE A NORMAL PART OF OUR SEXUAL NATURE

During our *Foundationalization Process*, we developed certain individual characteristics that were influenced by the experiences we acquired while being exposed to females, males, or other genderless beings similar to ourselves. Although no sexual association was attached to the characteristics we were exposed to, we recognized them as *feminine* and *masculine* human traits. We also recognized that *genderless humans* possessed some of both characteristics.

Each of our individual propensities was *foundationalized* by observing the *human* traits in others. Our observations were not always of *perfect* advanced human beings. We had the technological capabilities at that time to observe these traits in *imperfect humans* as we watched many different societies of people going through their own second stage of development in mortality upon *their earths*.

Each of us developed either more *feminine* traits or more *masculine* traits, depending on how we chose to spend our time during the *Foundationalization Process*. There were those of us who were more intrigued, for example, with the wars and carnage people caused each other in the *imperfect worlds* we observed. Some of us were intrigued by the chaos that *uncontrolled* free will caused human beings. Those who became interested in the *misuse* of free will eventually *foundationalized* with a more *masculine nature*. Others of us were more attracted to the gentle side of human nature and were *foundationalized* with more *femininity*. (Keep in mind, advanced *males* are those who oversee the misuse of free will in *imperfect* worlds. Advanced *females* want nothing to do with it.)

For this reason, when our *essence* is placed in a mortal *imperfect* body, regardless of whether it is a male or a female, the power of our *essence*, or the *foundationalized* experiences contained therein, subconsciously causes our brain to be geared more towards either *feminine* or *masculine* propensities.

This is why homosexuality occurs. Many of us find more comfort—more alignment—exhibiting *feminine* desires in the *imperfect* body than we do *masculine*, or vice versa. The majority of us are more comfortable accepting the sexual act between two women than we are between two men, because of the propensities of *femininity* around which most of us were *foundationalized*. However, homosexual men are naturally attracted to physical *masculinity*. The men to whom other males are attracted must also exhibit an overall *feminine* generality (compassion, kindness, gentleness, etc.), regardless of how masculine their body is, or the homosexual relationship will not work.

5. THE SEX ORGANS ARE THE EXTRA SENSORY RECEPTOR SYSTEM

Gender gives us an extra sensory receptor system apart from, but also comprised of, what we consider to be our basic senses of sight, smell, sound, taste, and touch. These sensory systems create the events of our experience and bring us physical (but not necessarily emotional) happiness. Because this *extra* system didn't exist when we were *foundationalized*, we have no alignment set in our *essence* that can give us a sense of balance pertaining to how this particular system should react to or act upon the environment.

In other words, we do not have a natural "sense" of what we need from our environment to satisfy the urges that this extra set of sensory organs creates. We do not have an "irritating" urge to satisfy our sense of sight, smell, sound, taste, and touch, because we have already set a balance (alignment) of what these senses can do for us. This *new sensory system* associated with our sex organs, however, does not have this *balance*. Therefore, we are driven incessantly to satisfy its urges. Because we lack an "alignment" for the use of sex organs, we are constantly seeking a balance that just isn't there! And that can be very irritating!

This can be very bothersome to us without us even knowing *why* it is! In our *imperfect* bodies, we don't consciously know why there is such a drive to satisfy it any more than we consciously know that we have an *essence*. However, once we understand that the *essence* provides the *balance of our humanity*, we then can begin to understand why sexual urges seem more powerful, and the need to satisfy them so much greater, than what is required by our other sensory receptor systems, whose alignment is maintained by the presence and power of our *essence*.

6. THE ORGASM CREATES THE ULTIMATE PHYSICAL EXPERIENCE

It is in our attempt to satisfy these *irritable* urges that we experience an energy level unlike any other event produced by the normal sensory receptors of our body. We call this experience an orgasm or sexual climax. Because we have no subconscious idea of what the potential of this *new sensory system* is, we don't have any intrinsic guidelines established to help us deal with the new energy levels created by our sex organs as we experience them. In other words, there seems to be no end or constraint when it comes to our ability to experience the sensations of a sexual experience. The more we have sex, the more we want it and the more intense and better it can become.

Eating an apple, for example, seems to have a capped limit on the amount of sensual pleasure we get from eating it, no matter how good it tastes. Sex doesn't seem to have a limit. The "new urge" gives us such a powerful physical sensation that our other senses seem unable to satisfy it. We do everything possible to *see*, *hear*, *taste*, *smell*, and *touch* something in our environment (usually another person or ourselves) in order to gain some sort of a balance (alignment) to these *new* energy levels. The result of using <u>all</u> our senses to satisfy this *irritating urge* is that, instead of just one of our senses being satisfied at one time, *all of our senses* are satisfied simultaneously when this balance (orgasm) is reached! That's why a sexual orgasm is the most powerful physical pleasure a human being can experience.

7. SEXUAL ENERGY CAN OVERPOWER FREE WILL

As we sense the *irritation* and begin the process of making it go away, or satisfying it, the irritation or urge gets stronger and stronger, forcing us beyond the capacity of our ability to stop the process by the power of our free will. Through the use of our free will, most of us can stop the feelings at the various energy levels being produced at any point of the process leading up to the satiation of the urges. However, none of us has the ability to stop once the process has begun to produce the powerful energy levels that are emitted right before the final burst of energy that finalizes the satisfaction. It is hard to stop an orgasm!

At the pinnacle of the sexual act (the process of satisfying the urge), we are *seeing*, *hearing*, *tasting*, *smelling*, and *touching* whatever our environment is providing us in a completely uncontrollable manner. We reach out to our environment in an effort to experience the ultimate end of what these energy levels are producing in our body. And until we reach that end, we will take advantage of what is available in our environment any way we can.

8. UNDEVELOPED SENSORY SYSTEMS INHIBIT THE SEXUAL URGE

Pre-pubertal mortals do not have these urges; therefore, there is nothing that needs to be satisfied. Children are curious of the *inequality* among themselves as they notice that boys have penises and girls do not. However, there is nothing that "irritates" their physical body at this stage of their physical development. Children expend all of their energy in satisfying hunger, sleepiness, and other physical discomforts, which are also associated with the construct of the *imperfect* body; but again, children have no sexual urge that creates discomfort.

The moment we are born, our body begins to mature to a certain pre-determined level mapped out in the "plans" of our *imperfect* DNA. These "plans" are not equal and the same for any of us in an *imperfect* world. Some of us mature earlier and faster than others. While our sensory receptor systems are maturing during our childhood years, they are more easily satisfied because it takes less energy to do so. But once these systems reach a certain level of maturity (the stage of human physiological development we refer to as "puberty"), these systems are not satisfied until they are used to their full potential.

Our eyes want to see the brightest colors and the sharpest contours of our environment. Our ears are pricked to hear all that makes a sound. Our taste buds are longing to be satisfied. Our nose craves the smells that we enjoy. We want to touch everything and anything we can get our hands on. We also begin to want sex, which again, is a coalescence of all of our physical senses.

9. AN IMPERFECT WORLD DOES NOT ALLOW US TO FULLY SATISFY ALL OF OUR SENSES

We base our desire to satisfy our senses on the unconscious memories, or "alignment" that was established in a *perfect* world where the sights, sounds, smells, tastes, and textures provided the *ultimate* human experience. In an *imperfect* world, when our sensory systems reach their full maturity and are *not* satisfied the way that they were during our *Foundationalization Process*, we are subconsciously seeking that "aligned" balance.

Because the *imperfect* world cannot provide us with anything close to the "ultimate human experience" of a *perfect world*, when our senses mature and are at their peak, they never seem to be satisfied. This inability to satisfy our senses creates what we experience as the more powerful sexual urges. These "urges" are simply all of our sensory receptors longing to be satisfied at the same time.

As we engage in the process of sex, all of our senses are affected. They are functioning at their full capacity, each seeking the fulfillment for which it was created. As the sexual process progresses, and the closer we seem to get in reaching that balance, the harder it is for us to use our free will to control the energy levels created by our senses. In an *imperfect* body in an *imperfect* environment, it is *impossible* to reach a complete balance between our brain and the "aligned" energy levels of the *essence*. In other words, we never completely satisfy our senses of sight, smell, sound, taste, and touch with the *imperfect* things that are available to us in an *imperfect* world.

To compensate for our inability to match our current sensory experience with that stored in our *essence*, we are continually motivated to satisfy the only one of our sensory systems that we can completely satisfy—our sexual sense. We appear to *completely* satisfy this sensory system because of our experiences in an *imperfect world*, where we first encounter the sexual sensory system. In our current world, we **consciously** set the *alignment* for what is satisfying and what is not. There is no stored level of sexual sensory balance from our previous perfect world.

10. WE ESTABLISH OUR SEXUAL TENDENCIES IN AN IMPERFECT WORLD

In our current mortal life, we have the ability to satisfy and complete the balance of our sexual senses BECAUSE WE SET THE ALIGNMENT ACCORDING TO OUR EXPERIENCE. We measure whether or not we are satisfied (whether or not the sexual experience is good) based on our past experiences in *this life*, without the influence of our *essence*. The expectations of our other senses are not satisfied by the poor imitations of the ultimate human experience provided by an *imperfect* environment. For this reason, when we experience "good sex," all other sensory experiences that do not make us feel like we did during this "good" experience, or those that don't allow us to feel the same energy pattern produced by a past sexual experience, do not completely satisfy us.

11. MALES MATURE SEXUALLY SLOWER THAN FEMALES

Generally, the sensory receptor systems of females reach their maturity about the age of 20 years. Males take a little longer and are usually fully mature sometime in their early 30's. Full maturity means that the *imperfect* body has developed to its greatest physical potential. It's at this time that a person can experience the greatest energy levels that their fully mature *imperfect* sensory receptors can produce.

This does not mean that one's ability to experience the satisfaction of sex gets less intense over time, because in most cases it does not. Not being sexually satisfied has nothing to do with the *imperfect* body not having the ability to reach its full potential of experiencing pleasure. Sexual satisfaction has all to do with the ability of the person to utilize the body and its senses to reach what they experienced in past sexual experiences. Past experience sets the parameters of sensory potential.

The more experience one gains in the process of sex, the better the person develops the ability to use the senses to reach the energy levels produced by the process. In other words, younger men, for example, can enjoy sex quite frequently, but are unable, because of lack of experience, to use their surrounding environment (their or their partner's body) to create the maximum powerful energy levels that are possible through the sexual experience.

Very few women are able to achieve the ultimate potential of the sexual experience—many because of the lack of experience or desire of their partner to help them achieve it. Most women go through mortal life believing that the height of their sexual potential has been reached, when it has not. Reaching closer to this potential usually occurs when they change partners to one who is more experienced or they take the time and patience to achieve the potential themselves through masturbation as they explore their own sexuality.

As is the case with all of our *imperfect* experiences in mortality, none of us will ever experience the ultimate human sexual experience. We cannot achieve it with an *imperfect* body. Our current bodies can only entice us to want to keep having sex in order to increase the levels of ecstasy of the experience. Nevertheless, these bodies cannot provide us the opportunity to achieve what most of us will never experience, unless we are Solarian human creators.

12. AS THE SENSORY SYSTEMS BREAK DOWN, THE SEX DRIVE DIMINISHES

As a person grows older, the body begins to break down and the sensory receptors do not function as well as they did when the body first reached maturity. Less energy is needed to satisfy the deteriorating sensory systems; therefore, the need for sex also diminishes proportionately. If, however, a person keeps the body in shape and limits its deterioration, the sexual process can be experienced late into one's life, though the frequency and need of the senses to be satiated will become less and less.

The *imperfect* body only allows a certain time frame wherein its sensory receptors are fully mature and able to function to their potential. But even functioning to its maximum sensory limits, an *imperfect* body will never be able to reach the balance necessary to bring the energy levels of the body in line with the *foundationalized* perfection of human sensory stimuli established in a perfect world. In an *imperfect* world, we will never see, hear, smell, touch, taste, and feel the way we could when we had a *perfect* body. Thus, we are continually unsatisfied on a subconscious level. Our *imperfect* body will eventually die, not having experienced the full potential of any of its senses.

13. OUR INABILITY TO FIND OUR SEXUAL BALANCE IS A CURSE

As is the same for all of our sensory systems, through each of our individual experiences, we set the level of potential for each. Sex is no different, except for one very important thing: Unlike our time going through our *foundationalization process*, there is not an advanced human being around all the time who can teach us all about sex and its potential. They are not available to guide us through the process of establishing the *perfect alignment* for this particular sensory system!

We are left to ourselves to determine what this alignment, or ultimate human experience, should be. Furthermore, we do not have a perfect environment in which to set the perfect foundation for this new sensory system. We are left to ourselves with an *imperfect* body in an *imperfect* world attempting to first, find the potential of sex, and then, reach that potential. So, instead of sex being a wonderful sensory experience that creates unlimited satisfaction (the feeling of joy), it becomes a curse to us in an *imperfect body*.

14. SEX CREATES INEQUALITY AND HUMAN SUFFERING

Sex becomes a curse because it creates inequality. Males experience it differently than females. Women seem to be more vulnerable to the negative effects of sex (rape, incest, prostitution). However, the finality of the sexual process in its *imperfect state* creates misery for everyone. As a result of sex, the woman gets pregnant and is forced to create a child that grows inside her body and comes out in an incredibly painful manner. Once the child has been produced by the woman, the man feels a sense of responsibility to provide for both mother and child, and is forced to do so in an *imperfect* environment, which does not provide anything without the expenditure of energy; i.e., work.

With an *imperfect body* in an *imperfect world*, the curse of having the ability to have sex is basically two-fold: One, we experience pain in childbirth; and two, we are forced to work for what we need in order to support not only our own life, but also the new life we created.

We can call it a curse because it causes us misery. It causes us misery because it does not match any of the experiences that we have recorded in our *essence.* These experiences were all *foundationalized* in an advanced *perfect* world, where the human body was created *outside* of the body of the female, and in an environment that provided everything we needed in abundance, without any of us having to work (expend our personal energy).

If we don't have to expend our energy on supporting another life, other than our own, or in forcing a newly created human body out of a hole in our own body (by the greatest expenditure of energy ever used by a human), then we can use all of our energy to satisfy the things that bring us *true personal* joy. We can satisfy our senses and concentrate our energy on being *who we are.* Furthermore, rearing children is certainly not an easy task. Parenting in an *imperfect world* takes away from our personal happiness, especially when the children reach their sexual pubertal years.

15. ONLY HUMAN CREATORS HAVE SEX ORGANS

Now we are presented with the dilemma mentioned previously that arose when we were advanced human beings, and which will again arise when we are ready to receive our advanced bodies once again:

ONLY THOSE WHO ARE SOLARIAN SERVANTS AND HAVE MADE THE CHOICE TO CREATE AND BE RESPONSIBLE FOR NEW HUMAN LIFE **HAVE THE SENSORY ORGANS THAT PRODUCE THE ENERGY LEVELS EXPERIENCED DURING THE PROCESS OF SEX**!

But, because all of us (regardless of whether we want to be served, to serve ourselves, or to serve others) were allowed to experience the *potential* of joy in having sexual sensory organs, we now know what this potential is capable of providing for our physical bodies. Having experienced what sex can do, it is a hard thing for any of us to willingly give it up forever!

Regardless of how we feel about maintaining our ability to experience sex, the rules and laws of the Universe have always been: **ONLY THOSE WHO CREATE NEW HUMAN LIFE AND BECOME SERVANTS TO OTHERS CAN EXPERIENCE SEX!** And why is this so? Because if we could have sex ***without*** the responsibility of the creation and development of another human being, why would any of us even *consider* being a creator and servant forever?

The ability to experience the incredible energy levels produced by the sexual sensory system of the human body **MOTIVATES US TO AT LEAST CONSIDER THE CHOICE OF BECOMING PARENTS AND PRODUCING CHILDREN.** In this way, the Universe continues to exist for the purpose for which it does: to provide human beings the experience of life. Again, if there was no motivation to become servants and serve others, why would any of us consider choosing it as our *humanity type*? Therefore, this answers the supposed unanswerable question of why *only* Solarian creators will be able to have sex in advanced human societies—it has universally been set in place to attract candidates for Solarian service.

16. OUR FOUNDATIONALIZATION PROCESS DID NOT ALLOW SEXUALITY

Because we were genderless while we were being *foundationalized* and choosing our "humanity type," we didn't have the ability to experience sex. We had to FIRST choose for ourselves what type of human being we wanted to be ***without*** being enticed to choose just because we wanted to be able to experience sex. In other words, we had to make the choice to serve others for THEIR SAKE and not for our own. Those of us who chose to become Solarian Servants did so out of a genuine desire and interest in satisfying the needs of others and NOT BECAUSE WE WANTED TO SATISFY OUR OWN SELFISH INTERESTS.

Not having had the actual physical pleasure, newly created humans without gender do not have any memories stored that would allow them to re-live sexual pleasure. Without actually experiencing it, yet knowing that it is a possibility, helps keep free will protected. As stated above, we must first desire to *serve for the sake of others* by our own free will without being swayed to consider an existence of service because our physical body entices us. **True knowledge** is impossible without personal experience. Even though we might have been told how wonderful something might be, we would never know for sure until we experience it for ourselves.

However, all of us perceived that when human beings engage in sex, the experience seemed incredible. In viewing the actions taking place on other worlds where mortals were going through their experience of an *imperfect* world, we witnessed human beings engaging in the act of sex and becoming satisfied thereby. We could tell that having sex provided energy levels that combined all human senses into a coalesced package of the "ultimate sensory experience."

However, we could also see the enormous amount of problems and responsibilities that having this power created. Yes, we saw how miserable human beings could become because they had this ultimate human power in an *imperfect* world, and also how great the responsibility was for those advanced beings who had the ability in a *perfect* world. We had to decide for ourselves what was best for each of us individually.

17. WE WERE ABLE TO SEE THE NEGATIVE EFFECTS OF SEX

We saw the inequality, the jealousy, the unfulfilled desires, and the lust associated with sex. We saw the way that free-willed beings exercise power and control over one another, not for the sake of another, but for the sake of the individual. We saw the way that leaders control their followers by regulating sex and causing free-willed humans to feel guilty and depressed for using their **free will** to satisfy the needs of their body without hurting another or impeding on another's free will. We saw these same leaders manipulate and convolute explanations of naturally occurring diseases, associated with and intended by our mutual creators for an *imperfect* world, into "*sexually transmitted*" diseases that further perpetuate a false sense of fear and anxiety. We saw the overwhelmingly pervasiveness of sex in all aspects of humanity. We saw exactly what we are currently experiencing in *our* world.

We saw very unhappy people unable to satisfy the full potential of their other sensory systems (sight, smell, sound, taste, and touch) in an *imperfect* environment provided by an *imperfect* world. We saw that the ONLY sensory system that they seemed to completely satisfy, according to the nature of their *imperfect* body, was their sexual one. We saw that the very motivation of most human beings in an *imperfect* world became centered on satisfying their sexual urges, which, again, were the only ones that they seemed to be able to satisfy to any degree of complete gratification.

To reiterate, because our sexual experience is limited *only* to our experience in an *imperfect* world, it seems to us as if we can actually satisfy our sexual urges; this is because we have no *essence*-based memory with which to subconsciously compare it. However, our experience with sex leaves us with the impression that there is much more to our sexual potential than what we know about. We come to this realization because the experience has the capability of reaching higher levels of ecstasy each time we engage in it.

Again, while we were being *foundationalized*, we were able to watch other societies of human beings develop on their *imperfect* worlds. As human life began to develop in these worlds, the first experience of sex always ended in the creation of a new human being—at least until humankind progressed enough to figure out how to have sex without having a baby. With the new freedom that came from being able to experience sex without any responsibility, and the advancement of technologies that allowed less stress and work to provide for the necessities of life, the frequency of the sexual act increased. As it increased, the people become more aware of their *inability* to reach the *full* potential of the urges that they created from exercising their uninhibited power to have sex.

Life in an *imperfect* world became all about having sex, which in *essence*, is simply the free-willed desire to satisfy the physical sense of the body! Nevertheless, as the society of humans with *imperfect bodies* became more liberated in their sexual experiences, they realized that something was still missing that kept them in a miserable state of existence. Although they could have sex when they wanted and with whomever they wanted without feeling guilt or filled with anxiety, and they had all of their basic necessities provided for with little or no expenditure of energy on their part, they were *still* very unhappy and miserable.

Imperfect societies that reach this point of sexual liberation and more civilized cultures (similar to that which has been reached by humans upon this earth *circa* 2012) begin to realize something important to their development as human beings. Subconsciously, they start to feel that no matter how much satisfaction they are getting out of the extraordinary physical sensations provided by their senses (although, as explained, only their sexual senses are being satisfied completely according to the restrictions of an *imperfect* world), the way that they are experiencing life is NOT THE WAY THEY EXPERIENCED IT WHEN THEY LIVED IN A PERFECT WORLD! They are not happy!

18. WE WILL NEVER REACH A FULL BALANCE OF HAPPINESS THROUGH SEX

As mortals, we will never be completely happy until we are able to match our present experience with what was *foundationalized* in our primordial life. No matter how much sex we have, no matter how many riches we have or worldly possessions, because these experiences weren't part of our *original foundationalization*, we can never find a fullness of joy in the *imperfect* world. We will never find this complete joy, UNLESS we are able to become the unique individual that we became in a world where we made the choice of *who we are*, without being forced to become someone we are not because of the expectations placed upon us by others.

In the end, most of us will figure out that it is better to give up sex and be happy with *who we are* rather than live forever in a state in which we are distracted from our personal balance. We will understand the connection between our imbalance and the sexual experience when it is associated with only serving ourselves or being served by others. We will one day concede that those who serve others deserve the pleasure—the only form of energy (physical pleasure) that *serves them* while they are serving everyone else.

19. SEX DISTRACTS US FROM BECOMING WHO WE REALLY ARE

The *imperfect* world allows sex to distract us from being the person *we really are*. If we were to get rid of sex, then our only motivation would be to express our individuality and find joy in being ourselves. But because the *imperfect* world was created and intended to provide us with an **opposition** to all that is perfect, sex is the only thing connected to our physical senses that we can count on to give us a full satisfaction of joy, if only for a moment. So, we have sex for a few minutes, but then are forced to once again confront a world where it is impossible to find a fullness of joy in anything else. Is it any wonder then why sex is such an integral part of our current *imperfect* experience of life? And is there any wonder why sex provides only a very short temporary escape from the *reality* of our misery?

20. THERE ARE TWO BASIC HUMAN NEEDS —PHYSICAL AND EMOTIONAL

Based on what we have discussed so far, we can conclude that we have two basic needs as a human being:

1. To satisfy all of our senses to their full potential, and
2. To exercise our free will as an individual and be *who we really are*.

The first one satisfies the needs of our body and the second satisfies the needs of our *essence*. We refer to these needs as our *physical* needs and our *emotional* needs, respectively. In a *perfect* world, we are able to satisfy both completely without any difficulty. This is because the basis for these needs was *foundationalized* when we lived in the *perfect* world.

However, we could never really appreciate what our bodies could do or who we had chosen to be, **until** we experienced the *opposite* of these things in an *imperfect* world. In our *imperfect* world, we are attempting to satisfy both our *physical* and our *emotional* needs. In our attempt to do so, we have created something that doesn't exist in a perfect world; we have created the human concept of and need for **love**.

In our *perfect* world, we became the center of our mother's attention and were provided a life experience where everything was centered on pleasing us—the Universe existed for us! Upon trying to reproduce this experience in our *imperfect* world, we seek to become the "one and only" and center of attention to others. We want to be loved at least as much as all others and have our personal needs met by those closest to us in our environment. How well we are able to match these experiences of equality and self-centeredness embedded in our *essence* defines the parameters of the meaning we give to **love** and the impact it has on our emotional security.

21. LOVE DOES NOT EXIST IN THE PERFECT WORLD

Whether we like to admit it or not, **love** causes both the *greatest* and the *least* desirable emotional experiences. It can bring great amounts of joy and tremendous amounts of pain. In contrast, nothing exists in a perfect world that has the potential to cause us both pain and sorrow. If so, it wouldn't be a *perfect* world.

Love is something we have invented as mortals to offset the lack of balance, or better, the unhappiness that we experience in an *imperfect* world. We use it to satisfy both our physical and emotional needs. Moreover, because we invented **love**, we also invented its opposite: **hate**. In our *imperfect* state, we have the ability to both **love** and **hate** the same thing. The fact that we can **love** something and then **hate** it with the same emotional intensity shows the futility and illusion of the emotion.

Love does not really exist. What does exist is how we perceive our environment. If our environment pleases us by providing us with the ability to fulfill our physical or emotional needs, then we accept it and **love** it. If it does not provide anything for us, we reject it and **hate** it. However, there is only one thing in our world that we can both **love** and **hate** with the same intensity: **each other**.

22. LOVE IS BASED ON WHAT OTHERS CAN DO FOR US

Because we exist to satisfy both our physical and emotional needs, in an *imperfect* world, sex is the first *measure* most often used to determine if a person is going to fulfill our needs. Because our physical bodies are craving sex, the sensation becomes a craving for **love** in our minds, as it is a constant urge that needs satisfying. In addition, because we individualize the emotion and direct it towards just one person, **love** becomes the determining factor of whether or not we involve ourselves with a specific person.

Do we love that person or not? Are we falling "in love"? As we analyze the emotion, we do not consider what **we** can do for the other person. We develop our "love" based on what the other person can do for **us**. Even in a situation where another might be in need of our assistance, we still base our emotional attachment to the experience on whether or not another's circumstance will somehow add to our own need to demonstrate our "love."

23. PHYSICAL ATTRACTION CAN DECEIVE US INTO THINKING WE'RE IN LOVE

All of us want our physical needs met. Because this physical desire is foremost on our minds, many times the first thing that determines whether or not we "love" a person is whether or not we are sexually attracted to him or her. Physical attraction is often the first thing that leads us to "fall in love," or feel that the object of our affection can satisfy the longing that our physical body craves. However, unlike all other animals, it is **not** the <u>only</u> thing that can cause us to make the determination that another can fulfill our needs.

Humans have other needs that also require satisfaction—our emotional needs. If a less-attractive person fulfills our emotional needs, we can indeed "fall in love" with him or her. Again, the value we place on everything in our *imperfect* world is based on whether or not it fulfills *our personal* needs.

However, no matter how hard we try to maintain a strong level of **love**, our physical bodies propel us to lust after sexually attractive people who we have conditioned ourselves to believe can satisfy our sexual needs. This leaves the less-attractive people at a disadvantage in our *imperfect* world. Most people in an *imperfect* world are **not** sexually attractive. And those who are "attractive" are usually less likely to satisfy emotional needs.

Therefore, NO ONE IN AN IMPERFECT WORLD CAN EXPERIENCE A FULLNESS OF JOY. It's just impossible! If it were possible, then the purpose for which we are going through our second stage of development in an *imperfect* world would be thwarted.

24. SOCIETIES THAT BECOME SEXUALLY CENTERED USUALLY END UP BEING EMOTIONALLY WRECKED

Not only are we distracted in our efforts to be *who we are* by our sex drive, but our **self-actualization** is also affected by our emotional need to be **loved** by others. To be loved, we are forced to do what we know will get someone to love us. We spend a great amount of energy trying to change *who we actually are* in order to make ourselves more physically or emotionally attractive. And as we concentrate more energy on becoming physically attractive, less energy is used to satisfy our emotional needs.

This is how societies become sexually centered and emotionally wrecked. Even our established relationships outside of our sexual natures do not provide us with continual and lasting satisfaction. Our family and friends more often than not let us down and cause us more emotional turmoil than those with whom we have no established bond. Yes, this *imperfect* world fulfills the purpose for its creation: it allows us the experience of everything that can make a human being miserable!

Therefore, no matter how much effort might be used to explain to another person *how* life *should* be lived in order to completely satisfy our emotional needs, the realization of complete satisfaction will never happen in an *imperfect* world—NEVER! And the more we accept the fact that we *cannot* change things as they are, and instead learn to understand *why* things are the way they are, the more we will be able to find peace as we go through the negative experiences intended for our mortal experience.

25. LOVE IS SIMILAR TO A MENTAL ILLNESS

If we were honest with ourselves, we would conclude that **love** is no different from many of the other mental disabilities that affect our balance and deter us from experiencing happiness. Although we might be able to arrive at this *reason*able conclusion, it cannot explain the phenomena of **love** and **sex** and why these seemingly "wonderful" human attributes cause so many problems. The answers to these "problems" are found in the acceptance and understanding of the human *essence*—what it is, how it works, and how it was formed.

26. WE VALUE RESPECT MORE THAN WE DO LOVE

The need for emotional balance is much greater for a human being in our quest for ultimate and lasting joy than the immediate satisfaction that we receive from the body through our sensory receptors. Because we had no sexual physical satisfaction from those with whom we were *foundationalized* in our primordial existence, we crave the satisfaction from what we *did* receive from other people in a *perfect* world.

And what was that satisfaction? We were not **loved** there, we were **respected**! This respect protected our free will and individuality. It is the *absence* of that **respect** in this *imperfect* world that causes all of our human emotional problems, particularly when we seek sex as its substitute.

27. ADVANCED SEXUALITY EXISTS ONLY FOR MERCURY COUPLES AND VENUS WOMEN

When we enter the advanced stages of human development, wherein we will remain forever enjoying our ability to experience life to its fullest, most of us will not have the ability to have sex, nor will we have the desire to do so. Once our *imperfect* bodies are replaced with *perfect* ones, we will once again not have sex organs or the cravings they produce. Although this seems to be an extreme measure for those who do not choose to be Solarian-type humans and create and be responsible for life, that is how it is and how it has always been throughout the Universe. It is *human reality.*

Sexuality in an advanced society of human beings is perfectly balanced and maintained so as to never cause the negative emotions associated with it in mortal worlds. Solarian (Mercury) couples have specifically structured DNA patterns that outline their sexual nature. Their bodies are genetically engineered so that they only crave sex with each other. Venus Mothers have sex at will—not from the will of the body, but the will of the *essence.* Although these eternal mothers have the sex organs that produce the stimulation and enjoyment associated with sexual pleasure, they do not have any of the other organs that create pregnancy, which consequently produce great pain in mortality. They have no ovaries or womb in which they create human bodies.

SUMMARY

No newly created human being is provided with a body that has sex organs. Having no gender during our *Foundationalization Process* in a *perfect* world keeps us from establishing a standard of what the *perfect* sensations generated by these sex organs should be. An *imperfect* body in an *imperfect* world, on the other hand, gives all of us sex organs of one kind or another, male or female, sometimes both. These organs at maturity create a constant need to be satisfied.

As these organs experience the energy created by the sexual experience, we have nothing to gauge against when it is good or when it is bad, as there is no standard recorded on our *essence,* and each experience we have with sex creates a unique pattern of energy levels that we record as a memory. Because none of the sexually produced energy patterns we experience in our mortal world match any previously recorded in our *essence*, we are subconsciously constantly craving to produce energy patterns that will match those THAT DO NOT EXIST (except from our current life)!

We experience complete joy when the energy patterns produced by our current experience in our *imperfect* world match those *foundationalized* in our *essence*. In other words, when we do what we did in a *perfect* human world, we feel a sense of balance that we recognize as joy. Sex was not foundationalized in that perfect world. For this reason, in this *imperfect* world we can have sex with a lot of people and experience great amounts of physical pleasure (or we can even create this pleasure for ourselves), but we are still left without being emotionally fulfilled once the physical effects of the experience wear off.

Although sex allows us to experience a physical energy that is unknown by any other form of life, even an energy that is the most powerful and satisfying experience we could ever imagine, we have to accept the many problems it creates. The stress it causes outweighs the benefits we gain from it.

Our advanced creators are both very wise and also merciful. They did not create us to suffer in any way or for any reason, except as pertaining to the reasons we experience suffering in this *imperfect* world in *opposition* to the experience of the perfect world. This is why there are eternal restrictions placed on sexuality. Without sex organs, we will not be affected by the physical experiences of sex recorded in our eternal *essence*. If a memory of a sexual experience is willed to the present mind of an advanced human, who does not have sex organs to act upon the experience, the event will be viewed and perceived as a little child views sex. And without the sexual urges, we will experience life as we did when we were little children, when sex was the last thing on our minds. What a wonderful time that was! Everything that was *a miracle...beautiful...happily, oh joyfully*, we will experience again!

The "Game" of Life

CHAPTER THIRTEEN

All life is an experiment. The more experiments you make, the better.

—Ralph Waldo Emerson

1. WE ARE IN THE "GAME" OF LIFE

In a sense, this mortal life can be compared to a "game" that was started by our creators. Hypothetically, in this "game," they gave each of us the exact same amount of money (let's say, one million dollars) and a time limit in which to spend the money and to interact with each other as we so choose. Each of our choices in how we spend the money will be influenced by our *foundationalized* individual *humanity type*.

Because they didn't set any ground rules for the game, we are compelled to depend upon our own intuition (what feels right) to figure out the rules as we go along. We are given the ability and discretion to set and follow whatever rules we desire. We can also change the rules according to our discretion. More often than not, it isn't long into the game before a *very few* take all the money from the majority and begin to control, not only all of the money, but also all the rules of the game.

When the time limit allowed for us to play the game is up, the advanced humans who prepared the game for us will return and bring with them a copy of the *universal rules for the "Game of Life."* These are the original rules that have always existed throughout the Universe to manage the never-ending "game" of human existence. As they explain how the "game" *is played by the rules*, we will realize that playing by these *universal rules* creates and maintains equality and peace among us. We will recognize these rules as those that we followed when we once lived in a *perfect world* as advanced beings.

Unfortunately for the few who have garnered all the money and control over "the game," they will realize that the cause of all human misery afflicted during the game was *personally caused by them*. Had they followed the *original* rules, they would have never allowed themselves to become unequal to anyone else by taking another's money, which was never theirs in the first place. They will realize that the rules and control that *they* maintained throughout "the game" were directly responsible for *how* it was played. Needless to say, those who make the rules for and control the resources of the *imperfect world* are responsible for much of the misery experienced in it.

If we consider that only about one percent (1%) of the humans upon this earth control the rest of the population and most of its assets, we can begin to see the great misappropriation of the earth's resources and the disparate representation of the rule of law that controls human behavior. Consider that currently there are about 7 billion people upon the earth at the writing of this book. This means that 70 million humans benefit disproportionately from the "game of life" than the other ninety-nine percent (99%). This is how "the game" is currently played on our earth.

2. WE WERE CREATED TO BE EQUAL

We have learned that we were created as equals in all things pertaining to our ability to support our individuality. In other words, each of us in our primordial existence had the same opportunities afforded to us to become who we made the choice to become. The environment there existed to make sure that we had the necessary means to do so, according to our individual desires.

In the beginning of our mortal existence upon this earth, our creators placed us in an *imperfect* world, yet in an environment where we were all equally capable of supporting our individuality. They did this so that we could see for ourselves what happens when free-willed human beings are left uninhibited to their own natures and to make their own decisions in relation to one another. This life became a probative experience (probationary period) where we are able to see for ourselves what each of us as an individual is capable of doing (and will do) with our free agency.

As explained previously, in our advanced primordial world we were able to observe what other humans did with their free agency as they went through their second stage of development (mortality) on their "earths." Many of us could not have imagined that we would do the exact same things with our free agency when it came our time to experience mortality. Even though Stellarian and Lunarian people realized that they would *never* have power and control over others, let alone the ability to create other humans, they still could not *imagine* that they would act as they observed other Stellarians and Lunarians acting in the *imperfect worlds* they were observing.

At that time, we didn't see how any human in the Universe could act contrary to the *universal rules* that supported humanity, and the most important aspects of being human—free will and individuality. Our creators smiled at us as some of us assured them that, "This kid is **not** going to mess up the peace and order of the Universe! Just you wait and see!"

3. LIFE SEEMS TO BE AN UNFAIR DISADVANTAGE

How are any of us supposed to know the rules of the "game" if they are stored as energy patterns on an *essence* that we don't even know exists? How are we supposed to "play the game" in equality and fairness to all (as the original rules stipulate) if we are unable to remember the rules and there is no one around to teach them to us or enforce them?

It doesn't seem fair that so many of us are going to "fail" at "playing the game" when our own creators made it impossible for us to know how to *play it right*! Furthermore, they set up the game so that it *would* be impossible to play by the rules, which rules would ensure us the peace and happiness that they experience in their *perfect world*! They *expected* and *wanted* us to "fail" so that we would learn from the experience! Therefore, if it was *expected* of us to "play the game" improperly, then is it not **true reality** that we are, in fact, "playing the game" correctly?

It seems confusing! On the other hand though, we know that there isn't an advanced human being in the Universe (who is responsible for the creation and development of new human life) who isn't completely fair and just in all that they do. So *why* and *how* did they set up "the game" in the first place and *what* have they done to help us play it?

4. GIVING UP SEX FOREVER DOESN'T SEEM FAIR

We have learned that there are three basic *humanity types*: 1) those who want to *be* served by others, 2) those who want to serve themselves, and 3) those who want to serve. We've also learned that only those who have chosen to serve others and be creators will have the ultimate power of creation and the ability to experience the unmatched sensory fulfillment provided by sex.

We have learned that, relatively speaking, very, very few of us will ever want to be eternal servants. But because we are all allowed to experience sex in this mortal world, it doesn't sit well with most of us to know that we will be deprived of this incredible power to utilize and fulfill the full potential of all of our human senses. It just *doesn't make sense* that all of us cannot have this ability, even if we don't choose to be eternal creators of and servants to others. Even though it doesn't make sense, it is still Universal *human reality*.

5. WE ENVIED OUR CREATORS, WANTING TO BE LIKE THEM IN EVERY WAY

Because our *Foundationalization Process* took place around those whom we recognized as our *parents* and *creators*, we developed a deep respect for them, whether we chose to be like them or not. The desire to have their qualities and power is a *natural* effect of being around them for such a long period of time. There isn't a human being in the Universe who can honestly say that having the power to control the elements and the ability to experience the benefits of sex forever is not something a human would consider "special." It is something that all of us would love to have!

Those who wanted to *be served* wondered why they just couldn't have the power to create with the simplicity of a thought instead of having to depend upon others to serve them. They sided with **those who wanted to *serve themselves***, who also had the same question.

Remember, those who *serve themselves* (Lunarian) have certain powers and abilities to manipulate their environment by themselves, but are restricted in doing so. They do not have the ability to control the basic components—protons, neutrons, electrons—that make up all matter. The specific Lunarian powers do not extend beyond the planet on which they reside. Lunarians need advanced technology, automation, and machinery to manipulate their environment according to their desires, whereas Solarians use the power of their thoughts to do anything anywhere in the Universe. Stellarians, on the other hand, have Solarians set up and do everything *for* them.

6. WE HAD AN ARGUMENT WITH OUR CREATORS

Our creators explained that only **those who wanted to *serve others*** would use the powers associated with creation correctly. Once this was explained and we fully understood the conditions and the restrictions of our free will, the very first argumentative discussion ensued in our perfect world:

"How do you (parents/creators) know, that just because we do not choose to have children and be responsible for them, we would misuse the power to control the elements?"

7. OUR CREATORS COULD NOT EXPLAIN WHY WE COULD NOT BE LIKE THEM

It was futile for our creators to argue with those of us who posed this question. They simply reminded us that we would find out in our next stage of development. They explained to us that only those who chose to be servants would find personal happiness in never violating the rules that govern human equality and peace. As mentioned above, many of us *thought* we would *never* violate the rules while "playing the game"; thus ensued the disagreement.

Our creators explained that those who *serve themselves* or *want to be served* would change the rules to benefit themselves and their own agendas. They would do this, not because these *humanity types* are any better or worse in any way than the service-oriented type, but because the Universal rules under which eternal servants operate could never provide Lunarian and Stellarian humans with the happiness they desire. Being responsible for another person's happiness is a time-consuming and sometimes monotonous duty. No part of this type of responsibility would fulfill the desires of Lunarian and Stellarian *humanity types*.

8. WE COULD ONLY BE CONVINCED THROUGH EXPERIENCE

The argument was not settled during our primordial existence. We were not fully convinced and didn't believe our first parents and their opinions any more than we believe our *imperfect parents* in this world. The only way for us to come to an understanding and become convinced for ourselves was to **find out for ourselves**.

Of course, once placed in an *imperfect world*, we would not be able to remember the argument; therefore, this life became the "day of our probation." We had to prove to ourselves what our creators were saying about us. We had to see firsthand how each of us would personally *act* when allowed the ability to create and have power over others and dominion over our environment.

Would we use it to have others serve us? Would we use it to serve ourselves? Or would we find our greatest *sense of peace and happiness* in the service of others, doing all that we do for the sake of others? Our probative experience away from the influence of advanced humans would prove that *who we are* is **truly the best for us**.

9. TIME AWAY FROM OUR CREATORS ALLOWS US TO VALUE OUR TRUE SELF

For this mortal probative period, we were given a world where we would be allowed the ability to have sex and have *limited* power and control over our environment. Here upon the earth, it appears to us (because we have no known interaction with them) that we are unsupervised by those whom we would recognize as ones we should obey and whom we know have ultimate power and always use it properly. If we could remember our life experience with our creators, there would have been no question that we would live more like we did when we were with them, because we would remember how wonderful it was to live that way. We would know without a doubt that there was an *overseer* monitoring the use of our free will, who would eventually step in and keep us from violating the rules. We would know that we could be monitored and watched at all times.

It's easier to understand this concept by using the example of comparing how employees of equal standing act when their boss is around and monitoring what they are doing, with how they act when their boss is gone on vacation for a few weeks and they know they are not being monitored. Would they continue to work with the same integrity, the same motivation, and always in the same emotional state as when their boss is present?

It would make sense that the ones, the very few, who continue to act the exact same way while their boss is gone as they do while the boss is around would be considered the most beneficial and productive employees. The others enjoy the aspect of "play" in the notion, "While the cat's away, the mice will play!"

Many people do not enjoy their job or their boss, and when there's an opportunity to violate the rules, whether that be from simply taking a longer break than allowed, to extorting money and materials from one's employer and justifying these actions in any way, most will do anything to make their employment seem more tolerable. (This example in no way reflects the integrity of a person who is a loyal employee even though he or she gains little to no happiness in the current employment opportunities to which humans are subjected while in an *imperfect* world. The example is only used to get a specific point across about our state of mind in the presence of *advanced human beings* and what our state of mind might be when we are not around *them*.)

The point is, we would never act true to our ***real*** **self** if we were aware that our parents/creators were monitoring our actions. Because the purpose of life in an *imperfect* world is to *prove to ourselves* who we *really* are, our knowledge of any humans outside of our earth is restricted. As far as we know for sure, there is no other life form in the Universe except that which is found upon the earth. And if there happens to be, none directly intervenes into our daily lives, as far as we know.

10. THERE IS NO SUCH THING AS "FAILURE"

In a situation where we are *expected* to fail, there can be no **real** *failure*. It was not intended for any of us to fail the experience of an *imperfect* life. How could we fail to fail? It is impossible! The *imperfect* world was set up to cause us to fail; therefore, it is not counted as a *failure* for us.

Even if we could fail, our personal measure of failure would determine our *personal success*. This success is not based on the *failure* of our actions, but rather on what we learned from it. Our consciousness is the continual effort of our *imperfect* brain trying to match the energy patterns/levels (memories) of our *essence*. When the energy we expend (our actions, thoughts, and experience) matches those stored in our *essence*, we *sense* a state of peace and equilibrium that we equate to the feelings of *joy* and *happiness*. If our actions, thoughts, and experience don't match those that are stored in our essence, then we feel anxious, sad, depressed, angry, lonely, etc. If we can accept our current life as a series of "failures," per seay, intended to teach us something about ourselves, then we will feel a whole lot better about our situation in an *imperfect world.*

Our overall motivation in life is to feel peace and happiness. Yet again, the overall purpose of an *imperfect world* is to give us the opportunity to experience the *opposite* of peace and happiness. Therefore, no matter what we do, we can *never* fail in this life. We can only learn from the experience. Our experiences in an *imperfect world* will forever allow us to recognize just how wonderful human existence can be. In the overall eternal picture of things, therefore, we were not created to fail. We were created so that we might have joy.

11. OUR "FAILURE" IS THE PURPOSE FOR THIS LIFE

We are now well into "the game of life" (*circa* 2012 upon the planet we call Earth), and near the end of the time allotted for us to "play the game." Generally, we can all agree that by our *continual failure* to find peace and happiness, we—as a group of humans—are succeeding quite well at the *real* purpose of life. As each of us individually is **unable** to find continual peace and happiness, we have won the game that all along we thought we were losing.

As explained previously, advanced human beings are monitoring our individual experiences as mortals. They intercede at times (unseen and unnoticed, and not how most people would like to believe) in order to ensure, not only that the "game is played" fairly, but that each of us has every opportunity we need to learn for ourselves. And what do we need to learn? That indeed it would be foolish to allow us to have the abilities of a powerful human creator. For this reason, we each live various lives while going through the time frame allotted to "play the game." At the end of "the game," all of those who questioned our creators in the first place will see for themselves exactly *why* their creators/parents were right.

12. MANY LIFETIMES ARE NEEDED TO HELP US UNDERSTAND OURSELVES

Most of us will be given the opportunity to live many times during our mortality in an *imperfect* world. During each lifetime, we will be placed where we need to be to help us gain proper experience and understanding about who we have chosen to be.

We will be female in some lives, male in others; born into wealth in some, poverty-stricken in others; dark-skinned in some, light-skinned in others; allowed physical beauty and strength in some, homeliness, deformities, and physical disabilities in others. Although sometimes the placement of our *essence* into a particular body is random, as most people can learn from the same experiences, the advanced beings who monitor our *essences* will always make sure that what each of us needs to *prove our humanity* is accommodated.

If we are prejudiced against dark-skinned people in one life, we may, for example, come back as a dark-skinned person. If we believe males are the more capable gender, we may come back as a woman. If we believe that people should respect and honor their own family, culture, and traditions, and maintain a patriotic concern for their own country, we may be born into a third-world country ripe with unrest and tyranny. If we have any propensity or feeling that we are better than another in any way, we may come back into a life where we will have the opportunity to experience life in the shoes of those we have judged as inferior to us.

If we condemn the murderer, the thief, the terrorist, the rapist, the pedophile, the drug user, the prostitute, or the mentally or physically challenged, we may be put into similar circumstances and environments that led our **equally eternal siblings** to use their free agency to commit what we judge to be atrocious crimes and behavior. And it can be guaranteed that most of us will do what they did if placed in similar circumstances.

There might be some wisdom in the often quoted, but hardly ever heeded counsel: "Judge not, that ye be not judged. For with what judgment ye judge, ye shall be judged: and with what measure ye mete, it shall be measured to you again." (King James Bible, Matthew 7:1–2)

13. ANY ACTION THAT DOES NOT SUPPORT AND RESPECT FREE WILL IS A MISUSE OF OUR FREE WILL

Keep in mind that we are meant to fail in life; and by our failures, or the experience of unhappiness, we learn more about ourselves. Remember the argument, *"How do you (parents/creators) know, just because we do not choose to have children and be responsible for them, that we would misuse the power to control the elements?"*

Part of the responsibility in controlling the elements that create the environments in which human beings exist is that everything is always done in equality and for the sake of others. Free agency is always encouraged and protected by those who control the Universe. Any thought, any action, any expenditure of energy that is *not* used to support this equality and free agency is a **misuse of power**.

Most people judge others or condemn others for exercising their own free agency. When we form a personal opinion of somebody or something that others might do with their free will, is this not an expenditure of our energy through thought and consideration? And when our judgment does not support the ability of another to exercise their free will as they desire, as long as their free will does not impede the free will of another, is this not a **misuse of power**? There are but few humans in an *imperfect world* who do not find a need in the pursuit of their own happiness to violate the free agency of another in some way. In so doing, they justify the **misuse of power**.

14. THE WEALTHY MISUSE FREE WILL

For just one example of many, consider this: Imagine a person is rich in material goods in this world and judges the poor as irresponsible or "second class." This person also does **not** do all that he or she can to ensure that all others have equal opportunities to have the material goods that he or she has (if they so desire). Therefore, in this scenario, this person demonstrates the **misuse of power**. These are those who subject others to be their servants and who desire that others serve their needs in their businesses and corporations. These are those who seek financial security and wealth by the sweat of another person's brow and not by their own—this means that others do the bulk of the physical labor while they benefit thereby without laboring for that which they earn.

Although some of these might argue that they were once poor and worked hard to get to the position of authority and power over those who work for them, they cannot deny that being poor and serving others made them unhappy—for this reason they desired to become rich!

If laboring for another makes a person unhappy, and that person desires to become wealthy and powerful so that they will not have to work hard anymore, is that not evidence of the *humanity type* that fits a person *who wants others to serve them* (Stellarian)? When the whole idea of wealth and success revolves around having others exist in a position of servitude to support this wealth and success, are the *humanity types* who desire these things not creating inequality; and therefore demonstrating a **misuse of power**?

15. NOTHING WRONG WITH THE DESIRE TO BE WEALTHY

In our creators' eyes, however, there is absolutely nothing wrong with a person wanting to become rich and having others serve them. Why would there be? We were given the opportunity during our *Foundationalization Process* to make the choice *to be served*, having an irrevocable guarantee to be able to have this choice fulfilled in every way.

However, those who chose this *humanity type* (Stellarian) ***cannot have the power of a creator***. And their "success" in an *imperfect* world in *failing* to support equality and free agency for all people, when they had the chance to wield power and authority over others, will prove the point to them.

Again, there are advanced beings who monitor the mortal lives of those going through their second stage of development. They will ensure that during one of their mortal lives, those who are of the Stellarian *humanity type* will be put in a position of wealth and authority over others, if not by their own choice and hard work, then by birth into a wealthy and "successful" family. And when they are experiencing wealth and power over others and finding a *sense* of happiness in doing this, these people can rest assured that they will *never* be granted the powers and abilities of human creators. No employer, for example, who gains personal happiness from the labors that others perform *for* them (no matter how much money they pay their employees in an effort to justify that it is okay that others *serve their needs*) *will ever* be allowed the power of a human creator.

16. WE CAN DO NO WRONG IN AN IMPERFECT WORLD

The same can be presented in thousands of scenarios of human experience in our *imperfect world*. If we find any justification or sense of joy in forming a personal opinion about somebody (judging another) who has free will equal to our own, we are **misusing the power of free will**. Any time we put our own needs above those of another, if it is within our control to provide equally for both, we are **misusing the power**.

From the moment we were left to ourselves in this *imperfect world*, without the ability to recall our associations with advanced humans, we began to take control of our environment. We use the power of our free agency to satisfy the inner longings of our subconscious by expending our energy in pursuit of balance between our conscious brain and our *essence*. We pursue our individual happiness.

The conflict and misery associated with human nature ensues because the vast majority of us can only find our balance in *serving ourselves* or *being served by others*. Thus it can be properly said that a world with all of its injustices, atrocities, and misery is indeed a *perfect world* for the intended purpose of its creation. It can also be said that those responsible for these injustices, atrocities, and miseries are doing no wrong—they are merely searching for and finding their personal balance.

17. WHATEVER MAKES US HAPPY IS RIGHT FOR US

How can any of us judge a wealthy person who has many servants and slaves to be doing wrong, when that person chose the *humanity type* of one who wants to be served by others? In an *imperfect* world, they may appear to be doing the *wrong* thing. But when they were *foundationalized* in a *perfect* world, they were doing the *right* thing, because they were granted the ability by their creators to choose to have others serve them. However, because it will have been proven that their choice of action causes inequality, before they get their perfect body, they must be convinced *why* they cannot be trusted with the power and abilities granted to a human creator.

Their actions in this *imperfect* world, or better, their individual pursuits of happiness here upon this earth, will provide the appropriate probative experience for them. It will be proven that their parents/creators were right: Only those who find their happiness in serving others can be trusted with the power that will maintain equality and peace among free-willed beings.

When those who desire wealth and success for themselves and their families live once again in ***their*** *perfect world*, they will have their servants (whether free-willed Solarians or programmed, advanced, android-like humans) who will serve them forever. And they will always remember that in pursuit of their own chosen happiness, they created injustices, atrocities, and miseries for others. They will be completely satisfied (i.e., happy) with their Stellarian status in the Universe and never desire the power of a Creator.

18. SOLARIAN TYPES DO NOT NEED MANY LIVES

Unlike the majority of people who have chosen to be *served by others* or *serve themselves*, Solarian humanity types (those who made the choice to be servants) are not required to have many mortal lives. They have nothing to prove to themselves. They weren't involved in the argument centered on why only Solarians (they) could have "special" powers and abilities.

Most of their lives involve coming into an *imperfect* world as children who have short lives ended because of the choices of the other *humanity types*. Whether they die because of hunger, disease, or physical abuse or trauma, the advanced human monitors place Solarian *essences* in bodies they know will not last long in an *imperfect* world. The people who kill the children, whether directly through war and carnage, or indirectly through poverty and neglect, need the experience of seeing children die and suffer because of the free-willed choices ***they*** make. This will prove to them that their need *to be served* or *to serve themselves* has the potential of causing others misery and sorrow.

Solarian servants made the choice to "serve others" in the capacity of martyrs so that others could learn from the experience. Well can it be surmised that there are but few (very, very few) human beings upon this earth who have not used another for their own gain. And again, when we use another to make ourselves happy, we fall into the category of desiring that others *serve us* in some capacity or that we *serve ourselves* without concern for the plight of another.

Those who are *true* Solarian *humanity types* find little balance in an *imperfect world.* They find no happiness in the reality that another has to be unequal to them so that they can find happiness. Because they can *only* find happiness in attempting to serve others for the sake of others, they cannot bear to have anyone suffer in any way to support their own happiness; and they continually find themselves so concerned about the plight of others, that their own lives are lost.

However, the *imperfect* life is not about them; it is always about others. For this reason, most only find their *essences* used for the bodies of children as explained above, and some for the sake of creating the opportunity for others to know and understand the *true reality* of *who they are* and *why they exist.*

19. OUR CHOSEN OVERSEER NEEDS ONLY ONE MORTAL LIFETIME

We discussed the necessity of one of the children assigned to each solar system to become the predestined *overseer* of the rest. Because this human being had no choice in his upbringing, and the rest of us realized that because of this he will never misuse his power and abilities, he has no need to participate in an *imperfect* world except but once. He must be placed in an *imperfect* world for two main purposes:

20. AN OVERSEER NEVER MISUSES HIS POWER UNDER ANY CIRCUMSTANCE

The first purpose is to prove to the rest of us that he was indeed *foundationalized* correctly for what he was intended to do. We must know that *he will always* support the Universal laws of humanity and never do anything contrary to these laws no matter what consequences he is forced to face personally. How could any of us accept such complete authority and control over our solar system, even over our individual free agency, if the one who was placed in a position of control over us didn't have to go through what we did? We could question, "How do we know for sure that our *overseer* wouldn't have misused his power as we did if he were placed in similar circumstances?"

We have no need to prove to ourselves if any other of our siblings, who chose to be Solarian, can be trusted with the power of creation, because they are **not** our overseer. They will have an overseer watching over their actions just like the rest of us.

21. WE NEED AN OVERSEER TO SUPERVISE THE WAY WE USE OUR FREE WILL

Another reason why the overseer came to this *imperfect* world was to prove to those who are *not destined* to be creators that—even if there was one among them to teach them the proper rules of "the game"—they would reject him. The people of the world would be shown that even if there was one upon earth who revealed all the truths of the Universe, which *imperfect* humans cannot remember on their own, this *one* would still be rejected. Because *universal truth* mandates total equality in all things and a profound respect of individuality and free will, anyone who teaches these *universal truths* would be perceived as a threat to the free will of those who want *others to serve them.*

It must be proven to us ***why*** an overseer is needed. We must unconditionally, without being forced, accept that this overseer has the right to exercise extraordinary power in supervision of our free agency, subjecting all of us to his supreme authority. While in an *imperfect* world, an overseer will never *improperly* exercise his power and authority over others, but will teach the simple truths that establish and promote peace and happiness for all people equally, thus giving us the chance to accept these truths without being forced. Because he and his message is usually always spurned and rejected by the majority, we will begin to understand *why an overseer must* use force in limiting the use of our free agency to fulfill the mandates of *universal human law*.

Again, we *succeeded* just fine, according to the premise of our *imperfect* world, by *failing* to recognize this overseer for who he was and to accept the simplicity of his message. If we cannot learn by ourselves to abide by the terms of our humanity, then we will be **forced** to choose to comply or terminate our existence as a human being. Moreover, because of our experience in condemning and rejecting our own overseer and his servants when given the opportunity, without them disclosing their *true identity*, we will finally be more willing to accept the necessary conditions that control our free will.

22. QUASI-OVERSEERS ARE SENT TO HELP US LEARN

There is always only ONE overseer per solar system. Who he is and the reason for his existence have been explained previously. None of us will have the excuse that, "*I would have surely accepted the overseer and his message had I heard about it during one of my lifetimes in the imperfect world. Therefore, how do you creators/parents know that I wouldn't have if I didn't have the opportunity to hear him or his message?*" Rest assured. Our creators have taken all of our excuses into consideration.

Because it is contrary to the very nature of our free agency to be controlled by another, it was necessary to see what would happen if we were given the chance to accept the Universal laws of humanity without being *forced* to accept them. Other Solarian servants (from our batch of children) are chosen to live in mortality at various times in our *imperfect* world to ensure that all of us have the opportunity during *at least one* of our lifetimes to learn the appropriate rules and hear the *same* message of peace and equality supported by our overseer. Each of the *quasi*-overseers comes at a certain stage of human development in our *imperfect* world, being placed strategically throughout the world in many different isolated human cultures.

In all of these situations though, there has always been *only ONE* who is prepared and given the permission by our creators to teach the people. This is to give us the experience of listening to the counsel of just ONE, instead of the possibility of the confusion that would occur if *more than one* free-willed person were assigned to teach the people in their *own* way.

There are not many of these *quasi*-overseers needed for any one world. They can come back in many lifetimes and do the same thing they did in a previous life, which is to teach the people the message of **real truth** and the proper way to live with each other. These others were and are treated the exact same way as the overseer was in his one lifetime experience; they were and are spurned and their message was and is rejected by the majority of *imperfect humans* for the same reasons *imperfect humans* rejected their own overseer.

23. WE CANNOT DECEIVE OURSELVES INTO THINKING WE CAN BE TRUSTED

Each time these *true messengers* are rejected by the people, we are further convinced *why* it is necessary that our free will is curtailed and monitored by someone besides ourselves. No matter how good our intentions, no matter how much control we *think* we have over our thoughts and actions, the fact that we have free will makes us all susceptible to the possibility of misusing our free agency to take away that of another.

Many of us will go through some of our lives convinced that we have done nothing to harm another or impede equality and the ability of another to exercise their free will as we exercised our own. It is not until all things are fully revealed and understood that we will know for sure if our chosen lifestyle and actions did indeed do no harm.

Most of us have very little concern for anyone outside of ourselves and those whom we choose to value with our "love." Those who concentrate all of their energy on their own family unit will never be immune from the possibility that their self- and family-centered actions have not caused another person an unequal situation in life. All we have to do is trace the ripple effect of any one of our actions back to its original source and we will be surprised about the many injustices caused to others because of that one action. For example:

24. OUR ACTIONS UNKNOWINGLY CAUSE INEQUALITY

More than likely the reader of this book is reading these words via some source of written communication, either from a book, a printed page, or from a computer screen. It takes basic natural resources from the earth to make the products or produce the apparatus upon which the reader is reading these words (i.e., paper and ink, or computer components). If the reader were to patiently dissect the means of receiving this information, one would find that someone (or many) along the way of production was taken advantage of and treated FAR less than equal to the reader.

In an *imperfect* world, matter does not materialize out of nowhere. The basic materials of all things come from some source provided by the earth. These resources must be gathered and processed into the parts of the things we use in our daily lives. There is no doubt that those who begin the process of gathering the materials from the earth needed for the product, and those who produce the product, are treated much differently than he or she who uses the product. If we gain some sort of happiness and enjoyment from the use of any product, and we do not produce it ourselves from start to finish, then we are indirectly **misusing the expenditure of our energy to create inequality for someone else**.

Again, in an *imperfect* world, it is almost impossible to avoid creating inequality. A fieldworker, for example, will never be granted the same importance as a medical doctor, although the medical doctor needs the fieldworker to pick his food just as much as the fieldworker needs the doctor to reset a broken limb. However, if the doctor does not want to ***misuse*** his free agency to create inequality, he or she should be anxiously engaged in trying to create equality between the medical profession and the fieldworkers. Why don't they both receive the same pay?

25. FORGIVENESS IS THE ESSENTIAL NATURE OF CREATORS

We do not always know what we do in this life that causes others to suffer; therefore, WE WILL NEVER BE CONDEMNED by our creators for following the *true feelings* of our desires and seeking to *be served* or for *serving ourselves*. Advanced humans created us and are responsible for us as the free-willed beings who turned out this way. It is their responsibility to make sure we have the environment necessary so that we can generate the experiences that will satisfy *who we are*.

From the most extreme mass murderer to the little old lady who judges the actions of her annoying neighbor, none will be made to suffer for following the dictates of his or her own conscience. What they will learn from their experience, however, is that they have chosen a course in life that confirms that they will never become like their creators/parents and share in their unique powers and abilities.

26. IMPERFECT FAMILY UNITS DESTROY EQUALITY AND ISOLATE US FROM OTHERS

One of the first things we did to create inequality in pursuing our own happiness in an *imperfect world* was to create the family unit. Family units cause us to separate and isolate ourselves from others. Not knowing any better, and motivated by the intense desire to have sex, males and females have their *own* children. In so doing, they feel a bond of attachment associated with those for whom they are responsible.

Whatever it takes to support this family unit, even at the expense of others or their natural environment, *imperfect* humans are sure to expend their energy in the support and protection of their *own family*. There wouldn't be any problem, *if* the environment always provided *equally* for each family unit. But the environment of an *imperfect* world is not set up to provide for everyone equally. Its natural resources are limited, causing each family to protect what it needs in order to survive.

27. OUR IMPERFECT WORLD IS CENTERED AROUND MONEY

Before long, establishing bordered homes, communities, cities, nations, and countries and killing others to protect one's own family became a justifiable and reasonable expenditure of energy—but still always a **misuse of power**. When the human race spread throughout the world, and the families it had formed took power and control over the limited natural resources of the earth, we had to find an appropriate way to place values on these resources. Therefore, we created money.

The introduction of money began to control every aspect of our expenditure of energy. Every waking thought and action has something to do with making enough money to support our families or ourselves. The concept of money introduced designated values for everything in our world. Along with the values we place on the material things of the world, we began to place values on each other according to what we owned and how well we earned and managed our money. The "game of life" became a game about money: how it is earned, how it is managed, and how it affects our daily lives. We have set up a world in which it is impossible to live without money.

There are those of us who know how to play the game of money so well, that even if everyone in the world were given one million dollars, the few who know and play the game well would have the millions belonging to others in their own pockets in a matter of just a few weeks.

28. MONEY CANNOT BUY HAPPINESS

No matter how wealthy a person is and no matter how much control and power one might have over others, finding continued happiness in an *imperfect* world seems impossible. It seems impossible, because it is!

No matter how hard we try, unless we have a perfect body in a perfect environment, we will never be able to match the experiences that are *foundationalized* in our subconscious *essence*. Emotional turmoil is the bane of our mortal existence. From the negative emotional situations that arise in an *imperfect* world, a wide variety of mental illnesses add to our mortal experience. Well can it be said that we are all mentally ill.

29. WE ARE ALL INSANE—THEREFORE, NONE OF US ARE

Let's take, for example, a man who walks down the street talking to himself. In his mind, a conversation is taking place between his *conscious* mind and something that appears to him to be coming from outside of his head. We judge this man to be "insane."

Yet, the majority of people, if honest, would admit that they have had conversations in their own heads. Most believe that they can communicate with unseen sources outside of themselves and therefore expend their energy (create the experience) attempting to communicate with something or someone who is not actually there. Because it takes place in the privacy of one's own intimate surroundings instead of out in public, it is considered to be a "sane" and appropriate thing to do.

But is it? How can the very same experience (that of having a conversation with someone or something that others cannot see) be "sane" in one instance and "insane" in another? It just doesn't make sense! And it certainly is not being fair and equal to those judged to be "insane"!

Therefore, any of us who judge another person as being insane, because he or she is not afraid to carry on intimate conversations with unseen entities outside of themselves in public, **misuse the power** that should maintain equality. The fact is, we are all equally insane! We all have *imperfect* bodies in an *imperfect* world.

30. LOOKING TO OTHERS TO LEAD US CAUSES INEQUALITY

Many of our societal problems can be traced to those who believe an outside source communicates with them and tells them what to do and what to tell others to do. Throughout our history, great masses of free-willed humans have been placed under the influence of charismatic leaders, who have effectively convinced the people that their "mental illness" is not a mental illness at all, but a divinely directed mandate given by the progenitor of the thoughts that come to them.

These human leaders **misuse power**, because they literally take away the free will of others and replace it with their own. Keep in mind, during our *Foundationalization Process*, not one of our creators told any of us (except for the one to be the overseer) what to think or how to act. We were taught to become our own individual self, not the product of another's experience, but that of our own.

But because we cannot remember these *foundational* experiences, we have become confused by our situation in an *imperfect* world and make ourselves susceptible to someone outside of ourselves telling us *who we are* and *why we exist*. We look to a leader or someone who we think knows more than us, about us, to guide us.

Many of these leaders and their groups have come and gone throughout our history, and many still exist today; yet none of them has ever been able to speak to all of humanity equally. None of them has been able to speak to our common sense and convince all of us that what they say is true *for everyone*. And, if what a leader teaches is not true *for everyone equally*, it is a **misuse of power** and creates inequality.

31. INEQUALITY IS CREATED BY THOSE WHO BELIEVE THEY ARE SPECIAL

There are many people who believe they have tapped into some cosmic force outside of their own body and that this *force* is available to all people equally. They claim that they have found the secret to retrieving this *force* and using it for their own purposes.

To protect their integrity and keep the rest of us from referring to them as "insane," they explain that the "force" is available to all of us equally, but that only a few of us are more "gifted" in the ability to access it more readily than others. In stating this, they are insinuating that we are *not all equal*, because the majority of us cannot "tap into" this *cosmic force* that only they understand and can "tap into."

Not one of these individuals has ever spoken to all of us equally and made complete sense out of our own inner longings and feelings (which, more often than not, completely disagree with what their "cosmic force" tells them). To create value for themselves and be compensated for this value, they write books, give seminars, and do anything else that will draw the free will of another to their own ways. They **misuse the power** because the solutions that they present are not universally agreeable to all people equally. In other words, their beliefs do not work for everybody; therefore, they are far from the **real truth**.

32. "SPECIAL ONES" CAN BE CURED LIKE ANY OTHER MENTALLY ILL PERSON

The same treatments we currently use to treat those whom we consider to be mentally ill can be used on those who believe they are somehow receiving outside communication. If anti-psychotic drugs were administered to those who make a claim of "inspiration" from outside of their own head, the delusional process by which they formulate their thoughts would abruptly end. Likewise, if a person making such a claim suffered physical damage to their brain, either from trauma or from natural deterioration of the brain tissue, the delusion of grandeur would also stop.

Current scientists have developed these drugs to treat those whom they consider to be "insane." But if seemingly "sane" people were to use the same drugs, they would likewise react the same way and all communication within one's own head, or from what appears to be coming from without (from *the cosmos*), would stop.

33. THE FEELING OF BEING "SPECIAL" COMES FROM OUR ESSENCE

The reason why so many of us believe that we receive communication from beyond our own brain is because of our lack of understanding of how our *essence* functions. This has been explained in the preceding chapters of this book.

All mental illnesses can be traced to our inability to properly balance the energy of our current experience with the patterns of energy established and subtly felt from our *essence*. This includes schizophrenia, bipolar disorder, and psychotic, eating, and anxiety disorders, to name just a few. It also includes those illnesses that are not categorized as those of one who is "insane," such as depression, fear, anxiety, insecurity, and being "in love."

The communications that go on inside of our heads and which often appear to be coming from another source outside of us are simply our *imperfect brain* being affected by the energy emissions of our *essence*. As explained previously, some of our brains are constructed differently than others, therefore allowing some of us to utilize the *essence* differently than others.

We have discussed how this occurs in those whom we have labeled "mentally challenged," such as savants and autistic people. And since many of us remain unconvinced that *we alone* are responsible for all of our thoughts and "in-head" communications, we cannot very well label others "insane," when many of us show the same characteristics.

34. THOSE WHO SEEK FOR ACCEPTANCE OF OTHERS WANT TO BE SERVED

Again, it is in an effort to have others serve us by honoring and respecting us that our humanity type is demonstrated. Those who set up followings of people whom they have convinced to listen to their views and understanding of life are merely seeking respect and honor from others. When they receive this respect and honor, they are being *served by others*. Those who pursue courses in life that make them famous and well-liked are also trying desperately to find those who will *serve their needs*.

Most people, however, do not need others' accolades and praises to find their own happiness. But they *do* need privacy and equality of resources to be able to pursue what makes them happy, distinct, and unique individuals. In all of our pursuits in life, none of us can be faulted for trying to achieve our own individual happiness, no matter what type of happiness that might be.

SUMMARY

The "game of life" in the *imperfect world* is set up so that we will *fail* in our efforts. But in our *failure*, we will have succeeded in solving our primordial argument with our parents/creators: *"How do you (parents/creators) know, that just because we do not choose to have children and be responsible for them, we would misuse the power to control the elements?"*

After going through mortality during our second stage of human development, we will know! With this understanding, we will be ready to accept the fact that we will never be able to experience sex again, nor will we be given the power to control the elements. We will be more than willing to accept *the way things are* in the Universe, the way things *have always been*, and the way things *will always be* in the future—**real truth** in worlds without end.

Imperfect Mortal Foundationalization

CHAPTER FOURTEEN

Parents wonder why the streams are bitter,
when they themselves have poisoned the fountain.

—John Locke

1. CONSISTENT HAPPINESS IS ELUSIVE ON EARTH

We have covered how we are all affected by the same mental disorders in some form or another. We've concluded that, consistent with the purpose intended by our creators, continual and consistent happiness eludes us no matter what we try to do in an *imperfect* world. To experience the full effect of mortality, it was intended for us to live various incarnations upon this earth. From each mortal life we experience, we gain further proof that the rules and laws of a *perfect world* are just and true.

We learn just how necessary and important these laws are in support of our free agency because we live during times when these laws are not enforced. The Universal and unchangeable laws of a *perfect human world* allow each person to be happy with the self each has chosen. They protect us from the free will of others. Upon living in an *imperfect* world, we are finding out just how elusive consistent and continual happiness is, unless the *perfect* rules and laws for human behavior are implemented.

Our various lifetimes in mortality, throughout the different time periods of human history upon Earth, further convince us that most free-willed beings *cannot* be trusted with the power and abilities that our service-oriented advanced parents/creators have.

We've learned through our lives' experience that, when given power over another's free will, most of us will seek to establish and protect *our own* individuality and free agency, in spite of how our choices affect other's free agency.

The most important thing that we have learned is that **nothing** we do during our mortalities upon this earth can be counted as a failure. This is because the success of living in an *imperfect world* is measured by our failure to find enduring happiness. This "failure" ensures that we will be forever appreciative of living in one of the infinite *perfect human societies* that exist throughout the Universe. There is no other purpose for the experiences of this life that are diametrically opposed to our happiness, which our advanced creators/parents allow us to go through for our own good.

2. IMPROPER PARENTING KEEPS US FROM TRUE HAPPINESS

It is vital to a proper understanding of *who we are* and *why we exist* to have a more complete comprehension of exactly *how* we learned to act so blatantly contrary to the way we were *foundationalized* by our creators. Why do mortal humans act so inhumanely? Why can't we figure out how to live peacefully and equally with each other by being humane in all that we do? We have made progress and advancements in improving our ability to live what seems to be a more civilized and advanced life than our ancestors. Why, then, is the pursuit of happiness in this life such an emotional battle? The answer to these questions lies in **how** we were *foundationalized* by our *imperfect* parents in an *imperfect* world.

A proper parenting manual is not available to guide *imperfect* mortals in the correct way to *foundationalize* other *imperfect* mortals. When it comes right down to it, mortal parents are directly responsible for the inability of their children to find happiness in life. But, if the parent is responsible for the way the child is reared, then the grandparent is just as responsible for the way the parent was reared, and so on and so on, back through our human ancestry. Tracing back the roots of *imperfect parenting* leads us again to our advanced creators. They placed us upon this earth without intervening and explaining how to *foundationalize* our children correctly. For a very good reason, they *didn't* tell us! If they had, we wouldn't have an *imperfect world* from which to gain the intended experiences we needed.

3. THE FAMILY UNIT PROVIDES THE FOUNDATION FOR THE IMPERFECT WORLD

After the *imperfect* human race had established itself upon this earth, it wasn't long before all those being born into mortality, to *imperfect parents*, entered the world into an *imperfect* and unequal situation. Some were born into great wealth and security, others into reasonable comfort and protections, but most into abject poverty and mortal danger. The main cause of this inequality is ironically what the *imperfect human race* believes to be its greatest strength—the family unit. We have already discussed how the perpetuation and support of these "units" causes us to disregard the needs of others in response to the needs and wants of our own *family*. Indeed, the "family" is the greatest strength of an *imperfect world*. These "units" will keep the human race forever **imperfect**!

4. WE ARE CONTINUALLY SEARCHING FOR HAPPINESS

We've discussed how our sex drive leads us to "love," and that these feelings motivate us to establish a *family unit* by creating a measure of value upon which we place our personal happiness. We've learned that "love" itself is another great contributory factor to our continual unhappiness. We've touched upon the concept of "money" and how it steals our hearts, controls our desires, and dominates our very existence. We've also determined that no matter how much money we have, we still do not experience continual happiness. Also, no matter how successful we are at satisfying our biological needs through sex and material things, there's a piece of the happiness puzzle still missing that doesn't have anything to do with the satisfaction of the natural senses of our physical body. We can have all of our physical senses satisfied, even to extremes, and still find ourselves out of balance with our *primordial foundationalization*. It was during this *Foundationalization Process* that we learned how to act humanely towards one another.

We are not experiencing anything close to what we experienced when we were created and *foundationalized* by advanced and perfect human beings. As individuals in an *imperfect* world, we are not respected and supported as we were when our creators helped us establish our ***true humanity***. Therefore, once our physiological needs are met in our *imperfect* world, we search endlessly to self-actualize. This means that we attempt to find our *true self,* to understand our individuality, to recognize our personality as our own, and to develop a sense of ease and balance with *who we are*.

5. INNER CONFLICT IS CAUSED BY UNREAL EXPECTATIONS

The conflict to find our *true self* is an endless battle within us. No one respects us for who we *really* are. Our *family units* have expectations already set for us before we are even out of the womb. The world expects us to be as it is, instead of each of us being able to be who we *truly* are as separate individuals. Because none of us can remember that we lived before our current incarnation, we are forced to accept the present conditions. These conditions become our only *known* reality.

Even when we meet the expectations of this preconditioned reality, we often feel out of balance. This occurs because our individuality and free will are not respected and supported as the memories in our *essence* reflect. (Remember, "Happiness" is simply the aligning of the energy patterns of our actions in our current experience with those already recorded on our *essence*.) Our *imperfect* mortal parents do not recognize us as an individual. They do not accept that we were *not* a member of their "family" in any of our previous lives, nor shall we be in any of our future lives. So the first cause of the unsettling feelings of "being lost" is the *foundationalization* we receive in this *imperfect* world from ***imperfect*** **parents** who haven't a clue what they are doing.

6. MORTAL PARENTS FOLLOW THEIR OWN PURSUIT OF HAPPINESS

Parents are seeking happiness just like their children. Children expect their parents to provide them with happiness, and parents expect the same of their children. Many people choose to become parents, not for the sake of the child, but for their own sake. They want a personal value that they are not receiving from an *imperfect* world. To offset the *imbalance* they feel, *imperfect* humans create a child that they *hope* will give them the value they desire. They create a *new human being* who they want to control and attempt to force to act as they (the parent) *need* the child to act in order to bring value to themselves. Once they have a child, parents try to give the child everything *they feel* will make the child happy. It makes *them* happy to give the child everything that the child wants, *because these actions are in balance with those experiences embedded in their essence*—it's the way they were treated by their *perfect* parents/creators.

In a *perfect* world, we were given everything we wanted by our perfect parents/creators, because it made *them* and *us* happy. In a *perfect* world, newly created humans are smiled upon, cooed to, and coddled. For this reason, it's a natural response for adults to smile and coo at newborn infants. It *feels* good when they do! It is natural for *imperfect* parents to respond to their children in ways similar to *perfect* parents on an advanced perfect world.

A mortal parent's desire to be attentive, nurturing, and provide for all of the child's needs naturally *feels* like the "right" thing to do. These actions balance with the energy patterns stored on the *essence*, thus justifying them as being *good*. However, they are **not** raising children in a *perfect world*, and many times, aggressive nurturing and too much catering can cause the child a serious disadvantage in an *imperfect* world.

7. WITH UNDERSTANDING, IMPERFECT PARENTS CAN HELP PREPARE THEIR CHILDREN FOR ADULTHOOD

Mortal children who receive too much attention and are treated as if the Universe revolves around only them, (which is exactly how each of us were *foundationalized* by perfect parents), have a hard time adjusting to the reality of this harsh world as an adult. Everything about an *imperfect* world is in opposition to how a loving parent rears a child.

There are those parents who isolate their children from the travesties and vicissitudes of the real world, only to produce emotionally insecure children and ones who do not adapt well as adults. When *imperfect* parents realize what our *true* purpose for being upon this earth in mortality actually is, they will be in a better position to prepare their children for the world into which they chose to introduce the child.

If our advanced perfect parents sent us here and expected us to experience the *opposite* of all that is perfect, then it would follow that a good and wise *imperfect* parent would prepare their children for the *imperfect* world as an adult. This preparation should be well thought out and planned. The perfect, *imperfect foundationalization* should be done in such a way as to aid the child in being able to find the self and enjoy *who they are*, even though the child lives in an *imperfect world*. This preparation should never include too much praise of the child, too much control, or too much *imperfect* **love**.

8. OVERPROTECTION ADDS TO OUR UNHAPPINESS

Our *imperfect* parents protect us from what they *believe* will cause us harm. What our parents *believe* will cause us harm and what actually would are often two completely different things. If mortal parents understood the ***true value*** of our existence in an *imperfect* world, they would not fear or worry so much for their child's safety. During our *imperfect foundationalization* years, we hear the word "No!" more than any other word of direction given.

In contrast, we never heard the word "No!" in a perfect world. Is it any cause of wonder, therefore, that our parents are *stressed* when they say the word "No!" They are stressed because the expenditure of energy created in formulating the thought that precedes the command of "No!" does not match (balance with) the *perfect* foundation of their own *essence*.

However, generally our parents have no choice but to tell us "No!" We live in an *imperfect* world where our bodies fall instead of float. In our current world, bees sting instead of tickle. We have to be careful of what we put into our mouths because of viral or bacterial infection. Our *imperfect* bodies are susceptible to infections. (There weren't, of course, any viruses or bacteria that would hurt us in a perfect world). To make matters worse, if our *imperfect* parents were to allow us to explore our environment and learn from our own experience, and develop our unique personalities according to the effort of our *essence* to express itself in our actions, our *imperfect* society would judge them as unsuitable parents and take us away.

9. IT IS NATURAL FOR US TO DESIRE TO BE PARENTS

Why did our parents decide to create us and bring us into a world that they very well knew would cause us considerable misery? Didn't they sit down and contemplate what they were doing? Didn't they realize that by our very nature we would rebel against their "No's"? Isn't one of our first contentions with our parents caused by our ability to stand up for ourselves and say "No!" to them when we are not allowed to do what we want? Did they stop and think that maybe adding another human being to the world would not really help anyone, except for maybe providing more cheap labor for those who need others to serve them? What were our parents thinking when they decided to create us?

Until more recent times, our parents didn't *think* much about having children. They gave in to their natural desires for sex, and children were the byproduct of satisfying their sensual needs. In addition, for most women and some men, the desire to have children is much deeper than just the physical desire for sex. There is a natural desire to be parents. Why? Because this is the experience recorded on our *essence*—we were all *foundationalized* by parents! None of us are immune from the feeling of happiness and value that a child gives us in looking up to us and needing us. The natural *urge* to find individual value and happiness is a product of us attempting to bring our current actions in line with the subconscious energy stored as past experiences in our *essence*. But once our natural desire to be a parent is satisfied and we become responsible for the children we create, the conflict begins when we have to figure out what to do with them in an *imperfect world*.

10. OUR PARENTS' FREE-WILLED CHOICE BROUGHT US INTO THIS WORLD

In more ancient times, the *conscious choice* to have children was also influenced by the necessity to have more physical bodies to help take care of the family unit—the more hands in the field, the easier the harvest. However, the *necessity* of having children solely to support the family unit diminished as technologies developed and replaced physical labor.

In more recent times, humans have the choice of whether to have a child or not, and the decision to (or not to) is largely motivated by purely selfish reasons. No child in an *imperfect world* is ever created for the sake of the child. Only advanced, perfect parents create a *new* human being for the sake of the *new human being*. We came into this world because our parents were seeking to satisfy their *own desires* of happiness.

11. OUR TRUE SELF IS LOST IN ESTABLISHED PREJUDICES

No one in the *perfect* world dictates to a free-willed child what it *should* do or who it *should* become. If any amount or any type of control were used in the *Foundationalization Process*, the individual would lose free will and become a product of the *will* forced upon that person by others.

In contrast, every *imperfect* parent has an established set of opinions, perceptions, prejudices, judgments, traditions, beliefs, and aspirations that they pass on to their children. These were often *foundationalized* in them by their own parents and the societies and cultures in which they live. No matter how much we rebel to protect our individual free will, our parents force their opinions, perceptions, prejudices, judgments, traditions, beliefs, and aspirations upon us.

Unfortunately (but according to the intention set forth for our mortality), in our *imperfect* body, our *imperfect foundationalization* has an enormous amount of power over our free will. Because our *imperfect* brains cannot fully access our *perfect essence*, the energy patterns (memories) stored in our brains are much stronger than the constant and subtle energy patterns stored in our *perfect* foundationalized *essence*. The energy patterns of our *imperfect* parents' teachings and example are stored forefront in our *imperfect* brain and are the main cause of the imbalance and unhappiness that we experience throughout our life. Consequently, our *perfect humanity* becomes lost in the subconscious realm of our dreams and imaginative thoughts.

In our present world, we can only *dream* of and *imagine* a world of equality where no prejudices, judgments, condemnations, forced opinions, beliefs, and traditions exist. But because we can dream about it and imagine it, this type of world *is* possible. However, to achieve this type of world in our *imperfect state*, we must use more energy of *thought* and force ourselves to rend the tapestry of *inhumanity* that our parents have woven to cover our ***true selves***.

12. OUR PARENTS ARE NOT TO BLAME

Before we discuss just how *improperly* our mortal parents *foundationalize* us, we need to understand and accept that it is NOT their fault! All normal parents would like to rear their children in a world of peace and harmony, one with no conflict or turmoil, and with an abundance of goods to take care of all of our human needs—parents dream and imagine too!

However, their experience in mortality has taught them otherwise. They have learned and convinced themselves that the *perfect world* is just a hope, a dream, an imaginative utopia that can never be. They do not blame the *imperfection* of our world on their own personal set of opinions, perceptions, prejudices, judgments, traditions, beliefs, and aspirations. In their minds, someone else caused all the problems. Because they do not believe that a perfect world is possible, they have become a major contributor to the reason *why it is not.* They have stopped trying to *imagine* what could be, because they have found personal security in accepting *what is.* What else could be expected from *imperfect* mortal parents?

13. IT'S IMPOSSIBLE TO BE A PERFECT PARENT IN AN *IMPERFECT* WORLD

We know that this mortality is a time for us to experience the *opposite* of all that is *perfect* so that we can learn to appreciate all there is about being human. Therefore, it makes sense why our creators would provide a situational environment upon this earth where it is *impossible* for anyone to be a *perfect* parent. First, none of us can remember what a *perfect parent* is supposed to be like. Second, we don't have the physical body or the resources to be this type of parent. And third, most of us chose *humanity types* that have nothing to do with *perfect parenting*. Because the majority of us *did not* choose the *humanity type* of a servant/parent who creates and serves children for the child's sake alone, it would *naturally* be contrary to our happiness to have children for any reason other than to serve our *own* needs.

Mortal parents are only doing what they were *foundationalized* by their *imperfect parents* to do, or what they are allowed by *imperfect societies of human beings* to do. These restrictions and parameters uphold the purpose of an *imperfect* world. Therefore, it is **impossible to fail** as a mortal parent. In fact, it would appear consistent with the purpose of our mortal life that the **more** misery and opposition to peace and happiness parents cause in a child's life, the more "successful" they are at fulfilling the purpose for which they are allowed to be parents in mortality.

14. HUMANITY WANES AS WE GAIN MORTAL EXPERIENCE

The reason why we can't seem to get it together in mortality and be consistently humane to each other is because of how we are *foundationalized* here. Little children are more humane than any of us. They easily smile when their basic needs are taken care of, and they have no preconceived notion of opinions, perceptions, prejudices, judgments, traditions, beliefs, or aspirations. Little children lack pretentious egos. Their greatest propensity for demonstrating proper humanity is their unconditional ability to forgive. They are incapable of holding a grudge, *until* they are taught how to by those who *foundationalize* them *imperfectly*.

A little child's *essence* is the "power source" that is responsible for generating their innocence and perfect humanity. But, as these little ones develop, what is recorded in their physical brain will eventually *veil* the energy levels that are produced by their *essence.* They will eventually become as *inhumane* as those who are responsible for allowing the energy patterns of *imperfect* experience to be stored in the forefront of their brains.

In other words, the energy patterns of their actions in mortality are mapped out in the structure of their *imperfect* brain as memories and experiences. This "mapping" or "imprinting" hinders their ability to be influenced and motivated by their *true and perfect essence.* Their ability to act *true to their inner self* becomes obstructed proportionately to the development of their *imperfect* brain. The more we learn and experience in the *imperfect world* of mortality, the less humane we become.

Now we can understand why the following lyrics make so much sense:

When I was young
It seemed that life was so wonderful
A miracle, oh it was beautiful, magical
And all the birds in the trees
Well they'd be singing so happily
Oh joyfully, oh playfully watching me

But then they sent me away
To teach me how to be sensible
Logical, oh responsible, practical
And then they showed me a world
Where I could be so dependable
Oh clinical, oh intellectual, cynical.

There are times when all the world's asleep
The questions run too deep
For such a simple man
Won't you please, please tell me what we've learned
I know it sounds absurd
But please tell me who I am

I said, now watch what you say
Or they'll be calling you a radical
A liberal, oh fanatical, criminal
Oh won't you sign up your name
We'd like to feel you're
Acceptable, respectable, oh presentable, a vegetable!

But at night when all the world's asleep
The questions run so deep
For such a simple man
Won't you please, please tell me what we've learned
I know it sounds absurd
But please tell me who I am, who I am, who I am, who I am.

Supertramp, "The Logical Song" (© 1979 A&M Records: Los Angeles, CA); *on* Breakfast in America [CD].

15. EARLY CHILDHOOD LEARNING INFLUENCES OUR IMPERFECT NATURE

We have acquired "logic" or "common sense" by which we make the decisions to act and allow ourselves to be acted upon during our life experience. Our *imperfect* **common sense** is a *collection* of the opinions, perceptions, prejudices, judgments, traditions, beliefs, and aspirations that we acquired while our brain was developing. In contrast, our ***true* common sense** was established in our *essence* and aligned during our perfect *Foundationalization Process.* During this primordial process, we were not exposed to *opinions, perceptions, prejudices, judgments, traditions, beliefs, and aspirations* that were not part of the *perfect* human world.

How can any part of the *imperfect common sense* "collection" we gain in mortality be consistent with *perfect humanity*, when every part of it was ***collected*** in an *imperfect world* and placed in an *imperfect* brain? How can <u>any</u> part of <u>anything</u> we experience in mortality be construed as important to our humanity, except the experience we gain?

Our parents and those who teach us and provide us with our "collection" do not understand that mortality **is** an *imperfect state of human existence.* Their only reality is the one that they are consciously aware of and can remember. And AGAIN, the reason *why* they cannot remember is so that we CAN HAVE THE EXPERIENCE OF AN *IMPERFECT* LIFE!

Everything we learn, everything we experience, and everything we <u>think</u> we know (even our entire "collection" of opinions, perceptions, prejudices, judgments, traditions, beliefs, and aspirations acquired while existing in mortality) will **never** be a part of our future in a *perfect* human world. But while we are here in mortality, these things are very important to us. The reason we suffer is because we allow and support this *imperfect collection* of personal encumbrances to our ***true humanity***, and they become very important to us.

16. PARENTS SEEK HAPPINESS THROUGH THEIR CHILDREN

Mortal parents not only seek love and respect from their children, but also the adoration and respect of others *because* of their children. When we as their children succeed in life, they beam with pride!

"*My son's a doctor!*" "*My daughter is the CEO of one of the richest and most successful corporations in the world!*" "*My son is President of the United States!*" "*My daughter is a successful actress!*" "*I have three sons who play professional sports!*" "*My daughter graduated from college at the top of her class—at HARVARD!*"…and so on, and so on, and so on.

17. IMPERFECT WORLDLY SUCCESS DOESN'T LEAD TO LASTING HAPPINESS

Any "success" in this *imperfect* life provides us with an opportunity to experience the **opposite** of all that is *right* about humanity. ***None*** of these "successes" will ever lead to a constant state of personal happiness or to a state in which **all** humans are treated equally. It is *impossible* to find any "successful" person in this world who is honestly fulfilled and completely happy. Although they have succeeded in life, in some other way they have failed their **true** humanity—something, by the way, that they are SUPPOSED TO DO during this second stage of our human development.

Let's take each accolade given above (and there are many others that would make any *imperfect* mortal parent proud) and look at it *through the eyes* of our advanced, perfect creators:

My son's a doctor!

Doctors do not *prevent* disease and injuries; they cure them, or attempt to. Few doctors will ever reveal the *true* reason why heart disease, diabetes, cancers, and most other diseases and illnesses occur. (More than likely, they were never taught *how* to prevent them either; and if all sicknesses were "prevented," then there would be no need for someone to "cure" them.) The **real** cause of most mortal sickness and its prevention has nothing to do with what a certified doctor has been trained to do. It has all to do with what we introduce into our bodies.

18. COOKED AND PROCESSED FOOD ARE NOT GOOD FOR US

What we eat directly affects how our *imperfect* body functions. Our creators did NOT teach us how to cook our food, nor did they intend for us to eat cooked food. There is no other creation (flora or fauna) upon this earth that cooks its food before it eats it. Our creators *did not* intend for us to process anything contrary to the natural state in which it is found. Heat destroys; it does not create. Any form of excessive heat causes the natural bonds of matter to distort and come apart so that they cannot fulfill the purpose for which they were created in the first place. Other animals whose DNA patterns are very similar to our own do not get heart disease, diabetes, cancers, and most other *human* diseases and illness BECAUSE THEY DO NOT COOK AND PROCESS THEIR FOOD!

Applying energy in the form of heat to any naturally bonded compilation of elements causes its very nature to change. When it changes, the purpose for which it was created (to give our body *proper* nutrition) is thwarted. The foods that are found naturally (not heated or processed) provide the perfect balance of enzymes, proteins, and other nutrients that our *natural* body needs. When we apply heat to them, many of these natural enzymes, proteins, and other nutrients are destroyed. This leaves nothing more than empty calories that give us enough energy to live, *until* we die from heart disease, diabetes, cancers, and most other diseases and illnesses.

19. INEQUALITY IS PREVALENT IN ALL EMPLOYMENTS

Doctors attend school for many years studying the mortal "successes" of their predecessors so that they will be able to cure us of our maladies and gain both monetary and egocentric value. The energy that they expend in attending school is provided to them by the food that they eat. This food is produced and processed by the rest of us (the majority), who haven't the ability or the means to go to school and become a doctor. The fieldworkers keep the fledgling doctors alive by providing them with food, so that one day the doctors can keep the fieldworkers alive.

It seems to be an evenly balanced *quid pro quo* relationship, right? Wrong! Instead, we have developed a system of the abstract accountability of values called "money." In this system, we justify paying the doctors in our society a lot more than we do the fieldworkers, because we *value* what they do in their doctor's office more than what is done during harvest time. This is ***not*** *equality* and respect for each individual and unique person with differing desires and abilities! Ironically, if the harvesters kept their food for themselves and didn't cook or process it, what value would doctors have then? The doctors usually don't eat what other doctors produce, in order to survive. Therefore, which profession is ***really*** more valuable to the human being?

20. CURING DISEASE DOES NOT IMPLY INTELLIGENCE

Some mortals who have been convinced that there is an existence beyond mortality claim that the degree of intelligence we attain in this life will put us that much further ahead in the next one. So, with rigorous effort and a sincere desire to "get ahead," they justify becoming a doctor, in this example, because there seems to be a great amount of "intelligence" acquired in becoming one. There is no such **real** thing as "intelligence"; there is only experience.

Some feel obliged by their personal *humanity* to use their knowledge and expertise to *save* the human race. Enormous amounts of time and *money* are spent in an attempt to cure the diseases of the impoverished of the world. But once they are cured, the disadvantaged have nothing to eat, no shelter in which to live, and no hope of a future except to continue living *without hope*. The *humanity* of the ill-informed doctor *causes* the continued misery of those they *believe* they are saving; thus, it is a demonstration of *imperfect humanity* of no ***real value*** to anyone but the doctor's own ego.

Unfortunately, for those "doctors" who believe this way, we have already described the *perfect* world and the *perfect* human body, neither of which requires anything, *not one thing*, a doctor can possibly learn during mortality (except for the mortal experience of opposition to our **true reality**). But for those who know how to pick food from the vine—now this type of "intelligence" will most certainly come in handy for those who serve themselves and who serve others.

Not to worry, Doctors! You will be *served* all the food you can eat when your desires to be *served* and given accolades for your accomplishments are provided for, in a *perfect* human world!

21. FINANCIAL PROFIT DIMINISHES HUMAN VALUE

My daughter is the CEO of one of the richest and most successful corporations in the world!

Chief Executive Officers (CEO's) of the richest and most successful corporations in the world (or any business or corporation no matter how large or small) expend their personal energy for one purpose and one purpose only: PROFIT! Their "intelligence" consists of knowing the way the "game of life" is played regarding the "*system of the abstract accountability of values*" called money. They know how to make money by utilizing the labor of others and controlling free will. Moreover, they know how to make *more* money through investments and interest, in addition to the money that others make for them.

Their *personal success* depends on the success of their corporation or business turning a profit from a product made from the resources available upon the earth or from the services provided by the *enslaved employee*. CEOs create a need for using the resources of the earth and then pay others to extract them from the earth and produce the satisfaction of the need they invented. The same goes for the service sector of corporations and business.

Profit comes from the following equation: NEED (minus) THE COST OF PRODUCTION OF THE RESOURCE TO MEET THE NEED (equals) PROFIT. The greater the "need" and the less "the cost of production," the greater the profit. Using this equation properly, a CEO becomes successful when he or she can maximize the need and minimize the cost to produce what will satisfy the need. Therefore, the *only* part of the equation that will ever be "minimized" is the cost of production. The "cost of production" is the means provided by the value of another human being, who is needed to produce what is required in order to satisfy the need.

Restated appropriately: **A CEO becomes successful when he or she can maximize the need while minimizing the value of the human beings who provide the means to satisfy the need**. In other words, they create a system of value called "wages" that can be kept low enough in relation to the "need" so that more profit can be made. When the "need" diminishes, the *successful* CEO will proportionately *decrease the value of the employee*, so as to maintain anticipated profit margins. The profit is ultimately determined by the *system of the abstract accountability of values called money*. The more **profit** the CEO can make for the corporation or business, the more successful he or she becomes.

Some readers might become confused by the way that we have presented the function and purpose of a CEO above. However, from this, none can honestly say that he or she does not understand how a *successful* CEO in our world adds to our mortal experience in exposing us to the *opposite* of *pure and true humanity*. How can **any** human being ever be considered **less important than the profit** made from the resources of this earth?

CEOs do a great job at what they do, both for their corporations and for providing us with another facet of an *imperfect human world.* What they do not consider (or maybe they do, but they don't want to spend too much of their energy contemplating it) is that our mortal world has a very *limited* amount of resources. They cannot suppose that all of us have an *equal opportunity* of creating our own corporation or establishing our own business and being successful at it by using the equation for profit we have presented above. If we were all equal

CEOs, who then would be left to process the resources to satisfy the "need," thus creating the profit? If we are all after the same *limited* resources, who then is going to be left out when they are all used up? Surely not the *successful* CEOs!

22. IMPERFECT GOVERNMENTS ARE SELF-SERVING

My son is President of the United States!

Nothing is more inconsistent with the basis of an equal state of humanity than the borders we have established on this earth, which divide us and isolate us from each other. These borders separate us into nations and races, ostensibly, to protect our individual FAMILY UNITS. Borders are an excuse to protect resources, money, opportunity, and ultimately the free will of a people who expect a certain lifestyle. Most people fear that all this will be lost or extremely diluted if the borders of *their nation* aren't protected.

We have already discussed the futility of the governments we have set up in an attempt to create peace and equality in our world. No government has ever worked and none ever will, *unless* its constitution *really* mandates (not in eloquently written declarations, but in very deed and action) that EVERYONE IS TO BE TREATED EQUALLY, and then implements this mandate!

To maintain the purpose for which this *imperfect world* exists, those who have chosen Solarian *humanity types* are seldom the heads of state, presidents of nations, or leaders of any kind. They would be in these positions, **if** we chose them to lead us (although some or many of them would refuse, as they do not like the praise or attention). Still, we do not choose these types of people by the voice of the majority, because most of us want to be served or to serve ourselves. We choose the type of government that typifies our own humanity type.

In other words, although politicians claim to *serve* the best interests of the people, in reality, their use of political power is generally motivated by self-protection and the support of special interests groups (which have nothing to do with equality for all people). Most governments in our mortal world *serve themselves* or cause *others to serve them*. And the epitome of the greatest self-serving government ever created in our mortal world, even the most powerful government that has ever existed on planet earth—the one that wants us to be subservient to it ("*ask not what your country can do for you—ask what you can do for your country*")—is the United States of America.

23. AMERICA'S DEMOCRACY IS THE BEST EXAMPLE OF AN IMPERFECT GOVERNMENT

The United States government provides us with the quintessential example of the **opposite** of a *perfect* government. All one needs is a proper investigation into the foundation and preservation of this government to find this to be true. Many Americans believe that our creators have condoned, "ordained," and "blessed" the United States of America. In some respects, they are right! Advanced humans could not have inspired a more appropriate institution that would have allowed us to experience the effects of an absolutely ***imperfect government***!

The United States is one of the youngest nations in our world. By the time the land upon which it has established its borders was discovered, the rest of the world had already gone through countless forms of governments. Each of these had previously failed to create continual peace and happiness. And although these pre-United States governments throughout the world did not create any semblance of *perfect* societies, they *did succeed* in providing many other examples of *imperfection*.

In spite of all of the failed governments, our creators knew that we could never be convinced of the beauty and perfection of an *advanced* human government that controls our Universe, **unless** we could experience a government based on what we all value more than any other human right we possess: free agency. There had never been a truer form of democracy (i.e., rule by those chosen by the voice of the majority) until the establishment of the United States of America. As mentioned previously, we needed to experience this type of "free" government to finally be able to accept that **FREE-WILLED HUMAN BEINGS CANNOT BE TRUSTED WITH POWER AND AUTHORITY OVER OTHERS**.

This probative stage of our human development will leave us ample evidence as to why we shouldn't be able to make our own laws and rule ourselves as free-willed beings. Although some will never agree with the rules and laws of the Universe that affect our free agency, these laws are what they are, what they have always been, and what they will always be forever.

Without the experience of a free democracy that is fueled by free will, we might be left with the excuse: "*How do you (creators) know that we are not fully capable of governing ourselves if given the chance?*" The United States of America is the chance we have been given. With this chance, we have proven that no matter how much freedom we are given (or at least believe that we have been given), free-willed beings left to themselves cause each other harm and inequality.

It is important to reiterate that,

> A free-willed being—who establishes who it is from the exercising of unlimited and uninhibited free agency—might one day determine for itself that its happiness should extend beyond maintaining the status quo forever. This being might determine that a little change here and there probably wouldn't hurt anything; in fact, it *might* create more happiness.
>
> The history of human government in our current world should be all the proof we need to understand that it is impossible to trust any one of us or a group of us to treat all people equally and establish the perfect government. None of us can be trusted with power and authority over others, because it is part of our human nature to change our environment to fit our *personal* preferences. However, the Universe is an environment that cannot be modified to adapt or react to the opinions and perspectives of any one individual or of a majority. **All** opinions and perspectives must be respected and protected. (See chapter 8, section 6.)

Again, the purpose for which we exist in an *imperfect* state upon this earth is to experience the **opposite** of everything that is responsible for our ultimate happiness. When this purpose is fulfilled, we will be able to look back on the way the United States was established and what it did with the power of its democracy. At that point, we will rejoice in its success in adding to the effectiveness of our lessons learned concerning *imperfect* government. Although our creators will be happy that we had the experience, they will never condone *one thing* that the United States of the America has ever done—not one thing!

So why in the world would a parent be proud that their son or daughter was President of the United States? Maybe it's because their mortal child's name might one day be vainly emblazoned on the hulls of America's great ships, which are built for one purpose and one purpose only: to destroy human life.

24. WE BECOME SUCCESSFUL ACTORS BECAUSE OF THE EXPECTATIONS OF OTHERS

My daughter is a successful actress!

The art of acting consists of individuals having the ability to present themselves as someone or something that they are not. This false persona is created according to the wants and desires of the audience who pays to see these actors perform.

In many ways, *everyone* in an *imperfect* world becomes adroit at creating a false persona and presenting themselves as someone or something that they are not. We do this to receive a *form of compensation* in return. This "acting" has few restrictions. It can apply to a person who is *acting* as if they enjoy their job and respect their boss in order to earn more money. It also applies to any other way that we "act" around others, so that we "fit in" and are accepted by our peers. The more *compensation* we receive in return for being something that we are not, and the more natural it becomes, the more we begin to believe that *we are* what we *really* are not. Most of us have become very proficient *actors* in our personal lives.

There are very few people in an *imperfect* world impervious to the propensity to lie about who they *really* are and what they *really* want to do with their free agency. We are conditioned from the time we are born to please our parents and others who establish *their* expectations for us. If we don't live up to *their* expectations, then we are punished, or at least not rewarded with any *form of compensation*. If we do not wear the right clothes, say the right things, or fulfill the expectations of our peers, we cannot belong to a "group" of people who *act* like they accept who we are, as long as we *act* like them.

We subdue our *true self* and hide it from others so we can be accepted. This *true self* is abused and forced into submission, first to our parents' expectations, and then to the various expectations of other people who are *not being who they really are* either! Fortunately for all of us, our *true self* is securely and safely protected in the construct of our *essence*. In addition, it is most fortunate that no other person can read our minds and know our true feelings, unless we make a conscious effort to reveal our *true self*. If we could read each other's minds, our mortal relationships would last no longer than just a few minutes.

Our identity—our *true self*—was *foundationalized* in a perfect world, where people existed who did not have any expectations of who we chose to be. We were respected regardless of our choices. This proper *foundationalization* environment was overseen by those who fully expected us to become individuals and to *not fit in* or become someone or something *outside* of how we personally chose to exercise our own free will.

Following our hearts and doing what we *really* want to do during the days of our mortality would ultimately bring us happiness and emotional balance. But again, this is not something intended for our mortal experienced-enhanced education of the *opposite* of what balances us and makes us happy. That's why it is so hard to tap into the energy levels of experience recorded in our *essence* and know who we *truly* are. This mortal life is to see what it's like to be a successful actor!

25. WE ALL LIVE DELUSIONAL REALITIES

Acting is just one of the many creative arts that humans have invented to escape the drudgeries of everyday life with its painful *realities* and the hopeless dreariness found in its monotony. We find no balance in an *imperfect* world, so many of us escape from *reality* into a world of subjective perception and thought we call "imagination." This *imaginary* world is generated by our *essence,* as has been explained previously. The false personas we create to define ourselves in a world without any definitive boundaries of who we should be, is our attempt to find our *true self.* Well was it philosophized by a human who was perceived as having more *common sense* than most:

> A human being is a part of a whole, called by us "Universe," a part limited in time and space. He experiences himself, his thoughts and feelings as something separated from the rest—a kind of optical delusion of his consciousness. This delusion is a kind of prison for us, restricting us to our personal desires and to affection for a few persons nearest to us. Our task must be to free ourselves from this prison by widening our circle of compassion to embrace all living creatures and the whole of nature in its beauty. (Albert Einstein, Letter of 1950, as quoted in *The New York Post* [28 November 1972].)

Can *acting* truly make one balanced and happy? The **real truth** would be revealed in an honest, personal, and intimate conversation with any of our well-compensated fellow humans who create fantasies for us. If they were honest, **not one** of these actors would admit that they are completely balanced and happy with who they are. Most are hiding behind drugs, alcohol, and the false personas they have created for themselves.

Few of us would ever tell our boss what we *really* felt about our job and their supervision. Why? Because our *imperfect* parents have taught us *how* to *act*, and we don't want to disappoint the countless hours of *acting lessons* they have invested into our (or maybe *their*) lives. Besides, we need the *money* that the acting provides!

26. COMPETITIVE "GAMES" OPPOSE LASTING HAPPINESS

I have three sons who play professional sports!

Few experiences are more diametrically opposed to balance and happiness than the competitive games we play. In these games, there are always two competing sides, whose only desire is to win. Nevertheless, when one wins, the other loses. The winner walks away from the event in happiness, while the loser walks away in misery and depression.

To add ironic substance to the purpose for which these games are played, the spectators join in by taking one side or another. The spectators' happiness is affected by the outcome of an event that they have no control over! The players, along with those who cheer for them, desire an outcome that they consciously do not want to admit because it is contrary to an acceptable form of *humanity*. They want to cause misery and unhappiness to others because it adds value to themselves. They want to win!

Upon the bedroom walls of many *imperfectly foundationalized* youth are the posters and pictures of their favorite athletes. One day, they dream, they will be just as much of a "winner" as their sports heroes.

Sporting events are not the only competitive games played in an *imperfect* world. War is also a "game" that is played in which the outcome creates a loser and a winner. Like a sporting event, the opposing sides in any war have a desire to win by inflicting more pain, misery, death, and destruction upon their opponent than their opponent inflicts upon them. There are millions of spectators who cheer on the "game of war" and are equally affected by the outcome of the contest.

In a sporting event, the emotional support that the spectators create is called "loyalty" to one's team. In war, this support is masked behind "PATRIOTISM." Patriotism couldn't be further from the pure concept and purpose of our *true* humanity. It divides us and causes us to justify the horrendous things we do to each other.

27. ADVANCED HUMANS RECOGNIZE NO HEROES

Not to be outdone, and even more powerful in the way that it affects our emotions, is the manner in which people honor and portray their "heroes" of war. Upon the fireplace mantle or proudly displayed on the walls of homes are photos, medals, and flags that represent the "heroes" for one side, but the mercenary terrorists for the other. Which one is truly a "hero"? Which one the "terrorist"? It depends on for whom we are cheering. No one is going to be convinced that his or her *loved* one is a terrorist, anymore than one will be convinced that this one is *not* a hero.

Advanced human beings take no sides. They see both sides, and respect and support the unconditional exercising of free will in an *imperfect* world. In their *perfected* view, no side wins and no side loses. The experience of "loss" (and the emotional burden that comes with it) is what our creators consider a "win" for the intent and reason *why we exist* in an *imperfect* world, which is vital for play and to win "the game of life."

Again, our creators name none of us as "heroes" and none of us as "terrorists," and none of us as winners and none of us as losers. They see all of us as little children trying to establish *value* for ourselves by *devaluing* each other. They smile; they weep tears of joy; sometimes they even laugh. But they are never *proud* of any one child over another. They have no heroes.

28. MORTAL EDUCATION IS USELESS TO ETERNITY

My daughter graduated from college at the top of her class—
at HARVARD!

Although a person might gain the whole world and have success in everything that he or she does, what value can be gained if one loses one's own identity in the process? There is not one thing that has ever been learned through the schools of education established in an *imperfect* world that will remain in a *perfect* world—

NOT ONE! Everything that we *think* we know today will be replaced with a different *reality* of tomorrow.

Consider, for example, a few courses of study given through the educational processes of our *imperfect* world:

29. MONEY PLACES INEQUITABLE ABSTRACT VALUES ON PEOPLE AND RESOURCES

Business: When it comes to equality, nothing on this earth has created more problems than money. Money is responsible for all poverty and inequality throughout the world. Yet no one can live in our current *imperfect* world without it!

When we were first placed upon this planet, there was no such concept as money. Nor were there values placed upon the earth's resources or each other. For a time, many human societies survived quite well sharing their labor and the resources of the earth to care for their needs. The introduction of placing a value on a useless stone, coin, or a piece of paper, whose value is an abstract measure supported only by the emotional motivation we give it, is the underlying cause of most of our *inequality* issues.

The social system that revolves around money places specific values on our free will and upon human life itself. Some of us are *worth* more to society than others. Those who are *worth* more are treated better and have a better chance at being accepted. "Finding our *true self*" and valuing who we *really are* has been replaced with the motivation to *prove* that we *are somebody* based on how successfully we position ourselves in a society that is based on how much money we have.

There is no money or system of exchange in a *perfect* world. Solarian advanced humans provide everything and anything one needs free of charge. This is possible because there are no limits to the resources in a *perfect* world. There is no need for CEOs, financial advisers, banks, businesses, corporations, or any other financial entity that has anything to do with money or the value or devaluation it creates.

30. MORTAL CREATIONS DO NOT SUPPORT LASTING HAPPINESS

Science and Engineering: From the ancient pyramids found in Egypt to the tallest skyscrapers erected in the largest cities, and from the formations of the world's tallest monuments to the smallest intricate components of nanotechnology, nothing a mortal can conceive and produce on this earth will stand the test of time. The continuing expansion of human understanding and intellect and the effects of natural catastrophe and disintegration render everything *imperfect human beings* create useless to the realization of continual and lasting happiness.

The perfect human society, along with the perfect structure of all things, has **always been**. Because a perfect knowledge of these things has *always* been, and those who know these things have *always* existed, what need would anyone have in learning something that does not need to be learned, because it hasn't *always* existed, except, again for the sake of comparing the two to see which one lasts and which one does not?

Not one thing that the greatest engineers in an *imperfect world* have created, are creating, or will create, will come close to those things that have **always been**. The advanced things that have **always been** do not deteriorate, sag, need maintenance or improvement, nor does any effect of nature change them.

Current structural, biological, genetic, or any other type of application of science in the design, planning, construction, and maintenance of any form of matter, are based on our *imperfect* knowledge of how the Universe works. The progress and advancements that are made seem to be miraculous in the way that they affect our daily lives. But because the foundation of their invention comes from *imperfect minds* in an *imperfect world*, **nothing** they produce adds to the lasting and continual happiness of the human race.

31. SYNTHETIC PRODUCTS DESTROY THE NATURAL EARTH

For example, one of the greatest inventions of the 20th century (that came from the process of chemical engineering) was the invention of plastics. There are many forms of plastics, rubber, nylon, and other synthetic products. With each form, engineers learn how to use them and to change them to suit the needs and wants of society.

Plastics are durable and degrade very, very slowly (if at all) naturally. Their use generates an increasing percentage of human waste that packs the landfills of the earth. Not only does the manufacturing of plastics often lead to large quantities of chemical pollutants, but even after they begin to disintegrate within the earth, they can release toxic combinations of gases that destroy the natural environment even thousands of years later.

Current scientific research has no idea what plastics will do after being subjected to natural disintegration over many, many years. Plastics haven't been around long enough to be observed as they break down in the landfills in which they are placed. This is the case with **everything** and **anything** that is unnaturally or synthetically produced, or in other words, made by the *imperfect* intellect of *imperfect* human beings.

32. IMPERFECT SCIENCE HAS IMPERFECT ANSWERS

To use another example, let's hypothetically say that the apple is the perfect food and that we want to preserve it so that it can be eaten at any time. *Imperfect* science comes up with an airtight *plastic* container that will preserve the apple for a time. In contrast, *perfect* science comes up with an apple peel, which is an outer layer that can also be eaten, and which preserves the apple far more efficiently than the plastic container.

The *perfect* scientists found that a slightly permeable container in which to store the apple allows just the right amount of energy exchange to take place between the succulent fruit inside and its surrounding environment outside, so that it maintains its original state. The apple is constructed so that it will not affect its environment negatively, but will benefit its environment, whether it is eaten by an animal or not. Furthermore, in a perfect world, the advanced apple grows to a preprogrammed ripeness and then remains that way forever until it is eaten.

Current scientific and engineering exploration of plants has led *imperfect* humans to discover ways to genetically change the structure of some foods so that they last longer. However, nothing they can produce matches the *taste* that a perfect piece of fruit is designed to give a human being. This can only be done by those who have a *perfect* knowledge of what a *perfect* apple is, how it has *always* been, and how it will *always* be.

Nature existed perfectly balanced long before the "wise ones" (our definition of *Homo sapiens*) started altering it. There is no pride to be taken in one's ability to create a substance that destroys nature (synthetic plastics, as just one of many examples).

33. ARTISTIC EXPRESSION DOES NOT EXPRESS REALITY

The Arts and Humanities: As we've discussed, our *imagination* is responsible for our creativity. This creativity is a reflection of our experience in a *perfect* world, which we cannot completely recall, but has nonetheless been recorded in our *essence*. We've also explained that our dreams are a disconnected and often random attempt of our conscious mind (our mortal brain) seeking to make sense of the subconscious and subtle energy emissions of our *essence*.

Humanities and art are the ways we attempt to express our creativity in order to make sense of things we do not understand. Abstract art, like all scientific theories and conclusions, does not reflect the reality of what we are ***really*** experiencing. The majority of people upon the earth, if they stopped *acting* and told the truth, would admit that not only do most scientific theories make little sense to their reason, but the abstract paintings produced by artists make even less sense.

If what an artist paints does not look like something seen in the visual world, an honest critic would state that a small child could have painted the same image. The abstract art displayed in prestigious art galleries throughout the world and valued sometimes in the millions of dollars, would appear to our more simple ancestors as the hodgepodge of an irresponsible brush. Nevertheless, to the artist and those who *act* as if they understand and appreciate the artist and his or her creations, they are a perfect reflection of what the artist is feeling inside.

Because these artists are attempting to find their *true self*, their artistic expressions with paint and brush, music, theater, and literature are indeed a *true* expression of what they have found themselves to be: incomprehensible.

34. WE USE MUSIC TO ESCAPE AND COPE WITH REALITY

In the case of musical artists, for example, the more *lost* the person is in knowing their *true self*, the further away their production of rhythm, song, and volume strays from the sounds found in nature. In contrast, in the simple, gentle song of a bird is found a symphony of breathtaking sounds that *pure* nature provides our sense of hearing. This beautiful sound comes from an authentic form of life (the bird) that acts according to its *true self,* although *it* has no "understanding" of the self or the free will to express itself in an *unnatural* way.

To lose ourselves and escape the reality of the *imperfect world*, we listen to one of two general types of music: one that makes us feel more balanced or one that throws us further *off* balance. When we listen to music that brings us more peace, we are attempting to *escape* the world. When we listen to music that creates more emotion, usually exciting our minds and our energy levels, we are trying to *cope* with a world that is full of stress. The former allows us an escape from *reality*. The latter elevates our emotions to match those of *reality* so that we can deal with it better.

The emotional effects of this second type of music prepare us to deal with the realities we are facing in an *imperfect world* by raising our energy levels to match those established by our society. For this reason, the pressures of adolescents and puberty (which lead into the responsibility of being forced to accept and live in a world that they did not create) generally lead the young to choose loud, nonsensical, or seemingly rebellious music as their choice. Once they realize, however, that there is not much they can do about the world in which they live (although many of them make valiant efforts to change it), their choice of music generally transforms into something that allows them to *escape* from reality, by placing them closer to the sounds produced in nature. For this reason, the more an *imperfect human* matures, the more they attempt to *escape* reality by listening to music that resembles the sounds of nature.

35. NATURE PRODUCES THE PERFECT SOUNDS

From the gentle breeze that sings through the treetops to the sound of a tiny insect's mating call, nature produces precise symmetrical patterns of sound. Each instrument that was created by advanced human beings to produce the music we listen to for escape reflects the symmetry of nature in the sounds it produces. If we were to break down the energy patterns created in the sound waves that all things produce, we would find that those that undulate in precise symmetrical fluctuations of perfect wavelengths generate the sounds that we truly enjoy. These sounds reflect the sounds around which we received our primordial *foundationalization*.

Plants, for example, produce symmetry in the form of their flowers, leaves, and stems. They are like nature's orchestrated ensemble of reeds and strings. When the wind passes over the construct of the plants, the energy transferred by the wind produces symmetrical vibrations based on how each petal, each leaf, or each stem affects the passing atoms, just as a violinist gracefully runs her bow across the strings of a perfectly tuned violin.

However, nothing produced by the arts or humanities in our *imperfect* world will come close to matching the perfected symmetrical rhythms that are found in a *perfect* human world. Try as we may to replicate *natural perfection* in our Arts and Humanities, we will never be able to match the beauty of sight and sound that is created by advanced human beings, which is a part of a *perfect* world.

36. HONORING OTHER'S ABILITIES SUPPRESSES OUR OWN

This does not mean that we will not continue to try. The problems arise, however, from our perception that what we have arrived at is as close to perfection as we will ever get. We listen to what others have produced and accept their rendition of perfection, because we believe that we do not have the ability to create our *own* individual concepts of perfection. This leaves us doubting ourselves and forces us to submit to the ignorance that we are not as good as the artists of our world. This is how we create inequality by the way we honor other's abilities. In honoring their abilities above our own, we suppress our own, because we have convinced ourselves that we do not have the same abilities.

Nevertheless, try as they may, there is not an artist in the world that can create the emotion that a little child feels as the child explores its environment and is affected by the shapes, the feeling, the sounds, the tastes, and the smell of each new experience. Little children are unaffected by the values placed on what the Arts and Humanities have given us in an *imperfect* world. They are truly the *only* ones who can rightfully claim an "Honorary Degree" from the "School of Life," which brings them consistent and lasting joy until they are sent to the ***imperfect schools*** *of mortal education*.

37. MATHEMATICAL EQUATIONS ARE INVENTED AS A RESULT OF IMPERFECT UNDERSTANDING

Mathematics: It has been said that mathematics is the *only* **real truth** available to humankind. Some suggest that mathematics gives the perfect solution to any established equation. The problem with mathematics, however, is not in the solutions it provides, but in the **equations** it produces.

An equation can be produced for anything. But where one equation exists, there is always another needed to support it. The invention of all mathematical equations, their values, their quotients, logarithms, sines, cosines, tangents, angles, circumferences, exponents, and the myriads of other mathematical terms, are all inventions of *imperfect* minds, created to explain what they don't understand.

Before any equation of mathematics is invented, the product or answer is first determined. Once the product or answer is agreed upon, then the *imperfect human*-made application of mathematics is **invented** *to fit the answer*. If the answer is flawed, or not **real truth**, then the equation that arrives at the answer is also flawed and useless in its application, except as far as it proves the falsehood upon which it is based.

38. MATHEMATICAL "RULES" ARE SUBJECTIVE

One might claim, for example, that one (1) banana plus one (1) banana equals two bananas. Upon further scientific observation, however, another might find that what one might perceive as one (1) banana, another might perceive as three (3) separate symmetrically equal parts. Therefore, the equation $1 + 1 = 2$ is not absolute, and can only be used if one accepts that a banana only consists of *one part.* The equation can correctly be changed to reflect another perceived reality of the banana: $3(x) = y$, where (y) is the whole banana and (x) are the parts thereof. Therefore, what one sees as two (2) bananas, another could see as six (6).

Then, still another *imperfect brain* comes along, attempts to outdo the first two, and devises a completely different equation based on a completely *different reality*: "The circumference of the relative parts must equal the mass divided by the square root of the energy released in the transformation of the flower into the fruit, thereby allowing the exponential values of the banana to be properly formulated to reflect its true nature, which is never 1 banana, but always 3."

Whatever one mathematician may come up with, another can create a "logical" equation to either prove him or her wrong or enhance the equation with other useless calculations, all leading to the same end: What "I" perceive is right, because what "YOU" perceive is wrong—the futility of abstract mathematics. The only thing that is important to most people is how to remove the peel from the banana and eat the sweet fruit therein. Nevertheless, even the energy it takes to remove the peel can be calculated by a precise formula and equation.

Furthermore, if a child is not taught to count, or is taught from birth that inside the banana peel there are three (3) distinct bananas, then it would be futile to try and convince the child that there is only one banana inside the peel. A mathematician can argue until he is blue in the face that there is only one banana inside the peel and never change the mind of a person who has always known bananas to be three equal parts inside of one peel.

(For those who are now interested: Peel a ripe banana and break the peeled banana in half. Force your index finger into the middle of one of the halves, and then you will have three separate, distinct, and symmetrical pieces of banana. Where there was once one [1], now there are three [3].)

39. THERE ARE NO QUANTITATIVE MEASURES IN A PERFECT WORLD

Quantitative measures are only as good as the comprehension of those who have been taught to understand and accept them as *reality*. In a *perfect* world, there are no quantitative measures. There is no counting, because there is no need. There is no reason for a person to attempt to invent a mathematical equation to solve problems, because there are no problems—things exist as they have always existed forever.

Some argue that, *without* mathematics, we could have never made the extraordinary advancements in technology that we have made as a human race. They maintain that humans cannot progress without being able to figure out their environment and utilize it for their betterment. They further argue that "figuring things out" means understanding and using the calculations of the mathematical equations they have formed to explain the constants found in nature.

Earlier in this book, we explained *how* and *why* the mathematical calculation that supports Albert Einstein's Theory of Relativity is not correct in all instances. It would take volumes of explanation, but each and every mathematical equation ever invented by the *imperfect mind* to explain the *imperfect world* could be countered with an explanation that renders it useless. Eventually, all forms of mathematics will be rendered obsolete by **real truth**.

Because few mortals understand the *true reality* of all things, there can be no absolutes in an *imperfect world*. The reality that everything that exists in the Universe has **always** existed in the same form somewhere else in the Universe is a *true* concept that our limited *imperfect minds* have a hard time fully comprehending. Nevertheless, this new way of looking at the Universe makes sense and will eventually prove the uselessness of the value we place on mathematics. Mathematicians cannot formulate an equation that supports the concept that everything in the Universe has *always* been.

Those who argue that the advancements in technology have made our lives better might reconsider how these "advancements" are used in our world today. Not only do we have a greater capability of destroying each other (as demonstrated by the use of atomic and other nuclear weapons) but the uses of our "advanced" technology, propagated by our mathematical equations, are diametrically opposed to the delicate equations found in the natural world. These *natural equations* existed long before mortals began to invent their own. In reality, the application of *imperfect* mathematics is destroying ourselves, and the world in which we live.

40. UNHAPPINESS PROVES THE UNIMPORTANCE OF WORLDLY SUCCESS

Now that we have a different perspective of the achievements that our mortal parents might want us to gain, is there any wonder *why* they are considered *imperfect parents*? The way that they foundationalize us in this mortal world continues to perpetuate and ensure that the purpose for our existence upon this earth continues to be exactly what our creators intended—to experience everything that is *opposite* of perfection.

Our mortal parents are only doing the best they know how to do. They motivate us to be successful in this world, because it is the only world they are familiar with and the only world they can remember. The pursuit of worldly success and the failures associated with not having success makes us very unhappy. Even when some of us become successful according to the standards set by our peers, few find lasting joy in this success. It seems that the more we succeed, the more we desire to succeed even further. Once the bar of success has been raised to a certain level, then it is no longer considered "successful" unless we reach further and exceed the bar. Thus, the "bar of success" is ever changing and being raised beyond anyone's preset expectations of its height. None of us can remain satisfied with the fruits of success when the definition of success is ever changing.

Not only is all that our mortal parents do good for us in the long run, but it is good for them in the short run. When *imperfect parents* see the *real* effects that worldly success has on their children and the rest of the world, they might be more apt to examine their expectation of success and see it as their failure in helping their children to find peace, happiness, and their *true selves*. Once we begin to realize that there is no ***true*** happiness in anything extrinsically motivated outside of the "self," we will be in a better position to accept success as only those things that satisfy the "self" and no one else. Keep in mind, continual and lasting happiness is the measuring stick of ***true success***.

There are those in this current world who *appear* to be successful. An honest inspection of the inner feelings of these would prove that *none* of their successes *outside of themselves* bring them lasting personal happiness. In fact, few (if any) have really achieved true happiness at all. This is all the proof we need to be convinced that worldly success is not important in the realization of the **true self**.

41. WE ARE NOT FULLY RESPONSIBLE FOR OUR IMPERFECT ACTIONS

Again, nothing we do in this life is considered to be a *failure* in the eyes of our creators. They are the ones who allowed this *imperfect* world for our benefit. The way things have been set up makes it *practically impossible* to create a *perfect* world wherein we can find the continual happiness that we desire. If we are not responsible for the *imperfection* of our natures, how can we then be responsible for our actions in an *imperfect* world?

Lunarian and Stellarian people who exercise their free will the only way that is consistent with their personal happiness cannot *fairly* be held accountable for the *seemingly* "terrible" things that they do to others. The things that they do are not *really* terrible! Their actions do, however, reinforce the evidence that their particular *humanity type* should never be allowed to wield power over others. Mortal life is the probationary time period in which these *humanity types* prove that they should not be entrusted with this kind of power. Therefore, their actions are consistent with the purpose for which they exist during their second stage of human development.

42. IN A PERFECT WORLD, THE HUMAN BEING CREATES THE EXPERIENCE

The most important question that can be asked to determine our individual responsibility for using our free will and acting thereupon is:

DOES THE EXPERIENCE CREATE THE HUMAN BEING OR DOES THE HUMAN BEING CREATE THE EXPERIENCE?

In a *perfect* world, the free will of the human being creates all experience; therefore, we are responsible for what we do. However, in an *imperfect* world, where free will is often impeded by the free will of another, the experience creates the "mortal person," thereby relieving us of much of the responsibility for our actions in this life. How can any of us be held completely responsible? Are we responsible for being born into a home where parents instill bigotry and prejudice into our cognitive paradigms, which consequently motivate our actions?

We did not ask to be created. We had no choice in the matter. The responsibility for having free will, in which we get to choose our actions and become who we are, lies solely with those who created us. This is why it is a crucial responsibility of advanced human beings to *foundationalize* newly created humans **correctly**. The way we are *foundationalized* lays a *foundation* for the way we choose to use our free will. This is the importance of being *foundationalized* correctly in a *perfect* human world. And because it was intended for us to experience the *opposite* of our *foundationalized humanity*, we can also see the importance of why we are allowed to be *foundationalized* **incorrectly** in an *imperfect* world.

SUMMARY

In our *imperfect world*, we started out as carefree children who found a great amount of happiness in our surroundings. This carefree nature lasted a very short time, until the stress of expectation began to shape us into *imperfect human beings*. As adults (aged little children), we find it hard to experience the happiness and stress-free life we once had as a little child. Nothing our *imperfect parents* taught us, nor anything else we have learned and experienced during our mortal life, brings us the childlike happiness we all desire. The only thing that we gain from an existence in an *imperfect world* (that can be considered continual and lasting) is the comparative experience we will one day depend upon to help us recognize what *true* joy is.

Recognizing the futility of worldly success in providing us with the happiness we desire, it shouldn't be hard for us to agree with a few things said by Albert Einstein, one of the most renowned (and widely accepted by the world as *successful* and *educated*) mortals that ever lived:

> We can't solve problems by using the same type of thinking that created them in the first place. …Common sense is the collection of prejudices acquired by age eighteen. …The only real valuable thing is intuition. …Education is what remains after one has forgotten everything he learned in school. …Two things are infinite: the universe and human stupidity; and I'm not sure about the universe. …As far as the laws of mathematics refer to reality, they are not certain; as far as they are certain, they do not refer to reality. …Great spirits have always found violent opposition from mediocrities. The latter cannot understand it when a man does not thoughtlessly submit to hereditary prejudices but honestly and courageously uses his intelligence.
>
> —Albert Einstein

Our struggles in life come from our inability to figure out exactly *who we are* and *why we exist* on this seemingly small and insignificant planet we call Earth. Our perceptions of each other and ourselves have been formed in ignorance. We fear each other and remain separated and isolated because of our inability to conclusively agree upon our similarities. Our similarities have all to do with the fact that we are each unique and independent individuals who has been endowed by our creators to pursue our uniqueness and individuality.

There is little doubt in anyone's mind that our world is far from the perfect one for which our hearts long. Our greatest hope should be that one day we can truly understand *who we are* and *why we are* here. If we can accept the wise purposes behind our *imperfect* world, we can embrace the experience rather than stress ourselves out because of it. We will begin to realize just how intricately connected we are with each other and with the rest of the Universe. We will realize that we are not alone in our struggle to find ourselves, but that everyone else is just as insecure, unsure, and confused about our *imperfect world* as we are. Every human being in the Universe had to go through the same second stage of human development in which we currently find ourselves. In unity, we can find the strength to endure our *misery*.

Knowing these **real truths** about HUMAN REALITY places us in a better position to make the choices that can change our world into a new world—or rather, back into the *perfect world* where we used to live. This hope of a *better* world is part of being a *mortal* human being. Making this hope a *reality* is part of being a *perfect* one!

Our True Reality

CHAPTER FIFTEEN

Reality is merely an illusion, although a very persistent one.

—Albert Einstein

1. WE ARE UNITING TO LEARN MORE ABOUT OUR WORLD

The human race seems to be moving towards a united world. Communication technology now allows us to find out all there is to know about the world in which we live. The Worldwide Internet is going to be (if it isn't already) the primary source that humans depend on for the information that educates them about our world, even about reality. Being "educated" means that one has acquired knowledge. "Knowledge" is the information that is stored in our mind that is easily accessible with little effort. It is a compilation of the facts, ideas, truths, perceptions, and principles that are responsible for how a person thinks. How we think motivates us to act. The knowledge that we have acquired thus far during our conscious mortal existence upon this earth cannot be of much value to our success as a united human race, because the resulting actions caused by our knowledge has not yet united us in peace and contentment.

2. NO AGREEMENT ON WHAT IS TRUE AND WHAT IS NOT

Unfortunately for our human race, there are very few (if any) facts, ideas, truths, perceptions, or principles upon which all of us agree. Some "wise ones" have concluded that there is no such thing as

real truth. They surmise that the basis of all human knowledge is the personal opinions and perceptions of individuals who have accumulated agreed-upon facts, ideas, truths, perceptions, or principles. With this accumulation of personal knowledge, each person then invents his or her *own* truth. Those who believe this way could be considered *wise* based on what we are allowed to know in our *imperfect* world. This is true because we are only capable of acquiring the knowledge that is necessary for us to fulfill the purpose for which we exist in an *imperfect world.*

Once we understand the purpose for *why we exist* though, it then becomes clear that all of the knowledge that we acquire in an *imperfect world* is useless in a *perfect* one. It is impossible in mortality to have everyone agree upon everything. Therefore, in protection of our personal opinions and beliefs, we create the *imperfect world*, which gives us the experience of opposition in all things.

3. NOTHING IN AN IMPERFECT WORLD IS TRUE REALITY

The challenge of our existence upon this earth is that we have forgotten everything about our *foundationalization existence* and have become as little children, who know nothing about their new environment. Little children left to themselves develop their own individual reality. They base it, not upon what *others* determine is reality, but rather upon what each of them as a free-willed human being creates as *their own.* Our realities change as our individuality is affected by an *imperfect* world. Our individual reality forms and is based on the "information" we receive during the experience of mortality.

The purpose of this life is for us to experience an existence that is the *opposite* of the ultimate human experience—one that brings complete and continual joy. Because of this, it should make sense that nothing that we learn upon this earth—not one fact, one idea, or one bit of mortal truth, perception, or principle—can possibly be ***true reality***. (The definition of *true reality* is the **real truth** created by the knowledge acquired by those humans in the most advanced human world, which we consider the *perfect human world.*)

4. REAL TRUTH NEVER CHANGES AND IS AGREED UPON BY ALL ADVANCED HUMAN BEINGS

Real Truth (with a capital "T") is anything upon which every (non-veiled/non-mortal) freethinking and free-willed human being in the Universe agrees. It is something that none of us in our perfected state, in complete honesty, could deny.

Real Truth never changes. Nothing can be added to it or taken away from it. It is the same throughout the entire Universe; and anywhere advanced, perfected human beings are found, there is no disagreement on its substance and its conclusive statement of fact.

5. DURING MORTALITY NO ONE KNOWS REAL TRUTH

Based on the above explanation of **real truth**, it should be easy for us to accept that one of the only realities of our mortal existence, upon which we can all agree, is that **no one** knows the **real truth**. We each convince ourselves that what we personally accept as truth is **real truth**. But, when forced to consider the truths of others and compare them with our own, the only protection of the integrity of our conviction is our stubbornness to accept that we might be wrong. We must accept the **real truth** that up until this time during our mortal life upon this earth, there has never been a hard, concrete "fact" that has not changed or had some other "fact" added to it or some part thereof reconsidered.

6. ADVANCED HUMANS KNOW REAL TRUTH

Real truth cannot change and has always been the same and will always be the same. Therefore, it can only be reasoned logically that the facts, ideas, truths, perceptions, and principles of the most advanced human societies in the Universe are closer to *true reality* than what is accepted as reality in less-advanced worlds. If we can reason that these advanced societies developed to a point of understanding and knowledge after billions of years of experience, then we can accept that what they know about human life is much greater than what we currently know or have the ability to find out.

Advanced humans are free-willed beings just like we are. It is their nature, as it is ours, to seek out all there is to know about everything there is to know in the Universe. Knowing this, we can then safely assume that what these advanced humans have found out is the **only real truth** that exists in the Universe. Moreover, if their conclusions of truth have remained unchallenged and unchanged for an infinite amount of years, we can be sure that their reality **is** the only ***true reality***.

Like us, they do not have a limit on their ability to create their own reality. But they have found a set of *facts, ideas, truths, perceptions, and principles* that has not changed their reality over the infinite amount of time they have existed. Because they have found nothing in the Universe that contradicts their *facts, ideas, truths, perceptions, and principles*, then there is nothing else that they need to learn or experience that would add to or change the knowledge and understanding that they have already acquired.

7. MORTAL EXPERIENCE COULD LEAD TO REAL TRUTH

If we, as a race of humans, continue to learn and grow in experience and knowledge, there is no doubt that, even in the short span of 100 years, we will be much smarter and more knowledgeable than we are today. This concept (that we are continually becoming more knowledgeable) *should be* a portion of **real truth** upon which we can all agree by using our collective common sense, in spite of our disagreeing personal realities.

No honest person can say that the mortal human species is not learning and acquiring more knowledge with each passing decade. Most experiences we are having today were not experienced by our ancestors of 100 years ago; nor will our experiences today be the same as those of our descendants another 100 years into the future.

8. REALITY OF TODAY IS NOT THE REALITY OF TOMORROW

The *facts, ideas, truths, perceptions, and principles* of today will not be those of tomorrow; therefore, the realities we accept today will not be the same realities of tomorrow. But if we continue to exist for an infinite amount of time into the future, it should seem reasonable to our minds that one day we could possibly know all there is to know about everything and reach a point where our reality no longer changes, thus becoming a ***true reality*** that supports **real truth**.

Unfortunately, more examples of a **real truth** that never changes, as it relates to our current world, cannot be provided, because we live in an *imperfect* world where our understanding is constantly changing.

9. REAL TRUTH HAS ALWAYS EXISTED AND WILL ALWAYS EXIST AS IT IS TODAY AND AS IT HAS ALWAYS BEEN

The **REAL TRUTH**, as presented in this book, is that there **have always been** human societies throughout the Universe that do not change, advance, or progress, except in the expansion of their own personal experience. Those who reside in these societies know all there is to know about everything there is to know in the Universe. There have always existed perfect humans who are this way, and there will *always* exist human beings who are this way.

It is very hard for mortals (*imperfect humans*) to comprehend the concept of eternal (always has been and always will be) life with their limited minds. The only way we can possibly make sense of the *true reality* that these quintessential human societies do indeed exist is by using what we know from our current experience. Thus, we have considered the idea that human beings with each passing day continue to advance and learn more and more about themselves, their world, and the very Universe in which they exist. Consider the possibility that one day, after millions more years of experience, after discovering technologies that make our current technologies seem "primitive" by comparison, we will finally arrive at a complete and unchangeable understanding of all things.

We can either accept the fact that the **real truth** found in advanced human worlds has *always existed*, and is the same yesterday, today, and forever and cannot be changed; or we can look at it differently and accept that we are currently continuing to advance, and that one day we will know all there is to know about everything. No matter which way we look at it, the ultimate *true reality* is that **REAL TRUTH does** exist! Finding it in an *imperfect world* meant to keep it hidden from us for our own sake, however, is the challenge.

10. A FALSE SENSE OF REALITY IS INFLUENCED BY THE REALITY OF OTHERS

There is not one bit of information taught in any textbook or in any of the most prestigious colleges or universities in the world, that is **REAL TRUTH** as advanced humans view it. The "truths" we have been *taught* to accept as "reality" (and for which we spend a lot of money to acquire) are the *imperfect* assumptions of *imperfect* minds. Those in this *imperfect world* who depend upon schooling, textbooks, historical documents, newspapers, news reports, magazines, the best books written by the most renowned contemporary authors, or the ever-expanding Worldwide Internet, will **never** find **real truth**.

These types of people are completely dependent on the prejudices formed in their mind by the *facts, ideas, truths, perceptions, and principles* of the current day or from past history. For most people upon the earth, the things mentioned above are their *only* source of knowledge. Even those who believe that they have an open-mind and think on their own are still stimulated by the thoughts and experiences of other *imperfect* people and the current or past accepted realities of the world in which we live.

11. CHANGE DEMONSTRATES THAT MORTALS DO NOT KNOW REAL TRUTH

Because we have experienced our own understanding changing with time, we are aware that knowledge must continually be renewed, or it will be lost or left behind to exist in the ignorance of the past. We cannot trust what has been written by others to be true, because an author can only present the truth as it is formed in his or her mind. And most assuredly, their *truth* has been prejudiced by the ignorance of time in an *imperfect* world.

In the attempt to find truth, mortals spend many hours of their lives researching and listening to the opinions of others. There are countless venues on the Internet, for example, where those who are trying to bring value to their own reality write, "It's a historical fact that…" There is no such thing as a "historical **fact**." There are only points of view given by authors who, more times than not, weren't even present during the event upon which they claim to be an authority.

It is an "historical fact" that the planet earth was flat. One can find many assertions upon historical records that this "fact" was true. To the people who lived at the time this "historical fact" was presented by the scholars and "wise ones," it was their *only reality*. Nevertheless, there has always existed a few who have disagreed with current reality and formed a completely different reality than what was universally accepted. These "few," though rejected out rightly during their own lifetimes, are later proven correct in the future.

12. THERE ARE TWO SOURCES OF MORTAL KNOWLEDGE

Mortals gain their knowledge from two main sources. As mentioned above, most get their knowledge from the opinions of others presented in the form of books, media, and Internet exposure. But there are a few who get it from a second source: their own consciences.

It was from within his own conscience that a medieval astronomer named Copernicus came up with the motivation to experiment on his *own* perception and formulate an idea that was diametrically opposed to the reality of his time. He just *knew* that the earth could not be flat. The idea of a flat earth did not sit well with him. It confused him, threw him off balance, and caused a subconscious uneasiness that forced him to question the truthfulness of the "fact."

No matter what the rest of the world thinks, a person can only gain value for him or herself as an individual if what is generated in the form of thought brings balance instead of confusion. Knowledge (in the form of energy) from any extrinsic (outside) source will always collide with the intrinsic (inside) nature that makes us different from all other animals; that intrinsic nature is the **human essence**.

13. WE ARE DECEIVED BY A FALSE SENSE OF BALANCE

Nevertheless, because our *imperfect* brains record experiences in mortality that contradict *true reality*, we can easily be deceived into believing we have found the comfort level that **real truth** would give us, when we have not. We can generate energy from thoughts that do not agree with our *essence*, but do agree with our *imperfect* brain. Many find a personal balance in these falsehoods, because it takes much less energy to conform to the energy patterns given off by the *imperfect brain* than it does to attempt to access the *essence* and conform to its energy levels.

This is where we need to compare the things that *seem* to give us personal balance and comfort with the parameters of **real truth**. Again,

> **Real Truth** (with a capital "T") is anything upon which every (non-veiled/non-mortal) freethinking and free-willed human being in the Universe agrees. It is something that none of us in our perfected state, in complete honesty, could deny. **Real Truth** never changes. Nothing can be added to it or taken away from it. It is the same throughout the entire Universe; and anywhere advanced, perfected human beings are found, there is no disagreement on its substance and its conclusive statement of fact. (See chapter 15, Section 4)

If another advanced and perfected person exists in the Universe, who does not agree with our *imperfect* belief or opinion of "truth," then our personal truth cannot be **real truth**, no matter what it is or how strongly we believe it. If what we accept as truth does not agree with the truth known by advanced humans with *perfect* brains, then our truth is wrong and a product of our *imperfect* brain.

14. WE ALREADY KNOW EVERYTHING THERE IS TO KNOW

Our *essence* was foundationalized in a *perfect world* where advanced human beings, who knew all there is to know about **real truth**, helped us to become individuals by allowing us to exercise our free will and learn from our surrounding environment. Our surrounding environment provided a *true reality*, because it was found in a never-changing world that provided *facts, ideas, truths, perceptions, and principles* that had existed forever.

This pre-earth existence allowed us, as newly created humans, to establish a *foundationalized alignment* of how things are, how they have been, and how they will always be, which never changes. We became PERFECT HUMANS living in a PERFECT WORLD! There is no way "perfection" can be improved upon.

15. OUR ESSENCE MOTIVATES US TO QUESTION REALITY

The existence of our *essence* gives us the ability to question reality and motivates us to do so. It is the "missing link" that philosophers and "thinkers" of times past and present could not explain as the "medium of conscious thought." It is what gives us the capacity to reason.

A generally respected philosopher, David Hume (*circa* 1735), made the following assertions of truth and reality:

> "When we look about us towards external objects, and consider the operation of causes, we are never able, in a single instance, to discover any power or necessary connexion [sic]; any quality, which binds the effect to the cause, and renders the one an infallible consequence of the other. …There is required a medium, which may enable the mind to draw such an inference, if indeed it be drawn by reasoning and argument. What that medium is, I must confess, passes my comprehension; and it is incumbent on those to produce it, who assert that it really exists, and is the origin of all our conclusions concerning matter of fact. …This question I propose as much for the sake of information, as with an

intention of raising difficulties. I cannot find, I cannot imagine any such reasoning. But I keep my mind still open to instruction, if any one [sic] will vouchsafe to bestow it upon me. …all arguments concerning existence are founded on the relation of cause and effect; that our knowledge of that relation is derived entirely from experience; and that all our experimental conclusions proceed upon the supposition that the future will be conformable to the past. …Without the influence of custom, we should be entirely ignorant of every matter of fact beyond what is immediately present to the memory and senses. (Hume, David. "An Enquiry Concerning Human Understanding." Vol. 37, Part 3. The Harvard Classics. New York: P.F. Collier & Son, 1909–14; Eighteenth-Century Studies.)

First we may observe, that the supposition, that the future resembles the past, is not founded on arguments of any kind, but is derived entirely from habit. (Hume, David. "The Treatise of Human Nature." Oxford University Press Warehouse. New York: Macmillan & Co., 1896, pg 134.)

And as this is the obvious appearance of things, it must be admitted; till some hypothesis be discovered, which by penetrating deeper into human nature, may prove the former affections to be nothing but modifications of the latter. All attempts of this kind have hitherto proved fruitless, and seem to have proceeded entirely from that love of Simplicity which has been the source of much false reasoning in philosophy. …The simplest and most obvious cause, that can there be assigned for any phenomenon, is probably the true one. (Hume, David. "An Enquiry Concerning the Principles of Morals." Cosimo, Inc., 2006, pgs. 140–1.)

---

16. STUDYING OTHER OPINIONS CAN MISDIRECT US AWAY FROM REAL TRUTH

The existence of an *essence*, exactly what it is, the way it works, and why and how it exists, is the "missing link" that the great thinkers and philosophers throughout the history of our earth have never found. A few in their humility, admit that they do not understand many aspects of human consciousness and reality; but in their attempt to bring value to their own reality (i.e., in their pride), most of them confuse those who study their words (thus the case of David Hume given above).

Instead of adhering to the gentle persuasion of humility and directing others to the actual *source* from which *they* formulated their *own* thoughts and conceived *their own* reality (a person's own conscience), **these thinkers made themselves the source**! When one becomes a source of learning and truth for others, those who study their words are limited to the misconceptions, prejudices, and *untrue* realities that these *thinkers* present as truth. They misdirect the energy produced by the minds of their students away from their students' own *essences* and towards the *thinkers'* understanding and conclusions. This stops the students from being able to find the **real truth** that has already been established within their *own essence.*

17. COMMUNICATION COMES FROM OUR THOUGHTS

If all the greatest *thinkers* got together, without their egos, and compared notes on the conclusions they have made through their considerations, they would probably come pretty close to **real truth**. Our creators knew of the possibility that by using our free will, even as *imperfect* mortals, we might someday get together and contribute our own little piece of the puzzle and solve the mystery of life before the intended time. Solving the *mystery* would have negated the purpose of living in a world where it wasn't meant for us to understand **true reality**, so that we could experience what it is like to live without it.

The greatest obstacle in our inability to help us put the pieces of the puzzle together is the way we relay information to each other—it is in the way that we communicate. When we were placed in our *imperfect* current world and given brains that couldn't easily access the memories of our past life in a *perfect* world, our advanced mothers provided the opportunity for us to learn some basic communication skills. Over the next few sections of this chapter, we will explain their involvement.

We will begin by discussing the interaction of our vocal cords with our nerves and brain. Our vocal cords are designed to produce sounds from energy transmissions received from our brain. The nerves leading to the vocal chords are directly connected to the part of our brain that is responsible for organizing energy patterns into experiences and memories (in other words, thoughts).

It is in this same part of our *imperfect* brain that we are able to experience the events of today or the memories of the past. We remember the past and relive the experience as if we are watching a projection of the events inside of our head. The *imperfect* brain allows us to relive these experiences consciously *without* any interaction of our sensory organs.

With an *imperfect body*, we are only able to *see* and *hear* things within the confines of this internal "movie theater"—much like the experience we have during a movie theater presentation of the early 21st Century. When we relive experiences, we *cannot sense* the sensations of smell, taste, or touch. For example, we can think of a rose and how the wind might sound passing over its petals, but we cannot *think* of its smell, how it feels, or how it tastes.

However, with a *perfect body*, our *essence* works in unison with our *perfect* brain to project a *full sensory experience* of all of the events of any of our lives at anytime we desire to recall them. For those of us who have tasted the bitterness of a rose petal, we need not eat another one to recall the "bitter" sensation—once will be enough! A *perfect* body allows us to relive the experience in real time (as if it is presently happening exactly how it happened in the past) so that we never forget or become complacent and accidentally eat a rose petal whose bitterness we have long forgotten.

As explained before, because the brain of an *imperfect* infant is not full of energy patterns (experience) yet, the source of energy that creates many infantile sounds and gestures comes from the subtle influence of the *essence*. For this reason, infants often smile even though they have never been taught how to. We were taught how to laugh and smile by perfect parents; and the memories of those experiences are stored as energy patterns in our *essence*.

18. MULTIPLE LANGUAGES KEEP US FROM UNDERSTANDING ONE ANOTHER

We have quoted from David Hume, above, because he wrote in the English language, the same language in which this book is written. Many other philosophers wrote in their native tongue, and then their words were translated into different languages. During the process of translation, the *true* meaning of what the author was trying to say is often distorted and lost. Nothing that has been translated out of the original language in which it was written can be accepted as the truth, as intended by the original author.

Language as a part of our *imperfect world* keeps the *real purpose* for why we are here intact. Language is a barrier that has been established by those who oversee our world to ensure that we don't come up with ***true reality***, when it is the opposition of ***true reality*** that we are here to experience. In other words, the many different languages that exist in our world were *intended* to keep us from coming together and finding **real truth**.

If we all spoke the same language, we could possibly combine our individual abilities to tap into our *essence* (which each contain all **real truth**), and come up with what we were taught when we were *foundationalized* in the perfect world. When one of us comes up with a piece of the puzzle to *true reality*, and another comes up with a different piece, our inability to speak the same language can keep us from being able to put the two pieces together. In this way, we cannot come to a knowledge of what we are *not* supposed to know while we are here.

19. DIFFERENT LANGUAGES AND DIALECTS WERE ENCOURAGED

In the beginning of our experience in this *imperfect world*, instead of setting up a universal language based on fundamental sounds, words, and phrases, we were allowed to come up with our own unique way of vocalizing what we wanted to communicate. This communication was not limited to words only, but also included visually transmitted sign patterns using different parts of our bodies to convey the meaning of our thoughts.

Because our mothers were advanced perfected humans of the Solarian type, they knew exactly what we meant before we acted out each sound or gesture that represented what we were thinking. They did not speak to us, but encouraged the formation of the sounds and gestures produced by our *imperfect bodies* that each of us assigned to our own thoughts.

Had they spoken to us, they would have introduced into an *imperfect world* a *perfect* form of communication, even that which we used during our *Foundationalization Process*. Again, this would have invalidated the purpose for which we live in an *imperfect* world. Had we heard them speak in the perfect human dialect, we would have simply mimicked the sound patterns made by their voices, much as children do today. But remember, the purpose of this life is to *not* be able to communicate our thoughts perfectly to each other.

20. THE FIRST COMMUNICATION WAS NOT COMPLEX

There were hundreds of thousands of people who were first created by our advanced mothers in this *imperfect world*. These now *mortal* children could not logistically associate with every single other child during the time these mothers spent with us before they went back to their own planet. Those children who associated in close proximity became familiar with the sounds and gestures of each other and subsequently developed a different form of communication (language) than those with whom they did not associate closely.

However, these first languages were simple and not as complex as our languages are today. Therefore, it was easy for us to learn the basic communication skills of the other people we did not associate with on a day-to-day basis. In addition, body language was a much greater part of the communication than it is today.

For example, if a person without complex language skills said, "Ugh!" few would be able to understand what that person meant. But if the person held out an apple and said, "Ugh!" simultaneously lifting their eyebrows and smiling, we would all know that "Ugh!" meant, "Here, do you want this apple?" If the person *did not* lift the eyebrows and *did not* smile, then the sound "Ugh!" probably means, "Here, take this!" The same word is used, but by changing the body language slightly, the word is given a completely different meaning.

21. THE WAY WE THINK AFFECTS OUR TRUE REALITY

Each of our experiences is a compilation of energy patterns that arrive at our brain from our individual sensory receptors. Our brain organizes the unique energy patterns it receives from each sensory system into a completed thought or experience. This *complete* compilation is then stored as a memory.

With each new experience in our *imperfect world*, our brains formulate new energy patterns that we did not have while we existed in a *perfect world.* While in an *imperfect* state, when we want to communicate with others, we search through the energy patterns of our experience and prepare a thought. The process of preparing a thought, or "thinking," is done in the same location in our brain that receives and organizes the energy patterns that are received from our senses.

"Thinking" is simply the attempt to reverse the process and send the energy patterns from our brain back to our sensory organs. In this way, we *think* we are hearing, seeing, smelling, tasting, and touching something that is not actually part of our current *true reality*. We deceive ourselves into believing we are sensing something that we are not because we are relying on our ability *to recall* the event instead of actually reliving it exactly as it occurred.

In contrast, as explained previously, with a *perfect* body, any of our thoughts become our ***true reality***, because the memory will create the exact same sensations that were created when we first experienced the event.

22. OUR THOUGHTS AFFECT OUR BODY LANGUAGE

Because our vocal cords are directly connected to the same location of the brain where sensory input is received, we are consequently able to produce sounds that reflect what we are thinking. In addition, our sensory organs react to our thoughts because they are receiving energy patterns, not from our surrounding environment, but from inside of our heads.

This is why we salivate when we simply *think* of eating something tasty. This is why our senses are affected and stimulated by various thoughts in our head that are not part of our current reality. However, when we communicate, we are sending the energy patterns of thought from our brain to our vocal cords; and whatever sound our vocal cords produce from the thought is one way in which we communicate what we are thinking to others.

The other way is through body language. In this way, our eyes, ears, mouth, nose, and hands are being stimulated by the energy patterns they are receiving from our thoughts. This is why it is possible to "read" a person's body language and tell what he or she is thinking before anything is vocalized.

23. BODY LANGUAGE REFLECTS OUR TRUE THOUGHTS

We cannot understand other languages, though all of us "think" of the same events in the same way. Each language associates different sounds made by the vocal cords to each event.

However, if we could sit inside the "movie theater," or the location in one another's brains where thoughts are formulated, we would have no communication barrier, and would then know *exactly* what each other is thinking. But our advanced mothers did not want it this way; so they allowed each of us to develop our own unique way of expressing our thoughts both vocally and through body language.

Can one imagine the difference in our world had our advanced mothers taught us the correct way to communicate with each other? In advanced worlds, there is only **one language** spoken. This perfect language provides a perfect communication of what is intended by our thoughts. Advanced humans never misunderstand what others say, what the body language means, or what is shown in the countenance of another.

One part of our body language that *is* the same in a *perfect* or *imperfect world* is the human smile. Given in sincerity, it means the same throughout the whole Universe—worlds without end!

24. WRITING IS THE POOREST FORM OF COMMUNICATION

The other form of communication we have developed in our *imperfect world* that did not exist (nor has it ever) in a *perfect world*, is writing. The ability to transfer one's thoughts onto a piece of paper negates the *human* experience of communication entirely. It is the way in which most of us are deceived into accepting another's reality that is not our own, and whose reality gained in an *imperfect world*, is not **true reality**.

It is easy, for example, to deceive a lover by the eloquent words of poetry and beautiful prose, when the poet could actually have desires for a completely different person. But when an unfaithful lover is confronted face-to-face, the true thoughts generated by his or her body language or speech are not so easily hidden.

25. THE WRITTEN WORD NEVER CONVEYS TRUE REALITY

It is easy to fall under the hypnosis of the written word. We can read something and invent in our mind whatever we want the true meaning of the words to be. We project a meaning into what we read according to what we have accepted as our personal reality, real or not.

We cannot possibly know the true intent of the words written by another human who has a completely different view of reality than our own. For this reason, those sincere and "wise" humans who knew ***true reality*** never left any of their *own* writings. They knew what could happen to the written word. Not only could it be misinterpreted, but also through translation and unauthorized editing, it could be changed to reflect something that the original author never intended.

It's very easy to change words that are written. It is not so easy to change a free-willed being's thoughts. Nothing that has ever been written can honestly and truly convey the exact thoughts of the person who wrote it. If the person who writes is available to provide commentary and explanation with his or her own vocal cords and body language, only then will the reader be able to receive a true reflection of what the author is trying to convey. Even then, the way our *imperfect brains* function, what is heard might not be perceived and received like the conveyor of the thought intended. Well has it been said, "A person hears what they *want* to hear."

26. WRITERS USE THEIR SKILL TO CREATE VALUE FOR THEMSELVES

Generally, people write literature to generate value for their own opinion. The more accolades they receive from those who read their works, the more value they gain for themselves. For this reason, writers are some of the most egocentric and insecure humans that exist. An author's purpose is not to serve others. One either serves oneself by projecting into one's writings what one is thinking as a catharsis of inner turmoil, or one seeks to be served by others in the platitudes of praise expected from those who read their writings.

27. ADVANCED HUMANS ONLY APPROVE OF THE WRITTEN WORD TO COUNTER WHAT HAS ALREADY BEEN WRITTEN

The ONLY reason why advanced Solarian humans ever allow the written expression of their thoughts is to help those who depend on or trust in the written words of others as a source of truth. They utilize the written form of communication when there is no other way to get people on this earth to consider that what has been written by other authors is **not** *true reality*. The best way, of course, would be to have them visit earth and teach us face-to-face, so that we could read their body language and ask them questions. Until the purpose for their non-intervention is complete though, they will not deal with us face-to-face. They will leave us to our own devices. If prudent, in their wisdom, they will attempt to help us *without* interfering with our free agency to choose our own course of action based on our own accepted knowledge.

This book, HUMAN REALITY—Who We Are and Why We Exist, is our creators' attempt to communicate **real truth** to us by utilizing a form of communication that we can understand and accept, if we so choose. Although it appears counterintuitive, there was no other way, other than through writing, for our creators to give our *imperfect* minds a chance to understand *true human reality*.

28. THE AUTHOR OF THIS BOOK WAS GIVEN THE KNOWLEDGE OF TRUE REALITY FACE-TO-FACE

For a wise purpose that will be explained later, our creators did not choose a great writer, philosopher, orator, statesman, or one who is set up as a "wise one" or leader of human thought. These types cannot be trusted with the power of supporting the free will and equality expected of human beings, whose existence and happiness is solely dependent on their free will and ability to create *their own* reality.

They chose a typical, common human being, one subjected to the same passions and desires as any other, and who lives as the least of all humans. No secular education or indoctrination contributed to the knowledge acquired by the author of this book. The author has no particular extraordinary skill or talent that would otherwise promise him worldly praise or glory. Simplicity and plainness best describe his lifestyle.

The author was given this knowledge face-to-face from advanced human beings. These advanced humans knew the author's life, his personality, and propensities. They knew that this author would never violate the purpose for which knowledge of **real truth** was received. They knew that in all things, the integrity and purpose for the second stage of human development upon this earth would be supported by this author. They intended for the voice of the weak and undesirable to confound the strong and the worldly acceptable. And at their discretion, the author will remain **ANONYMOUS**.

29. REJECTING MORTAL "FACTS" CAN HELP US FIND REAL TRUTH

As mentioned at the beginning of this chapter, the Worldwide Internet is becoming the main source for most of the information that forms a person's concept of reality. One of the most popular online encyclopedias is *Wikipedia*.

Wikipedia is a vast reference of comprehensive information available on most areas of knowledge. Anyone can go to this source and add to or change any of the information presented therein. It comprises the opinions, understanding, perceptions, principles, ideas, facts, truth, and beliefs of freethinking human beings—who essentially create their own reality and attempt to share it with others in the *Wikipedia* venue. It is used by students, teachers, and authors to reference "facts" that are more than likely not the **real truth**.

These types of centralized reference sites on the Internet will only add to the ignorance of the human race and keep the *imperfect brain* forever dependent upon the knowledge (real or not) acquired in an *imperfect world*. Until the human race learns to disregard all that it supposes to be true facts—which information has created a world full of human misery and despair—it will not be ready or able to find the **real truth** hidden in the depths of every human soul, which we now know as the *human essence*. We will not know a fullness of what is recorded in our *essence*, or that which would demonstrate our *true humanity* to help change our world into the *perfect world* that it should be, unless we reject all that keeps us from accessing what is recorded in our *essence*.

30. LITTLE CHILDREN KNOW ALL THAT MORTALS NEED TO KNOW

The simple reality that we are not supposed to know **real truth** should help us realize that the many different opinions of reality are really just that—opinions! Just because a person can utilize language skills and eloquently articulate their thoughts through speaking or writing, does not mean that they know any more about *true reality* than those who can't read, write, or express themselves through language.

In fact, little children who can't even speak properly know just as much or more about **real truth** than the oldest and "wisest" human on earth does. Little children have an easier time of experiencing joy—the *true* reason why humans exist—because they have not yet formulated a *false* sense of reality from their experiences in our *imperfect* world. They might not know much about our current world, but in reality, owing to the state that it is in, who would want to?

31. HAPPINESS IS MISSED WHILE WE ARE BUSY WORRYING

We experience joy through the stimulation of our senses by our environment. Thinking and contemplating about our world does not bring us joy; it wastes our time. While little children are involved in experiencing their surroundings and hearing, seeing, smelling, tasting, and touching everything around them, those of us who do not see ourselves as little children are *wondering* what it all means.

The only joy we experience through the process of thinking is when we formulate energy patterns that match those stored in our *essence*. This is where the euphoria of "Wow! Now I understand!" comes from. This is the "light bulb" that seems to turn on in our head. This is the "Eureka!" and the sense of satisfaction that comes when something finally makes sense to us.

32. OUR COMMON SENSE DOES NOT ALWAYS LEAD US TO REAL TRUTH

When we read or hear something that doesn't make sense, most likely it is not **real truth**. HOWEVER, if we have an established set of *facts, ideas, truths, perceptions, and principles* already prominent in our head, and if what we hear, **real truth** or not, does not match this *knowledge*, it can seem as if it does not make sense to us.

Again, this is the purpose of having an *imperfect* brain that can record its own experiences, apart from those recorded on the *essence*. Once we have recorded a compilation of *facts, ideas, truths, perceptions, and principles* in our *imperfect brain*, the energy levels of these memories are much easier to match with our current experience, thus deceiving us into thinking that what we do and think is **real truth**, when it is not.

It's harder to match these energy experiences (what we think and do) with our subconscious *essence*, because of the impact our *imperfect brain* has on the process of how we formulate a thought. If our brain didn't record any energy levels of experience (as is the case in a *perfect human body*), everything we think and do would automatically relate to those energy levels stored in our *essence,* and we would immediately feel if what we were thinking and doing was *true reality* or not. In fact, we would not experience anything that was not **real truth**.

Once more, if we were meant to immediately recognize what makes us happy and what does not, we would never choose a course of action that would lead to unhappiness, and this world is all about us experiencing unhappiness.

33. CONSISTENT AND LASTING JOY IS THE LITMUS TEST OF ALL CONCEPTS BASED ON REAL TRUTH

Based on what we have just learned, we now know that nothing we think or do in this world is *true reality*, UNLESS it brings us a consistent and lasting feeling of joy *without* impeding on the free will of others and causing them *not to* be able to experience the same consistent and lasting joy. Our bodies are set up to allow us to know if something is **real truth** or not. Ask yourself, "Does the thought or act create consistent and lasting joy, or not?"

When we judge the actions of another, for example, does it make us feel good, or not? Does holding any prejudice, bigotry, or condemning attitude toward another, bring us joy? When a thought comes into our head that another person is doing something "wrong," do the energy patterns created by the thought bring us joy, or consternation and frustration? One of the greatest contributors to our unhappiness is the way we view and judge each other.

34. STRESS IS A PHYSICAL REACTION TO IMPERFECTION

Stress is a mental or emotional strain on our physical body. It is caused by the energy patterns that we are creating through our actions and thoughts *not being able* to find a matching energy pattern either on our *imperfect brain* or upon our *essence.* Once we do something or think something enough times, we develop an energy pattern in our *imperfect* brain. Consequently, something that caused us stress in the past can now find a familiar energy pattern, which relieves us of much of the subconscious mental strain that takes place in finding a match.

Most people don't like change. They experience a stressful feeling when they are faced with an event that they are unfamiliar with, such as death, marriage, divorce, birth of a child, a new job, etc. With each new event, the subconscious mind attempts to match it to a previously recorded experience. The more mental stress we experience, the more our subconscious mind adapts to it until the stress itself seems to be the most comfortable situation for us to deal with.

35. FEAR AND STRESS COME FROM THE SAME SOURCE

Fear is also stress. When we first experience fear, it is simply our reaction to something unknown or something we have not yet experienced. There is little difference between what causes us to *fear* something and what causes us to *stress* about something. Once the energy pattern of an experience that caused us to fear or stress has been established in our brain, when the same experience occurs again, we do not feel the same degree of stress. This is because we don't have to expend much energy in searching for a match. **However**, in our *imperfect* brain, because we do not have the ability to recall our experiences immediately, we often re-experience the fear and stress we felt when we first recorded the energy patterns of the unknown experience.

For example, if we are stressed about or fearful of being left alone in the dark, it is because we have no experience of the incident recorded in the memories that we can recall. The next time we are left in the dark, because of the stress associated with our inability to see our surroundings, the memory that nothing negative came from the same experience of the past is blocked by our current experience of stress. The more time we spend in the dark, the more enhanced our mental capacity to deal with the experience becomes.

It is highly unlikely, however, for any *imperfect human* to not experience stress or fear, UNLESS that person learns to bypass the energy levels produced by the *imperfect brain* and relies solely on what is felt from the *essence*. And the reason why most people will never be able to accomplish this is because they are not even aware that there **is** an *essence* apart from their brain.

36. OUR EXPERIENCES DETERMINE THE DEGREE OF STRESS WE FEEL

The happiness and joy that we feel comes from our thought patterns finding a reflective energy pattern on our *imperfect brain* or in our *essence*. If, for example, a young girl was cooed and coddled, loved, and treated tenderly by her father, the experience *foundationalized* exactly what she later expects and needs from *any* man in her life. If she is not able to find a man that treats her like her father did, she will never be happy.

On the other hand, many young children experience tremendous stress in their early lives, most often from the actions of their parents. Because these experiences were *foundationalized* in them, they cannot find consistent and lasting happiness when someone is cooing and coddling them, or loving and treating them tenderly. They think and act in some way to find a balance that is consistent with the experiences of the more prominent energy levels established in their *imperfect brain*. Therefore, they cause stress on themselves and others in order to reach this balance.

37. WHY DO WE ACT SO INHUMANELY TOWARDS EACH OTHER?

This brings us to the ***true reality*** of why human beings seem to mistreat each other and do not act humanely, as they know they should, or better, as is established *subconsciously in their essence.* Why is there so much misery and suffering caused by human beings mistreating each other? Why do we allow the existence of abject poverty and inequality? Why are there wars and crimes that repulse the very sense of humanity that we think separates us from other animals?

Why does it appear that other species of animals treat those of their same species with greater equality and respect than the human species does, when we are supposed to be able to reason, and are the only life form that even understands what "acting humanely" actually means? With all of our intelligence, all of our advancements, and our unrestricted ability to imagine and be creative, why can't we change our *imperfect world* into a *perfect* one?

38. EXPERIENCING INHUMANITY IS THE PURPOSE OF THIS LIFE

The greatest minds that have ever set themselves to figure out life and humanity have never been able to answer these questions about human nature. They have studied and quoted each other time and time again, transposing one another's thoughts and theories and developing their own, trying to come up with a reasonable explanation to humankind's inhumanity. The only *part of* **real truth** that any of them has been able to come up with is the understanding that the *ultimate truth* of any phenomenon should make as few assumptions and speculations as possible.

Some of these so-called "great minds" created a term for this conclusion called "Occam's Razor." This proposal states that "all other things being equal, the simplest solution is the best." In other words, when none of these so-called "wise ones" can isolate the cause and effect of negative human nature, the theory that offers the fewest conjectures and the fewest number of reasons, **must** be the right one.

The easiest answer to the questions given above concerning why we can't treat each other humanely (which is also the simplest answer) is this: WE'RE NOT SUPPOSED TO! If we were supposed to, why would we have had to leave the *perfect world* where we were created and *foundationalized* as human beings?

39. OUR JUDGMENTS OF EACH OTHER ARE NEVER REAL TRUTH

Accepting that nothing in our world is ***true reality*** and that nothing we do in an *imperfect body* can be a mistake (because if we experience unhappiness in doing it, it is the proper experience for the purposes of this world), we are able to view our world in a completely different light. Our view of others should also change dramatically!

How can we judge what others do as being a reflection of their *true nature*, when the very makeup of their *imperfect brains* are responsible for the action? Who can be a *true* criminal when what they have done (from murder to petty theft and everything in-between) is simply a reaction to the environment in which they were placed according to the experiences they have received in a world meant for *imperfection*?

Shouldn't we then be able to forgive each other of our faults and mistakes as we each are unconditionally forgiven by those who placed us upon this earth? For example, if you had the same *imperfect brain* that came from the same *imperfect* DNA of the same *imperfect* parents, who then provided an *imperfect* foundation of experience that led one to become a murderer, would you act differently? How can any of us be sure that in these same circumstances we would not also use our free agency to kill another? If the events took place just the same as they occurred in the life of the one committing murder, we can't be sure what we would do!

Are we sure we wouldn't rape someone? Or steal from them? What if we were placed in a position of leadership and authority over others? How would we act? What would we do? How can any of us possibly know what we would do in any given situation unless we were all experiencing the same reality, at the same time, and in the same *imperfect* situation? Much truth rings true in a popular children's song:

> You think the only people who are people, are the people who look and think like you. But if you walk the footsteps of a stranger, you'll learn things you never knew you never knew. (Menken, Alan and Schwartz, Stephen. "Colors of the Wind." 1995.)

---

40. IMPERFECT REALITY ADDS TO OUR TRUE PURPOSE

If our *essence* was in the vicinity of Austria-Hungary, *circa* the 20th of April 1889, and it just happened to enter the *imperfect body* of one, called by his parents, "Adolf," and we experienced everything that he did, how do we know that we would not have made the exact same decisions that he made throughout his life? It would behoove the reader to research and find any early photographs of Adolf Hitler as a small child. Look at the pictures! Could any of us ever imagine that this innocent child might one day be responsible for the genocide of millions of people?

Hitler and those like him add to the *true purpose* for which we are here upon this planet. The *true reality* is that we don't know what we would have done in any particular circumstance except for those that we have actually experienced for ourselves (all of which we will be able to remember someday).

What we can finally understand though, is that no one else's experience is pertinent to our happiness. No one else's reality is our own. And the greatest realization of all is that **we, alone, create our only TRUE REALITY**! Therefore, our goal should be to match our **TRUE REALITY** with that of the advanced human beings who placed us upon this earth. Upon doing so, we will find **REAL TRUTH**!

SUMMARY

The purpose of our existence upon this earth is to experience the opposite of the perfect state in which we were *foundationalized*, and in which we will live forever. Because of this, it was never intended for any of us to go through life without acting contrary to our innate *humanity*. We needed the understanding that comes from experiencing an opposition in all things.

Everything about our existence as mortal, *imperfect humans* was designed and is supported by advanced human beings, who have been helping newly created humans become as advanced as they are for a very long time. For a wise purpose, they do not intercede and attempt to change our wars, arguments, prejudices, hypocrisies, opinions, facts, ideas, truths, perceptions, or principles. They allow us to exercise our free will and invent any perception of reality we desire. With this free agency, we are realizing that those things that we have accepted as our current reality cause us to act towards each other and react to each other ***in****humanely*.

Because it was their *intention* to have us experience life in an *imperfect world*, they do not judge us or condemn us for acting the only way our *imperfect body* allows us to act. To them, we are like little children who fight and hit each other and take each other's toys because we want what they have. We are as emotionally unstable in our environment as spoiled children are in theirs. They know that one day we will grow up to be *adults* just like them and look back on our childhood and smile, because we will realize that it was a very important part of our development and purpose.

Nevertheless, just because they forgive us for what we do in an *imperfect human state* of existence, does not give us an excuse for not figuring out what does and does not make us happy when we have the power to exercise our free agency. We have been allowed in these latter times of our development on this earth to have the power and knowledge to solve our own dilemmas without the intervention of advanced beings. The problem is, our human nature invents excuses why we do not.

The Excuse of Human Nature

CHAPTER SIXTEEN

Man's cleverness is almost indefinite, and stretches like an elastic band, but human nature is like an iron ring. You can go round and round it, you can polish it highly, you can even flatten it a little on one side, whereby you will make it bulge out the other, but you will NEVER, while the world endures and man is man, increase its total circumference.

—H. Rider Haggard

1. MORTALITY TEACHES US MORE ABOUT OURSELVES

We are living upon the earth without the ability to remember anything outside the scope of what we learn from our current lifetime experience. Because we are human beings, we are affected by the subconscious energy of our *essence*. We are the only life form upon the earth that is affected by the *essence* in such a way that it causes us to *imagine*, *ponder*, *wonder*, and *reason* about ourselves and the world around us. The way that we imagine, ponder, wonder, and reason not only makes us unique, but also motivates us to act any way that we choose. Our actions (without being able to consciously remember anything beyond our current existence) have shaped the societies and cultures of human life. The *life* that we have established upon this earth for ourselves has caused us and the natural world in which we live a significant amount of misery and continual strife.

Human nature has overcome and controls the majority of *ordinary* nature. Through using our free will and our unique mental capacities, we have created a *reality* that seems completely contrary to what was intended for our natural world. Usually what we perceive as reality is a *reality* of our own creation. But it cannot be our ***true reality***, because it is not our *true* nature to cause ourselves misery and strife. It is our **true nature** to be happy.

We are continually searching for this happiness and utilize everything in our environment to find it. Thus, so it appears, our *true natures* are in direct conflict with what the *natural* earth has the potential and capability to provide for us. The way the *imperfect* earth is set up (in its natural state) cannot provide human beings with what they desire—as it does every other life form found upon it.

Those who are responsible for our existence and who placed us upon the earth, purposefully intended for us to experience the opposite of all that is perfect. It was deliberate—that while we are away from their influence and their direct and continual intervention—that we not experience *true reality* in regards to *perfect human nature*. During our time upon this earth, no one controls what we do or how we do it, except for us. Being left to ourselves, we impede each other's free will and cause ourselves and others much misery and suffering.

We are here to experience an opposition to our *true humanity*. In the situations presented to us during mortality, we are able to see which course of action our *humanity type* would choose in any given situation. We learn what makes each of us feel comfortable and what causes us depression and discord. When faced with a situation, each *humanity type* reacts differently. We experience similar circumstances as everyone else at one time or another while existing upon the earth in various human incarnates. In doing so, we learn more about the uniqueness of our *true self*. Once we recognize *who we are*, we are able to accept *who we are* and remain comfortable with the choice we have made. This is what one would call "self-actualization."

2. WE CAN RECOGNIZE OUR HUMANITY TYPE BY OBSERVING OUR OWN ACTIONS

When placed in a set of random, similar circumstances, we do not all act in the same manner. We have already concluded that in a *perfect* world none of us could have known how we would act with our free agency under certain circumstances, until we were placed in those particular circumstances. During our *Foundationalization Process*, we had the ability to observe the free-willed choices of others going through their second stage of human development in other mortal, *imperfect* worlds throughout the Universe. We couldn't have *imagined* that we would act the same as the mortal people we were watching on other earth-like planets. Though our advanced creators assured us that most of us would act the same, if placed in a similar set of circumstances, it was very hard to accept this reality about ourselves.

Our advanced creators DO KNOW how each of us would generally act when placed in any given circumstance. They do not know the *exact* reactions or actions we will make, but they can make a general and very accurate guess based on their vast experience over millions of years of watching human beings of different *humanity types* go through the same stages of human development.

As explained previously, it is from their vast experience of being with us in a primordial perfect world that our creators knew just how many and what size of planets to place in our solar system. They knew each of our individual *humanity types* and prepared the appropriate worlds for us according to these "types," which correspond to our own personal desires of happiness. From their limitless experience, they know what will make each of us happy.

3. OUR ACTIONS PROVE WHY OUR FREE WILL NEEDS TO BE CONTROLLED

Our understanding of the **true reality** of the universal and eternal nature of human beings was established while being *foundationalized*. During this time, we encountered a problem with the issue of not being able to have sex (the ultimate human ability to utilize the body for its greatest sensory fulfillment) unless we chose the Solarian/service-oriented humanity type. We also learned that equality and respect for free will was the most significant part of being a *human being*. Therefore, we also found it difficult to accept that, after our life as an *imperfect mortal*, most of us would not have the power and control over our environment (i.e., all matter) that only Solarian humans possess.

These dilemmas arose during our *foundationalization* when we were around our creators while having the ability to exercise our free will according to our own desires. They told us that we could become anything we wanted. We were not forced to meet any pre-set expectations of behavior, except when our behavior affected the free will of another. We wondered why all of us couldn't have the same power to control the elements as our creators, whether for the sake of serving ourselves (Lunarian humanity type), or so that we could create and command our environment to serve us (Stellarian type).

None of us could completely understand why we couldn't have what our parents had regardless of our choice of *humanity type*. It just didn't make any sense! And it would never have made sense had we not been placed in a position of power upon this earth, similar to the position that our creators are in upon their advanced *perfect* human world. In our current situation, we all have the ability to have sex. And although we cannot control the source of all matter, we do have the ability to control our environment to a much greater extent than any other creature found upon earth.

Without our free will being controlled, and having similar powers to Solarian humans, we have effectively demonstrated over the course of human history upon this earth how we use this power. Our history convincingly proves that without something intervening to control and oversee our *human nature*, we will never be able to fulfill the purpose for which we exist—to experience continual and lasting happiness.

4. WE CAN UNDERSTAND OURSELVES BY HOW WE ACT

How we use our free will on earth is the key to understanding and solving the dilemmas (why we can't all have sex and have equal power as our creators) we were faced with during our primordial upbringing. Our experiences in an *imperfect world* help us to realize what would happen if we had power to exercise our own free will without restriction.

What would we do with this power? Would we use it to serve others? Serve ourselves? Or to have others serve us? What would we do if we had more knowledge, strength, control and power than others? How would we wield this power over them? We could never have answered these questions unless we were provided the opportunity to exercise our free will according to the "power" of our individual *essence* (in other words, the *humanity type* we chose for ourselves after billions of years of existence in a perfect human society).

Here is the key to the answers:

- *If we are comfortable and content with how we act, then we are acting in accordance with our essence and* ***true humanity type****.*
- *If we are not completely comfortable with our actions, then we are not acting in conformity with our* ***true humanity type****.*

It's really that simple!

Again, the "power of our essence" reflects who we *really are*, or better, who we chose to become during our *foundationalization* period. Our *essence's* power does not reflect who we have become, who we *act* like, or who we *think* we are in our current *imperfect* world. It only reflects *who we* ***really*** *are.*

An *imperfect* world will never allow us to *know our true selves*, as we do not have the ability to access all of the memories of our past lives. But it *will* allow us, according to the power of our *essence*, to know how we feel (comfortable or not) *when we act.* Existing in an *imperfect world* allows us to come to know and accept ourselves better by providing an experience where we temporarily forget *who we are.* This world provides opportunities for us to act in opposition to our true nature.

If during mortality we knew without any doubt that we were Solarian, for example, we would force our actions to align with our

Solarian nature. We would not experience what it is like to *not act* like a Solarian, thus negating the purpose for our time in an *imperfect* world—to experience an opposition in all things. We must have the opportunity to act contrary to our *true nature* during this probationary time so as to learn to appreciate and enjoy being who we *truly* are forever. If we didn't have a contrasting experience to our self, how would we ever appreciate forever who we have chosen to be?

5. OUR IMPERFECT MORTAL ACTIONS DO NOT ALWAYS REFLECT WHO WE REALLY ARE

In review of what we know so far, we realize that anything we do becomes an actual pattern of energy that is stored in our *essence.* We know that when what we do balances with (or matches) an energy pattern found in our *essence*, we feel peace and contentment. On the other hand, when we act a certain way and create an energy pattern that does *not* match any found in our *essence*, we feel frustration, irritability, and unhappiness.

We also understand that an *imperfect body* has a brain separate from our *essence.* This *imperfect brain* also records all the experiences of an *imperfect world* as accessible memories, though our conscious access to these memories is limited. Science recognizes these "recordings" and sometimes defines them as specific *dendrites* formed on the surface of our brain.

We also know that the *imperfect* brain acts as a "veil" that generally prohibits the energy of the *essence* from being consciously recognized and used in our daily cognitive processes, or better, during our normal thinking patterns. We have learned that when we relax our minds, the power produced by our *imperfect brain* is reduced to a point where a small portion of the *essence's* energy is able to leak through to the place in our brain where we formulate our thoughts. We've referred to this place earlier as our inner "movie theater." This is where we experience random and often disconnected events we call "dreams" or "visions."

We have learned that our "SELF" is a compilation of the experiences recorded in our past, the experiences we have today, and all those which will be recorded in our future. But the most important thing we have learned is that WE ARE **NOT** WHAT OUR IMPERFECT **BRAIN** RECORDED, RECORDS, OR WILL RECORD! **We are** what is recorded on our HUMAN ESSENCE.

6. OUR MORTAL BODIES DO NOT DETERMINE WHO WE ARE

A family of eight siblings with the same DNA patterns will most likely produce different *humanity types*, depending on the *essence* that enters into the body of each child. This is why human beings with similar *imperfect bodies*, and who experience the same upbringing, will nevertheless act or react differently when faced with similar situations. Some children cry when a toy is taken away from them; some fight to take the toy back; and still others find another toy to play with without responding negatively to having a toy taken from them.

One of the examples our creators have allowed in our *imperfect world* to get this point across is in the case of identical twins. This paradigm will leave us without excuse for understanding the power the individual *essence* has over our actions. Each identical twin has the exact same body as its sibling, but neither acts exactly the same. How could this be if only our physical brains are responsible for *who we are*? In the case of *identical* twins, both brains are from *identical* DNA patterns, but each *essence* that entered each body upon birth was uniquely different from the other.

7. WE ARE PROVIDED REAL EXAMPLES OF OUR HUMANITY'S POTENTIAL

Another example that has been allowed in our *imperfect world*, so that we can understand the phenomena of the power of the *essence* and how it motivates our actions, is in the case of individuals with Down syndrome. These people have been given specific physical bodies that appear more similar in nature than any other human body other than identical twins. Our creators specifically engineered this type of body for an important purpose. They made the Down syndrome brain in such a way that the emotions of these individuals are **more** affected by the power of their *essence* than those of the "normal" *imperfect* brain.

In other words, the "veil" is a little bit thinner in the head of a Down syndrome person. It is rare, if not impossible, to find a Down syndrome person who judges others, exhibits bigotry, possesses prejudice, or in any other way uses his or her individual free will to affect the free will of another. Of all of the people upon the earth, Down syndrome people are the most satisfied with their environment. Their nature is more like our *perfect nature* than any other human example given in an *imperfect world.*

They do not seem to contribute to our world, as they have no incentive to gain knowledge, money, possessions, or any other item of "success" that most of us have placed value upon and continually desire. If they do desire any of these things, it is because the conditioning is forced upon them throughout their life. This conditioning is not natural for them, but must be patiently reinforced *in them* over their lifetime, which is generally much shorter than the average mortal. Nevertheless, the desire for anything a *normal* human being desires from the world is not part of their ***true** human nature.*

These types of individuals do not seem to add to our society in an *imperfect world*—but in reality, they are truer to their *foundationalized humanity type* than the rest of us. They are the most *humane* people that exist. Their mental abnormality allows the energy levels of their *essence* (where our *true* humanity is stored) to have greater influence over their actions. Although they are inhibited in their desire for worldly things, they *do* desire what all of us do: to be valued, accepted, and respected. They want to be loved.

These abnormal body types are a part of our education and probation upon this earth. They demonstrate the potential of a human being by showing how it is possible to respond to and treat one another. They provide us with an example of what we *could* become if we learned to adjust our actions to be more in line with our *essence.* We are not Down syndrome and do not act like them. Our *imperfect world* won't allow us to act like them. If we did, we would not be able to take care of ourselves and our basic human needs. Ironically and for good purpose, we have an example of *how* to act in a world where we *can't* act the way that we should.

8. WE ACT DIFFERENTLY IN THE EXACT SAME SITUATIONS

Some of us kill to defend ourselves, while others do not fight back and are instead killed. Some of us fight to protect ourselves and our possessions, when others instead run and give up their possessions. Some of us express our feelings by crying, while others of us get angry in the same circumstances. Some of us hate others and form personal prejudices, while a few of us accept everyone for whatever they choose to be.

The various lives we live during our time on earth allow us to be placed in a wide variety of different circumstances. In the end, when we are able to remember (not only all of our experiences during our various incarnates in mortality, but also all of our primordial experiences during our *foundationalization*), we will be amazed at how we acted. When we once thought that there was no way we would act the same way as others did in a particular situation, we will be forced to accept that we did indeed act very similar. It will be a very humbling and self-actualizing experience.

9. THE UNDERLYING CAUSE OF OUR ACTIONS IS OUR HUMANITY TYPE

Every choice we make that leads to an action can be broken down into one of the three main categories that express each *humanity type*: 1) it is done for our sake alone; 2) it is done to get a response from another; or 3) it is done for the sake of another. Although there are many different degrees of action, there is no *free-willed* action that does not fit into one of these three main categories.

The following are a few of many, many examples of each different *humanity type*. In order to help the reader understand some of the unique attributes of each, specific human situations experienced in an *imperfect world* are used below. Keep in mind that these situations are not the *only* ones that reflect each type. To list them all would be too voluminous and tedious to read.

10. STELLARIAN ACTIONS NEED OUTSIDE STIMULI TO PRODUCE HAPPINESS

In the category of a Stellarian person—one who wants to be served—the action produces an energy that is not absorbed immediately by the individual. The energy produced must be reacted upon by an outside source of energy. Something outside of the Stellarian person uses its own energy to combine with the energy produced by the Stellarian act and reflects the combination back to the Stellarian, who **then** absorbs the *combined* energy.

An example of this is seen in the experience of being a stage actor. If an actor does not receive the applause (energy) back from an audience (an outside source), he or she will not be happy with him or herself. The audience takes the energy produced by the actor (the action itself) and combines it with the energy of appreciation, which is then reflected back to the actor.

Therefore, all of those who need anything outside of themselves to provide them with praise, glory, accolades, awards, or any other type of notoriety—and they are consistently and lastingly happy in receiving them—are Stellarian humans. Those who cause trouble or drama in their lives, feeding off the negative attention they receive, and are not completely comfortable unless they are receiving this attention, are also Stellarian humans.

11. LUNARIAN ACTIONS AND REACTIONS ARE ALWAYS SELF-SERVING

Every Lunarian action generates a reaction of some kind. As explained previously, each of our actions produces specific energy patterns. An action is the release of energy into our surrounding environment. In the category of a Lunarian person—one who serves oneself—the reaction, or the energy that is released, is isolated to the individual and absorbed only by the person who generated the energy (acted) in the first place. No one else is affected by the act.

An example of this would be owning a home that one maintains not to please one's neighbors, but only to please oneself; wearing clothes to please oneself, in spite of what others might think of the particular style; or acting in any way that satisfies one's own conscience without feeling one bit uncomfortable if others disagree with the action.

12. SOLARIANS ACT FOR THE SAKE OF OTHERS

A Solarian person—one who serves others—acts and generates an energy that is **only** absorbed by others. None of the generated energy (the act) is absorbed or affects the Solarian personally.

This type of person feels more comfortable if their acts of kindness and nobility are not known by others. They also do not act in order to receive a personal special feeling of accomplishment in serving another. Most *imperfect humans* feel compassion, which causes them to experience a negative imbalance that then motivates them to act. They are motivated to act, not because it is in the best interest of another, but it is in their *own* best interest so that they do not feel a negative imbalance.

Although ***true*** Solarian acts are usually considered to be great personal sacrifices in the eyes of Lunarians and Stellarians, to a Solarian, they are not sacrifices at all, but necessary components of experience that give them joy.

There is one exception to this rule—sex. The ability to have sex is the ability to generate enormous amounts of energy and absorb this energy back into oneself or combine the energy with that produced by another, where both people then absorb the *combination* of the energy created. This is why the sexual experience (even in mortality) is so physically overwhelming. The sex organs produce energy levels unmatched by the energy produced by the rest of our sensory organs. But as explained, ONLY Solarian people will have sex organs to produce these kinds of energy patterns. Is it any wonder then, why those who are not Solarian would question the fairness and equality of why they are not allowed to have sex organs?

13. THE UNIVERSE EXISTS ONLY TO SERVE HUMAN BEINGS

As explained, the Universe exists solely for the human being—the ultimate life form. It does not exist for the benefit of any other form of matter. All other forms of matter exist exclusively to compliment and satisfy the human experience.

There are no Klingons, aliens, one-eyed, enormous, two-headed scaly beings, or any other weird looking creatures of unknown origin anywhere in the Universe that are free-willed and have the ability to *imagine* and *reason*. These types of fantasized creatures exist because of human *imagination*.

Good examples of human imagination and reason inventing **real** non-free-willed creatures can be seen in the wide varieties of animals, birds, and insects on this planet. Every creature that is not human is created with *human* imagination—these creatures can look however their creator wants them to look as long as they fulfill the purpose for which they are created.

The human being is the most advanced life form in the Universe. All of the energy of the Universe exists to serve humans. Every action and every reaction occurs because a human being makes it happen. All actions and reactions occur to serve human life in some way. This is how it has always been, this is how it is, and this is how it will always be—worlds without end.

14. SCIENCE FICTION BASED ON AN IMPERFECT WORLD

We should now understand how important it is that **only** those who use the Universe for the purpose for which it exists are allowed to have the power to control it. If it were not this way, then the same things we are experiencing upon this planet would be happening in all other parts of the Universe. There would be intergalactic wars and bloodshed where one species of intelligence overwhelms and subdues or destroys a less-advanced species.

All of the science fiction we have created and imagined in our world *could be* our reality in an *imperfect world*. We base science fiction on how we act and react to each other in this world, as this is the only point of reference of perspective we have from which to draw our creative conclusions. In other words, those who create science fiction draw on the energy patterns provided by their *imperfect brain*. Because these *thought* energy patterns (i.e., experiences) match the *inhumane* way in which we treat each other upon this earth, is it any wonder why they have such vivid imaginations regarding science fiction?

15. THE UNIVERSE IS CONTROLLED BY ADVANCED HUMANS

We can rest assured, however, that **only** people who use their free will to serve others without expecting anything in return are entrusted with the power of the Universe. This is why the Universe appears to be in such an exact and consistent order. This is why we have not encountered, nor will we ever, the alien creatures we have invented in our heads and in the virtual fantasy worlds of our computer games and movies. The only beings we have to fear are ourselves and every other *imperfect* human who exercises their free will without regard to our own.

16. EXPERIENCE PROVES WHY FEW SHOULD HAVE POWER OVER ALL THINGS

With the **real truth** we are learning throughout this book, we can now have a better appreciation for this life and the reason *why* we are here. We are witnessing what happens when power and control are given to Lunarian and Stellarian *humanity types*. We are seeing the effects of free will that are being used to serve oneself or to be served by others.

As mentioned in chapter eight, we have never had a government that serves the interests and needs of all people equally. In some instances, we have been given the chance to vote for those whom we want to serve us. We have had the freedom and liberty to exercise our free will to have anything we want or to be anything we want in this world. Despite these "freedoms," we are still experiencing the negative effects that occur to our happiness when the improper *humanity types* wield power over us.

17. SOLARIANS ARE UNCOMFORTABLE BEING LEADERS

In this *imperfect world*, there has never existed a Solarian *essence* that has inhabited the body of any leader, judge, or any other person who exercises authority over another for any reason, UNLESS the person in fulfilling the role of a leader or judge is completely unhappy and frustrated with the position they are forced by circumstance to hold over others. It is, and will always be, inconsistent with a Solarian nature to take away the free will of another human being, **unless the person's act of free will is taking away the free will of another**.

18. ADVANCED HUMANS DO NOT WIELD POWER AND CONTROL OVER OTHERS

Some argue that we need "righteous" judges and leaders to exercise their authority for the *good* of the human race. But what "good" has come to the human race, where one leader or judge has exercised authority over another's free agency? Those who judge others and exercise authority over them continually cause human suffering to those whom they judge and control. The sentences and judgments administered by those who are currently in power upon this earth have done very little to stem the tide of hopelessness, misery, and discord felt by the human race. And these judgments certainly do not serve the person upon whom they are placed.

Even in the case of exercising judgment upon a murderer, for example, no *real* justice is administered. The victim doesn't receive any justice, nor do those who have been affected by the victim's death. Those affected usually live with constant pain and with a vindictive attitude, both which take away their peace and happiness. A Solarian *humanity type*, on the other hand, would never be comfortable with him or herself without the conditions of complete and unconditional forgiveness taking place for any act chosen by the free will of another.

Many leaders on earth have exercised their power and control over free agency by taking from the rich and giving to the poor—none of these has ever been Solarian. There are those who prosecute and punish those who take away the free agency of others through murder, theft, rape, incest, and many other seemingly inhumane acts—none of these acts can be done by a Solarian without a considerable amount of discomfort and remorse.

How do we know this? Because advanced Solarian humans are responsible for this world and they DO NOT INTERCEDE and take away the free agency of any person who commits a "crime" against another. They watch and respect free will, even when an adult rapes and kills a child! If mortal, a Solarian would never be consistently and continually happy in using his or her free agency to take away the free agency of another, no matter what the act was.

19. IMPERFECT AND INAPPROPRIATE LEADERS ARE EXPECTED IN AN IMPERFECT WORLD

Common sense tells us that if there are not leaders and judges upon this earth to protect people from others, the whole world would decline into chaos and anarchy. This is true. But isn't chaos and anarchy the complete opposite of the *perfect* human society? And are we not here to experience this opposition? On the other hand, the world has never known a time when all humans were unconditionally forgiven for all that they did. What would happen in such a world? No one in an *imperfect world* can answer this because none has yet experienced it.

Although these contrasting points of view are interesting to consider, neither leads us to a proper understanding of the *true reality*. What is really going on here upon the earth? If there are advanced human beings who are monitoring what is happening, WHY DON'T THEY STEP IN AND DO SOMETHING?

20. THE MOTIVATION BEHIND OUR ACTIONS IS MUCH DIFFERENT IN A PERFECT WORLD

Those who cause chaos, anarchy, or any inhumane act towards another are doing so because in this life their *imperfect situation* allows them to, whereas in a *perfect world* they wouldn't even consider it. In mortality they have the power to act according to their own free will. They can kill if they want. They can steal if they want. They can rape if they want. No one takes away their free will to do these things, if they want.

Although the leaders and the judges of this world prosecute, convict, and punish those who do these things, the fact remains that each person still has the free will to do what he or she wants in spite of what the consequences might be. In contrast of each situation (although humans retain their free will in both instances), humans act *perfectly* in a *perfect world* and inhumanely in an *imperfect* one. There is one major difference as to *why*: the **motivation** behind the use of free will is much different in each world.

21. AN IMPERFECT BODY MOTIVATES US TO ACT AGAINST OUR TRUE HUMANITY

People do what they do because they are motivated by a physical or emotional need. Using an extreme example, a person rapes another because the rapist seeks to fulfill a need that he or she has at the time. These actions are completely motivated by the needs and desires of an *imperfect body* in an *imperfect* environment. Though some argue that the cause of rape is a need for control, they are only correct in assuming that the rapist seeks *control* in the ability to satiate sexual motivation. If the rapist had no sexual urges, they would not rape. If it was just *control* that the person desired (and many *imperfect* humans do), then they would do other things such as pursue roles of authority over others, as in law enforcement, politics, business, or becoming a spiritual leader or even a parent.

For another example, many young girls, who find that they have little control over their own environment or their own lives, seek to become pregnant and produce a child, whom they believe they will be able to *control*. These girls are motivated by the need to control something in a world that overwhelmingly controls their free will.

With our mortal bodies, we are allowed to have sex. We are driven to have sex by the very hormones that our sex organs produce. Most humans will do whatever it takes to satiate this need. This includes the subtle motivations we have to wear make-up, obtain cosmetic surgery, or lie about who we *really are*, to having a reason and incentive to rape another person. Whatever it takes to fulfill our sexual need, we have the free agency to do it in this world. And these motivations come from our needs in an *imperfect* body.

However, if the need, the reason, and the incentive were taken away, what then would stimulate the action? In a *perfect world,* there are no physical or emotional needs that are not fulfilled. Consequently, there is no motivation in a *perfect world* to act against our humanity.

22. THE NEEDS OF THE IMPERFECT BODY MUST BE MET

In an *imperfect world*, we have physiological needs that must be met, and these physical needs often create secondary, but powerful, psychological needs. We have physical needs to breathe, eat food, drink water, and excrete the parts of the foods and liquids that our body does not process completely. We need sleep. Most need sex.

As these needs act upon us, our bodies are subject to the laws of nature and seek to maintain a state of equilibrium. Every one of our cells seeks a state of homeostasis because the need for equilibrium is preprogrammed into them. Our *imperfect* bodies depend on our surrounding environment to take in and let out everything needed in order to maintain this state of balance. Obviously, our needs are not always met in this *imperfect world* with our *imperfect bodies*.

23. A PERFECT BODY ELIMINATES PHYSIOLOGICAL NEEDS

But what needs would there be if we had a *perfect body*? We've already explained that the perfect body is *not subjected* to the surrounding environment. Instead, the "laws of nature" are subjected to the *perfect body*. We've discussed how our *essence* is an energy factory that takes the parts used in the basic structure of all matter from its surrounding environment and turns them into the energy that we need for the *perfect* body.

In the *perfect world,* we do not need to breathe, eat food, or drink water. The only excrement that leaves our body is in the form of the parts of the basic structure of all matter we took in, in the first place. In other words, the perfect body "inhales." This "inhaling" is similar to osmosis, wherein the basic elements of matter are diffused through the semi-permeable membrane from which the *perfect* skull is constructed. It can then be said that it "exhales" through reverse osmosis. Supported by the power of our *essence*, the *perfect* body maintains its own homeostasis no matter in what environment it finds itself in the Universe.

24. WITH NO WORRIES ABOUT OUR PHYSIOLOGICAL NEEDS, OUR MOTIVATION TO ACT CHANGES

In eliminating our physiological needs, many of the motivations of human nature are eliminated, including powerful psychological motivators. In a *perfect world*, the survival instinct will no longer be the greatest human stimulant. Survival of the *fittest* will no longer have any meaning to humans who are all *equally fit.*

No longer will there be the "haves" and the "have nots." Hunger through poverty in all of its ugly forms will cease to exist. The hoarding of the limited resources of our environment will be a thing of the past. How can a person horde the *unlimited* resources of the Universe that are freely available to all?

The *perfect* body will only use the materials of the Universe that it needs. It inhales (as explained above) the components of elements, utilizes them for the enjoyment of the human, and then exhales them again out into the surrounding environment, keeping everything in an ordered pattern of homeostasis.

Every "crime" against another person in attempting to satisfy the needs of our *imperfect body* will be gone. How, for example, can a person with no sex organs (and thus no essential hormones that stimulate the desire for sex) commit rape? *Why* would they and *how* would they?

A *perfect* body leaves no human desiring something that is not readily available in unlimited abundance. There are no human physiological needs in a *perfect* world.

25. OUR PERSONAL SECURITY IS VERY IMPORTANT

Nevertheless, there are other important needs that all human beings have, even those possessing a *perfect* body. We all have a need to feel completely safe and secure in our environment. We need to know that no other person can hurt us. We need to know that no one can take away our free agency to use our body in the way that we choose to use it.

There can never be a moment when a *perfect* human being can feel personally threatened or have a sense of fear of the unknown. We must have unconditional free agency, along with the assurance that this agency will always be protected. And we must know all there is to know about everything in the Universe, thereby not fearing anything.

26. THE IMPERFECT BODY COMPENSATES FOR OUR PHYSIOLOGICAL NEEDS

In our *imperfect* bodies, if we go without food and water for a day, our bodies adjust and we soon hardly notice that we are hungry or thirsty. If our body is subjected to the extreme conditions of weather, it will adjust to the point that we become accustomed to the cold or heat over time.

Although our body adjusts and calms our mind to the fact that our physiological needs are not being met, the *imperfect body* is going to die! For this reason, people feel calm during the last stages of hypothermia and heat exhaustion. All they want to do is sleep. The desire to sleep is the body telling the brain, "You don't want to experience what is going to happen next, so go to sleep!" It is the merciful way that our *imperfect* bodies are constructed so that we would not experience or remember the trauma preceding death to which our *imperfect bodies* are often subjected. Few people who experience a *physically* traumatic event can remember the pain or even the last few moments leading up to the trauma. But when a person experiences an **emotionally** traumatic event, the memory is much stronger than other memories stored in our brain. Emotional stress is a greater contributor to our unhappiness than the lack of fulfilling our physiological needs.

27. WE NEED TO FEEL VALUED AND ACCEPTED

Emotional needs account for the greatest source of happiness and unhappiness in our lives. They include the need of intimate relationships with family and friends. They include the romantic relationship that is developed beyond the physical part of sexual intimacy. Many people have sex with each other, but the consistent and lasting happiness really comes in the day-to-day experiences one shares with their partner long before and long after the sexual need is met.

These needs are what we associate with "love," as we have discussed previously. The more the person, animal, or thing meets our emotional needs, the more "love" (value) we feel towards it. These emotional needs also include the need of self-esteem, which relates to the need to be treated equally and with the same respect as others. Because of the respect we received in the primordial world, as recorded in our *essence,* we have a constant need to feel confident that we are equal with everyone else.

28. HAVING OUR EMOTIONAL NEEDS MET IS IMPORTANT TO HAPPINESS

Physiological needs, therefore, take a back seat to our emotional needs. Some people deny themselves food and water so that their bodies will be just the right size and shape to fulfill the need to be accepted by others. Some deny themselves sleep so that they can accomplish things that others might see as worldly or material "success."

Each of us at one time or another has used our body and its senses to *act* in a way that is not consistent with our *true nature* so that others would accept and respect us. All of the misery we experience in this life, including all the misery we cause each other, can be traced to our emotional needs not being met or to our desire to have these needs met. These emotional needs were *foundationalized* within us by the way we were treated in our primordial world by our Solarian creators/parents.

29. IN A PERFECT WORLD OUR EMOTIONAL NEEDS ARE ALWAYS FULFILLED

Emotional needs cause us to desire to become what the *imperfect world* expects and respects, but not who we *truly* are—an individual pursuing our own happiness apart from everyone else. If we could fulfill all of our needs, we would find our *real* SELF! Then, all of our actions would be motivated by *who we really are* and not by whom we think we "need" to be in order to have our emotional needs met.

A *perfect world* either provides for all of our needs or takes away the need altogether. Everyone is treated equally. Everyone has equal understanding about the Universe (this comes through the eons of time spent during our first stage of development—our *Foundationalization Process*). We have nothing to fear because there is no unknown. And the greatest assurance of our personal security, or that which assures us that no other being will ever impose upon our free will, is the knowledge that there is a powerful *overseer* who guarantees each of us this security.

30. MORTAL ACTIONS THAT ARE NOT REFLECTIVE OF OUR TRUE SELF CAUSE UNHAPPINESS

How we feel about what we do (meeting our emotional needs) directly exposes one of the *humanity types* we have discussed. However, not all of our actions in an *imperfect body* are consistent with our *true self*; therefore, they do not always reflect our humanity type correctly. And when they don't, our emotional needs are not met and we suffer the consequences.

The way that we can tell if our actions reflect who we *really are* is if we gain consistent and lasting happiness from the experience. We might gain an immediate gratification through a particular experience, but we will never gain a consistent and lasting happiness, unless the action matches who we *truly are*.

This is why we mentioned above that a Solarian individual in an *imperfect* body *could* be a leader or a judge, but would never find consistent and lasting happiness from the experience. Likewise, a Lunarian or Stellarian individual might find a moment of happiness in an action that serves another, but never for a consistent and lasting period of time. They might have a compassionate thought for a suffering child and write a check to a charitable organization that ostensibly serves the child's needs. But the Lunarian or Stellarian would not find a continued and lasting life of service to the child amenable to their core happiness.

In this same example, they might write a check and find joy in doing so every month, *without* taking any action to find out *why* the child is in poverty in the first place and doing all that is possible to end the poverty. But a *true* Solarian person would analyze the poverty of the child and *not* intervene, IF it would ruin a situation of learning and accountability for those responsible for the child's poverty. Furthermore, the Solarian would not feed the child one day and then forget about the child's hunger the next. In other words, a Solarian would act in everyone else's best interests, in addition to the child's.

IF it was appropriate to do so and in the best interests of all other humans affected by the child's poverty, the Solarian would give up their life to improve the child's situation. They would have to, or they wouldn't be able to find any consistent and lasting happiness in existing if they knew a child lived in a state of poverty. Without giving up their own life, they will never find consistent and lasting happiness living in a world where poverty and inequality exist.

31. THE WRONG PEOPLE ARE NOW IN POWER

Most humans upon this earth are of the Lunarian type. They want to serve themselves and not be responsible for the happiness of others. And although they are fewer in numbers, Stellarians are typically more well-known. Stellarians generally wield the power in politics, business, entertainment, culture, and social organizations, and are the ones who commit most of the crimes against other people. They are the ones who use the greatest amount of energy to seek to be seen, heard, accepted and acknowledged by others. They need to be served by others.

In all that they do, however, including here in mortality, Stellarians (as well as everyone) are never condemned by their creators for having chosen the course of happiness of being served by others. They have this right, and it is the responsibility of the advanced Solarians to serve them in all of their needs, and allow Lunarians every opportunity to serve themselves.

However, the lessons of our *imperfect world* will prove to the rest of us and to them (Stellarians and Lunarians) that they *should not be given* any power or control over the free will of others or the matter that makes up all things in the Universe. During mortality, we experience what they do with this power and control. They support and perpetuate an *imperfect* world and would even continue to do so if placed in a *perfect* world, thus causing it to fall into *imperfection*.

32. IT IS HARD FOR STELLARIANS TO FIND HAPPINESS

Stellarians are the most unsatisfied with the overall environment of an *imperfect world*. Mortality is not set up to allow Solarians to be their servants, nor are the human societies of an *imperfect world* conducive to a service-oriented atmosphere. Stellarians are the most insecure of all human beings and turn to many forms of physical and emotional manipulation in their quest to receive the outside stimuli they need to be happy.

Some of the *physical manipulations* that they use are the stimulants that directly affect how they think. Drugs, both natural and synthetic (which include alcohol, wine, and the other intoxicants that affect our brain, and also "medicines" created by "wise" scientists and prescribed by "wise" physicians), place the partaker in a position where they no longer crave extrinsic stimulation. However, Lunarian and even Solarian people in *imperfect bodies* will often also use these same types of physical stimulants to manipulate their brain into a state where they, too, no longer are aware of the fact that they are unable to find consistent and lasting happiness in an *imperfect world.*

33. EMOTIONAL MANIPULATION IS USED TO GET GAIN

Stellarian humanity types most often use *emotional manipulation* to gain some sort of outside stimuli. Although Lunarians and Solarians also are prone to the use of emotional manipulation from time to time in their *imperfect bodies*, each does it for a different reason (i.e., as described previously in the way energy patterns are exchanged between each individual and their surrounding environment). Lunarians will use emotional manipulation to serve their own needs, and Solarians will use it to serve the needs of others.

In the value system of "love," for example, a Stellarian will strike back at their lover if the lover (the object of their affection) uses his or her free will and desires not to be with the Stellarian any longer. Stellarians find a temporary emotional balance in believing that they can cause just as much pain and sorrow to their unfaithful partner as was caused to them. They use emotional manipulation, and sometimes physical manipulation, to create an extrinsic stimulus that serves their needs.

A Lunarian, on the other hand, is more likely to walk away from the broken relationship and internalize the pain. They do not seek revenge, but would rather not have anything to do with the person again.

The Solarian, rare as they are, will find joy that their lover has found a greater prospect for happiness in someone else. However, it would seem highly unlikely that the partner of a Solarian person would ever want to leave or find someone better at "loving" them, since the Solarian is a service-oriented person.

34. HUMAN BEINGS HAVE EGOS

One *imperfect* school of psychological thought breaks up human motivation into three separate categories: the Id, the Ego, and the Superego. According to this "school of thought," the Id is associated with the need to satisfy our physiological and emotional needs and can best be paralleled with the concepts of the needs of our *imperfect body* as discussed in this book.

The Superego can best be associated with what we learn through experience. It is connected with the moral part of us that develops due to the rules and restraints placed on us by our parents and by the expectations placed upon us by others. It is the closest to expressing a definition of our *true* humanity. It can be paralleled to how we are *foundationalized* in the beginning of our existence, either improperly in an *imperfect world*, or properly (something we can't remember) in the *perfect* one.

The Ego is associated with the Superego (our humanity), or the way we perceive other people and our environment. The Ego attempts to control the desires of the Id and tries to bring balance to a person's life by conforming one's actions with the Superego.

Humans are the only animals that have an Ego. They are the only beings who are aware of themselves and can make decisions about their behavior. "Is this going to bring me happiness or not?" The Ego is responsible for this decision-making process. It is what separates us from animals (although we still sometimes *act* like animals).

Although they do not have an Ego, all animals have an Id and can possibly develop a Superego. Just as we are trained up in the way that we should behave, animals can also be trained to act a certain way, thus developing a Superego similar to humans. This is why some animals become great pets. They develop a *human*like Superego.

However, again, only humans develop an Ego and can act upon it. This is because of their unique free will.

35. WE STRIVE HARDEST TO PROTECT OUR OWN EGO

It is the Ego that all human beings try hardest to protect. We seek balance between the needs of our body (Id) and the expectations of our parents, peers, and others outside of our self (Superego).

With what we now know about our *essence*, it can be understood that our Ego is constantly trying to create experiences that match those in our *essence*. This is why people who need others to serve them seem to be more "**ego**tistical" than others. They are constantly craving outside stimuli in order to feel balanced.

36. PSYCHICS, CHANNELERS, AND MYSTICS ARE PRODUCED FROM STELLARIAN NEEDS

The opportunities to be a political leader, judge, business icon, spiritual leader, movie star, artist, or one of the many other positions associated with worldly success and glory, are few and far between. Those Stellarians who don't live up to the expectations needed to fall into one of these categories will make up their *own* position in the world in order to bring value to themselves.

Stellarians create a sense of "self" that relies on outside stimuli. They may even create a world of mysticism and the unseen. These include, but are certainly not limited to, those who believe they are psychic, channelers, or who claim that they can read others' thoughts and feelings. These also include those who feel the foreboding presence of what they describe as "evil," or who otherwise take the negative experience of *reality* and create an *imagined* entity that exudes this negativity.

37. THE ENERGY OF OUR THOUGHTS CAN BE FELT BY OTHERS

All of our thoughts are forms of generated energy that are emitted from our physical body. In other words, when we *think,* we are releasing energy into our surrounding environment. Along with our ability to release energy outside of ourselves, we also have the ability to be affected by the energy of our environment. For this reason, we can *feel* the energy generated by another person (part of non-verbal communication, even beyond ordinary "body language").

This ability to subtly sense the emotional disposition of another is equal in all <u>normal</u> *imperfect* brains, and does not give those who make claims to psychic powers any more of an advantage than the rest of us have. However, those who make supernatural claims *do* learn how to take advantage of their *normal* ability to sense human emotion. With this practiced and cultured ability, "psychics" can elicit feelings and reactions from others. This leads them to ascertain what they convince themselves the other person is thinking, or something that might have happened in that person's past.

Nevertheless, any *normal* person can do this with practice. And psychics are only one example of those who believe that they are a "chosen one" with whom *concealed* aliens or advanced beings from other, unknown realms or worlds communicate *unseen*.

38. BELIEVING ONE IS MORE SPECIAL THAN ANOTHER DISREGARDS TRUE REALITY

A rare few people are indeed "chosen." ***True*** chosen messengers actually ***see with their physical eyes and perceive with their other physical senses*** the other human beings with whom they communicate. These **few** know the *true reality* of all things. This is how one can tell the difference between those who *believe* they are a *chosen one*, and those who *truly* are. Those who *truly* are, can provide the answers to life's mysteries so that the mysteries make sense. Those who are not, make up excuses as to why they cannot provide the answers to the mysteries of life.

True chosen ones will also always give the credit for their knowledge to their having spoken face-to-face with an advanced human in a *true physical body*. The mysteries of life are simply all those things that advanced human beings know that those in mortality cannot remember. No *true messenger* in an *imperfect body* can know what advanced humans know without being given the knowledge from an advanced human being.

A *true* messenger can answer any question about *human reality*, whereas a self-proclaimed, but false, "chosen one" cannot. Although there are many people on earth who make claims of communication with those on other worlds, there are *very, very few* who actually do. A *true messenger's* communication with those on other worlds pertains to all humans and would never create a following or a separation between human beings. A message of **real truth** would always support unconditional equality and fairness. Those who **falsely** make claims of having some supernatural power or ability that others do not, do not support **real truth**, and rather create inequality.

When confronted with skepticism from the majority, Stellarians will hold fast to their egos and protect their claims of *false reality* with just as much energy as they used in creating the reality in the first place. It is hard to convince a Stellarian that their reality is of their *own* making, because in doing so, they lose personal value. Their ego is threatened.

However, a Lunarian or Solarian who has developed these false "Stellarian" propensities will never be consistently happy abiding in their claims. These often come to a proper realization of what is taking place in their mind. When confronted with the **real truth** that all of these experiences are really happening in their own mind, they are more apt to change their perception about themselves (because they don't have the same need as Stellarians). Hence, they find a greater balance and joy in knowing that they are not any more "special" than anyone else.

39. OUR EMOTIONAL NEEDS CREATE FALSE REALITIES

The **real truth** will show that what Stellarian people claim they can do is *actually* the truth! However, their perception of what is *actually* taking place is skewed by their inability to consciously explain how their personal phenomenon works. All they know is that it does!

What they do not realize is that *every one of us* has the same capabilities that they have. We are all psychics and channelers and can read each other's thoughts and feelings (through non-verbal body language, as explained previously). With a little practice and concentration, we could also convince others of our own unique powers.

We have all felt a foreboding presence of some sort or another, though many choose to describe that feeling as simply a negative experience and not necessarily an "evil" one. And as presented for the first time in this book, we are all capable of receiving energy patterns or frequencies from the advanced human beings who created our solar system and placed us here. But we are always assured that not one of us will receive any special treatment. Advanced beings react with all of us in exactly the same way (and these energy patterns will never be negative ones, if from an advanced Solarian).

40. ALL HAVE THE ABILITY TO EXPERIENCE PHENOMENA

The difference in the phenomena experienced by those who need to be served by others (Stellarian) and by the other humanity types (the majority of the rest of us) is that Stellarians CONCENTRATE A GREAT DEAL OF ENERGY on doing what all of us could do if we applied the same concentration of energy to the effort. Most of us simply choose not to. Every phenomenon created in a person's mind can be shared by or created by everyone else equally. It all depends on how much effort we put into creating it.

41. TRUE REALITY SUPERSEDES OUR PERSONAL REALITIES

An understanding of these types of human emotional, self-imposed phenomena relegates the phenomena to an understandable basic part of *who we are* and *why we exist*. Unfortunately for those who need the outside stimuli of praise and the other means of compensation from others (whether monetary or emotional), the revelation of the **real truth** will force them to seek some other form of stimuli to serve their needs; or they will reject the **real truth** altogether and continue to maintain their status as *someone special*.

Whether they can accept it or not, ***true reality*** **creates the same potential reality for all free-willed beings equally**. Any personal reality that one might invent for oneself, all of us, if we desired and made the effort, could create the exact same reality. This **real truth** ("unfortunately" for Stellarians) does not support the emotional need of those who constantly crave to satisfy their own.

42. DREAMS AND PERSONAL REALITIES ARE CREATED FROM THE SAME SOURCE

There is not a person in this *imperfect world* who has not experienced a dream in some form or another. These experiences are "dreams" when we are asleep and "visions" when we are awake. Sometimes people focus on what appear to be psychological phenomena through a "visualization technique" by meditating or concentrating on something that they want to accomplish for themselves.

A careful study of what we have already presented in this book will reveal that the experiences associated with the phenomena of the mind are produced in the part of our *imperfect brain* that coordinates the energy patterns of our senses into thoughts. It has been described as our inner "movie theater."

It is here where we formulate and experience our dreams and visions. It is in this location where we generate the energy patterns of our thoughts. This includes the thoughts of psychics and channelers (two examples of many who claim that they can read others' thoughts and feelings), those who feel the foreboding presence of what they describe as "evil," and those who believe that they are a "chosen one" with whom unseen aliens or advanced beings from another unknown world communicate. It is here where their levels of concentration are projected. In this part of the brain, **they create their own reality apart from the *true reality* that affects everyone equally**.

43. PERSONAL REALITIES SEEM AS REAL AS OUR DREAMS

When these phenomena claimants expend energy from their *imperfect brain* in the form of concentration, the "veil" that is produced by their brain becomes thinner, allowing more movement of energy from the *essence*, although the energy is often skewed and misinterpreted because of the veil that still exists. As explained previously, the "veil" is simply the inability of the *imperfect brain organ* to access and properly arrange the energy patterns given off by the *essence* into rational and conscious thought.

Nevertheless, when a person concentrates enough energy into the "projection room" that shows what is seen in our inner "movie theater," more energy from the *essence* seeps through. They then begin to perceive and think things that create a "reality" that only they are able to experience. These new perceptions and realities become their **conscious dreams**. These new personal realities can be just as disconnected to *true reality* as any of our subconscious dreams, but to the conscious mind they might seem very real.

44. PERSONAL REALITIES ARE EXPERIENCED IN THE MIND

Most people do not create dreams until their brain shuts down and the energy emissions of the *essence* seep through when they are not concentrating on anything in particular. When we are conscious and "thinking," our *imperfect brain* creates energy patterns that block the energy given off by the *essence*.

In fine, all of the experiences of the mind are made up *in the mind* and experienced there. Psychic feelings, channeling voices, reading others' thoughts and feelings, sensing "evil," or feeling we are "specially chosen" are all **consciously made-up thoughts**. Dreams are subconscious thoughts. Nonetheless, whether our thoughts are experienced subconsciously or consciously, they are all simply that—**only our thoughts**! And just like our dreams appear to be real while we are dreaming, any thought we can generate can appear just as real while we are awake.

We all have taken a situation and twisted it into a reality that we *want* to be true, even though it is not. We can manipulate the situation with our *imperfect* mind into pieces of "evidence" that support what we *want* to believe. Once we have convinced ourselves that the evidence taken from the situation is real, although it is not, we will hold our *new reality* to be the **only** reality.

45. WE CAN CONTROL PRETENDED REALITIES

For one of many, many examples, let's take the situation of a man secretly hiding his telephone conversations from his wife. When she comes into the room, he might turn away from her and speak more softly. If his wife inquires into his unusual behavior, he might come up with an excuse that the wife knows cannot be true. But what is the *true* reality of the situation? Is the man cheating on his wife or is he planning a surprise for her?

We have learned that our *imperfect* minds make it very difficult for us to know the **real truth**, as this is a part of our intended experience in mortality. Our experiences in the past also cause personal insecurities. If, using the above example, the wife was cheated on in the past, or she cheated on her husband and hid personal telephone conversations from him, she has an experience that her mind can recall to create evidence that supports her *pretended reality* (perception of the situation).

Volumes could be filled with these kinds of examples. Both emotional and physical destruction have been caused because of the *imperfect* way we often form our personal perceptions. The most important thing for us to understand is that we are **susceptible** to these feelings and should make an effort to control and limit (if we desire) what *personal realities* we create in our minds that are not ***true*** *realities*. Again,

> **Real Truth** (with a capital "T") is anything upon which every (non-veiled/non-mortal) freethinking and free-willed human being in the Universe agrees. It is something that none of us in our perfected state, in complete honesty, could deny. **Real Truth** never changes. Nothing can be added to it or taken away from it. It is the same throughout the entire Universe; and anywhere advanced, perfected human beings are found, there is no disagreement on its substance and its conclusive statement of fact. (See chapter 15, Section 4.)

46. WE CAN PROVIDE OUR OWN EMOTIONAL"THERAPY"

The easiest way for us to prove our personal realities is to seek the perception from others who might not agree with us. What do they have to say about the situation? This has led to the current explosion of people attending therapy sessions, where a trained therapist invalidates many made-up personal realities. Although these sessions might serve some positive purpose, they are often expensive and not available to everyone equally. Therapists even need therapy! The best therapy, therefore, is understanding more about our *imperfect* state and learning to control our minds by the power of our own *essence*, which contains all *true reality* just as everyone else's.

The reader may now be curious to find out the techniques that can be used to tap in to the power of the *essence* in a way that can keep one from inventing realities that are not true. What can be done? How does one do it?

Although understanding our weaknesses can force us to confront them and, by the power of our free will, overcome them to some degree, if we could do it all of the time, then the purpose for which we are here in mortality would be thwarted. We need to experience what it is like to have an *imperfect* body so that we will appreciate the *perfect* one we will possess forever. Therefore, a presentation of these techniques is beyond the scope of this book. But with a little less concentration on the things that cloud the *imperfect brain*, we will have the needed energy to tap in to the essence, although never with complete accuracy while in mortality.

47. THOSE WITH FALSE REALITIES WILL DEFEND THEM

Some claim that they have experienced the ability of another individual to know things about them that no one else could have known. These include those who aren't even aware that they have the same powers. They claim that one so endowed with special powers talked to one of their dead ancestors or loved ones and were told things that only that ancestor or loved one could have possibly known.

What these, thus convinced, do not realize, however, is that for as many times as demonstrations of special mind powers have succeeded, they have failed much more often. But the person who gains self-esteem from "*personal special powers*," is never going to tell a new source of outside stimuli (a prospective believer) about the times when their powers failed to work. They will defend their "powers" for the sake of protecting their Ego.

48. SPECIAL POWERS ARE NOT PART OF OUR INTENDED EXPERIENCE

Except in the cases we have previously discussed in relation to autism, savants, and other *abnormal* anomalies of the brain, NO PERSON IS GIVEN OR CAN DEVELOP A SPECIAL POWER OR ABILITY WITH AN IMPERFECT BODY that everyone else is not also **equally** capable of developing if they applied the same concentration to acquiring it. It is impossible for the *imperfect brain* to function in any other way than how it was intended. Because all of us are here in mortality to experience the opposite of human perfection, why would any of us have an unfair advantage over another?

If, in fact, our creators had ever created inequality by granting some of us advantages and powers that others did not have, then they would have created the opportunity for excuse:

"If you had just given me the power to read thoughts, speak to the dead, see in the future, see in the past, or experience the sensations of 'evil' and divine intervention, then I would have never acted like I did with my imperfect body! So how do you, creators/advanced beings, know that I cannot be trusted with the power to control the elements and the ability to have sex when you provided a playing field that was unlevel and unfair?"

49. EVERYTHING IS FAIR AND EQUAL TO ALL

Our creators never have been, nor will they ever be, respecters of persons. We are treated equally in all things. There are no "special" or "chosen" people or those more "worthy" or "righteous" than another (except as explained above in the case of a **true messenger**). Our creators have established a world for our second stage of development that will allow us to fulfill the purposes they had in mind for our experience in this world. They are giving us the experience of life that we chose to have so that we could prove ourselves to our SELVES. Everything that exists in our *imperfect world* will one day be revealed as being fair and just to us all. In the end, we will have no excuse.

50. ADVANCED BEINGS ONLY INTERCEDE FOR THE SAKE OF ALL EQUALLY

As mentioned previously, there are times when advanced beings intercede into our affairs upon this earth by communicating to the mind of a person. But as we discussed, this ONLY happens when their intercession will do something that will help all of us equally and not just the one who is receiving the communication. If advanced beings want to commission a mortal to do their will, they will ALWAYS make the commission face-to-face with the person. It will NEVER be done in the chosen one's own mind.

To preserve the right we all have to free will, advanced human beings do not, nor can they, control our minds. They can send energy impulses of thought that are suggestive in nature, just as we can give our opinion to others with our external voice of what one should or shouldn't do. Once the transmission is received by the individual, that person **must then decide** if he or she will accept the opinion given by the *unseen* and *unperceived* Solarian servant or not.

The way that these advanced beings communicate with mortals is so subtle and non-invasive that the person receiving the communication will not be able to tell the difference between one of their own thoughts and a suggestive thought directed at their mind from an advanced *monitor*. Again, these advanced forms of communication with *imperfect minds* are very subtle, so as not to affect the free will of the person receiving the communication. Our *imperfect minds* are very capable on their own of creating conversations inside of our head that *only* happen between us and our own mind.

51. BELIEVING IN OUTSIDE INFLUENCES TAKES AWAY PERSONAL RESPONSIBILITY

Those who believe or convince themselves that they are receiving communication from a "higher source," are not. If a person thinks he or she is "chosen" or "special" and is in direct communication with someone outside of themselves, their free agency has been affected. By having this "feeling," they will feel stimulated and motivated to act on the impulses of intuition because they believe it is coming from a "higher power" other than their own mind. They will relieve themselves of any personal responsibility for their thoughts and actions. They become a puppet to their own impulses, which, more often than not, impinge upon the free will of others.

Unfortunately, for those so inclined to these "feelings," one day they will learn that everything they did when they *believed* they were serving an extrinsic "higher power" is a direct reflection of their *true self.* They will be solely responsible for their actions and have no excuse that some outside force (of either good or bad) compelled them to act.

52. THERE IS NO SUCH THING AS A "HIGHER POWER"

There is no such thing as a "higher power," or better yet—our individual *essence* IS our personal "higher power." As discussed previously, all human beings are *equal* when it comes to the knowledge stored in our *essence.* By the time our primordial *foundationalization* ended when we lived in the solar system of our creators, we knew all they knew, even all there was to know about the Universe and how it related to us. This knowledge was necessary so that we could choose the correct humanity type for ourselves.

Keep in mind that we lived there for what we would equate with our *imperfect* minds as being billions of years! It would have been unfair to not receive a full education of everything there is to know about being a human before making the choice of which humanity type bests suits us. Not knowing what someone else knew would have left us with the excuse, "*But if I had only known!*"

As discussed previously, some abnormal *imperfect* brains *are* capable of tapping into the power of the *essence* (savants, autistics). But these few people will never make an excuse that someone or something outside of themselves was responsible for their extraordinary abilities. If a "higher power" is responsible for their *special* ability, then that same power is also responsible for their *inability* to tie their shoes without outside help.

53. BODY TYPE DOES NOT AFFECT PERFECT KNOWLEDGE

The ONLY differences among **advanced**, **perfected** humans are the abilities they have according to the body type they possess. An "ability" has no reflection on one's knowledge and experience. In contrast, some of the greatest *imperfect minds* in our current world are vastly inhibited in their physical abilities.

The renowned physicist Stephen Hawking is a good example of a person who has a lot of *worldly* knowledge with very limited ability to use it. If it were not for the technology available to him, he would not be able to utilize what he knows. (However, keep in mind that what Hawking knows is not **real truth**. His mortal knowledge is based on theory and speculation and his study of reality is based on what others before him have conjectured combined with what he adds to their *imperfect* conclusions. But his *essence* is just as powerful and filled with just as much **real truth** as any other human's in the Universe.)

54. MOST PEOPLE WANT TO SERVE THEMSELVES

We have discussed various types of mortals who, by being true to themselves and what brings them happiness, become those who need outside stimuli to serve their needs. These are the typical Stellarian humanity types. (And they are just as *perfect* as the other humanity types.)

Now we will discuss what the majority of people do who are the Lunarian type—those who want to serve themselves. These types are prone to be the followers of the Stellarian types in an *imperfect world*. This is the reason why most mortals are *followers* instead of *leaders*. They would rather follow another person so that they do not have to expend the energy themselves.

Lunarians find more balance in internalizing their emotions and coming up with a conclusive response to their environment that satisfies just them. They have no need, stimulus, or motivation to share what they believe (or better, what satisfies them) with others. Some of their credos would be, "To Each His Own"; "Leave me alone and I'll leave you alone"; "I respect what you think, so respect what I think"; and "I'll do my thing, you do your thing."

55. MOST FIND COMFORT IN BELONGING TO A GROUP

Lunarians do things that make a personal statement about themselves that does not require an outside response to their actions in a positive or negative way. They are not comfortable when the "spotlight" is on them. They find most social interactions bearable when they can dissolve "into the woodwork" and be a part of what everyone else is doing. They can never lead others because they would find no joy in telling others what to do, when they themselves don't know what is even right for them while residing in an *imperfect* world.

Lunarians are constantly searching within to find out *who they are*, because they are honest with themselves and accept the conclusion that they do not know who they *really* are. They try many different things in life to see what works and what does not. These join forces with others who are like-minded and experience a "groupthink" mentality.

They are prone to avoid conflict with others (especially the Stellarian types), and join together in various types of group settings, which satisfies their immediate need to understand themselves. They listen to different "leaders" and decide which ones meet their current emotional needs.

Once joined with a particular "group," they avoid critical thinking and do not find any need to analyze the reality that their group provides to them. They become comfortable with their choice of a particular group and avoid expressing any viewpoint that is not consistent with others in their chosen group, even when their own personal balance is affected by the consensus of group thought.

56. MOST PEOPLE GAIN FROM BEING LED BY OTHERS

Lunarians make the best soldiers, employees, political bureaucrats, and spiritual followers, who promote and support a "higher authority" other than themselves. They are all satisfied with the role of submitting to a higher authority, as long as their subservience is rewarded by the "higher power." Soldiers feel a sense of accomplishment when awarded with a medal or a higher rank; employees value the promotion and wage increase; and bureaucrats like the acknowledgement and platitudes received of their superiors; and spiritual followers feel accepted and valued when they are complying with the commands of a supernatural entity. All these gain personal satisfaction when their superiors ("higher authority") receive the honor and glory that they believe *they* made happen.

57. WE GAIN PERSONAL VALUE FROM OUR GROUP

Lunarians seek out any type of "group" that a Stellarian leader has established. Some of these groups have agendas that create much of the misery we experience in our *imperfect world.* Gangs of marauders and terrorists (armies and navies to some) can be supported by Lunarians seeking some kind of group affiliation, which gives them a reason for their existence. They gain compensation from their group either through monetary value or an emotional value within the group's leadership structure. Although they tend to aspire to higher ranks within their particular group, they usually feel less comfortable becoming the head of the group.

58. GROUPTHINK MENTALITY HIDES THE TRUE SELF

This groupthink mentality can be one of the most dangerous parts of human nature. Not wanting to be seen as a fool, and seeking to avoid embarrassment or angering other members of the group, Lunarians stifle their inner humanity and make irrational decisions, or support those choices of their leaders. They are easily convinced that the *right* way is the appointed and accepted *leader's* way.

Outside of the influence of the group they have chosen for themselves, however, a Lunarian often questions the validity of what the group is doing. When alone, a Lunarian is more inclined to act responsibly and more *humanely* (more in accordance to the alignment of our human *essence*) than when they are with their chosen group. Alternately, the power of groupthink can cause a Lunarian to act completely opposite of how they would normally act *outside* of the group. Most of the wars, genocides, and human atrocities are a result of the Lunarian (the majority) groupthink syndrome.

59. GROUPS PRODUCE A UNIFYING ENERGY

When groups of people join together with a specific, unified purpose, they generate powerful levels of energy through groupthink mentality. When thus united, those in the group sense extraordinary feelings of emotional personal power.

Attending a sporting event, for example, generates enormous amounts of energy, which affects the overall emotional and physical state of an individual. The "fans" generate these energy patterns based on how well their chosen side is doing in the contest. Whether winning or losing, the cumulative energy released into the environment of the event is undeniably felt by all those in attendance. In this example, a Lunarian type will feel right at home with the negative feelings of losing or the positive feelings of winning.

A Stellarian type will attempt to become the center of attention in the audience and stand out as a more enthusiastic fan than the others, thus feeding off the energy created by the crowd. In complete contrast, a Solarian would always feel a sense of uneasiness and sorrow for the side that is losing. Regardless, Solarians are least affected by groupthink mentality.

60. GROUP ENERGY AIDS THE GROUP'S COHESIVENESS

The strong energy generated by groups of people leads to the cohesiveness of the people within the group. It also causes the people to desire that others outside of the group join them to feel the same energy that they are experiencing inside the group. Likewise, when a member of the group leaves, there is a sense of sorrow and alienation shared by the cohesive energy of the group members who remain.

All belief systems in an *imperfect* world produce groupthink mentality. These groups are usually started by a charismatic Stellarian who is looking for someone in his or her environment to satiate his or her inner longing for attention and praise. Like an over-enthusiastic fan, group leaders feed on the desires of the group and motivate the members of the group to explore and expand their agreed-upon belief system.

61. GROUP COHESIVENESS CAN CAUSE HUMAN MISERY

As indicated above, this human phenomenon of groupthink mentality is responsible for the justification and support of wars, carnage, and genocide of others who are outside of "the group." Members of "the group" can turn off their humanity and cheer for the destruction of anyone outside of their group just as easily as a sports fan can turn off human compassion and consideration for the visiting team; there is no emotional difference.

The greater the cohesive bond (the energy generated) of "the group," the easier it is for its members to turn off any concern for anyone outside of the group. These cohesive bonds form first between the individual and whomever provides value to the person (the people they "love") then continues with the bonds formed with the family unit, then with the community, then with the nation, and then with the rest of the world.

The formation of bonds outside of the individual causes great problems with humanity. One's family, community, and nation become more important than another's family, community, and nation. And in the defense of one, the destruction of the other is justified.

62. GROUPS THAT DO NOT SUPPORT FREE WILL ARE A CONSTANT THREAT TO FREE WILL AND HUMANITY

Because we *Homo sapiens* ("wise ones") are continually trying to find ourselves, we are responsible for the creations of the many "groups" in our *imperfect world.* We are usually unable (with our *imperfect brains*), or at least unwilling, to realize which groups benefit the overall human race and which ones do not. The litmus test, however, is quite easy:

Because the greatest part of existing as a human being is the ability to exercise our free will, **any and all groups that inhibit this free will in any way cannot be good for our humanity**. The worst groups are those where free will is not allowed at all or is extremely restricted.

These groups control what their members think and do and threaten banishment and sometimes even death, to anyone who leaves "the group" and uses his or her free agency to think differently. These groups are led by authoritarian (Stellarian) leaders who have convinced their followers that *only they* know what is right for humanity, not allowing their members any choice in the matter. This type of groupthink mentality is in complete opposition to how our humanity was *foundationalized* in the beginning. It is the greatest threat to our peace and happiness.

63. THERE ARE NO GROUPS IN A PERFECT WORLD

During our foundationalization, our Solarian creators had no expectations of us. They let us become separate and unique individuals, exercising our free will to become who *we* wanted to become, not who *they* wanted us to become. In a *perfect world*, there are no "groups," just individuals experiencing their own *personal happiness*. Once we are again in a *perfect* world, the need to question *who we are* and *why we exist* will no longer be part of our emotional makeup.

In the *perfect* world, we will know that we exist for ourselves. We will know that the Universe exists for each of us individually. And we will have a firm and unwavering understanding that we were created by Solarian people who are obligated by their own nature to serve every one of our *individual* needs. Living in this world (as was the case in our original *perfect* world), we will become a "group" of one, an "army" of one, and a "gang" of one. We will become who we *truly* are and will not need anyone else to tell us *who we are* or who we should be—we will become our *true* selves!

SUMMARY

Although we will never be condemned for the experiences we have in our *imperfect body*, we will one day acknowledge that our actions here upon this earth proved who we really are and why the majority of us cannot be trusted with power and control over others.

We will acknowledge all of our prejudices and bigotry towards others that we developed by exercising our uninhibited free will. We will acknowledge that we did not think of others like we thought of ourselves, nor did we treat others as we would have wanted to be treated if we were them. We will acknowledge the times we cared more about ourselves and those who we valued (our loved ones) more than we did those whom we did not value.

We will be left to contemplate the pervasive and convincing *truth* that we are *who we are*. Our actions in the approximate 100 lives we will have lived, without knowing who we were before, will convince us of what we do with uninhibited free will and the ability to have sex. Most of us will no longer question whether or not we should be granted the power and ability of a creator. And with some frustration, most of us will realize and accept that we will never have the ability to have sex again.

But before this day of reckoning, we need to go through one more stage of human development that will further solidify *who we are* and leave us with even less of an excuse for our actions. We need an experience where we can fully concentrate on *who we are* and learn to be as comfortable with ourselves as possible. We need to experience what it is like to live in a **perfect world** with an *imperfect body*.

Preparing for a New World

CHAPTER SEVENTEEN

It doesn't matter how long we may have been stuck in a sense of our limitations. If we go into a darkened room and turn on the light, it doesn't matter if the room has been dark for a day, a week, or ten thousand years—we turn on the light and it is illuminated. Once we control our capacity for love and happiness, the light has been turned on.

—Sharon Salzberg

1. WE NEED MORE PROOF OF WHO WE REALLY ARE

We have discussed how we prove our *humanity type* by the actions we decide to take while living in an *imperfect world* with an *imperfect body*. Forced to live with an *imperfect* human nature and to experience the vicissitudes of life that it creates, we may remain unconvinced that we would act differently than our creators would under the same circumstances. We still might claim the excuse that the motivations and consequences of our actions are directly associated with the misery and inequality of an *imperfect world*. We may still remain unconvinced that we would misuse the power of our free will if exposed to better human conditions.

Would we act the same in a **perfect world** with a **perfect body**, where we were allowed to have unlimited use of our free will (along with the ability to have sex), but where all of the basic necessities of life were provided for us without labor or charge? How do we know that, if placed in better circumstances, we wouldn't feel just as comfortable being around Solarian advanced humans as we are around those of our same *humanity type*?

There must come a time when we become convinced beyond a shadow of a doubt that who we have chosen to be is indeed who we *truly* are, and that the restrictions placed on this *humanity type* are completely fair and just. We must be provided with the experience of living in a *different* world than the one in which we currently find ourselves—one that will finally help convince us of the truth.

2. A NEW WORLD WILL HELP US TO SELF-ACTUALIZE

During the next stage of our development (the final stage before we return to becoming the *perfected, advanced humans* that we are), we will still have an *imperfect body* and retain, if we choose, the ability to enjoy sex. However, in this *new world*, all of our physiological and emotional needs will be provided for. With the advanced technology that will be brought to this earth, we will be able to access the energy emissions of our *essence*. Although our *imperfect brain* still won't fully allow it, through the advanced technology of advanced beings, we will come to know a lot more about our past lives. This technology will allow us to plug into our *essence* and transfer the experiences into images that our *imperfect* senses can assimilate and react to. Upon accessing more of our past experiences, we will know ourselves better and observe the choices we have made in the past. (More on this later.)

On this *new earth*, different locations will be established for the different humanity types. There will be a cultural center, or a State (or country) set up, which will provide a place for Solarians to congregate and do what brings them lasting and consistent happiness. A Lunarian State and a Stellarian State will also be formed where those people of those humanity types can live freely to do what makes them happy. Everyone upon the earth will be able to freely travel to these different parts of the world and experience firsthand what it is like to live amongst humans of each *humanity type*. Upon so doing, we will realize where we find ourselves most comfortable living.

3. CONVINCED OF OUR HUMANITY TYPE, WE WILL GET A CORRESPONDING PERFECT BODY

The ultimate end and purpose for this *new society* will be for us to finally understand *who we are* and *why we exist* and to accept the conditions set for the *humanity type* that we have chosen. When we are ready to accept these things, by the choice of our own free will, we will once again receive a **perfect body** that will be ours forever. Before we discuss more about this new earth and society though, in order to better understand its purpose in our development, we need to consider the state of humanity leading up to this significant change.

4. SOCIETAL PROBLEMS ARE WIDESPREAD AND INCREASING

This book was published *circa* 2012. At this time, the cultures and societies that have developed upon the earth are experiencing instability and a general disposition of hopelessness. The monetary systems that control trade and commerce, which all people are dependent upon, are going through unprecedented changes in the way that they are managed and controlled to influence and stabilize society.

Social problems continue to rise as more and more people find themselves questioning authority and the laws that govern their lives. The disparity between the rich and the poor is increasing, causing the value placed upon human life to decrease as the rich find little use for those who once provided the labor to support their lifestyles.

5. TECHNOLOGY IS DIMINISHING HUMAN VALUE

The cause of the problems that face the human race at this time can be attributed in large part to the extraordinary advancements made in industry and technology. However, the actual technology and industry are not causing the problems. The people who control them are.

Computer technology is replacing human reason. There is no longer a need for a *real* person to use his or her brain to solve the problems and issues facing the manufacturing and production industries.

A few keyboard strokes on the right computer with the appropriate software program installed can solve most problems that were once worked out by the conscious reasoning of human beings. Human ingenuity and the use of free will and reason to acquire knowledge is becoming a relic of a past era. A correctly programmed computer is replacing the human mind in all aspects of life on planet Earth.

Robotics and animation have replaced the need for labor in many of the factories that produce goods. Computers are integrated into the service sector, taking away the need for the personality and wisdom of a human being. No longer can a person call a company's customer service department without hearing a computer-generated message first.

Advancements in production and manufacturing have *devalued* the majority of the human race. A person no longer uses his or her unique free will to provide a product or service that others need, thereby creating a demand that will ultimately *increase* the value of the individual. Instead, personal ingenuity is outperformed by automation and technology of huge corporations that have the ability to offer the same products and services much more efficiently and for a much lower price.

The world is slowly but progressively losing its humanity!

6. IMPERFECT TECHNOLOGY RUINS THE ENVIRONMENT AND CONTROLS OUR FREE WILL

These advancements are not only *devaluing* the human race, but they are affecting the natural balance of the earth's delicate environment. Whenever an interaction takes place between synthetic (artificially made to resemble something natural) products and the natural world, the natural world loses. Synthetic materials are not created by advanced humans with the knowledge to create materials that work well with a natural environment. Rather, they are created by *imperfect* scientists and developers who do not worry about what their creations will do to the natural world, but instead how much money can be made from them.

For this reason, the earth is being polluted with synthetic products that do not break down easily and upset the delicate balance of our natural world. The advancements in science and technology are made artificially by chemical syntheses that attempt to resemble natural realities. Artificial body parts are being used to replace natural ones. Synthetic pharmaceuticals are developed in an attempt to mimic natural plants. The genes and DNA of the natural world are being manipulated and changed to meet the demands of a changing world, to such an extent that the natural world can no longer provide us with what we need to be happy.

We seek for more and more technology. We depend on it. We lust after it. Consequently, we have allowed it to control our lives.

7. THOSE WHO CONTROL MONEY RESTRICT FREE WILL

Those in power and those who profit from these advancements in technology are the ones responsible for their use. They are responsible for what advanced technology does to other human beings and to the natural world. These are the merchants and political powers of the earth. These are those who seek power, glory, and authority over other people. These are those who control the one thing that all of us have become dependent upon for our survival—MONEY—the abstract means of value we have allowed to be placed upon the resources of the earth and upon each other.

There is not a person upon the earth who can buy or sell unless he or she utilizes the economical systems based upon money. Because all of us are dependent upon money to survive, our free will is manipulated, controlled, and restricted by those who manage money's value, exchange, and availability.

8. THE HUMAN RACE WORSHIPS MONEY

The abstract value we place on money has increasingly become the *only* system by which we assess our worth. Human beings are valued by the money they have, the money they make, and the possessions that money has given them. This causes us to continually expend most of our energy in using money, or in thinking about how much we have or do not have, and how we can get more.

We are tormented day and night by our experiences with the abundance of money or the lack thereof. Money has left its mark upon us. The *image* of success and the values it has created in our minds pollute our *true* humanity and cause us to disregard the emotional balance that we call happiness. It has definitely left its mark upon us. The very number we have ascribed to the value of money has created an economic system the likes of which the world has never known before.

This economic value system we have created can be likened to a "Great Beast of burden" upon whose back the inhabitants of the earth ride, having a cup of wine in one hand, being drunk with the material things of the world. But the people of the world do not see where this *Great Beast* is taking them. Nor do they care. As long as they are enjoying the ride and are drunk with pleasure, or are attempting to get drunk, why should they worry about it?

9. WE HAVE SOLD OUR HUMANITY FOR MONEY

We are not being true and faithful to our humanity. Our *essence* contains our humanity and was established in us before we were placed in this world. Our humanity is being pushed further and further back into our subconscious mind, where we pay less and less attention to it. The worries and cares of the world and the aspirations of becoming as the world expects us have clouded our minds. The energy needed to keep a proper balance between the energy levels of our *perfect essence* and our *imperfect brain*, which is responsible for our conscious thoughts, is being wasted. The energy is wasted on our constant craving for worldliness.

A *sign* of our humanity is a constant desire for the welfare of others. A *token* of our humanity is our willingness to do whatever is necessary to live in peace and harmony with others. The *sign* and *token* (the *essence* of our humanity) were given to us by our mothers, who were responsible for ensuring that our humanity was *foundationalized* correctly. And it was! We just can't remember that it was. Because we can't remember, we sell our *sign* and *token* for money.

Our politicians have *sold* their humanity for glory, power, and personal gain. The bureaucrats who support them have *sold* their humanity in exchange for a title and a government pay grade that is reflected in their paycheck. Unethical and corrupt behavior is justified because of the attitude that, "It's my job!" Soldiers kill because it is "their job," and they have sold the *sign* and *token* of their humanity for the pay and accolades they receive from their commanding officers. Police officers, prosecuting attorneys, judges, and correctional administrators have sold their *sign* and *token* for money. They are blind to the social problems caused by their actions and justify what they do by exclaiming, "I'm just doing my job!" Sales people, not only of material goods but also of emotional goods and services, justify their abuse of humanity because it is "their job." It is how they earn their money and how they are *paid* (not just monetarily).

Throughout the world, people justify acting against what they know to be right because it is "their job" to do it. They justify their lack of humanity exclaiming, "Someone has to do it! If I don't, someone else will, so why shouldn't I get the **money**?" No longer is it part of humanity to treat others how one would want to be treated. This antiquated rule of humanity has been replaced with do unto others as they do unto you, or *before* they do it unto you.

10. LEADERS FAIL TO USE POWER TO BENEFIT OTHERS

The leaders of our world who seek and maintain power over others have been given the chance to prove to themselves what they will do with such power. They have the power to utilize their humanity in a way that benefits the rest of us without upsetting the delicate natural balance of our world and at the same time provide for the needs of all people equally.

In these current times, the United States of America, for example, has the ability to feed **the entire world** through the technological advancements and the economic systems that it controls. It has the power to provide clean, sound shelter to all inhabitants of the world. It has the power to provide everyone with the best in health care. It has the power to do many things for the good of *all* humanity.

But it does not! Instead, it sells its *sign* and *token* of humanity, or better, places a higher priority on MONEY than on people! The people of the United States have placed themselves and their own importance above all others of the world. Being an "American" means more to them than what "*being an American*" is doing to the rest of the world. The "American Dream" and its dependence on money and consumerism stand in the way of utilizing the great technological advancements of today (and the many that will be coming in the near future) to solve the whole of humanity's problems.

11. WE HAVE THE ABILITY TO PROVIDE FOR ALL EQUALLY

The leaders of the United States of America have *no excuse* why they cannot use their power for the benefit of all Americans equally or even for the entire world. Until now, not at any time during the history of the human race upon this planet has humankind had the ability and technology to produce the products and services that would increase our state of contentment. The ability to do this was reserved for the latter days of the second stage of our development upon this earth *without* the intervention of more advanced human societies.

As discussed previously, our creators purposefully ensured that the technologies and advancements we are experiencing today were not discovered in the past, because they knew what *imperfect human nature* would do with these technologies. They knew that once the mortal human race was allowed to discover what they have today, they would be able to destroy themselves and the planet upon which they live.

One would reason that over time we would learn how to be more humane and use our free agency to create peace upon earth. But since the beginning of history, nothing has changed. We are still treating each other in inhumane ways despite our advancements in technology. We are learning that no matter how much power we are allowed to have, most of us will never use it correctly for the benefit of all people equally.

12. THOSE WHO CRAVE POWER DEMONSTRATE HOW THEY MISUSE IT

The reason why our creators are allowing such advancements today is to take away the excuse of those who wield the power and domination of these advancements. Again, another very important purpose for this *imperfect world* is to show us that few free-willed human beings can be trusted with the power of an advanced creator, something we all desired in the beginning. If we were never given the **power and ability** to do what is for the good of humanity, how could it be proven that we would misuse this power?

Because those who are in power upon this earth *now* have the ability (through advanced technologies) to improve the state of humanity, **if** they do not use their power to do so, they will have proven to themselves and to the rest of us that they **cannot** be trusted with this power. Subsequently, these Stellarians and Lunarians will have proven to themselves what their advanced, perfect mothers tried to tell them all along during their *Foundationalization Process*: You cannot be trusted with this type of power. Many of us might have argued the point then, but we will have no argument after experiencing what we did with the power during our second stage of development in mortality.

13. WE ARE SEEING THE UNHAPPINESS OUR SEXUAL NATURES CAUSE US

The other point of contention we had with our primordial parents was concerning the issue of sex. We wondered, "Why can't we *all* have the power and ability associated with sex?" During these current times upon this earth, we are allowed to exercise our sexual desires unlike at any other time in our history.

Sex is no longer taboo. It is a natural and perfectly rational use of our bodies. It has become very enjoyable, especially in light of the fact that the act no longer has to end in producing a child. The means of contraception will increase and advance like everything else in our world. The moral value that has inhibited sex is decreasing, as it should, so that all of us can freely exercise our ability to experience the amazing power and sensory fulfillment of sex.

Humans were created to experience joy from utilizing the senses of our body. As we have discussed in this book, our body has specific organs that support our senses and allow us the ability to experience joy thereby. We have also discussed how our sex organs provide us with an additional way that we can utilize *all of these senses at once.* There is no justifiable reason why any *imperfect* human should not be allowed to use all of their senses as their creation intended, at any time they choose.

However, in so doing, protection of individual free will must be strictly enforced. No one is justified in enjoying the sensory fulfillment of their sex organs with another person who is not capable of choosing for themselves whether or not they wish to participate in the act of sharing the sexual experience. This includes, but is not limited to, young children, the mentally disabled, and those who are raped or forced beyond their will to resist. Bestiality is also a direct violation, not of free will (because animals don't have any), but of the rules our creators have established for all living creatures in how their bodies react sexually within each individual species.

Rules and laws encompassing morality must be respected and maintained, but limited only in the prohibition of impeding the free will of another. Any form of sexual behavior that does not take away the free will of another, should be protected and supported, as a personal choice of action. A person should not be judged in any way based on his or her sexual orientation or persuasion. We all have the right to enjoy the mortal bodies we have been given and we should all protect each other's right to do so as we each choose individually.

Through this liberation of our sexual abilities, we are learning about the problems that sex can cause to our emotional balance. As sexual abilities become more individualized and liberated, we are learning to disassociate the act of sex from our deep personal emotions. The act *seems* to be no different from eating or satisfying the rest of our bodily senses. Yet, no matter what is "seems," we are still affected emotionally by sexual experiences.

When acted upon with free will, the sexual act causes nothing but happiness, albeit temporary, while it is being experienced. Even so, the reality still exists that, one day, *only* those who choose to perpetuate the human race will be able to experience sex with their *perfect* bodies. The rest of our *perfected* bodies will not have the organs to do so. And without the organs, we will not be able to relive any sexual experiences. Those sexual experiences of the past will be as useless to our enjoyment then, as they are to little children who observe sexual activities of mortal adults—they are of no concern to the child whatsoever. The reality of losing the ability to have sex will always be something that we will never completely understand and it will never make sense to us. Nevertheless, it is the way things *have always been* and will continue to be throughout the Universe. And through our experiences upon this earth, we will be given the opportunity to concede this and accept that it must be.

14. UNHAPPINESS IS THE CONSEQUENCE OF OUR LACK OF HUMANITY TOWARDS OURSELVES AND EACH OTHER

Unhappiness is the effect of continually disregarding the power of our human *essence*. *Misery is the natural* ***physical*** *byproduct* of producing energy levels through our actions that oppose those given off by our *essence*. Unhappiness and misery are caused from the inhumane things we do to ourselves and to each other, including the things that we **don't** do for others.

As discussed throughout this book, the cause of our misery is that we cannot readily recall who we *really* are, and are left to ourselves upon this earth without the intervention of those who helped us establish our humanity in the first place. It had to be this way so that we could experience misery; and the purpose of this second stage of our development has been overwhelmingly successful.

15. WE WERE NOT CREATED TO ALWAYS BE UNHAPPY

Even so, we were *not* created to live in continual misery and without the hope for happiness and lasting peace. What a cruel and unfair proposition to suppose that advanced humans gave us life and the free will that made us conscious of our self, only to let us continually exist in unhappiness! What sadistic person would do such a thing?

Why would they create us in a *perfect* human world with all we need to exercise our free agency to do anything we desire, only to have us meet an end of our existence in a world full of human suffering, misery, and hopelessness? Would any of us create a child, knowing that we were introducing the child into a life that ended in death (nonexistence), and that, until the child meets that end, it is going to suffer through all sorts of miserable circumstances? If we could not *imagine* ourselves doing this, how could it be possible for anyone to suppose that advanced human beings could do it?

16. A PERFECT WORLD MAKES US FULLY RESPONSIBLE FOR OUR ACTIONS

Our *imperfect world* must be transformed into a *perfect* one, where we will no longer be able to blame our actions on our environment. We need the opportunity to continue to exercise our free will and have complete power over our environment, instead of the environment controlling us. We need this experience so that we can better understand *who we have chosen to be.* As mentioned previously, only in a *perfect* world can free-willed people be completely responsible for their actions.

Therefore, to allow us this experience, we need to exist in a *perfect world* with an *imperfect body*. Only then can the excuses we might come up with for our actions be exposed and eliminated.

17. WHY IS THE REAL TRUTH BEING REVEALED NOW?

We have discussed why it is necessary that *true reality* be kept from us during our probationary period upon this earth. We have explained why we cannot have full access to the memories of our past lives, and a great deal of our present life. So, if this is the purpose for mortality, then ***why*** are these **real truths** being revealed in this book at this time? Better yet, *how* is *true reality* being revealed to us? Who is this author? How do we know that the author hasn't made everything up that is written in this book just for the author's own personal gain? Who gave the author the knowledge and authority to do these things?

18. KNOWING THE REAL TRUTH ELIMINATES ALL EXCUSES

This book, a *true* explanation of *Human Reality*, is being published *circa* the year 2012 for one reason: to eliminate further excuse that many will have as to why they should not be allowed the powers and abilities of Solarian humans. Before the publication of this book, a person could have easily complained to our creators that mortality wasn't a fair test.

Some might have claimed:

> *You didn't want us to know true reality so that we would experience the opposition of happiness. You set us up to fail! We understand that you did not openly intervene into our lives so that we could prove to ourselves what we would do if we didn't think anyone was watching us. But why didn't you give us the* ***real truth*** *and still allow us to exist in a state where we didn't think anyone was watching over us? We might not have failed,* ***if*** *we had only known the* ***real truth****!*

As we will discuss later, this excuse will be eliminated when we are allowed to live in a *new world*, patterned after the *perfect* world where we were *foundationalized*, yet still have all the powers, abilities, and probative experience that we are allowed with our *imperfect* body.

19. THE YEAR 2012 IS AN IMPORTANT TIME PERIOD

There is a set time given to this earth when our creators will reveal themselves to the world. That time is about 135 years, plus or minus a few years, from the time that this book is published. We know this, because the advanced beings who oversee this solar system have explained this time period to those "selected ones," who were given all the answers to *human reality* and provided them to us, so that a *full* understanding of **real truth** could benefit us all.

There have been some interesting theories and beliefs associated with the year 2012. Some believe it will be the end of the world as we know it. Others believe it will be the beginning of a *new* world—a better world.

All of these speculations were invented in the minds of some people, who were able to tap into the power of their *essence* and attempt to formulate an explanation of what they felt. As discussed previously, they have created their *own* personal reality, which is no different from their dreams. None of these theories is correct.

20. THERE IS UNIVERSAL OPPORTUNITY TO KNOW THE REAL TRUTH

Every human *essence* assigned to this solar system will have the opportunity to live in mortality during the time that the fullness of ***true reality*** is available to the entire world equally. There are roughly 15 billion people assigned to this solar system. A typical lifespan for a human being now upon this earth is approximately 72 years. Therefore, it is reasonable that during two generations (about 144 years) of human beings numbering 7.5 billion in population, the entire 15 billion of us will have an opportunity to live upon the earth when the **real truth** is available, without a sure knowledge that other advanced humans exist in other parts of the Universe.

None of us will ever have the excuse that we were not given the chance to prove our *humanity type* during a time that the fullness of **real truth** was upon the earth—during a time when we were free to act with our free will without knowing that we were being watched over by other advanced human beings. Remember, if we *really*, *really* knew we were being observed, our free will would be impeded, and we would never act *true* to our *humanity type*. However (and this is very, very important to keep in mind), although **real truth** is being made available to all of us, this does not take away the free agency of a person to reject it or to not even search for it.

21. MANY PEOPLE WILL REJECT THE REAL TRUTH BECAUSE OF PRIDE

This book contains the presentation of ***true reality***. It will be published and made available to everyone upon the earth. With the current technology of the Internet and the advanced technology of worldwide communication that is coming in the near future, every human being will have access to the **real truths** presented in this book for the very first time in human history.

Again, although this book will be made available to everyone equally, this does not mean that it will be accepted by everyone equally. Because it points out the fallibility of **every** idea, **every** concept, **every** perception, and **every** thought produced by *imperfect* human minds in an *imperfect world*, many will be offended at its revelations. Many will scoff at the idea that they know nothing of **real truth**. They will find it very hard to accept that all they have believed and learned throughout their life is a false or misleading representation of *perfect human reality*.

Yes, personal pride and egocentricity (the very things that were instilled in our *essences* during our primordial *foundationalization*) will keep many from even reading this book. Many who believe they *already* have the truth will not be searching for anything; therefore, by their choice, they will never discover this book. Nevertheless, this book will still be made available for all equally. This is so that none will ever have an excuse for why they did not find it and allow it to affect their free-willed choices.

22. WE WILL HAVE NO EXCUSE FOR REJECTING THE TRUTH

None of us will have the excuse that the **real truth** was not made available to us during our probative state when we were left to ourselves without advanced human intervention. At the end of our second stage of human development in an *imperfect* body, we will be able to look back over our past lives, one of which (for the majority of us) is guaranteed to include the years between 2012 and 2145, or thereabouts. We will observe what we did during each of our lifetimes and will be left with no excuse or justification for any of our actions—NONE WHATSOEVER!

23. ONE MORTAL HUMAN IS GIVEN A FULL UNDERSTANDING OF ALL THINGS

As explained previously, advanced humans have intervened at times during our probative state to ensure equality and fairness to all. Sometimes they decide upon a person to whom they reveal their *true identity* (as a human being, although advanced) and teach this individual ***true reality***.

The way this is completed is very simple. As explained, all of us have a complete universal knowledge of all things recorded in our *essence*. Our *imperfect physical brain* "veils" this knowledge, or rather, prohibits us from accessing it. An advanced being has the ability to create a pathway through this "veil," which more fully connects one's *imperfect* brain to one's *essence*.

With this actual, physical connection, this one individual then has the capability to access memories and understanding stored on their *essence*. With this unique ability, the individual can then carry out the purpose for which he or she was given the capability. This is how (and is the **only way**) an *imperfect* mortal person gains an understanding of the mysteries of human existence, even as complete an understanding of all things as any advanced human being found anywhere in the Universe has.

24. THE ONE SELECTED WILL ONLY USE A KNOWLEDGE OF REAL TRUTH TO BENEFIT EVERYONE EQUALLY

We now know *how* the knowledge of *true reality* is given; but the more important question might be *how* the advanced beings decide upon a person to whom to give this power. In addition, how can the rest of us know of a surety that this person has actually been properly selected, and is not just creating a *personal reality* for him or herself, as do those who claim "psychic" or "spiritual" powers, as discussed previously?

The answer lies in the understanding that this knowledge will ONLY be given to a person with a Solarian *essence*. This person will **never** use that power for gain, either monetarily or to gain the respect of others. A person belonging to this *humanity type* will *never* allow a group of people to *follow* him or her or set up a groupthink mentality, wherein those who believe in the "selected one" isolate and separate themselves from the rest of society. Everything these "selected ones" do will benefit the **entire** population of the world **equally**. These will never claim to know, nor will they ever reveal, any information about another person in mortality that they would not reveal about everyone else UNLESS, upon so doing, everyone else in the world benefits thereby. They will never use their understanding of ***true reality***, unless it serves the purposes of *serving* the whole world equally.

25. THOSE SELECTED RECEIVE THEIR COMMISSION FROM AN ADVANCED BEING FACE-TO-FACE

These "selected ones" will *never* claim that they receive information about how they should use their *new ability* (their purpose) from any outside source that they cannot see with their physical eyes and hear with their physical ears. This "outside source" *must* be in human form and be as recognizable as any other human being. It cannot, nor will it ever be, an ethereal manifestation of any kind. The source must be an actual, physical advanced human being.

Advanced human beings have bodies of flesh and bone—nothing else! The reason why it is important for a person to receive proper instruction face-to-face with an actual human being is because of the ability of the *imperfect* brain to deceive a mortal, as explained previously in this book. Thoughts can be created by our *imperfect* mind. Speaking face-to-face with an advanced human being—who communicates in the familiar way that humans are accustomed to receiving information (i.e., from mouth to ear)—ensures the ones "selected" that they are not making things up in their *own* mind. There can be no misunderstanding when a directive is given from the voice box of an advanced being to the ears of a mortal "selected one."

In summary of this important concept concerning those who are "selected" to know **real truth**:

A "selected one" must **actually** be visited by an advanced human being from another galaxy or solar system. The advanced being must **physically** make adjustments to the "selected one's" brain to allow access to the *essence*. "Selected ones" will only be mandated to do something that will affect all the people of the world equally *WITHOUT impeding anyone's free will.* Along with the commission comes the ability to confound anything that is **not real truth**, or that does not make sense to a normal person. The "selected one" can answer any question about *human reality.* If **all** of these criteria are *not* met, then the person who makes any claim to "special" insight or understanding coming from a "higher source," other than themselves, is making up a *personal reality* in their own head through their imagination.

26. THOSE SELECTED CAN ANSWER ANY QUESTION ABOUT THE TRUE MEANING OF LIFE

The greatest determining factor of whether or not an individual was *truly* selected to do a *specific* work for a particular purpose is whether or not they can explain **all of the mysteries of life**. Can they answer any and all questions about *who we are* and *why we exist*? Although their answers might often be rejected by the world, do their answers make *perfect* sense to the average human intellect?

Most importantly, does everything they teach as *true reality* (or **real truth**) negate everything known, believed, opined, reasoned, and set forth in an *imperfect world*? (Keep in mind that what we have come up with in our *imperfect* world is far from *true human reality*.) Does what they teach help us create a better world for all and give one a comfortable feeling that what they teach is fair and equitable to all?

(This is creating a balance with what we already know but can't remember that is stored in our *essence*.) Does what they teach us help us better understand *who we are* and *why we exist*?

27. MOST DO NOT LIKE WHAT SELECTED ONES TEACH

The *imperfect* world as a whole has a hard time accepting the *true* "selected ones" because what they reveal usually negates all previously learned "knowledge." These "chosen ones" are hated, ridiculed, blasphemed, and receive very little accolade or praise (something they could care less about anyway) from the majority of the people of the world.

Whenever one of these individuals has existed among the human race, they have usually been killed by those whose self-image and value were threatened by their message and knowledge. Their deaths have usually been caused by those who are threatened by the **real truth**. These include the leaders, politicians, judges, psychics, and channelers, and all others who have convinced themselves and others that they have *special* powers that place them in a position of power or authority over others. And because the majority of the people in an *imperfect world* receive their own personal value from one of these leaders, etc., the people are going to follow the suggestion given by their leaders. Their leaders will convince them that anyone claiming to have the extraordinary power of being able to explain **real truth** that disagrees or contradicts *their truth*, must be eliminated.

28. THE PLACEMENT OF SELECTED ONES COINCIDES WITH THE CONSEQUENCES OF HUMAN NATURE

These "selected ones" are chosen at certain time periods throughout the history of the human race upon this earth, although there have been times when no mortal was *selected* to reveal any portion of **real truth** anywhere upon the earth. "Selected ones" come and go as the advanced beings who monitor our world see fit.

The "chosen" individual's presence among us usually coincides with some transitional period of our second stage of development. These "transitional stages" are determined by what we do with our free will.

29. WE GO THROUGH SEVEN TRANSITIONAL STAGES IN OUR IMPERFECT BODIES

In general, there are seven (7) "transitional stages" that we go through during mortality. These should not be confused with the three (3) main stages of human development. These seven "transitional stages" only occur during mortality (the *second* stage of human development), generally as has occurred during this earth's mortal existence:

Stage One

Our *imperfect bodies* were created and given to us. These bodies gave us the power to reproduce at will. We were taught the primary rules of humanity and were sent forth into the world to use its resources to support our *imperfect bodies*. We were given the power to act and be acted upon according to the natural laws of the earth.

Stage Two

Because we weren't taught to write, our first ancestors had no way to pass on the information about how to treat each other (these "primary rules of humanity"). We soon learned that we not only had power and dominion over the natural world (because of our advanced intellect in comparison to the rest of the animals found upon the earth), but we also had power over each other—the strong over the weak. Thus, during Stage Two, the first homicides in the form of warfare occurred in protection of a person's belief system and the limited resources of the earth.

Stage Three

During this stage, and because of the increasing means of warfare used for self-protection, we learned that the resources of the earth were ***not*** unlimited and needed to be controlled. We began to place abstract values on the things of the earth and upon each other. It was during this stage that the concept of "money" began to affect our humanity.

Stage Four

During the fourth stage, we learned to organize ourselves into civilizations, nations, and communities that supported what we learned and experienced in the first three stages. We learned to use our free will to support ourselves and our families, protect them through warfare, and gain more abundance than others. We justified this, ostensibly, because our abundance favored our chosen groups (families, communities, and nations) and ourselves.

Stage Five

Some people who were protected within the separate and isolated borders of civilized nations had the ability and great privilege to do nothing more than think all day long. This stage produced what the *imperfect mind* would relate to as the renaissance of human thought. It gave some the ability to refine their methods of trying to figure out what this life was all about. No human being who is forced to hard and continuous labor to support their life can focus their energy on considering *who we are* and *why we exist*. This can only happen when one can free up their energy and allow the energy of the *essence* to affect their thoughts.

From this stage came "great" philosophers, orators, writers, and others. None of these came from a life situation where they didn't have enough time to utilize human *reason* and *imagination* to contemplate *human reality*. These were soon honored and respected, and often envied for their *easy* lifestyle. With this honor and respect, they began to take away the free will of the human mind and replace it with invented realities of *imperfection* coming from their own minds. They had nothing better to do in life but sit around and create value for themselves.

"Taking away free will" in the sense mentioned above, indicates that what people were being taught and what they readily began to accept, gave them less of a chance to understand *true reality* on their own. The institutions of education, colleges, universities, and places where one pursued worldly honor and respect through diplomas and awards began to take the place of ***true reason*** and ***true humanity***. In these institutions of learning, the *imperfect understanding* invented in the minds of those who the world chose to accept as "wise ones" was continuously recycled, reinvented, and circulated in the human mind until the *invented vain and foolish imaginations* of *imperfect* humans seemed to be (and still are) the only accepted reality.

Stage Six

This is the stage of technological and industrial invention. It was during this transitional stage that our creators finally allowed us to act upon our *imperfect reason and thought processes* to produce whatever we could come up with on our own. During the previous transitional stages, this ability was monitored and hindered (as explained previously) to prevent the introduction of too much technology on earth that would have contributed to the premature end of the human race. Had the advanced *monitors* not intervened in deterring the thoughts of our ancestors, those before us would have discovered electricity and the technology we are experiencing today in their own time. As explained, if this had been allowed to happen, the human race would have destroyed itself a long time ago.

Stage Seven

We are near the beginning of this transitional stage. At the beginning of this stage, we will make the transition from being *imperfect humans* in an *imperfect world*, to *imperfect humans* in a ***perfect world***. We will then experience what it is like to live as *imperfect humans* in a *perfect world*.

This stage will be ushered in by our own free will and choice to make our world a better place for all humans to live equally, or it will be ushered in against our free will by the advanced human beings who oversee this solar system. As mentioned, to give us the opportunity to do this ourselves *without* their intervention, we are being given a complete understanding of ***true reality*** through this book. In the next chapter, an exact plan that will work for us without hindering anyone's free agency will be presented. By following this plan, we have the potential to unite the world and establish a foundation of humanity that we have never been able to accomplish before. It would be the first step in changing our world from what it currently is into a *new world*.

30. "SELECTED ONES" GIVE US THE CHANCE TO UNDERSTAND HOW OUR ACTIONS AFFECT US

Except for Stage One, before each "transitional stage" occurred, one mortal individual was selected and assigned to do a particular work that would equally benefit the entire human race, according to each particular culture to which the "selected one" was sent. The "benefit" gives the people of the earth the opportunity to prepare themselves for each stage. If these "selected ones" had not been placed appropriately, then mortals would have had an excuse as to why they acted the way that they did.

For example, someone was *selected* to warn us about the genocide that would occur if we started exercising dominion over other human beings (Stage Two). Someone was there to warn us about the inequality and poverty that was going to occur if we started placing abstract values on the things of the world and each other (Stage Three). Someone was there to warn us what would happen if we isolated ourselves into families, communities, states, and nations, and put up imaginary borders, walls, and fences to protect our selfish interests

(Stage Four). Someone was there to warn us about creating our own *personal realities,* and then forcing others through mental manipulation (through the written word and specialized oratory skills) to accept these untrue realities as **real truth** (Stage Five). Someone was there to warn us about what would happen when we began to develop industry and technology (Stage Six). And finally, someone (the author of this book) was chosen to warn us about what was about to happen to our world, because we didn't listen to those who preceded him or her, in preparation for transforming our world into a *perfect* one (Stage Seven).

Always keep in mind that every intercession upon this earth by our creators has to do with leaving each individual with no excuse. Because of these warnings given during the time away from the influence and control of advanced human beings, individuals will have no excuse for why they used their free agency the way that they did.

31. THE NUMBER OF THOSE SELECTED TO WARN HUMANITY VARIES DURING DIFFERENT TIME PERIODS

Because there were no worldwide communication connections throughout the earth during the first six (6) transitional stages, there was more than just one selected for each transitional period. There was usually *one* for *every* culture that existed on earth; but in each culture, there was always *only one.* From these *selected ones*' teachings of **real truth** (of what they were **allowed** to reveal at the time) came many of the mythologies, legends, and traditional belief systems that we have today, most of which inhibit free will and our ability to know the **real truths** that were actually taught by them.

We currently have the capability of having information provided to all parts of the world equally. Because of this, there is *only one* who needed to be assigned to be a "voice of warning" to the people of the world at this time. In preparation for the seventh and last transitional stage of human development upon this earth, and with modern technology and its continued development, the message of this *one* will be made available to all people in all parts of the earth. This *final* message will supersede, transcend, and encompass all other teachings of **real truth** given before it. It will reveal all things to the human race that have been hidden from them since the foundation of this world. It will truly become a marvelous work and a wonder for the inhabitants of this earth.

32. THE EGYPTIAN AND MAYAN CULTURES LEFT EVIDENCE

Our creators allowed some tidbits of empirical evidence to be established to help prove the truth of what has just been revealed in this book (i.e., concerning advanced beings' interaction with the human race upon this earth). Some of these evidences came from the ancient Egyptian and Mayan cultures. A "selected one" lived among the people of the ancient Egyptian (Eastern Hemisphere) civilization at the beginning of the *second* transitional stage; and at the beginning of the *fourth* transitional stage, a "selected one" lived among the Mayan (Western Hemisphere) civilization.

These particular "selected ones" not only taught the primary rules of humanity, but also gave these people some ideas and perspectives of science and technology that exist in a *perfect world.* These cultures of people gleaned knowledge of advanced civilizations from the "selected ones" sent among them. With the tidbits of information they received, the people developed ancient technologies that baffle modern-day anthropologists and other *respected* intellectuals who make an attempt to understand where these ancient people received their knowledge.

33. THE EGYPTIANS HAD A RECIPE FOR CEMENT

For example, the Egyptians came up with a recipe for an advanced type (for that time) of cement, which they used to create the blocks from which they formed their Great Pyramids. These pyramids were constructed by using a prefabricated block form into which was poured this "special" cement mixture. The prefabricated form was very lightweight and allowed the Egyptians and all those who knew of the cement "recipe," to make one layer of blocks, then carry the form up to the next higher level. The form was put into place on the next level and then the laborers mixed the cement and transported it with buckets to construct the next level of the pyramid.

Once hardened, the mixture resembled a solid block that rivals any manmade cement of today. The overall shape of the pyramid points towards space, where the ancient people were taught that advanced human beings lived. Because the Egyptians revered their leaders as "advanced humans" who were chosen to lead them, the pyramids were constructed as their tombs and pointed towards the direction where the people believed their leaders went when they died.

Current scientists, archeologists, and geologists (and all others who have placed a title next to their name to create personal value from their research) are puzzled as to how the Great Pyramids were made in the middle of the desert. They are baffled because they do not know the "recipe." All they need to do is to ask a "selected one." The one selected would then decide if revealing the "secret recipe" would benefit the entire human race or not.

34. WHY THE MAYAN CALENDAR ENDS IN THE YEAR 2012

The ancient Mayan culture also built pyramids like the Egyptians. However, the most puzzling thing about this Western Hemispheric culture is that the Mayan Calendar ends at the year 2012. The reason it ends at this year has also mystified the intellectuals of modern times. Only one *selected* to have this knowledge, however, would know *why* this is.

The Mayans were taught about the Seven Transitional Stages of human development. The one who was selected to teach them the specifics of each part of these stages of development was among them when Mayan leaders established their own calendar of time. The Mayans were taught that the end of ignorance concerning *true reality* was set for what would calculate out to be the year 2012, according to modern calendars. They were taught that ALL THINGS WOULD BE RESTORED to the people of the earth by the time this year took place on earth.

The Mayans erroneously assumed that if all things would be restored at that time, i.e., if all **real truth** was to be explained to the people of the world, then the advanced beings who knew these things would also come. They assumed that the world as they knew it, in all its *imperfection* and misery, would end once the *true reality* or the **real truth** was available to the people of the world. At that point, they figured there would be no need to keep track of time, especially when the calculation and management of time was only needed in an *imperfect world*.

They got one thing right! The **real truth will be available** to all the people of the world by 2012 (that is the purpose of this book). But the thing they didn't fully understand was what the people of the world would do once they received the **real truth**. It was their hope that everyone would rejoice once the advanced human beings finally gave us the definitive answers to the questions of *who we are* and *why we exist*. The Mayan people did not realize what state the *imperfect* human mind would be in their future. They knew nothing of the pride, arrogance, and stubbornness that are associated with egocentric human beings who do not consider ***true reality*** and who have fallen so far from it.

The ancient Mayans could not have imagined that, although the **real truth would be available to human beings**, the majority would have a very hard time accepting truths that counter everything they have believed since birth (even that which has influenced their parents and their ancestors from the beginning of this *imperfect world*). They would have never *imagined* that the majority of the world would likely reject the **real truth**, opting instead to continue to accept the *imperfect reality* to which they had become accustomed.

35. THERE IS NO COMPLETE OR REAL TRUTH IN ANY ANCIENT TEXT

The *ones selected* to warn humanity left tidbits of **real truth** with the people to whom they were sent. These "tidbits" were not a full disclosure of what the "selected ones" taught, but what the people retained of their teachings. Because the *selected ones* were instructed to not leave any written evidence of what they taught, the "tidbits" the people retained were often misinterpreted and changed. Most *selected ones* were eventually killed by the political and spiritual leaders who were losing their personal value and influence among the people who were listening to the *selected ones*. Although most of what the selected ones taught became corrupted, some of the truths they left behind can be found in distorted semblance in the mythology and belief systems passed down through subsequent generations of the many ancient cultures of the world.

No *true* "selected one" would leave anything in writing, **unless** instructed (face-to-face) to do so in order to counter the published writings of false teachers who deceived the people into believing that they were "selected," when they were not. As discussed previously, the worldly leaders could have changed their words to reflect what they, the leaders, wanted their followers to believe. Because no verifiable writings were left, what the "selected ones" actually taught was transformed into disjointed fragments of **real truth** mixed in with the *vain and foolish imaginations* of the leaders. From these imaginative realities came forth many written manuscripts that are currently accepted throughout the world as "truth."

Billions of people believe in ancient documents written by those whom they believe were actually "selected ones." However, no ancient document or manuscript meets the criteria of what would have been written by a *true* "selected one," as outlined above. No ancient document supports the unconditional right of free will and presents counsel that supports this right; in other words, none gives a perfect outline of how humans should treat each other. No ancient written document appropriately and concisely solves the human dilemma: *WHO AM I* and *WHY DO I EXIST*?

Therefore, any and all ancient texts are nothing more than the disjoined fragments of **real truth** mixed in with the vain and foolish imagination of *imperfect human understanding*.

36. A NEW WORLD WILL EITHER COME BY WAY OF US OR BY OUR CREATORS' INTERVENTION

One day, the world as we currently know it will change drastically. This change will not come from the cataclysmic events of destruction often portended by those with vain and foolish imaginations who don't know *true reality*. (It's not that any part of *human imagination* is foolish, but only that those who make a claim that their *imagination* is **true reality,** when it is not, become fools.) Our world will also not change because some unknown "alien" creatures come to the earth to destroy it and take us captive. It will change because of one of two reasons:

First, the drastic change could come when we collectively finally accept the *true reality* that each individual is equally responsible for all of the problems facing humanity, and in this acknowledgment **do all we can** to eliminate these problems. Second, if not by us, then the advanced human beings who placed us here and who are responsible for this solar system, will come to earth, reveal themselves to the whole of humankind, and make the necessary changes themselves.

Although certainly not impossible, the probability of the former happening, *based on our past actions*, is highly unlikely **(but still possible and desirable)**. The latter is the more probable, and will be the solution, if somehow we cannot unite and accomplish it ourselves.

37. THE PREPARED OVERSEER HAD TO BE PROVEN

We have discussed the necessity of an "overseer," who was *foundationalized* differently from the rest of us, so that he could fairly and equitably "oversee" our solar system. We have discussed how it was important for us to learn to trust this "overseer" so that we would be able to accept him as the ultimate and perfect dictator of the Universal laws that have always governed perfect human societies.

But how could we trust such a person to rule over our free will if that person's own power and free will had not been tested like our own? In other words, how would we know that this "overseer" was *foundationalized* correctly so that he wouldn't misuse his power and knowledge and make mistakes in governing us?

To prove himself to us, he was sent to the earth to experience mortality just like the rest of us, at the exact meridian of the Seven Transitional Stages of human development. His *essence* was placed in an *imperfect body* during the middle of the Fourth transitional stage when the *first* of the greatest human civilizations was established upon the earth. This great empire covered one fourth of the known world and had more power and authority over humankind than any other before it or any other after it, until the formation of the United States of America. This was the Great Roman Empire.

38. OUR OVERSEER WAS TESTED JUST LIKE US

All of the essential circumstances needed to test our "overseer" were present during the time of this Great Empire. It had to be proven whether or not he would misuse his power and abilities to treat any of us with inequality, no matter how we misused our *humanity*. The Roman culture was flourishing with money, prestige, education, families, communities, and every other idea that the *imperfect* human race had produced and valued.

How would this "overseer" use his free agency during this time period? If his own life was threatened by another, would he use his power to destroy his enemy? Would he judge another for the lifestyle that person chose to live? Would he do anything unbecoming of a *perfect overseer* whom we all would need and who we could respect and accept as our Supreme Head?

Although the few ancient manuscripts written about this person cannot be trusted as the "**real truth**" concerning his life upon this earth, this person did indeed exist. He had to! There was no other way for us to truly know if he could be trusted above all others unless he went through the same probative experience as those for whom he was created and *foundationalized* to be responsible and oversee.

39. OUR OVERSEER PROMISED TO ONE DAY TRANSFORM OUR WORLD

This "overseer" taught the same things that the "selected ones" sent into the world before him taught, and the same things the "selected ones" who were sent after him taught. Of course, he was killed by those whose personal value and public clout were threatened by his teachings and way of life.

Before he was killed, however, he told those close to him that one day he would return to the earth, but at that time with a *perfect body*. His body would have all the power of the advanced creators who created him, plus abilities to do things that not even our creators can do. When the *time was right*, he promised that he would come to the world again and usher in the beginning of a *new world*, patterned after the one where we lived previously—even a *perfect world*!

40. ADVANCED HUMANS WILL COME TO THE EARTH WHEN WE NEED THEM

The "right time" for the "overseer" to come is when we have exhausted all of our energy trying to create a *perfect* world through *imperfect* means, or we simply refuse to try. He and many other advanced human beings from the solar system where we were first created will come to this earth when the human race is on the brink of destroying itself and the whole of the natural world (unless humankind turns itself around, contrary to what might be expected based on its past *inhumanity*).

Unless, we discovery our *humanity* for ourselves, they will come when we have learned that few of us are capable of being trusted with power and authority over anyone else but ourselves. They will come at a time when the whole world is wondering WHAT IS ALL THIS ABOUT? WHO ARE WE? WHY DO WE EXIST? WHY CAN'T WE SEEM TO DO ANYTHING RIGHT ON THIS EARTH TO CREATE PEACE AND HAPPINESS AMONG US? When we have figured out just how *imperfect* our ways are, and are humble enough to realize that we need help, they will come and save us from ourselves.

41. ADVANCED BEINGS WILL TRANSFORM OUR WORLD INTO A PERFECT ONE

Advanced humans will bring with them the advanced technology that is needed to repair the destruction that we have caused to our natural world. They will come with technology that overrides and nullifies all the so-called "advanced technologies" we have invented in our *imperfect world.* They will completely shut down and destroy any weapon of destruction that can take a human life. No weapon will work, no gun or missile will fire, and **nothing** will operate if its purpose is to harm a human life.

They will introduce the means to produce food, clothing, shelter, and all the basic necessities of life, **without** harming the natural environment and **without** charging a price for them. They will eliminate poverty by providing everything a person desires for their individual happiness **without** charge. They will eliminate inequality by explaining that in a *perfect human world*, all people are equal, regardless of what they choose to do with their free agency, as long as what they do does not affect the free agency of another. In *essence* (pun intended), they will reiterate everything written in this book.

42. FREE AGENCY WILL REMAIN UNIMPEDED

These advanced humans are going to do all of the above activities without infringing upon our free agency, EXCEPT for making all weapons of war, and anything else that will harm a human being, useless and obsolete. They will not allow any human being to kill another human being. However, they are not going to interfere in the cultures and belief systems of the world. If a person wants to continue to believe any particular way, they will not prohibit a person from doing so. They will, however, teach the **real truth** to those who are willing to listen to what they have to say about the *perfect* worlds that exist in other parts of the Universe—the worlds that they came from…that we came from!

43. THE REAL TRUTH WILL EXTINGUISH HUMAN PRIDE

Those coming to earth will not impede our free will to think as we want to think and to believe as we want to believe. We will not need to accept *their ways* just because *they* say that *their* ways are better than our own. Nevertheless, because of the way they will come to the earth, many will want to hear what they have to say.

The "overseer" assigned to this solar system will be their spokesman. What comes out of his mouth will be like a "sharp two-edged sword." In other words, the things he will say will be taken one of two ways (thus the use of the metaphorical *two*-edged sword): a person will either rejoice in what he says, or else one's pride, ego, or self-value will be cut asunder and cause that person misery, weeping, and a constant state of frustration.

44. THE MERCHANTS AND THEIR WARES, ALONG WITH ALL MONEY, WILL LOSE THEIR VALUE

The merchants of the earth are going to wince in turmoil, because everything that they sell to make a profit will be of no worth. Although they can continue to attempt to sell their wares on the open market for money, who in their right mind is going to pay for the merchants' inferior products when far more superior advanced products provided by the newly arrived advanced beings are available *for free*?

Money will eventually become obsolete. The advanced human beings will "set up shop" and produce the wares that exist in the most advanced human worlds, free of charge. A merchant may want the antitrust and anti-monopoly laws enforced so that their products do not lose their value to unfair competition; but there will be no sheriff to deliver a summons and complaint. All military and police, and any other legal enforcement means (their weapons) used to control commerce, will be useless against these advanced beings.

When confronted with the rule of law created by *imperfect* people in an *imperfect* world, these advanced beings will respond:

> "This earth is part of the Universe. The Universal Rule of Law supersedes any law you have created upon this earth. Your judges, your lawyers, and your officers of the court and law have no jurisdiction over us. They can rule those who still desire to give them their power and authority. But they and their laws have no power over us or the rest of the Universe, or any of those here upon this earth who wish to follow us and our law."

45. IMPERFECT SYSTEMS OF JUSTICE AND PUNISHMENT WILL BE OVERRIDDEN

Because the Universal Rule of Law prohibits any person from impeding upon the free will of another, for any reason except to protect free will, any *earthly* rule of law that does not support free agency in this manner will become obsolete. The prisons will be forced open, and all the prisoners subjected to the inferior laws and their consequences created by *imperfect* humans will be released from custody.

The freed murderers, rapists, thieves, and all others who have committed crimes against the "law of the land," while in an *imperfect* world, will become subject to the Universal Rule of Law. Once released from custody, outrightly forgiven, and taught **real truth**, those who were once *abased* by the very laws that held them captive will rejoice that they are now *exalted* to the same equal level of humanity as those who put and held them in custody. The power of these advanced beings will permeate throughout the earth and will prohibit any person's free agency of being violated in any way.

46. THE ACQUIRED KNOWLEDGE OF DOCTORS, SCIENTISTS, AND HISTORIANS WILL ALL BECOME USELESS

With their knowledge and power, the advanced humans will heal all people of their infirmities, both physical and mental. These advanced beings will reveal what is done and how it is done in *perfect* human worlds. The learning and knowledge of doctors, psychologists, scientists, and researchers—even all those who have dedicated their lives to understanding the reasons why humans do what they do and why things are the way they are in this world—will become obsolete.

There will no longer be the written histories of the past. These often *false* and misstated historical documents will be replaced with actual advanced video-like footage of any event that occurred at any time on our planet. Instead of going to a library full of now-useless books containing erroneous and subjective information, the **real truth** will be available for all **to see with their own eyes**. Once seen, a person will then be left to form his or her own perception of any particular event that occurred on the earth. History will be that which each person personally perceives of any event. We will come to understand just how ridiculously useless our mortal system of education is to our *humanity* and to our ***true reality***.

47. ALL WORLDLY KNOWLEDGE WILL BECOME OBSOLETE

The kings, presidents, government heads, statesmen, judges, lawyers, doctors, scientists and the educated, even all those who "think" they have some power over others or some special knowledge that is needed by the people of the world, will groan in agony. They will realize that these advanced humans have brought with them understanding and technologies that supersede and negate everything they once thought was of value to the human race. They will soon learn that nothing—ABSOLUTELY NOTHING—that was or is produced in an *imperfect world* holds a candle to what these advanced beings bring to our earth from their *perfect worlds*.

48. WE WILL HAVE THE ABILITY TO ACCESS THE MEMORIES OF OUR PAST

The advanced technology the advanced human beings will bring includes the ability to allow a person to bypass the "veil" of the *imperfect* brain and access all of the experiences recorded on one's *essence*. We will be able to view any and all of our past experiences easier than we can view home movies stored on our current computers with a few simple clicks. With the advanced technology of what could be called "***L****ife* ***E****xperience* ***A****dvanced* ***R****etrospection* ***N****avigation* (**LEARN**)," our past life experiences will play back in our brain more vividly than any dream we currently have while asleep.

We will relive all that we did. We will have the ability, while utilizing the **LEARN** technology, to know who we were in the past, and most importantly, how we acted with our free will. Access to **LEARN** will increase our understanding of *who we are* and *why we exist*, thereby allowing us to become comfortable with our chosen *humanity type*.

49. UNCONDITIONAL UNIVERSAL EQUALITY WILL BE ESTABLISHED

All belief systems will be invalidated with *true reality*. Those who think they are special and have "gifts" they value in and of themselves, will stand embarrassed, and be emotionally punished. The emotional punishment will be twofold: 1) by the realization that they deceived themselves and 2) by the looks of disbelief and irreverence they receive from those who once believed in their imaginary special "powers" and "gifts."

The people of the earth will begin to understand how equal and fair we were all treated by our creators during the days of our probation upon this earth, and that no one had an unfair advantage in any way over another. We will see each other as equals. We will understand the equal human value between an illiterate derelict found in the dirtiest slums on earth and those who are the most educated persons of wealth, whose mansion walls are decorated with certificates and degrees of useless *imperfect world* education. We will then know just how equal we all are, even when compared to advanced human beings.

50. THE MOST POWERFUL HUMANS SERVE EVERYONE ELSE

The idea that will "cut the sharpest"—for the good of the majority and the bad of the minority—is the realization that these newly arrived advanced beings are OUR SERVANTS! The first person who attempts to honor them or give them thanks or platitudes will be met with a stern, but loving rebuke, "You were not created to serve us. We are here by our own choice to serve you."

Those who were convinced that somewhere in *human reality* there exist those with all the riches who have multitudes of servants and the power and control of the Universe, will be greatly disappointed to discover that the GREATEST AND MOST POWERFUL HUMAN BEINGS AMONG US ACT AS IF THEY ARE THE LEAST OF US ALL. They are **our** servants! We are their masters! They do what we want them to do for the sake of our happiness. They do not give us orders! They take *our* orders!

Then shall the poor rejoice! Then shall the meek rule the world! Then shall those who were once exalted above others feel belittled in the presence of those whom they once ruled, controlled and abased. Those whom they once belittled will be exalted—not over them, but equal to them. The least among all the humans of an *imperfect* world will rise up and take their place in equality and honor alongside everyone else. There will be no more "least," as there will be no more "greatest."

51. OUR OVERSEER'S ETERNAL PARTNER WILL IMPUGN ALL PREJUDICE

When our particular overseer (he who is assigned to our solar system) comes with these other advanced humans in their perfected glory as our servants, he will bring with him an example of one of the greatest ironies of *imperfect* human judgment and perception. There at his side will be a perfected woman whom the world will come to know as one who was once a mortal prostitute.

Yes, the one who became close to and bonded with this advanced human overseer during his pre-mortal life, and was picked by the overseer as his eternal partner, was once a mortal prostitute who roamed the streets in her hometown looking for someone who would pay her for sex. With this one irony, all human judgment will be relegated to the abyss of human misperception and ignorance, which was forced upon us by "moral values" established in our *imperfect world*.

Then those who once threw rocks at, arrested, and persecuted any prostitute who lived during their mortal lifetimes, will wish that the rocks would fall off the mountain tops and cover them up to hide their deep embarrassment. All those who ridiculed another for their lifestyle, their sexual orientation, or the color of their skin will be greatly uncomfortable. Anyone harboring any prejudice or insensitive judgment will feel self-conscious when they see advanced beings of all different skin tones, sexual persuasions, and personalities—all helping to turn this *imperfect world* into a *perfect one* like the one they came from.

52. WE WILL JUDGE OURSELVES

These advanced beings will not judge us. There will be no tribunal set up to try each one of us according to how we treated each other as mortals. The only judgment that will exist is our own personal judgment. Once we have finally been taught the **real truth**, we will begin to see the foolishness of our ways. The only punishment for anything that we have done with our free agency will be *the way we will perceive ourselves* and what we have done.

Those of us who once thought we could be trusted with the power and abilities of our creators will (or should by then) humbly admit that, based on our experiences while upon this earth, we *should not* be trusted with the power that they possess. In their presence, we will have the example of exactly how Solarian servants act with the power they possess. We will then more fully understand the purpose of an *imperfect world* in allowing us the opportunity to witness what Lunarians and Stellarians do with *their* free will. What they do is far different from the actions of a Solarian. We will *finally* be able to accept *who we are* and will no longer desire to be someone we are not.

53. UNIVERSAL LAW WILL CREATE THE PERFECT WORLD

Our world will be transformed into a perfect human society by advanced beings who will put our earth under the jurisdiction of Universal Law—the rule of law that exists in all other *perfect worlds* that are found throughout the Universe. All earthly governments will eventually fall. All human-made institutions that have caused us to separate from each other and form groups of intolerance and hate will fall. All prejudices and beliefs that put one person above another will fall.

Each individual person will become more precious than anything else in the Universe. Each of us will become rulers of our own individual kingdom with powerful servants to serve our every need. The Universe will once again "revolve" around each of us as it did from the moment we were first created in a *perfect world*. Each of us will see ourselves as the greatest being in the Universe—because we are!

The only source of unhappiness will come from our inability to accept who we have chosen to be. But once we have had opportunity to live in a world where there are no expectations placed on us of who we *should* be, we will be able to accept ourselves for who we *really* are. Once self-actualized, we will be happy with *who we are* and will be forever content with who we have chosen to be.

SUMMARY

Living in a *perfect world* with an *imperfect body* is a vital step towards our self-actualization. We experienced life in a *perfect world* with a *perfect body*, but we had no substantial realization of what "perfect" actually meant.

Living in an *imperfect world* with an *imperfect body* gives us the comparative experience that we need to appreciate all there is about being human. **We can thereby know what "perfect" means!** Human beings in their most advanced form are *perfect*. We will always be—as other humans like us have always been—the most *perfect* life form in the Universe.

Although it is very hard to be convinced of our *perfection* based on our experiences in this *imperfect world*, once we gain the experience of living in a *perfect world* with an *imperfect body*, we will finally have no doubt about it.

Everything that transpires in our personal Universe is to help us gain a better appreciation of our individual human existence. We have about another 135 earth years to figure out just how *perfect* we can be and begin to reflect *who we truly are* in our actions. If we have not done it by then, those who are very much like us, but who have already been convinced of the benefits of *human perfection*, will return to our solar system, intervene into our lives, and help us come to the same realization that they have:

ALL HUMAN BEINGS ARE EQUAL AND ARE THE PERFECT AND ULTIMATE LIFE FORM IN THE UNIVERSE!

Making the Future a Reality Today

CHAPTER EIGHTEEN

I am a citizen of the world.

—Diogenes Laertius

1. WE NEED THE LESSONS OF AN IMPERFECT LIFE TO PROGRESS

The purpose of any lesson is to gain some useful knowledge, sense, or other learning during a particular, structured time period. A lesson is valuable when it teaches something not previously understood or accepted. The best lessons often come from direct experience.

The lessons we needed to learn during an *imperfect* mortality (the second stage of human development) have been outlined throughout this book. We needed the direct experience of an *imperfect world* that would allow us to experience the opposite of all things that exist in a *perfect* one. We needed to experience what would happen if left to ourselves in control of our body and our surrounding environment. To enhance the experience, we were allowed unconditional free will and similar, but restricted, powers that advanced human beings possess. Besides the ability to dominate our environment and use it according to our free will, we were given the power to create other *imperfect* human beings by enjoying the physical sensations of sex.

We needed an effective lesson presented in the appropriate learning atmosphere to help us understand why very few of us would use our power and free will as our advanced creators do—in the service of others. In the primordial world, where we were first created and lived as advanced humans, we struggled to understand and accept this universal fact of human life. If we gain the knowledge or sense of that which we did not previously understand or accept, then the lesson has been successful and "schooling" is no longer needed.

2. WE LEARN VALUABLE LESSONS BY ATTENDING THE "SCHOOL OF LIFE"

The "school" that we attend where important human-based lessons are taught is known as *mortality* in an *imperfect world*. This is an existence where we have forgotten what we learned before attending our first day of school; or rather, we are not allowed to have a direct recollection of anything outside of the immediate "school yard." It was intended for us to use all of our faculties and energy in studying and learning what is taught during school. Without being concerned for what happens outside of school, we are in a better position to learn the lessons and repeat them over and over and over again until we learn what was intended from the lesson.

What we learn from experiencing the same lesson repeatedly impacts our ability to understand and accept the intended purpose for the lesson. As mentioned previously, each of us acts according to our *humanity type*, regardless of how many times our *essence* is in a mortal body. Each time we attend "school," we follow the same course of study and always achieve the exact same grade on the lessons we are given. In other words, no matter how many times we have lived upon this earth, each of us responds to our surrounding environment similar to the way we would respond in all of our incarnations under the same circumstances. Our circumstances, however, change during each new life. These changing circumstances provide us with many different lessons. A wide variety of different lessons reinforces the overall purpose for which we attend "school." Regardless of our different circumstances, we will always act according to our *humanity type*. The vital lesson that was intended to be learned from our placement in this *imperfect world* is:

WE ARE WHO WE ARE! And it is okay to be *who we are*.

3. OUR ADVANCED TEACHERS MAKE SURE ALL OF US GRADUATE

The curriculum and lesson plans used to teach us the lessons we need were prepared and are given to us by advanced teachers. These *unseen* instructors have already attended the *same school* and received the appropriate grades that allowed them to become "school teachers." They know what they are doing. They've taught numberless classes of different "student bodies" for eons of time. They know what scholastic environment and curriculum is necessary for each individual student.

Their failure rate at teaching the students what they need to learn is 0%. The teachers have a perfect record and guarantee graduation. Every student graduates who chooses to accept the diploma, as promised at the beginning of school. The "diploma" is: continued and everlasting life residing as a human being in our own individual part of the Universe. It is the guarantee that each of us will have the ability and unlimited resources to pursue our individual desires of happiness in a *perfect* human environment. Although we all have the opportunity to graduate and receive the diploma, there is the possibility that a few will not be willing to agree to certain conditions of their personal humanity and refuse to accept their diploma. (This has already been touched upon and will be further explained later.)

4. WE CAN PASS THE FINAL TEST ANY TIME WE ARE READY

The way that the **real** "school of life" is set up is different from the *imperfect* schools set up by *unaccredited* and *unqualified* teachers and professors tenured in teaching useless, *imperfect* curriculum. (As explained throughout this book, nothing we learn in this *imperfect world*, except for what we learn from the experience of it, is of any use to an advanced human being living in a *perfect world*—ABSOLUTELY NOTHING!)

In our *imperfect* schools, we are *forced* to follow the prerequisites and requirements of specified "credit hours" in order to obtain a degree or diploma. But in the "school of life," where *true reality* is the only course of study, students will be ready to graduate and receive their diploma whenever they have learned the overall vital lesson intended by life's schooling. At any point during the course of study, the students can demonstrate their aptitude of understanding by taking a "final test" to see if they have gained the knowledge expected from the lessons. If they pass the test, then school is adjourned and we are finally *sent home* to enjoy all that we have learned.

5. IF WE CAN'T PASS THE TEST, WE WILL BE GIVEN THE ANSWERS

The last section of the "Teachers' Handbook" on how to present the lessons of life instructs the teachers to come to the earth and *give us* the answers to the test, if we fail to learn them on our own. They will do this when they can see that the students have failed to learn from their lessons and instruction—no matter how much patience was shown and how many times the lessons were given during class time.

Keep in mind, it is intended that everyone graduates who attends the "school of life." Therefore, if we don't learn the lessons by ourselves that prepare us for graduation, then the advanced teachers are required to GIVE US THE ANSWERS TO THE TEST! (This way, they can maintain their success rate of 100 percent.) Whether we like their answers or not, we must accept that the answers are correct and a true reflection of the vital lesson intended for our life upon earth. We must accept **WHO WE ARE**.

6. THE FINAL TEST ENSURES THAT WE RECEIVED A COMPLETE EDUCATION

The test of the "School of Life" covers the lessons we are supposed to learn during our time in mortality. The three main sections of the test are as follows:

- **WHAT APPRECIATION OF HUMAN EXISTENCE DID WE GAIN FROM THE LESSONS OF LIFE?**

- **WHAT DID WE DO WITH OUR UNCONDITIONAL FREE AGENCY?**

- **DO WE UNDERSTAND AND ARE WE COMFORTABLE WITH OUR CHOSEN HUMANITY TYPE AND ANY ATTACHED RESTRICTIONS?**

7. THE SCORE WE RECEIVE ON THE TEST IS OUR PERSONAL HUMANITY TYPE

There are many *subsections* (different experiences we go through during mortality) to these three main *sections* of the test. Each subsection has many multiple-choice questions with only three possible answers, **all of which are correct**! Each multiple-choice question pertains to a different *humanity type.* If we answer the questions honestly, we will pass the test of our humanity. The score we receive is the *humanity type* that pertains to each of us. *The test **proves** who we are.*

The test seems reasonably simple and straightforward. It's impossible to fail! One would think that if all the students just answered the questions honestly, then there would be no purpose in continuing to attend school. But, even before we attended our first day of school, we were shown the test and all of the questions. Nevertheless, none of us could answer any of them honestly, because we hadn't yet received any of the lessons that would teach us the correct answer. In other words, each of us chose our individual *humanity type* and the parameters and restrictions of each. But we were still not convinced of why we shouldn't be trusted with the advanced powers of the Solarian (service-oriented) humanity type. Each of us thought,

"Though others might misuse the power, surely **I** would never!"

We hadn't yet had the experience of being allowed this power; therefore, we couldn't answer if indeed the *humanity type* we had chosen for ourselves was going to satisfy us forever.

Even so, after going through thousands of years of mortal schooling, most of us, if given the test during school, would still be susceptible to cheating. How could we cheat on a test where there are no incorrect answers? We cheat by not being honest with ourselves and choosing an answer that is *not* what we learned from our lessons in life. If we cheat, the advanced instructors who grade the test will know, because they know each of us and have a record of how we answered the questions when the lessons were given to us during classroom instruction.

8. WE CANNOT CHEAT ON THE FINAL TEST

To properly understand the above analogy of the "school of life," it is necessary to again reiterate what we have already discussed as to the content of the "test": None of us wants to give up the option of unlimited human power to control the elements at will; and none of us wants to give up sex. It is part of our basic human nature to believe that we can be entrusted with *anything* that any other equal human being can.

In being denied these ultimate human powers, we may think that, because we are being told that we are not trustworthy, it must follow that we are unequal to others who *can* be trusted. Although this is not the *real truth,* and is diametrically opposed to the Law of Equality, even sensing the *possibility* of human inequality causes us to experience confusion, because such inequality is diametrically opposed to our *human foundationalization*.

Yet, we know that if we don't mark the answers to the questions on the test that correspond to a Solarian-creator humanity type (those who serve others), we will never have these abilities. Therefore, it's our mortal human nature to want to cheat and mark the answer that corresponds to the *humanity type* that we would *prefer*, rather than the one *who we really are*. Nevertheless, it is impossible to cheat on the test when each student taking it has an advanced instructor who knows which answer is the honest one and is standing over the student and is watching every answer that is marked.

While going through mortality, however, none of us will know with absolute certainty which *humanity type* best suits our individual desires for happiness. There are too many different parameters and variables to consider when analyzing each of the choices we make as we are confronted with different situations during mortality. For example, a Solarian *humanity type* would never feel comfortable protecting his or her own interests when the interests of others are threatened. But because the person is unaware of his or her true *humanity type* while mortal, the choice each makes might be completely different from the choice he or she *might have made* if everything involved in the presented situation were completely understood.

9. TOGETHER, WE CAN ALL GRADUATE EARLY

As mentioned before, if we do not answer the questions honestly, or if we are stuck on one because we do not want to admit to the correct answer, our advanced instructors will eventually give us the correct answers. At any time during the "school year," we can ask to take the final test; and if we answer it honestly, we can end the rigors and daily grind of attending school. The only thing that prevents us from doing this is our free will.

There is one catch to ending school early: WE MUST ALL DO IT TOGETHER. No one in our "graduating class" can be left behind. As a group, we must be willing to take the final test together and answer the questions honestly. We can do this by helping each other learn the lessons.

We can study together and set up a schoolroom atmosphere that allows even the slowest learner to understand the answers to the questions. In other words, together, we must set up a world in which we are able to explore *who we are.* We must help each other find our individuality, so that we can be happy with whom we have chosen to be. As discussed previously, we presently cannot explore our individuality, because we are required to use all of our energy being concerned about our basic necessities, our personal security, and the expectations the world has placed on us.

There are, however, some who belong to our "group" who have already unconditionally accepted their humanity type. They have received their *perfect* body and reside on a planet in a solar system close to our own. These few have unfinished work that they started when they were among us as mortals. But, for a purpose specifically designed to help the rest of us prepare for graduation, they did not complete their work while among us. Their work was not finished while they were mortal because the final phase of their specific work extended beyond their time in an *imperfect* body.

These are some of the "selected ones" discussed earlier, who are now ready for "graduation" and have received their perfect body in order to help the rest of us become ready. They are also part of our "group," or batch of children, and will continue to help us unseen, as do our advanced creators. Because they do not want to be worshipped or seen as in any way unequal to the rest of us, they do not make themselves known. They work only through other *mortal* "selected ones" for the sake of all of us equally.

10. GRADUATION REQUIRES PROPER HUMANITY

One of the main purposes for this book is to help unify us, and to inspire us as a group (which includes all human beings upon earth) to stand up and proclaim that we are ready to take the final test and answer the questions honestly, thereby ending school. In other words, if we learn the lessons intended for us by our creators, we would transform our world into one of peace and security, wherein happiness is no longer a pursuit, but rather a guarantee. If we can do this together, then we do not need to wait for advanced beings to do it for us. We can end this *imperfect world* earlier than expected and as outlined in our creators' plan for this solar system.

We can cut the purpose of this life short by doing what our creators would do if they were here. To do this, we must prove our *true* humanity. Our "true humanity" is the concept of absolute equality and the ability to exercise unconditional free will (restricted only when our free will inhibits another's), which we were taught during our *Foundationalization Process* in our primordial world. We must prove that we can be trusted to exist peacefully with each other and to treat each and every human being with respect and equality. And we must prove that we can do it without being coerced by the presence of advanced human beings, whom we would want to emulate just because they're more "advanced" than we are. We must all be willing to take the final test on our own!

11. THE RIGHT ATMOSPHERE FOR LEARNING THE LESSONS

The first thing we have to do to "graduate early" is to set up an atmosphere of learning, where each of us can equally focus all of our concentration on our lessons instead of on our physical struggle to survive. Once the appropriate learning environment is set up, the lessons we learn will lead us to self-actualization, or knowing *who we are*. This will then afford us the opportunity to live according to our individual desires of happiness.

This "atmosphere" requires that we unite as a world and break down the nations and borders, races and cultures, and belief systems and opinions that divide us and isolate us from each other. If we cannot unite and help each other amicably, we will never be able to answer the questions on the test correctly. Consequently, we will need to wait for our *instructors* to give us the answers.

12. THE WAY WE TREAT EACH OTHER PROVES THAT WE ARE NOT READY

Most human beings are prejudiced by their *imperfect* ***mortal*** *foundationalization*. We do not know how to respect every human being as our equal. Fear keeps us chained to foundationalized prejudices against others and causes us to mistreat each other. We care only about ourselves and those whom we love (those who bring value to us).

Our mortal security lies in the prejudices that create the familial and friendship bonds and in the resources of the earth (i.e., money) that support these bonds. If our family and loved ones are secure, then our personal value is also safe and protected. Everyone else on earth becomes a possible threat to our security. This causes us to become apathetic towards the plight of other human beings living outside of the high walls of our secure emotional and often physical fortresses. We do not allow the poverty and insecurity of other people to affect our emotional state.

We have been conditioned by our prejudices to ignore what happens to anyone else outside of those who give us our personal value and security. We have allowed ourselves to justify human devaluation because of individual aggrandizement. We are currently failing the test of our *true* humanity. We are not acting as we know we should, as aligned in our *essence*. But, as has been discussed earlier, our failure is actually our success in realizing that most of us are incapable of being the *humanity type* who gains lasting personal peace and happiness by serving others.

13. OUR LEADERS ARE KEEPING US FROM OUR LESSONS

Up to this point of time in this *imperfect world*, we have failed to establish lasting peace and happiness. We are all capable of doing this by conforming our actions to the *foundationalized* experiences recorded in our *essences*, which created our *humanity* in the beginning. But, because we have denied our own humanity for so long, we can see how hard it would be to now unite and change our world. We see the apparent futility in attempting to transform our world into one where our *only* pursuit is our sense and knowledge of our own individuality (which futility is a vital lesson we need to learn). We've placed the ability to self-actualize far behind the constant need to conform to the expectations of our *imperfect world.*

The leaders who hold power over us physically and emotionally, or rather, those who **we allow** to hold power over us, stand in our way. Because our political leaders have power over us through their means of weaponry, we cannot rise up as a unified group and physically take our power back. It takes only a few soldiers who have "sold their humanity for money," and who know how to use the current technology of weaponry, to subdue millions of people. Furthermore, if we use the sword to get rid of the sword, it will only lead to continual bloodshed. Therefore, although we cannot realistically take back the control that our governments hold over us physically, we **can** unite and free ourselves from the emotional control we have allowed them to have over us. And we **can** stand united in emotional power to persuade, **even demand,** our governments to change their course.

14. OUR DIFFERING BELIEF SYSTEMS KEEP US FROM PASSING THE TEST

This physical and emotional control over us by our leaders was obtained (and is sustained) by "inspiring" us with the divisive feelings of patriotism and territorialism towards the differing nations and cultures in which we are divided. This control, however, is also sustained by taking advantage of belief systems that shape our values, affect our emotions, and regulate how we treat each other.

Even if we were all of the same nation and culture, we would still judge each other according to the belief systems that indoctrinate our minds and establish our personal prejudices. We would still treat those of varying belief systems differently than those who belong to our own accepted "group." We would still trade the right to free will and individual expression for the restrictive parameters set by the leaders of these belief systems, and to whom we have given power over our *true* humanity. These leaders take advantage of our *true humanity* for their own personal gain and cause us to become like them.

15. WE ARE BEING GIVEN THE INFORMATION WE NEED TO PASS THE TEST

This book, *HUMAN REALITY—Who We Are and Why We Exist*, is intended to help us regain the emotional power we have lost to our national patriotism and to the belief systems that keep us isolated and separated from each other. Throughout these pages, it has been explained that we are all **equal** in the eyes of our creators. It has been revealed that our patriotic perceptions and belief systems are **not real truth**. It has been explained that in the *perfect*, *advanced* human world, no institutions or powers exist that confine our humanity inside borders of any kind (physical or emotional). No national borders promote logistic separation of the human race. No emotional borders restrict our right to exercise our free will according to the dictates of our own conscience, as long as what we do does not inhibit the free will of another.

It has also been revealed that those who are responsible for our existence (i.e., our advanced creators/parents) are not our leaders, **but our servants**. We were created so that we might experience the same sense of complete happiness that all advanced humans experience throughout the Universe. It is our creators' responsibility to assure us this happiness. In fine, it has been explained that everything about our *imperfect world* is OPPOSITE to that *perfect world*, and thus IMPERFECT!

16. THE REAL TRUTH SETS US FREE TO FINALLY LEARN WHAT WE NEED TO LEARN

Because of the **real truth** that has been given throughout this book, we no longer have to remain shackled with the vain and foolish chains of ignorance, prejudice, and inequality by which our leaders have us bound. The **real truth** is the **key** to the lock that holds these chains securely around us. We must use this "key" to unlock the lock, remove the chains, and set ourselves free! If we cannot set ourselves free, it is because we refuse to recognize the "key" for what it is and use it to unlock the chains that bind us. It is because we refuse to acknowledge the **real truth**. If this is the case, then we must wait for the arrival of those who have the "key" to the lock.

If we cannot do it ourselves, advanced human beings will one day arrive and free us from our chains. And when we are free, oh how great will be our joy! When they arrive, they will take the key and unlock our chains. And with the lock and chain in hand, they will lay hold upon human ignorance, prejudice, and inequality and bind up everything that is contrary to *true humanity* and lock it up forever.

17. WE CAN SOLVE THE PROBLEMS OF HUMANITY

If we choose to use the "key" of **real truth** and unlock the chains to *set ourselves free*, we can then do what is necessary to transform this world by ourselves, without the intervention of advanced human beings. If we accomplish this feat, we will have demonstrated the incredible power of our own humanity and proven the power of our own free will, which is the power of advanced human beings. We would, thereby, advance our humanity!

From this accomplishment, we would develop a sense of self-esteem and self-appreciation that is vital to a proper understanding of *who we are*. Alone (as the human race), we would correctly answer the questions of the "final test" that have been given in the "school of life." And we could rest assured that the advanced human beings who created our solar system would show up—not to embarrass us because of our ignorance, but to embrace us and congratulate us for doing what very few "graduating classes" of other solar systems have ever done.

18. OTHER WORLDS HAVE PASSED THE TEST EARLY

There have been some (a very small percentage of) human beings who have gone through their second stage of development in an *imperfect* world, and have been able to establish lasting peace and happiness before more advanced beings interceded to show them the way. These passed the test before the answers were given to them! They ended poverty and inequality among themselves and helped each other self-actualize. At about the same time in their own transitional stage (as our current time), when technology was introduced and allowed upon their own "earth," they were in a position to do what needed to be done—and they did it! We are now in the same position. We have no excuse for our failure because it **has been done** before!

Because every other "graduating class" of every other solar system in the Universe was given the instructions on how to set up the proper learning environment so that all students could graduate early, we are now being given, as set forth below, what we need to do on our own earth at this time. We will not be left with the excuse of, "Oh, if only we would have known what to do!"

WE ARE NOW BEING TOLD!
HERE IS WHAT WE ARE BEING TOLD:

19. TECHNOLOGY CAN SUPPORT US IN OUR "STUDIES"

We must utilize the technology available to us to provide the basic necessities of life to all human beings equally. We must make sure that all students have enough nutritious food so that they can study properly. We must ensure that all wear the proper school uniform (clothing) so they don't have to come to school appearing unequal to everyone else. We must ensure that all students have a safe, warm, clean home to return to after school, where they can do their homework. We must make sure that if a student gets sick or has an accident, he or she is cared for promptly and properly. We must provide all of these things without affecting the natural balance of our environment. And in doing all of this, we must maintain and protect everyone's free will!

20. IF WE DON'T SUPPORT HUMANITY, IT WILL CONTINUE TO DISINTEGRATE

Some might suggest that this utopian, idealistic proposal is impossible in our current world. These "some" are unequivocally WRONG! Not only can we do it, we can do it in a matter of just a few years! We can do it without disrupting the free market, or rather, the free will of those who want to make a profit and enrich themselves. In fact, we can help those who have a right to their free will and want to be wealthy, become even wealthier, simply by supporting the proposal! We can do it without introducing major changes into the way our world currently operates. And if we DON'T DO IT, our world will disintegrate further and further into a state of turmoil, depression, uproar, and chaos, unlike during any other time in the history of our *imperfect world*.

21. HERE IS HOW WE CAN DO IT!

We can do it! HERE'S HOW:

(NOTE: The following descriptions are outlines of specific programs and named [with acronyms] for each purpose, as might be found in the United States, where the plan could be most immediately established and implemented. There is much more to each program than what is presented herein. By using common sense, the reader will be able to ascertain other important needed aspects of each of the following programs, which are needed to implement them both in America and throughout the world.)

I. FOOD

To provide food to everyone, give every human being "FOOD AUTHORIZATION CREDITS for EVERYONE" (FACE). These credits are stored on cards and will be accepted at any grocery store or food outlet anywhere in the world. However, they *will not* allow an individual to purchase anything but **good**, **nutritious** food.

A worldwide commission will be established that consists of the world's top health and nutrition officials. This commission will authorize which foods can be acquired with the FACE card. Nothing that causes the human body any harm will be acceptable; this means no soft drinks, no processed foods, no candy, and no deserts—nothing that negatively affects a healthy body. If a person wants other foods that are not purchasable with the FACE card, that person must go to work and earn the money to buy what he or she desires.

The FACE Service (FACES) will be responsible for the quality and safety of the food it authorizes. It will oversee quality inspectors, whose primary job will be to inspect the production of all of the food that is authorized.

Here's an example. A farmer who wants to grow a food product that is acceptable for the FACE program must apply to FACES to get the product approved. An inspector will visit the farm and inspect the means of production and the quality of the product. If it does not meet FACES standards, the farmer's application will be denied. The inspectors will ensure safety and quality from the farm, to the grocery outlet, to the mouth of the consumer.

Any packaged product manufactured by any company will have to go through the same strict approval process. To avoid commissioner or inspector fraud and corruption (possibly by the acceptance of a "kickback payment" to encourage the approval of a particular product), any violation of FACES rules will be viewed as a *crime against humanity* and punished appropriately. Both FACES commissioners and inspectors will be compensated sufficiently to make their job a suitable career choice for which the most educated people will compete.

The FACE will also be accepted at any *authorized* buffet restaurant, for those who do not have the desire or ability to prepare food. The card will authorize a daily purchase amount. These authorized restaurants will be inspected and approved based on the quality of the food they offer, which must also be nutritious. After meeting this threshold standard, competition among restaurant entrepreneurs will lead to contests, in effect, to see who will have the best tasting food and most inviting atmosphere in which to entice those with FACE cards to dine.

Using current market trends for buffet-type restaurants as an example, one spends about US$10 dollars for an all-you-can-eat meal. These restaurants are obviously making a profit in offering a meal for that price, and compete among the several restaurant chains to gain customers. Because their customer base will expand significantly once the FACE program is in place, there will be greater competition to offer the most nutritious foods and to win the FACES' contract.

The same scenario of competition will exist among the other food producers who ship their products to grocery outlets. The rules that govern FACES will not allow monopolization by any one company. The one who offers the **best** food at the **best** price will get the authorization. Authorizing any particular food or restaurant will be as simple as a few key strokes on the FACES' central computer, similar to how credit card companies typically monitor the use of credit cards.

With the increased competition to create a business that produces food products and services that meet FACES' approval, the quality and presentation of nutritious food will increase significantly through free market competition. The food producers will continue to be paid by the food retailers just as they are in our current free markets. The food retailers who are authorized to accept the FACE card will be reimbursed similar to the way that the United States Department of Agriculture (USDA) reimburses the retailers who accept its Food Stamps. The USDA food stamp program is a practical example of how the FACE program would work (although not allowing non-nutritious foods to be purchased).

Because we are accustomed to eating what we want, when we want, and because we can only purchase good, nutritious foods on this plan, the **incentive to work will increase**. Those who choose not to work will only be eating the foods that will ultimately increase their overall physical health. No longer will a person with integrity hold a sign that reads, "Will Work For Food." If one *does* hold such a sign, there will be no remorse felt by the rest of us in passing by without giving up our money.

Additionally, no one can abuse the FACE program by purchasing too much food and trying to sell it for money. Those to whom one might sell the food will exclaim, "*Why should I pay you money for food that I can get free just like you did*?"

There will be no extensive application process or monitoring of personal means and finances to obtain a FACE card. If you are a human being, you get a card! If you are rich or poor, you get a card! The money that a person would usually spend on food will be redirected into purchases that support a free-market economy. A person who utilizes FACE will have more money to buy other things that support their individuality.

Because our current economy is already a worldwide conglomerate, where the economic structure of one nation directly affects that of all other countries, it would not be hard to implement the FACE program throughout the world. If food retailers knew that 5 million starving Africans were going to be carrying their own FACE card, they would scramble to set up their businesses for profit in Africa, thereby hastening the process for these people to start using their cards. In time, the world's food production would increase, not only to match the quality and nutrition levels set by FACES, but by the demands of the card-carrying people. Food production and retail grocery stores and restaurants would replace weapons manufacturing as the number one profitable business in the world. Just imagine that!

(NOTE: Before explaining how the FACE program will be financed, the other programs that will offer us the other basic necessities will first be discussed. When the other programs have been presented, it will then be shown in detail where the money is going to come from to finance them. It is important to mention this because most readers' minds are going to be prejudiced by the question of "money." One must continue to read on with an open mind and first learn about the other programs. The reader can be assured that the "money" to implement all of these programs is available, once a proper understanding of the concept of "money," how it is created, and how it is controlled is considered. Read on with a "hope" that we can do these things and that you [the reader] will grasp a greater understanding of this than if your mind remains closed because of the *imperfection* of your current experience. We **do** have the ability to *perfect* our experience!)

II. SHELTER

Each person will be given a "HOUSING ASSISTANCE VOUCHER for EVERYONE" (HAVE). This voucher will be used to rent a HAVE Service (HAVES)-approved residence. The voucher can also be used for long-term payments of motel or hotel accommodations, in the case of an emergency housing need.

The government will reimburse the landlord, corporate property management company, or hotel and motel chain according to the average rent of any particular area. The owners of the properties must obtain HAVES preapproval before a HAVE will be honored. HAVES inspectors will ensure that the property is safe for residency.

This program will be very similar to the U.S. Department of Housing and Urban Development's Section 8 program—the differences being that everyone who wants a voucher will receive one; and the voucher will pay 100% of the market rent instead of a set amount based on the income of the person. The size of the rental unit will also help determine the rental amount.

Families with children will need only one voucher (HAVE) per family. The amount approved will depend on the number of children under the age of 18 years, and will also depend upon the number of bedrooms required. Once a person reaches the age of 18, he or she will be eligible for his or her own HAVE. A property owner will only receive **one** HAVE per rental unit, regardless of how many adults and children live there. Because the owner must pre-approve their renters, they can make restrictions on the occupancy according to their maintenance needs.

HAVES inspectors will be the main employees of this program. They will be trained to inspect residences and ensure safety. Only upon their approval will a property owner be approved to receive reimbursement of a HAVE voucher. Each residence will be inspected annually. The people who utilize the HAVE program will also be able to contact an inspector if any violation by property owners arises. The property owner can also evict any tenant for violation of applicable landlord/tenant laws.

Property owners are guaranteed payment for each voucher (HAVE) they receive for the rental of their property. Strict criminal penalties will be enforced to discourage fraud. If convicted of any HAVES' rule violation, the property owner will be banned from the program for a set time period, or continually, according to the severity of the violation.

The HAVE assistance program will help people find homes in the area in which they wish to reside, and will also assist property owners with any of their problems. The renters will be responsible for the proper upkeep and care of the residence. Those who continually violate general rules of reasonable care of the property will be penalized. These penalties will include being remanded to "Managed Family Facilities," where a family will be able to live, but will have their freedom restricted until they learn how to properly care for property. These Managed Family Facilities will be set up for instruction rather than punishment. However, those who cannot be trusted to take care of HAVES-subsidized homes, and have repeatedly proven their unwillingness to do so, will be *forced* to live in these secure, structured, and managed facilities.

Each home will be allotted a certain number of HAVES energy credits, which will provide the residence with electricity and gas, depending on the rental unit's size and the number of people residing in the unit. The property owners will be responsible for garbage disposal, sewer, and water. Compensation for these basic utilities will be included in the acceptable market value of the rental property, set by the owner and approved by a HAVES' inspector.

The HAVES program can be used to acquire ownership of any property. If a person wishes to own their own home, they must participate in the free market system. However, by utilizing HAVES, a young couple, for example, will be able to save for a substantial down payment on their own home. If the couple chooses to utilize the HAVE program until they have saved enough money to buy their own home outright, that will be their choice.

The free market will flourish, because people will be spending the money they would normally have to spend for housing, on other things. Construction companies and land developers will rush to build HAVES-approved housing, because they will know that the rent is guaranteed. Competition between companies will lead to better quality housing for everyone, because the people get to **choose** where they live. If a person is living in an approved HAVES residence and a better one is built elsewhere, nothing will prohibit the person from moving to the better unit.

Engineers, architects, and developers will bid on the major contracts needed to house the people of the world (just as they did to develop the vast city of Las Vegas, Nevada, USA, in the middle of the desert)! Technology will support the development of quality housing anywhere in the world. Wherever there are people who need a home, they will have one through the HAVE program. And when the people have the means to pay for their own privately owned home, others will willingly take their money for a personal profit by providing them with one.

III. HEALTH CARE

"HEALTH and UNIVERSAL MEDICAL ASSISTANCE NEEDS for EVERYONE SERVICE" (HUMANES) (similar to the U.S. Medicare/Medicaid systems) will provide physical and mental health care for everyone. Through the HUMANES program, people will choose their own doctor, hospital, dentist, pharmacist, psychologist, therapist, etc., according to their personal needs and wants.

The best doctors and the best hospitals will see the most patients; therefore, **they will make the most money**. HUMANES will appoint a commission to determine the proper amount to compensate health care providers for their services. HUMANES will ensure that anyone who provides good health care will be compensated **very well** for their services.

Nothing is more valuable to a well-fed, well-housed, well-clothed person than their health. Therefore, health care providers will be compensated sufficiently to affect the most efficient and advanced health care for all people. Again, people get to *choose* who their doctor is or which hospital they wish to go to for treatment, without restrictions. Health care providers will be drawn into the forefront of free market competition. No other government-backed career will earn more than health care professionals, thus enticing those who want to become wealthy with an incentive and the means to do so.

Each person will have a HUMANE card that will identify the person and have his or her medical records encrypted upon a microchip in their personal card. No matter where one chooses to go, they will have their medical records with them. A Universal Medical Database will be established that has a complete record of everyone's medical records and history. If someone loses their card, their medical information will be readily available. Of course, all of this will be strictly confidential. A simple swab of the mouth, a fingerprint, or an iris scan will access any human being's medical records.

HUMANES commissioners can oversee the health care that is provided for any individual. With a centralized database, the ability for health care providers to cheat the system will be eliminated. These commissioners will decide what medical, pharmaceutical, dental, and mental health services will be universally provided to ensure the health and welfare of all people equally.

HUMANES will not pay for unnecessary medical attention such as cosmetic surgery or other non-essential services that do not pertain to the general health of the individual. However, cosmetic surgery reconstruction for natural deformities or those caused by accidents will be covered; those pertaining to the vanity of the individual will not.

Any abuse of the HUMANES program will be considered a *crime against humanity* and punishable according to the severity of the crime. Some current health care providers overbill and charge for unseen patients. If a health care provider is convicted of HUMANES abuse, they will lose their ability to participate in the program and be subject to other criminal penalties.

People will not be able to abuse the program because the covered procedures will be understood and outlined specifically for them. In fact, if the above FACE program is in effect, most people will be eating a lot healthier, thus limiting their need for general health care at all. The money alone saved in not allowing the purchase of "junk food" (as is currently the case with the food stamp program), and the resulting beneficial effects on the body, will be enough to pay for the health care professionals who want to get rich providing health care to others.

The viability of the HUMANES program comes from the desire of health care professionals to be compensated properly for their services. When they know they are going to be valued and compensated according to their needs and wants, they will do whatever it takes to provide quality health care. Some will continue to desire participation in the program for the sake of caring for the wellbeing of the people of the world. But, as current human nature is, the better the pay, the better the care. Again, the way HUMANES will be set up will result in competition, which creates quality in a free market system.

IV. CLOTHING

Most people living in civilized communities and countries of the world have closets full of extra clothing. CLOTHING ASSISTANCE RESOURCES for EVERYONE SERVICE (CARES) will be set up to provide clothing to anyone in need. Used clothing receptacles will be placed in the communities of the world, where people can deposit their unwanted clothing. CARES will establish a way to collect this clothing, wash it, and place it in CARES distribution facilities throughout the earth, where the clothing will be free of charge to anyone needing it. If any clothing is not obtained within a period of one year, it will be sent to a CARES recycling center that will recycle the clothing into other products that are in demand in the free market system. The recycled clothing will eventually make enough money to pay for the rest of CARES needs.

V. EDUCATION

EDUCATION and QUALITY UNIVERSAL ASSISTANCE for LEARNING (EQUAL) will be available to all human beings free of charge. No government can place a value on education. It should be available to all people of the world equally. However, the requirements for graduation can be enhanced and improved by making it difficult for a person to gain a certificate or degree in any particular field, to ensure that these degrees are not misused.

For example, those who wish to become a doctor will be required to comply with a strict regimen of medical school education that will ensure quality doctors. Because medical school will be free to anyone wishing to attend, the importance of receiving a degree will be restrictive and left for those with sincere intent, thus ensuring quality medical professionals.

Because education will be free, the pool of human intellect will grow. This will create competition between the schools and a greater quality of educated people. Most importantly, each human being will be allowed to learn those unique things that support his or her own individuality. People will finally be left with no excuse as to why they did not receive an appropriate education with an emphasis on their personal elective field.

Nevertheless, those who do not desire to go through the regiment of strict educational requirements needed to obtain a degree will not have to. Because their basic human needs will be provided for, they can go to school, or not, depending on what makes them happy.

It has been explained that everything we have learned up to this point in our existence upon this earth has nothing to do with an advanced, *perfect*, human world. However, we are still living in *imperfection* and are subjected to the lessons of this world. Whatever we want to learn about *imperfection* will aid us in the final resolution of understanding the comparative values between *perfection* and *imperfection*. Therefore, we should be encouraged and supported in learning all we would like to know about our mortal world.

School administrators, professors, and teachers will be paid appropriately according to current free market trends. Although these service providers are not as necessary to basic human physical needs as health care providers are, they *are* important for the emotional state of human beings living in a free market world. They should be compensated based on their ability to retain students in their classrooms. Because education will be free, schools will be in competition to hire the best teachers that will attract the most students. Schools will have to offer the classes that the students want. The demand for education will create the supply in education as it does in all other aspects of a free market economy.

Private schools will remain under private, for-profit management. They will be paid much as they are in the current U.S.

Public School System. If an educational entrepreneur wants to establish a school that will attract students and provide educational disciplines that meet EQUAL guidelines, then let them compete with those thus established. Daily attendance will be tracked and schools will be paid based on student attendance. Students will have an "Education Card," much like a credit card, that can be used to pay for their education. Any abuse of EQUAL by school administrators or teachers will result in the charge of a crime against humanity, and be appropriately punished.

VI. THE WAY TO PAY FOR FACES, HAVES, HUMANES, CARES and EQUALS IS EASY

How will we pay for these programs? It's all about MONEY!

We are the ones who establish the abstract values we have place on each other and on the resources of the earth. We control how much money is printed to represent these values. We can print as much money as is necessary to support the value of human life. We can assign a number (a value) to anything we want. The more money that is made available, the more chance there is that it will be spread proportionately among the people of the earth according to their *wants*—as their *needs* will already be provided for.

An **International Anti-Inflation Law** (I.A.L.) will be established. This will be vital so that the printed money will be able to stabilize the markets and spread throughout the people of the earth. The governments of the world can implement anti-inflationary rules by which all nations must abide. The laws will (and should) allow a person to become wealthy by making a profit on the product or service they provide to the world within the free market, but with restrictions.

Anti-inflationary laws will not inhibit a person from making a profit, but will prolong the time by which one can create that profit. For example, if the I.A.L. allows only 1% inflation per year, a company can only raise their prices 1% each year. Because we now have a worldwide economy (hypothetically under these proposals), every other company is under the same price controls. This creates a fair advantage for a company that presently can only raise its prices by 1% while its suppliers and manufacturers are allowed to increase their prices at a greater percentage. The profit will come in the *demand* that the company creates for its products and services.

---

22. HAVING OUR NEEDS PROVIDED FOR WILL IMPROVE HUMAN LIFE

The implementation of FACE, HAVE, HUMANE, CARE and EQUAL will eliminate the need for unions or other protective measures currently used by employees who are *forced* by necessity to work for their survival. No longer will a person be *forced* to work for a company that is not treating its employees fair. Because a person's basic needs are already being met, if labor is needed, a company will have to compete for human labor and maintain a business atmosphere that will attract new employees and entice tenured employees to stay with the company.

Regardless of what critics might say, humans will NOT become lazy when they have their basic necessities provided for without having to work. Our natures will not support a life of happiness when we are subjected to *just living* and breathing. We need to explore life. We need to create the value of our individuality. However, it must be accepted that all humans are **not** created equal in this *imperfect* world. Many people do not have the mental, physical, or emotional capacity to engage in the same type of employment as the rest of us. It is no fault of their own, but the fault of an *imperfect* natural body.

For many of us (but certainly not all) our basic necessities on this earth were provided for during our *mortal foundationalization* years as children. Our parents and society forced us into slavery to the established economic systems of the world when *they* determined, not that we were ready, but when *they* were ready to stop supporting us. What's fair in that? Did we ask to be born into poverty? If given the choice, wouldn't we have chosen to be born into wealth? And *none* of us would have ever agreed to being forced to be a slave to an economic situation that we had nothing to do in creating.

23. MANY YOUTH CRIMES WILL BE ELIMINATED

The implementation of FACE, HAVE, HUMANE, CARE and EQUAL will significantly reduce prostitution, drug use, and a great majority of other crimes. Because we have the technology to implement these programs, and now understand how they will work, we make ourselves responsible for these crimes.

There is not a young girl in this world who would allow herself to be sexually abused by men, if her basic necessities were provided for. Most of the prostitution in our *imperfect world* is a direct result of poverty. Parents force their young children into prostitution to feed the other members of their families. We now have no excuse for allowing this physical and emotional destructive form of life to continue.

Now, with what has been presented in this book, we have the ability and **the plan** to stop this and all other forms of **inhumanity**. If we don't, we all deserve to suffer the consequences.

24. WE WILL CREATE A HOPE THAT LEADS TO PEACE

Once the plan is implemented, the people of the world will regain hope and trust in other people. They will begin to see themselves as a valuable part of humanity and start to act accordingly. The effects of caring for the basic necessities of each human being that exists upon this earth (whose lives began not by choice, but were forced upon them by others) will bring about an emotional change in the people of the earth that has never been experienced before during the recorded human history of this earth.

This, in turn, will effectuate a peace and happiness that will resonate throughout each home, community, and nation. It will unify the human race under one simple rule of *true humanity*:

WE HAVE PROVIDED FOR OTHERS WHAT WE WOULD WANT PROVIDED FOR US IN SIMILAR CIRCUMSTANCES!

25. A UNITED RACE WILL BECOME THE ONLY CHARITY

Guilt is brought upon us from the subtle energy emissions of our human *essence* (when we act contrary to our *true foundationalized humanity*). We will no longer feel guilty when we pass by the beggar or the homeless person living on the street. We will no longer feel emotionally obligated to charities and foundations that are (*ostensibly*) set up to solve poverty and inequality. (They are really set up so that their founders and administrators can personally profit—either monetarily or in praise and glory—from the plight of the needy.) There will be no need for charities or organizations that pull at our heartstrings. WE WILL BECOME THE CHARITY! We will create a new Worldwide United Foundation (www.wwunited.org) that forces our leaders to make sure that not one of us ever again goes without food, shelter, clothing, health care, or education.

26. THE POWER TO DEMONSTRATE OUR TRUE HUMANITY

We can unite ourselves by our *true humanity* and demonstrate our capacity to value all human beings equally for who and what we *really* are! **We are advanced human beings going through an important stage of our personal development**. Whether we accept this or not, if we continue to fail to treat each other as if this were the case, then *REAL* advanced humans will one day come to our earth and, by giving us the "answers to the test," will force us to face *who we **really** are.*

27. A WISE VIEW OF OUR CURRENT ECONOMIC SYSTEMS

One of the true "selected ones" (human messengers here on earth who represent advanced human beings) witnessed the various economic systems that have come and gone throughout the course of human history upon this earth. He was also privy to information about what generally occurred in other human civilizations found throughout our Universe—civilizations where others were also going through their second stage of development in *imperfect worlds*. Without disclosing his *true identity* to others of his day, he gave a figurative narrative of what would happen to *us* in modern times.

This *selected one* likened the global economic systems, which have tremendous power and control over our lives, to a woman arrayed in purple and scarlet color, and decked with gold and precious stones and pearls, having a golden cup in her hand full of the abominations and filthiness in how she (these economic systems) affects the people of the earth. Her name remains a *mystery* to the people of the earth, meaning that no one understands exactly how these economic powers work.

He compared her (the economic systems) to a harlot, who entices people to sleep with her for money. She is the "Mother of Harlots" and the *mystery of her name* and works is demonstrated by the abominations rendered by those who wield power upon the earth. These are those who print money, fix interest rates, and calculate and manipulate the value of the different currencies of the nations of the world. These are those who establish rules and laws governing the use of money. These are those who have sold their humanity for money and misuse their power by benefiting themselves and those like them instead of all of the people of the earth equally.

This *selected one* allegorically presented those who have benefited from the inequality and suppression of others, even the kings and politicians of the earth, as committing fornication with the harlot, and the merchants of the earth becoming rich through the abundance of her delicacies.

28. WHEN ADVANCED BEINGS COME TO THE EARTH

This *selected one* continued his allegory, explaining what usually happens when advanced beings intervene into the affairs of an *imperfect world* and begin to set up a *perfect world patterned after the one where we used to live.* He allegorically presented the kings and politicians of the earth, who have committed fornication and lived deliciously with the harlot, bewailing her, and lamenting for her, when they see her fall and "burn" from the symbolic "fire" of the knowledge of **real truth**.

This "fire" is the knowledge and power of the advanced technology of a *perfect* human world, where money does not exist and all people are treated unconditionally equal. The expertise and technology of these advanced beings will replace the systems of commerce and trade of free markets, where supply and demand outweigh human value.

29. THE LEADERS AND MERCHANTS WILL BE "BURNED"

The profound above-mentioned allegorical discourse presents the current economic policymakers standing afar off and witnessing the "smoke of her burning" from the "fire" brought to the earth by advanced human beings. They will stand in embarrassment and fear of the people of the earth, who will then see them (all politicians, kings, and merchants) for who they really are.

The people will see how they were manipulated and deceived by these power brokers. The personal value, power, glory, and honor the leaders of the nations of the earth once had among the people will "burn up," along with their policies and laws. Their merchandise of gold, silver, precious stones and pearls, and that of fine linen, silk, and scarlet, and all other manner of products will be of no value compared to that which the advanced humans will bring to our earth.

The merchants of these things, who were made rich by their *fornication* with the figurative "whore of all the earth," shall stand afar off with the kings and politicians of the world, weeping and wailing. They will cry,

> "Alas, alas, this great system of profit we have established to enrich ourselves and our families, in one hour so great riches have completely lost their value!"

The souls of humankind will no longer have a value placed upon them by these merchants, kings, and politicians. The people of the earth will all be equal to each other, and equal to every other human being found throughout the Universe.

SUMMARY

The human beings found in this solar system are the graduating class of *circa* 3150 B.C.E. We have the knowledge now to do what needs to be done so that we can all graduate together.

We need to take *control* of our earth and of the leaders whom we elect to wield power over us. We must stand together and demand that the power that we give these leaders is used to benefit all of us equally. We must value each student that is receiving an education in the "School of Life" as we would want to be valued, no matter what economic situation is forced upon each individual. We must demonstrate the *power* of our humanity! We must act as we know we must, as we know we can, to bring our emotional state in line with what is *foundationalized* in our subconscious memories. We must listen to our *common sense*! We must protect each other by standing together as *equal* human beings!

We have the power and ability to make the future a reality today! We are **human beings**—the GREATEST LIFE FORM IN THE UNIVERSE! Let's start acting humanely!

Chances are, however, that fear, pride, and prejudice will keep us from doing what we have to do. If we fail the test of our own humanity, we will have to wait upon our creators to save us from ourselves. When they finally come to this earth, whether to save us from ourselves or to congratulate us on our humanity, they will give to all of us what they already enjoy…

…a PERFECT HUMAN WORLD!

Living Forever in our Perfect Worlds

CHAPTER NINETEEN

Imagine there's no heaven
It's easy if you try
No hell below us
Above us only sky
Imagine all the people
Living for today...

Imagine there's no countries
It isn't hard to do
Nothing to kill or die for
And no religion too
Imagine all the people
Living life in peace...

You may say I'm a dreamer
But I'm not the only one
I hope someday you'll join us
And the world will be as one

Imagine no possessions
I wonder if you can
No need for greed or hunger
A brotherhood of man
Imagine all the people
Sharing all the world...

You may say I'm a dreamer
But I'm not the only one
I hope someday you'll join us
And the world will live as one

—John Lennon

1. WE MUST ACCEPT THE CONDITIONS OF OUR HUMANITY TYPE

Once the *perfect world* is set up on this earth among mortals who still possess *imperfect bodies*, there will yet be much to do before our solar system is transformed into the *perfect* place for us to live forever in peace and happiness. As mentioned previously, the most important part of our learning experience upon this earth, without being aware of or interacting with other more advanced humans, is to accept *who we are*. Once we are able to accept *who we are* in relation to everyone else, we will be given a *perfect* body that complements our *humanity type* as described in previous chapters of this book.

But, as mentioned, although the human race *will* one day be aware of advanced beings and have a complete understanding of ***true reality***, it will still be hard for those who are not Solarian *humanity types* to give up their ability to experience sex. On the other hand, based on our experiences throughout our mortality, it will be easy for the majority of us to accept that those who do not want to serve other humans should not be granted the power to control and manage the elements. Again, it will not be so easy for many to accept that they must give up the sensory receptor system and the organs associated with the ability to have sex, which allows a human being to experience more physical pleasure than any other sense. And until we are able to accept this, if our chosen *humanity type* is not a Solarian creator, we will not be ready to receive a *perfect* human body.

The human race will be allowed many, many years of existence in a *perfect world* with continued *imperfect bodies* so that we can have all the experience we will need to convince us of the justice and purpose of all the eternal laws of the Universe. Eventually, without having our free agency obstructed, most of us will submit to the rule of Universal law and the authority of those who administer it for the benefit of the entire human race in all parts of the Universe.

2. OUR IMPERFECT PERCEPTION OF BEAUTY IS PRIMARILY BASED ON SEXUAL DESIRE

In our *imperfect* state, we enjoy looking at each other and ourselves and experiencing the overwhelming aesthetic beauty that the human body provides our senses. A beautiful woman, for example, will naturally be reluctant to give up her feminine shape because upon so doing, she will no longer appear "sexy." We will learn that in a *perfect* human world, beauty is not associated with sex (except in the case of Solarian couples and mothers who will choose their respective partner's body or their own based on what each finds sexually attractive). Upon learning this **real truth**, many who still have an *imperfect body* that can experience sex will feel a perplexing dissonance as they contemplate all of their past mortal experiences involving sex and the way physical beauty played a role in these experiences.

While living in a *perfect world* with an *imperfect body*, men and women will be able to construct their bodies to their own personal perception of beauty. Just as women (and some men) currently strive to perfect the application of make-up to their faces and get plastic surgery to enhance their beauty, with the advanced technology that will be available, women and men will look as *perfect* as they desire. With this ability, sex will become even more of a prevalent part of our human nature than it currently is.

A *perfect world* and the government that will be set up to govern *imperfect* humans will no longer mandate how a free-willed, maturely responsible human being exercises his or her sexuality. However, the same problems that are associated with sex currently will continue to affect human society. Lust, jealousy, physical cravings, infidelity, and all else that causes humans to experience emotional duress because of sexual desire will be just as prevalent then as they currently are in an *imperfect* world. These emotional problems will continue to exist despite a society that supports all human beings' right to enjoy the physical benefits of sex, no matter how they choose to experience it.

The *imperfect* perception of beauty is based largely on the influence of the body's sexual nature. In other words, our *imperfect bodies* are conditioned to lust and to desire sex from the most *beautiful* specimens of our species. As one considers his or her chosen *humanity type*, one will wonder what his or her perception of beauty will be like once he or she has chosen to give up the ability to have sex. Those who know that their *humanity type* does not allow sexuality will wonder what will happen once they have received their perfect body. Will they remember how wonderful it was to have sex and how it felt to be "sexually attractive"?

It would seem cruel to take away a person's beauty, in regards to sexual attraction, and then have them vividly remember forever, not only the *beautiful*, *attractive* body with which they experienced sex, but the incredible physical feelings of the act itself. Our creators are not that malicious. Here's how it works in ***true reality***:

3. THE SEXUAL EXPERIENCES RECORDED WHILE IN MORTALITY WILL NOT BE RELIVED OR RE-EXPERIENCED

According to the *perfect order* and unconditional fairness of all things, our *imperfect bodies* are created with merciful purpose. The nature of our eternal and *perfect essence* also plays a major role in that purpose.

When our *imperfect body* is sexually aroused, there is an actual physical change that overcomes it. This is felt throughout the body and is caused by our sex organs and the sensory receptor system associated with sex. Although the experience as a specific event is recorded in the *essence*, without a physical body that has the appropriate sex organs, the memory cannot be relived or re-experienced as a *sexual* event. When, therefore, a person receives a *perfect* brain and is able to recall any past experience with vivid reality, as if the event were happening all over again for the first time, the sexual experience of any past event will become an obsolete part of that person's ***true reality*** (although a recollection of the event will remain). It will be as if we are dreaming of an event and watching a person other than ourselves acting out an experience in which we had no ***real*** participation.

The sexual experiences we have while mortal are recorded in and can ONLY be remembered by our *imperfect brain* connected with the nerves and sensory receptors of our *imperfect body*! The sexual energy produced by the *imperfect body* during sexual arousal and the satiation of this arousal IS NOT RECORDED IN THE *ESSENCE* THE SAME WAY IT IS RECORDED IN OUR IMPERFECT BRAIN!

The *human essence* is designed to complement the *perfect human body*, not an *imperfect* one. Upon being foundationalized in a *perfect* human world, none of us (as newly created humans) had any sex organs; therefore, we lacked any *foundationalized* sexual experiences with which to compare and associate any future feeling of balance that we would recognize as joy and happiness. As mentioned previously, we had the ability to observe other human beings going through their second stage of human development on their "earths," who were participating in the act of sex. These were not "our" experiences; these were "theirs." We didn't understand anything about what they were doing.

We did observe that the sex act seemed to provide tremendous amounts of physical pleasure to the participants. But we also witnessed all of the societal problems that sex created for the *imperfect* humans. We observed the act and reacted to it as a little child would upon seeing mom and dad having sex—the physical reaction of the adult parents, though odd, doesn't affect a child in any way. It is not until the morals and ethics of an *imperfect world* infect a child's mind, as the child's body matures and becomes sexually stimulated, that the child is negatively affected by the *true* nature of sex.

4. THE PERFECT SEXUAL EXPERIENCE ELIMINATES NEGATIVE EMOTIONS

With a perfect body, we will have the ability to recall any experience as though it happened a moment ago, but will be unable to <u>relive</u> any of our past sexual experiences with a genderless body. Not being able to re-experience the past sexual events recorded in our *essence* serves two main purposes: The most important purpose is so that when Lunarians, Stellarians, and those Solarians who do not want to be responsible for children receive their *perfect* body, they will not be burdened with reliving the extraordinary sensory experience associated with sex. They will, therefore, not miss what they cannot relive or re-experience.

Again, although the actual event will be remembered, it will never be *relived* as it was experienced, thus making it an obsolete part of a person's overall human experience. In contrast, remembering how a flower looked and smelled, for example, will always be relived precisely as it was first experienced. This happens because the *perfect body* maintains its sight and smell sensory receptors and the organs (eyes and ears) that contribute to these senses.

The second purpose why those without sex organs will not be able to re-experience the sexual component of past events is to assure those who become Solarian mates that neither partner, in their *perfected body*, will have a desire to have sex with any other person but their chosen partner. None of their *mortal* sexual experiences they had in their past *imperfect* bodies can be relived; so, *only* those sexual experiences they will have with each other in their *perfect bodies with perfected sex organs* will be re-experienced through recall.

In the perfect bodies of parents/creators, the *perfected sexual sensory system*, which includes *perfect sex organs*, creates energies and sensory stimulations that an *imperfect body* cannot create, and vice versa. In other words, all of the energy created by an *imperfect* sexual sensory system is incompatible with a *perfect sexual sensory system*. The energy levels of the sexual events stored on the *essence* while living in an *imperfect body*, therefore, cannot be reused (relived) by the *perfected body*.

Solarian partners will be able to recall the events of sexuality that are recorded on their *essence*, but their *perfected sexual sensory receptors* will not respond to the energy. Remembering a past sexual event for a gendered Solarian would be similar to having a dream about a brother or a sister having sex—not an observation that would cause any sexual arousal.

In a *perfect world with perfect bodies*, all negative human emotions associated with sex are eliminated. Because our sexual experiences are only able to be experienced in our physical *imperfect* brain, once our mortal life is over, thus ends the ability to relive sexual experiences of that person. (The experience is recorded on the essence, but the *sexual component* of the experience is not.) Those Solarians who are given perfect bodies with sex organs will not be affected by any *mortal* sexual experience, EXCEPT those they experience while in their *perfect* bodies.

Because the *perfect* body's brain does not *store* memories (as explained previously), the experience of sex in a *perfect* world is recorded in the *essence*. The power of the *essence* enhances the sexual experience beyond anything any *imperfect* human is allowed to experience. Because gendered Solarians can remember all sexual experience (that take place in their *perfect* bodies) as if the event happened a moment ago, every sexual experience will be a continuation of the last, making the experience an increasingly enjoyable event forever. This is something Solarian *humanity types* have to look forward to in relation to their chosen *humanity type*. Although those who know they will become genderless, because of their choice of a *humanity type*, will find it hard to acknowledge and accept, nevertheless, this is mandated as such by the Universal rule of law.

5. WITHOUT SEX, OUR PERCEPTION OF BEAUTY CHANGES

Once people are ready to accept their perfected body, they will be assured that giving up their ability to have sex will not be important to their overall happiness. They will be assured that, regarding their sexual natures, they will become as little children and have no more interest in sex than little children in mortality currently do. Their inability to have sex will not affect their ability to interact with their environment and experience a fullness of joy through all their other *perfected* senses.

Because most humans will lose their ability to have sex, their perception of beauty will also be affected. They will be choosing their own body based on their personal preference of what is beautiful to them personally, but now as seen through the "eyes of a child." Children do not base their perception of beauty on sex, but on comfort and familiarity. For this reason, children are comfortable around even the most unattractive parents.

Solarian people who will continue to have sex will base their body selection on sexual attributes that please themselves and those with whom they will be sharing their sexual experiences. But, again, those who will *not* be having sex will base their body selection on what is most familiar and comfortable to them based on their past experiences.

As explained previously, our first primordial bodies were created, not according to *our own* perception of beauty, but according to *our advanced Solarian mother's*. She picked how *she* wanted us to look as *her* child. We lived with her in *her* world for eons of time in comparison to the few thousand years we have lived in an *imperfect world*, where our body type was chosen by the natural selection of our DNA patterns. Having this (or better *our mother's*) perception of beauty *foundationalized* in our *essence*, it is not hard to figure out which body will be the most comfortable and familiar to us. Of course it will be the one we had for the longest time during our existence!

6. ASEXUAL BEINGS WILL GENERALLY DESIRE THEIR PRIMORDIAL PERFECTED BODY

Those who do not choose a perfect body based on sexual preferences will usually choose the body that their advanced mother created for them. We will know about this body by having our *imperfect* brain hooked up to "LEARN" (as explained in chapter 17, section 48). With this retrospect, the way that we looked in all of our lifetimes will be "relived" so that we can make a free-willed choice of what we want our eternal body to look like. IF one chooses a body different than the one their primordial mother chose for the person, then, by all means, the person will receive the body of their own choosing. But generally (and naturally), most of us will agree with the *perfect choice* of our advanced and perfected mother.

We will observe all of our incarnations upon this earth and in our primordial state and will be able to see how we lived and what we looked like for the billions of years (according to *imperfect* earth time) that we went through our human *Foundationalization Process*. Most of us will realize that our mothers only created bodies that were consistent with what all humans perceive as the ultimate beauty. Most of us, therefore, will accept without reservation the type of body our mothers created for us.

Once we receive our perfect body, when we look at our reflection in a mirror, the energy of the experience will match perfectly with the vast amounts of experiences stored in our *essence*, which were stored when we saw our refection while in our mother's perfect world. As explained previously, when our current experiences match those *foundationalized* in our *essence*, we feel the effects of incredible joy and happiness. We will all be very happy with the bodies we choose for ourselves—forever!

7. SEXUAL LIBERATION DOES NOT INCLUDE SEX AGAINST OTHER'S FREE WILL

Because all of us will still have *imperfect bodies* until we are ready to accept our *perfect one*, we will continue to have the ability and use of sex organs and enjoy them in fulfillment of sensory satiation. The physical act of sex will no longer be seen as anything other than pure enjoyment, just like the use of any of our other senses. There will be no moral taboos or restrictions placed on sexual behavior. There will be no sexually transmitted disease or unwanted pregnancies. People will use their sex organs at will, but strictly within the parameters of the Universal Rule of Law that protects the free will of others.

Anyone prone to rape, incest, or sexual promiscuity involving the young (the "young" are those who do not have a fully developed awareness of their own free agency and of their obligation to protect the free will of others) will have their sex organs removed. Many of those who are prone to any behavior that might violate the free will of another will acknowledge their personal propensity to act this way and ask to have their sexual desires terminated. If those prone to these behaviors do not make the choice for themselves to voluntarily give up their sexual abilities, and they cannot control their sexual nature, then (under the direction of a Solarian government servant) they will be forced to give up the ability to have sex. This does not mean that these types are necessarily ready to accept their *perfected*, eternal body. Generally, however, those who realize that they are prone to misuse their sexual abilities, or that their sexual propensities cause them unhappiness, usually choose to be given their *perfected* Lunarian or Stellarian body, thus eliminating any further misuse of their sexuality.

8. SEX WILL CONTINUE TO BRING US SORROW, EVEN IN A PERFECT WORLD

Although sex will become as prevalent in a *perfect world* with an *imperfect body* as enjoying a piece of candy, free of physical complications, the same negative emotional effects that are currently associated with sex will continue. Jealousy and infidelity will continue to plague our happiness. Possessiveness and anger will continue to be the result of our inability to understand that the desire to have sex is directly associated with our free will to satisfy the longings of our physical senses and has nothing to do with our *true* self-value. The need to be valued for more than just a "sex toy" will continue to create insecurity and affect our self-esteem.

Even in the *perfect world*, a lot of the infidelity in a personal relationship will come, as it does now, when a person finds more joy in having sex with another person than the one to whom the person has promised fidelity. According to the laws that govern free agency, the person desiring another should be relieved of the fidelity obligation so that he or she can exercise unconditional free will. However, only a Lunarian or Stellarian *humanity type* would find personal peace and happiness in breaking a promise of fidelity to be better served by another or to serve themselves. A person with a Solarian *humanity type*, who makes a vow of fidelity, will remain true to the spirit of the promise and never act to bring unhappiness upon another, not in thought or in deed.

9. EXPERIENCING SEX IN A PERFECT WORLD HELPS OUR UNDERSTANDING

During the time that we experience an *imperfect body* in a *perfect world*, we will come to realize just how much our sex drive affects our overall happiness. Even when everything else about our world is *perfectly* adapted to cater to our individual desires of happiness, sex will continue to cause us unhappiness.

Our creators allow all people, regardless of *humanity type*, to continue to experience sex before they choose to receive a perfected body that cannot have sex. They want us to understand the main reasons why allowing **all** *humanity types* to have sex would upset the balance of order that is established throughout the Universe for our happiness. If our creators took away the sex drive of those who chose not to be responsible for the creation of human life, without allowing them to experience it in a *perfect world*, they would never fully understand the problems it can cause. They would have forever had the excuse, "How do you know I would misuse my sexuality if I was able to experience it in a *perfect* world?"

While being foundationalized in our mother's *perfect world*, we did not have gender; thus, we were not able to experience how the sex drive would affect us. Even so, having the ability during our existence in an *imperfect world* will still not convince us that being permitted to have sex would lead to our unhappiness.

We would continually argue that it wasn't the actual "sex drive" that caused us unhappiness, but rather the consequence of living in an *imperfect world*. To dismiss this argument forever, we are allowed to have sex throughout the time we exist in a *perfect world*, thereby convincing us that, whether we live in a *perfect world* or not, the need to satisfy the urges created by sex organs will bring us much more misery than the few minutes of ecstasy we enjoy from the experience. With the ability to experience sex in a *perfect world*, it will be much easier for Lunarians and Stellarians (and even those Solarians who do not want to be responsible for creating new human beings) to accept that the desire and ability should be taken away from them.

10. EXPERIENCE CONVINCES US OF WHAT WE SHOULD NOT BE ALLOWED

Again, the two main issues we had with the Universal Plan of Happiness were 1) that most of us would *not* have the power that our parents/creators have; and 2) the realization that most of us would not have the ability to have sex, the most powerful sensory fulfillment possible with a human body. Every possible opportunity is afforded us to help us find a personal sense of peace and comfort with this *reality*. To get this peace, we must acknowledge that although we will not experience a fullness of all human potential, that which we *will* be capable of experiencing with the body allowed by our *humanity type* will ultimately bring us all the happiness we will ever desire.

11. CULTURE CENTERS WILL BE BASED ON THE DIFFERENT HUMANITY TYPES

Before we accept our *perfect* body, however, the most important part of our existence in an *imperfect body* is to be able to **fully** accept *who we are*. To help us do this in a *perfect world*, the *imperfect* people upon the earth will be divided according to our particular desire of happiness.

Although advanced Solarian servants will oversee this division, the people of the earth will naturally begin to separate themselves into diverse cultures according to their different *humanity types*. Lunarians will naturally create a large area of the earth where they are able to serve themselves; Stellarians will tend to congregate in areas of the earth where their needs can best be served; and the Solarians will gather in their own cultures, where they can best serve the needs of others.

12. STELLARIAN CULTURES SUPPORT THE NEED TO BE RECOGNIZED

Stellarians will be those who continue to place themselves in positions where they receive the accolades of others. They will live as the extremely wealthy do in our current world, with an entourage of servants at their beck and call. Under the direction of Solarians (utilizing the most advanced robotic/android specialists available), servants will cater to all aspects of a Stellarian lifestyle, which is always based on what the individual desires.

Stellarians will have cultures and societies where they will continue to be actors, athletes, and other performers, for example, whose forms of expression are intended to generate an extrinsic acknowledgment of their abilities.

Stellarians will continue to *be served* by the applause and congratulatory compliments of others. They will continue the theater and other venues of entertainment where they place themselves in a position to receive extrinsic energy from other humans. Both Solarians and Lunarians will visit these Stellarian cultures and communities according to their own *humanity type*. Lunarians will visit Stellarian cultures to be entertained (serve themselves), just like most *imperfect* humans do in today's world.

Solarians will visit Stellarian cultural centers only to support with accolade the needs of the entertainers they desire to serve. The only real value, in fact, that a Solarian will ever receive from being entertained by a Stellarian is knowing that, by being present and involved in the Stellarian lifestyle, Stellarians receive what they need. This act is very similar to that of a parent or grandparent attending a play or a sporting event that they aren't intrinsically interested in, but who do so at the bequest and support of the child's self-esteem.

13. LUNARIAN CULTURES ALLOW UNCONDITIONAL PERSONAL EXPRESSION

Lunarians will be left largely to themselves to live in their own houses with their own parcels of land, which they can cultivate and form however they wish to serve their own best interests. With the advanced technology that will be available upon the earth at that time, there will be no place upon this planet that will not be habitable. Advanced technology and power can control atmospheric pressure, which in turn can manipulate all weather conditions. Wherever a Lunarian wants it to rain, it will rain however much is needed. Advanced technology and knowledge will allow Lunarians to do whatever serves the individual needs of each.

14. SOLARIAN CULTURES PRODUCE AND REAR THE CHILDREN

Solarian cultures will largely be those responsible for rearing children. Except for the servants who have no gender and serve the needs of the human creators, by choice, most other Solarians will continue to have children.

All human *essences* assigned to this solar system will inhabit an *imperfect body* upon this earth during the time of a *perfect world.* The only exceptions to this rule are those who will have already received their perfected body. But even those who have received their eternal bodies, who are assigned to this solar system, or better, are a part of our particular *group* or batch of humans, will be again upon the earth during this time.

Because all of the *essences* assigned to this solar system need mortal bodies, there will continue to be the creation of *imperfect* bodies by Solarian parents. No matter whether the parent is a Solarian in a *perfect body* or a Solarian humanity type in an *imperfect body*, all people born during this time period will be given an *imperfect body*. And each person will possess this body until he or she decides for him or herself that it is time to accept their *humanity type* and the restrictions placed upon it. However, during this time, the *imperfect bodies* will all be produced asexually with advanced technology.

The ability and free will to produce a child will still be available at this time to all *humanity types*; it will not just be limited to Solarian people. However, over time, because all of us will then understand the

Universal Rule of Law and how things are done in advanced human societies, those who do not want to be responsible for *improper foundationalization* will not choose to be parents.

The Solarian cultures will seem very boring and monotonous to Lunarian and Stellarian people. Yet, being around children always brings some semblance of joy to almost any person. Lunarians and Stellarians, therefore, will visit Solarian cultures just to see little children and enjoy their presence, much like grandparents do now who know that, at the end of the day, they can relinquish the responsibility of the child to the parent after enjoying the child's presence.

15. WE HAVE A SET TIME LIMIT TO MAKE OUR DECISION

None of us will receive a *perfect* body **UNTIL** we have the sense of peace and comfort that will come from accepting our chosen *humanity type*. We are the ones who decide when we are ready, as long as we are, in fact, truly ready. We will exist in an *imperfect body* in a *perfect world* for as long as it takes us to come to a personal affirmation and acceptance of *who we are*.

However, our creators cannot wait on us forever. There is a set time when the days of our probation in an *imperfect body* will end. There is a time limit given to our second stage of human development, at which time we will be required to either accept the consequences of who we have chosen to be or reject the Universal law and order that has always existed. We have a choice. And we can even choose a *final* death.

Although there will be very few who will use their free agency to deny their own existence and reject the state of *true reality* that exists throughout the Universe, those who *do* will experience the **only** *permanent* death that will ever be associated with human life. Their very *essence*, in which is recorded all of their life experiences—the very *essence* of who they are—will be disassembled.

Once the elements that make up the *essence* have been returned to their basic atomic structure of protons, neutrons, and electrons, that human being will cease to exist forever, never again to live or relive any experiences of the past. Once disassembled, there is not a power in the

Universe that can bring back the person who was. The compilation of events experienced while in a human body will no longer exist. That person, that unique human individual, will cease to exist forever!

16. REJECTION OF UNIVERSAL LAW SUBJECTS US TO A MERCIFUL DEATH

This *ultimate death* is both just and merciful. It supports justice, because these types of people will only cause unrest and contention for the rest of the human race, whom will have already accepted the way things are as mandated by the Universal Rule of Law (or better, the Universal Plan of Human Happiness). It is merciful, because these individuals will never understand what they have given up, because they simply won't exist to remember or understand anything!

There will be many of our batch of humans who will have violated every law of humanity (some in the most egregious ways) while dwelling in an *imperfect body*. However, no matter what any of us has done, all will be unconditionally "accepted." But one who denies the very *essence* of their humanity, which is set forth by the laws and order of the Universe, cannot be "allowed" to exist. These must pay the ultimate penalty for rejecting the conditions set for all of humanity throughout the Universe. They will simply not exist.

17. WE CAN MAKE THE CHOICE TO BECOME PERFECT AT ANY TIME

Although there is a time limit to finally agreeing to and accepting the conditions set forth that pertain to our particular *humanity type*, there is no restriction on how *early* we can make the decision to accept our perfect body. We can make our decision at any time while in this temporary *perfect world* preparatory to the **final** *perfect world* (on one of the planets of our Solar System) to which we will be assigned forever. Once we understand *true reality* and are ready to accept *who we are*, there will be advanced humans among us who know how to create the *perfect* body for each of us. At any time, any of us can make the decision to effect the transformation.

By the time these advanced humans come to our world, our scientists will have already solved the mystery of aging. They will have isolated the genetic patterns that cause our bodies to begin to deteriorate once we have reached our prime. With precise genetic engineering, they will eliminate death that comes by old age. Before the perfect world begins, although people will continue to die from war, disease, accident, and suicide, no *imperfect body* in the future will grow old and die.

Once the advanced human beings come to our world and begin to implement the *perfect world*, there will be no more war, disease, accident, or suicide. At that time, there will be no more "death" (the separation of our *essence* from our physical body) except in the case of one who so chooses it, as described above, and the "separation" that takes place when we receive our final *perfect body* (explained in detail below).

18. SCIENCE WILL DISCOVER THE PERFECT BODY

Before advanced humans come to this earth, science will make great advancements in the medical field that will help keep us alive, but it will not have the technology or understanding to create the *perfect body*. However, because of their continued research and development in the area of the physiological sciences, scientists and researchers will come to understand how a perfect body *could* work to bring the greatest happiness to a human being without the negative effects of an *imperfect body*. They will do this by isolating the human head from the body, keeping it alive artificially, and providing energy pulsations directly to the brain that will bring extraordinary amounts of pleasure, all that any human being would desire.

The person whose head is detached from the body will still continue to see, hear, taste, smell and feel the sensations of touch on their head and whatever other sensations are sent to their brain through the stimulus of energy pulsations generated by a computer. The person will be able to enjoy any situation as *real* as any of the dreams we produce in our heads. But they will not be experienced as "dreams," but as ***real experience***. The bodiless person will eat, for example, but after the food passes the sensory receptors of the nose, mouth, and tongue, the food will then pass through a tube into a waste receptacle.

The person can eat whatever, whenever, and the quantity that they want, without ever being subjected to obesity and other results of improper eating. The artificial blood and oxygen sent to the brain to keep it alive will be kept clean and at a level of purity that will allow the brain to function as well as any brain inside the head of a full-bodied person.

But no matter how advanced science becomes, it will only be able to experiment and work with an *imperfect brain* and its limitations. Science will never understand the structure of the human *essence* or the ability of the human *essence* to react with a *perfect* human body. Although scientific experimentation and advancements will inspire human imagination to consider the potential of human perfection, only advanced Solarian humans will have the knowledge and the power to create the quintessential *perfect human body*.

19. ADVANCED BEINGS KNOW WHEN WE ARE READY

Only advanced creators know how to create a *perfect* brain that receives its energy from the *essence*. Only *they* know how to create a body with an extensive system of nerves that will deliver this energy to all parts of the body. And, most importantly, only *they* know when each of us has become fully convinced of *who we are*. If a person claims that they are ready to receive their *perfect* body, and they are not, the advanced beings will know and will not allow the person to receive it.

A person who is a Lunarian humanity type, for example, will never be able to deceive the advanced humans responsible for creating our perfect bodies into creating a Solarian body type for them, just so that they can have sex. Solarians can read all *imperfect* minds by accessing the stored energy of the *essence*. They know all there is to know about each of us. They exist to help us gain the most happiness out of our own existence, but also to maintain the perfect order that has always existed in our Universe. They will never do anything to us or for us that would not be the best thing for our happiness or the happiness of all other humans throughout the Universe.

20. OUR ADVANCED, PRIMORDIAL MOTHERS CREATE OUR PERFECTED BODY

As explained previously, at any time while in the *perfect* world that is to come to pass upon this earth, an *imperfect* person can decide to receive a perfect human body. The procedure and transformation from an *imperfect* body to a *perfect* one is carried out anywhere we choose to have it done. Some will choose to have it done in the privacy of their own home. Others will choose to have it done in the peaceful environment of nature. Some will have it done with their friends, family, and familiars present. Others will have it done alone.

Two advanced Solarian servants attend to the procedure. In addition, there is one other person present—the advanced mother/creator who created our first human body and *foundationalized* us as humans! She will be called from her world to attend each and every one of her children's transformation from an *imperfect body* back into a *perfect one*! This reunion of mother and child will prove to be the most profound and important part of our existence. And it will mean as much to our advanced mother as it will to us.

Our advanced eternal mothers are the ones who will use their Solarian power to create our *perfect adult* body, using the same procedure they used when they created our *primordial infant* body. They know each of us and have stored in their own *essence* the exact combination of the molecular construction of the primordial body they created for us in the beginning. If we have chosen some other body type other than the one which they created for us, our mothers will know of our desires and create the body as we desire it to be. Every part of our body will be restored or constructed to its *perfect* frame. Once our *essence* enters this body, we will already have the stored experience of how it functions with our free will, so it will not be necessary to reacquaint us with how to use these bodies. For this reason, we do not need to be created as infants as we were in our primordial state, when we had no recorded experience of how to use a human body.

21. OUR BOND WITH OUR MOTHER IS FINALIZED

The *perfect* body is created right before our eyes. In a completely conscious state, we see it all happen. Once created, our mothers will cause our *imperfect body* to recline suspended in the air, as if in an invisible lounge chair. The mother then takes the hand of the one going through the transformation, and with the same loving smile that we first saw upon her beautiful face when we first came into existence, the mother will have us close our eyes. The last thing we will see with our *imperfect* eyes is the first thing that we saw with our *perfect infant* eyes when we were first created: our eternal mother's impenetrable smile! And once again, it will be the first thing we see, but this time with *perfect adult* eyes!

The moment we close our eyes, by the gentle command of our mother, our new body reclines itself in the same position as our old body. We are instantly "put to sleep" for as long as it takes our mother to position herself next to our *perfected* body. Our mother then commands our *essence* to leave our old *imperfect* body and enter our *perfected new* one. She takes the hand of our *perfected* body and watches us open our eyes in our new *perfect body*!

There have been very few moments in our existence when we have experienced true "tears of joy." At this time, we will share them with our mothers. The emotional power of their *essence* reunited with our own will cause an energetic embrace unlike anything we have ever felt before. The transition from our *imperfect state* to our final ***perfect state*** will then be complete. We will **once again** be advanced humans like our creators! Our mothers will have fulfilled the responsibility they took upon themselves when they first decided to create us. They will have given us what they have and what we desire—eternal life and happiness!

Although we will long to remain with our mothers, we will realize that they have other children to attend to. Now vertical and standing, either suspended in air (because we now have the ability) or upon the ground, we will embrace our mothers before they leave. What an embrace! What an emotion that will be!

22. INSTRUCTIONS ON HOW TO ACT AROUND IMPERFECT PEOPLE ARE GIVEN TO US AS PERFECT BEINGS

At the same time that our *essence* is floating over to our new body, our old body will be taken apart, molecule by molecule, each element dissolving into the basic particles that make up all matter. This will be completed by the command of one of the two other advanced humans attending our transformation from *imperfection* to *perfection*.

After our mother has left, the *two* advanced beings attending the transformation will instruct us on some specific matters concerning the rules we must abide by while still existing with other people who remain in their *imperfect bodies*. Interacting with *imperfect* humans is something we have never done before while possessing a *perfect* body; therefore, we don't have any experience to recall, regarding how we should act. After a short briefing that entails specific ways that our new body can affect the free will of another, we will either be left to ourselves, if alone, or with those who attended our transformation. Never will we ever attend a party like the one we will experience once we have finally become an eternal, perfected human being!

23. ETERNAL PARTNERS ATTEND EACH OTHER'S TRANSFORMATION

In the case of a Solarian creator/parent transformational process, there is a slight difference in the transformation process, if the person is going to be in an eternal partnership as a male or a female. In this case, the body created for each partner is dependent upon the desire of sexual attraction of his or her mate. The mother, who is also present, uses her Solarian mind to search the *essence* of the partner not going through the transformation at the time, and immediately tunes into what he or she wants his or her partner to look like.

The body is created just as all other *perfected* bodies are created. Once created, there are kind smiles and gentle laughs in humor, as for the first time the partner being transformed sees what their mate longed for after considering all of their mortal experience. What kind of man or woman was most attractive to your partner? Now you will know!

The mother takes her position next to the *imperfect body*, and on the other side, holding the other hand, is the person's eternal mate. As is the case with all other humans, each eternal partner must make the choice to receive his or her *perfected body* when each is fully ready to do so. Consequently, most Solarian partnerships usually decide to receive their perfected bodies at the same time.

24. WE HAVE A PERFECT RECOLLECTION OF WHO WE ARE

Our *perfect body* can recall any past event and relive it (except for sexual experience, as previously explained) as if it happened just a moment ago. We will use the energy provided by our *essence* to recall past experiences just like we currently use our *imperfect brain* to remember things of our past. The biggest difference is that our *perfected* brain will never fail to bring up a memory instantaneously!

A *perfect brain* has no memories of its own, but exists only as a physical location where we can bring in the energy patterns stored as memories from our *essence* and put them where they can be brought to life by our *perfected* sensory receptors. This occurs in our "inner movie theater," as explained in an earlier chapter of this book.

Past memories will not bombard our brain with continual recollections of the past any more than they do to our *imperfect brain*. Our *essence* is like a fine-tuned memory chip that has all of our experiences organized and categorized, so that the moment something in our current environment "sparks" a memory, the energy pattern that formed the memory is automatically found and sent to our brain for the composition of a thought.

The *essence* has what can best be described in modern terms as a highly sophisticated and advanced "search engine." The source of energy that initiates the "search" comes from the *essence* itself. When we focus our thoughts, the *essence's* "search engine" is empowered and instantly scans the stored energy patterns, from which we then choose what we want to "think" and "relive" at that moment.

25. ALL OF US WILL LIVE TOGETHER UPON THE EARTH UNTIL THE END OF THE "SCHOOL OF LIFE"

These procedural transformations from *mortality* to *immortality* will continue to take place until every human being upon earth—even every human being assigned to this solar system—has received their *perfect body*, except the very few who deny the reality of who they are and who will subsequently be disassembled. By the time the last person receives their body, the earth will be very populated. There will hardly be a space where there are no humans. However, it won't be as populated as some might think.

The most advanced technology in architecture, food production, water renewal, and every other basic necessity needed to support human life will be available at that time. There are about 15 billion humans assigned to this solar system. The landmasses of the entire earth cover about 57.5 million square miles. Thus calculated, each person would have about 107,000 square feet (approximately 2.5 acres) of personal space. (The average home size is 2500 square feet.) Using these basic calculations and taking into account the technology that will be utilized, it is easy to visualize how all of us could fit comfortably upon the earth at the same time.

26. THE PLANETS WILL BE PREPARED FOR OUR HABITATION

Until we are <u>ALL</u> secure in our *perfect* bodies, according to our *humanity types*, advanced human beings cannot finalize the transformation of the other planets of our solar system into our individual eternal habitations. They cannot do this, because they do not know exactly how many of the 15 billion people are going to choose to NOT continue as advanced human beings. They have a good idea, based on their vast experience and knowledge, which made it possible for them to determine the size of the planets of our solar system in the first place. Nevertheless, they do not know for sure because of human free will.

The planets will be divided perfectly according to each of our individual desires of happiness. There will not be any part of any planet that is unclaimed or not utilized. Mercury will be for the Solarian couples; Venus for the Solarian mothers; Earth for Solarian servants; Mars, Jupiter, and Saturn for Lunarians; and Uranus, Neptune, and Pluto for Stellarians (using the names of our current known planets as examples **only**).

The main asteroid belt located between Mars and Jupiter will coalesce its asteroids and become a whole new planet. Upon this new planet, the overseer of our solar system will reside with his eternal mate. According to the way scientists have named the planets of our solar system, the new planet could be appropriately called "Episkopos." The reader can do his or her own research into this word ("Episkopos") to find out why this word would be an appropriate name for this yet-to-be-organized planet, upon which the overseer of our solar system will reside forever.

27. WE WILL EACH OWN OUR OWN PIECE OF THE UNIVERSE

The formation of our solar system has already been explained. With their advanced technology, and conferring with each of us according to our personal desires, the advanced humans who have overseen the formation of our solar system from its inception will ensure that the planets become our eternal homes. We will participate in the construction of our allotted space upon the planet where we will reside, just as a homeowner would do when working with an architect and a general contractor in building their personal dream house.

We will finally own a piece of the Universe that we can call our own. No one will ever evict us, nor will we ever give our space to another. It will be our Eternal Home!

28. OUR PERFECT WORLD IS ONLY LIMITED BY OUR IMAGINATION

The specifics of what these planets will look like and what our *Eternal Home* will look like will depend on each of us. Using our imagination correctly, we can visualize exactly what we would want our home to look like.

Before we came to this earth, we already knew what we wanted, based on our vast experience in seeing other worlds and observing all different varieties of environments in which human beings exist throughout the Universe. The *perfect* world we came from has been discussed previously. From the descriptions given, and by using your own intuitive, free-willed imagination, you can create your own world in your mind's eye. And just as easy as it is to form the thought of your *perfect world* through your imagination, our advanced creators and servants will one day help you create *in reality* your very own **perfect world**!

SUMMARY

Our creators know each of us a lot better than we currently know ourselves. The design of the Universe is to support each of us in our journey to become the ultimate life form in this Universe—a **perfected human being**. We must be given every opportunity to understand our self and to accept *who we are*, separate from everyone else, but in relation to the Universe as a whole.

These advanced beings' knowledge of human nature helps them to help each of us construct an individual life plan that aids us in achieving the goal of ultimate humanity. They've heard all of the excuses that any of us could possibly make about not being treated fairly or equally to everyone else. It is their responsibility, work, and mission to ensure our eventual immortality and eternal life as a human being. Our happiness is of utmost importance to the success of their mission. They have never failed. And they never will!

They have prepared us for immortal life and a world that we can call our own. In this world, we will live forever. In this world, we will experience the ultimate sensation of our humanity. In this world, we will be eternally filled with JOY and HAPPINESS!

In this world, we are **WHO WE ARE**…

and we know **WHY WE EXIST**!

It is our **HUMAN REALITY**!

—Worlds without end.

EPILOGUE

TRUE REALITY *is things as they were, as they are, as they are to come, and how they have always been—worlds without end.*

—Anonymous

Human societies exist throughout the Universe. There are an endless number of these societies, each located on its own planet, in its own solar system, and in its own galaxy. The life forms that live in these societies are *human beings*, whose appearance is similar to our current physical form. Human beings have always existed and they always will exist. Throughout the Universe, human beings are going through different stages of human development. These "stages" can be viewed as time periods of the **past**, **present**, and **future**. The ultimate state of human existence is in a *perfect* society around *perfect human beings*. Humans somewhere have always lived throughout the Universe in this essential and *perfected* state. This state provides a human being with a *perfect* existence, which might be described as continual and lasting happiness. This *human state* is as *perfect* and infinite as the Universe itself.

Human beings exist in these societies in a state of quintessential happiness that complements the physical nature of their particular life form. This "happiness" is a state of ideal balance between the surrounding environment (the Universe itself) and the human body. *Perfect* happiness occurs when the human body's sensory systems of sight, touch, smell, taste, sound, thought, and sex (for some) are absolutely satiated. The main objective of all human societies is to perpetuate the human race and this "happiness."

With highly advanced knowledge and technology that cannot be enhanced in any way, new human beings are created in these *perfect* worlds. The way of life experienced in these worlds cannot be improved upon to afford any greater degree of "happiness" than what is already experienced by advanced human beings. This ultimate human experience is the purpose for which the Universe exists.

The Universe, therefore, exists for human beings. It always has and it always will. There are no other life forms found anywhere in the Universe as complex as human beings. There are also no other life forms that are consciously aware of their existence; nor are there any who form a relationship with their environment and with each other, as humans are capable of doing. Most importantly above all other attributes of life, **only** humans have the power of **free will**.

It stands to reason that *something* in the Universe must be the highest form of intelligence and possess the highest level of power. With this intelligence and power, any life form would utilize its existence and its environment to benefit itself. Because humans are the highest form of intelligence, they take advantage of every other life form and matter that exists. It is *because* of human beings and for their sake that all other forms of matter are organized and created. The Universe is a **human Universe**, and all things exist *for* and are created and maintained *by* human beings.

Because newly created humans are born into a *perfect world* initially, they have no sense or knowledge of their *perfect* situation. They are completely unaware of how wonderful it is to exist as a human being. They are oblivious and naïve with respect to the extraordinary benefits of being the highest life form in the Universe. Their primordial environment serves all of their intended human needs and provides all that is necessary for their "happiness." They have the power to act upon and react to their environment according to their own free will.

However, living in a *perfect* human society, in which they begin to exercise their unique free will, newly created humans do not know *how to* use their exclusive powers of free will to act upon or react to their environment. They do not know how to walk, to float, or to fly, or in any other way to use their own energy to control the matter from which their *perfect* human body was created. They have no experience; therefore, they do not have a past that would provide them with the experience to know how to exist as a human being.

They do not know how to think or what to think; and left to themselves *without* guidance, they would be at the mercy of their surrounding environment. Their environment would act upon them, taking away their free will and forcing them to adapt to the will of their environment, instead of the other way around. Advanced, perfected human beings teach the newly created humans how to control their environment according to free will. They teach by example and demonstration exactly how to become the *perfect human being*. Because the newly created humans have no other experience from which to draw up on to form individual choices, they are "required," in effect, to become humane, as are their *perfected* creators. In this way, our humanity is established.

Our ***human***ity is the way that we, as human beings, choose to act upon and react to our surrounding environment. Our *humanity* ***type*** is our personal choice, completely unfettered by the wishes of our advanced parents, whose only desire is that we choose the *type* that will bring us the most happiness. Our advanced parents assure us that we will be supported in whatever humanity type we choose for ourselves. Their responsibility insures that each newly created human being establishes the humanity that makes each person one of the most ultimate life forms in the Universe.

Because our primordial parents are responsible for our ***foundationalized humanity***, they ensure that *how* we use the power of our free will *does not* impede upon the free will of any other human being or frustrate the overall balance of the natural environments found in the Universe. They also ensure that the use of our free will does not disrupt the way things have always been done in the Universe—they assure Universal order.

We often share the same environment (planet, solar system, or galaxy) with many other humans. We can do whatever we want to our surrounding environment, as long as what we do does not inhibit another human being from doing what they want to do in the same environment. Our free will to act cannot affect our shared environment in a way that others cannot also act upon it with their own free will. We are all equally powerful in the use of our environment, according to what we determine brings us the most joy—"joy" being the effect of "happiness."

During the *Foundationalization Process* of our humanity, we developed a sense of *self* apart from everyone else. This "self" is who we chose to become. It makes us a unique individual, different from any other human being who has ever existed or who will ever exist in the Universe.

Every human being that existed before our creation has *always existed to us*. We will never know of a time in *our own existence* when others did not exist. Likewise, all things being equally relative, *we have also always existed*, because we will never remember a time when we did not exist. Although our current *imperfect brain* cannot totally grasp and rationalize the concept that we have always existed, and that other humans have always existed, once we receive again our *perfect* human body and live in a *perfect* society, we will understand the concept completely.

We existed in a *perfect world* for eons of time, learning all there is to know about being human and about *human perfection*. Once our creators determined that we were ready, it was then time for us to have the opportunity to experience everything that is the **opposite** of *human perfection*. In experiencing a contrast to our *true human nature*, we could establish an appreciation for *who we are*. We would also learn to accept that there must be some limits and controls to the exercising of human free will.

Once we knew all there was to know about ourselves and everything there was to know about our Universe, we were ready to move on to our very *own* planet, in our *own* solar system, in our *own* galaxy. It is here where we would be able to stake our personal claim to a part of the infinite Universe.

After we were properly foundationalized, our parents helped us to create the right amount of planets at just the right size, to accommodate each of our individual needs and wants in our new solar system. (Or rather, we influenced our creators according to our individual needs and wants, and they used their power to do the actual creating.)

Each solar system is placed in a galaxy of many other solar systems that fall under the jurisdiction and responsibility of individual creators. Although there are just as many galaxies in the Universe as there are creators (an infinite number), only *one* galaxy and *one* solar system within that galaxy pertains to us, unless we choose to become creators ourselves and create our own galaxy of infinite solar systems.

Before the planets of our solar system are formed into *perfect worlds* like the one where we were created, one of them—Earth—was utilized to allow an *imperfect world* to develop without, or with very little, advanced human intervention. We (*the* collection of each our ***essences***, *of whom each of us* ***actually*** *is*) were placed on this world so that we could experience what happens when there is *no control* over our free will or the natural environment. We were given a body that conformed to the environment of an *imperfect world*; therefore, it is in an *imperfect* body that we cannot remember anything about what we learned before we were born upon earth. Unrestrained in the use of the power of our free will to control our environment and ourselves, we could then experience the effects of our individual humanity.

We prove to ourselves what happens when certain *humanity types* gain power and control over others. We see what happens when others exercise dominion and power over us by taking away our free agency, sometimes because of the physical need to survive, but often because of personal greed. Living on earth, we see what happens when free-willed humans protect their own right to exercise their free will in spite of what their actions do to another. In our *imperfect world*, we are forced to experience widespread inequality.

Here on this *imperfect world*, we experience what happens when we are allowed the ability to exercise all of our sensory systems, which includes the ability to create new life through sex. We see what happens when we foundationalize newly created beings incorrectly. We also experience what it is like to be subjected to the influence of our environment through natural disasters, sickness, and the wild forces of the plant and animal kingdoms that afflict us and cause us misery and physical pain and suffering.

This *imperfect world* provides us with every experience that is opposite of the *perfect human world*. We can *only hope* for a more perfect world while living upon this earth, because we do not have the ability to remember anything about our existence except what we experience upon this earth. And because we cannot remember anything beyond our current existence, we don't understanding *why* we even *hope* for a better world. But we do! "Hope" is the intrinsic measure of our humanity, or better, that which we feel can be possible in spite of the improbabilities that seem to be part of our present experience. (See chapter 1, section 36.)

Once our creators have determined that we have experienced enough opposition, they will come to our solar system with smiles on their faces and joy in their hearts that our time here upon planet earth has been successful for each of us. Once they explain to us the purpose for which we exist, and more thoroughly, *why* they allowed us to exist this way without knowing of them or being aware of their intervention, then we will smile and laugh with them. Then we will understand!

We will see the great importance of our time in an *imperfect world*, and we'll be surprised to learn that everything we have accomplished, everything we have learned, everything we have thought, everything we have aspired to be, even everything we have desired to possess, are all **nothing** compared to what we had once before in a *perfect human world*. We will learn that everything about our world is *imperfect* and that nothing that created this *imperfection* will ever exist in our future. We will understand this even before the planets of our solar system are transformed into *perfect human worlds* like the one where we used to live.

We have something that no other life form upon our earth possesses. We have an **imagination**. Although we are often convinced that the use of our imagination is not a part of our ***true reality***, it still remains our only source of information of what a *perfect human world* could possibly be like. Our **imagination is our connection to our past experience and to our future potential**.

We have progressed in the way that we control our surrounding environment and get it to do what **we** want it to do by using our imaginations. Technology is simply the end result of using our free will and imagination. We utilize technology to (hopefully) improve our world and its social and physical environments. We want these environments to benefit our human natures. As technology seems to advance faster than our current ability to imagine, we are beginning to see that the *imagination* of our past is becoming the ***true reality*** of our future. For this reason, this book has only explained a basic, miniscule part of our complete **HUMAN REALITY**. The rest of what any of us could possibly want to know about ourselves and the primordial, advanced world in which we were first created, or the world that would be *perfect* for each of us, is accessible through the <u>proper</u> use of our **imagination**.

Because *imagination is a product of human free will*, it also must have some specific limits and controls in place in order for it to serve us properly in better understanding our ***true reality***. Because each of us has an *essence* in which is recorded all of our unique *personal* past experiences, we cannot expect that the conclusions of our *own imagination* supersede all those of others. We must accept that our imagination is NOT ***true reality***, but a conscious effort each of us is personally trying to make in order to make sense out of what we *feel* is right for us. We must be willing to accept that we have an *imperfect brain* that cannot fully access what is recorded in our *essence*. And we must accept the purpose for which we currently have an *imperfect brain*.

We live upon this earth purposefully to experience the opposite of all that would otherwise make us very happy. It was intended to be this way for our development and learning. Nevertheless, we have our free will and, by way of this book, we now have a better understanding of how to use our unique human power to change our world and form it into one that will benefit all of us equally. We have forgotten (or better, we can't remember) just how powerful we really are as human beings. We let others rule over us and control us. We let others set expectations for us and tell us *how* **we** *should* be.

This is our final chance to get our act together and prove our *humanity*. Having humanity, how can we sit by and watch billions of our fellow human beings suffer the effects of poverty, when we know there is a simple way to provide equally for every human being upon this earth (www.wwunited.org)? How can our *humanity* endorse the punishment of others who, like ourselves, are only doing the best they are capable of doing in an *imperfect body*? How can our *humanity* continually support and justify the killing of other human beings, for any reason? How can our *humanity* justify the destruction of our natural environment and the squander of its limited resources, just because we *think* we have a greater need to fulfill our own needs than those of others?

We can *hope* for a better world of peace, equality, and plenty for all, because we once lived in one. We lived in a world where each individual was given the power and ability to exercise free will for the sake of the individual's own balance and happiness. Can we **imagine** all the people living life in peace? Can we **imagine** a *perfect* human world? Yes we can! We can, because we lived in one before; and the experiences we had there are recorded in our *essence*.

Don't take the chance of not considering and heeding the ***true realities*** presented in this book. Don't make an excuse of why you didn't open up your mind. Don't blame your inability to **imagine** on a stifled *false sense of reality* that was not formed *by* **you**, but *for you* by others. Don't take the chance that your personal *humanity type* (that which you **truly have become** by acting with the power of your free will) is responsible for any part of our *imperfect human world*.

Before other, more advanced human beings come to this earth to save us from ourselves, we now have the opportunity to demonstrate our **true humanity**! Each of us has the power to become who we each chose to become. We cannot let any other take that power from us! We must be *who we are*!

How can we claim individuality and personal responsibility when all that we know comes from outside of our **true self**? We must claim victory in the ongoing battle within us between who **we really are** and who the *imperfect world* expects us to be. We must not give up the battle for free will. It is free will that makes a human being. It is free will that brings us balance and happiness. If we lose our free will, we will lose ourselves!

And at last, keep this in mind,

None of us can run away and hide from the ***true reality of who we are***. One day, we will once again receive the *perfect* human body in which we will finally be able to remember all of our experiences, from our primordial creation throughout our many lifetimes upon this earth.

With this *perfected* body, we will finally and completely understand…

HUMAN REALITY—WHO WE ARE and WHY WE EXIST!

Worldwide United
FOUNDATION

www.WWUNITED.org

ONE world
ONE solution
ONE people
ONE DAY!

NOTE from the publisher: Pearl Publishing, LLC holds all legal rights to this book. Pearl Publishing, LLC is a small publishing company that the anonymous author of this book has assigned as the author's agent. It is the author's desire, as well as the publisher's, to attempt worldwide distribution of this book. Because Pearl Publishing, LLC has few resources and connections to facilitate a major release and promotion of this book, it has legal authority to offer and assign the rights of this book to any other publisher that might find this book a worthy and profitable cause. Again, the author's sole purpose and desire is to make the book known and available to the entire world. Any publishing company or representative interested in owning the rights to this book can contact Pearl Publishing, LLC for further information. 1-888-499-9666

About The Author

Because **real truth** embodies all things as they are, as they were, and as they always will be, no one can take personal credit for its authorship. **Real truth** just is!

The author of **HUMAN REALITY, Who We Are and Why We Exist** wants no part of the accolades or compensation (monetary or otherwise) that might be associated with this presentation of **real truth**.

The author has transferred the legal and copyrights of this work to the publishing company that has agreed to publish and market this book. Any royalties or profits from its sale are the sole property of the publishing company and managed at its own discretion. The purpose for allowing a publishing company such comprehensive rights is to improve the marketability and availability of this very important work; therefore, allowing as much exposure to it as possible according to current publishing and marketing trends.

Any human being could have written this book, if that person were allowed full access to all of his or her past memories. But because our current *imperfect* human brains do not allow such access, the information was given through this author. The author was chosen and authorized by those who know **real truth** to present it in the form of this book, written in the English language. Any subsequent translations of this book into a language other than English, imposes the risk of losing some of the authenticity of its *true* meaning.

No matter who one might speculate or infer wrote this book, the author will always remain…

—Anonymous

LaVergne, TN USA
22 October 2010
201801LV00003B/43/P

9 780978 526481